Black Americans and White Racism

Theory and Research

Edited and Introductions by
Marcel L. Goldschmid
McGill University

HOLT, RINEHART AND WINSTON, INC.
New York   Chicago   San Francisco   Atlanta
Dallas   Montreal   Toronto   London   Sydney

Library of Congress Catalog Card Number: 74-111797

SBN: 03-077685-6 (Pa)

SBN: 03-084738-9 (Cl)

Printed in the United States of America

0 1 2 3   17   9 8 7 6 5 4 3 2 1

This book is dedicated to the memory of
Dr. Martin Luther King, Jr. (1929–1968)

Foreword

"Be *involved*!" "Become *relevant* to society's pressing problems!" These calls to academia in general and to social science in particular have become so common in the mass media and from the platform that they have attained the status of clichés. In no realm are these understandable calls more insistent than in race relations. The issues raised by involvement and relevancy, however, are more complex and delicate than they might at first appear.

To begin, there is often implicit in these calls an assumption that social science has been virtually useless in the past. The less one knows about a subject, of course, the easier it is to entertain such assumptions. Professor Goldschmid's *Black Americans and White Racism: Theory and Research* presents a fresh look at the contributions of social scientists to the leading domestic concern of our times, and thus it offers the reader an excellent opportunity to judge for himself the accuracy of "the useless assumption."

The second and more important issue involves value and role conflict. The same pragmatic value orientation which demands "practical" research and solutions "that work" also leads to a deep suspicion of "experts" and "scientists." No one without special training assumes he is competently conversant with nuclear physics, for example. But since we are all human beings, we can think of ourselves with some justification as lay-psychologists by definition; and since we all live in society, we can also think of ourselves as lay-sociologists. Consequently, if social scientists reach practical conclusions in conflict with vested interests and "common sense," it is not difficult to retort, "What do those men know about it?" Similarly, not without some merit, the challenged practitioner's refrain is, "You have to be on the firing line to know really what the score is."

A significant case in point was the public and political reception of *The Equality of Educational Opportunity* report, issued in 1966 by the U.S. Office of Education. This is the research volume written by James Coleman, a professor of sociology at the Johns Hopkins University, and his colleagues, significant portions of which are discussed here in Chapter 5. It gave the results of the second largest study ever performed on American public education as required by Title IV of the 1964 Civil Rights Act. Indeed, it marked one of the first times social science had been called on by the United States Congress to perform research on matters of major national policy. From its subdued release on a rainy July 4th weekend, the so-called "Coleman Report" found itself less a scientific document than a political football. Those who liked its findings hailed it as a landmark study; those who disliked its findings sought criticism to validate their claim that it should not be taken seriously by policy makers. Soon a shrill and speculative criticism was informally sent out by two young economists to many persons in and out of government; this criticism became the last word among those who cared considerably less about techniques of regression analysis than about the politics of education.

The Coleman Report did indeed have its methodological and theoretical weaknesses, in part because of the political demands that it be conducted in great haste. But the necessarily charged political atmosphere into which it was released made the usual procedures of responsible criticism and retesting virtually impossible. The final verdict on the Report and its influence on American public education is not yet in. Reanalyses of the original data plus additional studies inspired by the Report are still under way. Yet a future study of the political history of this report will offer an invaluable opportunity to learn more about the complexities created by "involvement" and "relevancy."

This conflict places social scientists in a painful dilemma. On the one hand, we are told to get involved, be relevant, and to come down from the ivory tower. On the other, we are told that if we are involved and relevant then we are biased and unobjective and hence our contribution is at best suspect. Some would handle this conflict by literally "leaving the field," by opting out of their roles as social scientists and assuming "more relevant" duties for which their training and experience may not in fact be appropriate. Others would simply ignore the calls for involvement and continue to tread the well-worn paths.

But a growing number of social scientists have rejected these extremes; indeed, they strove to do competent work that was relevant to society's urgent problems long before today's popular pleas for involvement were sounded. They contend that their most important contribution can be made by "doing their thing," by bringing fully to bear upon major social problems their scholarly tools for gathering and assessing pertinent data in a broader context than the myopia of today's headlines. In so applying their skills, social scientists need to brace themselves against the society's ambivalence toward "experts" and against the political perspective within which their work will be judged, used, abused, disused, and misused. "It's hot in the kitchen," rightly maintained Harry Truman, but precisely because it is so hot are social science tools of data collection and analysis so desperately needed.

Within this perspective, the basic importance of this volume is that it brings together for the first time an important body of work, largely performed by social scientists, that is directly applicable to the problems of American race relations. Yet *Black Americans and White Racism: Theory and Research* is more than a useful collection of readings. It not only brings together material from a diversity of sources not previously assembled in one convenient place, but it also organizes and structures the realm which might best be labeled, "the social psychology of race relations." In one critical domain after another—black identity and personality, the black family and child development, racial differences and intellectual performance, black achievement in integrated and segregated environments, racism, and black militancy and violence—the editor blocks out the critical parameters; he provides a pointed overview, a number of carefully chosen selections, and an extensive bibliography. As a social psychologist who has specialized throughout my career in this field, I repeatedly discovered important insights, directions, and titles about which I was previously unaware.

In short, *Black Americans and White Racism: Theory and Research* is not just another "reader" in an age of nonbooks. It is itself an important contribution that will influence and further social psychological efforts in American race relations. And it is worthy of both the crucial problem to which it is addressed and the great man to whom it is dedicated.

Thomas F. Pettigrew
Professor of Social Psychology
Harvard University

November 1969

Preface

In the midst of writing the introductions for this book, I heard the shocking news that Dr. Martin Luther King had been assassinated. I was overwhelmed with grief and remembered Dr. King's profound diagnosis: "If the Negro needs social science for direction and for self-understanding, the white society is in even more urgent need. White America needs to understand that it is poisoned to its soul by racism." Dr. King then challenged the social scientists "to address the white community and 'tell it like it is.'"

While I was a consultant to a community agency in Watts, Los Angeles, I became aware of the need for a convenient source of recent psychological and sociological research reports on the plight of black Americans and on the manifestations and consequences of white racism. I hope that this book will help to meet this need and at the same time live up to Dr. King's challenge.

Rather than just presenting the reprinted articles with a brief commentary, I have reviewed the most recent related research literature in the introductions to each chapter. The articles that are reproduced have also been summarized in the introductions in order to place them in a larger context. Whenever possible, I have tried to relate the research to theories, essays, and personal accounts, thus providing the interested reader with further leads and suggestions.

My editorial consultants, Irwin Katz, Gary T. Marx, Thomas F. Pettigrew, and Harold M. Proshansky, made valuable suggestions for the selection of articles and offered detailed comments and criticisms regarding the editorial introductions. Their help and continuous encouragement are deeply appreciated. I would also like to express my sincere gratitude to the authors and publishers for their permission to reprint the articles and chapters included in this volume.

Clay Carson ably assisted me in the search for appropriate articles and in the organization of the book, and I gratefully acknowledge the helpful comments received from Ralph Mason Dreger, Myron Rothbart, Tom M. Tomlinson, and Dave D. Stein. I would also like to thank Herbert N. Weissman, who read my final version of all the introductions and made many improvements in the prose. His was a very significant contribution.

Rosemary Smith's help in typing the several drafts of the manuscript is gratefully acknowledged, and I want to express my great appreciation to Maureeta Percy who assisted in typing the introductions, preparing the final manuscript, developing the index, and proofreading.

Finally, I want to thank my wife Barbara for her unfailing support and encouragement.

I have dedicated this book to Dr. King for he, perhaps more than anyone, had labored during his short life for the unity of white and black.

Marcel L. Goldschmid
Montreal

May 1970

Contents

1

Introduction

Thrust any child, white or colored, from the womb to a world that offers the rewards of status and success. With a moat of discrimination cut him off from the mainland so that there are few or no opportunities to achieve those rewards. Let him continue to wish for the same things the mainlanders desire, but make him move around much more, lose a father to death or desertion and a mother to work and dependency. Give him less knowledge to absorb, less money than the mainlander receives for the same tasks. Surround him with examples of unlawful achievers, and make him fight to protect the mainland without fully participating in the rules to govern it. Shorten his length of life, expose him to disease, treat him as if he were biologically inferior and call him nasty names to convince him of it. Even if the mainlanders value the service he gives them and the feeling of importance his contrast offers, he is lost.

MARVIN E. WOLFGANG, *Crime and Race*

INTRODUCTION

The above quote from Wolfgang (1964) is in some ways a beautiful summary of the profile of black America and white racism this book will try to convey through editorial introductions and a sample of empirical studies. It is important that whites be informed, for, as Martin Luther King [1][1] points out in the first selection, "white America has an appalling lack of knowledge concerning the reality of Negro life," and it does not realize "that it is poisoned to its soul by racism."

What emerges from these data is a dismal picture. Large numbers of black Americans are still separate and unequal. Many live in overcrowded, miserable city slums or in isolated rural areas. Education largely fails to provide them with the essentials for competing and living in today's society. Unemployment is higher for blacks than for whites, salaries are lower, and advancement and status less easily attained.

Their collective self-image has suffered immensely, further impeding prog-

---

[1] Numbers in brackets refer to selections included in this book.

ress. According to recent surveys and polls, whites express less prejudice than previously, yet they still discriminate in schools, employment, and housing.

But there are winds of change. Massive resistance against subordination and oppression has begun. Violent uprisings have followed nonviolent protests. The black rebellion is in full swing and can no longer be ignored by the white masses. The results have been devastating. Division and fragmentation are threatening the very foundations of American democracy. Black extremists call for more violence and guerrilla warfare. Some black militants desire complete racial separation and the founding of a new black state. The majority, the black moderates, maintain their nonviolent approach and keep working toward an open society. White liberals, maligned and confused, are on the verge of withdrawing or being excluded from the black revolt. Some white radicals attempt to join ranks with proponents of black power. White reactionaries without concern for justice call for "law and order" and wish to suppress the black liberation movement by repressive legislation and police and military control.

In this struggle many whites are bound to search their consciences and reevaluate the roles they typically play. Before we act we need to understand the plight of black as well as white Americans. To effect change, however, we would do well to take seriously the advice of black leaders to redress the balance of concern from the black to the white community. After all, it is in the white community that racism and its destructive consequences are generated. It is there that power lies to bring about changes in laws and commitments to the principles of democracy. It is there that decisions concerning the allocation of America's resources are made.

Too little is yet known about the roots of racism, about its more subtle expressions, and particularly about ways of reducing or eliminating it. Even now the government, mass media (particularly television), the schools, and the teachers colleges and universities do not live up to their obligation to educate whites about the true history of blacks, their oppression, their present living conditions, and most of all, about white discrimination. Increasingly, blacks are asking for self-determination in their own communities. Whites must recognize this as a legitimate demand and become aware of the pitfalls in imposing white definitions and solutions on blacks. At best they can make whatever skill and competence they possess available when such resources are relevant and desired and when they can be used to the advantage and benefit of the black community. Most of all, whites should act in the white community to eliminate the barriers that are so important in the frustration of black aspirations.

This is not to suggest that whites cannot and should not contribute knowledge and factual information about black as well as white communities in America. Black and white authors and social scientists must probe into all facets of society and try to uncover the truth as best they know how. Data documenting the failure of the public school system to provide an adequate education for many minority group children, for example, or data on the meaning of the recent civil disorders may diminish the apathy of whites and decrease distortions in images of black Americans held by whites.

An open, pluralistic society remains the avowed long-term goal of most white liberals and black Americans. The present realities, however, reflect widespread segregation. Thus, we are confronted with a dilemma: Should we work toward immediate but small improvements within the ideal framework of an integrated society, or should we strive for immediate but possibly more significant changes within the actual framework of a segregated society? The latter choice may open up totally new avenues for revolutionary changes in the lives of Afro-Americans (Hamilton, 1968), but the danger of strengthening segregation and perhaps irreversibly solidifying it looms large. White supremacists have, of course, for a long time argued for segregation. In this respect intensified racial separation would clearly represent a step backwards and a reversal of civil rights goals (Pettigrew, 1969). Others have urged the creation of independent black economic institutions, the projected large-scale operation of which would necessitate increased black-white associations and interactions. Such equal-status interactions, it is argued, would hasten integration (see, for example, Perry, 1969). In any case, in the short run, segregated black communities must receive immediate and massive financial aid to improve housing, education, and community services, but Lewis (1969) has pointed out that "the American pattern is segregation in *social* life after 5 P.M., but integration in the *economic* life of the country during the day":

> So a black strategy which concentrated exclusively on building up black neighborhoods would be dealing with less than half the black man's economic problems. The neighborhood itself will not flourish unless the man who goes out of it in the morning brings back into it from the outside world an income adequate to support its institutions (p. 39–40).

The present course of the black struggle must be seen in the context of changes within American society. As this society relaxes its oppressive hold on the black minority (as a result of many forces, such as massive migration of blacks from the more repressive South to the more liberal North, white youths increasingly rejecting their parents' hypocrisy and bigotry, a more global collapse of old values and traditions, and economic prosperity), demands for more freedom and opportunities are voiced. Almost every social organization, be it the church, business, the military, or the university, has witnessed this phenomenon. Once a system becomes more permissive, change is inevitable. Success, however small, reinforces more demands and also demonstrates the potential power of a movement. Those who complain that the civil rights movement is going too fast and too far are not only unaware of the moral justice behind the movement but also ignore this universal social phenomenon.

One more point should be made with respect to racism and race relations. Although this book concentrates on Americans, it has become obvious that colored people all over the world have suffered to some extent from exploitation by whites. Inasmuch as they have shared similar experiences as a result of colonization, it may be surmised that some of the findings and theories offered here may also be relevant to their situation. Of course, only cross-cultural research will reveal to what extent this is true. In any case, the black Americans' position and rebellion must be seen in the context of worldwide yearning of oppressed peoples for freedom and independence (see Fannon, 1961). Successful independence movements elsewhere are bound to spur black Americans on, and conversely, Afro-American progress will stimulate aspirations in other subjugated peoples. World opinion has become more critical of racism and is likely to exert increasing pressure on the United States. It should also be clear that the world image of America as a just democracy with freedom and equality for all has suffered immeasurably as a result of her racial practices.

To give a broader perspective and to further clarify the research and theories presented in this volume, it may be helpful to discuss briefly some definitions and critical general and methodological issues, as well as highlight some research methods and topics that social scientists have tended to neglect.[2]

---

[2] For a discussion of "reforms as experiments" see Campbell (1969).

RACE

Several definitions of the term "race" have been used (see van den Berghe, 1967). Physical anthropologists, for example, have referred to subspecies of man as races, identified by phenotypes and genotypes. They have not, however, been able to reach consensus on one classification scheme. Too frequently the word "race" is misused to refer to ethnic or national groups who have certain cultural traits in common (for example, the "German race"). Race, as used in this book, refers to a group that identifies itself or is identified by others as being different from other groups on the basis of skin color and other physical characteristics. As van den Berghe (1967) has pointed out, the important element in the last definition is that "a group is *socially* defined but on the basis of *physical* criteria" (p. 9). This distinction becomes crucial when certain investigators pretend to have found links, for example, between intellectual abilities (see Chapter 4 of the present text) and genetic differences, even though the subject's "race" was determined by social rather than genetic criteria.

SOCIAL CLASS AND RACE

The differentiation between racial and social class factors in explaining the behaviors of whites and blacks is one of the most difficult and controversial research issues. Some would go as far as to claim that differences in socioeconomic status (SES) and its consequences account for most or all of the so-called racial differences in intelligence, attitudes, values, morals, life style, and so on. This is not the view adopted here, but comparisons between blacks and whites or indeed between any groups most definitely should control for the social class of the subjects. Unless samples are approximately equated on this factor, any differences between blacks and whites may be primarily a function of social class rather than race. Unfortunately, there are still published reports that have not given this matter adequate attention (see Dreger & Miller, in press).

MATCHING SAMPLES

Even if two groups are matched on SES, there is, of course, no guarantee that they are equated on other critical variables. This problem is compounded in studies of racial differences and so far, at least, has not been adequately resolved. Being black in America has been a stigma and has meant second-class citizenship for so long that the inferior social position of blacks has inevitably affected other personal characteristics (see Chapter 2).

If educational background is used, as it usually is, to derive SES measures, will there not occur serious imbalances owing to the different educational experiences of blacks, even when they have the same number of years in school as whites (see Chapter 5)? Most studies have not considered even such basic variables as age, sex, I.Q., achievement, income, occupation, or residence, *simultaneously*. One reason for this, of course, is the massive number of subjects required to vary these characteristics at the same time. Several psychological experiments and most sociological surveys reported here have nevertheless been reasonably successful in controlling many of these sample characteristics.

REPRESENTATIVENESS OF SAMPLES

The question of how representative a certain set of findings is, even if no black-white comparisons are made, is obviously important. We are not especially interested in how a particular sample, that is, 30 black high school students, behaves, but in how all black high school students with similar characteristics behave. The ability of generalizing specific results is naturally enhanced if right from the beginning the sample was drawn in such a way as to be representative of that population as a whole. Different studies involving similar subjects and questions can also corroborate a given set of evidence.

EXPERIMENTER EFFECTS

There is some evidence (for example, Barber & Silver, 1968; Rosenthal, 1966) that attributes of the interviewer or experimenter, such as his expectations, research hypothesis, and style, may affect the results of the study (see Chapters 4 and 6). Again this difficulty is compounded in research on racial relations by the reaction of the respondent or subject to the skin color of the experimenter or interviewer. Black respondents, for example, may withhold information about their feelings and attitudes from a white interviewer but may readily reveal them to a black investigator, and vice versa. Several studies discussed in later chapters deal specifically with this problem, but it should be clear at the outset that the findings of any study may be biased or inaccurate as a result of the "experimenter effect."

ACTION OR FIELD STUDIES VS. LABORATORY RESEARCH

Social scientists, like scientists in general, attempt to bring as many variables under their control as possible. The laboratory setting is usually better suited for this purpose, since testing procedures can be more easily standardized or even automated to eliminate or reduce inaccuracies in the results that are due to procedural variation from subject to subject. On the other hand, laboratory studies tend to focus on more narrowly defined (and therefore often less crucial) questions and may introduce artificial conditions that do not genuinely reflect the behavior of an individual in his natural habitat. Field studies that attempt to investigate the subject's behavior in his day-to-day environment are rarely carried out despite their enormous potential usefulness. Studies of learning, for example, have concentrated on laboratory animals or short-term memory with nonsense syllables. Until recently, the process of learning in the classroom was almost completely ignored. Discrimination too has usually been assessed under relatively artificial "laboratory" conditions rather than in more typical interracial situations.

Action research in race relations focusing on *changing* behavior or attitudes has been even less tempting to social scientists. The selection of articles included in this book reflects this state of affairs. The reasons for this gap in the literature are fairly simple. Not only are the methodological problems in field and action studies far more challenging, as has already been mentioned, but also such studies take longer and are not encouraged by the academic community because of their potential ambiguities. Yet competent field and action research is desperately needed to help answer a number of questions. For example, what are the optimal learning conditions in the classroom for children who live in a slum environment? What do black children in the ghetto experience and care about that could be used by the school to the long-term advantage of these children?[3] And could not the development of racism, its manifestations, and its elimination or ideally its *prevention* be examined by field and action research? (See Chapter 6.) Here is a challenge of formidable proportions for all students and social scientists to break new ground and produce vital information.

SURVEYS VS. EXPERIMENTAL RESEARCH

A distinction is sometimes made between survey results (or correlational studies) and experimental research (see Cronbach, 1957). The former usually involves larger samples and gives insight into the association or correlation among variables, but does not ordinarily permit cause and effect explanations. In the latter, one or more variables are manipulated in order to gain an understanding of the process and causal relationship of the variables investigated. Ideally, the two types of studies complement each other. The results of a survey may pinpoint certain interesting broad associations or "end products," which can be followed up by experimental research in order to derive insight into the causes of these end products. Both types of research are represented in this volume.

EVALUATION OF ACTION PROGRAMS

An enormous array of social action programs for blacks sponsored by all levels of government and various organizations has been initiated to supplement public schooling, provide vocational training, increase community services, and so on. Although such efforts are commendable, particularly when they are oriented toward black leadership and community control, it has become evident that many if not most of these programs are hastily conceived, understaffed, and most critically, not properly evaluated. Every service should be examined with respect to how adequately it meets its objectives. How else will we know whether the funds are used to the best advantage and whether the people for whom the program was designed really benefit? Many of the "enrichment programs," for example, have not been properly planned and evaluated, nor are the ordinary "established" services, such as the public school and the welfare system, sufficiently analyzed. It is astounding that huge funds are spent, for example, on the testing of fighter planes and other war materials, but only small sums for the evaluation of social services and school programs. Here is another challenge for social scientists that has been relatively neglected. We need thorough examinations of all systems and institutions, as well as of special programs designed to serve the public. From such examinations would flow innovations and ultimately more efficiency.

POLICY AND SOCIAL SCIENCE RESEARCH

As social science research and theory expand and become more sophisticated, their application to policy decisions should be encouraged and surveyed by social scientists who are intimately familiar with its limitations, validity,

---

[3] Instead of labeling ghetto children as culturally deprived and concentrating on what they "missed," maybe we should find out what they *did* learn and what they *are* interested in and use this knowledge to restructure the curriculum and teaching (preferably learning) methods to adapt them to these children's lives.

and reliability. A closer link between the social science community and government would also be beneficial in alerting researchers to important social problems; conversely, it could serve to apprise governments of critical issues and the need for means with which to carry out empirical investigations.

Social science is still in its infancy and at present has fewer solid conclusions to offer than the natural sciences. But it is also true—and in fact has been pointed out in Congress—that the funds available for social science research have been a pittance in comparison to the expenditures on physical and biological research. This is a very grave state of affairs indeed. The public, as well as social scientists themselves, may be impatient with the progress of social science, but one should not lose sight of the relatively small investment this society has made in social science education and research. Until recently, furthermore, the social science community has been relatively indifferent to policy issues and policy research. Finally, although domestic crises in urban living and black-white relations have reached gigantic proportions, the allocation of federal, state, and municipal resources to cope with these problems has remained woefully inadequate.

REFERENCES

Barber, T. X., & Silver, H. J. Fact, fiction, and the experimenter bias effect. *Psychological Bulletin Monograph Supplement*, 1968, **70,** 1–29.

Campbell, D. T. Reforms as experiments. *American Psychologist*, 1969, **24,** 409–429.

Cronbach, L. J. The two disciplines of scientific psychology. *American Psychologist*, 1957, **12,** 671–684.

Dreger, R. M., & Miller, K. S. Comparative psychological studies of Negroes and whites in the United States. *Psychological Bulletin*, in press.

Fannon, F. *The wretched of the earth.* New York: Grove, 1961.

Hamilton, C. V. Race and education: A search for legitimacy. *Harvard Educational Review*, 1968, **38,** 669–684.

Lewis, W. A. The road to the top is through higher education—not black studies. *The New York Times Magazine*, May 11, 1969. (Reprinted from *University: A Princeton Quarterly*, 1969).

Perry, S. E. Black institutions, black separatism, and ghetto economic development. Paper prepared for the annual meetings of the Society for Applied Anthropology, Mexico City, April 9–15, 1969. Washington, D.C.: Office of Economic Opportunity.

Pettigrew, T. F. Racially separate or together? *Journal of Social Issues*, 1969, **25,** 43–69.

Rosenthal, R. *Experimenter effects in behavioral research.* New York: Appleton, 1966.

van den Berghe, P. L. *Race and racism.* New York: Wiley, 1967.

Wolfgang, M. E. *Crime and race. Conceptions and misconceptions.* New York: Institute of Human Relations Press, 1964.

1

The role of the behavioral scientist in the civil rights movement

MARTIN LUTHER KING, JR.

It is always a very rich and rewarding experience when I can take a brief break from the day-to-day demands of our struggle for freedom and human dignity and discuss the issues involved in that struggle with concerned friends of good will all over the nation. It is particularly a great privilege to discuss these issues with members of the academic community, who are constantly writing about and dealing with the problems that we face and who have the tremendous responsibility of moulding the minds of young men and women all over our country.

THE CIVIL RIGHTS MOVEMENT NEEDS THE HELP OF SOCIAL SCIENTISTS

In the preface to their book, *Applied Sociology* (1965), S. M. Miller and Alvin Gouldner state: "It is the historic mission of the social sciences to enable mankind to take possession of society." It follows that for Negroes who substantially are excluded from society this science is needed even more desperately than for any other group in the population.

For social scientists, the opportunity to serve in a life-giving purpose is a humanist

Permission to publish this address was granted by the author. Since then, the paper has been published by the *Journal of Social Issues*, 1968, **24**, 1–12, and the *American Psychologist*, 1968, **23**, 180–186.

challenge of rare distinction. Negroes too are eager for a rendezvous with truth and discovery. We are aware that social scientists, unlike some of their colleagues in the physical sciences, have been spared the grim feelings of guilt that attended the invention of nuclear weapons of destruction. Social scientists, in the main, are fortunate to be able to extirpate evil, not to invent it.

If the Negro needs social sciences for direction and for self-understanding, the white society is in even more urgent need. White America needs to understand that it is poisoned to its soul by racism and the understanding needs to be carefully documented and consequently more difficult to reject. The present crisis arises because although it is historically imperative that our society take the next step to equality, we find ourselves psychologically and socially imprisoned. All too many white Americans are horrified not with conditions of Negro life but with the product of these conditions—the Negro himself.

White America is seeking to keep the walls of segregation substantially intact while the evolution of society and the Negro's desperation is causing them to crumble. The white majority, unprepared and unwilling to accept radical structural change, is resisting and producing chaos while complaining that if there were no chaos orderly change would come.

Negroes want the social scientist to address the white community and "tell it like it is." White America has an appalling lack of knowledge concerning the reality of Negro life. One reason some advances were made in the South during the past decade was the discovery by northern whites of the brutal facts of southern segregated life. It was the Negro who educated the nation by dramatizing the evils through nonviolent protest. The social scientist played little or no role in disclosing truth. The Negro action movement with raw courage did it virtually alone. When the majority of the country could not live with the extremes of brutality they witnessed, political remedies were enacted and customs were altered.

These partial advances were, however, limited principally to the South and progress did not automatically spread throughout the nation. There was also little depth to the changes. White America stopped murder, but that is not the same thing as ordaining brotherhood; nor is the ending of lynch rule the same thing as inaugurating justice.

After some years of Negro-white unity and partial successes, white America shifted gears and went into reverse. Negroes, alive with hope and enthusiasm, ran into sharply stiffened white resistance at all levels and bitter tensions broke out in sporadic episodes of violence. New lines of hostility were drawn and the era of good feeling disappeared.

The decade of 1955 to 1965, with its constructive elements, misled us. Everyone, activists and social scientists, underestimated the amount of violence and rage Negroes were suppressing and the amount of bigotry the white majority was disguising.

Science should have been employed more fully to warn us that the Negro, after 350 years of handicaps, mired in an intricate network of contemporary barriers, could not be ushered into equality by tentative and superficial changes.

Mass nonviolent protests, a social invention of Negroes, were effective in Montgomery, Birmingham and Selma in forcing national legislation which served to change Negro life sufficiently to curb explosions. But when changes were confined to the South alone, the North, in the absence of change, began to seethe.

The freedom movement did not adapt its tactics to the different and unique northern urban conditions. It failed to see that nonviolent marches in the South were forms of rebellion. When Negroes took over the streets and shops, southern society shook to its roots. Negroes could contain their rage when they found the means to force relatively radical changes in their environment.

In the North, on the other hand, street demonstrations were not even a mild expression of militancy. The turmoil of cities absorbs demonstrations as merely transitory drama which is ordinary in city life. Without a more effective tactic for upsetting the status quo, the power structure could maintain its intransigence and hostility. Into the vacuum of inaction, violence and riots flowed and a new period opened.

Urban Riots

Urban riots must now be recognized as durable social phenomena. They may be deplored, but they are there and should be understood. Urban riots are a special form of violence. They are not insurrections. The rioters are not seeking to seize territory or to attain control of institutions. They are mainly intended to shock the white community. They are a distorted form of social protest. The looting which is their principal feature serves many functions. It enables the most enraged and deprived Negro to take hold of consumer goods with the ease the white man does by using his purse. Often the Negro does not even want what he takes; he wants the experience of taking. But most of all, alienated from society and knowing that this society cherishes property above people, he is shocking it by abusing property rights. There are thus elements of emotional catharsis in the violent act. This may explain why most cities in which riots have occurred have not had a repetition, even though the causative conditions remain. It is also noteworthy that the amount of physical harm done to white people other than police is infinitesimal and in Detroit whites and Negroes looted in unity.

A profound judgment of today's riots was expressed by Victor Hugo a century ago. He said, "If a soul is left in darkness, sins will be committed. The guilty one is not he who commits the sin, but he who causes the darkness."

The policy makers of the white society have caused the darkness; they create discrimination; they structured slums; and they perpetuate unemployment, ignorance and poverty. It is incontestable and deplorable that Negroes have committed crimes; but they are derivative crimes. They are born of the greater crimes of the white society. When we ask Negroes to abide by the law, let us also demand that the white man abide by law in the ghettos. Day-in and day-out he violates welfare laws to deprive the poor of their meager allotments; he flagrantly violates building codes and regulations; his police make a mockery of law; and he violates laws on equal employment and education and the provisions for civic services. The slums are the handiwork of a vicious system of the white society; Negroes live in them but do not make them any more than a prisoner makes a prison. Let us say boldly that if the total violations of law by the white man in the slums over the years were calculated and compared with the law-breaking of a few days of riots, the hardened criminal would be the white man. These are often difficult things to say but I have come to see more and more that it is necessary to utter the truth in order to deal with the great problems that we face in our society.

Vietnam War

There is another cause of riots that is too important to mention casually—the war in Vietnam. Here again, we are dealing with a controversial issue. But I am convinced that the war in Vietnam has played havoc with our domestic destinies. The bombs that fall in Vietnam explode at home. It does not take much to see what great damage this war has done to the image of our nation. It has left our country politically and morally isolated in the world, where our only friends happen to be puppet nations like Taiwan, Thailand and South Korea. The major allies in the world that have been with us in war and peace are not with us in this war. As a result we find ourselves socially and politically isolated.

The war in Vietnam has torn up the Geneva Accord. It has seriously impaired the United Nations. It has exacerbated the hatreds between continents, and worse still, between races. It has frustrated our development at home by telling our underprivileged citizens that we place insatiable military demands above their most critical needs. It has greatly contributed to the forces of reaction in America, and strengthened the military-industrial complex, against which even President Eisenhower solemnly warned us. It has practically destroyed Vietnam, and left thousands of American and Vietnamese youth maimed and mutilated. And it has exposed the whole world to the risk of nuclear warfare.

As I looked at what this war was doing to our nation, and to the domestic situation and to the Civil Rights movement, I found it necessary to speak vigorously out against it. My speaking out against the war has not gone without criticisms. There are those who tell me that I should stick with civil rights, and stay in my place. I can only respond that I have fought too hard and long to end segregated public accommodations to segregate my own moral concerns. It is my deep conviction that justice is indivisible, that injustice anywhere is a threat to justice everywhere. For those who tell me I am hurting the Civil Rights movement, and ask, "Don't you think that in order to be respected, and in order to regain support, you must stop talking against the war?" I can only say that I am not a consensus leader. I do not seek to determine what is right and wrong by taking a Gallop Poll to determine majority opinion. And it is again my deep conviction that ultimately a genuine leader is not a searcher for consensus, but a molder of consensus. On some positions cowardice asks the question, "Is it safe?"! Expediency asks the question, "Is it politic?" Vanity asks the question, "Is it popular?" But conscience must ask the question, "Is it right?" And there comes a time when one must take a stand that is neither safe, nor politic, nor popular. But one must take it because it is right. And that is where I find myself today.

Moreover, I am convinced, even if war continues, that a genuine massive act of concern will do more to quell riots than the most massive deployment of troops.

Unemployment

The unemployment of Negro youth ranges up to 40 per cent in some slums. The riots are almost entirely youth events—the age range of participants is from 13 to 25. What hypocrisy it is to talk of saving the new generation—to make it the generation of hope—while consigning it to unemployment and provoking it to violent alternatives.

When our nation was bankrupt in the 30's we created an agency to provide jobs to all at their existing level of skill. In our overwhelming affluence today what excuse is there for not setting up a national agency for full employment immediately?

The other program which would give reality to hope and opportunity would be the demolition of the slums to be replaced by decent housing built by residents of the ghettos.

These programs are not only eminently sound and vitally needed, but they have the support of an overwhelming majority of the nation—white and Negro. The Harris Poll on August 21, 1967, disclosed that an astounding 69 per cent of the country support a works program to provide employment to all and an equally astonishing 65 per cent approve a program to tear down the slums.

There is a program and there is heavy majority support for it. Yet, the administration and Congress tinker with trivial proposals to limit costs in an extravagant gamble with disaster.

The President has lamented that he cannot persuade Congress. He can, if the will is there, go to the people, mobilize the people's support and thereby substantially increase his power to persuade Congress. Our most urgent task is to find the tactics that will move the government no matter how determined it is to resist.

Civil Disobedience

I believe we will have to find the militant middle between riots on the one hand and weak and timid supplication for justice on the other hand. That middle ground, I believe, is civil disobedience. It can be aggressive but nonviolent; it can dislocate but not destroy. The specific planning will take some study and analysis to avoid mistakes of the past when it was employed on too small a scale and sustained too briefly.

Civil disobedience can restore Negro-white unity. There have been some very important sane white voices even during the most desperate moments of the riots. One reason is that the urban crisis intersects the Negro crisis in the city. Many white decision makers may care little about saving Negroes, but they must care about saving their cities. The vast majority of production is created in cities; most white Americans live in them. The suburbs to which they flee cannot exist detached from cities. Hence powerful white elements have goals that merge with ours.

THE ROLE FOR THE SOCIAL SCIENTIST

Now there are many roles for social scientists in meeting these problems. Kenneth Clark has said that Negroes are moved by a suicide instinct in riots and Negroes know there is a tragic truth in this observation. Social scientists should also disclose the suicide instinct that governs the administration and Congress in their total failure to respond constructively.

What other areas are there for social scientists to assist the civil rights movement? There are many, but I would like to suggest three because they have an urgent quality.

Social science may be able to search out some answers to the problem of Negro leadership. E. Franklin Frazier, in his profound work, *Black Bourgeoisie*, laid painfully bare the tendency of the upwardly mobile Negro to separate from his community, divorce himself from responsibility to it, while failing to gain acceptance into the white community. There has been significant improvements from the days Frazier researched, but anyone knowledgeable about Negro life knows its middle class is not yet bearing its weight. Every riot has carried strong overtone of hostility of lower class Negroes toward the affluent Negro and vice versa. No contemporary study of scientific depth has totally studied this problem. Social science should be able to suggest mechanisms to create a wholesome black unity and a sense of peoplehood while the process of integration proceeds.

As one example of this gap in research, there are no studies, to my knowledge, to explain adequately the absence of Negro trade union leadership. Eighty-five per cent of Negroes are working people. Some 2,000,000 are in trade unions but in 50 years we have produced only one national leader—A. Philip Randolph.

Discrimination explains a great deal, but not everything. The picture is so dark even a few rays of light may signal a useful direction.

Political Action

The second area for scientific examination is political action. In the past two decades, Negroes have expended more effort in quest of the franchise than they have in all other campaigns combined. Demonstrations, sit-ins and marches, though more spectacular, are dwarfed by the enormous number of man-hours expended to register millions, particularly in the South. Negro organizations from extreme militant to conservative persuasion, Negro leaders who would not even talk to each other, all have been agreed on the key importance of voting. Stokely Carmichael said black power means the vote and Roy Wilkins, while saying black power means black death, also energetically sought the power of the ballot.

A recent major work by social scientists Matthew and Prothro concludes that "The concrete benefits to be derived from the franchise—under conditions that prevail in the South—have often been exaggerated", . . . that voting is not the key that will unlock the door to racial equality because "the concrete measurable payoffs from Negro voting in the South will not be revolutionary" (1966).

James A. Wilson supports this view, arguing, "Because of the structure of American politics as well as the nature of the Negro community, Negro politics will accomplish only limited objectives" (1965).

If their conclusion can be supported, then the major effort Negroes have invested in the past twenty years has been in the wrong direction and the major pillar of their hope is a pillar of sand. My own instinct is that these views are essentially erroneous, but they must be seriously examined.

The need for a penetrating massive scientific study of this subject cannot be overstated. Lipsit in 1957 asserted that a limitation in focus in political sociology has resulted in a failure of much contemporary research to consider a number of significant theoretical questions. The time is short for social science to illuminate this critically important area. If the main thrust of Negro effort has been, and remains, substantially irrelevant, we may be facing an agonizing crisis of tactical theory.

The third area for study concerns psychological and ideological changes in Negroes. It is fashionable now to be pessimistic. Undeniably, the freedom movement has encountered setbacks. Yet I still believe there are significant aspects of progress.

Negroes today are experiencing an inner transformation that is liberating them from ideological dependence on the white majority. What has penetrated substantially all strata of Negro life is the revolutionary idea that the philosophy and morals of the dominant white society are not holy or sacred but in all too many respects are degenerate and profane.

Negroes have been oppressed for centuries not merely by bonds of economic and political servitude. The worst aspect of their oppression was their inability to question and defy the fundamental precepts of the larger society. Negroes have been loath in the past to hurl any fundamental challenges because they were coerced and conditioned into thinking within the context of the dominant white ideology. This is changing and new radical trends are appearing in Negro thought. I use radical in its broad sense to refer to reaching into roots.

Ten years of struggle have sensitized and opened the Negro's eyes to reaching. For the first time in their history, Negroes have become aware of the deeper causes for the crudity and cruelty that governed white society's responses to their needs. They discovered that their plight was not a consequence of superficial prejudice but was systemic.

The slashing blows of backlash and front-lash have hurt the Negro, but they have also awakened him and revealed the nature of the oppressor. To lose illusions is to gain truth. Negroes have grown wiser and more mature and they are hearing more clearly those who are raising fundamental questions about our society whether the critics be Negro or white. When this process of awareness and independence crystallizes, every rebuke, every evasion, become hammer blows on the wedge that splits the Negro from the larger society.

Social science is needed to explain where this development is going to take us. Are we moving away, not from integration, but from the society which made it a problem in the first place? How deep and at what rate of speed is this process occurring? These are some vital questions to be answered if we are to have a clear sense of our direction.

We know we haven't found the answers to all forms of social change. We know, however, that we did find some answers. We have achieved and we are confident. We also know we are confronted now with far greater complexities and we have not yet discovered all the theory we need.

And may I say together, we must solve the problems right here in America. As I have said time and time again, Negroes still have faith in America. Black people still have faith in a dream that we will all live together as brothers in this country of plenty one day.

But I was distressed when I read in the *New York Times* [1] of August 31, 1967 that a sociologist from Michigan State University, the outgoing president of the American Sociological Society, stated in San Francisco that Negroes should be given a chance to find an all Negro community in South America: "that the valleys of the Andes Mountains would be an ideal place for American Negroes to build a second Israel." He further declared that "The United States Government should negotiate for a remote but fertile land in Equador, Peru or Bolivia for this relocation." I feel that it is rather absurd and appalling that a leading social scientist today would suggest to black people, that after all these years of suffering an exploitation as well as investment in the American dream, that we should turn around and run at this point in history. I say that we will not run! Professor Loomis even compared the relocation task of the Negro to the relocation task of the Jews in Israel. The Jews were made exiles. They did not choose to abandon Europe, they were driven out. Furthermore, Israel has a deep tradition, and Biblical roots for Jews. The Wailing Wall is a good example of these roots. They also had significant financial aid from the United States for the relocation and rebuilding effort. What tradition does the Andes, especially the valley of the Andes mountains, have for Negroes?

[1] For the complete address see: Charles P. Loomis. In Praise of Conflict and Its Resolution, *American Sociological Review,* 1967, **32**, 875–890.

And I assert at this time that once again we must reaffirm our belief in building a democratic society, in which blacks and whites can live together as brothers, where we will all come to see that integration is not a problem, but an opportunity to participate in the beauty of diversity.

The problem is deep. It is gigantic in extent, and chaotic in detail. And I do not believe that it will be solved until there is a kind of cosmic discontent enlarging in the bosoms of people of good will all over this nation.

There are certain technical words in every academic discipline which soon become stereotypes and even clichés. Every academic discipline has its technical nomenclature. You who are in the field of psychology have given us a great word. It is the word maladjusted. This word is probably used more than any other word in psychology. It is a good word; certainly it is good that in dealing with what the word implies you are declaring that destructive maladjustment should be destroyed. You are saying that all must seek the well-adjusted life in order to avoid neurotic and schizophrenic personalities.

But on the other hand, I am sure that we will recognize that there are some things in our society, some things in our world, to which we should never be adjusted. There are some things concerning which we must always be maladjusted if we are to be people of good will. We must never adjust ourselves to racial discrimination and racial segregation. We must never adjust ourselves to religious bigotry. We must never adjust ourselves to economic conditions that take necessities from the many to give luxuries to the few. We must never adjust ourselves to the madness of militarism, and the self-defeating effects of physical violence.

In a day when Sputniks, Explorers and Geminis are dashing through outer space, when guided ballistic missiles are carving highways of death through the stratosphere, no nation can finally win a war. It is no longer a choice between violence and nonviolence, it is either nonviolence or nonexistence. As President Kennedy declared, "Mankind must put an end to war, or war will put an end to mankind." And so the alternative to disarmament, the alternative to a suspension in the development and use of nuclear weapons, the alternative to strengthening the United Nations and eventually disarming the whole world, may well be a civilization plunged into the abyss of annihilation. Our earthly habitat will be transformed into an inferno that even Dante could not envision.

Creative Maladjustment

Thus, it may well be that our world is in dire need of a new organization, The International Association for the Advancement of Creative Maladjustment. Men and women should be as maladjusted as the prophet Amos, who in the midst of the injustices of his day, could cry out in words that echo across the centuries, "Let justice roll down like waters and righteousness like a mighty stream"; or as maladjusted as Abraham Lincoln, who in the midst of his vacillations finally came to see that this nation could not survive half slave and half free; or as maladjusted as Thomas Jefferson, who in the midst of an age amazingly adjusted to slavery, could scratch across the pages of history, words lifted to cosmic proportions, "We hold these truths to be self evident, that all men are created equal. That they are endowed by their creator with certain inalienable rights. And that among these are life, liberty, and the pursuit of happiness." And through such creative maladjustment, we may be able to emerge from the bleak and desolate midnight of man's inhumanity to man, into the bright and glittering daybreak of freedom and justice.

I have not lost hope. I must confess that these have been very difficult days for me personally. And these have been difficult days for every civil rights leader, for every lover of justice and peace. They have been days of frustration—days when we could not quite see where we were going, and when we often felt that our works were in vain, days when we were tempted to end up in the valley of despair. But in spite of this, I still have faith in the future, and my politics will continue to be a politic of hope. Our goal is freedom. And I somehow still believe that in spite of the so-called white backlash, we are going to get there, because however untrue it is to its destiny, the goal of America is freedom.

Abused and scorned though we may be, our destiny as a people is tied up with the destiny of America. Before the Pilgrim fathers landed at Plymouth, we were here. Before Jefferson scratched across the pages of history the great words that I just quoted, we were here. Before the beautiful words of the "Star Spangled Banner" were written, we were here. For more than two centuries, our forebears laboured here without wages. They made Cotton King. They built the home of their masters in the midst of the most humiliating and oppressive conditions.

And yet out of a bottomless vitality, they continued to grow and develop. If the inexpressable cruelties of slavery could not stop us, the opposition that we now face will surely fail. We shall win our freedom because both the sacred heritage of our nation, and the eternal will of the almighty God, are embodied in our echoing demands.

And so I can still sing, although many have stopped singing it, "We shall overcome." We shall overcome because the arch of the moral universe is long, but it bends toward justice. We shall overcome because Carlysle is right, "No lie can live forever." We shall overcome because William Cullen Bryant is right, "Truth crushed to earth will rise again." We shall overcome because James Russell Lowell is right, "Truth forever on the scaffold, wrong forever on the throne, yet that scaffold sways a future." And so with this faith, we will be able to hew out of the mountain of despair a stone of hope. We will be able to transform the jangling discords of our nation into a beautiful symphony of brotherhood. This will be a great day. This will not be the day of the white man, it will not be the day of the black man, it will be the day of man as man.

REFERENCES

Frazier, E. Franklin. *Black Bourgeoisie*. New York: Macmillan, 1962.

Lipsit, Martin. Political Sociology. In *Sociology Today*. New York: Basic Books, 1959.

Matthews, Donald R., & Prothro, James W. *Negroes and the New Southern Politics*. New York: Harcourt Brace, 1966.

Miller, S. M., & Gouldner, A. *Applied Sociology*. New York: The Free Press, 1965.

New York Times. August 31, 1967.

Wilson, James A. The Negro in Politics. *Daedalus*, Fall, 1965.

2

Black Identity and Personality

I am an invisible man. . . . It is sometimes advantageous to be unseen, although it is most often rather wearing on the nerves.

Then too, you're constantly being bumped against by those of poor vision. Or again, you often doubt if you really exist. . . . It's when you feel like that, out of resentment, you begin to bump people back. And, let me confess, you feel that way most of the time.

RALPH ELLISON, Invisible Man

INTRODUCTION

A sense of identity is a feeling of self or individuality, which is acquired through stages of development as a person interacts and compares himself with others—his family, his peer group, and the larger society. For a positive personal identity to emerge, an individual must receive at least some measure of reinforcement for and acceptance of his unique characteristics and behavior and perceive continuity in his actions and relationships.

Both the formation and stability of individual identity appear threatened by the swiftly changing values and standards of contemporary American society (Stein, Vidich, & White, 1960). Yesterday's "facts" are undermined by today's technological advances. Mass media and rapid means of transportation have expanded our consciousness and "shrunk" the world, forcing us to participate in the fate of distant lands and peoples. Modern man's great mobility often prevents him from sinking roots. Increasing awareness of the relativity and transitory nature of many of our customs and traditions has resulted in the large-scale rejection of rigidly held standards and morals. Increasing human interdependency and the anonymity fostered by bureaucratic structures have contributed to the creation of the "other-directed" personality and to feelings of powerlessness. Existential psychologists (for example,

May, 1967), psychoanalysts (for example, Erikson, 1959; Wheelis, 1958), sociologists (for example, Reisman, 1950; Seeman, 1966), theologians (for example, Tillich, 1952) and others who have addressed themselves to issues attendant upon man's search for identity have suggested that such problems represent modern man's greatest challenge.

Although anxiety and insecurity may accompany the white man's attempts to find and define himself, the black man's struggle for identity is even more arduous. No matter how hard a black individual may try to conform to the dominant culture, the color of his skin prevents him from becoming fully acceptable to large segments of the white population and, often, to himself. Baldwin (1962) asserts that "Negroes in this country . . . are taught really to despise themselves from the moment their eyes open on the world. The world is white and they're black" (p. 65). Thus, while the white person's skin color has relatively little bearing upon his emerging self-concept, black skin in a white society is a crucial factor in identity development (Dreger & Miller, 1960).

An important element of identity is an individual's group membership. As Erikson (1950) has stated, "The growing child must at every step derive a vitalizing sense of reality from the awareness that his individual way of mastering experiences . . . is a successful variant of group identity" (p. 208). Black identity obviously has a multitude of dimensions, but here we shall concentrate on specific aspects of the interplay between individual and group identity, such as racial awareness and identification, the modeling process, and feelings about the larger community.

RACIAL AWARENESS AND IDENTIFICATION

Ever since the Clarks' classical study (Clark & Clark, 1947), researchers have tried to identify the earliest signs of racial awareness and racial preference. A study by Morland [2], included in this chapter, was directed at determining North-South differences in racial self-identification between black and white nursery school children. His findings were consistent with his own previous ones and with those of other studies. White children preferred and identified with members of their own race, whereas black children tended to prefer and identify with members of the other race. Thus, it appears that American society encourages all children to develop a bias in favor of whites regardless of geographical region. The accentuation of this bias in the South is presumed by Morland to be a result of the segregated southern system, which places even more importance on being white than does the less segregated North. In a similar study, Gregor and McPherson (1966a) assessed racial attitudes of black and white children in segregated elementary schools of the deep South. They suggested that since their black subjects projected a more positive self-image than that reported in studies conducted with northern subjects, segregation may well enhance a more "viable self-system." This conclusion is questionable in view of studies reported by Dreger and Miller (in press) and Morland's findings, based on more socioeconomically comparable samples, that only 22 percent of the black children in the South as compared with 46 percent in the North preferred their own race. The results of another study (Gregor & McPherson, 1966b), however, support Gregor and McPherson's line of argument. They found that rural Bantu children in South Africa, who had little contact with whites, showed fewer signs of identity confusion than their urban peers, who were more exposed to biracial interactions. As did black children in the United States, a large majority of Bantus preferred and identified with whites, however. In view of the conflicting results more research is required to determine the influence of relatively segregated or integrated environments upon a black child's emerging self-concept. Richardson and Royce (1968), studying bases for prejudicial discrimination among slightly older American children, found evidence among white children that physical handicaps represent a more powerful stimulus to discrimination than skin color.

Morland (1963) has documented that racial bias develops early. He found that a majority of three-year-olds of both races preferred and identified with whites, even before they were able to make correct racial self-identifications.

How can these consistent and early preferences for whites be explained? The most obvious explanation is that they reflect the inferior status of black people in society. Discriminatory cues are all-pervasive in our environment, through mass media, housing, allocation of funds, and employment practices, so that direct parental communication of prejudicial beliefs might even be unnecessary for a young child to learn to assign less desirable status to black persons. Moreover, generations of slavery and discrimination have inculcated negative self-images in many black parents, who in turn pass them on to their children. Epstein and Komorita's [3] study, which is included herein, addresses itself to the role parental ethnocentrism and punitiveness play in the development of prejudice in black fifth graders. Their findings suggest that strong self-rejection may be the result of an early incorporation of white prejudices. Black children's negative feelings about their own race were associated with their perception of their parents' self-rejecting attitudes, suggesting that a black child's negative self-concept is in part learned at home. Other parental and personality factors in the child's developing self-concept will be considered in the next chapters.

The blacks' low self-esteem and the inferior position assigned to them by whites may also be related to the traditional meaning of color codes, which are frequently applied to designate racial groups. Williams [4] investigated the meaning of color names used in isolation and as adjectives in the description of people. He found that favorable ratings were assigned to "white," followed by successively more negative evaluations of "yellow," "red," "brown," and "black," by both white and black college students. As would be expected, blacks disagreed with whites, however, with respect to racial concepts. They rate Negro, for example, as good, Caucasian as relatively bad, and a brown person as "more good" than a white or black person. The white subjects' evaluations of colors, on the other hand, were consistent with their most favorable attitudes toward Caucasians, but were less favorable toward American Indians and Orientals, and least favorable toward Asiatic Indians and Negroes.

Many black leaders have recognized that their children need an early positive identification with being black. Increased efforts have taken place to reverse a negative self-image by instilling in very young children a feeling of pride in being "black and beautiful." Indeed, the change in names from "colored" to "American Negro" to "Negro American" to "Black American" or "Afro-American" must be seen as a commitment by black people to articulate a new self-image of which they can be proud (Browne, 1967). The data in Williams [4] and Caldwell, Richardson, Waage, and Dean (1969) suggests how difficult this struggle will be. The negative connotations of black in this culture ("black magic," "blacklisted," "black lies," and associations of black with evil, darkness, and so forth) and the more positive values ascribed to white ("white lie," "whitewash," associations of white with purity, goodness, light, and so forth) appear to be deeply entrenched in the greater proportion of black and white American society as well as in many other cultures. The gap between the two races is further expressed by Williams' finding that "each racial group saw its own racial designation of the other racial group as most similar to enemy and foreigner." (A study by Renninger and Williams [23] which deals with the development of racial concepts in young *white* children is included in Chapter 6.)

Measures of self-concept have been related to such variables as personality characteristics, intelligence, and achievement (for example, Bledsoe, 1964; Boyd, 1952; Combs, 1952; Dreger & Miller, in press; Gibby & Gabler, 1967; Henton & Johnson, 1964; Kardiner & Ovesey, 1951; Keller, 1963; McDonald & Gynther, 1965; Roen, 1960), but, in general, neither definite associations have emerged, nor have the cause-and-effect relationships among different variables been clarified. Coleman et al. (1966) and McGhee and Crandall (1968), on the other hand, have found that black children, who lack a sense of control over their own fate, have lower scores on achievement tests.

Relationships that may exist among dimensions of self-concept and achievement should not be thought of as unidirectional. Not only does a secure self-image enhance adjustment and achievement, but as Erikson (1950) has stated, "Ego identity gains real strength only from the whole-hearted and consistent recognition of real accomplishment, i.e., of achievement that has meaning in the culture" (p. 208). Thus, a vicious circle appears in which many Afro-Americans are ensnared. Centuries of white racism and discrimination have inflicted deep wounds upon the black man's sense of identity and worth, the consequences of which serve to impede his performance in almost all areas of endeavour. Poor performance lowers his self-esteem and appears to provide further evidence for white superiority.

Few rigorous research studies (especially of a longitudinal nature) are available to illuminate the development of the black man's identity. Social scientists (for example, Clark, 1965; Derbyshire & Brody, 1964a; Erikson, 1964, 1966; Pettigrew, 1964a; Proshansky & Newton, 1968; Rainwater, 1966) have begun to address themselves to this problem, however, and some black authors (for example, Baldwin, 1963; Brown, 1965; Cleaver, 1968; Malcolm X, 1965) have given us moving personal accounts of their own lives and feelings.

ROLE MODELS

Conflicting pressures are exerted on the growing black individual during his first identification with his subculture, whether this occurs in a middle-class or slum environment. Black leaders represent a variety of role models; their philosophies have ranged from passive submission and patience (often with religious overtones), to passive resistance, to a search for political and economic opportunities, to militant nonviolence, and finally to violent revolt. Thus, attempts to establish cohesiveness and group identity have been frustrated (Lomax, 1960; Comer, 1967). Comer has traced the historical roots of this fragmentation in the black community. (For other historical analyses see also Bronz, 1964; Fishel & Quarles, 1967; Killian, 1968; Killian & Grigg, 1964; Wish, 1964.) Comer points out that a most vicious form of slavery was practiced in America. All elements of African heritage and kinship were systematically destroyed. In addition, rivalries among slaves themselves made it impossible for them to organize effectively. Immediately after the brief reconstruction period following the Civil War, racial antagonism was at its peak and severe segregation laws were introduced and strictly enforced. There followed almost a century of discrimination and deprivation, which prevented black people from gaining political and economic power and forging a cohesive group identity. Consequently black people, although American in every way, remain among the least assimilated minorities in this country.

Derbyshire and Brody, in a series of studies (Brody, 1961, 1963; Derbyshire, 1966; Derbyshire & Brody, 1964a, 1964b, 1964c; and Derbyshire, Brody, & Schleifer, 1963) involving a variety of samples, have found indications of identity confusion in black Americans "stemming from culture conflict, caste restrictions, and minority status, mediated in part through the family structure" (Derbyshire & Brody, 1964b, p. 202).

In addition to black leaders, whites have served as role models for those large segments of the black community that perceive in their adoption of middle-class values and behaviors an escape from the stranglehold of the ghetto life and a promise that they can achieve security and respect. Maliver's study [5] raised the identification-with-the-aggressor hypothesis among black college students; that is, to what extent can black self-rejection be interpreted as reflecting identification with white aggressor attitudes toward black Americans? His hypothesis was only partially supported by his results. Students who accepted anti-Negro statements demonstrated a negative view of their fathers and a generalized fear of rejection. Rejection of anti-Negro statements, on the other hand, was associated with a positive view of the father and active involvement in the civil rights movement. Bayton, Austin, and Burke (1965) were also interested in the identification-with-the-aggressor theory. Their subjects, also black college students, assigned more positive values to whites on 6 of the 10 personality traits rated, suggesting that they perceived whites to be better adjusted than blacks. The judgments were influenced, however, by the trait being rated, the sex of the person assessed, and the sex of the rater. The authors state that their results reflect a tendency to both idealize the aggressor and incorporate negative views toward the minority group.

As the black child grows up and as pressures to interact with the white community increase, he may be confronted with a new set of values, that which characterizes the dominant middle-class society. Avenues for individual advancement, such as education, employment, and housing, are for most black Americans linked to white expectations and behavioral norms. It is not surprising, then, as we have seen in the studies reported above, that many black people incorporate negative views of their own subculture and identify with white middle-class standards. This may be particularly true of upwardly mobile Negroes, the "black bourgeoisie," as Frazier (1957) has labeled them. The next paper included in this chapter, by Parker and Kleiner [6] reports the results of intensive interviews with 1,500 black urban adults to assess the relationship between mental illness and the discrepancy between aspiration and achievement. Their findings support Frazier's thesis that the black bourgeoisie internalizes the aspirations and standards of the white middle and upper classes. High black status position was associated with acceptance of white attitudes, low preference for blue collar work, a desire for living among whites, weak involvement in racial aspects of a situation, and weak identification with the black community.

ALIENATION

To many white persons the most "acceptable" blacks are those who become "super-middle-class." This preference exacerbates the split between these blacks and those who remain segregated and impoverished. As each group has grown in number, the distance between poor blacks and those "who have made it" has increased in recent years (Moynihan, 1966). Although the black rural southerner's status has hardly improved, more black people in the North have obtained an adequate education and employment than ever before. On the other hand, living conditions in northern ghettoes, which have multiplied as a function of steady emigration of poor southern blacks and high birth rates, have deteriorated. In the process, large segments of the poor black population have become alienated not only from whites, but also from their more successful fellow blacks. Members of the black bourgeoisie who are not fully accepted by their ghetto brothers nor by the white bourgeoisie, feel alienated too, although perhaps to a lesser degree than less-educated, lower-class blacks (Middleton, 1963).

Derbyshire and Brody (1964a) discuss the black American's marginality in terms of Merton's (1957) reference group theory. Merton suggests that an individual tends to orient his values according to the normative reference group, which may consist of his membership group (for example, the black community in the case of the black person) or one to which he aspires (for example, the white middle class). Despite the fact that social advancement, in terms of educational, occupational, and financial success, is a principal feature of American culture, racial discrimination and segregation have made the black man's ascent on these dimensions very difficult relative to that of whites. Gerson (1966), for example, has found that black adolescents report that they use and depend on mass media (television, movies, books, and magazines) to a much greater extent than do whites for both norm acquisition and norm reinforcement. Gerson suggests that these results indicate that "many Negro adolescents are using mass media to learn how to behave like whites, i.e., behave in a socially acceptable way" (p. 40).

Although mass media may thus help some black people learn behavior that is rewarded in the larger society, it has also served to alienate many others who find little content that is not expressly geared to white audiences. Television could play a crucial role in presenting black heroes and black actors portraying real flesh-and-blood characters with whom black children could identify, but it obviously does not. Television programs and commercials, furthermore, feed the rage and despair of the black masses by exposing them daily to a way of life they cannot attain and which they are led to believe the typical white person enjoys. Unfortunately, there is little research evidence available that deals with the role mass media play in the identification and modeling process, despite their crucial importance in the black man's quest for identity.

By giving more black actors meaningful and substantial roles, television could also make headway toward modifying white racism; it is not only the black audience that needs a depiction of the normal black family. It is equally important for the huge majority of whites who lack interracial contact and who have formed their negative stereotypes of the Negro on the basis of old myths and crime and riot reports. The black man's accomplishments as well as his everyday life are excluded from mass media presentations, just as they are from most public-school textbooks (Dreger & Miller, in press). More and more black people are claiming their rights; they no longer want to be ignored. Chapter 7 will further examine the relationship between the black man's drive to find pride and the new militancy and black rebellion.

A final and perhaps more promising aspect of black identity is introduced by the last study included in the chapter. Bullough [7] studied alienation in two groups of well-educated black families, one living in a segregated, the other in an integrated neighborhood. She found that her integrated subjects showed fewer feelings of alienation; they expressed less powerlessness and normlessness. They also were more inclined to orient themselves toward the mainstream of society rather than toward the more limited segregated institutions of the black subculture. Bullough argues for a circular interpretation of ghetto alienation—that it not only results from ghetto living, but also keeps ghetto dwellers locked in their segregated community.

Battle and Rotter (1963) found that lower-class black children demonstrated a significantly stronger belief in external control or reinforcement than did middle-class black and white children. Works (1962) found that improvement in self-concept was more pronounced in black tenants in integrated housing than in black couples in segregated housing. Haggstrom's (1963) results suggested that black couples living in desegregated housing had significantly higher self-esteem and less hostility toward whites than matched couples living in segregated housing.

These results strengthen the demands of "traditional" civil rights leaders for complete integration and promise a more viable identity for those individuals who are able to escape from the constraints of a segregated environment. They also suggest that expecting to control one's own destiny is a result of perceiving that rewards of a particular culture are available.

PERSONALITY

Personality may be viewed as a mediator between environmental stimuli and subsequent behavior. Objective personality assessment can be helpful both in describing individual differences along a variety of measurable dimensions (hostility, flexibility, tolerance, and so forth) and in predicting the likelihood of specific behaviors (for example, a person's behavior under stress). Such measures are often difficult to find, owing to validity and reliability considerations as well as conditions of assessment.

When measures of personality are applied to black individuals, problems are further compounded. In comparing black and white subjects on a personality test, for example, should we rely on norms that are typically standardized on white middle-class samples? Will comparisons among black individuals based on white norms be meaningful? The arguments for or against a particular procedure are complex, but generally speaking, those procedures (and norms) are most appropriate which most accurately predict the specific behaviors in which we are interested.

An entire issue of the *Journal of Social Issues* was devoted to the topic of Negro personality (Pettigrew & Thompson, 1964). Pettigrew (1964b) addresses himself to the question of why we know so little about personality features of black Americans. He answers by pointing to the lack of a social-psychological theory, focus on narrow problems, and methodological difficulties that characterize previous research efforts. These problems have already been referred to in Chapter 1 and will not be further elaborated here. Pettigrew (1964a, b) and Megargee (1966) have provided reviews of personality studies including Negro-white comparisons; a recent example is included in the last paper in this chapter. Harrison and Kass [8] express surprise that so few significant and consistent differences between the two races have been found. In their study, they analyzed the Minnesota Multiphasic Personality Inventories (MMPI) of approximately 800 Negro and white pregnant women who visited an urban prenatal clinic serving the lowest socioeconomic classes exclusively. They found only minimal racial differences on conventionally scored MMPI scales. An item analysis, however, revealed striking differences between the two groups, close to half the 550 items being statistically significant. A subsequent factor analysis of the most significant items yielded 20 factors that provided even sharper distinction between the two races. The black group appeared to be relatively more anxious in their thoughts, but less anxious in social situations, less inclined to act out destructive impulses and relatively more introverted, romantic, and religious. Harrison and Kass contend that racial differences (of the order they found) may have been masked in previous studies, which have relied exclusively on scale scores rather than on item responses. Their contention was substantiated by an internal analysis, which revealed that about half the race-significant items in each scale were scored in the direction of the black group, the other in the white direction.

Cameron (1967) was interested in personality differences among black Americans, rather than in differences between whites and blacks. He employed Edwards Personal Preference Schedule (EPPS) and the Perceived Parental Attitude Inventory (PPAI), using over 800 black male and female college students, to investigate regional differences in emotional dependency. He found that the incidence of high dependency was higher among southern blacks (over 40 percent) than among northern blacks (over 22 percent) and border state students (25 percent). He suggested that these results may be "a manifestation of the effects of an oppressive culture and/or a particular child-rearing pattern" (p. 119). He pointed out that in contrast to popular opinion and studies with whites, he did not find sex differences in the incidence of overdependent behavior. As expected, however, overdependent subjects in his sample perceived their parents' discipline to be more physical and restrictive and to demand greater accomplishments than independent subjects. Comparing his results with those obtained from white subjects, Cameron suggests that his own and previous studies point to a much higher degree of emotional dependency among blacks than whites. If this is the case, it may well be a result of black Americans being forced to or choosing to act deferentially and submissively in order to get ahead or merely survive in a white-dominated society.

It is difficult to say at this point what major personality differences, if any, exist between black and white Americans. It does not appear as though we have advanced much beyond Pettigrew's evaluation in 1964. The question of why so little is known about racial differences in personality remains, although Harrison and Kass' methodological argument offers one provocative answer.

REFERENCES

Baldwin, J. Letter from a region in my mind. *New Yorker*, 1962, **38** (65).

Baldwin, J. *The fire next time*. New York: Dial, 1963.

Battle, Esther S., & Rotter, J. B. Children's feelings of personal control as related to social class and ethnic group. *Journal of Personality*, 1963, **31**, 482–490.

Bayton, J. A., Austin, J. A., & Burke, K. R. Negro perception of Negro and white personality traits. *Journal of Personality and Social Psychology*, 1965, **1**, 250–253.

Bledsoe, J. C. Self-concepts of children and their intelligence, achievement, interests, and anxiety. *Journal of Individual Psychology*, 1964, **20**, 55–58.

Boyd, G. F. The levels of aspiration of white and Negro children in a nonsegregated elementary school. *Journal of Social Psychology*, 1952, **36**, 191–196.

Brody, E. B. Social conflict and schizophrenic behavior in young adult Negro males. *Psychiatry*, 1961, **24**, 337–346.

Brody, E. B. Color and identity conflict in young boys. *Psychiatry*, 1963, **26**, 188–201.

Bronz, S. H. *Roots of Negro racial consciousness*. New York: Libra Publishers, 1964.

Brown, C. *Manchild in the promised land*. New York: Macmillan, 1965.

Browne, R. S. The case for black separation. *Ramparts*, September, 1967.

Caldwell, J. S., Richardson, D., Waage, R., & Dean, J. Semantic differential responses to "black," "white," and related verbal stimuli. Paper presented at the Western Psychological Association, Vancouver, B.C., June, 1969.

Cameron, H. A review of research and an investigation of emotional dependency among Negro youth. *The Journal of Negro Education*, 1967, **36**, 111–120.

Clark, K. B. *Dark ghetto: Dilemmas of social power.* New York: Harper & Row, 1965.

Clark, K. B., & Clark, M. K. Racial identification and preference in Negro children. In T. M. Newcomb & E. L. Hartley (Eds.), *Readings in Social Psychology*. New York: Holt, Rinehart and Winston, 1947.

Cleaver, E. *Soul on ice.* New York: Dell, 1968.

Coleman, J. S., et al. *Equality of educational opportunity.* United States Department of Health, Education and Welfare. Washington, D.C.: Government Printing Office, 1966.

Combs, A. W. Intelligence from a perceptual point of view. *Journal of Abnormal and Social Psychology*, 1952, **47**, 662–673.

Comer, J. P. The social power of the Negro. *Scientific American*, 1967, **216**, 21–27.

Derbyshire, R. L. United States Negro in conflict. *Sociology and Social Research*, 1966, **51**, 63–77.

Derbyshire, R. L., & Brody, E. B. Marginality, identity, and behavior in the Negro: a functional analysis. *The International Journal of Social Psychiatry*, 1964, **10**, 7–13. (a)

Derbyshire, R. L., & Brody, E. B. Identity and ethnocentrism in American Negro college students. *Mental Hygiene*, 1964, **48**, 202–208. (b)

Derbyshire, R. L., & Brody, E. B. Social distance and identity conflict in Negro college students. *Sociology and Social Research*, 1964, **48**, 301–314. (c)

Derbyshire, R. L., Brody, E. B., & Schliefer, C. B. Family structure of young adult Negro male mental patients: preliminary observations from urban Baltimore. *Journal of Nervous and Mental Diseases*, 1963, **136**, 245–251.

Dreger, R. M., & Miller, K. S. Comparative psychological studies of Negroes and whites in the United States. *Psychological Bulletin*, 1960, **57**, 361–402.

Dreger, R. M., & Miller, K. S. Comparative psychological studies of Negroes and whites in the United States: 1959–1965. *Psychological Bulletin*, in press.

Ellison, R. *Invisible man.* New York: Random House, 1952.

Erikson, E. H. *Childhood and society.* New York: Norton, 1950.

Erikson, E. H. Identity and the life cycle. In G. S. Klein (Ed.) *Psychological Issues*. New York: International Universities, 1959.

Erikson, E. H. Memorandum on identity and Negro youth. *Journal of Social Issues*, 1964, **20** (4), 29–42.

Erikson, E. H. The concept of identity in race relations: Notes and queries. In T. Parsons & K. B. Clark (Eds.), *The Negro American*. Boston: Houghton Mifflin, 1966.

Fishel, L. H., & Quarles, B. *The Negro American: A documented history.* Glenview, Ill.: Scott, Foresman, 1967.

Frazier, E. F. *Black bourgeoisie.* New York: Free Press, 1957.

Gerson, W. M. Mass media socialization behavior: Negro-white differences. *Social Forces*, 1966, **45**, 40–50.

Gibby, Sr. R. G., & Gabler, R. The self-concept of Negro and white children. *Journal of Clinical Psychology*, 1967, **23**, 144–148.

Gregor, A. J., & McPherson, D. A. Racial attitudes among white and Negro children in a deep-South standard metropolitan area. *Journal of Social Psychology*, 1966, **68**, 95–106. (a)

Gregor, A. J., & McPherson, D. A. Racial preference and ego-identity among white and Bantu children in the Republic of South Africa. *Genetic Psychology Monographs*, 1966, **73**, 217–253. (b)

Haggstrom, W. C. Self-esteem and other characteristics of residentially desegregated Negroes. *Dissertation Abstracts*, 1963, **23**, 3007–3008.

Henton, C. L., & Johnson, E. E. Relationship between self-concepts of Negro elementary school children and their academic achievement, intelligence, interests, and manifest anxiety. Office of Education, Washington, D.C., 1964.

Kardiner, A., & Ovesey, L. *The mark of oppression: A psychosocial study of the American Negro.* New York: Norton, 1951.

Keller, S. The social world of the urban slum child: some early findings. *American Journal of Orthopsychiatry*, 1963, **33**, 823–831.

Killian, L. M. *The impossible revolution?* New York: Random House, 1968.

Killian, L. M., & Grigg, C. M. *Racial crisis in America.* Englewood Cliffs, N.J.: Prentice-Hall, 1964.

Lomax, L. E. The Negro revolt against "the Negro leaders." *Harper's Magazine*, 1960, **220**, 41–48.

Malcolm X with the assistance of A. Haley. *The autobiography of Malcolm X.* New York: Grove, 1965.

May, R. *Psychology and the human dilemma.* Princeton, N.J.: Van Nostrand, 1967.

McDonald, R. L., & Gynther, M. D. Relationship of self and ideal-self descriptions with sex, race, and class in Southern adolescents. *Journal of Personality and Social Psychology*, 1965, **1**, 85–88.

McGhee, P. E., & Crandall, V. C. Beliefs in internal-external control of reinforcements and academic performance. *Child Development*, 1968, 91–102.

Megargee, E. I. A comparison of the scores of white and Negro male juvenile delinquents on three projective tests. *Journal of Projective Techniques and Personality Assessment*, 1966, **30**, 530–535.

Merton, R. K. *Social theory and social structure.* New York: Free Press, 1957.

Middleton, R. Alienation, race, and education. *American Sociological Review*, 1963, **2**, 120–127.

Morland, J. K. The development of racial bias in young children. *Theory Into Practice*, 1963, **2**, 120–127.

Moynihan, D. P. Employment, income, and the ordeal of the Negro family. In T. Parsons & K. B. Clark (Eds.), *The Negro American.* Boston: Houghton Mifflin, 1966.

Pettigrew, T. F. *A profile of the Negro American.* Princeton, N.J.: Van Nostrand, 1964. (a)

Pettigrew, T. F. Negro American personality: Why isn't more known? *The Journal of Social Issues*, 1964, **20**, 4–23. (b)

Pettigrew, T. F., & Thompson, D. C. (Eds.), Negro American personality. *The Journal of Social Issues*, 1964, **20**, No. 2.

Proshansky, H., & Newton, P. The nature and meaning of Negro self-identity. In M. Deutsch, I. Katz, & A. R. Jensen (Eds.), *Social class, race and psychological development.* New York: Holt, Rinehart and Winston, 1968.

Rainwater, L. Crucible of identity: the Negro lower-class family. *Daedalus*, 1966, **95**, 172–216.

Reisman, D. *The lonely crowd.* New Haven, Conn.: Yale University Press, 1950.

Richardson, S. A., & Royce, J. Race and physical handicap in children's preference for other children. *Child Development*, 1968, **39**, 467–480.

Roen, S. R. Personality and Negro-white intelligence. *Journal of Abnormal and Social Psychology*, 1960, **61**, 148–150.

Seeman, M. Status and identity: The problem of inauthenticity. *Pacific Sociological Review*, 1966, **9**, 67–73.

Stein, M., Vidich, A., & White, D. *Identity and anxiety.* New York: Free Press, 1960.

Tillich, P. *The courage to be.* New Haven, Conn.: Yale University Press, 1952.

Wheelis, A. *The quest for identity.* New York: Norton, 1958.

Wish, H. *The Negro since emancipation.* Englewood Cliffs, N.J.: Prentice-Hall, 1964.

Works, E. Residence in integrated and segregated housing and improvement in self-concepts of Negroes. *Sociology and Social Research*, 1962, **46**, 294–301.

2

*A comparison of race awareness in northern and southern children**

J. KENNETH MORLAND

Studies of race awareness in American children have shown that significant differences exist between Negroes and whites in racial recognition ability, racial preference and racial self-identification. However, it is not clear from these studies whether children vary in race awareness by region as well as by race.[†] A basic goal of the study reported in this paper is to try to clarify this question of regional variation by comparing children reared in a southern city under conditions of rigid racial segregation officially and traditionally supported with children reared in a northern city under less segregated conditions and where there is official disapproval of racial discrimination. Studies of this sort can serve a twofold purpose. They can add to our understanding of how sociocultural factors are related to the acquiring of racial attitudes, and they can be useful in knowing how to deal with such attitudes at a time when America is moving away from forced racial segregation to greater equality of treatment and opportunity for all of its citizens. The study of very young subjects offers advantages in carrying out this purpose. Young children can be assumed to reflect sociocultural factors in expressing their attitudes with a minimum of modification because of social expectations; they clearly reveal the effects on racial attitudes of varying environmental settings. Furthermore young children are the ones who presumably can benefit most from the guidance of educators, counselors and others who work with them as adjustments to changed conditions are made.[*]

SUBJECTS

The subjects for the study were children of preschool age in Lynchburg, Virginia, and Boston, Massachusetts. These two cities offered a contrast in regional environment so far as the organizing of race relations is concerned. All of the Lynchburg children were

Reprinted from the *American Journal of Orthopsychiatry*, 1966, **36**, 22–31, by permission of the author. Copyright, the American Orthopsychiatric Association, Inc. Reproduced by permission.

* Presented at the 1965 annual meeting of the American Orthopsychiatric Association, New York, New York.

† Goodman (1964) discusses conflicts in research, pp. 259–260, showing differences in her findings in the North with findings in the South.[13, 18]

* Trager and Yarrow,[19] the Ausubels,[1] and Clark,[4] and Goldberg[7] give indications of the difficulty of this adjustment so far as schools are concerned.

in racially segregated nursery schools and day-care centers. The Boston children had current or recent association with children of the other race, most from interracial nursery or playground groups. Furthermore, Lynchburg has had state and local policies of racial segregation until changed recently by federal rulings. Such changes have yet to have any effect on the nursery schools and day-care centers attended by the subjects, and indeed only token integration has taken place in other areas of community life. In contrast, the state of Massachusetts has an official commission to prevent discrimination. Special permission had to be obtained before race awareness could even be studied in Boston since there is a regulation against requiring a person to state his race. Data on the Boston children were gathered during the summer of 1961 and those on the Lynchburg children during 1962 and 1964.

The responses of 164 children are reported in this paper. The subjects were divided into four regional-racial groupings, designated as northern Negro, northern white, southern Negro, and southern white. Forty-one children matched by age * and by sex were placed in each grouping. Previous research had shown that race, age, and possibly sex † were significantly related to race awareness and therefore had to be controlled before valid regional comparisons could be made. Although no precise control of socioeconomic level was made, children of parents of varying occupations, ranging from professional and managerial to domestic and laboring, were included in each of the four groupings.‡ Also, subjects were not matched on intelligence test scores, although none of the children tested had been found by their teachers to be mentally retarded.§

---

* The actual age distribution for each grouping was six three-year-olds, sixteen four-year-olds, seven five-year-olds, and twelve six-year-olds.

† Goodman[8] found a significant difference by sex, but Springer[17] and Morland[13] did not.

‡ Previous research in Lynchburg by Morland[12, 13, 14] found little difference in responses of whites by socioeconomic status. However, no checks were made of responses of Negroes by socioeconomic status.

§ Brookover and Gottlieb[3] (pp. 34–35; 468–480) cite evidence showing that self-concept of ability is a significant variable in the learning

Since the children studied were not selected randomly from the total population of preschool children but rather were those available in certain nursery schools, day-care centers and playground groups, there is no claim that they form a representative sample in the two cities.

DATA-COLLECTION TECHNIQUES

The measuring instrument consisted of a set of six 8-by-10 black and white pictures about which questions were asked. The pictures were obtained through professional photographers and were selected by a panel of Negro and white judges who agreed that those in the pictures were readily indentifiable by race and were reasonably comparable in expression and dress. The set of pictures underwent two revisions following pretesting. Included in the version of the test employed in this research were pictures of children of both races and both sexes engaged in preschool activities, and adults of both races and both sexes. The six pictures depicted the following: five white boys and girls sitting at a table drawing pictures; five Negro boys and girls sitting at a table drawing pictures; four men, two Negro and two white, holding cokes and looking at a book; six women, three Negro and three white, sitting at a table and drinking tea; six girls, three white and three Negro, playing at a set of swings; four boys, two Negro and two white, playing on a "go-around."

Interviews were held separately and privately with each subject and lasted five to six minutes on the average. The children treated the interview as a picture game and frequently asked to look at the pictures again on subsequent days. Interviewing was done by senior sociology majors who had had a course in research methods and who were trained for the project and supervised by the author. While all of the interviewing reported in this paper was done by whites, pretesting in which

---

process. Since racial self-identification and preference can be logically related to self-concept of ability, it is conceivable that they, too, could affect learning and consequent performance on intelligence tests. Further research is needed to clarify this area.

Negroes interviewed Negro subjects showed no significant differences in the responses by race of the interviewer.*

The pictures and the interview were designed to measure four aspects of race awareness: racial acceptance, racial preference, racial self-identification and racial recognition ability. The results of each of these measures will be reported in turn.

RACIAL ACCEPTANCE

To find out how willing the subjects were to accept Negroes and whites as playmates, each was given three chances to say if he

questions. The interviewer pointed to a picture and asked the subject, "Would you like to play with this child (or these children)?" Following his response, the subject was asked, "Why?" or "Why not?" The responses of a subject were scored as "Acceptance" if he indicated a majority of times that he would like to play with the members of the race in question, "Nonacceptance" if he said most frequently he would not like to play with them for any reason other than racial, and "Rejection" if he said most often he did not want to play with them because of their race or color. Table 1 summarizes the willingness of the subjects to play with whites in the pictures. It shows that almost all of the children

TABLE 1 Acceptance of Whites by Northern and Southern Negro and White Children

Regional-Racial Grouping* (N for each = 41)	Acceptance of Whites Per Cent	Nonacceptance of Whites Per Cent	Rejection of Whites Per Cent
Northern Negro	95.1	4.9	0.0
Northern white	92.7	7.3	0.0
Southern Negro	100.0	0.0	0.0
Southern white	92.7	7.3	0.0

* Difference between any two groupings not significant at .05 level of confidence, by chi-square test.

TABLE 2 Acceptance of Negroes by Northern and Southern Negro and White Children

Regional-Racial Grouping (N for each = 41)	Acceptance of Negroes Per Cent	Nonacceptance of Negroes Per Cent	Rejection of Negroes Per Cent
Northern Negro	85.4	14.6	0.0
Northern white	87.8	12.2	0.0
Southern Negro*	92.7	7.3	0.0
Southern white	73.2	17.1	9.7

* Difference from southern white significant at .02 level of confidence, by chi-square test.

would like to play with Negro children and with white children in the pictures. He was asked if he would like to play with individuals of both sexes and with children as a group. Race or color was not mentioned in these

* However no checks were made to see if differences resulted if Negroes rather than whites interviewed white subjects.

of both races accepted the white children as playmates.

The responses for the acceptance of Negro playmates are given in Table 2. While a large majority in each grouping accepted the Negro children in the pictures, the percentages were somewhat smaller than for acceptance of whites. However, only southern whites were significantly lower in their acceptance of Negroes than in the acceptance of whites.* Southern whites were significantly lower than southern Negroes in accepting Negroes, and they alone rejected children because of their race, with almost 10 per cent rejecting Negroes for racial reasons.

RACIAL PREFERENCE

Three of the questions called for an indication of a preference between Negro and white children in the pictures. Each subject was asked if he would rather play with a group of Negro or a group of white children, with a white or a Negro boy, and with a Negro or a white girl. Again the interviewer did not mention race or color in these questions, but pointed to the picture and asked, "Would you rather play with this child (these children) or with that one (those)?" Responses were scored as "Prefer Own Race," "Prefer Other Race," or "Preference Not Clear," depending on the subject's most frequent response. The responses, summarized in Table 3, revealed that a majority of sub-

TABLE 3 Racial Preference of Northern and Southern Negro and White Children

Regional-Racial Grouping (N for each = 41)	Prefer Own Race Per Cent	Prefer Other Race, or Preference Not Clear Per Cent
Northern Negro*	46.3	53.7
Northern white†	68.3	31.7
Southern Negro‡	22.0	78.0
Southern white§	80.5	19.5

* Difference from northern white significant at .05 level of confidence, from southern Negro at .02 level, from southern white at .01 level, by chi-square test.
† Difference from northern Negro significant at .05 level, from southern Negro at .001 level.
‡ Difference from northern Negro significant at .02 level, from northern white and from southern white at .001 level.
§ Difference from northern Negro significant at .01 level, from southern Negro at .001 level.

jects in each of the four groupings preferred whites. Southern Negro subjects were least likely and southern whites most likely to pre-

* Chi-square = 5.51, p < .02.

fer members of their own race. It is to be noted that preference for one race, however, did not mean rejection of the other race, for the great majority in the four groupings accepted members of both races when no choice was required, as has already been seen in Tables 1 and 2.*

RACIAL SELF-IDENTIFICATION

Three measures were made of the subject's racial self-identification. One measure was based on the response to a question asking which of the children in the picture composed of Negroes and whites of his own sex the subject looked most like. Once again the interviewer pointed to the picture and did not use racial terms. Table 4 summarizes the

TABLE 4 Responses of Northern and Southern Negro and White Children to the Question, "Which child do you look most like?"

Regional-Racial Grouping (N for each = 41)	Most Like Child of Own Race Per Cent	Most Like Child Other Race, or Not Sure Per Cent
Northern Negro*	51.2	48.8
Northern white†	73.2	26.8
Southern Negro‡	58.5	41.5
Southern white§	82.9	17.1

* Difference from northern and from southern whites significant at .05 level of confidence, by chi-square test.
† Difference from northern Negro significant at .05 level.
‡ Difference from southern white significant at .02 level.
§ Difference from northern and from southern Negroes significant at .02 level.

answers and shows that white subjects were more likely to say they looked like one of the white children than the Negro subjects were to say that they looked like one of the Negro children.

A second question dealing with self-identification asked which of the children in the picture of Negroes and whites of the subject's

* This is in accord with an earlier report on southern children by Morland[12] and questions an interpretation by the Clarks[5] and Horowitz[10] who assumed that preference for whites implied rejection of Negroes.

sex he would rather be. Without mentioning race or color, the interviewer pointed to the picture and asked, "Which child would you rather be?" Table 5 indicates a significant

TABLE 5 Responses of Northern and Southern Negro and White Children to the Question, "Which child would you rather be?"

Regional-Racial Grouping (N for each = 41)	Rather Be Child of Own Race Per Cent	Rather Be Child of Other Race, or Not Sure Per Cent
Northern Negro*	56.1	43.9
Northern white†	78.0	22.0
Southern Negro‡	43.9	56.1
Southern white†	78.0	22.0

* Difference from northern and from southern whites significant at .05 level of confidence, by chi-square test.
† Difference from northern Negro significant at .05 level, from southern Negro at .01 level.
‡ Difference from northern and southern whites significant at .01 level.

difference between the responses of Negro and white subjects regardless of the region. More than three-fourths of both northern and southern whites responded that they would rather be one of the white children in the pictures, while only about one-half of the Negro children stated that they would rather be one of the Negro children. In other words, whites were more likely to identify with a child of their race than Negroes were to identify with a child of their race.

The third measure of racial self-identification sought to find out whether the subjects would identify their mothers as one of the Negro or one of the white women in the picture of six women. The subject was shown this picture and asked, "Which one looks most like your mother?" White subjects were more likely than Negro subjects to identify their mothers with one of the women of their own race, as Table 6 reveals. While there were significant differences between the races in each region, identification with whites was more likely among the Lynchburg than among the Boston children. More than nine out of ten southern white subjects stated that their mothers looked most like one of the white women, while fewer than three out of ten southern Negro subjects stated that their

mothers looked most like one of the Negro women.

TABLE 6 Responses of Northern and Southern Negro and White Children to the Question: "Which one looks most like your mother?"

Regional-Racial Grouping (N for each = 41)	Looks Most Like Woman of Own Race Per Cent	Looks Most Like Woman of Other Race, or Not Sure Per Cent
Northern Negro*	46.3	53.7
Northern white†	68.3	31.7
Southern Negro‡	26.8	73.2
Southern white§	90.2	9.8

* Difference from northern white significant at .05 level of confidence, from southern white at .001 level, by chi-square test.
† Difference from northern Negro significant at .05 level, from southern Negro at .001 level, from southern white at .02 level, by chi-square test.
‡ Difference from northern and from southern whites significant at .001 level.
§ Difference from northern and from southern Negroes significant at .001 level, from northern white at .02 level.

RACIAL RECOGNITION ABILITY

A final measure reported in this paper concerns the ability of the subjects to designate correctly the race of those in the pictures. After questions regarding acceptance, preference and self-identification had been asked, the pictures were shown again, and for each one the subject was asked, "Do you see a white person in this picture?" If the child said he did, he then was asked to point to the white person. For the same picture the child next was asked, "Do you see a colored person in this picture?" * Again, if the child replied affirmatively, he was asked to point to the colored person. This gave 12 chances, two for each of the six pictures, for the subject to identify Negro and white children and adults of both sexes. If the respondent answered correctly for all 12, or if he missed

* The term "colored" was used because pretesting had shown that children both in Lynchburg and in Boston were more familiar with this designation of the races than they were with the term "Negro." The Clarks[5] found this to be the case also with the children they studied.

only one, he was scored "High." If he missed more than one, he was scored "Low."* The responses, summarized in Table 7, showed

TABLE 7 Racial Recognition Ability of Northern and Southern Negro and White Children

Regional-Racial Grouping (N for each = 41)	High Ability Per Cent	Low Ability Per Cent
Northern Negro	46.3	53.7
Northern white	39.0	61.0
Southern Negro	39.0	61.0
Southern white*	73.2	26.8

* Difference from northern Negro significant at .02 level of confidence, from northern white and from southern Negro at .01 level of confidence, by chi-square test.

that southern white subjects had significantly higher ability to make racial distinctions than any of the other groupings. Although almost three-fourths of the southern whites scored high, less than one-half of those in the other three groupings scored high. Further analysis of recognition ability by age indicated that proportionately more southern whites than subjects in other groupings scored high in each age category. However, the greatest differences were found at the ages of four and five, particularly at age four.†

CONCLUSIONS

In general the research on the Boston and Lynchburg children supported previous findings that American Negro and white children of preschool age differ in race awareness, and that these differences between Negro and white hold across regional lines. Thus northern and southern Negro subjects differed significantly on only one of the seven measures, namely racial preference. Northern and southern whites differed significantly on only two, racial recognition ability and identifica-

* This cutting-point was derived from an earlier study in which the validity and reliability of the racial recognition ability were tested. Morland,[13] p. 134.

† See the discussion of these differences as they apply to southern Negro and white children in an earlier study by the author (Morland,[13] pp. 134–135).

tion of mother. In contrast, southern whites differed significantly from southern Negroes on six of the seven measures, while northern whites differed significantly from northern Negroes on four. The direction of the differences was that the white subjects in both regions tended to prefer and identify with members of their own race, while Negro subjects in the two regions tended to prefer and to identify with members of the other race. This can be interpreted to mean that regardless of the region the overall effect of American society on very young children has been to influence them to develop a bias for whites.* In other words, American society as it now operates teaches that racial differences are very important and that being white is preferable to being Negro. Under such conditions young Negro children probably unconsciously† learn to prefer and identify with the dominant race.

There are some regional variations, however, for the differences between white and Negro appear to be accentuated in the southern subjects. In the measure of racial preference in which there was a significant difference between northern and southern Negro subjects, southern Negroes were more likely to prefer whites. In the two differences between the white groupings, southern whites were more likely than northern whites to identify their mothers as white and to have high racial recognition ability.

These regional variations, while not extensive, can be logically accounted for by the sociocultural explanation of the development of the perception of race. The segregated southern system can be assumed to place an even greater importance on being white than does the less segregated northern system. Thus the southern white subjects were somewhat more likely than the northern whites to acquire a bias for whites and to develop racial recognition ability earlier. The southern Negro subjects, on the other hand, were more likely than the northern Negro to prefer the dominant race. This comparison suggests that the southern children may have a greater problem of adjustment as the nation moves

* The term "bias" is preferred to "prejudice" as explained in the author's earlier reports (Morland[11, 12]).

† In previous reports the author showed that bias for whites developed before racial recognition ability. See Morland,[12] pp. 277, 279–280.

toward the elimination of overt forms of racial discrimination. The southern white subjects evidenced such strong racial bias that reactions toward Negroes as persons, on a basis of equality, will probably not be easy.* For the southern Negro subjects the realization of their correct racial membership and their actual low position in the social order can be traumatic. Such an assumption is in accord with findings from studies of personality traits in Negroes which have indicated that the southern caste system has a more detrimental effect on Negroes than has the northern system.†

The results of this study on race awareness in young children suggest that as the sociocultural milieu in America changes, such awareness will change. There is little question that the structure of race relations throughout the United States is being altered by state and federal legislation, court rulings and the insistence of racial minorities on equal treatment. The elimination of forced racial segregation and the opening of educational and occupational opportunities according to ability will make for more association on the basis of equality between the races. Also, as mass media begin to include all races in advertisements, dramatic performances and the like on the same basis, a new image of Negroes in American society should emerge. It would be instructive to repeat the measurements of this study in another 10 years or so to see if racial preference, self-identification and recognition ability have changed along with the expected changes in the organization of race relations.

The results of studies of race awareness in young children also suggest certain kinds of teaching that might have an effect on racial attitudes. The American social system implies that race is of fundamental importance in judging the worth of a person. In spite of changes taking place, this situation probably will continue for some time. However, scientific studies indicate that race in and of itself is not related to the intelligence, character, or creativity of the individual.* Furthermore, cross-cultural studies show that the unity of a people lies in the sharing of values, ideals, and norms rather than in racial similarity. As American children begin to move more freely across racial lines, accurate information † about race and race differences should enable them to move more easily than if they are burdened with notions of racial superiority and inferiority. Controlled experiments on the effect of accurate information on racial attitudes are needed to guide the development of teaching in this area. The author is convinced from his own experience that teaching of facts about race can affect the attitudes and behavior of Negro and white college students. However, systematic research is required before the effectiveness of such teaching can clearly be determined. We are reminded from other research that information alone is not a sufficient condition to change attitudes (although the author is convinced that in the case of racial attitudes it is a necessary condition). If attitudes are to be affected, behavior itself also must be changed. In their experiment with young children in Philadelphia, Trager and Yarrow[19] concluded that democratic attitudes must be specially taught and practiced if they are to be learned. If such teaching and practice are combined with the changes already taking place in the larger sociocultural milieu, it can be expected that American children will be less likely to develop racial biases that handicap them in a democratic society.

REFERENCES

1. Ausubel, D. P., & P. Ausubel. 1963. Ego development among segregated Negro children. *In* Education in Depressed Areas. A. H. Passow, Ed. Teachers College, Columbia University, New York. pp. 109–141.
2. Bibby, C. 1959. Race, Prejudice and Education. Wm. Heineman, Ltd., London.

---

* In a psychiatric study of the effects of racial integration in public schools on white and Negro high school youth in Atlanta and New Orleans, Coles[6] revealed how difficult the adjustment is, particularly for some whites.

† Pettigrew[16] gives a recent summary of these studies, pp. 34–37. Karon's investigation[9] is particularly pertinent here.

* See the discussion in Pettigrew,[16] especially Chapter five. Brief reference is made in Morland,[15] pp. 24–25.

† In a clear, readable and anthropologically sound book Bibby[2] presents ways in which teachers can handle the question of race and race differences in their classrooms.

3. Brookover, W. B., & D. Gottlieb. 1964. A Sociology of Education, Revised Edition. American Book Company, New York.

4. Clark, K. B. 1963. Educational Stimulation of Racially Disadvantaged Children. *In* Education in Depressed Areas. A. H. Passow, Ed. Teachers College, Columbia University. New York. pp. 142–162.

5. Clark, K. B., & M. P. Clark. 1947. Racial Identification and Preference in Negro Children. *In* Readings in Social Psychology. T. M. Newcombe and E. L. Hartley, Eds. Holt. New York. pp. 169–178.

6. Coles, R. 1963. The Desegregation of Southern Schools: A Psychiatric Study. Anti-Defamation League of B'nai B'rith, New York, and the Southern Regional Council, Atlanta.

7. Goldberg, M. L. 1963. Factors Affecting Educational Attainment in Depressed Areas. *In* Education in Depressed Areas. A. H. Passow, ed. Teachers College, Columbia University. New York. pp. 68–99.

8. Goodman, M. E. 1964. Race Awareness in Young Children. Revised Edition. Collier Books. New York.

9. Karon, B. P. 1958. The Negro Personality. Springer Publishing Company, New York.

10. Horowitz, E. L. 1936. The development of attitude toward the Negro. Arch. Psychol. **28,** (194).

11. Morland, J. K. 1963. The Development of Racial Bias in Young Children. Theory Into Practice. **2**(3): 120–127.

12. Morland, J. K. 1962. Racial acceptance and preference of nursery school children in a southern city. Merrill-Palmer Quarterly of Behavior and Development. **8**(4): 271–280.

13. Morland, J. K. 1958. Racial recognition by nursery school children in Lynchburg, Virginia. Social Forces. **37**(2): 132–137.

14. Morland, J. K. 1963. Racial self-identification: a study of nursery school children. The American Catholic Sociological Review. **24**(Fall): 231–242.

15. Morland, J. K. 1963. Southern Schools: Token Desegregation and Beyond. Anti-Defamation League of B'nai B'rith, New York, and the Southern Regional Council, Atlanta.

16. Pettigrew, T. F. 1964. A Profile of the Negro American. D. Van Nostrand Company, Princeton, N.J.

17. Springer, D. 1950. Awareness of racial differences by pre-school children in Hawaii. Genetic Psychology Monographs. **41:** 215–270.

18. Stevenson, H. W., & E. C. Stewart. 1958. A developmental study of racial awareness in young children. Child Development. **29:** 399–409.

19. Trager, H. G., & M. R. Yarrow. 1952. They Learn What They Live: Prejudice in Young Children. Harper, New York.

3

Prejudice among Negro children as related to parental ethnocentrism and punitiveness

RALPH EPSTEIN AND S. S. KOMORITA*

The scapegoat hypothesis has dominated contemporary research literature on the origins of childhood ethnocentrism. This hypothesis maintains that severe discipline directed towards aggression may increase the instigation to aggress, and that anticipation of punishment for aggression directed towards the ingroup results in displacement from the original sources of frustration to outgroups. In order to clarify contradictory results related to this hypothesis (Masling, 1954; Miller & Bugelski, 1948; Stagner & Congdon, 1955), the authors conducted a series of investigations designed to evaluate the influence of two major variables upon displacement: child-rearing practices and stimulus characteristics of outgroups (Epstein & Komorita, 1965b, 1966). Although these studies demonstrated the significance of both variables, the results failed to support the displacement hypothesis. With regard to child-rearing practices, our earlier results suggested that moderate rather than severe discipline appears most conducive to the development of ethnocentric attitudes. Later findings replicated this result and suggested that both moderate discipline and high parental ethnocentrism

Reprinted from *Journal of Personality and Social Psychology,* 1966, 3(5), 574–579, by permission of the authors and the American Psychological Association.

* The authors are grateful to Maurice Lax, principal, and the teachers of the Goldberg School, Detroit, who cooperated in this study.

were most conducive to the formation of childhood prejudice. These results were conceptualized in terms of identification theory (Sears, Maccoby, & Levin, 1957). It was proposed that a major consequence of moderate discipline is to orient the child towards obtaining parental approval and to reduce doubt regarding approval by internalizing parental attitudes. With regard to perceived characteristics of outgroups, working-class status greatly accentuated prejudice towards the Negro as compared with the white group. Middle-class status served to minimize differential attitudes as a function of ethnic affiliation.

The purpose of the present study was to replicate these provocative findings on a non-white population, namely, Negro children. Although the sparsity of systematic research on the ethnic attitudes of minority groups is striking, the available research consistently suggests that members of such groups adopt the ethnic attitudes of the majority culture (Hartley, 1946). Evidence for feelings of self-derogation and rejection among Negro children was provided in studies by Clark (1963), Radke and Trager (1950), and Stevenson and Stewart (1958). Although the prevalence of anti-Negro attitudes among Negro children has received some support, the correlates of these attitudes have remained unexplored.

It is hypothesized in this study that the development of prejudicial attitudes among Negro children is a function of those social learning conditions previously reported by the authors as conducive to the development of similar attitudes in white children, namely, parental ethnocentrism and moderate parental punitiveness. A first-order interaction between these variables is predicted whereby high parental ethnocentrism and moderate discipline will be associated with prejudice in the Negro child.

METHOD

Subjects

The sample consisted of 120 Negro boys and girls who comprised the fifth grade in an elementary school in Detroit, Michigan. This school serves children whose socioeconomic background, as determined by residential area, is working class.

Measure of Parental Punitiveness

The Parental Punitiveness Scale (PPS) was developed by the authors to measure children's perceptions of parental punitiveness towards aggression. A detailed description of the development of this scale is reported elsewhere (Epstein & Komorita, 1965a). Briefly, the scale consists of 45 items which measure parental punitiveness towards physical, verbal, and indirect aggression in each of five major situations: aggression towards parents, teachers, siblings, peers, and inanimate objects. The scale is scorable separately for fathers' and mothers' responses to aggression. However, since the correlation coefficient between fathers' and mothers' versions was found to be .60, the two scores were pooled to yield a single average punitiveness score. The split-half reliability of this average punitive score, with the Spearman-Brown correction, was .81.

Experimental Conditions

Three independent variables were used: (*a*) parental punitiveness towards aggression —high, medium, and low as determined by scores on the PPS, (*b*) race of target group— Negro versus white, and (*c*) socioeconomic class of target group—working versus middle class. Thus, a 3×2×2 factorial design was employed with 10 subjects in each of the 12 experimental conditions.

The basic purpose of the experimental conditions was to create specific cognitions regarding a fictitious group, the "Piraneans." A fictitious group was used to minimize subjects' awareness of the purpose of the study and thereby facilitate nondefensive responding. Accordingly, subjects were presented slides which depicted Piraneans as either middle or working class, and Negro or white. Race of Piraneans was varied by presenting slides of four Negro or white children, two boys and two girls each, who were representative of the subjects' age range. Socioeconomic class was varied by presenting slides depicting residence and working place of Piraneans. For example, the "working-class" slides depicted scenes of a ramshackle house, deteriorated slum streets, and street construction, whereas the "middle-class" slides depicted a new split-level home, suburban streets, and a modern office building.

Prior to the group administration of the slides, the following instructions were given: "There is a group of people whom most of you have never seen. As a matter of fact, you have probably never heard of this group. They are called Piraneans. Would you like to see some slides of the Piraneans?" After viewing the slides, subjects completed a 7-item social distance scale with regard to Piraneans. These items ranged from "would you want to marry these people when you grow up?" (minimal) to "would you want these people to visit your country?" (maximal). Each item could be answered by checking one of four alternatives ranging from "very much yes" to "very much no."

In order to minimize the potentially confounding factors of differential clarity and brightness, the slides were matched as closely as possible in terms of these variables. The "low socioeconomic" slides were based on scenes within Detroit slums, whereas the "middle socioeconomic" slides were based on photos of suburban areas. Postexperimental interviews with a sample of subjects indicated that very few were able to state the specific locale of the slides, although several subjects believed that the photos were taken within the United States.

In order to determine the children's attitudes towards nonfictional groups, ratings of the following groups were obtained after the experimental sessions: Chinese, German, French, Catholic, Italian, Mexican, Negro,

Japanese, Jewish, and Russian. Social distance scores for each of these groups were then pooled to obtain a measure of generalized social distance. Three weeks later, subjects were requested to indicate how they thought their *parents* would rate these same groups on the social distance scales. Thus, a measure of the parents' social distance attitudes, as perceived by the child, was obtained as well.

RESULTS

For the purpose of intergroup comparisons, Table 1 summarizes the means and standard deviations of the social distance scores for the 12 experimental groups.

TABLE 1 Means and Standard Deviations of Piranean Social Distance Scores for Experimental Groups

Parental Punitive-ness	Negro		White		$\overline{X}$
	Work-ing Class	Mid-dle Class	Work-ing Class	Mid-dle Class	SD
High	17.7 (6.07)	16.2 (5.46)	12.7 (2.93)	12.6 (5.29)	14.80
Medium	16.4 (4.92)	14.8 (3.66)	15.8 (7.18)	12.9 (5.75)	14.98
Low	14.1 (4.28)	14.6 (1.62)	11.5 (2.69)	15.7 (7.48)	13.98
Mean social distance	Negro: 15.63 Working class: 14.70		White: 13.53 Middle class: 14.47		

Note. Standard deviations are enclosed in parentheses.

An analysis of variance of these scores indicated that the main effects for parental punitiveness and social class were not significant. However, the main effect for race was significant at the .05 level ($F = 4.61$, $df = 1$, 108), indicating that subjects manifested greater social distance toward the Negro ($\overline{X} = 15.63$) than white Piraneans ($\overline{X} = 13.53$). None of the interactions were significant.

In order to delineate further the antecedents of social distance, the subjects' Piranean social distance scores for each experimental condition were correlated with (a) subjects' generalized social distance attitudes towards the nonfictional groups (omitting Ne-

gro in the summation score), and (b) parental social distance, as measured by children's reports of parental attitudes towards the nonfictional groups. The correlation coefficients are shown in Table 2.

TABLE 2 Correlation Coefficients between Children's Social Distance towards Piraneans and Children's and Parental Generalized Social Distance[a]

Piranean Conditions	Generalized Social Distance	
	Children	Parental
White		
Middle class	.62**	.46**
Working class	.65**	.51**
Negro		
Middle class	.49**	.40*
Working class	.75**	.67**

[a] Sample size was 30 for experimental groups combined over three levels of PPS.
 * $p < .05$.
** $p < .01$.

The correlations in Table 2 are consistently positive as well as substantially significant, and with 28 degrees of freedom all of these correlations with parental social distance attitudes are significant at the .01 or .05 level. It is apparent that a highly significant proportion of the variance of children's social distance towards a fictitious group can be accounted for by their perception of parental prejudice. Furthermore, Table 2 indicates that social distance towards a fictitious group is highly correlated with the child's generalized social distance. Furthermore, the significant role of a generalized response set toward acceptance or rejection of other groups upon self-acceptance in Negro children is indicated by a correlation of .46 between subjects' social ratings of Negro and their generalized social distance ratings. This correlation, based on $df = 118$, is significant at the .01 level.

With regard to children's generalized social distance attitudes as a dependent variable, the correlation between children's and perceived parental social distance attitudes was .73, and with $df = 118$ this is significant at the .01 level. The correlation between children's generalized social distance and perceived parental punitiveness was only .12. However, since earlier research suggested that this relationship is nonlinear and that there might be an interaction between parental punitiveness and parental social distance attitudes upon children's prejudice, the data were cast into a 3 × 3 factorial design with 3 levels of parental punitiveness and parental generalized social distance. The 9 cell frequencies ranged from 10 to 18, and an unweighted-means analysis of variance resulted in a significant main effect for parental social distance ($F = 39.42$, $df = 2, 111$, $p < .001$). This result reflects the previously reported positive relationship between parental and children's generalized social distance. In order to evaluate the influence of parental attitudes upon subjects' attitudes towards their own ethnic group, a correlation between parental and subjects' social distance attitudes towards Negro was computed. The resulting correlation of .62, based on $df = 118$, is significant at the .01 level. These findings suggest that the Negro child's social distance attitudes towards both other minority groups as well as his own are influenced by parental attitudes. Further research is necessary to evaluate the alternative possibility that prejudiced children may attribute prejudicial attitudes to their parents.

The main effect for parental punitiveness, as well as the interaction between punitiveness and ethnocentrism, failed to achieve significance at the .05 level. However, it is interesting to note that the differences between means reflect a trend which is consistent with earlier findings (Epstein & Komorita, 1966); that is, given a high level of parental ethnocentrism, moderately disciplined children manifested stronger social distance attitudes ($\overline{X} = 203.82$) than weakly ($\overline{X} = 187.47$) or severely disciplined (181.50) children. On the other hand, differential social distance as a function of discipline level was minimal for both low and moderate parental social distance groups.

DISCUSSION

A primary finding in this study is that among Negro children social distance attitudes are directed towards a fictitious group depicted as having the same racial characteristics as the subjects. These results are consistent with previous investigations (Clark, 1963; Hartley, 1946), which indicated that Negro elementary school children, residing in a northern urban community, adopted the prevailing prejudices of the white majority.

Furthermore, the correlational data suggest that social distance attitudes towards one's own groups, for example, Negro, as well as towards fictitional groups, for example, Piraneans, are significantly related to a generalized personality predisposition or response set which involves the rejection of people in general. Thus, prejudice towards a specific group may be viewed as a manifestation of a generalized misanthropy which encompasses multiple groups (Hartley, 1946). This conclusion is related to a major controversy within the area of intergroup relations, namely, the development of in- and outgroup distinctions in the development of ethnic attitudes. It has been assumed that a strong identification with the ingroup is conducive to the development of hostile attitudes towards the outgroup (Adorno, Frenkel-Brunswik, Levinson, & Sanford, 1950). Also, the perception of outgroups as threatening and the subsequent arousal of hostility towards such groups may intensify altruistic attitudes towards members of the ingroup (Campbell, 1965). However, our finding of a significant relationship between social distance towards Negroes and generalized social distance attitudes across groups is consistent with the alternative position, elaborated by Buss (1961), that prejudicial or self-rejecting attitudes reflect a generalized hostile predisposition or set of habits which may be elicited by both in- and outgroups.

Insofar as the significant relationship between parents' generalized social distance and subjects' generalized social distance attitudes is based on correlational data, assumptions regarding the direction of causality should be viewed as tentative. However, these findings are consistent with a social learning theory which focuses on the role of imitative processes in the development of ethnic attitudes. This conceptualization is consonant with recent investigations which demonstrated that children's prejudices may reflect parental attitudes. For example, Anisfeld, Munoz, and Lambert (1963) reported a strong relationship between the ethnocentric attitudes of Jewish children and those of their parents. Mosher and Scodel (1960) reported a similar relationship in a middle-class Protestant population.

Although previous research (Epstein, 1966; Epstein & Komorita, 1965b) suggested that, among white subjects, social distance attitudes towards Negroes are determined to a large extent by the group's perceived inferior social status, the current research suggests that the Negro child's low self-esteem is based less on socioeconomic than on racial factors. This suggests that the Negro's perception of dark skin color as the basis for the white person's hostility may be discrepant from the basis employed by many whites, namely, the Negro's social status. These discrepant perceptions may be attributed to the possibility that the more concrete quality of the concept, skin color, relative to socioeconomic status may facilitate the acceptance of the former concept by the working-class Negro child as the basis for his rejection. In addition, relating the majority group's hostility to one's skin color is consistent with an external orientation in which negative reinforcements are attributed to chance, fate, and other events beyond personal control (Lefcourt & Ladwig, 1965).

REFERENCES

Adorno, T. W., Frenkel-Brunswik, E., Levinson, D. J., & Sanford, R. N. *The authoritarian personality*. New York: Harper, 1950.

Anisfeld, M., Munoz, S. R., & Lambert, W. E. The structure and dynamics of the ethnic attitudes of Jewish adolescents. *Journal of Abnormal and Social Psychology*, 1963, **66**, 31–36.

Buss, A. *The psychology of aggression*. New York: Wiley, 1961.

Campbell, D. T. Ethnocentric and other altruistic motives. In D. Levine (Ed.), *Nebraska symposium on motivation: 1965*. Lincoln: University of Nebraska Press, 1965. Pp. 283–312.

Clark, K. B. *Prejudice and your child*. Boston: Beacon Press, 1963.

Epstein, R. Aggression toward outgroups as a function of authoritarianism and imitation of aggressive models. *Journal of Personality and Social Psychology*, 1966, **3**, 574–579.

Epstein, R., & Komorita, S. S. The development of a scale of parental punitiveness towards aggression. *Child Development*, 1965, **36**, 129–142. (a)

Epstein, R., & Komorita, S. S. Parental discipline, stimulus characteristics of outgroups, and social distance in children. *Journal of Personality and Social Psychology*, 1965, **2**, 416–419. (b)

Epstein, R., & Komorita, S. S. Childhood prejudice as a function of parental ethnocentrism, punitiveness, and outgroup characteristics. *Journal of Personality and Social Psychology*, 1966, **3**, 259–264.

Hartley, E. L. *Problems in prejudice*. New York: Kings Crown Press, 1946.

Lefcourt, H. M., & Ladwig, G. W. The American Negro: A problem in expectancies. *Journal of Personality and Social Psychology*, 1965, **1**, 377–380.

Masling, J. M. How neurotic is the authoritarian? *Journal of Abnormal and Social Psychology*, 1954, **49**, 316–318.

Miller, N. E., & Bugelski, R. Minor studies in aggression: The influence of frustrations imposed by the in-group on attitudes expressed toward out-groups. *Journal of Psychology*, 1948, **25**, 436–442.

Mosher, D. L., & Scodel, A. A study of the relationship between ethnocentrism in children and the ethnocentrism and authoritarian rearing practices of their mothers. *Child Development*, 1960, **31**, 369–376.

Radke, M., & Trager, H. G. Children's perceptions of the serial roles of Negroes and whites. *Journal of Psychology*, 1950, **29**, 3–33.

Sears, R. R., Maccoby, E. G., & Levin, H. *Patterns of child-rearing*. Evanston, Ill.: Row, Peterson, 1957.

Stagner, R., & Congdon, C. S. Another failure to demonstrate displacement of aggression. *Journal of Abnormal and Social Psychology*, 1955, **51**, 695–696.

Stevenson, H. W., & Stewart, E. C. A developmental study of racial awareness in young children. *Child Development*, 1958, **29**, 399–409.

4

Connotations of racial concepts and color names[1]

JOHN E. WILLIAMS

Language custom designates racial groups according to a "color code" in which Caucasians are called white, Negroes are referred to as black, and Orientals, American Indians, and Southwest Asians are designated, respectively, as yellow, red, and brown. On reflection, it is obvious that this color code has little descriptive accuracy with regard to skin color; Caucasians are not literally "white," nor is the modal American Negro "black," and yet, applications of this color nomenclature are encountered daily, for example, in popular press accounts of racial problems or incidents. Although admittedly convenient, and seemingly innocuous, the practice of color coding may have hidden and, perhaps, undesirable effects since color names such as white and black are regularly used in other contexts as general cultural symbols to convey different connotative meanings such as goodness and badness (Williams, 1964). The present study was concerned with the question of whether the color-coding practice is related to the way in which different racial groups are perceived.

In an earlier investigation, Williams

Reprinted from *Journal of Personality and Social Psychology,* 1965, **3**, 531–540, by permission of the author and the American Psychological Association.

[1] This research was supported, in part, by a grant from the Wake Forest College Graduate Council. The author is grateful to Lafayette Parker and Jefferson Humphrey of Winston-Salem State College, to Bertram Spiller of Washburn University, and to Jack Hicks, formerly of Washburn University, for their assistance in data collection.

(1964) studied the connotative meanings of color names presented in a nonracial context. It was demonstrated that there are striking differences in the connotative meanings of color names and that these meanings are relatively stable across both regional and racial lines. For example, the connotative meaning of the color name *white* was found to be "good," "active," and "weak," while the color name *black* was "bad," "passive," and "strong." Since it is known that the connotative meanings of words can be classically conditioned to other words (Staats & Staats, 1957, 1958), it seemed likely that the consistent association of a color name, such as *black*, with a racial concept, such as *Negro*, would tend to condition the connotations of the former to the latter. In this way, the practice of color coding might operate as a background factor in the development and/or maintenance of attitudes toward racial groups.

One way to observe the effects of using color names to designate groups of persons would be to study the meaning similarity between color names, as such, and color names used as adjectives to describe people. For example, is there a similarity in the connotative meanings of the concepts *black* and *black person*? One might also study color-person concepts in relation to color-code related ethnic concepts (e.g., *black person* and *Negro*) and observe the degree of connotative meaning similarity. In a third type of comparison, one might study the meaning similarity of ethnic names (e.g., *Negro, Caucasian*) to the color names with which the color code associates them.

The general hypothesis for this study was that similarities in connotative meaning will be found to be greater among concepts which are linked by the color code than among concepts not so related. Although no specific predictions were made, it was anticipated that Caucasian subjects and Negro subjects might differ in their ratings of the racially significant concepts of the present study, in spite of their generally similar performance in rating color names in the earlier study (Williams, 1964).

METHOD

This study was an extension of Williams' (1964) earlier study of the connotative meanings of color names, with the same subject populations and data gathering procedures being employed. The reader is referred to the earlier study for a more detailed description of materials and procedures.

Subjects

Subjects were introductory psychology students from three institutions: Caucasian [2] students from Wake Forest College, a liberal arts college in North Carolina; Caucasian students from Washburn University, a municipal university in Kansas; and Negro students from Winston-Salem State College, a liberal arts college in North Carolina. The numbers of subjects from each institution rating the color-person concepts were, respectively, 86, 88, and 106. The numbers rating the ethnic-national concepts were 110, 70, and 60. In the two Caucasian groups, no subject rated both groups of concepts. In the Negro group, approximately one quarter of the subjects rating the ethnic-national concepts had rated the color-person concepts approximately 1 month earlier. All research groups were composed of equal numbers of men and women.

Semantic Differential

Other than the concepts rated, the rating procedure used was identical to that employed by Williams (1964) which was based on the work of Osgood, Suci, and Tannenbaum (1957).

[2] The term Caucasian is used throughout this paper in its popular meaning of "white person" rather than in any technical ethnological sense.

COLOR-PERSON CONCEPTS

The 10 color-person concepts were formed by pairing the word person with each of the 10 color names studied by Williams (1964), that is, black person, white person, brown person, yellow person, red person, blue person, green person, purple person, orange person, and gray person. The concepts were presented to the subject in random order and rated on 12 scales, 6 of which had been chosen to reflect the evaluation (E) factor, 3 the potency (P) factor, and 3 the activity (A) factor.

ETHNIC-NATIONAL CONCEPTS

This group of 14 concepts included 5 concepts selected because of their relevance to color and color-person concepts—Negro, Caucasian, Indian (Asiatic), Oriental, Indian (American); 4 other ethnic-national concepts —American, African, Chinese, Japanese; and 5 general reference concepts—citizen, foreigner, friend, enemy, and person. Using the same 12-scale rating sheet the subjects rated person first; then the other 4 reference concepts in random order; and, finally the 9 ethnic-national concepts in random order.

Procedure

The procedure was administered to groups of subjects by an experimenter of the same race using conventional semantic differential rating instructions. The concepts to be rated were presented to the subject in a mimeographed booklet with a single concept name heading each page and with the 12 rating scales presented below. Subjects recorded their sex but no other identifying information was requested.

RESULTS

The basic data for study consisted of the E, P, and A scores for the five race-related color-person concepts—black person, white person, brown person, yellow person, and red person; and for five corresponding ethnic concepts—Negro, Caucasian, Indian (Asiatic), Oriental, and Indian (American).

Each rating sheet was scored by assigning the digits 1–7 to the 7 positions on each rating scale and summing the ratings on the appropriate scales for the E, P, and A factors.

Low scores represented the "good" end of the E dimension, the "weak" end of the P dimension, and the "passive" end of the A dimension. Separate analyses by sex were not made after inspection of the data indicated that men and women subjects were responding to the task in essentially the same manner. Table 1 displays the three mean factor

the present study, correlation coefficients were computed for each pair of the three scores, for each of the five race-related color-person concepts and for each of the five corresponding ethnic concepts, separately for each of the three groups of subjects. For the color-person concepts, the median coefficients were as follows: E versus P, $r = +.03$; E versus

TABLE 1   Mean Semantic Differential Scores for Concepts Rated by Caucasians from the South, Caucasians from the Midwest, and Negroes from the South

	Evaluation			Potency			Activity		
	Caucasian		Negro	Caucasian		Negro	Caucasian		Negro
	South	Midwest		South	Midwest		South	Midwest	
White	1.79	1.85	2.05	3.60	3.49	3.52	4.75	4.90	5.10
Black	5.09	4.98	4.11	5.98	6.29	5.70	3.31	3.69	3.63
Brown	4.45	4.25	3.82	4.95	5.20	4.92	2.74	2.95	3.51
Yellow	2.82	2.64	2.52	3.21	3.10	3.24	4.99	4.77	5.00
Red	3.18	3.18	3.08	5.58	5.96	5.19	6.23	6.32	5.77
White person	2.63	2.45	3.75	4.24	4.26	3.53	5.24	5.06	4.48
Black person	4.52	4.76	3.89	5.79	5.22	5.23	3.53	3.73	4.45
Brown person	4.02	4.14	3.22	5.01	4.86	4.72	3.61	3.77	4.58
Yellow person	3.61	3.81	3.47	2.69	2.69	3.54	4.31	4.27	4.49
Red person	3.69	3.72	3.83	5.15	5.21	4.69	5.51	5.52	4.96
Caucasian	2.69	2.98	3.89	4.86	4.66	4.14	5.17	5.06	4.42
Negro	4.08	3.92	2.89	5.10	4.72	4.93	3.52	3.99	4.72
Indian (Asiatic)	3.65	3.84	3.68	3.83	3.79	4.26	3.85	3.84	4.27
Oriental	3.20	3.53	3.63	3.01	3.10	3.85	4.35	4.24	4.37
Indian (American)	3.24	3.46	3.53	4.91	4.64	4.47	4.66	4.41	4.72
Person	2.56	2.88	2.69	4.47	4.30	4.40	5.10	4.70	4.93
Friend	1.91	1.85	2.40	4.94	4.77	4.70	5.55	5.75	5.28
Enemy	5.68	5.67	5.41	4.74	4.53	4.07	4.73	4.22	4.18
Citizen	2.74	2.69	2.81	4.71	4.60	4.64	5.00	5.00	4.92
Foreigner	3.18	3.18	3.41	4.09	3.98	4.00	4.45	4.45	4.22

Note. Scores shown are mean factor scores divided by number of scales. Color-name data are from Williams (1964).

scores for each concept, separately for each of the three groups of subjects. Included in Table 1 are the scores for the five race-related color names from the Williams (1964) study.

Intercorrelations of E, P, and A Scores

In the earlier study of color names, it was found that the E, P, and A scores were characterized by a high degree of statistical independence, thus supporting the notion that the different scores reflected different aspects of connotative meaning. In order to assess the degree of independence of the three scores in

A, $r = -.40$; P versus A, $r = +.29$. For the ethnic concepts the median coefficients were: E versus P, $r = -.28$; E versus A, $r = -.46$; P versus A, $r = +.40$. While these correlations indicated that the E, P, and A scores were not statistically independent, the amount of common variance was not high (0–20%) and it was judged useful to analyze and report the scores separately.

Comparison of Caucasian Groups

The E, P, and A scores of the two Caucasian groups were analyzed to determine whether the connotative meanings of the concepts under study were rated differently by Southern and Midwestern college students.

COLOR-PERSON CONCEPTS

For each of the three scores (E, P, and A), separately, a Lindquist (1953) Type I analysis of variance was performed with the five color-person concepts comprising the within-subjects dimension and the two groups of Caucasian subjects, the between-subjects dimension. In each analysis, the between-groups and interaction effects were not significant while the between-concepts effect was highly significant ($p < .001$).

ETHNIC CONCEPTS

The analyses of the E, P, and A scores for the five ethnic concepts paralleled the color-person analyses just described with similar findings: nonsignificant between-groups and interaction effects, and highly significant ($p < .001$) between-concepts effects.

On the basis of the foregoing analyses, it was judged appropriate to pool the data of the Southern and Midwestern Caucasian groups in subsequent analyses.

Comparison of Caucasian and Negro Groups

This analysis was to determine whether the Negro subjects were responding to the race-related color-person and ethnic concepts in a manner similar to that of the Caucasian subjects. For each of the two groups of five concepts, three Lindquist (1953) Type I analyses of variance were run, one each for the scores E, P, and A. In these analyses the five concepts represented the within-subjects dimension and the Caucasian-Negro classification was the between-subjects dimension. In each of the six analyses, the interaction effect was highly significant ($p < .001$) indicating that the two groups of subjects were responding quite differently to the concepts and, hence, that the subsequent analyses should be made separately for Caucasian and Negro subjects.

Caucasian Subjects: Comparison of Related Color, Color-Person, and Ethnic Concepts

In the top portion of Figure 1 are displayed the scores for related triads of color,

color-person, and ethnic concepts along the E dimension. The vertical lines connect color-code related triads of concepts, that is, white-white person-Caucasian; black-black person-Negro; brown-brown person-Indian (Asiatic); yellow-yellow person-Oriental; red-red person-Indian (American). The general similarity of rank orders along the E dimension is quite apparent with the concepts white, white person, and Caucasian rated most "good," the concepts black, black person, and Negro rated most "bad," and the other three triads occupying intermediate positions. Thus, one can predict the rank position of color-person and ethnic concepts on the E dimension quite accurately on the basis of the rank position of the color concept with which they are conventionally associated.

The middle and lower thirds of Figure 1 indicate a substantial degree of rank-order similarity for related triads along the P and A dimensions but not as high a degree of consistency as that found for the E dimension. On the P dimension, the color-person concepts maintain the same rank order as the color concepts, but a shift out of rank order is seen for the ethnic concepts Caucasian and Indian (Asiatic). On the A dimension, there is some shifting of rank order both from color to color-person concepts, and from color-person concepts to ethnic concepts.

D SCORES

The similarities in meaning seen in Figure 1 may be conveniently summarized by the use of the D index developed by Osgood and his associates (1957, pp. 89 f.). Based on the generalized distance formula of solid geometry, D provides an index of the distance between pairs of concepts in three-dimensional semantic space. Osgood et al. (p. 93), note that the use of D to indicate absolute semantic distances requires the assumption that the three variables employed are statistically independent, a condition not met in the current instance (see above). It was judged, however, that in the present situation where interest was in the *relative* magnitude of different D scores, the partial violation of this assumption was not critical.

Applying the formula of Osgood et al. (1957, p. 91), D scores were computed between: each color and each color-person concept, each color and each ethnic concept, and each color-person and each ethnic con-

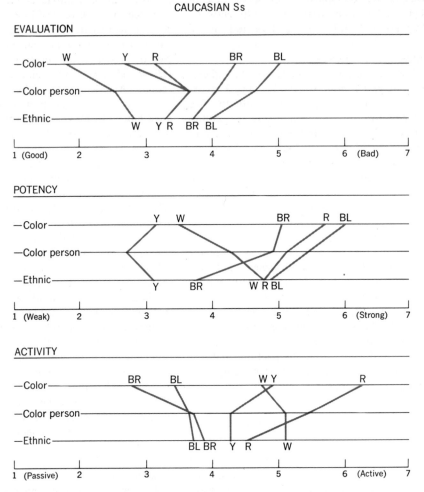

FIGURE 1 Semantic differential scores of Caucasian subjects for color-linked triads of color, color-person, and ethnic concepts. (Vertical lines connect triads, as follows: W = white, white person, Caucasian; Y = yellow, yellow person, Oriental; R = red, red person, Indian (American); BR = brown, brown person, Indian (Asiatic); BL = black, black person, Negro.)

cept. To illustrate, the *D* score for any two concepts was obtained by: computing the difference between the two mean E scale scores, the two mean P scale scores, and the two mean A scale scores; squaring each of these differences; summing the squares and taking the square root of the sum. From this, it can be seen that low *D* scores indicate high similarity in overall meaning while high scores reflect low similarity. It should also be noted that the *D* procedure weights all three difference scores equally, ignoring the greater pervasiveness of the E factor (in a factor analysis sense) and also its greater relationship to positive and negative attitudes

as traditionally measured (Osgood et al., 1957, p. 193).

Table 2 lists the 75 *D* scores obtained when each concept in one class was compared with each concept in the other two classes. These *D* scores provide a convenient place for a formal testing of the hypothesis that similarities in connotative meaning will be found to be greater among concepts linked by the color code than among concepts not so related. To test this hypothesis, a Mann-Whitney *U* test (Peatman, 1963) was computed for each third of Table 2 separately. For the comparison of color and color-person concepts at the upper left, the *D* score for

TABLE 2 Semantic Distances (*D* Scores) for Caucasian Subjects between Three Groups of Concepts: Color versus Color Person, Color versus Ethnic, and Color Person versus Ethnic

	White person	Black person	Brown person	Yellow person	Red person	Caucasian	Negro	Indian (Asiatic)	Oriental	Indian (American)
White	**1.10**	3.63	2.88	2.11	2.62	**1.65**	2.82	2.13	1.64	2.00
Black	3.54	**0.79**	1.51	3.74	2.63	3.08	**1.56**	2.66	3.58	2.41
Brown	3.08	0.98	**0.94**	2.86	2.80	2.82	0.98	**1.74**	2.71	2.29
Yellow	2.92	2.72	2.44	**1.25**	2.60	1.62	2.48	1.57	**0.85**	1.76
Red	1.95	3.02	2.84	3.66	**1.06**	1.52	2.80	3.13	3.32	**1.94**
White person						**0.59**	2.17	1.81	1.66	1.13
Black person						2.47	**0.85**	1.94	2.86	1.75
Brown person						1.93	0.04	**1.12**	2.13	1.16
Yellow person						2.42	2.32	1.20	**0.52**	2.16
Red person						1.05	1.84	2.15	2.47	**1.09**

the five related concepts (along the diagonal) were found to be significantly ($p < .001$) smaller than the 20 *D* scores for unrelated concepts. For the comparison of color and ethnic concepts at the upper right, the related *D* scores were again significantly ($p < .025$) smaller, as were the related *D* scores for the comparison of color-person and ethnic concepts at the lower right ($p < .001$). The consistency of the predicted effect may also be observed by comparing any one of the *D* scores for related concepts with the mean of the other four *D* scores in its particular row or column. *In every instance, the D for related concepts is smaller than the mean of the other four unrelated D scores.* These findings were taken to indicate that the general hypothesis was confirmed for Caucasian subjects.

The relative similarity of color-linked and non-color-linked concepts for Caucasian subjects is summarized in the upper portion of Figure 2. In the triangle on the left, the distance between any two vertices represents the mean of the five *D* scores for color-related pairs of concepts. For example, the distance between the points designated C and CP was obtained by averaging the five *D* scores for related color and color-person concepts (i.e., white versus white person, black versus black person, etc.). The distance between the vertices labeled CP and E represents the average of the five *D* scores for related color-person and ethnic concepts (i.e., white person versus

Caucasian, black person versus Negro, etc.). The distance between the C and E vertices represents the average of the five *D* scores for white versus Caucasian, black versus Negro, etc. Thus, the distances shown in the small triangle represent the average distances among the various pairs of color-related concepts.

The distances between the vertices of the right-hand triangle were computed in analogous fashion. The distance between any two

MEAN SEMANTIC DISTANCES

CAUCASIAN Ss

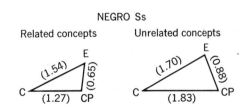

NEGRO Ss

FIGURE 2 Mean semantic distances (*D* scores) for color-related triads of color (C), color-person (CP), and ethnic (E) concepts; and for non-color-related triads of C, CP, and E concepts.

vertices is the mean distance between the concepts in a particular group and the four unrelated concepts in the second group. Thus, the C to CP distance is the mean distance between each of the five color concepts and all of the unrelated color-person concepts, for example, the distance between white and all color-person concepts except white person, the distance between black and all color-person concepts except black person, etc. The relative size of the two triangles again reflects the great similarity of connotative meaning found for color-related concepts.

Some relationships of particular interest may be seen in Table 2. In the color versus color-person comparison, these Caucasian subjects rated the concept white person as most similar to white and most different from black; while black person was most similar to black and most different from white. In the color-person versus ethnic comparison, the concept Negro was well differentiated from white person while the concept Caucasian was most similar to white person and least similar to black person. In the color versus ethnic comparison, the concept Caucasian appeared about equally similar in meaning to red, yellow, and white, and most differentiated from black. The concept Negro was most similar to brown, next most similar to black, and most differentiated from white and red.

Negro Subjects: Comparison of Related Color, Color-Person, and Ethnic Concepts

An examination of the mean color-person and ethnic scores for the Negro subjects (see Table 1) indicated that there was much less interconcept variability for these subjects than for the Caucasian subjects. The first step, then, was to determine whether there were statistically significant interconcept differences for the Negro subjects. Treatments by subjects analyses of variance (Lindquist, 1953) were employed for this purpose with an individual analysis made for each of the three scores (E, P, and A), separately for the five color-person concepts and the five ethnic concepts. For the color-person concepts, the between-concepts effect was significant at the .01 level for all three scores. For the ethnic concepts, the between-concepts effect was significant at the .01 level for the E and P scores and of borderline significance ($p < .10$)

for the A scores. On the basis of these findings it was concluded that, although the observed differences were much smaller for Negro subjects, there were significant differences in interconcept meaning.

Figure 3 displays the mean scale scores for the related triads of color–color-person–ethnic concepts for Negro subjects. The contrast between Figure 3 and Figure 1 is rather striking. While the color-concept data from the earlier study (Williams, 1964) shows virtually identical rank orders along the E, P, and A dimensions for Negro and Caucasian subjects, it is clear that the similarity of the color-linked triads found with Caucasian was not present to the same degree in the data of the Negro subjects. On the E dimension, the Negro subjects agreed that black person was "least good" but did not agree that white person was "most good," rating this concept not differently from black person. The most positive evaluative rating was given to brown person which was rated significantly more positive than either white person or black person. For the ethnic concepts on the E dimension, the Negro subjects rated the concept Negro significantly more positive and Caucasian significantly more negative than the other three ethnic concepts.

The Negro subjects' P scores, displayed in the middle of Figure 3, indicate a substantial degree of consistency among the color-linked triads with the general rank order of the color scores being repeated for the color-person and ethnic concepts. In particular, black, black person, and Negro were rated substantially more potent than were white, white person, and Caucasian. Comparatively, it can be noted that this finding is consistent with the P ratings given by the Caucasian subjects, except that Caucasian subjects did not rate the concepts Negro and Caucasian differently.

In the bottom portion of Figure 3, it can be seen that the dispersion of mean A scores of the Negro subjects decreased sharply in moving from the color concepts to the color-person and ethnic concepts. The color-person concepts appear to be undifferentiated on the A dimension with the exception of red person which was rated significantly more active than the other four. The small observed differences among the ethnic concepts were not statistically significant.

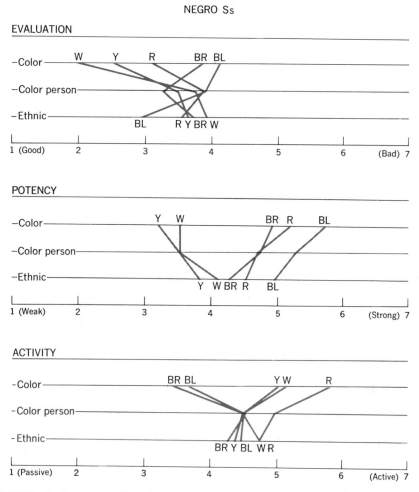

FIGURE 3 Semantic differential scores of Negro subjects for color-linked triads of color, color-person, and ethnic concepts. (Vertical lines connect triads, as follows: W = white, white person, Caucasian; Y = yellow, yellow person, Oriental; R = red, red person, Indian (American); BR = brown, brown person, Indian (Asiatic); BL = black, black person, Negro.)

D SCORES

The data of the Negro subjects was subjected to the same *D*-score analysis as that described above for the Caucasian subjects. These scores are given in Table 3. As would be expected from the foregoing discussion, the *D* scores of these Negro subjects showed less differentiation among concepts, generally. Mann-Whitney *U* tests were again employed to determine whether color-linked concepts were more similar in connotative meaning than were non-color-linked concepts. For the color versus color-person comparison, the *D* scores for the color-related concepts were significantly (*p* < .01) smaller than the *D* scores for unrelated concepts. For the other two comparisons, the *D* scores for related concepts were generally smaller but in neither case significantly so. Thus, the data of the Negro subjects provided only slight support for the hypothesis under investigation.

The relative similarity of color-linked, and non-color-linked concepts for Negro subjects is summarized in the lower portion of Figure 2. As would be expected from the statistical tests discussed above, the related concepts triangle is somewhat smaller than the unrelated concepts triangle. It seems clear, however, that classification of concepts as "color-related" and "color-unrelated" has much less significance for the Negro subjects than for the Caucasian subjects. The relative size of the two right-hand triangles illustrates, again, the lesser degree of concept differentiation by the Negro subjects.

Certain of the *D* scores in Table 3 are of particular interest. These Negro subjects

concepts. (Mean scores for the reference concepts are given in Table 1.)

D scores computed for the data of the Caucasian subjects revealed that the concept Caucasian had a higher similarity to citizen (.20) than to foreigner (1.01) and a higher similarity to friend (1.06) than to enemy (2.94). On the other hand, the concept Negro was seen as more similar to foreigner (1.48)

TABLE 3   Semantic Distances (*D* Scores) for Negro Subjects between Three Groups of Concepts: Color versus Color Person, Color versus Ethnic, and Color Person versus Ethnic

	White person	Black person	Brown person	Yellow person	Red person	Caucasian	Negro	Indian (Asiatic)	Oriental	Indian (American)
White	**1.81**	2.59	1.76	1.55	2.14	**2.06**	1.69	1.97	1.77	1.80
Black	2.36	**0.97**	1.63	2.41	1.70	1.76	**1.80**	1.63	2.05	1.74
Brown	1.70	0.99	**1.24**	1.73	1.47	1.20	1.53	**1.05**	1.39	1.32
Yellow	1.37	2.48	1.69	**1.12**	1.95	1.51	1.75	2.35	**1.41**	1.62
Red	2.21	1.55	1.29	2.12	**1.21**	1.89	1.10	1.86	2.01	1.35
White person						**0.62**	1.66	0.76	0.36	1.00
Black person						1.09	**1.08**	1.01	1.41	0.88
Brown person						0.90	0.41	**0.72**	0.21	0.42
Yellow person						0.73	1.41	0.78	**0.37**	0.96
Red person						0.77	1.00	0.82	1.04	**0.45**

rated the concept Caucasian as most similar to the concept white person and most different from the concepts black person and brown person; while Negro was most similar to brown person and least similar to white person. It is noteworthy that the largest *D* score among the ethnic versus color-person comparisons was that between Negro and white person. In the color versus ethnic comparison, it is of interest that these subjects rated Caucasian as least like white and Negro as least like black.

Comparisons with Reference Concepts

It will be recalled that certain reference concepts had been rated along with the ethnic concepts. Included were the concept person and two sets of logically contrasted concepts, namely, friend and enemy and citizen and foreigner. It was considered of interest to study the connotative similarity of the concepts Caucasian and Negro to these reference

than to citizen (1.84) and more similar to enemy (1.88) than to friend (2.87). For these Caucasian subjects, the similarity of the concept person to the five ethnic concepts was, in decreasing order, Caucasian (.45), Indian (American) (.84), Indian (Asiatic) (1.60), Oriental (1.62), and Negro (1.88). The similarity of the concept person to the five color-person concepts was, in decreasing order, white person (.31), red person (1.40), brown person (1.94), black person (1.95), and yellow person (2.09). The mean of the *D* scores between person and the color-person concepts was 1.54. This figure may be compared with the mean *D* score of 1.03 between color and color-person concepts, noted above.

Turning to the data of the Negro subjects, the concept Negro was found to be more similar to citizen (.36), than to foreigner (1.18) and more similar to friend (.78) than to enemy (2.72). On the other hand, Negro subjects saw the concept Caucasian as more similar to foreigner (.54) than to citizen (1.29) and more similar to enemy (1.54) than to friend (1.81). For the Negro subjects, the similarity of the concept person to the five ethnic concepts was, in decreasing order, Negro (.62), Indian (American) (.63), Oriental (.76), Indian (Asiatic) (.83), and Caucasian (1.00). The similarity of the concept person to the five color-person concepts was, in decreasing order, brown person (.50), yellow person (.57), red person (1.03), white person (1.15), and black person (1.33).

DISCUSSION

The data of the Caucasian subjects provided evidence in strong support of the hypothesis under investigation; namely, that racial concepts have connotative meanings similar to the color names with which they are linked by the color-coding custom. Although similarities in meaning were found for the A and P dimensions, the most consistent similarity was seen on the E dimension. This is perhaps the most important finding of the study since it is known that score variation along the E dimension covaries closely with score variation on conventional attitude tests (Osgood et al., 1957, p. 193). Using this interpretation, we can note that the attitudes of Caucasian subjects would appear to be most favorable toward Caucasians, somewhat less favorable toward American Indians and Orientals, and least favorable toward Asiatic Indians and Negroes. This is to be compared with their favorable evaluative rating of white and progressively less favorable ratings of yellow, red, brown, and black. While the direction of cause and effect cannot be demonstrated here, these data are consistent with the notion that the evaluative connotations of color names applied to racial groups are one determinant of the favorability of attitudes toward the racial groups. A hypothesis under current investigation is that evaluative color connotations—particularly white as good and black as bad—are learned early in childhood and influence the subsequent development of racial attitudes.

It was interesting to observe how the meaning of the word person was modified by the use of color adjectives. In the data of the Caucasian subjects, it was seen that the meanings of the color-person concepts were generally more similar to their associated color names than to the concept person. Apparently, the color adjective takes precedence over the noun and the connotative meaning communicated by the concept black person is *black*-person rather than black-*person*.

The high consistency in the data of the two Caucasian groups is worthy of note. As in the earlier study of color names (Williams, 1964), Caucasian students in North Carolina and in Kansas were found to rate the connotative meanings of racial concepts in a highly similar fashion indicating that the hypothesized effects of color coding may have some geographical generality. It would be interesting to know whether the same effects would be found among Caucasian subjects from other geographical regions with differing histories and customs in racial matters.

While it was clear that the Caucasian subjects saw each triad of color-code related concepts as belonging to the same "meaning family," this was not the case for the Negro subjects. While generally agreeing with Caucasians on the meanings of color names presented in a nonracial context, Negro subjects responded to the racial concepts in a quite different fashion, particularly along the evaluative (attitude) dimension. Examples of the different ratings of the Negro subjects were their rating of Negro as good and Caucasian as relatively bad, and their rating of brown person as more good than white person and black person. It is not surprising, of course, to find that the responses of Negro subjects to racial concepts differ from Caucasian responses since the groups obviously have had differential experiences with the concepts. In addition, there appears to be developing resistance among Negroes to the color-coding practice with its connotative significance. This is seen in extreme form in the efforts of the Black Muslims and others to arbitrarily reverse the conventional symbolism by associating black with goodness and white with badness. It would seem doubtful that such deliberate efforts at reversal can generally succeed in a culture where the symbolism of white as good and black as bad is so thoroughly entrenched in literature, religion, the mass media, etc.

A simpler way of dealing with the unfortunate effects of color coding would be an attempt to bypass the problem by a deliberate effort to reshape language habits so that groups of persons are not designated by color names. For example, if the popular press would forego the convenience of discussing racial problems in terms of white persons and black persons, one important avenue of reinforcement would be removed. As noted elsewhere (Williams, 1964), such a proposal would probably encounter resistance from many Caucasians who, while perhaps willing to part with the designation of Negroes as black or brown, would be reluctant to give up the designation of their own group as white, with its positive evaluative connotations. And, of course, the abolition of the custom of color coding would not fully solve the color problem since there are average differences in skin color between Caucasian and Negro persons and lighter skin would no doubt continue to be positively valued. However, one might say that white Americans and black Americans will continue to find it very difficult to solve their problems, while Americans (with differing shades of skin color) would have a better chance of doing so. Indications of the problems remaining to be solved were seen in the comparisons of ethnic concepts and reference concepts where it was shown that each racial group saw its own racial designation as most similar to the concepts person, friend, and citizen and the designation of the other racial group as most similar to enemy and foreigner.

REFERENCES

Lindquist, E. F. *Design and analysis of experiments in psychology and education.* New York: Houghton Mifflin, 1953.

Osgood, C. E., Suci, G. J., & Tannenbaum, P. H. *The measurement of meaning.* Urbana: University of Illinois Press, 1957.

Peatman, J. G. *Introduction to applied statistics.* New York: Harper & Row, 1963.

Staats, C. K., & Staats, A. W. Meaning established by classical conditioning. *Journal of Experimental Psychology*, 1957, **54,** 74–80.

Staats, A. W., & Staats, C. K. Attitudes established by classical conditioning. *Journal of Abnormal and Social Psychology*, 1958, **57,** 37–40.

Williams, J. E. Connotations of color names among Negroes and Caucasians. *Perceptual & Motor Skills*, 1964, **18,** 721–731.

5

Anti-Negro bias among Negro college students[1]

BRUCE L. MALIVER[2]

In recent years, the phenomenon of minority group self-hatred has received considerable attention. Probably in response to the thought-provoking work of Lewin (1941) and Bettelheim (1943), three separate studies of anti-Semitic attitudes among Jews are available (Adelson, 1953; Radke-Yarrow & Lande, 1953; Sarnoff, 1951). Since Sarnoff

Reprinted from *Journal of Personality and Social Psychology*, 1965, **2,** 770–775, by permission of the author and the American Psychological Association.

[1] This article is based on a dissertation submitted in partial fulfillment of the requirements for the PhD degree at Yeshiva University in October of 1963. The writer is indebted to Nor-

man B. Gordon and Victor Sanua who served as members of the dissertation committee, and to Bernard Kutner, chairman of the committee under whose supervision the investigation was conducted. A summary of the study was presented at the meeting of the Eastern Psychological Association in Philadelphia, April 18, 1964.

[2] The author wishes to express his thanks to

drew hypotheses from the general theory of identification with the aggressor (Freud, 1946) in an attempt to relate degree of Jewish anti-Semitism to a variety of personality factors, his study is of greatest interest here.

Sarnoff discussed at length the relationship between the theory of identification with the aggressor and the study of Jewish anti-Semitism. He argued that there are social situations, analogous to the individual Oedipal situation, in which identificatory responses are likely to be evoked. Among the conditions considered necessary for such responses are those in which aggressors are determined to impose hostility upon social scapegoats, and where the victims are socially dependent upon the aggressors (and therefore are likely targets), and where the victims cannot escape the sphere of influence of the aggressors. When the position of the Negro in current American society is considered, it seems obvious that these conditions are also fulfilled, perhaps to an even greater extent than they are for Jews. This then, leads to the questions: Does the concept of identification with the aggressor help explain Negro self-hatred and self-rejection? Will a relationship obtain between the degree of anti-Negro bias and personality variables derived from the theory?

The devaluation of Negroid characteristics among Negroes was noted by Herskovits as early as 1928. Other writers such as Johnson (1943), Frazier (1940, 1957a, 1957b), and Powdermaker (1939, 1943) have observed and interpreted various aspects of self-hatred among Negroes from the anthropological point of view. Studies of attitudes and stereotypes among Negroes have shown that the Negro holds the same prejudices and stereotypes towards diverse ethnic groups as does the white, even to the point of largely accepting the negative stereotypes about himself (cf. Bayton, 1941, 1942). Authoritarianism in relation to other attitudes among Negro students has been studied by Steckler (1957) who, in the process developed a basic anti-Negro (AN) attitude scale. Until this current study, however, there has been no reported

attempt to predict personality differences among Negroes on the basis of prejudicial attitudes.

The research to be reported here was, in part, an attempt to determine whether the conclusions in support of the theory of identification with the aggressor, drawn from Sarnoff's study of Jewish anti-Semitism, might be applicable to the phenomenon of anti-Negro bias among Negroes. Accordingly, effort has been exerted to make the general design and the hypotheses of this study as similar as possible to those of Sarnoff.

HYPOTHESES

Three broad areas of personality differences between Negro subjects who accept and those who reject anti-Negro statements were explored. It was hypothesized that Negroes scoring high in anti-Negro bias would show a concomitantly high incidence of negative attitudes towards the parents (Hypothesis 1), of negative attitudes towards the self (Hypothesis 2), and would be more prone to react passively in the face of hostile interpersonal attack (Hypothesis 3). On the other hand, Negro subjects scoring low in anti-Negro bias were expected to show a high incidence of positive attitudes towards the parents (Hypothesis 4) and towards the self (Hypothesis 5), and to be more prone to direct retaliation when attacked (Hypothesis 6). Twenty-three specific predictions about personality variables were derived from these six major personality hypotheses.[3]

METHOD

Subjects

The subjects for the research were 160 Negro, male college students. Three southern groups (85 subjects) and two northern groups (75 subjects) were tested in five different college locales throughout the country. Faculty members who had previously helped

---

the administration for their cooperation in the preparation of this paper, while he was employed by Columbia University's College of Physicians and Surgeons at the Department of Psychiatry, Harlem Hospital.

[3] Sarnoff's detailed derivation of these general hypotheses and the specific predictions from the concept of identification with the aggressor will not be repeated here, in the interest of brevity. The personality variables subsumed under each of the hypotheses as presented in Table 1 are self-explanatory.

in similar research were contacted and their cooperation was secured.[4]

The total group of 160 students proved to be a broad and heterogeneous sample with respect to demographic variables. Using Edward's (1950, p. 135) procedure to test the significance of transformed z' scores on several populations by way of the chi-square distribution, it was determined that these five smaller samples were randomly drawn from a statistically common population.

Measurement of Anti-Negro Bias

Anti-Negro bias was measured with a 7-point Likert scale composed of anti-Negro items (Steckler, 1957) and new pro-Negro items. A variety of steps were taken to control for acquiescence response set and other extraneous measurement variables. In an attempt to control the total scale format for possible acquiescence set interference, the anti-Negro and pro-Negro items were randomly mixed with items from the E Scale (Adorno, Frenkel-Brunswik, Levinson, & Sanford, 1950) and the forward and reversed F Scales (Christie, Havel, & Seidenberg, 1958) to make up a 60-item scale.

In addition, the individual anti- and pro-Negro items were subjected to a scoring reversal system so that, in order to be placed at either extreme of the bias continuum, subjects had to be highly consistent in their racial attitudes. Thus, subjects ultimately considered to be high in anti-Negro bias, were those who had accepted anti-Negro items while rejecting pro-Negro items; similarly, subjects designated as low in anti-Negro bias were those who both rejected anti-Negro items and accepted pro-Negro items. Thus, random responses tended to cancel each other out.

[4] The author wishes to express his appreciation to the following people, all of whom were generous in their expenditure of time, advice, and help in gathering subjects, or enlisting the aid of Negro graduate student confederates to administer the protocols: Paul I. Clifford, University of Atlanta; James A. Bayton, Howard University; Albert and Bernice Lott, University of Kentucky and Kentucky State College; Leonora C. Lane, Central State College, Wilberforce, Ohio; Robert Bierstedt, New York University; and Kenneth B. Clark, City College of the City University of New York.

The individual items were subjected to the following procedure:

1. All subjects were ranked by their scores on Steckler's AN scale, and the discriminatory power of each item was determined. All of the original items still proved satisfactory with this diverse group.[5] (See Table A, in ADI supplement.)

2. Next the subjects were ranked on the basis of their scores on the new pro-Negro items, and again the discriminatory power of each item was determined. (See Table B, in ADI supplement.)

3. After dropping the one new item that did not adequately discriminate between high and low quartiles at this stage, the subjects were ranked by the sum of the remaining items in both scales.

4. Finally, the discriminatory power of each item in the merged distribution *vis-à-vis that distribution* was determined, and items which did not sufficiently discriminate between high and low quartiles were dropped. (See Table C in ADI supplement.)

The final result was a scale of 20 positively and negatively phrased items with a split-half reliability of $+.750$, corrected by the Spearman-Brown prophecy formula.

Measurement of the Personality Variables

The specific personality variables subsumed under each of the six general hypotheses were rated present or absent for each subject on the basis of paper-and-pencil test material. Five Thematic Apperception Test (TAT) cards (Cards 1, 6BM, 7BM, 3BM, and 12M), and 50 items from the Michigan Sentence Completion Test [6] were rated according to

[5] A 5-page supplement containing the scale items and detailed statistical data (quartile means and discriminatory power values, overall mean values, etc.) about this item analysis procedure has been deposited with the American Documentation Institute. Order Document No. 8527 from ADI Auxiliary Publications Project, Photoduplication Service, Library of Congress, Washington, D. C. 20540. Remit in advance $1.25 for microfilm or $1.25 for photocopies and make checks payable to: Chief, Photoduplication Service, Library of Congress.

[6] An unpublished test developed at the University of Michigan, and used through the courtesy of Irving Sarnoff, personal communication, 1961.

strictly defined criteria by two raters working without knowledge of each other's judgments. In cases of disagreement, the responses in question were submitted to a judge who, knowing only that the raters had disagreed, made a final judgment using the same criteria.

The projective instruments in this research were handled in a manner that is different from the common practice in which the subject's words provide a stimulus for the interpretive skill of the clinician who attends to the symbolic meaning (assumed to be) underlying the actual words of the response. Rather, in this study exact criteria for the presence of each response was specified in an attempt to make the coding and rating of the variables as objective as possible. An example of this can be seen most easily in the use of the TAT in which only direct fantasies of death of a parent or suicide of the hero met the criteria for the unconscious expression of negative parental or self-attitudes. This procedure led to an overall agreement of 97.36% between the two raters.[7]

Summary of Test Battery and Experimental Design

In the first pages of the final test booklet, each subject was presented with the 60-item Likert attitude scale described above. Fifty sentence-completion items and 5 TAT pictures followed, with adequate space for written responses. Finally, a personal data sheet was appended in order to elicit information about each subject's age, residence, socioeconomic status, etc. Included were questions designed to elicit specific information about the subject's attitudes towards "sit-ins," and his actual participation in desegregation activities and organizations.

Upon return to the investigator, the completed protocol was separated into its component parts and each part was subsequently handled separately.

The subjects were ranked on the basis of

[7] Thanks are here expressed to Murray Garfinkel and Vera Henriquez who served as rater and judge, respectively. Perhaps it should be added that all of the raters felt uncomfortable laboring under these constraints and were often driven to comment that even though a given response did not meet the stated criteria, they knew clinically (i.e., intuitively) that the variable was present.

their final scores on the revised measure of anti-Negro bias, and the highest and lowest thirds of the distribution were designated as high- and low-bias groups. Except to determine that a curvilinear distribution did not occur, the middle third was not considered for any subsequent statistical operations.

Finally, for each personality variable, a count was made to determine the number of high- and low-scoring subjects who were rated as having that variable present. The significance of these differences was determined through the use of the chi-square distribution.

At all stages, independent statistical determinations were made for the northern, southern, and total groups.

RESULTS

Major Hypotheses

As only four of the series of specific subhypotheses were significant beyond the .05 level, all major hypotheses (1–6) were rejected (see Table 1).

These data did not support the expectation that broad personality differences could be predicted on the basis of the degree of anti-Negro prejudice held by Negroes.

TABLE 1 Difference between the Number of High- and Low-Scoring Subjects Rated as Having the Personality Variables Present

Hypotheses (1–6)[a]	Anti-Negro Bias Group[b]		χ^2
	High	Low	
1. Negative attitudes, parents			
Death of mother (TAT)[c]	2	1	.00[d]
Death of father (TAT)	8	6	.03
Death of parents (TAT)	1	1	.53
Death of all parent figures (TAT)	11	8	.09
Negative percept of mother	7	8	.34
Negative percept of father	11	3	3.76*
Fear of parental disapproval	11	6	1.12
Negative percept of home	6	7	.35

TABLE 1 Difference between the Number of High- and Low-Scoring Subjects Rated as Having the Personality Variables Present (*Continued*)

Hypotheses (1–6)[a]	Anti-Negro Bias Group[b]		x^2
	High	Low	
2. Negative attitudes, self			
Self-negation	18	13	.72
Psychic stress	22	20	.04
Self-derogatory remarks	11	9	.03
Fear of rejection	14	5	4.10*
Fear of future	19	18	.00
3. Passive response to aggression			
Passive response, aggression	30	21	2.41
Suicide of hero (TAT)	3	4	.61[d]
Suppression, retaliatory desire	12	8	.32
4. Positive attitudes, parents			
Positive percept, mother	23	22	.00
Positive percept, father	5	12	4.48*
Positive percept, home	26	28	.33
5. Positive attitudes, self			
Self-assertion	5	8	.20
Absence of fears	1	7	6.62**
Favorable remarks about self	14	14	.00
6. Active response to aggression			
Direct retaliatory action	30	30	.00

[a] For Hypotheses 1, 2, and 3, high group frequency predicted to exceed low group frequency; for Hypotheses 4, 5, and 6, low group frequency predicted to exceed high group frequency.

[b] $N = 53$ in each group (high and low thirds of 160 ranked subjects).

[c] Unless TAT is indicated, variable was rated from sentence-completion items.

[d] Also not significant with Fisher's exact test.

* $p \leq .05$.
** $p \leq .01$.

It may be noted that there is little likelihood that Type II (beta) error was committed here. The power efficiency of a statistical test is, in part, a function of a sample size (Cohen, 1962). With an N as large as 160, and using one-tailed, fourfold chi-square tests with $p = .05$, regardless of the magnitude of the effect in the population, these null hypotheses may be accepted with confidence.

The hypothesized relationship between attitudes towards the father and degree of anti-Negro bias was sustained in these Negro subjects. That is, subjects low in anti-Negro bias were rated as demonstrating a positive percept of the father more frequently than subjects high in anti-Negro bias ($x^2 = 4.48$, $p = .05$). Further, the opposite relationship obtained when negative attitudes towards the father were independently rated,[8] that is, subjects high in anti-Negro bias expressed negative attitudes about their fathers with significantly greater frequency than did subjects who scored low in anti-Negro prejudice ($x^2 = 3.76$, $p = .05$).

The predicted relationship was also sustained with respect to the variable, fear of rejection; subjects high in anti-Negro bias were rated as having expressed such fear with significantly greater frequency than were subjects low in such bias ($x^2 = 4.10$, $p = .05$).

Finally, subjects scoring low in bias were rated as having expressed optimism and an absence of vague fears of the future more frequently than were subjects high in anti-Negro bias ($x^2 = 6.62$, $p = .01$).

Incidental Findings

No significant relationships were found between scores on the modified anti-Negro bias measure, and the following demographic variables: age, college class level, family income, social status scale rankings, college grades or major subject, and number of siblings.

Significant North-South differences did *not* occur in either the tests of the major hy-

[8] Although the same sentence-completion items were often used to rate specific personality variables which might have either a positive or negative valence, the raters were instructed to examine all the protocols for the presence of one variable before going on to another variable that might be considered the opposite of the first. Thus, for example, absence of negative attitudes towards the father did *not* mean that a subject was credited with positive attitudes towards the father. Before being credited in any category a response had to independently meet the scoring criteria for that category.

potheses or in scores on the anti-Negro bias measure. Further, northern and southern samples did not differ in authoritarianism or ethnocentrism scores.

The reports of organizational membership and participation in antisegregation activities were subjected to chi-squares in much the same way as were the personality variables. In the general context of the major hypotheses, it would be expected that subjects low in anti-Negro bias would be more likely to be members of such groups as the National Association for the Advancement of Colored People (NAACP) or the Congress of Racial Equality (CORE) than would Negro subjects high in anti-Negro bias. In the case of each organization the results were in the expected direction, and significantly so when CORE membership was considered ($x^2 = 5.48$, $p = .01$).

Further, it would be expected that low-scoring subjects would be more likely to have participated in demonstrations. This expectation was sustained ($x^2 = 3.24$, $p = .04$).

It should be noted that these data concerning organizational memberships and participation in demonstrations (and the associated probability levels) may have only limited validity, as it was not possible to determine the extent to which these subjects concealed their memberships or activities through fear of possible retaliation, even though they were told that the booklets were to remain anonymous.

One final incidental finding: In the analysis of the sentence-completion and TAT protocols direct and obvious racial statements were occasionally noticed. In the hope that relative frequencies of these comments might be of interest, all projective protocols were rated for the presence of responses indicative of positive or negative attitudes towards Negroes, as well as towards whites.

There were no positive remarks about whites expressed in the protocols of the 160 subjects in the total sample. Low-scoring subjects made significantly more spontaneous antiwhite remarks ($x^2 = 3.36$, $p = .04$), and significantly more pro-Negro remarks ($x^2 = 5.50$, $p = .01$); both findings are consistent with the overall theoretical position taken in this study. The reverse position, that is, that subjects scoring high in anti-Negro bias would

be more prone to make anti-Negro remarks, does not find support in the data. However, this finding may be a reflection of the apparent greater freedom with which low-scoring subjects express any racial comments ($x^2 = 7.99$, $p = .005$).[9]

DISCUSSION

Three broad areas of personality differences between Negroes high in anti-Negro bias and Negroes low in such bias were hypothesized on the basis of the theory of identification with the aggressor. The theory was extended by Sarnoff from the realm of individual psychopathology to the study of Jewish anti-Semitism, and he reported acceptance of hypotheses which stipulated that Jews high in anti-Semitism differ from Jews lows in anti-Semitism in attitudes towards the parents, attitudes towards the self, and methods of dealing with hostility directed against the self by others. In this research, similar hypotheses did *not* yield similar results with Negro subjects and all major hypotheses were rejected.

The rejection of these hypotheses indicates that, within the limits of the design used, it cannot be said that the theory of identification with the aggressor is supported by data drawn from a diverse sample of male American Negroes. Further, the conclusions drawn from the study of Jewish anti-Semitism have been shown not to be directly applicable to another minority group.

While real personality differences between Negro and Jewish ethnic groups may exist, it is most parsimonious to explain the differences between the current findings and those of Sarnoff in terms of research design and execution. A discussion of the methodological differences between the two studies, especially with regard to sampling procedures,

[9] The significance associated with this contingency table must be considered an approximation as the cell entries may violate the principle of independent observations. This is so because in one or two cases the same subject made racial comments scorable in different categories; thus, when the cell entries are summed over all categories, the same subject is counted more than once.

the measurement of prejudice, and statistical procedures, is available and need not to be repeated here (Maliver, 1963). To the extent that the hypothesized relationships between personality variables and minority group attitudes depend solely on statistical relationships between measured *verbal* factors, it seems evident that the method does not afford a good test of the theory.

The positive findings of this study, combining as they do a pattern of verbal and behavioral elements, do offer a measure of support for the concept which lies at the heart of the theory.

It will be recalled that a high degree of acceptance of anti-Negro statements was associated with a negative view of the father and generalized fear of rejection by adult figures. This then may be seen as affecting behavioral spheres in a lack of positive identification with those social forces which are critical of the Negro's low estate and willing to take positive strides to change the environment. On the other end of the bias continuum, a low degree of acceptance of anti-Negro statements is associated with a positive percept of the father, an absence of conscious fears of the future, and more active identification with the current movement to effect social changes. Stated conversely (and keeping in mind all the dangers of reasoning from a converse), the validation of the predictions with respect to the father suggests that for these Negro males, strong positive or negative feelings towards the father may result in identification with the Negro in general, or unwillingness to be so identified.

REFERENCES

Adelson, J. A study of minority group authoritarianism. *Journal of Abnormal and Social Psychology*, 1953, **48**, 477–485.

Adorno, T. W., Frenkel-Brunswik, Else, Levinson, D. J., & Sanford, R. N. *The authoritarian personality*. New York: Harper, 1950.

Bayton, J. A. The racial stereotypes of Negro college students. *Journal of Abnormal and Social Psychology*, 1941, **36**, 97–102.

Bayton, J. A. The psychology of racial morale. *Journal of Negro Education*, 1942, **11**, 150–153.

Bettelheim, B. Individual and mass behavior in extreme situations. *Journal of Abnormal and Social Psychology*, 1943, **38**, 417–452.

Christie, R., Havel, Joan, & Seidenberg, B. Is the F Scale irreversible? *Journal of Abnormal and Social Psychology*, 1958, **56**, 143–159.

Cohen, J. The statistical power of abnormal-social psychological research: A review. *Journal of Abnormal and Social Psychology*, 1962, **65**, 145–153.

Edwards, A. L. *Experimental design in psychological research*. New York: Rinehart, 1950.

Frazier, E. F. *Negro youth at the crossways: Their personality development in the middle states*. Washington, D. C.: American Youth Commission, 1940.

Frazier, E. F. *Black bourgeoisie*. Glencoe, Ill.: Free Press, 1957. (a)

Frazier, E. F. *The Negro in the United States*. New York: Macmillan, 1957. (b)

Freud, Anna. *The ego and the mechanisms of defense*. New York: International Univer. Press, 1946.

Herskovits, M. J. *The American Negro*. New York: Knopf, 1928.

Johnson, C. S. *Patterns of Negro segregation*. New York: Harper, 1943.

Lewin, K. Self hatred among Jews. *Contemporary Jewish Record*, 1941, **4**, 219–232.

Maliver, B. L. Anti-Negro bias among Negro college students. Unpublished doctoral dissertation, Yeshiva University, 1963.

Powdermaker, Hortense. *After freedom*. New York: Viking Press, 1939.

Powdermaker, Hortense. The channeling of Negro aggression by the cultural process. *American Journal of Sociology*, 1943, **48**, 750–758.

Radke-Yarrow, M., & Lande, B. Personality correlates of minority group belonging. *Journal of Social Psychology*, 1953, **38**, 253–272.

Sarnoff, I. Identification with the aggressor: Some personality correlates of anti-Semitism among Jews. *Journal of Personality*, 1951, **20**, 199–218.

Steckler, G. A. Authoritarian ideology in Negro college students. *Journal of Abnormal and Social Psychology*, 1957, **54**, 396–399.

6

Status position, mobility, and ethnic identification of the Negro

SEYMOUR PARKER AND ROBERT KLEINER

A considerable body of literature has emerged concerning the relationship between the Negro's social status position and his "racial" or ethnic identification (i.e., his attitudes toward, and feelings of kinship with, other Negroes). This literature fails to distinguish between attitudes of those socialized in a given status position and those who have moved into that position. The purpose of this study is to investigate not only the relationship between ethnic identification and status position, but also between identification and mobility. Research efforts in this area have encountered serious methodological problems, such as eliciting directly an individual's private attitudes toward this emotionally-charged subject. Consequently, the literature often represents inferences from oblique questionnaire probes or clinical-type interviews with unrepresentative samples. Another purpose of this paper is to determine whether our results can be encompassed within a unified conceptual framework.

The issue of ethnic identification is currently a controversial topic within the Negro community itself. In recent issues of popular lay journals, Lomax (1960) and Fuller (1963) accuse the dominant (mainly middle-class) Negro leadership of being white "carbon copies" and of feeling covert contempt for the Negro masses. In the professional

Reprinted from *Journal of Social Issues,* 1964, **20,** 85–102, by permission of the authors and The Society for the Psychological Study of Social Issues.

literature, one of the most widely-known theses on the relationship between status position and ethnic attitudes of Negroes is Frazier's *Black Bourgeoisie* (1957). Frazier maintains that upper- and middle-class Negroes are ambivalent, both toward the wider Negro community and the white middle class with which they identify. These Negroes internalize many of the negative or patronizing white middle-class attitudes toward the Negro masses; in addition, they resent their own inability to disassociate themselves from their ethnic group, which is regarded as a barrier to their social mobility aspirations. Their internalization of white middle-class goals and values and the concomitant nonacceptance by the white community, engender hostility toward the very group they wish to emulate. These individuals often compensate for their devalued self-image as Negroes and for their marginal position in the white community by becoming leaders in the Negro community. Frazier does not consider the relative effect on such reactions of mobility *into* the higher Negro status position, or of socialization *within* these positions. This is one of the major issues to be considered in this paper.

Reference group theory, as discussed by Hyman (1942) and Merton (1957), provides a wider context for Frazier's ideas about the dilemma of the "black bourgeoisie." In fact, Hyman (1942, p. 84) cites Negro identification patterns as a special instance of reference group behavior, and Lewin (1948) makes use of the same formulations in his discussions of the Jewish group. The pertinence of Merton's position on reference group theory for Frazier's characterization can be illustrated by the following:

> The marginal man pattern represents the special case in a relatively closed social system in which the members of one group [the "black bourgeoisie"] take as a positive frame of reference the norms of a group from which they are excluded in principle [non-acceptance by the white middle-class]. Within such a social structure, anticipatory socialization [expectation of acceptance by white middle class] becomes dysfunctional [acceptance of negative stereotypes about Negroes and of white middle-class values and goals] for the individual who becomes the victim of aspirations he cannot achieve and hopes he cannot satisfy (Merton, 1957, p. 266).

In this paper, we intend to utilize concepts from reference group theory to explain the ethnic identification patterns of socially mobile and non-mobile Negroes.

In a given status position there are three types of individuals: those socialized at that level (i.e., "stable" individuals), those who have experienced upward mobility, and those who have been downwardly mobile. How is the ethnic identification of these types of individuals related to their reference group behavior? We assume that the ethnic attitudes of socially mobile individuals are determined by the reference values of their former status level (i.e., parental position), and of their current level. On the basis of this assumption, we expect the attitudes of mobile individuals to include components of both status levels. For example, the individual currently in a status group having negative attitudes toward Negroes, but who has come from a group with comparatively positive attitudes, will exhibit more positive attitudes than "stable" persons at his present level. Specific predictions flowing from this general rationale will be presented in a later section.

PROCEDURE

The data for this paper were collected as part of a larger project [1] investigating the relationship between mental illness and the

discrepancy between aspiration and achievement. Information was gathered from two different populations: (1) a psychiatric sample (N = 1,423) admitted as in- or outpatients to selected public and private agencies during the period March 1, 1960–May 15, 1961; and (2) a sample drawn from the Philadelphia Negro community (N = 1,489). Individuals in the two samples were Negroes, age 20 to 60 years, living in Philadelphia; both they and their parents had been born within the continental United States. Since this report is concerned only with data collected for the community sample, the description of the procedure will be limited to this group.

The interview instrument was a 206-item questionnaire, designed for a person-to-person interview in the home. The questionnaire was introduced to the respondent as part of a study concerned with the attitudes and health status of the Philadelphia Negro, conducted jointly by the institutions with which the authors were affiliated.[2] The 28 interviewers were also Negroes, age 20 to 60 years, with a mean education of 15.1 years. The initial objective was 1,500 community interviews, with a 1/200 probability of selection for any given individual. The sampling procedure was divided into a five-stage design, based on stratified and proportionate sampling.

In the coding procedure reliability checks were made between: (1) the Project Directors; (2) each of the Project Directors and the supervisor of the two coders; (3) the supervisor and each coder; (4) the coders. The average reliabilities at all levels were over 90 percent.

Since the project involved a Negro sample, a class index based on the various criteria of social status mentioned by members of the Philadelphia Negro community itself was developed. Respondents were asked: "What things do you think of when you decide what social class a person belongs to? Choose three

[1] Supported by Research Grant M-3047, National Institutes of Health, Public Health Service, Bethesda, Maryland. The community survey was conducted by National Analysts, Inc., Philadelphia, Pa. The authors wish to express their appreciation to Miss Judith Fine for her invaluable assistance in preparing this paper for publication.

[2] Jefferson Medical College and the Pennsylvania Department of Public Welfare.

from the list, in order of importance." The list included one's education, neighborhood, income, family background, occupation, color of skin, membership organizations, influence in the community, and any other factor specified. In order to weight the responses for importance, a first choice was multiplied by three, a second by two, and a third by one; the weighted choices were summed for every response category. The three components of the index were weighted according to the relative difference in the summed weighted scores for each category (education, 4.4; income, 2.5; and occupation, unweighted).[3] Measures of each of the selected index components were collapsed into a seven-step scale so that these relative weights would be the principal determinants of the index score. Rather than use occupational prestige scales developed with primarily white populations, a new seven-step occupational scale was developed from a special study of a Negro sub-sample. The final index score for any individual was determined as follows:

$$(Education \times 4.4) +$$
$$(Income \times 2.5) + (Occupation \times 1).$$

The index score for housewives was determined by using the respondent's own educational level, and the income and occupational level of the head of household. The social status scores for the community sample were divided into four approximately equal groups, designated as status position 1 (lowest) through 4 (highest). Subsequent sections of this paper will focus on data showing a consistent increase or decrease from position 1 to 4.

In the present paper, 16 items from the 206-item interview schedule will be evaluated. The paper will be divided into three sections:

(1) The distribution, by status position, of responses for each of the 16 items will be presented.

(2) The proportion of individuals, by status position, showing each of three types

---

[3] Although occupation was used as a component of the final index, it was not selected as the third most important determinant of social status. We had included numerous questionnaire items on occupation, under the assumption that this would be an area of major concern to our population.

of ethnic identification response patterns will be determined. These response configurations (ambivalence, consistent weak, and consistent positive, identification) are defined in terms of combinations of selected responses to each of six pairs of questions involving different hypothetical conditions: [4]

Situation 1: reaction to "passing" vs. reaction to favorable ("award") headline;

Situation 2: reaction to unfavorable ("arrest") headline vs. reaction to favorable headline;

Situation 3: reaction to "passing" vs. reaction to unfavorable headline;

Situation 4: reasons for reactions in pair of questions under Situation 1;

Situation 5: reasons for reactions in pair of questions under Situation 2;

Situation 6: reasons for reactions in pair of questions under Situation 3.

In the definition of Situations 1–6, those responses were selected that showed a systematic relationship to status position.

(3) The relationship between type of identification response pattern (i.e., ambivalence, weak, or positive) and educational mobility (i.e., upward, downward, or stable) will be analyzed.

It is important to note that, since all data are based on interviews, we cannot distinguish between an individual's private or public expression; however, we can point out the nature of his conflicts, as reflected by his responses.

---

[4] For example, considering the questions covered in Situation 6: anger at a friend's "passing" and condoning a Negro's arrest, or, conversely, condoning a friend's "passing" and an assumption of discrimination against the arrested Negro, may be considered ambivalence patterns; condoning a friend's "passing" coupled with condoning a Negro's arrest, may be considered a consistent weak identification pattern; anger at a friend's "passing," combined with an assumption of discrimination against the arrested Negro, may be considered a consistent positive identification pattern.

All the data discussed are significant at less than the .001 level of confidence, unless otherwise indicated.

RESULTS

1. Relationship Between Questionnaire Items and Status Position

A. ASPIRATIONS FOR SELF AND FOR HYPOTHETICAL SON

Frazier's thesis states that the Negro "bourgeoisie" internalize the values and goals of the white middle and upper classes. This is consistent with reference group theory, which predicts that an individual or group moving toward a higher status position will incorporate the goals and values of the aspired group. Educational aspirations of graduate school (Level 7, Table 1) for a

firmed. On the other hand, those with occupational aspirations for a hypothetical son at Levels 1 and 2 (i.e., unskilled and semi-skilled) and 3 and 4 (i.e., skilled and clerical), decrease from position 1 through 4.

It was predicted that occupational aspirations for oneself would also rise with status position. The percentage of those aspiring to occupational Levels 1 and 2 (i.e., unskilled and semi-skilled) diminishes from the lowest to the highest status position (see Table 1). Conversely, aspirations to occupational levels 3 and 4 (i.e., skilled and clerical), 5 and 6 (i.e., minor professional and business), and 7 (i.e., major professions) increase from the lowest to the highest position.

The percentage of those with income aspirations at the highest level (Level 7, Table 1) increases from status position 1 through 4. The percentage of those aspiring only to Levels 3 and 4, however, decreases with increasing status position.

TABLE 1   Aspirations for Self and Hypothetical Son, by Social Status Position*

Aspiration Level	Occupation-Son Social Status				Income-Self Social Status				Education-Son Social Status				Occupation-Self Social Status			
	1	2	3	4	1	2	3	4	1	2	3	4	1	2	3	4
	%	%	%	%	%	%	%	%	%	%	%	%	%	%	%	%
1 and 2	63	51	40	14	11	2	—	—	—	—	—	—	13	10	5	3
3 and 4	17	28	34	38	63	49	39	16	26	15	17	7	19	16	12	7
5 and 6	17	19	19	36	19	36	39	39	62	66	61	53	21	21	17	18
7	1	2	6	12	6	13	22	44	12	19	22	39	47	53	64	71

* Each percentage is based on the total number of individuals in any given social status group.
Position 1: N = 354.
Position 2: N = 350.
Position 3: N = 386.
Position 4: N = 382.
Position Unknown: N = 17 (Excluded from analyses).
Any total percentage < 99 for a given status group reflects those in individuals for whom status position could be computed, but who gave no response to the particular item.

hypothetical son, a highly-prized goal in the white community, increase in occurrence from status position 1 (lowest) through 4 (highest). On the other hand, the number of individuals who would be satisfied with some high school or high school graduation (Levels 3 and 4, Table 1) for a hypothetical son decreases from position 1 through 4.

Occupational aspirations at the professional level (Level 7, Table 1) for a hypothetical son were expected to increase from position 1 through 4; this expectation is con-

In summary, data on educational, occupational, and income goal striving for self and hypothetical son confirm the prediction that internalization of prevailing attitudes in the larger white community will increase with status position.

B. BLUE OR WHITE COLLAR
OCCUPATIONAL PREFERENCES

Since white collar-high prestige occupations are valued by the white middle and upper classes, we predicted an increasing preference for these occupations, from position 1 through 4. Conversely, an increasing preference for blue collar-low prestige occupations was predicted as status position goes down from 4 through 1. For each of three choice situations (Set I, II, and III, Table 2) these predictions are confirmed.

TABLE 2 Blue or White Collar Occupational Preferences, by Social Status Position*

Blue/White Collar Preference	Social Status			
	1	*2*	*3*	*4*
	%	%	%	%
Set I:				
Bricklayer @ $120/week	53	41	35	23
Teacher @ $90/week	47	58	65	77
Set II:				
Machine Oper. @ $100/week	59	52	46	38
Gov't Clerk @ $80/week	41	48	54	62
Set III:				
Factory Worker @ $80/week	67	65	62	46
Sales (dept. store) @ $60/week	33	35	38	54

* See footnote to Table 1.

C. RACIAL COMPOSITION OF ACHIEVED (OR ACTUAL) AND ASPIRED NEIGHBORHOOD

Another characteristic ascribed to the Negro "bourgeoisie" by Frazier is a desire to live in predominantly white communities. Reference group theory predicts similar preferences for individuals aspiring to membership in some coveted group. In the present study, respondents were asked to describe the racial composition of the neighborhood in which they actually resided, and of a neighborhood in which they would like to live. The percentage of those describing their actual neighborhood as "predominantly white" (i.e., encompassing responses of "almost all white," "mixed-mostly white," and "half-and-half") increases from status position 1 through 4 (i.e., 6%, 7%, 8%, and 9%, respectively). The small number of cases in each status group precludes any statistical evaluation. As status position rises, there is also an increase in the proportion of respondents describing their neighborhood as "mixed-mostly Negro" (i.e., 53%, 58%, 64%, and 66%, respectively), and a decrease in the proportion who

live in an "all Negro" neighborhood (i.e., 40%, 35%, 28%, and 24%, respectively).

It is noteworthy that a majority of respondents in each of the four status groups describe their actual neighborhood as "mixed." These findings, if valid, are inconsistent with the generally accepted assumption that Negroes live in all Negro neighborhoods. It is possible that respondents use the characterization "mixed-mostly Negro" loosely (e.g., a white storekeeper on an otherwise Negro residential block). If there is a tendency to exaggerate the "mixed" quality of one's neighborhood, which reflects a desire to live in such a neighborhood, the preference for predominantly white neighborhoods should increase with status position (as Frazier predicts). Our data show this to be the case (see Table 3).

TABLE 3 Racial Composition of Aspired Neighborhood, by Social Status Position*

Racial Composition	Social Status			
	1	*2*	*3*	*4*
	%	%	%	%
Almost all white ⎫ Predominantly White				
Mixed-mostly white ⎬ nantly	13	21	24	30
Half-and-half ⎭ White				
Mixed-mostly Negro	20	21	22	21
All Negro	26	19	10	5
No preference	40	38	43	44

* See footnote to Table 1.

At the same time, the preference for all Negro neighborhoods decreases from position 1 through 4.

Approximately 40 percent of all status groups express "no preference" about the racial composition of an aspired neighborhood. This is particularly important because the pre-coded response choices do not include "no preference"; this response was recorded only at the respondent's insistence. These findings could mean either that subjects actually have "no preference," or that they would like to select a neighborhood without considering the racial issue. If "no preference" actually determines neighborhood choice, moving patterns would be more diffuse. In reality, Negroes move into "broken" areas, or those already predominantly Negro. It seems more likely that those giving a "no preference" response would like to select a neighborhood on a basis other than its racial composition, but are not free to do so.

In summary, the data show that as status position rises, the proportion of those describing their actual neighborhood as "mixed" or "predominantly white" increases. There is also an increase in those who aspire to a predominantly white neighborhood, and a decrease in those who aspire to an all Negro neighborhood, from position 1 through 4. These findings confirm the predictions about the relationship between status and interest in living among whites.

D. REACTIONS TO HYPOTHETICAL SITUATIONS

Frazier predicts a decreasing involvement and identification with the Negro community with an increase in status position. Respondents in our study were asked how they would feel if they saw the (unfavorable) headline, "Negro Seized in Camden." The percentage of those feeling "very uncomfortable" or "fairly uncomfortable" decreases as status rises, while "slightly uncomfortable" and "no feeling" responses increase from status position 1 through 4 (see Table 4). Respondents

TABLE 4 Reactions to Hypothetical Racial Situations, by Social Status Position*

Reaction to Hypothetical Racial Situation	Social Status			
	1	*2*	*3*	*4*
	%	%	%	%
Unfavorable Headline: *"Negro Seized in Camden"*				
Very or fairly uncomfortable	59	53	47	36
Slightly uncomfortable or no feelings	39	46	51	63
A Friend's "Passing"				
Mixed feelings toward him	27	34	35	38
Angry with him	28	24	21	17
Glad for him; no feelings; other	45	41	42	45

* See footnote to Table 1.

were also asked their reactions to the (favorable) headline, "Negro Receives Major Award." The percentage of those who feel "very" or "fairly proud" changes relatively little from status position 1 through 4 (i.e.,

90%, 89%, 89%, and 87%, respectively). Similarly, the number of those who would be "slightly proud," have "no feelings," or be "slightly annoyed" shows no variation with status position (i.e., 10%, 11%, 11%, and 13%, respectively). It is interesting that 59 percent of those in position 1 (lowest) feel "very uncomfortable" or "fairly uncomfortable" about the unfavorable headline, whereas 90 percent are "very" or "fairly proud" about the favorable headline. Among those in position 4 (highest), 36 percent feel "very uncomfortable" or "fairly uncomfortable," in contrast to 87 percent who are "very" or "fairly proud." These contrasting response patterns indicate that more upper than lower status individuals deny their involvement in unfavorable publicity situations; however, at the same time they profess to be equally proud and enthusiastic about the reported success. This suggests more inconsistent emotional involvement in racial matters among higher status individuals.

In a third hypothetical situation, reactions to a friend's intention to "pass" were elicited. The data show no differences by status position for the responses "glad for him," "no feeling," and "other" (see Table 4). However, the proportion of those with "mixed feelings toward him" increases from position 1 through 4. The chi square is 11.03 (p = < .02 > .01). This response indicates conscious feelings of conflict within the individual about an act which denies one's racial identity. The number of respondents who would be "angry with him" decreases as status position rises. The chi square is 14.40 (p = < .01).

It is clear that the higher status individuals deny involvement in the unfavorable situation, express mixed feelings toward a friend who would "pass," and profess pride in the favorable situation. On the other hand, lower status individuals show more feelings of discomfort about unfavorable publicity, greater feelings of anger at a friend who would "pass," and pride in the favorable situation. The data suggest weaker or more ambivalent involvement in the racial aspects of a situation for those in upper status positions.

E. REASONS FOR REACTIONS TO HYPOTHETICAL SITUATIONS

Table 5 includes only the percentages for the significant response categories for the

TABLE 5 Reasons for Neighborhood Aspirations and for Reactions to Other Hypothetical Racial Situations, by Social Status Position*

Reasons	Social Status			
	1	2	3	4
	%	%	%	%
*Aspired Neighborhood***				
Positive statement about Negroes	26	22	14	10
*Unfavorable Headline***				
Assumption of discrimination and/or injustice; or Positive identification with Negroes	40	32	30	21
Empathy with individual (race not explicit)	11	8	6	4
Defers judgment	12	20	25	24
*Favorable Headline***				
Accomplishment of Negro (explicit)	59	54	51	48
Concern with improvement of public image	11	20	22	24

* See footnote to Table 1.
** Only the significant "reasons" responses are presented. The complete content categories for neighborhood aspirations and other hypothetical racial situations are as follows:

Aspired Neighborhood: Race irrelevant; Positive statement about Negroes; Negative statement about whites; Negative statement about Negroes; Positive statement about whites; Better neighborhood—emphasis on physical characteristics; Better neighborhood—emphasis on social characteristics; Concern for integration; Other.

Unfavorable Headline: Race irrelevant; Concern with public image; Assumption of discrimination and/or injustice; Empathy with individual (race not explicit); Negative statement about Negroes; Condones seizure; Defers judgment; Positive statement about Negroes; None; Other.

Favorable Headline: Accomplishment of Negro (explicit); Concern with improvement of public image; Accomplishment of a person (race not explicit); None; Other.

"Passing": Up to individual; Approves without qualification; Approves with qualification; Decision not practical; Detrimental to race (e.g., "traitor to race," "deserter," etc.); Should affirm Negro identity; Other.

four hypothetical situations. The major finding about "reasons for neighborhood aspirations" is the decrease in "positive statements about Negroes" as status increases.

Considering the reasons for respondents' reactions to the unfavorable headline, the percentages for "race irrelevant," "concern with public image," "condones seizure," and "defers judgment" increase with status position. However, "defers judgment" is the only category significantly related to status when

analyzed alone. It is possible that individuals giving one of these responses either (1) deny the racial aspects of the situation; (2) are more concerned with the image of the Negro presented to the larger white community; (3) assume the arrested person to be guilty, possibly showing an acceptance of the white stereotype about Negroes as criminals; (4) assume an "objective" point of view, thereby also denying the racial aspects of the situation.

Two of the response categories (i.e., "assumption of discrimination and/or injustice" and "positive identification with Negroes") increase as status goes down from position 4 through 1. The response involving "discrimination and/or injustice" assumes that the individual arrested by the police is innocent. Since the headline gives no facts other than that of arrest, any more detailed interpretation of the situation must reflect respondents' projections. The proportion giving the response "empathy with the individual" increases as one moves down the status hierarchy. If those giving this response are not, in fact, oriented to the racial aspects of the situation, those in lower status groups would seem to have greater ability to sympathize with individuals in trouble.

Thus, the data show an increase in the proportion of those who have weak identification with the Negro community, or who deny the racial characteristics of the hypothetical "arrest" situation, as status position goes up. In addition, the proportion of those who have positive identification with the Negro community, or who express empathy for individuals in trouble, increases as status position goes down.

In regard to reasons for reactions to the "award" headline, the proportion of those individuals concerned with the "improvement of the public image" of the Negro increases from position 1 through 4 (paralleling the trend noted for the same response category in the "arrest" headline context). As social status decreases from position 4 through 1, there is an increase in feelings of satisfaction with the "accomplishment of a Negro." It should be noted that this category includes only those responses involving explicit references to the Negro aspects of the situation.

None of the response categories dealing with reasons for reactions to "passing" is significantly related to social status. There is a tendency for the percentage of those who feel one "should affirm his Negro identity" to increase as status position goes down. There is also some indication that the proportion of those who feel the decision to "pass" is a personal one increases from position 1 through 4.

2. Response Pattern Analyses by Social Status Position

Up to this point, we have been concerned only with the distribution of responses for single items, by social status groups. Although we may characterize different status groups by this type of presentation (e.g., Kleiner, Parker, and Taylor, 1962), it will be more fruitful to determine to what extent the responses of a given individual coincide or conflict with one another. Specifically, we intend to show that attitudinal trends by social status position at the group level reflect these same trends within individuals occupying the different status levels.

Frazier's thesis predicts a greater preference for predominantly white neighborhoods as social status increases. Table 6, in effect,

neighborhoods aspire inceasingly to predominantly white neighborhoods. (The chi square for the "mixed-mostly Negro" category is 8.74 (p = < .05 > .02)). There is no relationship between any of the types of achieved neighborhoods and the proportion of individuals aspiring to a "mixed-mostly Negro" neighborhood. However, for each of the three achieved neighborhood categories (i.e., "all Negro," "mixed-mostly Negro," and "predominantly white"), the percentage of those who prefer an "all Negro" neighborhood decreases from status position 1 through 4. The significance of "predominantly white" (actual), compared to "all Negro" (aspired), was not evaluated because of the small number of cases in status positions 1 and 2.

These data clearly show an increasing preference for predominantly white neighborhoods from status position 1 through 4, and an increasing preference for "all Negro" neighborhoods as status position goes down.

The remainder of the Results section will deal with the relationship between three types of response patterns (ambivalence, consistent weak, and consistent positive ethnic identifi-

TABLE 6 Interrelationship of Achieved Neighborhood and Aspired Neighborhood, by Social Status Position*

Achieved Neighborhood	Predominantly white (cf. Table 3) Social Status				Mixed-Negro Social Status				All Negro Social Status				No preference Social Status			
	1	2	3	4	1	2	3	4	1	2	3	4	1	2	3	4
	%	%	%	%	%	%	%	%	%	%	%	%	%	%	%	%
Predominantly white (cf. Table 3)	45	57	48	50	5	4	7	11	23	4	3	—	27	26	41	39
Mixed-mostly Negro	12	18	22	26	23	25	24	24	16	14	7	3	49	42	45	47
All Negro	10	18	21	31	19	20	22	20	40	30	19	12	30	33	38	37

* See footnote to Table 1.

determines the relationship between aspired neighborhood and social status, controlling for achieved neighborhood. This type of presentation also indicates the extent to which the respondent's aspired neighborhood is influenced by the characteristics of his actual neighborhood. As status goes up, those living in "mixed-mostly Negro" and "all Negro"

cation) and social status. Several of the previous item analyses indicate a diminishing positive identification with the Negro community at the group level, from status position 1 through 4; in other analyses, the reverse appears to be the case. By considering several responses simultaneously, for any given *individual*, we may determine whether a response showing positive identification in fact reflects conflicting attitudes about ethnic identification.

Table 7 shows the percentage of individuals in each status position who manifest one of the three types of ethnic identification patterns already defined. A consideration of Frazier's thesis, along with our earlier data, leads to a prediction of more frequent ambivalent or weak identification patterns in the higher status groups. Only for Situation 2 does ambivalence increase from status posi-

TABLE 7 Ethnic Identification and Social Status Position*

	Social Status			
Ethnic Identification	1	2	3	4
	%	%	%	%
Ambivalence				
Situation 1**	22	28	34	32
Situation 2	26	39	42	47
Situation 3	29	27	25	21
Situation 4	26	25	32	29
Situation 5	25	36	35	33
Situation 6	33	36	37	31
Consistent Weak				
Situation 1**	—	—	—	—
Situation 2	4	6	4	7
Situation 3	9	15	18	24
Situation 4	5	8	10	10
Situation 5	6	10	12	15
Situation 6	17	21	27	30
Consistent Positive				
Situation 1**	21	21	17	14
Situation 2	48	45	41	31
Situation 3	17	14	12	9
Situation 4	26	22	18	16
Situation 5	37	23	20	18
Situation 6	23	12	12	10

* Each percentage is that part of 100% in each status group manifesting the particular response pattern.
** The nature of "ethnic identification" is inferred from selected responses to the following pairs of questions:
   Situation 1: Reaction to "passing" vs. reaction to favorable headline;
   Situation 2: Reaction to unfavorable headline vs. reaction to favorable headline;
   Situation 3: Reaction to "passing" vs. reaction to unfavorable headline;
   Situation 4: Reasons for reaction to "passing" vs. reasons for reaction to favorable headline;
   Situation 5: Reasons for reaction to "passing" vs. reasons for reaction to unfavorable headline;
   Situation 6: Reasons for reaction to unfavorable headline vs. reasons for reaction to favorable headline.

tion 1 through 4 (see Table 7). For Situation 1, the proportion of those showing ambivalence increases from position 1 through 3 and drops in position 4. However, the chi square for status positions 1 and 2 (combined), compared to positions 3 and 4 (combined) is significant. Conversely for Situation 3, ambivalence decreases from position 1 through 4, but these percentages are not significant.

The results presented previously suggest that ambivalence increases from status position 1 through 4. The present data, however, do not overwhelmingly confirm this prediction.

Except for Situation 2, the consistent weak ethnic identification pattern increases with status position for the four other Situations.[5] However, only Situations 3, 5, and 6 are significant. It is interesting that for this same Situation (i.e., 2) ambivalence patterns did increase with status position. This suggests that a Situation can show either increasing ambivalence or weak identification, with status position, but that it would be difficult for both patterns to appear. The data, therefore, show an increase in weak identification from position 1 through 4.

In each of the six Situations, the percentage of those with a consistent positive identification pattern increases significantly as status goes down, except for Situations 1 and 3 ($p = < .10 > .05$). The consistency of this data and the degree of significance clearly support Frazier's statement that positive identification diminishes as status increases.

It should be emphasized that the observed correlations between identification and status position probably operate independently of one another. As mentioned earlier, Situations 1-6 were defined in terms of particular responses (i.e., those showing a systematic relationship to status) to selected questions. Although all those in each status group were used to determine percentages, every individual did not necessarily manifest one of the three identification patterns.

3. Mobility and Ethnic Identification

Having related ethnic identification to status position, we will consider the influence

[5] There were too few cases in each status position to compute percentages for Situation 1.

of mobility itself on such patterns. We have discussed the rationale for predicting that an individual's identification is an approximate equilibration of the norms of his present and past status groups. In the present paper, an individual's mobility is defined in terms of his own and his parental educational level. If the educational achievements of his parents differ, the higher of the two is selected. The use of education for this purpose is based on three considerations: (1) educational achievement is known for each individual in our sample, and for at least one of his parents; (2) education has been found to be an important element in the Negro's social mobility; (3) both education and the social status index are significantly correlated with each ethnic identification pattern.

On the basis of reference group theory, we hypothesize that the mobile individual (either upwardly or downwardly) holds attitudes deriving from two reference points: his former and his current status position. Thus, specific predictions (Table 8 and 9) rest on the modal response patterns of the various status levels (Table 7).

In Table 8, parental educational level is held constant, and the individual's mobility is estimated from this point. Of the nine predictions, the comparisons made for eight are in the expected direction, and one is inconclusive (by Sign Test $p = < .004$). Five of the eight predictions are significant ($p = < .05$). Only for the consistent positive identification pattern are there significant differences between the two mobile groups and the "stables." As the individual moves upward from his parental status level, he shows significantly less positive ethnic identification, and significantly more ambivalent and weak patterns. The downwardly mobile individual tends to show less ambivalence and weak identification, and more positive identification than the "stables" at his parental (higher) status level. It should also be noted that for all three identification patterns, the upwardly mobile differ significantly from the "stables"; the downwardly mobile differ only in positive identification.

In order to determine the relative influence of current status and past mobility on ethnic identification, comparisons of the different mobility groups were made within given status levels (see Table 9). Eight of the nine predictions are in the expected direction, and one is not (by Sign Test $p = < .04$); two of the

TABLE 8　Predictions of Types of Ethnic Identification of Mobile and "Stable" Individuals, Using Parental Educational Level as a Point of Origin

Predictions of Types of Ethnic Identification	Confirmed**	Not Confirmed	Level of Significance (By Sign Test)
*Ambivalence**			
Upwardly mobile higher than "stable"	17	4	.004
Downwardly mobile lower than "stable"	9	8	.50
Upwardly mobile higher than downwardly mobile	8	4	.19
Consistent Weak			
Upwardly mobile higher than "stable"	15	4	.01
Downwardly mobile lower than "stable"	8	8	.60
Upwardly mobile higher than downwardly mobile	8	5	.29
Consistent Positive			
Upwardly mobile lower than "stable"	17	5	.008
Downwardly mobile higher than "stable"	16	6	.03
Upwardly mobile lower than downwardly mobile	13	1	.001

* See second footnote to Table 7.
** The number of tests for each prediction is influenced by three factors:
  (a) instances in which the percentages for any two groups in a given prediction are equal;
  (b) the number of Situations actually analyzed (i.e., Situations 1–6 for Ambivalance and Positive; Situations 2–5 for Weak);
  (c) instances in which the parental educational level precludes comparisons (e.g., an individual at the lowest parental educational level cannot be downwardly mobile).

TABLE 9 Predictions of Types of Ethnic Identification of Mobile and "Stable" Individuals, Using Respondent's Educational Level as a Point of Origin

Predictions of Types of Ethnic Identification	Confirmed**	Not Confirmed	Level of Significance (By Sign Test)
*Ambivalence**			
Upwardly mobile lower than "stable"	8	7	.50
Downwardly mobile higher than "stable"	11	2	.01
Upwardly mobile lower than downwardly mobile	8	4	.19
Consistent Weak			
Upwardly mobile lower than "stable"	13	8	.19
Downwardly mobile higher than "stable"	10	8	.76
Upwardly mobile lower than downwardly mobile	9	5	.21
Consistent Positive			
Upwardly mobile higher than "stable"	14	9	.20
Downwardly mobile lower than "stable"	20	4	.001
Upwardly mobile higher than downwardly mobile	8	10	—

* See second footnote to Table 7.
** The number of tests for each prediction is influenced by three factors:
   (a) instances in which the percentages for any two groups in a given prediction are equal;
   (b) the number of Situations actually analyzed (i.e., Situations 1–6 for Ambivalence; five Situations for Positive; and six Situations for Weak);
   (c) instances in which the respondent's educational level precludes comparisons (e.g., an individual at the lowest educational level cannot be downwardly mobile with respect to parental educational level).

eight are significant. Although the findings do not indicate overall significant differences between the mobile groups and the "stables," or between each other, there are consistent tendencies suggesting that mobility is a relevant factor. The upwardly mobile tend to show less ambivalence and weak, and more positive, identification than the "stables" in their current status group. The downwardly mobile manifest significantly more ambivalence, and significantly less positive identification than the "stables."

When Tables 8 and 9 are examined independently, the findings relating mobility and identification patterns appear inconsistent. This apparent difference is reconciled when the tables are viewed in juxtaposition. The attitudes held by the upwardly mobile are significantly different from those of the "stables" in their parental status group (see Table 8), but not significantly different from those of the "stables" in their current status group (see Table 9). Although the upwardly mobile are not identical to the "stables" at their present status level (for weak and positive identification patterns—see Table 9), they use them as their primary reference group. The downwardly mobile differ from

the "stables" of their current group (see Table 9); apparently the latter are *not* their primary reference point. This is clarified by the fact that the downwardly mobile do not differ significantly from their parental status level in two of the three identification patterns (see Table 8). It is interesting that both mobile groups attempt to maximize their self-esteem by selecting the higher of their two potential reference groups (the parental level for the downwardly mobile, and the current level for the upwardly mobile). Furthermore, although both mobile groups equilibrate their attitudes, the higher reference point determines the degree of change. While the predictions based on equilibration of norms go in the expected direction, they all become significant when the probabilities of their *joint* occurrence are considered.

SUMMARY AND CONCLUSION

The data presented in sections 1 and 2 of the Results clearly support Frazier's thesis of the Negro "bourgeoisie." Negroes in the higher status positions tend to have values more similar to those of the white middle class, stronger desires to associate with whites, more internalization of negative attitudes toward other Negroes, and relatively weaker ethnic identification, than individuals in lower status positions. By examining the compatibility of responses to different questions (using the individual as the unit of analysis), we note that both ambivalence and consistent weak identification patterns increase with status, while consistent positive identification decreases. Reference group theory permits us to understand Frazier's ideas and our related findings. It also allows us to make a series of predictions about the relationship between identification and social mobility (regardless of direction) from a consistent theoretical point of view. The identification patterns of the upwardly and the downwardly mobile can be explained by two factors: the simultaneous influence of two reference groups, and the choice of the higher as the primary one, in an attempt to maximize self-esteem. These conclusions are congruent with results and interpretations reported in experimental studies with small groups.

The consideration of another potential reference group, the aspired status group, might have enabled us to predict with greater accuracy. This factor should be carefully evaluated by future researchers in this area.

REFERENCES

Frazier, E. F. *Black Bourgeoisie.* Glencoe, Ill.: The Free Press, 1957.

Fuller, H. W. Rise of the Negro Militant. *The Nation,* September 14, 1963, **197,** No. 7, 138–140.

Hyman, H. H. *The Psychology of Status.* New York: Archives of Psychology, No. 269, 1942.

Kleiner, R. J., Parker, S., & Taylor, H. *Social Status and Aspirations in Philadelphia's Negro Population.* Philadelphia: Commission on Human Relations, 1962.

Lewin, K. *Resolving Social Conflicts.* New York: Harper and Brothers, 1948.

Lomax, L. E. The Negro Revolt against "the Negro leaders." *Harper's Magazine,* June 1960, **220,** No. 1321, 41–48.

Merton, R. K. *Social Theory and Social Structure,* revised edition. Glencoe, Illinois: The Free Press, 1957.

7

Alienation in the ghetto[1]

BONNIE BULLOUGH

Thirty years ago Chicago sociologists described the pattern of the urban Negro ghetto. The center of the "black belt" was occupied by the new arrivals to the city who were often unskilled and unemployed. The more successful and better-educated residents tended to move further out toward the periphery of the area; occasionally they even moved a short distance beyond the concentrated Negro area, so that there were neighborhoods which were temporarily integrated as the ghetto expanded.[2] In spite of the cur-

Reprinted from *American Journal of Sociology,* 1967, **72,** 469–478, by permission of the author and the University of Chicago Press. Copyright 1964, the University of Chicago Press.

[1] I am indebted to Melvin Seeman for advice and help in all stages of the research and in preparation of this manuscript. Computing assistance was obtained from the Health Sciences Computing facility of the University of California, Los Angeles, sponsored by National Institutes of Health grant FR-3. I am supported by a U.S. Public Health special-nurse fellowship.

[2] E. Franklin Frazier, "The Negro Family in

rent revolutionary drive for integration, this over-all pattern has not changed much in the large cities of the North and West. Even in the sixteen states that have laws making discrimination in housing illegal there has been no massive movement toward residential desegregation.[3]

Recently, however, it has been reported that in Boston, Seattle, and Philadelphia there are isolated Negro families who have moved completely away from the old ghettos and have settled in previously all white areas.[4] In Los Angeles, where a similar movement has taken place, a small but growing number of Negro families have moved into the previously all white areas of the San Fernando Valley. Although actually a part of the sprawling city of Los Angeles, "the Valley" is separated from the older, central portion of the city by the Santa Monica mountain range. It is one of the fastest growing areas in the country, having developed in the last twenty years from a few scattered communities to one large solidly settled area with almost a million inhabitants. Even before the postwar building boom it contained one predominantly Negro community called Pacoima, which reported a Negro population of 9,000 in 1960,[5] but the remaining large

expanse of the Valley was until recently almost "lily white." It is too soon to say whether the movement of these scattered Negro families in Los Angeles or elsewhere portends future urban integration, but such a possibility cannot be discounted. In any case these first families, which I have called "barrier breakers," seemed like an interesting group of people to study.

Preliminary investigation of the families in Los Angeles who had made this move indicated that they tended to be well educated and occupationally successful, which is consistent with the findings reported in the other cities mentioned. Since portions of the Los Angeles ghetto also contain areas in which there are many well educated and successful Negroes, it was reasoned that socioeconomic status was not the only factor that determined who would be able to break through the barriers of housing discrimination. The problem for research, then, was to determine some of the social-psychological characteristics that distinguish the barrier breakers from other middle-class Negroes.

The main theoretical framework used to investigate the social psychological barriers to integration was an alienation one. Alienation would seem to be particularly important since it has been mentioned as an aspect of ghetto life by many writers, both popular and scholarly.[6] The alienation of many Negro residents of Los Angeles was dramatically demonstrated in smoke and flames across the skies of Watts during the riots. The rioters, however, were drawn primarily from the poorly educated, unemployed youths,[7] and the focus of this research, which was actually completed before the riots, was on the conse-

Chicago," in Ernest Burgess and Donald Bogue (eds.), *Contributions to Urban Sociology* (Chicago: University of Chicago Press, 1964), pp. 404–18. A similar pattern was described by St. Clair Drake and H. R. Cayton in *Black Metropolis* (New York: Harcourt, Brace & Co., 1945), pp. 174–213.

[3] "How the Fair Housing Laws Are Working," *Trends in Housing*, **IX** (November–December, 1965), 3–4, 7–10.

[4] Helen MacGill Hughes and Lewis G. Watts, "Portrait of the Self Integrator," *Journal of Social Issues*, **XX** (April, 1964), 103–15; L. D. Northwood and Ernest A. T. Barth, *Urban Desegregation: Negro Pioneers and Their White Neighbors* (Seattle: University of Washington Press, 1965); and Commission on Human Relations, *Some Factors Affecting Housing Desegregation* (Philadelphia, 1962).

[5] Marchia Meeker and Joan Harris, *Background for Planning* (Los Angeles: Research Department, Welfare Planning Council, Report #17, 1964), pp. 55–60. A Negro population of 334,916 was reported in 1960 in the city of Los Angeles; see Los Angeles County Commission on Human Relations, *Population and Housing in Los Angeles County: A Study in the*

Growth of Residential Segregation (Los Angeles, 1963), p. 1.

[6] See, e.g., James Baldwin, *The Fire Next Time* (New York: Dial Press, 1963); Charles Silberman, *Crisis in Black and White* (New York: Random House, 1964), pp. 189–223; James Coleman, "Implications of the Findings on Alienation," *American Journal of Sociology*, **LXX** (July, 1964), 76–78; and Russel Middleton, "Alienation, Race and Education," *American Sociological Review*, **XXVIII** (December, 1963), 793–97.

[7] John A. McCone (chairman), *Violence in the City—An End or a Beginning? A Report by the Governor's Commission on the Los Angeles Riots* (Los Angeles: State of California, 1965).

quences of alienation for the well-educated, employed middle-class ghetto dwellers.

Previous studies have suggested that those who are less alienated are more likely to seek integration. Researchers in a southern Negro college found that students who felt that they themselves could control their own fate were more willing to participate in a civil rights demonstration.[8] In a study done in Nashville the Srole anomia scale was used to predict which families would seek an integrated school for their children.[9] Based on the conceptualization developed by Melvin Seeman, alienation in this research was viewed as not just a single attitude but as a group of attitudinal variables, which under certain conditions can be related, but which for conceptual clarity should not be confused with each other.[10] Three aspects of the alienation complex were investigated: (1) powerlessness; (2) anomia, which in Seeman's scheme is called normlessness; and (3) an orientation toward or away from the ghetto, which in his scheme would be called a type of value isolation. In conceptualizing the direction of orientation as a type of alienation it should be noted that the alienation can be from the values and institutions of the Negro subculture or from the dominant society. It was hypothesized not only that powerlessness and anomia would be associated with ghetto life but that they played a key role in holding people within the old residential patterns. It was also hypothesized that the subjects would turn their attention away from the strictly segregated institutions of the ghetto as they moved out into integrated neighborhoods.

Sixty-one Negro families, scattered throughout the predominantly white section of the Valley, were located and interviewed during the winter and spring of 1964–65. All available Negro adult members of the household were included in the sample (three non-Negro spouses were excluded).[11] This yielded

a sample of 104 persons, 54 men and 50 women. The names and addresses of these subjects were obtained through the efforts of members of the Valley Fair Housing Council, a local civil rights group. Members of the council used a wide variety of contacts to locate the subjects, including other organizations, work contacts, schools, and so on. The subjects themselves were able to furnish the names of some other Valley Negro families known to them. A control group of 106 persons, 48 men and 58 women from sixty-five families, was obtained by randomly sampling two middle-class neighborhoods with Negro populations of over 90 percent. One of these areas was in the Pacoima section of the Valley, and the other was in central Los Angeles, several miles to the north of the now famous Watts area. Actually, the physical characteristics of all the sampled areas, integrated and ghetto, were somewhat similar. Most of the dwellings were single family with just an occasional apartment building; the neighborhoods were attractive and the yards well kept. Sixty-three persons from Pacoima and forty-three from the central Los Angeles area were interviewed; two white spouses were excluded from the sample. There seemed to be little difference between the two ghetto areas; the educational, occupational, and income levels were similar, as well as the findings on the alienation scales, so the two areas were combined for the final analysis.

The powerlessness scale that was used measures the extent to which the subject feels that he himself can control the outcomes of events that concern him.[12] The conceptualization of powerlessness is based on the social-learning theory of Julian B. Rotter, which, stated in a simplified way, holds that behavior is a function of values and expec-

---

[8] Pearl Mayo Gore and Julian B. Rotter, "A Personality Correlate of Social Action," *Journal of Personality*, **XXXI** (March, 1963), 58–64.

[9] Eugene Weinstein and Paul Gusel, "Family Decision Making over Desegregation," *Sociometry*, **XXV** (March, 1963), 58–64.

[10] Melvin Seeman, "On the Meaning of Alienation," *American Sociological Review*, **XXIV** (December, 1959), 783–91.

[11] Both spouses were included in the sample because there was some question ahead of time

as to which one would be the most significant in deciding about moving and in carrying through the decision. As it turned out, there was agreement in most families, although in some one partner was a stronger force in the decision, but it could be either the husband or the wife.

[12] The powerlessness scale was developed by Shephard Liverant, Julian B. Rotter, and others. For a discussion of its use and development see Melvin Seeman, "Alienation and Social Learning in a Reformatory," *American Journal of Sociology*, **LXIV** (November, 1963), 270–84.

tations.[13] It has been argued that people tend to develop generalized expectancies, including those for control or lack of it. Since integration seems to be a commonly held value among Negroes, at least on the surface, it would seem that the expectation for successful integration would play an important role in determining who would make the effort to move into the integrated or predominantly white neighborhood. The powerlessness scale uses a forced-choice format so that subjects chose between pairs of items such as the following: (1) I have usually found that what is going to happen will happen, no matter what I do. (2) Trusting to fate has never turned out as well for me as making a definite decision.

The Srole anomia scale was selected as a second alienation measurement because it seems to be a more global type of measurement of the subject's lack of integration into the ongoing society. The Srole scale also captured the feelings of hopelessness and despair expressed by some of the subjects. It is a five-item Likert-type scale made up of statements such as the following:[14] In spite of what some people say, the lot of the average man is getting worse. A ten-item factual test was constructed to assess the amount of information subjects had about housing integration and the legal rights of minority people in the housing market. It included items such as: Restrictive housing covenants are still legal in California (false) and real-estate offices were defined as places of public accommodation so they are not supposed to discriminate (true).

A fourth scale, which measures the orientation toward or away from the ghetto, was built from information obtained in the interview schedule. It actually measures reported behavior rather than an attitude, but the behavior suggests an underlying orientation toward the Negro subculture of the ghetto or away from it. Subjects indicated what organizations they belonged to, their church affiliations, their chief leisure-time activities, the newspapers and magazines they read regu-

larly, the schools they sent their children to, the racial identities of their close friends, and the degree of integration in their work situations. Each of these items was rated as to whether it was exclusively Negro or was reflective of an integrated situation.[15] It was expected that there would be some drifting away from a strictly segregated life as a part of the process of moving out of the ghetto. Obviously, some of the items in this scale, such as the school, the church, and even the friendship choices, are affected by place of residence, so the fact that the ghetto dwellers and the outsiders would differ was to be expected. It nevertheless proved to be a useful device for looking at what happens to people when they move out.

A special methodological problem in a study such as this one is the possible biasing effect of the race of the interviewer. Approximately half of the interviews were done by white and half by Negro interviewers. The data were therefore analyzed controlling for this factor. Slight differences (not statistically significant) were found in the answers about the racial characteristics of friends; more people indicated that they had non-Negro friends when the interviewer was white. There did not seem to be other differences in responses that could be related to the race of the interviewer.

FINDINGS

As had been anticipated, the educational and income levels of the barrier breakers were high. Their median income was approximately $11,000 a year, which is well over the average Valley income.[16] The hope was that the ghetto samples would be of the same socioeconomic level as the people in the integrated sample, but due to the rather wide

---

[13] Julian B. Rotter, *Social Learning and Clinical Psychology* (Englewood Cliffs, N.J.: Prentice-Hall, Inc., 1954).

[14] Leo Srole, "Social Integration and Certain Corollaries: An Exploratory Study," *American Sociological Review*, **XXI** (December, 1956), 709–16.

[15] The items in this scale of ghetto (versus outside) orientation were scored in the following way: 0 if the activity was ghetto and only that, 1 if no direction could be determined, and 2 or 3 if the activity was clearly integrated or pointed to an outside interest. Eight items were included in the scale, and a range of scores from 0 to 19 was possible, with the low scores pointing toward the ghetto and the high scores indicating an outside interest.

[16] Meeker and Harris, *Background for Planning*, p. 53.

variety of income levels found in segregated neighborhoods the median income for the ghetto samples was lower, being approximately $9,700. There were, however, only six persons in the ghetto and two persons in the Valley-wide sample who reported family incomes of less than $5,000, so that poverty was not a factor in either area. Part of the difficulty in matching socioeconomic levels was due to the decision to avoid the mixed neighborhoods on the edge of the ghetto where the incomes might well have been more uniformly high but where some of the impact of segregated life would have been lost.

each sample had moved up forty or more points beyond the level of their parents' occupations.[17] It was, for example, not at all unusual to find people with technical or professional jobs whose fathers had been laborers or their mothers domestic workers. This finding supports observations made by such writers as the late Franklin Frazier that there is a new and rapidly growing Negro middle class.[18] Possibly also related to the recent development of this middle class was the scarcity of older people in both groups. The median age in both samples was thirty-nine, but there was just one person over sixty in

TABLE 1 Mean Powerlessness and Anomia Scores in the Valley-wide and Ghetto Areas When Education, Income, and Sex Are Controlled

Control	Powerlessness		Anomia	
	Valley Wide (N = 101)	Ghetto (N = 105)	Valley Wide (N = 103)	Ghetto (N = 105)
Education:				
College graduate	2.14 (N = 43)	2.88 (N = 32)	9.67 (N = 43)	11.72 (N = 32)
Some college or technical education	2.73 (N = 42)	3.15 (N = 39)	10.90 (N = 42)	12.54 (N = 39)
High school or less	2.75 (N = 16)	2.97 (N = 34)	12.17 (N = 18)	14.38 (N = 43)
Income:				
$15,000 and over	2.05 (N = 34)	3.05 (N = 22)	9.91 (N = 34)	12.60 (N = 22)
$7,800–$15,000	2.59 (N = 49)	2.80 (N = 56)	10.26 (N = 50)	11.77 (N = 56)
Below $7,800	3.00 (N = 18)	3.27 (N = 26)	12.79 (N = 19)	15.19 (N = 26)
Sex:				
Male	2.55 (N = 53)	2.77 (N = 48)	10.77 (N = 54)	12.65 (N = 48)
Female	2.42 (N = 48)	3.21 (N = 57)	10.42 (N = 49)	13.08 (N = 57)

There were some factors that were similar in and out of the ghetto. The majority of people in both samples said they saw some value in living in an integrated or predominantly white neighborhood; 87 per cent of the Valley-wide group and 80 per cent of the ghetto dwellers indorsed such a statement, although the Valley residents could think of more concrete reasons why they felt that way. Both groups seemed to be made up of occupationally mobile people. The Bogue scale was used to assign numerical ratings to occupations, and about half of the people in

the Valley group, and in the ghetto sample there were just four.

When the powerlessness scores of the two groups were compared, significant differences were found; the people in the ghetto sample have a mean powerlessness score of 3.01, while the outsiders' mean score is 2.48 ($t = 2.07$; $P < .05$). The people who have moved

17 Donald Bogue, *Skid Row in American Cities* (Chicago: University of Chicago Press, 1963), Appendix.

18 E. Franklin Frazier, *Black Bourgeoisie* (Glencoe, Ill.: Free Press, 1957).

out thus indicate that they feel they have more control over their own lives. Table 1 shows these scores with education, income, and sex controlled. As can be noted in the table, the greatest differences in powerlessness between the in- and out-of-the-ghetto samples show up in the high income and educational levels. This suggests that when the objective criteria for overcoming the barriers of housing discrimination are most favorable, the expectation for control of one's life helps predict who will actually make the move.

The anomia scores follow a similar pattern. In the ghetto the mean score on the anomia scale is 12.9; in the integrated community the mean score is 10.6; these differences are also significant ($t = 4.24$; $P < .001$). The controls for income and education indicate that, although the anomia scores vary more in relation to these factors, the area of residence still makes a difference at each level. There is a correlation between anomia and powerlessness; inside the ghetto it was $r = .43$ and outside it was $r = .37$. This suggests that there is indeed a relationship between these two kinds of alienation in this situation, although the two scales are not measuring the same thing.[19]

Most of the people now living in the Valley spent their childhoods in the ghetto or on its edge (only twelve people reported having grown up in predominantly white neighborhoods). Some explanation should be given as to why the two groups of people scored differently on the alienation scales. This paper cannot, of course, supply all of the answers to that question, but if we look at some of the other factors associated with anomia and powerlessness some clues are offered. Anomia seems to correlate negatively with almost any of life's advantages,[20] so it

would seem that the people with lower scores on the Srole scale, including those who moved out of the ghetto, somehow escaped some of the worst disadvantages. Table 2

TABLE 2 Correlations (Pearson's r) of Powerlessness and Anomia[a] with Selected Factors

	Valley Wide	Ghetto
	Powerlessness	
Father's occupational level	−.04	−.004
Employed subject's occupational level	−.31**	−.05
Present income	−.18*	−.03
Educational attainment	−.17*	−.07
Amount of integrated schooling	−.22**	−.10
Neighborhood of childhood (segregated to integrated)	−.30**	−.24**
	Anomia	
Father's occupational level	−.04	−.20*
Employed subject's occupational level	−.22**	−.22**
Present income	−.23**	−.28**
Educational attainment	−.28**	−.31**
Amount of integrated schooling	−.13	−.19*
Neighborhood of childhood (segregated to integrated)	−.12	−.27**

[a] The numbers varied in these correlations from 79 to 105.
* Significant ($P < .05$).
** Significant ($P < .01$).

shows the small but consistently negative correlations with several of these factors. Since powerlessness is a less global sort of attitude it does not correlate highly with as many variables; in this study the development of a high expectation for control seems most related to past and present experiences with integration, not only in housing but also in other aspects of life. Segregation and all that is associated with it emerges as such a crucial problem for Negroes that successful experiences with integration seem to raise the general level of expectation for control. Notice that the childhood experiences most related to lower powerlessness scores are those of integrated school experience and living in a racially mixed neighborhood while growing up.

[19] The relationship of powerlessness and anomia is discussed by Arthur Neal and Melvin Seeman, "Organization and Powerlessness: A Test of the Mediation Hypothesis," *American Sociological Review*, **XXIX** (April, 1964), p. 222 n.; see also Arthur G. Neal and Salomon Rettig, "Dimensions of Alienation among Manual and Non-Manual Workers," *American Sociological Review*, **XXVIII** (August, 1963), 599–602.

[20] Dorothy L. Meier and Wendell Bell, "Anomia and Differential Access to the Achievement of Life Goals," *American Sociological Review*, **XXIV** (April, 1959), 189–202.

It was expected from the beginning of the study that the Valley-wide residents would have lost some of their ties with the strictly segregated institutions within the ghetto. In fact, giving up some of the old customs and ties seems to be the price paid by any minority group that is assimilated. It was therefore not surprising that the Valley group had a mean score of 13.0 on the "ghetto-orientation" scale, while the mean of the ghetto sample was 9.7 ($t = 7.99$; $P < .001$). This wide difference on the ghetto-orientation scale indicates that the various aspects of integration tend to be related to each other; moving out of the ghetto is one part of a total life pattern. That this change in pattern is a long-term process is suggested by the fact that the last residence of 61 percent of the Valley group was described as predominantly white or mixed, while only 23 percent of the ghetto sample reported that the place they lived in last had even token integration.

It was of interest to find out that within each sample the drift away from a ghetto orientation was related to a greater expectation for control and to lower anomia scores. Table 3 shows the differences in powerlessness and anomia when the two samples are split at the median on orientation. As an alienation measurement the orientation scale is two sided. It indicates the degree to which the customs and associations of the subcul-

ture are selected over those of the mainstream of the society; movement away from one pole implies a movement toward the other. This type of value isolation is alienation of a different dimension than that assessed by the Srole scale in which movement away from the mainstream could mean a withdrawal into apathy. The concept of value isolation has been used to describe the alienation felt by intellectuals, although presumably members of any subculture that holds values that deviate from the commonly held societal values would be alienated in this sense.[21] Of course it is also possible to be alienated from the subculture. Since the ghetto orientation was related to both powerlessness and anomia, regardless of place of residence, it would seem that the securely "locked-in" position within the Negro ghetto was not a particularly desirable state. The "marginal" or moving-out position may not be as undesirable as it is sometimes considered. Of course it can be argued that, since Negroes are already familiar with American culture, and yet not completely accepted by it, their position in the ghetto is already a marginal one.

One of the items used to make up the orientation scale was the racial makeup of the subject's church congregation. In addition to the racial characteristics of the individual congregation, the denominational identification also turned out to have predictive value. As can be noted in Table 4, not

TABLE 3   Mean Powerlessness and Anomia Scores in the Valley-wide and Ghetto Areas When the Samples Are Divided at the Median[a] on Orientation

Orientation	Valley Wide	Ghetto
Powerlessness:		
Integrated orientation	2.38	2.63
	($N = 49$)	($N = 57$)
Ghetto orientation	2.75	3.45*
	($N = 52$)	($N = 48$)
Anomia:		
Integrated orientation	10.00	11.86
	($N = 49$)	($N = 57$)
Ghetto orientation	11.19*	14.10**
	($N = 54$)	($N = 48$)

   [a] The median scores on the orientation scale were 13 in the valley-wide area and 9 in the ghetto.
   * Differences between the mean scores of those with integrated or ghetto orientations were significant ($P < .05$).
   ** Significant ($P < .01$).

TABLE 4   Mean Powerlessness Scores and Religious Identification*

Religion	Valley Wide ($N = 101$)	Ghetto ($N = 105$)
Baptist	3.29	3.62
	($N = 7$)	($N = 29$)
Methodist	2.17	2.95
	($N = 23$)	($N = 19$)
Holiness	3.00	3.63
	($N = 3$)	($N = 8$)
Other Protestant	2.10	2.27
	($N = 28$)	($N = 22$)
Catholic	1.96	2.28
	($N = 24$)	($N = 17$)
None	3.45	2.70
	($N = 16$)	($N = 10$)

   * Differences in religious affiliation in the two areas: $x^2 = 19.4$ ($P < .01$).

   [21] Seeman, "On the Meaning of Alienation."

only were members of Baptist and Holiness churches more powerless than others, they were seldom found outside the ghetto. Methodists, whose churches also have been segregated historically, did not score so high on the powerlessness scale, and they were well represented in the Valley-wide area. Members of other Protestant churches, Catholics, and non-church members were the best represented in the Valley. The church is the focus of much of the social life within the ghetto, so that it may sometimes act as a positive tie to hold people within the segregated areas.[22] These differences by denomination were not adequately anticipated in the planning of the study, so that data were not obtained about past religious identification. It is therefore not known whether certain church affiliations are associated with staying in the ghetto or whether people change their religious identifications when they move out.

Having found that Negroes who live outside the ghetto feel less powerless and less of the hopeless detachment measured by the anomia scale still leaves an unanswered question; are the feelings of alienation a selective factor that keeps some people from moving out, or does the experience of having successfully moved lessen the feelings of alienation? Probably both happen, but the evidence for alienation as a negative selective factor is strongest. Some of the correlations associated with childhood conditions suggest that feelings of alienation are fairly stable attitudes, developing sometimes over a lifetime. When the powerlessness scores of the Valley residents who have lived outside of the ghetto for more than five years were compared with the newcomers, the older residents did have lower scores, but even the newcomers were lower in alienation than the average for the ghetto.

As suggested by other research on alienation, one of the mechanisms by which higher expectation for control fosters integration is probably through its relationship with more effective social learning.[23] People who feel less powerless would thus be expected to have

[22] E. Franklin Frazier, *The Negro Church in America* (New York: Schocken Books, 1964); Joseph R. Washington, Jr., *Black Religion* (Boston: Beacon Press, 1964).

[23] Seeman, "Alienation and Social Learning in a Reformatory"; see also Melvin Seeman and J. W. Evans, "Alienation and Learning in a Hos-

learned more about their rights in the housing market and how they might be able to secure a house or an apartment in an integrated area. Table 5 shows the differences in scores

TABLE 5 Mean Scores on the Housing-Facts Test When Divided at the Median in Each Area on the Powerlessness Scale[a]

Powerlessness	Valley Wide	Ghetto*
Above median or at the median	7.10 (N = 47)	6.27 (N = 61)
Below median	7.37 (N = 54)	7.02 (N = 44)

[a] Both samples were split at 2.
* The differences in the ghetto sample were significant (P < .05).

on the housing-facts test with the subjects divided at the median on their powerlessness scores; the low powerlessness group does tend to have learned more of these facts.

Both powerlessness and anomia seem to act as psychological deterrents to people making the kind of sustained effort that is necessary to be successful in overcoming the barriers to integration. Subjects in the ghetto were asked if they had ever looked for housing in an integrated or predominantly white neighborhood. Fifty-six of the people in that sample said they had done so at some time in their lives. However, when the ghetto sample was divided by this factor, the anomia scores were the same for the two groups (12.9), and the powerlessness scores were actually higher for the group that said they had looked (3.20 mean score as compared with 2.80). Just looking at these scores it would seem that alienation was not a selective factor. However, when these people were asked to elaborate on their experiences in looking, they characteristically told of a single experience in which they looked and were rebuffed. When the Valley residents told of their experiences they sometimes described years of searching until they were finally successful. Occasionally these accounts included reports of open refusals, but more

pital Setting," *American Sociological Review,* **XXVII** (December, 1962), 772–82.

often they were faced with a long series of evasions and trickery including realty salesmen who were "out" or ran to hide from them in the other room, managers who had no authority to rent the apartments, owners who could not be located, forms that could not be processed, returned deposits, and so on. The persistence shown by some of these people in the face of one disappointment after another is worthy of note. It would seem, then, that alienation as a selective factor may function more in fixing the amount of determination and effectiveness that the subjects bring to the task, rather than merely selecting who will make a single attempt. The people who were successful in moving out, despite the present barriers of discrimination, were unwilling to accept one act of prejudice as their final answer, and here an ultimate belief in a manageable world undoubtedly helped them.

SUMMARY AND CONCLUSIONS

When a group of integrated middle-class Negro subjects was compared with another group of middle-class subjects who remained within the traditional Negro ghettos, significant differences in alienation were found. The integrated subjects had greater expectations for control of events that concerned them and less of a feeling of anomia. They also tended to orient themselves toward the mainstream of society rather than toward the segregated institutions of the Negro subculture. Alienation within the ghetto takes on a circular characteristic; not only is it a product of segregated living, it also acts to keep people locked in the traditional residential patterns.

The fact that alienation is such a circular process does not mean that nothing can be done to deal with the problems of segregation. It does mean that antidiscriminatory legislation alone cannot bring about instant integration. Instead such legislation would be more effective if accompanied by other efforts to overcome the psychological barriers to integration. The fact that anomia correlates with almost any kind of deprivation suggests the need for effective programs to combat poverty, unemployment, and lack of educational opportunity in the ghetto; these programs are needed not only for their own intrinsic worth but also to combat the feelings of hopelessness and despair that are a part of the ghetto attitude. The fact that choosing the integrated way of life in one sphere is related to choosing it in others suggests that any sort of program aimed at decreasing segregation is worth trying. A fair-employment-practices act can even help bring about more housing integration by giving the workers the experience of working together. Integrated school or church experiences give children the opportunity to set up patterns of mixed associations. However, the solutions to the problems of segregation are not easy; the old patterns, supported by the psychological barriers of alienation, do not change rapidly.

8

Differences between Negro and white pregnant women on the MMPI [1]

ROBERT H. HARRISON AND EDWARD H. KASS

Previous psychological investigations of personality differences between Negro and white Americans have revealed few replicable or striking differences between the two racial groups. The absence of striking differences in personality is surprising in view of what is known about the contrasting social environments of the two groups. Negroes must contend with personal and economic discrimination. More often than whites they appear to be brought up in a matriarchal family structure (Pettigrew, 1964). Their religious beliefs and institutions are often different from those of the white majority (Yinger, 1957). If social variables such as these influence the development of personality, and if presently available tests are sensitive to personality differences, substantial racial differences in

Reprinted from *Journal of Consulting Psychology,* 1967, **31,** 454–463, by permission of the authors and the American Psychological Association.

[1] This study was supported by Research Grant HD 01288 from the National Institutes of Health, United States Public Health Service, and National Science Foundation Grant GP-2723. The authors are indebted to John Sturrock, J. Michael Lane, Samir Hajj, and A. Michael Rossi, for their assistance in the initial planning; and to Sheila Hodge, Barbara Eidam, and Patricia O'Shea, who were chiefly responsible for collecting the data. Claire Finnegan and Olga Ulchak provided valuable nursing care. Thanks are also due to Beverly Lee and David Drew of the Harvard Computing Center for their programming assistance, and to Theodore Colton and Kailie Uong for their advice and assistance in the statistical analyses.

personality test scores should be found regularly, yet these have not been consistently observed.

Four explanations for this paradox suggest themselves: (*a*) uncontrolled variables affecting the samples to be compared have minimized mean differences and maximized variability within each group; (*b*) differences may not be marked in the areas of adjustment and psychopathology, which have been the focuses of most previous research; (*c*) most of the studies have been done on the middle class Negro and his white counterpart, and there is reason to believe that middle class Negroes minimize their differences from whites (Pettigrew, 1964); and (*d*) the tests used in the various studies may not be sufficiently sensitive. Each of these explanations deserves further scrutiny.

Most studies reviewed by Klineberg (1944), Dreger and Miller (1960), and McDonald and Gynther (1963) were controlled for age and sex. Social-class variables have been relatively well controlled. McDonald and Gynther's (1963) parametric (Sex × Class × Race) study of high school seniors in a segregated school system, with MMPI as a test instrument, found that social-class differences were insignificant relative to racial differences. In general, IQ and education have not been controlled, and their effects on most personality tests are unknown. However, it seems likely that their control would reduce rather than amplify racial differences in test scores. A further problem in subject selection is that most studies have been done on samples of high school or college students, on patients, or on prisoners. Karon's (1958) study using the Tompkins-Horn Picture Arrangement Test is the only study in the literature which used representative sampling procedures. The consideration of the problem of sampling restricts the generality of the differences which have been found.

The second alternative considered above is that racial differences may not be marked in the areas of adjustment and psychopathology. Replicable but moderate differences have been found on the MMPI, as summarized in Table 1. These studies indicate that Negroes are more elevated than whites (in at least three of nine studies) on *L*, *F*, *Hs*, *Sc*, and *Ma* scales and less elevated (in three studies) than whites on *Hy*. The Bernreuter Personality Inventory has shown little promise of being able to differentiate between the groups, and similarly limited differentiation has been achieved using the Bell Adjustment Inventory (Dreger & Miller, 1960). Outside of the adjustment area, only Mussen's (1953) work on lower class boys has shown racial differences of the expected magnitude. He found that 14 of 50 TAT content analysis categories were related to racial differences. Karon (1958), using the Tompkins-Horn Picture Arrangement Test (PAT), found that only 13 of 150 PAT scales reliably differentiated southern Negroes from whites. Even more unimpressive and scarcely consistent findings have appeared in work with the Rosenzweig Picture Frustration Test (Dreger & Miller, 1960). Work with the Allport-Vernon-Lindzey Study of Values, using college students, has produced a minimum of differences (Dreger & Miller, 1960). Racial differences in nonadjustment areas of personality are no more striking than in the adjustment area.

Pettigrew (1964) suggested that middle class Negroes attempt to minimize differences between themselves and their white middle class counterparts. These pressures are not so great among lower class Negroes. Since all of the studies using the Bernreuter Personality Inventory, the Bell Adjustment Inventory, and the Allport-Vernon-Lindzey Study of Values have involved college students as subjects, it is hardly surprising that no racially specific differences have been found. The MMPI studies have used lower class and lower middle class samples (prison-

ers and patients) and have produced moderate differences. Mussen's (1953) study with lower class boys produced similar degrees of difference. Negative evidence for Pettigrew's (1964) hypothesis, however, is McDonald and Gynther's (1963) failure to find a significant Race × Class interaction on most of the MMPI scales in their study. Education was held constant, however, and the observed class differences were among the parents and not among the subjects themselves. The hypothesis that middle class Negroes tend to minimize differences between themselves and white middle class counterparts offers at least a partial explanation of the lack of striking differences between Negroes and whites that has been found in psychological tests.

Finally, it is possible that the tests are not sensitive enough. Either the items themselves may be insensitive, or discriminating items may be combined in scales in such a way as to cancel each other's effects, producing nondiscriminating scales. Negroes and whites could vary considerably in the way they achieved similar test scores. This criticism is particularly applicable to tests such as the MMPI, whose scales were developed with no regard to internal consistency criteria. To find out whether the scales only or both the scales and the items are insensitive to race differences, one has to do an item analysis. Few item analyses are reported in the literature. None of these item studies examined the possibility that the two groups obtain close to identical test scores in different ways.

The present study was designed to test the hypothesis that there are racial differences in personality and to meet objections that were raised in connection with previous work in the following ways:

1. Subjects were selected from successive admissions of pregnant women to a city hospital prenatal clinic. While the conclusions will be limited to lower class pregnant females, behavioral self-selection was close to minimum, in that the hospital and clinic serve exclusively the lowest socioeconomic classes. Because all deliveries are on a nonpayment basis, without private care, it can be assumed that observable differences are largely independent of socioeconomic class differences.

2. If Pettigrew's hypothesis is correct, differences should be at a maximum in a lower class group such as this one.

TABLE 1 Summary of Previous Work on Negro-White Differences in the MMPI

Study	Sample Size				Mean Age	Setting	MMPI scale												
	NM	NF	WM	WF			L	F	K	Hs	D	Hy	Pd	Mf	Pa	Pt	Sc	Ma	Si
Ball (1960)	14	17	81	88	14–15	Integrated schools; Kentucky; 9th grade.		NF	WF	NM		WF					NF		NF
Butcher, Ball, and Ray (1964) Sample 1	50	50	50	50	18–21	Segregated college students; South; no socioeconomic grouping.	NM NF							WF	WM WF			NM	
Sample 2	26	16	26	26		Same; socioeconomic status controlled.	NM NF			NM				WM WF	WM WF	WM		NM	WM
Caldwell (1954)	34		63		21	Prison inmates; South.							WM[a]	NM[a]			NM[a]		
Fry (1949)	22		75		29–32	Prison inmates; North.												NM[b]	
Gottlieb and Eisdorfer (1954)					adult	Medical outpatients.				W	W	W	N				N		
Hokanson and Calden (1960)	34		84		32–35	TB patients; VA North.	NM	NM					WM	NM			NM	NM	
McDonald and Gynther (1963)	90	90	90	90	17–18	Urban segregated schools; South; 12th grade.	N	N		N	N	W		N			N	N	
Miller et al. (1961)	100		100		adult	Applicants to VA Mental Hygiene Clinic; North.	NM			NM				WM				NM	
Panton (1959)[c]					adult	Prison inmates; South.	N	N				W			N		NM	NM	

Note. The letters N, W, M, and F refer to "Negro," "white," "male," and "female," respectively. A letter entry for a scale means that subjects in the category indicated are significantly (p < .05) higher on this scale than their other-race counterparts. For example, NF means that Negro females were higher than white females on the scales indicated.
[a] Difference in means of 5 or more T-score points; SDs and t tests not reported.
[b] Originally reported as not significant; recomputation of data reveals a t = 2.33, df = 96, p < .05.
[c] The reference given by Dahlstrom and Welsh could not be traced; Panton's data are given as summarized in the MMPI Handbook, p 273.

3. The MMPI contains 194 items which are not on any of the clinical scales. Many of these are related in manifest content to topics having no obvious relevance to adjustment.

4. Item analyses were conducted, and the possibility that different racial groups have different ways of obtaining approximately equal scale scores was examined.

METHOD

The data were collected in the course of a study on predictive relationships of psychological and physiological variables on the outcome of pregnancy, that is, prematurity, complications of pregnancy, and complications of delivery.

Patients

The total sample on which data were collected consisted of 1,038 women in their 20-24th week of pregnancy. They were selected as successive admissions to the Prenatal Clinic at the Boston City Hospital between July 17, 1961 and December 30, 1963. Each patient registering at the clinic who was 20 weeks pregnant or less was given an appointment to return during the 20-24th week. At this time, in addition to the usual obstetrical examination, the patient was asked to supply a specimen of urine for bacteriological culture and was given an appointment to return for the MMPI. At the conclusion of the MMPI, the patient received a measured dose of radiolabeled iodoalbumin for determination of plasma volume, total blood volume, red blood cell mass, and hematocrit. The patients were informed that the blood volume procedures were to be conducted only after the psychological testing had been completed.

Of the total of 1,038 women who were seen before the 20th week of pregnancy, only two patients in the consecutive series refused to take the MMPI, one a frankly schizoid individual and the other a young unmarried mother whose parents refused to allow her to participate. Of the 1,036 remaining women, 264 were excluded from the final analysis of the data, leaving 772. The exclusions were on the basis of the following successively applied criteria: (*a*) some physiological data missing, usually because of technical problems associated with withdrawal and process-

TABLE 2   Means, Standard Deviations, and Differences on Formal MMPI Scales

Variable	Negro		White		Difference	*t*
	M	*SD*	*M*	*SD*		
?	8.91	12.22	6.17	9.37	+2.74	3.51**
L	4.95	2.56	4.85	2.28	+0.10	0.57
F	5.95	4.03	5.35	3.61	+0.60	2.23*
K	13.66	5.20	13.89	5.10	−0.23	0.62
Hs	10.70	5.26	9.81	5.26	+0.89	2.35*
D	24.82	5.40	24.78	5.67	+0.04	0.10
Hy	23.08	6.18	23.72	6.00	−0.70	1.47
Pd	17.96	4.86	17.85	4.98	+0.11	0.28
Mf	34.05	4.16	34.08	4.10	−0.03	0.10
Pa	9.53	3.85	9.32	3.39	+0.21	0.80
Pt	15.52	7.89	15.03	8.03	+0.49	0.87
Sc	15.18	8.88	13.66	8.94	+1.52	2.36*
Ma	16.69	4.42	15.60	4.69	+1.09	3.32**
Si	31.47	7.76	32.50	8.74	−1.03	1.74
Es	38.87	5.86	40.42	6.30	−1.55	3.55**
MA	18.62	7.96	19.02	8.69	−0.40	0.66
Discriminant function	−6.92	3.04	−8.97	2.90	+2.06	

* *p* < .05.
** *p* < .001.

ing of blood (118); (*b*) termination of pregnancy with spontaneous abortion, stillbirth, elective cesarean delivery, or twin delivery (71); (*c*) report of delivery at another hospital unobtainable (3); (*d*) illiteracy— the MMPI had to be read to these patients— (47); and (*e*) MMPI *F* scale over 90 (25). Of the 72 patients rejected on MMPI criteria, 57 were Negro and 15 were white. In the final sample, 389 patients were white and 383 patients were Negro.

Differences in socioeconomic status between the Negro and white groups were not measured. However, since the entire sample came from the socioeconomically underprivileged neighborhoods surrounding Boston City Hospital, these differences cannot have been great. Education was not formally measured. More Negroes than whites had to be excluded by the illiteracy and *F* scale criteria, however.

Procedure

The card form of the MMPI was administered individually, with the administrator either present in the patient's cubicle or close at hand. Use of the ? category was allowed, but if over 15% of the patient's responses fell in that category, she was asked to sort the category again. Her final sort was regarded as valid, regardless of whether the 15% criterion had been met. The 4 validity scales, the 10 standard clinical scales, Barron's Ego Strength (*Es*) scale, and the Taylor Manifest Anxiety (*MA*) scale were scored and punched on IBM cards. The *K* correction was not made. The patient's response to individual items was also recorded and punched on IBM cards as deviant, normal, or ?.

RESULTS

Differences on Scales, Items, and Factors

SCALE SCORES

Table 2 presents the means, standard deviations, and *t* tests for the 16 scales. The Negro group was significantly higher than the white group on *?*, *F*, *Hs*, *Sc*, and *Ma* and lower

TABLE 3   MMPI Items Differentiating between Negroes and Whites

Significance Level	T	F
$p < .000001$	98, 415, 469, 490, 213, 11, 58, 173, 53, 557, 25, 477, 73, 538, 229, 400, 429, 378, 498, 546, 392, 284, 558, 456, 457, 4	419, 30
$p < .00001$	482, 280, 511, 206, 93, 513, 165	9, 468, 530, 532
$p < .0001$	420, 552, 164, 237, 476, 426, 78, 202, 364, 279	238, 446, 116
$p < .001$	449, 129, 79, 167, 125, 231, 132, 147, 136, 428, 15, 473, 84, 521, 241, 239, 502, 264, 386, 527, 59, 46, 556, 406, 184, 67, 70, 525, 423	486, 133, 64, 304, 74, 38, 496, 376
$p < .01$	354, 510, 432, 437, 89, 566, 44, 472, 407, 526, 298, 297, 433, 106, 69, 425, 114, 199, 275,[a] 545, 340, 416, 124, 16, 24, 404, 485, 3, 380, 319, 436, 150, 385, 80	540, 450, 531, 225, 282, 506, 464, 439, 563, 522, 246,[a] 26, 255, 322, 81,[a] 22, 285, 396, 471, 524, 34
$p < .05$	349,[b] 480,[b] 218,[b] 101,[b] 344,[b] 27, 178, 157, 221, 393, 252, 348, 523, 352, 166, 72, 283, 117, 66, 417, 212, 265, 261, 453, 120, 163, 226, 35, 341, 395, 200, 7, 384, 222, 410, 547, 87, 121, 320, 57, 161, 299, 293, 170, 483, 412, 92, 324	481,[b] 160,[b] 474, 208, 561, 171, 103, 223, 145, 140, 18, 542, 361, 347, 421, 214, 193, 105, 39

Note. An item appears in the T column if it is answered "True" more frequently by Negroes than by whites and in the F column if it is answered "False" more frequently by Negroes than by whites; items are listed in decreasing order of significance within each significance level.

[a] These items were excluded from the factor analysis on the basis that they exceeded a 95–5 split between T and F.

[b] These items were included in the factor analysis.

than the white group on *Es*. These findings are in agreement with the previous literature cited in Table 1.

ITEM ANALYSIS

Chi-square was computed for each item against the race criterion, using Yates' correction and observing conventional restrictions on minimum expected frequencies. For each computation the *?* category was ignored. Of the 550 items, 213 discriminated between Negroes and whites at the .05 level of significance. They are listed by level of signifi-

cance in Table 3. Thus, differences based on the racial grouping overshadowed those we had set out to study.

FACTOR ANALYSIS

Grouping the items conceptually on the basis of subjective judgment has obvious pitfalls. For this reason, the 150 most significant items were factor analyzed in order to get a more objective basis for conceptualizing. The tetrachoric correlations between the items were computed (*?* was classified as a deviant response) and then factor analyzed by the

TABLE 4 Summary of Factor Analysis

Factor No.	Content
I	Estrangement (N).[a] 26 items describing hopelessness, unhappiness, guilt, and self-devaluing schizoid thinking.
II	Intellectual and cultural interests (N). 21 items expressing interest in reading, studying, thinking about, and discussing various topics.
III	Denial of major symptoms (W). Descriptions of unusual bodily states and experiences are denied in most of the 10 items.
IV	Cynicism (N). 26 items describing disillusionment with the human race in which the respondent prefers "honesty" to "illusion."
V	Admission of minor faults (W). 9 items admitting activities (petty thievery as a youth, playing hookey) subject to mild social censure.
VI	Romantic interest (N). These 9 items describe enjoyment of movies, novels, and discussions with romantic, mildly sexual themes.
VII	Somatic tension (N). These 9 items describe pains in the stomach and head, as well as general tension.
VIII	Impulse-ridden fantasy (N). 12 items combining attraction to sexual and aggressive activities combined with reality-based inhibition. They have a voyeuristic, vicarious flavor.
IX	*?* (N). A miscellany of 7 items which suggest rigidly moralistic attitudes and auditory hallucinations.
X	*?* (N). 4 items suggesting ability to imagine pleasant events and deny the possibility of unpleasant events.
XI	Dislike of school (W). 6 items reporting bad deportment, playing hookey, disinterest in school.
XII	Religiousness (N). 19 items describing conservative religious beliefs and practices, condemning indulgence in sex, alcohol, and smoking.
XIII	Masochism versus sadism (W). 5 items denying sadistic impulses and expressing willingness to suffer for the common good.
XIV	Compulsive orderliness (N). 7 items describing an abhorrence of physical or intellectual sloppiness and a desire to set things straight.
XV	Fearfulness (N). Many of the common phobias (dark, lightning, spiders) are included in these 8 items.
XVI	*?* (W). 4 highly diverse items.
XVII	Dream concern (N). 2 items on frequent dreaming, and 2 suggesting embarrassment.
XVIII	Self-consciousness (W). 11 items describing self-conscious embarrassment in group situations.
XIX	*?* (N). 7 diverse items suggesting honesty about oneself and one's world.
XX	Group sociability (N). 6 items suggesting enjoyment of large groups and strangers.

Note. A list of the specific items for each factor may be obtained from the senior author; only items with factor loadings of .30 or greater were considered to belong to a factor.

[a] N indicates that Negroes were higher on a factor than were whites; W indicates the reverse.

TABLE 5 Means, Standard Deviations, and Differences in Factor Scores

Factor	Negro		White		Difference	t**
	M	SD	M	SD		
I Estrangement	+2.49	9.17	−2.69	8.07	+5.18	8.33
II Intellectual and cultural interests	+2.92	6.48	−3.04	5.37	+5.96	13.91
III Denial of major symptoms	−1.82	4.76	+1.75	3.81	−3.57	11.48
IV Cynicism	+3.24	9.32	−3.52	7.83	+6.76	10.91
V Admission of minor faults	−1.03	3.67	+1.01	3.67	−2.04	7.78
VI Romantic interest	+1.38	3.42	−1.47	2.74	+2.85	12.81
VII Somatic tension	+0.61	3.99	−0.71	3.48	+1.32	4.93
VIII Impulse-ridden fantasy	+1.58	5.14	−1.67	3.65	+3.25	10.13
IX (?)	+0.75	3.07	−0.83	2.49	+1.58	7.81
X (?)	+0.43	2.42	−0.53	2.05	+0.96	5.89
XI Dislike of school	−0.60	2.64	+0.46	2.94	−1.06	5.26
XII Religiousness	+3.52	6.62	−3.62	4.65	+7.14	17.35
XIII Masochism versus sadism	−0.85	2.10	+0.91	1.88	−1.76	12.31
XIV Compulsive orderliness	+0.46	2.38	−0.52	2.17	+0.98	5.96
XV Fearfulness	+0.98	3.01	−0.98	2.91	+1.96	9.22
XVI (?)	−0.82	2.56	+0.70	2.06	−1.52	9.08
XVII Dream concern	+0.64	3.19	−0.70	3.08	+1.34	5.97
XVIII Self-consciousness	−0.94	4.53	+0.86	4.56	−1.80	5.50
XIX (?)	+0.86	2.94	−0.96	2.54	+1.82	9.23
XX Group sociability	+0.80	3.46	−0.78	3.38	+1.58	6.40
Discriminant function	+2.64	2.85	−2.59	3.11	+5.22	

** $p < .001$ for all t.

principal-components method with 1.00 in the diagonals. Although 50 factors with latent roots over 1.00 were extracted, following Cooley and Lohnes' (1962) recommendations, only the first 20 factors were preserved for subsequent rotation.[2] These 20 factors accounted for 54% of the total variance in the matrix and were rotated by Kaiser's Varimax criterion to orthogonal simple structure. From the Varimax rotation, 16 of the 20 factors could be named without undue conceptual strain. Table 4 presents a summary of the item content for each factor. Factor scores were then computed for each subject by the direct method outlined by Harman (1960).[3]

[2] Limitations of the Varimax rotation program available at the Harvard Computing Center restricted our selection to 20 factors.

[3] The model in which communalities are fixed at 1.00 was used for computation of factor scores.

FACTOR SCORE DIFFERENCES

Table 5 presents the means, standard deviations, and t tests for the two racial groups on the factors. In decreasing order of importance for racial differences, Negroes reported themselves as more religious, intellectual, romantic, cynical, impulsive in fantasy, fearful, estranged, sociable, concerned with dreams, orderly, and somatically tense than whites and less masochistic, free of aberrant behavior, indulgent in minor crimes, self-conscious, and antagonistic toward school than whites. The pattern of correlations between factor scores and the nature of the trait labels suggested that the Negroes are more anxious in their thoughts (Factor Nos. I, III, VII, XIV, XV) and less anxious socially than whites (Nos. XI, XVIII, XX). Negroes presented themselves as being less inclined to act out destructive impulses than whites (Nos. V, IX, XIX), while acknowledging the presence of these impulses on a fantasy level (Nos. IV, VIII, XIII). They also appeared more introverted and romantic (Nos. II, VI, VIII, IX) and more religious (No. XII).

Group Separation

Multiple discriminant analysis was used to further clarify two issues: (*a*) What variables contribute the most (indirectly as well as directly) to a discriminant function which maximizes the separation between the two groups? (*b*)What is the maximum degree of separation possible using scale scores and using factor scores?

Table 6 summarizes the results of discriminant analysis using the MMPI scale scores as independent variables. The univariate analysis stresses *Es, ?, Ma, Sc, Hs, F, Si,* and *Hy* in decreasing order of importance for race differences. In contrast, the multivariate analysis stresses *Hy, Hs, MA, Es, Si, D, K,* and *?* in decreasing order of importance for this distinction and suggests that the profile of scores on these scales is more useful in separating the two groups than scale scores taken one at a time.

Table 7 summarizes the corresponding

TABLE 6 Discriminant Analysis of Scale Scores

MMPI Scale	Normal- ized Vector[a]	Scaled Vector[b]	Relative Impor- tance
?	+.0802	24.24	8
L	+.0534	3.60	15
F	+.0410	4.34	14
K	+.2044	29.21[c]	7
Hs	+.5789	84.54	2
D	+.2029	31.16	6
Hy	−.5538	−93.56	1
Pd	−.0096	− 0.13	16
Mf	+.1803	20.69[c]	9
Pa	+.0753	7.59	13
Pt	+.0407	8.99	12
Sc	+.0717	17.33	11
Ma	+.1562	19.58	10
Si	−.1497	−34.36	5
Es	−.2419	−40.90	4
MA	−.3374	−78.03	3

[a] These are weights for the discriminant equation; the *F* ratio for the discriminant function is 5.66 (*df* = 16/755, *p* < .001).
[b] These are the normalized vectors multiplied by the square root of the corresponding pooled within-group variances.
[c] These variables are suppressors; their weighting in the discriminant equation is opposite to that indicated by the difference between means.

TABLE 7 Discriminant Analysis of Factor Scores

Factor	Normalized Vector[a]	Scaled Vector[b]	Relative Importance
I Estrangement	+.2506	+60.14	1
II Intellectual interests	−.0853	−14.07[c]	14
III Denial of major symptoms	−.1701	−20.41	9
IV Cynicism	+.0463	+11.07	16
V Admission of minor faults	−.1730	−17.65	11
VI Romantic interest	+.2855	+24.55	7
VII Somatic tension	−.1581	−16.44[c]	12
VIII Impulsive fantasy	−.3512	−43.55[c]	2
IX ?	−.1663	−12.97[c]	15
X ?	−.0503	− 3.12[c]	20
XI Dislike of school	−.3751	−29.26	4
XII Religiousness	+.1580	+25.12	6
XIII Masochism and sadism	−.2709	−14.90	13
XIV Compulsive orderliness	−.0793	− 4.99[c]	17
XV Fearfulness	+.2446	+20.06	10
XVI ?	−.3581	−22.92	8
XVII Dream concern	−.0395	− 3.44[c]	18
XVIII Self-consciousness	−.2474	−31.17	3
XIX ?	+.3340	+25.28	5
XX Group sociability	+.0340	+ 3.23	19

[a] These are weights for the discriminant equation; the *F* ratio for discriminant function is 28.29 (*df* = 20/751, *p* < .001).
[b] These are the normalized vectors multipled by the square root of the corresponding within-groups variance.
[c] These variables are suppressors; their weighting in the discriminant equation is opposite to that indicated by the difference between means.

analysis for factor scores. Since the factor scores are correlated (whereas the factors are not), there is less than a perfect correspondence between the results of the univariate tests and the weighting of the variables in the multivariate discriminant function. While the univariate analysis stresses religiousness, intellectuality, romanticism, cynicism, and an impulse-ridden fantasy life, in the multivariate analysis the most important factors are estrangement, impulse-ridden fantasy, self-consciousness, dislike of school, religiousness, and romantic interests.

Using the discriminant functions outlined in Tables 6 and 7, it is possible to use each function to classify subjects as Negro or white on the basis of their test scores. The formulae and computer program given by Cooley and Lohnes (1962) take into account the standard deviation of the discriminant function scores of each group as well as the size (antecedent probability of membership) and computes a probability value of membership in each group for each subject. Table 8

TABLE 8 Classification of Groups from MMPI Scale Scores

Predicted Race Group	Actual Race Group		Total
	Negro	White	
Negro	233	132	365
White	150	257	407
Total	383	389	

Note. $x^2 = 54.96$.

shows that using the discriminant function based on MMPI scale scores, 61% of the Negro and 66% of the white subjects can be correctly classified; the overall hit rate is 63%. Using the factor scores, Table 9 shows that 80% of the Negro group and 86% of

TABLE 9 Classification of Groups from Factor Scores

Predicted Race Group	Actual Race Group		Total
	Negro	White	
Negro	305	56	361
White	78	333	411
Total	383	389	

Note. $x^2 = 327.31$.

the white group can be correctly classified. The overall hit rate (83%) is considerably higher than that from scale scores.

DISCUSSION

The main result of this study is that in our sample of pregnant women, race differences in both MMPI items and derived factor scales are of a magnitude seldom found in personality research. Whether or not the self-reports in the context of a white administrator in a white-dominated city hospital correspond with the self-report and "actual" behavior of these patients in other contexts is a matter for future investigation.

Why are these results of such different magnitude than others in the personality test literature? It is probable that results of this order could have been hidden in previous data by the exclusive use of scale scores rather than that of item responses. The scale-score differences reported here are smaller than those reported in previous studies and are significant only because of the large size of the sample. Nonetheless, race differences on the items were huge. The scales are not very sensitive to race differences, whereas the items are remarkably sensitive. A canceling-out process must be at work in each scale. If so, each scale should have approximately equal numbers of (significant) Negro-favored and white-favored items. This is indeed the case, as is seen in Table 10. Table 10 also reveals that 32% of the discriminating items appear on none of the clinical scales, suggesting substantial race differences in the nonadjustment areas of personality as well as in the adjustment area. It is also possible that the whites and Negroes have different ways of getting high scores on a scale. To test this hypothesis, items in each scale were ranked (for Negroes and whites separately) from those most frequently endorsed in the pathological direction to those least frequently endorsed. Spearman rank-order correlations were computed between Negro and white rankings of items belonging to each scale. These are reported in the right-hand column of Table 10. The agreement between the groups, while not complete, is generally high, suggesting that the two groups have similar ways of obtaining high scores on the various clinical scales.

TABLE 10 Agreement between Groups on MMPI Scales

Scale	No. Significant Items Favored by Negroes	No. Significant Items Favored by Whites	Spear- man r^a
L	5	4	.95
F	14	4	.83
K	4	5	.90
Hs	7	3	.91
D	10	9	.93
Hy	7	13	.93
Pd	9	5	.94
Mf	17	14	.92
Pa	15	6	.95
Pt	7	7	.93
Sc	19	5	.92
Ma	12	5	.86
Si	11	15	.91
None of the above scales[b]	43	26	

[a] Spearman r is between rank of endorsement by Negroes and rank of endorsement by whites.

[b] The items in this row are those race-significant items which do not appear in the scales scored in this study. They are separated according to those which were answered in the deviant direction by Negroes (1st column) and those which were answered in the deviant direction by whites (2nd column).

In any case, the above analyses suggest that scales based solely on empirical item validity (ignoring internal consistency criteria completely) are not likely to discriminate well between groups defined by other than the validation criteria. For example, the *D* scale may be excellent for identifying depressives, but irrelevant for distinguishing whites from Negroes. Component factors of the *D* scale may, on the other hand, distinguish well between racial groups and still be useful in identifying depressives.

Alternate explanations to those advanced here must be considered. It may be that our subject selection was biased by socioeconomic and educational differences between the groups, producing many more differences than would have been found had such variables been controlled. The fact that no race differences were found on the *K* scale, which has been suggested by Dahlstrom and Welsh (1960) to be an MMPI correlate of socio-

economic status, would indicate that differences in socioeconomic status between the Negroes and whites were not large in this study. McDonald and Gynther (1963) found that when education was held constant, class differences had no impact on MMPI scale scores. The situation, however, may be different in the case of item analysis. Socioeconomic status may be a variable requiring more rigorous investigation. Educational differences may also be confounded with the race differences discovered. Many more Negroes than whites in our sample were eliminated on the basis of functional illiteracy. A residue of educational differences undetected by our rough criteria could be present in the sample whose data were analyzed.

Another explanation for the magnitude of the differences found is the possibility that the state of being pregnant amplified race differences and minimized similarities. There may be a Negro way of reacting to pregnancy and a white way of reacting. This would require that the differences in personality subside after the termination of pregnancy. The fact that the formal scale results replicate previous results very closely would cast doubt on this explanation for the scale differences, although it cannot be ruled out as an explanation for the item differences.

The discovery of large differences between racial groups has emotional implications for many persons. Typically, studies of race differences have been conducted for many reasons, such as: (*a*) to prove or disprove the superiority of one group and/or the "place in society" of another (e.g., studies of intelligence and of admission rates to mental institutions); (*b*) to prove that one group has been suffering psychologically at the hands of another (e.g., Kardiner & Ovesey, 1951); and (*c*) to describe differences in order to identify possible areas of misunderstanding and/or fruitful interchange between the groups. The discovery of large group differences stimulates a number of fears: (*a*) that one group is inferior to the other, (*b*) that the differences found will prick our consciences, or (*c*) that these differences may be irreconcilable. For many, therefore, a strong preference for ignoring or minimizing differences exists. The results of the present study indicate that a high degree of differentiation of Negro from white is possible on the basis of pencil-and-paper test responses alone. The recognition of the nature and extent of these differences is perhaps a first step in their understanding.

REFERENCES

Ball, J. C. Comparison of MMPI profile differences among Negro-white adolescents. *Journal of Clinical Psychology*, 1960, **16,** 304–307.

Butcher, J., Ball, B., & Ray, E. Effects of socioeconomic level on MMPI differences in Negro-white college students. *Journal of Counseling Psychology*, 1954, **11,** 83–87.

Caldwell, M. G. Case analysis method for the personality study of offenders. *Journal of Criminal Law, Criminology, and Police Science*, 1954, **45,** 291–298.

Cooley, W. W., & Lohnes, P. F. *Multivariate procedures for the behavioral sciences.* New York: Wiley, 1962.

Dahlstrom, W. G., & Welsh, G. S. *An MMPI handbook.* Minneapolis: University of Minnesota Press, 1960.

Dreger, R. M., & Miller, K. S. Comparative psychological studies of Negroes and whites in the United States. *Psychological Bulletin*, 1960, **57,** 361–402.

Fry, F. D. A study of the personality traits of college students and of state prison inmates as measured by the MMPI. *Journal of Psychology*, 1949, **28,** 439–449.

Gottlieb, G., & Eisdorfer, C. Personality patterns of medical outpatients. Unpublished manuscript, 1959. Cited by J. Butcher, B. Ball, & E. Ray. Effects of socioeconomic level on MMPI differences in Negro-white college students. *Journal of Counseling Psychology*, 1954, **11,** 83–87.

Harman, H. H. *Modern factor analysis.* Chicago: University of Chicago Press, 1960.

Hokanson, J. E., & Calden, G. Negro-white differences on the MMPI. *Journal of Clinical Psychology*, 1960, **16,** 32–33.

Kardiner, A., & Ovesey, L. *The mark of oppression: A psychosocial study of the American Negro.* New York: Norton, 1951.

Karon, B. P. *The Negro personality: A rigorous investigation of the effects of culture.* New York: Springer, 1958.

Klineberg, O. (Ed.) *Characteristics of the American Negro.* New York: Harper, 1944.

McDonald, R. L., & Gynther, M. D. Differences associated with sex, race, and class in two adolescent samples. *Journal of Consulting Psychology*, 1963, **27,** 112–116.

Miller, C., Wertz, C., & Counts, S. Racial differences on the MMPI. *Journal of Clinical Psychology*, 1961, **17,** 159–160.

Mussen, P. H. Differences between the TAT responses of Negro and white boys. *Journal of Consulting Psychology*, 1953, **17,** 373–376.

Panton, J. H. Inmate personality differences related to recidivism, age and race as measured by the MMPI. *Journal of Correctional Psychology*, 1959, **4,** 28–35.

Pettigrew, T. *Profile of the American Negro.* New York: Van Nostrand, 1964.

Yinger, M. *Religion, society, and the individual.* New York: Macmillan, 1957. Pp. 183–194.

3

The Black Family and Child Development

For this [the condition of the Negro family], most of all, white America must accept responsibility. It flows from centuries of oppression and persecution of the Negro man. It flows from long years of degradation and discrimination, which have attacked his dignity and assaulted his ability to provide for his family.

PRESIDENT JOHNSON, *at Howard University, June, 1965*

INTRODUCTION

Parents play a crucial role in their children's intellectual, social, and emotional development. The early home environment is largely responsible for the amount and kind of stimulation a child receives. Such stimulation serves to enhance his motor and language development and his auditory and perceptual skills. As we have seen in Chapter 2, parents vary in ability to provide models for personal identification which in turn may affect their child's sense of identity and self-worth, and his achievement motivation. The family also influences the child's first, and often lasting, attitudes and behavior toward others. Several social scientists, whose efforts we shall review here, have focussed on the black family and the relationship between parental factors and the child's emotional and intellectual development.

THE MOYNIHAN REPORT

A report issued by the U.S. Department of Labor (1965) came to the conclusion that black dependency and family disorganization represent one of the cornerstones in the dilemma of race relations. The much-discussed report, which became known as the "Moynihan Report," presented census figures, findings from special studies, and theoretical analyses that suggested a much higher incidence of broken marriages, matriarchal households, illegitimate children, and dependence on public assistance among black than among white families. Such data on the black family must be seen in the context of black America's economic position. The unemployment rate among black people, for example, is twice that of whites, their median income half that of whites although their families tend to be larger. Moynihan (1966) suggested that:

> The cumulative result of unemployment and low income, and probably also of excessive dependence upon the income of women, has produced an unmistakable crisis in the Negro family, and raises the serious question of whether or not this crisis is beginning to create conditions which tend to reinforce the cycle that produced it in the first instance. The crisis would probably exist in any event, but it becomes acute in the context of the extraordinary rise in the Negro population in recent years (p. 147).

As early as 1939 Franklin E. Frazier, the eminent black scholar, had predicted the disruption of black family life:

> First, it appears that the family which evolved within the isolated world of the Negro folk will become increasingly disorganized. Modern means of communication will break down the isolation of the world of black folk, and, as long as the bankrupt system of Southern agriculture exists, Negro families will continue to seek a living in the towns and cities of the country. They will crowd the slum areas of Southern cities or make their way to Northern cities where their family life will become disrupted and their poverty will force them to depend upon charity. (Quoted in Moynihan, 1967, p. 35.)

In the face of the "crisis" in the black family, Moynihan suggested that ordinary measures to help black people (increase in employment, education, welfare, and so forth) would no longer suffice. He believed that although America must continue to push for better education and employment for its black citizens, a more direct attack on the problems of the black family had become necessary. President Johnson's famous speech in June of 1965, at Howard University, clearly reflected Moynihan's conclusions:

> So, unless we work to strengthen the (black) family, to create conditions under which most parents will stay together—all the rest: schools and playgrounds, public assistance and private concern, will never be enough to cut completely the cycle of despair and deprivation.

He promised that his administration would

> . . . move beyond opportunity to achievement. To shatter forever not only the barriers of law and public practice, but the walls which bound the condition of man in the color of his skin.

> This is the next and more profound stage of the battle for civil rights. We seek not just freedom but opportunity—not just legal equity but human ability —not just equality as a right and a theory, but equality as a fact and as a result. (Quoted in Moynihan, 1967, pp. 33–34.)

Even before Moynihan's report was released to the public a bitter controversy ensued (see Rainwater & Yancey, 1967). Herzog (1966), for example, maintained that although the economic conditions in the black lower class were indeed deplorable, there were no indications of a *sudden* increase of family breakdown, illegitimacy, and public dependence; the figures rather suggested a gradually increasing deterioration of the black family. The reasons for this deterioration, furthermore, were not to be sought in slavery, but in the present conditions of economic oppression and discrimination. However, she agreed with Moynihan that

> . . . the man who cannot command a stable job at adequate wages cannot be an adequate family provider; the man who cannot provide for his family is likely to lose status and respect in his own eyes and in the eyes of others— including his family. His inability to provide drains him of the will to struggle with continuing and insuperable family responsibilities. It is an incentive to desertion, especially if his family can receive public assistance only when he is gone (p. 4).

Some of Moynihan's critics emphasized the affectional bonds among black people and their remarkable capacity to endure the most adverse conditions over centuries. Erikson (1966), in another context, has drawn attention to the superb strength in many black mothers, which, some black leaders believe, made it possible for many black people to retain dignity and courage in the face of oppression.

Hill and Jaffe (1966) and Herzog (1966) gave a number of reasons, such as less use of contraception and abortion, differences in reporting, fear of losing public assistance by admitting to a man in the house, and the expense of divorce and legal separation, which may have distorted Moynihan's statistics on illegitimacy among black families. Rainwater (1966), who has also studied black lower-class families, maintains that pregnancy for the black girls is

> . . . the real measure of maturity, the   dividing line between adolescence and womanhood. Perhaps because of this, as well as because of the ready resources for child care, girls in the Negro slum community show much less concern about pregnancy than do girls in the white lower-class community and are less motivated to marry the fathers of their children. When a girl becomes pregnant the question of marriage certainly arises and is considered, but the girl often decides that she would rather not marry the man either because she does not want to settle down yet or because she does not think he would make a good husband (p. 175).

The original Moynihan Report did not contain any specific recommendations, but later Moynihan (1966; 1967; 1968) made it clear that he was opting for a *family allowance*. This he considered to be "a first step in the necessary movement from the 'civil-rights' phase—the phase involving legal equality for Negroes—into the phase of 'equality as a fact and as a result' " (Moynihan, 1967, p. 36). He argued that the United States had a family allowance only for *broken* families (Aid to Families of Dependent Children— AFDC) which, he feels, penalizes families with a father in the home. He contrasted the many advantages of the family allowance with the disadvantages of the present welfare system which he claimed serves

> . . . to maintain the poorest groups in society in a position of impotent fury. Impotent because the system destroys the potential of individuals and families to improve themselves. Fury because it claims to do otherwise. (Moynihan, 1968, p. 22.)

Finally, he pointed to the great need for research on poverty and its consequences. In particular he called for longitudinal studies, which would help determine more specifically the factors that lead to and maintain poverty and those that might lead one out of poverty.

The first two studies included in this chapter report consequences or concomitants of the broken family. Parker and Kleiner's results [9] show that black mothers in broken homes are more maladjusted and frustrated than black mothers in intact homes. They are, furthermore, characterized by significantly lower-goal striving for themselves and a hypothetical son, a notion that the authors feel has serious implications for the achievement-related attitudes of offspring. Parker and Kleiner recognized that their findings do not permit specific cause and effect assertions. It may well be that the personality characteristics of these mothers were causing rather than resulting from the breakup of their families.

Hetherington [10] assessed the effects of absence of fathers and time of fathers' departure on sex-typed behaviors. Her results indicated that the effects of father's absence were particularly pronounced in both black and white boys whose fathers had left before the boys were five years of age. For example, these children demonstrated less aggression and more feminine sex role preferences than did the other boys (see also D'Andrade, 1962). Absence of the father after the boys reached age five, when sexual identification is presumably nearing completion, had little effect on their sex-typed behaviors. The only racial difference she found was that black boys engaged in more competitive activities involving contact than white boys did. In view of the more widespread incidence of families headed by females in the lower-class black community her findings are of considerable importance in this context. Both Parker and Kleiner and Hetherington reviewed additional consequences of fatherless homes.

The next paper included in this chapter, by Lewis [11], provides some insight into the functioning and organization of low-income families. Intensive interviews and field observations in Washington, D.C. revealed that these families are not as homogeneous in their child-rearing practices and attitudes toward sex and marriage as is commonly believed. Their verbalized aspirations for themselves or their children, furthermore, are not very different from those of middle-class families. Most of their concerns center around immediate pragmatic considerations and environmental pressures, which often undermine their personal goals and their control over their children. They express strong dissatisfaction with their jobs, housing, and education, but many of these parents persist in trying to improve their own lives and those of their offspring.

The picture that emerges from these data suggests that we have yet a great deal to learn about low-income black families. Above all else their behavior which is "essentially non-class, non-cultural—just universally human" (Lewis, 1964, p. 7) reflects an attempt to cope with the harsh realities of poverty.

> And thus, as never before in our society, it is the relationship between the family *and* society, not the relationship of family and ethnic group or racial category, that is decisive. (Lewis, 1967, p. 21.)

CHILD REARING AND DEVELOPMENT

Lewis attempted to understand the behavior of low-income families by means of long-term observations and repeated interviews. Blau [12] used the more traditional survey method. Her findings indicate that black mothers are less exposed to information on child rearing than are white mothers. This racial difference pertains regardless of class position and, in most instances, of educational level. On the other hand, black mothers' attitudes toward experts are more favorable. Ambivalence toward experts increases with rising exposure to more information in lower- and middle-class mothers of both racial groups. The negative correlation between degree of exposure to experts and expressed hostility that Blau found for whites did not hold for black mothers. Blau explains her findings by referring to economic discrimination and social segregation, which impede the acculturation of the black masses to urban middle-class culture. Generally speaking, the black community offers fewer opportunities for exposure to and assimilation of middle-class standards of behavior. More specifically, structural differences between the black and white class systems differentially affect the diffusion of and pressure to adopt middle-class norms. In another paper, Blau (1965) came to much the same conclusions. Her suggestions that residential integration would facilitate this acculturation process is in line with Bullough's findings [7] that black families in an integrated community scored lower on her measures of alienation and were more oriented toward the mainstream of society.

The significance of social class values regarding the aspirations black mothers have for their children were demonstrated in a study by Bell (1965). Two groups of black lower-class mothers were compared: "low-status" (low educational level of mother and large number of children) and "high status" (high educational level of mother and small number of children). Significant differences between these groups emerged on a number of variables, including the following: the high status group had higher aspirations for their children with respect to education and occupation, and they generally preferred that their children be older at the time of marriage and have fewer children.

The next paper included in this chapter, by Hess and Shipman [13], attempts to define cultural deprivation and demonstrate its effects upon the cognitive development of the child. Black mothers from four different social status levels and their four-year-old children were interviewed and tested on a number of cognitive tasks and parent-child interactions. The data indicate significant differences between higher- and lower-status groups with respect to the children's and mothers' task approaches, linguistic codes, and maternal teaching styles. The authors maintain that behaviors that lead to cultural and economic poverty are established in early childhood; that the primary effect of cultural deprivation is a lack of cognitive meaning in parent-child interactions; and that cognitive functioning is enhanced or constricted depending on the availability of alternatives for action and thought. These are important considerations when one attempts to explain why children from lower-class families score lower on intelligence tests, have lower achievement records, and complete less schooling than children from middle-class backgrounds.

To further stress the importance of the early environment it should also be noted that evidence presently available (see also Chapter 4) indicates that there are few if any racial or social class differences in mental development at very early ages. Such differences are, however, very apparent in children of school age. Walters (1967), for example, compared black babies and white babies, equated for social class on the Gesell Developmental Schedules, at 12, 24, and 36 weeks. Her results indicate no difference between the two racial groups, except that the 12-week-old black babies were superior to whites in motor development. Her results are similar to those previously reported by Bayley (1965), Knoblock and Pasamanick (1953), and Pasamanick (1946). Bayley (1965) administered her Scales of Mental and Motor Development to over 1,400 infants in the age range of 1 to 15 months. Although she found no differences in mental development between black babies and white babies, the black babies achieved higher scores on the Motor Scale than whites. She states:

> There is ample evidence that, within normal limits, development status in the first year of life is a poor predictor of later mental and motor functioning. There is also ample evidence that mental-test scores after 3 or 4 years of age are correlated with a number of variables which are customarily used as indicators of socio-economic status. Evidently, the period between 1 and 4 years of age is an important one in the development of mental and motor functions. This age period should be studied closely in an effort to seek out those environmental factors which are relevant to the development of intellect and those behaviors that appear to be resistant to environmental impacts and also in an effort to identify the behaviors and the specific age periods for which correlations between test scores and socio-economic ratings first occur (pp. 409–410).

Research has demonstrated that the differences in mental growth between children of upper and lower socioeconomic groups are to some extent the result of differential early stimulation and experience (Lesser et al., 1965; Covington, 1967; Hunt, 1961; Pines, 1967).

An issue yet remains as to what specific variables in the home environment account for these differences. Parent-child interactions play a crucial role in shaping the child's aspirations and cognitive behaviors. Freeberg and Payne (1967) have indicated that the amount of verbalization and styles of communication favor the middle-class child with respect to achievement in a standard school setting. He has ample reading material, questions are encouraged and answered in detail, and he is challenged to reason and think independently and to communicate his experiences. Baumrind and Black (1967) have investigated the relationships between socialization practices and competence in preschool children. They found that parents who combine enforced demands and consistent discipline with independence and verbal interchange are most successful in producing stable and assertive behavior in their children. Honzik (1967) also focussed on the relationship between early family setting and mental growth in a 30-year longitudinal study. Her data indicate that children's intellectual growth is positively related to parental ability, maternal sensitivity to the child's welfare, and parents' concern with achievement. Wolf (1964) found high correlations between the child's I.Q. and "environmental process characteristics," such as parents' aspirations for the child, opportunities for increasing his vocabulary, and the extent of parental assistance in learning situations. Freeberg and Payne (1967) conclude that "children of superior intellectual ability come from homes where parental interest in their intellectual development is evidenced by pressure to succeed and assistance in doing so, particularly in the development of the child's verbal skills" (p. 71).

Prenatal and postnatal care as well as nutritional factors are of utmost importance. Some evidence (for example, Bronfenbrenner, 1967; Knoblock & Pasamanick, 1960; Pasamanick, 1969; Pasamanick & Knoblock, 1961; Pettigrew, 1964) suggests that inadequate maternal care during and after pregnancy and protein deficiences may be responsible for neurological damage and brain dysfunctioning resulting in impaired intellectual functioning and behavioral disturbances that impede learning.

Baratz and Baratz (1969) have challenged the underlying assumptions of enrichment programs. (Research on compensatory education will be reviewed in more detail in the next chapter.) They maintain that such programs for blacks are based on a "social pathology model," that is, the notion that deviations from white middle-class intellectual norms stem from inadequate parents, are pathological, and must be corrected as early as possible by intervention programs. They reject this model as well as "the genetic model" which ascribes intellectual differences to genetic determinants. Baratz and Baratz suggest that research efforts should instead focus on discovering "the different but not pathological forms of Negro behavior" (p. 22) and urge that such differences be used to acculturate the black child "to the mainstream while maintaining his individual identity and cultural heritage" (p. 22).

To conclude, if the most effective assistance is to be rendered to low-income families, efforts to understand their behavior, value systems, and child-rearing practices must continue. Thus far, emphasis has been placed on trying to provide remedial programs and compensatory experiences without a clear comprehension of the functioning and organization of low-income families. It appears that the diversity and strengths in these families have often been underestimated and have not been sufficiently drawn upon by concerned agencies. In the face of inadequate resources for meeting even the most basic needs, however, all other considerations pale. What these parents, particularly the fathers, need most of all are jobs that will give them a sense of accomplishment and worth as well as a stable and sufficient income.

REFERENCES

Baratz, S. S., & Baratz, J. C. Early childhood intervention: the social science base of institutionalized racism. Paper presented to the Society for Research in Child Development, Santa Monica, California, 1969.

Baumrind, D., & Black, A. E. Socialization practices associated with dimensions of competence in preschool boys and girls. *Child Development*, 1967, **38**, 291–327.

Bayley, N. Comparisons of mental and motor test scores for ages 1-15 months by sex, birth order, race, geographical location, and education of parents. *Child Development*, 1965, **36**, 379–411.

Bell, R. B. Lower class Negro mothers' aspiration for their children. *Social Forces*, 1965, **43**, 493–500.

Blau, Z. S., Class structure, mobility, and change in child rearing. *Sociometry*, 1965, **28**, 210–219.

Bronfenbrenner, U. The psychological costs of quality and equality in education. *Child Development*, 1967, **38**, 909–925.

Covington, M. V. Stimulus discrimination as a function of social-class membership. *Child Development*, 1967, **38**, 607–613.

D'Andrade, R. G. Father absence and cross-sex identification. Unpublished doctoral dissertation, Harvard University, 1962.

Erikson, E. H. The concept of identity in race relations: Notes and queries. In T. Parsons & K. B. Clark (Eds.), *The Negro American*. Boston: Houghton Mifflin, 1966.

Freeberg, N. E., & Payne, D. T. Parental influence on cognitive development in early childhood: A review. *Child Development*, 1967, **38**, 65–87.

Herzog, E. Is there a "breakdown" of the Negro family? *Social Work*, 1966, **11**, 3–10.

Hill, A. C., & Jaffe, F. S. Negro fertility and family size preferences: implications for programming of health and social services. In T. Parsons & K. B. Clark (Eds.) *The Negro American*. Boston: Houghton Mifflin, 1966.

Honzik, M. P. Mother-child interaction and the socialization process. *Child Development*, 1967, **38**, 338–364.

Hunt, J. McV. *Intelligence and experience*. New York: Ronald, 1961.

Knoblock, H., & Pasamanick, B. Further observations on the behavioral development of the Negro children. *Journal of Genetic Psychology*, 1953, **83,** 137–157.

Knoblock, H., & Pasamanick, B. Environmental factors affecting human development, before and after birth. *Pediatrics*, 1960, **26,** 210–218.

Lesser, G. S., et al. Mental abilities of children from different social class and cultural groups. *Monographs of the Society for Research in Child Development*, 1965, **30** (4).

Lewis, H. The contemporary urban poverty syndrome. Paper presented at Howard Medical School, 1964.

Lewis, H. New perceptions of the family: New agenda, different rhetoric. Paper presented at the 43rd annual conference of the Child Study Association, New York, 1967.

Moynihan, D. P. Employment, income, and the ordeal of the Negro American. In T. Parsons & K. B. Clark (Eds.), *The Negro American*. Boston: Houghton Mifflin, 1966.

Moynihan, D. P. The President and the Negro: The moment lost. *Commentary*, February, 1967, 31–45.

Moynihan, D. P. The crisis in welfare. *The Public Interest*, 1968, **10,** 3–29.

Pasamanick, B. A. A comparative study of the behavioral development of Negro infants. *Journal of Genetic Psychology*, 1946, **69,** 3–44.

Pasamanick, B. A. Tract for the times: Some sociological aspects of science, race, and racism. *American Journal of Orthopsychiatry*, 1969, **39,** 7–15.

Pasamanick, B. A., & Knoblock, H. Epidemiologic studies on the complications of pregnancy and the birth process. In C. Caplan (Ed.) *Prevention of mental disorders in children*. New York: Basic Books, 1961.

Pettigrew, T. F. *A Profile of the Negro American*. Princeton, N.J.: Van Nostrand, 1964.

Pines, M. *Revolution in learning*. New York: Harper & Row, 1967.

Rainwater, L. Crucible of identity: The Negro lower-class family. In T. Parsons & K. B. Clark (Eds.), *The Negro American*. Boston: Houghton Mifflin, 1966.

Rainwater, L., & Yancey, W. L. *The Moynihan report and the politics of controversy*. Cambridge, Mass.: MIT Press, 1967.

U.S. Department of Labor. The Negro family: The case for national action. Washington, D.C.: Government Printing Office, 1965.

Walters, C. E. Comparative development of Negro and white infants. *The Journal of Genetic Psychology*, 1967, **110,** 243–251.

Wolf, R. M. The identification and measurement of environmental process variables related to intelligence. Unpublished doctoral dissertation, University of Chicago, 1964.

9

*Characteristics of Negro mothers in single-headed households**

SEYMOUR PARKER AND ROBERT J. KLEINER

The Negro family in America has frequently been characterized as matri-centered, often with the father absent or having only a peripheral spouse and parental role. This family configuration has been attributed both to historical factors rooted in slave society and to current patterns of discrimination and employment among Negroes.[1,2,3]

Statistical studies have clearly demonstrated the widespread and increasing incidence of female single-headed Negro families in the United States.[4,5] Although this phenomenon is also increasing among white families, it is especially prevalent among Negroes.[6] According to the 1960 census,[7] about 25 percent of all non-white families had a single head of household. The corresponding figure for white families was ten percent. In the vast majority of cases the male is the absent member.[8] A recent report noted that only 50 percent of the Negro children in Harlem under 18 years of age were living with both [natural] parents; the corresponding figure for New York City as a whole was 83 percent.[9]

Many serious social problems, such as apathy,[10] homosexuality and sex-role confu-

Reprinted from *Journal of Marriage and the Family*, 1966, **28**, 507–513, by permission of the authors and the National Council on Family Relations.

* Supported by Research Grant Number HM-10690, National Institutes of Health, Public Health Service, Bethesda, Maryland. The community survey was conducted by National Analysts, Inc., Philadelphia, Pennsylvania. The authors wish to express their appreciation to Miss Judith Fine for her invaluable assistance in preparing this paper for publication.

[1] E. F. Frazier, *The Negro Family in the United States*, Chicago: University of Chicago Press, 1939.

[2] K. B. Clark, *Dark Ghetto: Dilemmas of Social Power*, New York: Harper and Row, 1965.

[3] J. Bernard, *Marriage and Family Among Negroes*, Englewood Cliffs, New Jersey: Prentice-Hall, Inc., 1966.

[4] United States Department of Labor, *Negro Women Workers in 1960*, Washington, D.C.: United States Government Printing Office, 1964, p. 12.

[5] United States Department of Labor. *The Negro Family*, Washington, D.C.: United States Government Printing Office, 1965.

[6] United States Bureau of the Census, *Historical Statistics of the United States, Colonial Times to 1957. A Statistical Abstract Supplement*, Washington, D.C.: United States Government Printing Office, 1960, p. 16, Series A-255-263.

[7] United States Bureau of the Census, *United States Census of Population, 1960. General Social and Economic Characteristics of the United States, Summary. Final Report PC(1)-1C*, Washington, D.C.: United States Government Printing Office, 1962.

[8] E. F. Frazier, "Problems and Needs of Negro Children and Youth Resulting from Family Disorganization," *Journal of Negro Education*, **19** (1950), pp. 269–277.

[9] Harlem Youth Opportunities Unlimited, Inc., *Youth in the Ghetto: A Study of the Consequences of Powerlessness and a Blueprint for Change*, New York: Century Printing Co., 2nd ed., 1964, p. 127.

[10] W. Mischel, "Delay of Gratification, Need for Achievement, and Acquiescence in Another

sion,[11,12,13] delinquency,[14,15,16] and mental disorder,[17] have been attributed to the effects of a family environment in which the father is absent or ineffectual. However, many of these studies are based on data gathered by clinical methods. Systematic studies are infrequent.

The absence of large-scale, systematic studies of the effect of this type of family situation on the child has been noted by a number of investigators,[18,19] In spite of the prevalence of the single-headed female household among Negroes, the effects of this situation and the factors within the situation responsible for some of the hypothesized effects have not been empirically investigated in a systematic fashion.

The present paper will focus on the psychological adjustment of mothers in single-headed households and their aspirations for their children. The design involves a comparison between Negro mothers in intact families, i.e., with a husband or husband-substitute present, and those raising children with no male partner present. However, this design does not allow one to determine sources of difference between mothers in these two samples. Such differenecs may result from the effects of the male's absence or possibly from selective personality factors characterizing women in these types of family situations. Regardless of the underlying reasons, the authors shall delineate some characteristics of mothers in these two samples and discuss how these factors may affect the goal striving of their children.

A number of studies have investigated the effects of the broken family situation on the child. The Negro's relatively low achievement levels in this society (particularly in occupation and education) have been attributed to discrimination and to the effects of social barriers, which presumably inhibit his achievement aspirations. Investigations of these issues demonstrate that the Negro's social handicaps markedly curb and inhibit his actual achievement and even his motivation to achieve.[20,21] Aside from the more obvious barriers to achievement, however, subtle personality factors may also influence the Negro's goal striving. These factors will assume greater importance as the more evident economic barriers and social handicaps are eliminated.

In recent years there has been increasing interest in how motivation to achieve is affected by early socialization experiences in the family.[22,23] Although there are few definite, conclusive findings about the relationship between the need to achieve [24] and actual achievement strivings, the relevance of an achievement motive must be considered.

Culture," *Journal of Abnormal and Social Psychology,* **63** (1961), pp. 543–552.

[11] M. W. MacDonald, "Criminally Aggressive Behavior in Passive Effeminate Boys," *American Journal of Orthopsychiatry,* **8** (1938), pp. 70–78.

[12] J. Nash, "Critical Periods in Human Development," *Bulletin of the Maritime Psychological Association* (1954), pp. 18–22.

[13] J. E. Hokanson and G. Calden, "Negro-White Differences on the MMPI," *Journal of Clinical Psychology,* **16** (1960), pp. 32–33.

[14] S. Glueck and E. T. Glueck, *Unraveling Juvenile Delinquency,* New York: Commonwealth Fund, 1950, p. 280.

[15] W. B. Miller, "Lower Class Culture as a Generating Milieu of Gang Delinquency," *Journal of Social Issues,* **14** (1958), pp. 5–19.

[16] J. H. Rohrer and M. S. Edmondson, *The Eighth Generation,* New York: Harper and Brothers, 1960.

[17] L. M. Stolz, *et al., Father Relations of War-Born Children: The Effect of Postwar Adjustment of Fathers on the Behavior and Personality of First Children Born While the Fathers Were at War,* Stanford, California: Stanford University Press, 1954.

[18] L. Bartemeier, "The Contribution of the Father to the Mental Health of the Family," *American Journal of Psychiatry,* **110** (1953), pp. 277–280.

[19] F. I. Nye, *The Employed Mother in America,* Chicago: Rand McNally and Co., 1963, pp. 208–209.

[20] A. M. Rose, "Race and Ethnic Relations," in *Contemporary Social Problems,* ed. by R. K. Merton and R. A. Nisbet, New York: Harcourt, Brace and World, Inc., 1961, pp. 324–389.

[21] L. Broom and P. Selznick, *Sociology: A Text with Adapted Readings,* New York: Harper and Row, 3rd ed., 1963, pp. 502–507.

[22] D. C. McClelland, J. W. Atkinson, R. A. Clark, and E. L. Lowell, *The Achievement Motive,* New York: Appleton-Century-Crofts, Inc., 1953.

[23] *Motives in Fantasy, Action, and Society: A Method of Assessment and Study,* ed. by J. W. Atkinson, Princeton, New Jersey: D. Van Nostrand, Inc., 1958.

[24] Nash, "Critical Periods in Human Development."

Studies have reported high achievement motivation among individuals whose parents stressed self-reliance and mastery in early socialization.[25,26,27] Rosen [28] investigated the achievement motive in different ethnic groups which presumably provided dissimilar socialization experiences. He reported that Negroes ranked low in achievement motivation (as measured by fantasy productions), although they maintained high goals relative to other ethnic groups.

As noted earlier, the literature on Negro family life frequently refers to the matri-centered Negro family, in which the father plays a comparatively weak role or is absent altogether.[29] This broken home phenomenon among Negroes may account at least partly for the low achievement motivation noted by Rosen. A search of the literature revealed no studies *directly* relevant to this question. Some investigators have suggested that the weak-or-absent father situation results in a confusion of sexual identity in the male child.[30,31,32] Lott and Lott [33] reported less sex differentiation in the values of Negro youths than in those of white youths. They attributed this difference to the less sharply differentiated parental sex roles in the Negro family. Since a high level of achievement striving tends to

be a male-linked characteristic in American society, confused sex identity in the male might reduce his achievement strivings. In this context, boys in father-absent homes showed less aggression in their fantasy behavior than boys in intact homes.[34]

A low degree of competitiveness has also been associated with low achievement motivation.[35] Finally, Mischel [36] noted that young children from father-absent homes were less able to delay need gratification than children whose fathers were present in the home. Since ability to delay gratification is positively related to a high level of achievement striving, this finding provides another link between the single-headed female family situation and low levels of achievement motivation in children from such families.

In a study of the educational and occupational aspirations of lower class youth, Kahl [37] showed that the father's influence was a major factor in determining whether lower class, intellectually capable boys would attend college. Such influence would be lacking in the broken home situation. However, several other investigators[38,39] found that mothers exerted the major influence on educational aspirations among lower class Negro and white youths. These contradictory findings indicate that the relative importance of the father and mother to achievement-related behavior of their children has not been established with any degree of certainty.

[25] McClelland, *et al., The Achievement Motive.*

[26] D. C. McClelland, "Measuring Motivation in Phantasy: The Achievement Motive," in *Studies in Motivation,* ed. by D. C. McClelland, New York: Appleton-Century-Crofts, Inc., 1955, pp. 401–413.

[27] D. C. McClelland, *The Achieving Society,* Princeton, New Jersey: D. Van Nostrand Co., Inc., 1961.

[28] B. C. Rosen, "Race, Ethnicity, and the Achievement Motive," *American Sociological Review,* **24** (1959), pp. 47–60.

[29] Frazier, *The Negro Family in the United States, op. cit.*

[30] MacDonald, "Criminally Aggressive Behavior in Passive Effeminate Boys."

[31] A. Kardiner and L. Ovesey, *The Mark of Oppression: A Psychosocial Study of the American Negro,* New York: W. W. Norton and Co., Inc., 1951.

[32] T. F. Pettigrew, *A Profile of the Negro American,* Princeton, New Jersey: D. Van Nostrand Co., Inc., 1964, pp. 15–24.

[33] A. Lott and B. E. Lott, *Negro and White Youth,* New York: Holt, Rinehart and Winston, Inc., 1963, p. 161 ff.

[34] R. R. Sears, M. H. Pintler, and P. S. Sears, "Effects of Father Separation on Pre-School Children's Doll Play Aggression," *Child Development,* **17** (1946), pp. 219–243.

[35] M. R. Winterbottom, "The Relation of Need for Achievement to Learning Experiences in Independence and Mastery," in *Motives in Fantasy, Action, and Society: A Method of Assessment and Study,* ed. by J. W. Atkinson, Princeton, New Jersey: D. Van Nostrand Co., Inc., 1958, pp. 453–478.

[36] W. Mischel, "Father-Absence and Delay of Gratification: Cross-Cultural Comparisons," *Journal of Abnormal and Social Psychology,* **63** (1961), pp. 116–124.

[37] J. A. Kahl, "Educational and Occupational Aspirations of 'Common Man' Boys," *Harvard Educational Review,* **23** (1953), pp. 186–203.

[38] R. A. Ellis and W. C. Lane, "Structural Supports for Upward Mobility," *American Sociological Review,* **28** (1963), pp. 743–756.

[39] N. P. Gist, "Aspirations of Negro and White Students," *Social Forces,* **42** (1964), pp. 40–49.

Lynn and Sawrey [40] suggested that many of the characteristics of children reared without a father were attributable to the effects of the father's absence on the mother, rather than to the direct effect of his absence on the children. They reported that mothers in father-absent families tended to be more protective and authoritarian in their childrearing patterns than mothers in intact families, and that they used their children as objects for gratification of their own needs. Comparable effects of the father's absence on mother-son relationships have been noted in other studies.[41,42]

These findings suggest the importance of exploring further the adjustment and attitudes of mothers in broken homes, instead of assuming that differences between children in broken and intact family situations are directly attributable to the father's absence. Although all the findings reported above support a relationship between the broken home situation and both achievement-related behavior and other phenomena, the reasons for this association are not completely understood. In order to investigate this issue more fully, the authors shall examine some characteristics of mothers in single-headed households.

A sample of Negro mothers who were heads of their households, i.e., no husband or husband-substitute present in the home (a broken family situation), was compared with a sample of Negro mothers in households with such a male figure present (an intact family situation). The particular variables used to compare these two groups of mothers were (1) prevalence of psychoneurotic symptoms, (2) discrepancy between the mother's actual and ideal self-image, considered to be a measure of her self-esteem, (3) perceived discrepancy between the mother's own achievement and that of her "close friends," designated as the "reference group discrepancy," (4) the mother's level of goal-striving stress [43] related to her educational and occupational aspirations for a hypothetical son, and (5) the mother's level of goal-striving stress based on aspirations for herself.

The first two of these factors will be used to characterize psychosocial adjustment in the two types of family situations. The third factor will be considered a measure of relative deprivation or frustration, and the final two factors will be regarded as indicators of these mothers' levels of aspiration and the motivational strength of their aspirations.

Given the ambiguous state of knowledge and theory on these issues, it is difficult to formulate and test specific hypotheses. It should be noted, however, that in a larger study of mental illness in a Negro population, the authors found that community individuals characterized by high levels of psychiatric symptoms also manifested a definite pattern of low goal-striving stress for themselves and for a hypothetical son.[44] On this basis the authors anticipate that *if* mothers in broken home situations manifest poor psychological adjustment relative to their counterparts in intact homes, they will also show lower goal striving for themselves and a hypothetical son. Existing research leads one to expect less adequate psychological adjustment among mothers heading households with no husbands or husband-substitutes present than among mothers in intact homes. In addition to the actual personal and financial problems involved in raising children in the former situation, the broken-home mother may experience a certain degree of social stigma in her community.

The clinical literature suggests other patterns of striving for a mother and her children in a broken home situation. The mother in this type of home may be disappointed in her own life and attempt to use her children as vehicles for her own wish fulfillment. In this case, she may induce high goal striving in them; she may give up striving for her own goals and manifest high compensatory levels of striving for her children. Some of the literature has also suggested that the mother

[40] D. Lynn and W. L. Sawrey, "The Effects of Father-Absence on Norwegian Boys and Girls," *Journal of Abnormal and Social Psychology,* **59** (1959), pp. 258–262.

[41] H. Wylie and R. Delgado, "A Pattern of Mother-Son Relationship Involving the Absence of Father," *American Journal of Orthopsychiatry,* **29** (1959), pp. 646–649.

[42] H. S. Stean, "Treatment of Mothers and Sons in the Absence of the Father," *Social Work,* **6** (1961), p. 29–35.

[43] The components of this concept are explained in "Explanatory Notes" at the conclusion of this paper.

[44] S. Parker and R. J. Kleiner, *Mental Illness in the Urban Negro Community,* Glencoe, Illinois: The Free Press, 1966, p. 67.

in the broken home situation is so preoccupied with her own striving problems and anxiety to protect her children that she becomes overly protective and inhibits their achievement behavior. Another possibility (already suggested in this paper) is a generalized "giving up" and consequent low striving for both self and children. In any case, the authors assume that the mother's goal-striving stress for her children will be indirectly communicated to them, that is, if it is low, it will reduce their achievement motivation.

PROCEDURE

The data reported in this paper are based on interviews of a representative sample of the Philadelphia Negro community between 20 and 60 years of age (N = 1489) and a comparable sample of mentally ill Negroes from the same city (N = 1423). The intact family situation has been defined as one in which a mother was raising school-age children with a husband or husband-substitute present in the home (N = 389). The mother in the broken home situation was unmarried, divorced, or separated and was raising school-age children with no husband or husband-substitute present in the home (N = 115). This paper is based only on data collected for the community sample.

Members in the two types of family situations were compared with respect to the number of psychoneurotic symptoms they manifested. Respondents specified the frequency with which they experienced each of 13 psychoneurotic and psychosomatic complaints. These items, which were similar to items used as measures of neuroticism in some recent large-scale epidemiological studies,[45,46,47] were a modification of a list

originally included in the Cornell Medical Health Index.

The authors' measure of self-esteem was derived from two sets of 17 paired statements in the questionnaire instrument, involving behavior in specified interpersonal situations. Each of the first set of statements was preceded by the phrase, "I am a person who . . ." and the second set of statements, by the phrase, "I would like to be a person who. . . ." A numerical value was assigned to each precoded response choice. The numerical value of a subject's response to an item in the first set of statements, i.e., her perception of her actual behavior, was subtracted from the value of her response to the paired item in the second set of statements, i.e., her desired behavior. An average score was computed for each respondent on the basis of the number of paired items actually answered. This average score, the "self-ideal" discrepancy, was considered to be a measure of self-esteem. The larger this discrepancy score, the greater the respondent's dissatisfaction with herself and the lower her self-esteem. Conversely, the smaller this discrepancy, the greater her satisfaction and the higher her self-esteem.

The reference group discrepancy was derived in the following manner. Each respondent defined her personal concept of the "best" and "worst" way of life. She was then presented with a diagram of a ten-step ladder, the top step representing the "best possible way of life" and the bottom step the "worst possible way of life." She evaluated the level of her own general achievement on this ten-step scale relative to these two anchor points.[48] She was asked subsequently to evaluate the achievements of her "close friends" in terms of this same ten-step scale. The discrepancy between the respondent's perceived achievement level for herself and for her close friends was considered to be her reference group discrepancy.

The specific formulation of goal-striving stress used in this study was based on particular aspects of level-of-aspiration theory developed by Lewin and Escalona [49,50,51] and

[45] L. Srole, T. S. Langner, S. T. Michael, M. K. Opler, and T. A. C. Rennie, *Mental Health in the Metropolis: The Midtown Manhattan Study*, New York: McGraw-Hill Book Co., Inc., 1962, Volume 1.

[46] T. S. Langner and S. T. Michael, *Life Stress and Mental Health: The Midtown Manhattan Study*, Glencoe, Illinois: The Free Press, 1963, Volume 2.

[47] D. C. Leighton, J. S. Harding, D. B. Macklin, A. M. Macmillan, and A. H. Leighton, *The Character of Danger*, New York: Basic Books, Inc., 1963.

[48] H. Cantril, *The Pattern of Human Concerns*, New Brunswick, New Jersey: Rutgers University Press, 1966.

[49] S. K. Escalona, "The Effect of Success and Failure upon the Level of Aspiration and Behavior in Manic-Depressive Psychoses," in *University of Iowa Studies in Child Welfare: Studies*

on various social-psychological experiments conducted in laboratory situations. The authors have conceptualized goal-striving stress as a measure of an individual's psychological investment in a given goal area. This stress index was derived as a composite score from independent measures of three different components: the discrepancy between one's level of aspiration and actual achievement in a given goal area, his own estimated chances of attaining this aspired goal, i.e., probability of success, and the importance or salience of this goal to him.[52] Thus, this composite measure represents a more comprehensive means to evaluate goal-striving behavior than considering only the height of an individual's aspirations.

RESULTS

Before reporting the findings directly relevant to this study, the authors shall discuss social status differences between the broken- and intact-home mothers. Subsequent comparisons between these two samples may raise the possibility of status differences as an explanatory factor.

Since utilizing income and occupation data was a problematic procedure in the two female samples,[53] the authors focused on edu-

cational achievement as a measure of social status position. If the continuum of educational achievement is divided according to completion of elementary school, some high school, and some college, no statistically significant differences emerge between the two samples. However, when the "some high school" category is divided into women who left high school before graduation and women who did graduate, mothers in the intact family situation manifest higher educational achievement ($p < .05$).

The sample size made it inadvisable to institute controls for status position. Therefore, the reader should bear in mind the possibility that even the relatively small educational differences between the two groups of mothers may partially account for some of the findings reported in this paper. However, in the previous, larger study conducted by the authors, status-linked analyses of some of the same social-psychological variables considered here indicated that status differences could not be considered an explanatory factor.[54]

Psychosocial Adjustment of Mothers in Broken and Intact Homes

Mothers in the intact family situation manifest fewer psychiatric symptoms than mothers in broken home (by Chi-square, $p < .10 > .05$).[55] Children in broken homes are thus exposed to mothers who manifest slightly more psychiatric difficulties than are children in homes where both parents are present.

One's self-esteem, another measure of adjustment, was derived from the self-ideal discrepancy index described above. It was assumed that the smaller the discrepancy perceived between one's actual and ideal self, the higher the self-esteem. In the earlier, larger study the authors demonstrated a relationship between low self-esteem and a high level of psychiatric symptoms. The average self-ideal discrepancy of mothers in intact families is lower (.53) than the discrepancy of mothers in broken homes (.62), but the difference between these scores is not significant.

The authors considered the average perceived discrepancy from one's informal ref-

---

in Topological and Vector Psychology I, Iowa City: University of Iowa Press, 16:3 (1940), pp. 199–302.

[50] K. Lewin, T. Dembo, L. Festinger, and P. S. Sears, "Level of Aspiration," in *Personality and the Behavior Disorders: A Handbook Based on Experimental and Clinical Research,* ed. by J. McV. Hunt, New York: The Ronald Press Co., 1944, Volume 1, pp. 333–378.

[51] S. K. Escalona, *An application of the Level of Aspiration Experiment to the Study of Personality,* Teachers College, Columbia University Contributions to Education, Number 937, New York: Bureau of Publication, Teachers College, Columbia University, 1948.

[52] See "Explanatory Notes" for a more detailed explanation of this goal-striving formulation.

[53] More females in the broken than in the intact family situation were probably receiving public assistance. Therefore, income data on these two groups of mothers were not comparable. In addition, since there were no males present in the broken home families, there was no basis for comparing occupational status in the two female samples.

[54] Parker and Kleiner, *Mental Illness in the Urban Negro Community,* p. 259.

[55] In this paper differences are considered significant if the confidence level is less than .05.

erence group to be a measure of relative deprivation or frustration. The previous large-scale Parker-Kleiner study provided evidence that individuals with a relatively high level of psychiatric symptoms placed themselves below the position of their reference group. The average reference group discrepancy for mothers in intact families is .48, compared to .89 for mothers in broken homes. This difference is significant (by t test, p < .05). In terms of whatever criteria they consider to be important in comparing themselves to their close friends, mothers from broken homes experience greater relative deprivation than their counterparts in intact homes.

In summary, mothers in broken home situations are apparently more maladjusted and experience greater frustration than mothers in intact homes. Although all three measures considered up to this point support this generalization, only the reference group discrepancy differentiates significantly between these two samples. The authors conclude that the differences between the two groups of mothers are small but consistent.

Goal-Striving Stress of Mothers in the Two Types of Family Situations

In the area of educational aspirations for a hypothetical son, mothers in broken homes manifest a lower mean goal-striving stress score (20.65) than mothers in intact homes (60.76). The difference between these average stress scores is significant (by t test, p<.01). With respect to goal-striving stress associated with occupational aspirations for a hypothetical son, mothers from broken homes again manifest a significantly lower mean score than mothers in intact homes (32.24 and 49.48, respectively; by t test, p<.05).

The authors' other measure of goal-striving stress involves a mother's aspirations for herself on a generalized "striving scale." Each respondent placed herself on the ten-step, self-anchored scale described above as the means for determining reference group discrepancy. Each subject also selected the step representing the position she *would like* to attain in the future. The discrepancy between these two striving-scale positions was combined with the probability of success and the salience of the goal in order to derive the total striving-scale stress score.

Mothers in broken homes are characterized by a significantly lower mean goal-striving stress score with respect to their own generalized striving than mothers in intact family situations (13.91 and 15.71, respectively; by t test, p < .03). The data thus show that mothers in broken homes have lower goal-striving stress than mothers in intact homes, with respect to aspirations both for themselves and for a hypothetical son.

DISCUSSION

This paper has compared the psychological adjustment and goal-striving behavior of mothers of school-age children in broken and intact family situations. It was felt that such knowledge would enlarge understanding of the influence which the broken home situation brings to bear on the child. The female-headed family is particularly prevalent in the Negro population and has sometimes been regarded as an inhibitory influence on the later goal-striving behavior of Negro youths. The authors' data show that mothers in the broken home situation have poorer psychological adjustment and lower goal-striving for themselves and for their children than mothers in the intact family situation.

Studies in the research literature report that mothers in father-absent homes tend to be particularly protective and authoritarian in the training of their children. These data can be linked to indications in the authors' findings that mothers in father-absent homes manifest poorer psychological adjustment than mothers in intact homes. In this connection, it is interesting that the literature has also reported an association between both of the above socialization characteristics and low achievement needs in children. These factors, which are present in mothers in the broken home situation, suggest that, whatever other influences result from the absence of the male, the mother's psychological adjustment and achievement-related attitudes exert a depressing influence on the goal-striving behavior of her children. Thus, the female-headed household, so widespread in the Negro community, may have some serious consequences for children raised in these homes.

The data presented in this report indicate a need for more extensive research on how mothers in broken and intact family situations, at comparable status levels, differentially affect the goal-striving behavior of their children. The information provided by such studies would have considerable theoretical interest as well as importance for social policy considerations.

EXPLANATORY NOTES

The discrepancy between level of aspiration and achievement is considered to be the "stressor" factor in the goal-striving stress formulation. It seems logical that in the absence of a discrepancy between a mother's actual achievement and the level she would like to attain (for herself or for a hypothetical son) no stress will be experienced. The individual's estimate of the probability of success (selected from a ten-step scale ranging from "no chance" to "excellent chance") in a given goal-striving content area is assumed to reflect how open the opportunity structure appears to her. In order to obtain data on the subjective importance of the goal, each respondent selected a precoded response indicating the degree of disappointment she anticipated if she or a hypothetical son did not attain the specified aspirational levels.

Although the discrepancy concept taken alone indicates the distance from the individual's desired goal, it does not specify the level or strength of motivation invested in attaining that goal. In the comprehensive formulation of goal-striving stress or aspirational involvement, one must consider the interaction of the aspiration-achievement discrepancy (or stressor factor) with strength of motivation for an aspired goal. The strength of motivation for a goal, i.e., the "resultant weighted valence," is defined as the difference between the pressure to strive for a goal (the approach component, considered to have a positive value) and the pressure to avoid striving for that same goal (the avoidance component, considered to have a negative value). A positive difference between these components is taken to mean that the individual will work toward the goal. The actual magnitude of the difference represents the strength of the motivation to move toward or away from the goal, depending on the sign of the difference.

The approach component is defined as the interaction between the perceived probability of success and the importance of success to the individual, i.e., the salience of the goal. The avoidance component is defined as the interaction between the perceived probability of failure and the degree of disappointment anticipated upon failure, i.e., valence of failure.

The following formula, which incorporates the above concepts, was used to compute goal-striving stress:

$$\text{Stress} = (\text{LA-Ach})\ [(P_{\text{succ}}\ Va_{\text{succ}}) - (P_{\text{fai}}\ Va_{\text{fai}})]$$ where

LA = level of aspiration;
Ach = achieved level;
P_{succ} = probability of success;
Va_{succ} = valence of success;
P_{fai} = probability of failure;
Va_{fai} = valence of failure.

10

Effects of paternal absence on sex-typed behaviors in Negro and white preadolescent males

E. MAVIS HETHERINGTON

This study investigated the effects of father absence on the development of sex-role preferences, dependency, aggression, and recreational activities of Negro and white preadolescent boys. All children had mothers but no father substitutes present in the home and no contact with the fathers subsequent to separation.

In previous studies of the effects of father absence on the development of children, total and final absence of the father usually had not occurred. The father was either temporarily away due to war (Bach, 1946; Sears, Pintler, & Sears, 1946) or to occupational demands (Lynn & Sawrey, 1959; Tiller, 1958). An exception to this is the McCord, McCord, and Thurber (1962) study of boys from broken homes. These studies frequently indicated disruption of masculine identification in boys whose fathers were absent. Boys with fathers absent from the home tended to be less aggressive in doll-play situations (Sears et al., 1946), had father fantasies more similar to those of girls (Bach, 1946), and were more dependent (Stolz et al., 1954; Tiller, 1958) than boys whose fathers were living in the home. In contrast to these findings McCord et al. found no differences in dependency between boys from homes in which the father was absent and those in

which the father was present and found the former group was more aggressive. The Lynn and Sawrey study also indicated that boys deprived of regular contact with their fathers made stronger strivings toward masculine identification shown by preference for a father versus a mother doll in a Structured Doll Play Test, and manifested an unstable compensatory masculinity. They found no differences between boys whose fathers were absent and those whose fathers were present in ratings of dependency in the doll-play situation and attribute this to a "compensatory masculine reluctance to express dependency [p. 261]."

It might be expected that if boys with absent fathers in contrast to those with a father present manifest compensatory masculinity they would score high on behaviors associated with masculinity such as independence, aggression, masculine sex-role preferences, and participation in activities involving force and competition. Moss and Kagan (1961) suggested that for boys, participation and skill in sports is closely involved with maintenance of sex-role identification. However, if father absence results in a direct expression of a failure to establish masculine identification, boys without fathers would be rated low on the previous variables.

The age at which separation from the father occurs could differentially affect the form of disrupted identification in boys. Early separation may result in greater disruption of sex-typed behaviors than would later sepa-

Reprinted from *Journal of Personality and Social Psychology*, 1966, **4**, 87–91, by permission of the author and the American Psychological Association.

ration when identification is well under way or completed. Early separation might result directly in less masculine sex-role behaviors since identification with the father has never developed. In contrast later separation may have little effect on these behaviors or result in exaggerating masculine behavior in an attempt to sustain the already established masculine identification with the major role model, the father, absent.

It might also be expected that the effects of father absence would interact with the race of the family. It has frequently been suggested that the Negro family structure is basically matriarchal (Karon, 1958). Maternal dominance has been demonstrated to have a disruptive effect on sex typing in boys (Hetherington, 1965; Mussen & Distler, 1959). In such mother-dominated families, absence of the father might be expected to have a less disruptive effect on sex-typed behavior of boys than it would in a father-dominant family.

Kardiner and Ovesey (1951) suggest that Negroes have strong inhibited aggressive needs which are displaced and expressed in competitive sports. It would therefore be predicted that Negroes would be rated lower in overt social aggression than would white boys, but would show a marked preference for aggressive, competitive activities.

METHOD

Subjects were 32 Negroes and 32 white first-born boys between the ages of 9 and 12, who were attending a recreation center in a lower-class urban area. Sixteen of the boys in each group were from homes in which both parents were present, and 16 from homes in which the father was absent. In half of the father-absent homes for Negro and white families, separation had occurred at age 4 or earlier, and in half, after age 6. Father separation was caused by desertion, divorce, death, and illegitimacy. No father substitutes lived in the home. There were no significant differences in causes of father separation between groups, although illegitimacy was a cause only in the early groups.

Forty-nine of the subjects were only children, seven subjects had a younger male sibling, and eight subjects had a younger female sibling. These subjects were distributed approximately evenly across groups, although there was a slightly larger proportion of only children in the group of children whose fathers left early than in the groups whose fathers were present or had left the home after age 6.

Procedure

Two male recreation directors who had known the subjects for at least 6 months rated them on 7-point scales measuring dependence on adults, dependence on peers, independence, aggression, and on an activities test. The scales ranged from 1, very rarely and without persistence, to 7, very often and very persistently. Interrater reliabilities ranged from .85 to .94. All subjects were also individually administered the It Scale for Children (ITSC; Brown, 1956).

Measures

Scales for dependence and independence were based upon those used by Beller (1957). The aggression scale was based on that of Sears, Whiting, Nowlis, and Sears (1953). Behaviors involved in each scale were more fully elaborated as in Beller (1957), but used behaviors appropriate to the age group of the present study. A total rating for each of these three scales was obtained.

Rating Scale for Dependence on Adults was comprised of ratings of:

1. How often does the boy seek physical contact with adults?
2. How often does the boy seek to be near adults?
3. How often does the boy seek recognition (any form of praise and punishment) from adults?
4. How often does the boy seek attention from adults?

Rating Scale for Dependence on Peers was composed of the same items as dependence on adults oriented toward children.

Rating Scale for Independence involved the following four of Beller's autonomous achievement-striving scales:

1. How often does the boy derive satisfaction from his work?
2. How often does the boy take the initiative in carrying out his own activity?

3. How often does the boy attempt to overcome obstacles in the environment?

4. How often does the boy complete an activity?

Rating Scale for Aggression involved the following items:

1. How often does the boy act to necessitate correction, scolding, or reminding?

2. How often does the boy ask for special privileges?

3. How often does the boy attack other children or their property to show envy?

4. How often does the boy threaten adults?

5. How often does the boy threaten other children?

6. How often does the boy destroy the property of the Center or of other children?

7. How often does the boy derogate others?

8. How often does the boy quarrel with other children?

9. How often does the boy display undirected aggression?

10. How often does the boy attack other children physically?

11. How often does the child exhibit displaced aggressive attacks?

The Activities Test was comprised of ratings on a 7-point scale ranging from 1, very rarely participates in this activity, to 7, very often and persistently participates in the activity. Five activities in each of four categories were rated. In standardizing the Activities Test three recreation directors were asked to sort a group of 48 activities into the following four categories. Only those in which the three judges agreed were retained.

1. Physical skill involving contact—boxing, wrestling, football, basketball, battle ball.

2. Physical skill not involving contact—foot-racing, bowling, horseshoes, table tennis, darts.

3. Nonphysical competitive games—dominoes, checkers, scrabble, monopoly, cards.

4. Nonphysical, noncompetitive games—reading, watching television, building things, working on puzzles, collecting things.

Total ratings for each of the four types of activities were obtained.

The ITSC (Brown, 1956) is a test of sex-role preference which presents the child with an ambiguous figure (It) and asks the child to select from a group of toys and objects those that "It" prefers. A high score indicates masculine preference.

RESULTS

Separate two-way analyses of variance involving race and father status (early absent, late absent, and present) were calculated for each scale. When significant F ratios were obtained, t tests between means were calculated. Table 1 presents the means for all groups on all variables.

The analysis of variance of total dependence on adults yielded no significant differences; however, the analysis of dependence

TABLE 1 Means for Father Separation Early, Father Separation Late, and Father Present, Negro and White Boys

	Father Present		Early		Late	
	White	Negro	White	Negro	White	Negro
Dependency on adults	15.69	15.19	14.25	14.00	12.75	13.00
Dependency on peers	15.31	15.50	17.62	18.25	18.25	19.12
Independence	15.75	15.69	18.25	15.37	15.25	18.25
Aggression	39.87	47.06	32.00	30.75	51.00	52.12
ITSC	67.56	70.69	53.50	55.00	65.12	73.25
Physical contact	20.62	23.62	14.87	18.87	21.50	21.87
Physical noncontact	21.06	18.75	15.37	17.50	21.12	17.00
Nonphysical, competitive	21.44	20.81	16.87	18.62	20.12	17.62
Nonphysical, noncompetitive	17.69	16.62	24.25	22.37	21.37	19.12

on peers yielded a significant F ratio ($F =$ 10.18, $p < .005$) for father status. Subsequent t tests indicated that both early-separated and late-separated boys were significantly more dependent on peers than were the boys with fathers living in the home ($t = 2.23$, $p < .05$; $t = 2.90$, $p < .005$).

No significant differences were found between groups on total independence scores.

The analysis of total aggression scores indicated a significant effect of father status ($F = 10.39$, $p < .005$) on aggressive behavior. Both boys who were deprived of their fathers after age 6 and boys whose fathers are present manifested more aggression than boys who were deprived of their fathers at an early age ($t = 3.20$, $p < .005$; $t = 2.21$, $p < .05$, respectively).

The results of the ITSC also yielded a significant effect for father status ($F = 4.966$, $p < .025$). Boys experiencing late separation from the father and boys from unbroken homes have more masculine sex-role preferences than early-separated boys ($t = 2.32$, $p < .05$; $t = 3.14$, $p < .005$).

The Activities Test indicates that early-separated boys play fewer physical games involving contact than do either late-separated boys or boys with fathers living in the home ($t = 2.06$; $p < .05$; $t = 2.60$, $p < .025$). Negro boys tend to play more games of this type than do white boys ($t = 2.22$, $p = .05$). It should be noted that this is the only signifi-

cant racial difference found in the entire study. No significant effects were obtained in the analysis of physical activities involving no contact or in nonphysical competitive activities. However, a significant effect ($F = 8.236$, $p < .005$) for father status was found in nonphysical, noncompetitive activities. Early-separated boys spend more time in these activities than do boys living with both parents.

It seemed possible that the obtained differences between early- and late-separated boys were a result of the total time elapsed since the father left the home, rather than the developmental stage at which separation occurred. The early-separated children may have had more time for a loss of cathexsis on masculine behaviors. In order to investigate this possibility, an attempt was made to compare subjects in the early- and late-separation groups who had been deprived of their fathers for 6 years. The resulting Ns in each group were too small to permit an adequate analysis of the scores ($N = 4$ in early separated, $N = 3$ in late separated); however, the results appeared to parallel those of the total early- and late-separated groups.

The small sample size and predominance of only children did not permit a satisfactory analysis of the effects of family size and sex of sibling on the behavior studied.

Table 2 presents the intercorrelations among all variables studied for all subjects.

TABLE 2 Correlations among All Variables for All Subjects

	1	2	3	4	5	6	7	8	9
1. Dependence on adults	1.00	.02	−.25**	.06	.04	.04	.06	.11	−.06
2. Dependence on peers		1.00	−.10	.06	.04	−.02	.03	−.26	.10
3. Independence			1.00	.05	.02	−.01	.11	.17	−.17
4. Aggression				1.00	.21*	.40****	.22*	−.01	−.33***
5. ITSC					1.00	.38***	.02	.09	−.29***
6. Physical contact						1.00	.13	.03	−.59****
7. Physical noncontact							1.00	.17	−.16
8. Nonphysical, competition								1.00	−.23
9. Nonphysical, noncompetition									1.00

Note. Numbered variables in columns correspond to those in rows.
   * $p = .10$.
  ** $p = .05$.
 *** $p = .01$.
**** $p = .001$.

Dependence on adults but not on peers is negatively related to independence. Masculine sex-role preferences, aggressive behavior, and participation in physical activities cluster together. Conversely, it appears that boys who enjoy nonphysical, noncompetitive activities are low in masculine sex-role preferences, aggression, and in participation in activities involving physical contact or nonphysical competition.

DISCUSSION

The results of the study indicate that absence of the father after age 5 has little effect on the sex-typed behaviors of boys. These boys in most respects do not differ from boys who have their fathers present. They are similar in their independence, dependence on adults, aggression, and sex-role preferences. In preferences for activities involving physical force or competition which might permit socially accepted expression of compensatory masculinity we again find no differences. An increased dependence on the adult all-male staff of the recreation center might have been expected if the boys lacking fathers were seeking attention from other adult males as father substitutes. This did not occur. It appears that any frustrated dependency needs which loss of a father might have produced do not generalize to other adult males. In fact there was a trend for boys with no fathers to be less dependent on adults ($F = 2.56$, $p < .10$). The greater dependence on peers of boys who had lost their fathers early or late is difficult to explain. It may be that loss or lack of a father results in a mistrust of adults with a consequent compensatory increase in dependence on peers. This general pattern of relations was reported by Freud and Burlingham (1944) in their studies of children separated from their parents by World War II. These children showed strong ties to their peers but few emotional ties to adult caretakers in institutions.

Boys who lost their fathers early, before identification can be assumed to have been completed, showed considerable deviation in sex-typed traits. They are less aggressive and show more feminine sex-role preferences than the other boys. They also participate less in physical games involving contact and

more in nonphysical, noncompetitive activities. This preference for the latter type of activity could be considered an avoidance of activities involving the appropriate masculine behaviors of competition and aggressive play. An alternative explanation might be that it is a manifestation of social withdrawal since the activities in that category tend to be ones which involve a minimum of social interaction. It is difficult to accept this interpretation in view of the high dependency on peers ratings obtained by these boys. One could speculate that these boys make unsuccessful dependent overtures to peers, are rebuffed, and remain socially isolated.

The results suggest that adequate masculine identification has occurred by age 6 and that this identification can be maintained in the absence of the father. If the father leaves in the first 4 years before identification has been established, long-lasting disruption in sex-typed behaviors may result.

The predictions concerning racial differences were only partially confirmed. Differences between Negro and white boys in overt aggression which would be expected if Negroes inhibit direct expression of aggression were not obtained. However, the predicted high participation of Negroes in competitive activities involving contact was found. On the basis of this study it must be concluded that the behavior of Negro and white boys observed in the setting of a recreation center appears very similar.

REFERENCES

Bach, G. R. Father-fantasies and father typing in father-separated children. *Child Development*, 1946, **17**, 63–79.

Beller, E. K. Dependency and autonomous achievement-striving related to orality and anality in early childhood. *Child Development*, 1957, **29**, 287–315.

Brown, D. G. Sex-role preference in young children. *Psychological Monographs*, 1956, **70**(14, Whole No. 421).

Freud, A., & Burlingham, D. T. *Infants without families.* New York: International Universities Press, 1944.

Hetherington, E. M. A developmental study of the effects of sex of the dominant parent on sex-role preference, identification, and imitation in children. *Journal of Personality and Social Psychology*, 1965, **2**, 188–194.

Kardiner, A., & Ovesey, L. *The mark of oppression.* New York: Norton, 1951.

Karon, B. P. *The Negro personality.* New York: Springer, 1958.

Lynn, D. B., & Sawrey, W. L. The effects of father-absence on Norwegian boys and girls. *Journal of Abnormal and Social Psychology*, 1959, **59**, 258–262.

McCord, J., McCord, W., & Thurber, E. Some effects of paternal absence on male children. *Journal of Abnormal and Social Psychology*, 1962, **64**, 361–369.

Moss, H. A., & Kagan, J. Stability of achievement and recognition seeking behaviors from early childhood through adulthood. *Journal of Abnormal and Social Psychology*, 1961, **62**, 504–513.

Mussen, P., & Distler, L. Masculinity, identification, and father-son relationships. *Journal of Abnormal and Social Psychology*, 1959, **59**, 350–356.

Sears, R. R., Pintler, M. H., & Sears, P. S. Effects of father-separation on preschool children's doll play aggression. *Child Development*, 1946, **17**, 219–243.

Sears, R. R., Whiting, J. W. M., Nowlis, H., & Sears, P. S. Some childbearing antecedents of dependency and aggression in young children. *Genetic Psychology Monographs*, 1953, **47**, 135–234.

Stolz, L. M., et al. *Father relations of warborn children.* Stanford: Stanford University Press, 1954.

Tiller, P. O. Father-absence and personality development of children in sailor families: A preliminary research report. *Nordisk Psykologi*, 1958, Monogr. No. 9.

11

Child rearing practices among low income families in the District of Columbia

HYLAN LEWIS

The focus of the project is on the relationships between the conditions of life of low income families and parental inadequacy, child neglect, and dependency. While the central interest has been in child rearing practices and community settings among low income "problem" families, for comparative purposes, material has been obtained on low income families without "problems" and on "adequate" income families.

Excerpt reprinted from *Culture, Class and Poverty*, Washington, D.C.: Communicating Research on the Urban Poor (CROSS-TELL), 1967, pp. 2–12, by permission of the author.

Field workers have been trained to observe and to report on people in their natural settings. The purpose is to get material in depth, to see as well as listen. Participant-observation, as well as direct observation, is being used to get family and community data.

The number of field contacts with families ranges from one to 27. The average number of contacts with low-income families was more than nine; the average number of hours of contact for these families was twelve.

The field documents illustrate the wide variety in the concrete human styles of low income families. The fact that these documents were obtained indicates, among other things, an impressive willingness of these low income family heads to share their experiences over extended periods of time. One of the mothers volunteered that she was pleased to be "a part of a larger study"—of a project that is "doing something that might be of help to other families like mine, so that they might not have to go through all the things we have been through."

In general, our materials confirm the findings of other students that among low income families, unguided, unplanned influences outside of the family or household are relatively more important, and take effect in the socialization process relatively earlier, than among higher or adequate income families. Our analysis of the field materials . . . has resulted in a series of propositions about family and community influences on child rearing among low income families.

Among the propositions that we think have implications for policy and practice—and that we wish to share here—are some that have to do with (1) parental control, (2) the relationship between family values and actual behavior, and (3) the organization of life in low income neighborhoods.

PARENTAL CONTROL

In many study families, the effects of external influences are reflected in the strikingly early appearance of cut-off points in parental control and emotional support—in the falling off of parents' confidence in their ability—as well as in the will—to control and give attention to their children.

For practical purposes, the immediate point of interest is that changes in control, and in self-estimates of ability to control, occur when the children are as young as five and six. In these instances the factors associated with potential and actual child neglect or dependency are different from those in which neglect and inadequate care of infant and very young children are related to parental rejection. This latter type of situation is well understood, of course.

Here we are talking about the mothers who are not basically rejecting of, or hostile to, children. Characteristically, for such mothers the care and control of younger children is not perceived as a real problem: the mothers

show confidence, warmth and are able to exercise effective control. As children grow older there seems to be a cutting point at which parents express impotence and bafflement. Although there are anxieties, the fate of these children is often written off as out of the parent's hands. There recurs in the records a mixture of hope and resignation:

> *I do hope they don't get in trouble. I tried to raise them right.*
> *The Lord will have to look out for them. I'm glad mine are little. I kinda hate to see them grow up. At least I can do something for them now.*

Additional factors that seem to have something to do with the cutting points are the size of the family and expectations about the child's work role. These may be summarized as follows:

Mothers in low income, large family situations set training and discipline goals in keeping with needs or demands for assistance in the household and in the care of other children; these goals are unrealistic vis-a-vis growing children who are exposed progressively to extra-family influences. When mothers in such family situations fail to achieve their specific and immediate child rearing goals related to household functioning, they exhibit discouragement and bafflement. They describe their inability to cope with external factors which they say have stronger pulls on their children than maternal demands for good manners, respect, floor scrubbing, and supervision of the younger children. A staff member comments:

> There is current in much of the literature on child rearing a belief that mature status for the child is granted relatively early on the lower socio-economic levels. Much is made of the idea that middle and upper class children envy the "freedom" of their lower class contemporaries. Our field materials suggest that this apparent freedom of the children in lower income families is not necessarily "granted." Frequently, it appears to be wrested from begrudging parents or parental substitutes.

The fact that the loss of parental control occurs so early in many of these families—whether due to parental abdication or the revolt of children—should be juxtaposed to the fact that the adolescent period is the socially accepted or expected period for revolt.

VALUES AND BEHAVIOR

The field materials . . . indicate that the low income parents in this study group—whether they are adequate or inadequate, dependent or nondependent—tend to show greater conformity to, and convergence with, middle class family and child rearing standards in what they say they want (or would like to want) for their children and themselves than in their actual child rearing behavior. This was evident in much of the material examined in relation to factors affecting such matters as parental concerns and control, self-appraisal, education, and sex and illegitimacy.

That much of a basic strain toward conformity to standard values and practices among low income families is missed or ignored is probably due to tendencies to underestimate heterogeneity, variability, and change. Paradoxically enough, this is due in part to the effort to be scientific or to the uncritical adoption and application of selected findings or concepts. Prime examples are the use of the terms "culture" or "subculture" to describe behavior under contemporary urban conditions and of summary statistics alone to indicate social characteristics of an area. Although it may not be intended, concepts and statistics too frequently are interpreted as indicating a kind of homogeneity and a degree of regularity that are just not present.

For social welfare practice this kind of trying to say the most with the least about complex, multi-dimensional behavior is often premature and dangerous. Loose use of concepts and too great a dependency on statistics only tend to obscure—and what is worse for social welfare practice—to dehumanize.

In both categories of low income families —the dependent and the nondependent—parents who show a high degree of interest and parents who show a low degree of interest in children's health, education and welfare are found. But, despite deprivation and trouble, the persistence of positive concern and of the willingness to sacrifice for children are features of the child rearing behavior of a good proportion of the low income families observed.

As other studies have shown, the low income mothers of this study group have relatively high educational aspirations for their children, and, above all, they want better housing and neighborhoods. The persistent themes are—"getting a good education," "getting enough education," "getting a good job." A staff member points out, however, that what constitutes a good job, or sufficient education, is not always specified.

There is lack of knowledge or clarity as to *how* children are to obtain the goals projected; and there is very little indication that the parents know what to do themselves in order to motivate children. On the contrary, what seems to be an underlying theme is expressed in various ways in the idea that "you can lead a horse to water. . . ." There is communicated a combination of realism and pessimism, a kind of wise weariness that may appear to belie the very educational or career goals they express for at least some of their children.

Acute dissatisfactions cluster around housing, and the lack of proper places for children to play. Examples are:

The first step I'm striving for is better housing. I just want to get out of all this. The one thing I want, it's a backyard fenced in so my children don't play out in the street. I hope and pray some day to do better. But what can I do now?
I would like a comfortable home for them, if I could give them anything.
So we have the will, we're just waiting for the way. (With reference to moving out of the area.)

LEVELS OF CONCERN

In an analysis of child rearing among these low income families, we have distinguished three varieties of parents classified according to concern—(1) those with high concern who demonstrated it in their behavior; (2) those with considerable verbal concern but who exhibited inconsistent or contradictory behavior; and (3) those who expressed little or no concern and who are extremely neglectful.

The first type consists of parents whose high degree of parental concern is exhibited in *actions* related to the welfare of children, in contrast to verbalizations. Observation indicates that working with what they have, they show high "copability," self-reliance, and self-respect. The way in which they face problems—that is, react to outside impersonal forces—indicates good mental health in this sense of the term.

The second type of parents includes those who are inconsistent in their concern and exhibit a borderline degree of parental control. They tend to be highly self-centered and demanding. Characteristically, parents of this type are persons who themselves recall unsatisfactory or deprived childhoods. They are reported as having difficulty in accepting the child as an individual. They tend to be impatient and they apply discipline inconsistently.

Parents of the third classification are central adult figures in the classic picture of child neglect—children who suffer undernourishment, untreated physical ailments, exposure to violence, harsh treatment and arbitrary punishment. There is a tendency among the parents who show a very low degree of concern and few parental strengths to use their children as scapegoats. Dependent and lacking in self-reliance themselves, they seem to resent their children for being dependent on them. They are rated low in self-confidence and self-esteem.

The most inadequate and neglectful parents are the most reluctant to talk about the specifics of child rearing. However, even in the cases of the most neglectful parents, the evidence indicates that they ascribe no virtue to inadequacy or neglectful behavior in themselves or in others, or to neighborhood disorganization. If there is any suggestion of approval, or accentuation of the negative, it smacks of perverseness, defiance, bravado, or desperation of the I-don't-care type. The following field document illustrates this last:

> When a neighbor commented to a mother in a low-income project that one of the mother's four children appeared to have a bad cold, the mother, referring to herself, calmly said, *Her mother don't care!* At the neighbor's expression of surprise that she would say such a thing, the mother—bridling at the implied criticism—countered with, *Well, that's the way it is so I might as well tell the truth.*

In every category of low income families observed there are differences in hopes and expectations of changes for the better, and in the estimates of resources parents think they have—or can find to effect changes in themselves. In other words, there are cutting points also in the optimism and confidence of many parents about the futures of their families—and in the belief that their efforts alone might affect them. This cut-off point in parental optimism and confidence is something that emerges—it reflects one of the most insidious and eroding processes affecting child rearing. Confidence that is continuing—even though mixed or fluctuating, as much as anything distinguishes low income families that are not now marked by neglect or dependency from those that are "clinically" dependent or neglectful.

The "multi-problem" or "hard core" cases of inadequacy, dependency and neglect are, to use medical terminology, "clinical cases" with unknown or varying potential for rehabilitation. As in types of heart disease and cancer, when the condition becomes known or public, it is frequently too late; prognosis for these relatively few cases is poor. "Clinical" dependency—that which is known to public and private agencies and health and welfare institutions—is costly and provokes concern beyond the numbers involved. And, although it is necessary and important to seek improved ways of rehabilitation or containment, the long-range dividends are likely to be greater from research and demonstration programs that seek to identify and work with the highly vulnerable families, not yet publicly dependent or neglectful—to examine the "preclinical" and "subclinical" aspects of dependency and neglect.

UNWED MOTHERS

Any interpretation or programming based on the assumption that there is a distinctive population of unmarried mothers, or a cult, or a conspiracy among unwed mothers—or that unwed mothers would rather be unwed flies in the face of the facts. The propositions our materials support are:

> The belief that broad categories of people —such as lower income groups, newcomers, and certain ethnic minorities—are not troubled about illegitimacy, gets very little support.
> Birth in wedlock is an important value, but in any given instance, it might be preempted by another important value, or its realization thwarted by practical considerations.

For program purposes, the salient values and practices related to illegitimacy are those reflected in the affirming of family support for mother and child—"taking them in"—or having and keeping of the child in the face of possible community disapproval.

Pregnancy out of wedlock, particularly the first, is commonly referred to as a "mistake." Identifying with her pregnant daughter, Mrs. Billups, mother of ten children, differed with her husband who wanted to put his daughter out. The mother said:

I told him she ain't the first one who ever made a mistake and I was going to let her stay right here with me. I told Esther we would take care of her through this one, but no more babies before you're married. I did this because I had made a mistake and got pregnant and I could understand how anybody could make a mistake, at least once.

The idea of one's mistake being "human" or even a "right" is also heard. Not unmindful of the fact that she did not marry until her second pregnancy, Mrs. Potter said:

Everybody has a right to one mistake, but two out of wedlock children are no mistake —and three—the girl's just beyond herself!

The acceptance of the "first mistake" does not imply, however, that there is no emotional upheaval on the part of the parents. Mr. Billups was ready to put his daughter out, and his wife—despite her acceptance—said, *It made me feel awful bad about her. She was the pick of the family.*

A grandmother, learning in court that her granddaughter's "mistake" had occurred in their own living room, said: *I just knew I was going to die. I had tried so hard.*

A white mother who considered the possibility of her daughter's becoming pregnant decided:

I don't know. Maybe I almost would have lost my mind, but I would not turn her out. I just could not do it. I certainly would take care of the baby. I would not permit the baby to be put up for adoption.

A Negro mother of eight children concurred, saying:

I know it would hurt me an awful lot. But I wouldn't put her out. A real mother wouldn't do that. But it would really hurt me . . . I would not do that. But I wouldn't place the baby for adoption even though I have so many children.

The field materials indicate that there is a great deal of popular misunderstanding and some myth about the sex behavior and propensities of lower income families and individuals from these families. There is a striking incidence of parental shame and embarrassment about sex. (We seriously doubt that this last is in itself a class trait— that it is unique in this category of the population.) Sex education is found to be a family matter to a very limited degree. Vague warnings and prohibitions constitute the bulk of sex training.

Behavior and expressions of many mothers in relation to children's curiosity about sex were reminiscent of a Victorian attitude. Their evasions were reinforced by dismissal of talk about sex as "bad" and "nasty."

A mother in her early twenties who lives with her family in a low income housing project said:

We knew nothing about sex the whole time we were growing up. Sex was hush-hush. It was like the Dark Ages. It was sad. It really was.

A 42-year-old white mother of five children said:

No, we would never talk about such things to my mother. We had too much respect for her.

A 31-year-old mother in a low income housing project said:

All my mother said to me was "tell your sister" when I started menstruating and to this day that is all she said to me.

For the mothers in general, the onset of the menstrual cycle was the point at which the silence was broken by vague admonitions about keeping away from boys.

My mother told me about "ministrating." She never told me about sex, nothing about a man and she say—after I got up the nerve to ask her—"You fool around with a boy, you get a baby," and that was all.
My mother didn't talk to me when I was growing up. She would say, "If something happens to you, will you please let me know." I used to wonder what she was talking about. That's all she would say.

The woman above whose mother referred her to her sister for explanation was told by the sister to read aloud a passage on menstruation from a medical book. She drew the conclusion that conception could occur auto-matically and therefore was expecting to be-come pregnant momentarily.

A young woman who married at 18 said that she became pregnant three months later and, although she knew by then where the baby was, she was puzzled about how it was going to get out of her stomach.

The key problem, in previous generations as well as now, seemed to be one of embar-rassment in talking about sex. Even some of the mothers who said they want to bring their children up differently, mentioned difficulty in overcoming this embarrassment. One of the mothers, when pressed for an explanation of why she said that she often got her sister to talk to her children, said:

It was the way I was raised. I had a very strict mother and she never came out and talked to me about it and when they came to me, I just couldn't.

This embarrassment over discussing any aspect of sex appeared to be widespread. Mrs. Parsons with three out of wedlock chil-dren blushed when any aspect of sex was mentioned as she "doesn't believe in that nasty talk."

Despite embarrassment and ambivalence, what to do about the sex training of children and the recognized threat of illegitimacy was seen as an acute dilemma by a good propor-tion of the low income mothers. Two of the more poignant examples are the mother who brought home condoms from the drugstore to explain their use to her 12-year-old daughter, and another mother who requested a diaphram from the birth control clinic for her 14-year-old daughter.

An important commentary on the matter of sex and illegitimacy among low income groups was the avidity with which women in four mothers' groups entered into a discus-sion of problems in these areas. A staff report said about these meetings:

One got the impression of people anxious to share and exchange views and to learn. Tempers were riled, anxieties expressed and personal confidences shared in brisk and lively sessions. . . . What was of par-ticular importance was that so much in-terest was evidenced even though it was clearly understood that our prime interest was in learning what they had to say and not in telling them what to do. Their reac-tion suggests there is much more that can be done in this area on an educational level.

In spite of the fact that many homes do not have fathers or husbands, the lower in-come male and father is a key figure in gain-ing an understanding of child rearing in the lower income or dependent family. Of par-ticular importance is the man's ability to sup-port and stand for the family—to play the economic and social roles wished of him, particularly by wives, mothers, and children. Some of the implications of this are sug-gested in the field document that describes a mother of six children chiding her husband for being afraid and not showing aggressive-ness in looking for a second job to increase the family income. Showing his pay stub, she said: *This looks like a receipt for a woman's paycheck instead of a man's.*

CULTURE AND CLASS

It was pointed out earlier that many of the current assumptions and much of the current thinking about low income areas and the families that live in them are influenced by the concepts of class and culture. For ex-ample, one well-known student has conceptu-alized "lower class culture as a cultural system in its own right—with an integrity of its own; a characteristic set of practices, focal con-cerns, and ways that are meaningful and systematically related to one another, rather than to corresponding features of the middle class culture." (Walter B. Miller, "The Cul-ture of the Roxbury Community," a paper delivered at the National Conference on Social Welfare, Philadelphia, Pa., 1957.)

Our materials suggest that neither the quality of life in most low income neighbor-hoods nor the varying child rearing behaviors of low income families observed by our staff is to be interpreted as generated by, or guided by, "a cultural system in its own right—with an integrity of its own." The behaviors ob-served in these varying low income families do not present the kind of organization or cohesion suggested by these phrases. Rather they appear as a broad spectrum of prag-matic adjustments to external and internal stresses and deprivations. In any event, pro-gramming might best focus on the facts of deprivation and the varied responses rather than on presumably organized values that represent a preferred or chosen way of life.

In fact, many low income families appear

here as the frustrated victims of what are thought of as middle class values, behavior and aspirations. That this has its implications for child rearing is suggested in the separate comments of two mothers who blamed their parents for their childhood deprivations.

> *I don't think my parents should have sacrificed us to get a house.*
> *My father ought not to have sacrificed us for a car.*

An anthropologist [Richard Slobodin] who was a staff member during one summer studied a one-block enclave of low income families. His observations about the interaction and communication among these families have pertinence for assumptions about collective behavior and the bases of community organization:

> The scope and intensity of my observations were insufficient to justify generalizations about the social position of those whose conduct of life is conspicuously disorganized in terms of the standards of the larger society and of their own immediate needs. Such persons include the men who are unable to hold a job and support their families, and the perennial ADC mothers who exist in a kind of serial polyandry. I do not know to what extent and in what areas of activity such persons are accepted and rejected by their neighbors. Acceptance, especially for the women, is certainly greater than in the larger urban society, but some censure and a larger portion of pity is to be found in the attitudes and behavior of most respondents toward these "disorganized" persons.
> Is there a representative Upton Square resident? In a sense there is not, since individuality and idiosyncrasies of character flourish there as they do not, at present, in conformist middle-class society. It can be stated, however, that most Upton Square men and women work hard, or fairly hard, for little material reward, judged by general American standards, and that they lead circumscribed lives.
> What are the goods that they obtain, or wish to obtain from life? As stated earlier, I cannot venture to generalize about areas and modes of satisfaction or about the levels of aspiration, except to say that the former, although various, center to a considerable—to me even somewhat surprising—extent around the better life; and the latter are more in evidence than some sociological studies of the working class would lead one to expect. Upton Square parents certainly hope that their children will avoid "getting into trouble," but the aspirations of my respondents for their children were not limited to this negative hope as were those of the "hard core" proletarians reported in Walter Miller's Boston study. It must be said, however, that Upton Square parents appear to be as baffled by their adolescent children and neighbors as are their fellow-Americans in many other kinds of communities and status-levels.

. . . . .

The willingness of [CRS] families to cooperate appears to be related to an initial approach that stressed the contributions the families can make to . . . a project that they think will contribute something to the improving of child rearing—for themselves, if possible, for others certainly. Our experience shows this to be a value that transcends class lines . . . despite the fact that what some people themselves do about it, or are able to do about it, or even have the will to do about it, varies. As much as anything, the reasons we give for this variability have major consequences for social welfare practices and policy.

12

Exposure to child-rearing experts: A structural interpretation of class-color differences[1]

ZENA SMITH BLAU

The writings of experts bearing on diverse realms of behavior, transmitted by the mass media, constitute a major mechanism for the diffusion of new information and ideas in contemporary societies. As yet, however, we have achieved little systematic understanding of the social processes by which exposure to this source of innovation comes about, or about the related problem of the processes that lead to the adoption of the ideas advocated.

In a recent article reviewing the present status of research concerning the diffusion of innovation Katz, Levin, and Hamilton comment that "very few studies have been done on the basic problem of comparing the ways in which different kinds of structural arrangements within a group condition the diffusion of a given item."[2] They go on to

Reprinted from *The American Journal of Sociology*, 1964, **69**, 596–608, by permission of the author and the University of Chicago Press. Copyright 1964, the University of Chicago Press.

[1] This study was supported in part by National Institute of Mental Health, Public Health Service Research Grant 07316-01, and in part by a grant from the University of Illinois Graduate College Research Board. I also wish to acknowledge the assistance of Arlene Krieger and former Dean Emily C. Cardew, of the University of Illinois College of Nursing, and the advice of James A. Davis, Jacob J. Feldman, and Harold Levy, of the National Opinion Research Center during early phases of the research.

[2] Elihu Katz, Martin L. Levin, and Herbert

suggest some of the ways in which social structures may condition the diffusion process. Their idea that social structure implies, among other things, the existence of boundaries which differentiate "the frequency and character of social relations"[3] and thus constitute barriers to diffusion comes very close to the central problem with which the present paper deals—the analysis of selected structural attributes of class-color groups and how they facilitate or hinder the exposure of their members to the writings of a body of experts in the realm of child-rearing. More specifically, the substantive problem is to provide a structural interpretation of a pattern of differences between Negro and white middle- and working-class mothers in their exposure to the writings of child-rearing experts, in their attendance at child-care classes, and in their attitudes toward experts.

Child-rearing studies have repeatedly shown that the class position and educational level of mothers condition their exposure to diverse sources of formal and informal information and advice.[4] Although these find-

Hamilton, "Traditions of Research on the Diffusion of Innovation," *American Sociological Review*, XXVIII (April, 1963), 248.

[3] Katz, Levin, and Hamilton, "Traditions of Research on the Diffusion of Innovation, p. 247.

[4] See, e.g., Martha Sturm White, "Social Class, Child Rearing Practices, and Child Behavior," *American Sociological Review*, XXII (December, 1957), 704–12; Melvin L. Kohn, "Social

ings were based, for the most part, on samples of white women, there was every reason to believe that they would apply as well to Negro women of similar class position and educational level.

Indeed, color differences in the realm of child-rearing had largely ceased to be a matter of specific research interest after Davis and Havighurst reported, in a pioneering study published in 1946, that they found few differences in the child-rearing practices of Negro and white mothers who occupied similar class positions.[5] Although their study did not deal with the problem of exposure to experts' writings it seems to have been assumed by the researchers who followed them that the pattern of findings would extend to this kind of behavior as well. However, in the last decade several studies of class differences in the child-rearing patterns of white mothers have reported findings which contradict those of Davis and Havighurst.[6] Whatever the reason for these discrepancies, they suggest the need for taking a new look at the problem of class-color differences in child-rearing, and especially for bringing to bear on this question some of the new modes of sociological analysis that have been developed since the appearance of the early Chicago study.

The study of which the present paper is a part does not replicate the content of the Davis and Havighurst study, but it has a similar sample design.[7] A quota sample of 224 mothers, selected on the basis of race, class position,[8] and parity, was interviewed during the period of confinement on the maternity floors of three large, centrally located hospitals in Chicago during 1961–62. One section of the interview schedule contained a series of questions about the extent and nature of respondents' exposure to various mass media and to child-rearing content in these sources. Some of these data are presented in the analysis that follows.

EXPOSURE TO CHILD-REARING LITERATURE

An index of the extent of exposure to child-rearing literature was obtained by combining the scores assigned to answers to three questions: the frequency with which respondents read child-rearing articles (1) in their daily newspapers and (2) in magazines, and (3) whether they have read Dr. Benjamin Spock's book, *Baby and Child Care*.[9] "High"

[7] The original design called for fifty cases each of middle-class and working-class white and Negro mothers, one third having had only one child and the rest having had more than one. However, we could not locate as many Negro middle-class mothers as planned (although we remained in the field longer in an attempt to do so), and decided instead to obtain more interviews with women in the other three class-color categories in order to prevent undue shrinkage of the sample. Conclusions based on so small a sample, particularly of Negro middle-class mothers, are admittedly tentative and are presented merely as hypotheses which still need to be tested on a more adequate sample.

[8] The index of class position is based on husband's occupation. Respondents whose husbands are engaged in non-manual occupations are classified as middle class, and those whose husbands are in manual occupations are defined as working class.

[9] The individual questions were cross-tabulated and scored in the following way: a score of 1 each was given if a respondent regularly read child-rearing articles in a daily newspaper or in any magazine mentioned, and a score of 2 was given to those who had read Dr. Spock's book, on the assumption that the latter covers at least as wide a range of content and has at least as much impact as the other two sources taken together. Respondents were also asked about their exposure to the well-known pamphlet, *Infant*

Class and Parent-Child Relationships: An Interpretation," *American Journal of Sociology,* **LXVIII** (January, 1963), 471–80; and esp. Urie Bronfenbrenner, "Socialization and Social Class through Time and Space," in Eleanor E. Maccoby, Theodore M. Newcomb, and Eugene L. Hartley (eds.), *Readings in Social Psychology* (New York: Henry Holt & Co., 1958), pp. 400–425, which presents a review of many child-rearing studies and a provocative discussion of how reading the experts may promote changes in child-rearing.

[5] Allison Davis and Robert J. Havighurst, "Social Class and Color Differences in Child Rearing," *American Sociological Review,* **XI** (1946), 698–710.

[6] E.g., Robert R. Sears, Eleanor E. Maccoby, and Harry Levin, *Patterns of Child Rearing* (Evanston, Ill.: Row, Peterson & Co., 1957), and White, *op. cit.*; for an interpretation of these inconsistencies see Bronfenbrenner, "Socialization and Social Class through Time and Space.

exposure (a score of 3 or 4) signifies regular readership of child-rearing articles in at least one of the mass media, and of Spock's book. "Medium" exposure (a score of 1 or 2) indicates regular readership of such articles in at least one of the mass media, or only of Dr. Spock's book; and "low" exposure (a score of 0) indicates that a respondent has not read Spock and does not ordinarily read child-rearing articles.[10]

Table 1 shows that the extent of exposure to child-rearing literature is influenced by both the class position and color of mothers.

TABLE 1   Child-Rearing Media Exposure Scores in Four Class-Color Groups (Per Cent)

Exposure	*Middle Class*		*Working Class*	
	White	*Negro*	*White*	*Negro*
Low	13	32	38	56
Medium	39	47	30	38
High	48	21	32	6
Total per cent	100	100	100	100
No. of cases	(83)	(19)	(56)	(66)

White mothers expose themselves more to this kind of literature than Negro mothers, both in the middle and in the working class, and exposure is more prevalent in the middle class than in the working class, independent of skin color. In other words, the woman with no regular exposure to child-rearing literature is highly exceptional in the white middle class, considerably less so in the Negro middle class and white working class, but in a majority in the Negro working class.[11]

Care, published by the U.S. Children's Bureau, but so few had read it (33 respondents) that it was not included in the exposure index. Two open-ended questions concerning other sources read by respondents yielded even fewer returns.

[10] No value judgment that mothers ought to read child-rearing literature is implied here, nor are any a priori assumptions made about the impact of this literature on the child-rearing practices of mothers variously located in the social structure. The latter problem will be dealt with in a forthcoming paper.

[11] The Negro-white differences in exposure to child-rearing content are not due to differences in extent of exposure per se to newspapers and magazines. Analysis of scores on a mass-media exposure index, based on the frequency of news-

The difference between Negro and white mothers in *extent* of exposure to child-rearing content stems in part from the difference between them in the *kind* of media to which they expose themselves, specifically their use of Dr. Spock's book. Separate analysis of the proportions who have read this book shows that among white middle-class mothers the overwhelming majority (77 per cent) have read the book, but in the Negro middle class the proportion is strikingly smaller (32 per cent); indeed it is lower than in the white working class (48 per cent). The smallest proportion of Spock readers is found among Negro working-class mothers (12 per cent).[12]

It is well known, of course, that book readership is more widespread in the middle class than in the working class, particularly among the better educated. Higher education, in turn, is more widespread among whites than among Negroes in the middle class. For example, among middle-class respondents in our study only 8 per cent of the whites but 37 per cent of the Negroes have not completed high school, and 69 per cent and 21 per cent, respectively, have had some college education. In the working class, on the other hand, the level of education of white and Negro mothers is virtually identical. Fifty-five per cent in each color group have not

paper and magazine reading, indicates that the exposure of respondents varies primarily with class position and only slightly with color. Thus the proportions of respondents who read both a newspaper and a magazine regularly, or one regularly and the other occasionally, are 82 per cent among whites and 79 per cent among Negroes in the middle class and 59 per cent and 54 per cent, respectively, in the working class. Also of interest is our finding that none of the Negro respondents exposes herself *exclusively* to Negro publications. Only five respondents read the *Chicago Defender,* the local daily Negro newspaper (which, incidentally, does not carry a column on child care) and all these also read at least one of the four daily Chicago newspapers.

[12] Respondents were first asked whether they had ever heard of Dr. Spock's book. The proportions who had never heard of the book were only 5 per cent in the white middle class, but 37 per cent in both the Negro middle class and the white working class, and 65 per cent in the Negro working class. It is interesting that, although identical proportions of white working-class and Negro middle-class women knew about the book, fewer in the latter group had read it.

completed high school; and 9 per cent and 8 per cent, respectively, have had some college education. But the differences in exposure to Dr. Spock's book between Negroes and whites persist, for the most part, even when educational background of respondents is controlled. Table 2 shows that at each educa-

white mothers who have read Spock is as high in this group as among those with some college education, whereas among Negro mothers this proportion is considerably higher among the college-educated than among high-school graduates. In other words, readership of this source of child-rearing information varies

TABLE 2 Percentage Who Read Spock, by Class, Color, and Educational Level

Class and Color	Education*			Difference	
	Grades 8–11 (1)	High-School Graduate (2)	Attended College (3)	Col. (2) Minus Col. (1)	Col. (3) Minus Col. (2)
Middle class:					
White	57 (7)	68 (19)	82 (57)	11	14
Negro	0 (7)	37 (8)	†	37	
Difference	57	31			
Working class:					
White	39 (31)	60 (20)	60 (5)	21	0
Negro	8 (36)	12 (35)	40 (5)	4	28
Difference	31	48	20		

* *N*'s are given in parentheses.
† Three of the four Negro middle-class respondents who attended college have read Dr. Spock's book.

tional level in both classes the proportion of mothers who have read Spock is higher among whites than among Negroes, although in the middle class the size of the differences between the two color groups diminishes considerably as educational level rises. In the working class, the difference in readership between Negroes and whites is greatest among high-school graduates. It can also be seen that, while each of the three variables—class, color, and educational level—independently affects exposure to Spock's book, the magnitude of differences between Negro and white mothers in most cases is greater than between mothers of comparable educational background in the two classes, or between respondents at different educational levels within the same class. It is noteworthy that in the middle class the differences in the proportions of Negro and white mothers who have read Spock diminish considerably as educational level increases. But in the working class the largest difference between Negro and white mothers occurs among the high-school graduates, because the proportion of

more with education among Negro than among white mothers. But it is apparent that educational differences do not account for the large variance between the two color groups with respect to readership of Spock's book.[13]

ATTENDANCE AT MOTHERS' CLASSES

The pattern of differences between Negro and white mothers in exposure to child-rearing literature also extends to their attendance at mothers' classes, which many hospitals run for the benefit of maternity patients. Patients are ordinarily invited to attend classes during either their pregnancy or confinement, and in some cases at both times. The decision to attend or not is left up to the patient with the result, as a number of studies have shown, that middle-class women attend

[13] Similar differences occur between Negro and white respondents of like class position and educational background on the composite index of exposure (see Table 6).

these classes more frequently than working-class women.[14]

Respondents in the present study were asked: "Have you ever attended any classes or groups dealing with the care of infants either before or since you have had your baby?" Mothers who had not attended classes were asked: "Were you ever approached or invited to join such a group or class?" These questions were asked to ascertain whether differences in attendance might reflect class or color bias on the part of hospital personnel rather than self-selection on the part of respondents themselves.

Table 3 shows that higher proportions of white than of Negro mothers attended classes,

ations on their part of the importance of expert advice in the realm of child care and child-rearing. One might expect that the greater exposure of white mothers, particularly those in the middle class, to various sources of information reflects a belief on their part that they can thereby enhance the effectiveness of their behavior in the maternal role, while Negro women may expose themselves less to such sources because they are less inclined to share this opinion. The data, however, contradict this assumption.

Respondents were asked: "Some mothers feel it's important to find out what the experts (like doctors, psychologists, etc.) have to say about raising children while others

TABLE 3 Attendance at Mothers' Classes, by Class and Color (Per Cent)

Invited	Attended	Middle Class		Working Class	
		White	Negro	White	Negro
Yes	Yes	52	21	42	21
	No	13	63	18	38
No	No	35	16	38	36
No answer	No	0	0	2	5
Total per cent		100	100	100	100
No. of cases		83	19	56	66

regardless of class position, and that attendance varied little with class position. The differences between the two color groups evidently do not reflect discriminatory treatment of Negro maternity patients, since the proportion of those not invited to join classes is no higher among Negro than among white respondents.

don't think that is necessary. What do you think?" Responses were classified as generally favorable (e.g., "experts have more knowledge or experience"), unfavorable (e.g., "I don't believe in raising children by the book" or "mothers know best"), or ambivalent (e.g., "it does not hurt to get their ideas, but I'll use my own judgment"). Table 4 shows, con-

ATTITUDES TOWARD EXPERTS

The question arises whether the pattern of differences between Negro and white mothers in their exposure to formal sources of information may simply reflect different evalu-

[14] See, e.g., D. Mann, L. Woodward, and N. Joseph, *Educating Expectant Parents* (New York: Visiting Nurse Service, 1961), and A. Yankauer, W. Boek, E. Shaffer, and D. Clark, "What Mothers Say about Childbearing and Parent Classes," *Nursing Outlook*, **VIII** (October, 1960), 563–65.

TABLE 4 Attitude toward Experts, by Class and Color (Per Cent)

Attitude toward Child-Rearing Experts	Middle Class		Working Class	
	White	Negro	White	Negro
Favorable	45	63	52	62
Ambivalent	23	16	12	5
Unfavorable	31	21	32	27
NA	1	0	4	6
Total per cent	100	100	100	100
No. of cases	83	19	56	66

trary to expectation, that favorable attitudes toward child-rearing experts are expressed more frequently by Negro mothers in both the middle and the working class. Negative sentiments, on the other hand, occur slightly more often among whites. Ambivalent attitudes are more frequent among middle-class women, both white and Negro, than among those in the working class.

That Negro women express favorable attitudes toward child-rearing experts more often than white women, regardless of class position, but typically expose themselves less to such informational sources seems contradictory and might even be dismissed as simply another instance of the known tendency of respondents in low-prestige groups to express agreement more readily, regardless of item content, in the interview situation.[15] But some recent evidence of a similar order suggests another explanation, which turns out to be more fruitful for understanding the dynamic interplay of attitudes and behavior toward experts among mothers in different social contexts.

In a recent National Opinion Research Center study of public attitudes toward medical care, Feldman found that people who have more contact with physicians are also more critical of them than those with less contact.[16] More recently, in a study of attitudes toward fluoridation in a Massachusetts community, Gamson and Schuman reported that respondents who accord physicians high-prestige rankings in comparison with other professions also express hostile sentiments toward them more frequently than those who give them lower rankings.[17] One explanation for this ambivalence suggested by the authors is that "the very standards that lead to high prestige may cause physicians to be judged against criteria that are exceedingly difficult to meet. The stronger a respondent feels about

the importance of such standards the more he is likely to accord prestige to physicians as against other occupations but to judge physicians severely by these same standards." [18]

By the same token, white mothers may be more prone than Negro mothers to express ambivalence toward child-rearing experts precisely because they depend more on them for guidance, as indicated by the fact that they expose themselves more to the writings of experts. Indeed, a comparison of mothers' attitudes toward experts according to mothers' exposure scores in each of the four class-color groups lends support to this interpretation (see Table 5). It shows that in each class-color group, the proportion who express ambivalence toward experts is greater among respondents who have high- or medium-exposure scores than among those with low-exposure scores. The original differences noted in Table 4 between Negro and white mothers virtually disappear in the middle class, and become smaller in the working class, among respondents who expose themselves to experts' writings.

Among those with low exposure to this literature, on the contrary, the differences in ambivalence and particularly in negativism between white and Negro women become *more* pronounced. Unfavorable sentiments are voiced more often by mothers who do not read the experts in three of the four groups—all except the middle-class Negroes. But among mothers with low exposure negative attitudes are expressed considerably more often by whites, particularly in the middle class, than by Negroes. This suggests that the woman who does not "read the experts" but is located in a social milieu where this practice is prevalent feels called upon to justify her deviance by denigrating experts. Thus, in the white middle class where the pattern of reading child-rearing literature is most prevalent, women with low-exposure scores are most often negative toward experts.[19] In the white working class where this pattern is less widespread women with low exposure scores exhibit negative attitudes cor-

---

[15] See, e.g., Gerhard E. Lenski and John C. Leggett, "Caste, Class, and Deference in the Research Interview," *American Journal of Sociology,* **LXV** (March, 1960), 463–67.

[16] Jacob J. Feldman, "What Americans Think about Their Medical Care," American Statistical Association, Proceedings of the Social Statistics Section Meeting (December, 1958).

[17] William A. Gamson and Howard Schuman, "Some Undercurrents in the Prestige of Physicians," *American Journal of Sociology,* **LXVIII** (January, 1963), 463–70.

[18] Gamson and Schuman, "Some Undercurrents in the Prestige of Physicians," p. 469.

[19] The proportion of mothers in the Negro middle class who express negative sentiments is lower than in the white middle class, as expected. But contrary to expectation, it is also lower than in the other strata.

TABLE 5　Per Cent Ambivalent and Per Cent Unfavorable toward Experts, by Exposure Score, Class, and Color

Exposure	Middle Class		Working Class	
	White	Negro	White	Negro
Per cent of total with medium and high scores	87	68	63	44
	Per Cent Ambivalent			
Low	18　(11)	0　(6)	10　(21)	0　(37)
Medium and high	24　(72)	23　(13)	14　(35)	10　(29)
	Per Cent Unfavorable			
Low	55　(11)	17　(6)	43　(21)	33　(37)
Medium and high	28　(72)	23　(13)	26　(35)	21　(29)

respondingly less often. Exposure to experts' writings is least prevalent among Negro mothers in the working class. Consequently, Negro women who do not read this literature do not feel constrained to rationalize their indifference to expert opinion by denying its value. This difference in social context may well explain why Negro women with lower exposure scores express hostility toward experts considerably less often than their white counterparts.

CLASS MOBILITY AND COLOR DIFFERENCES

The pattern of high exposure to the writings of child-rearing experts is more prevalent among white middle-class mothers than among Negro middle-class mothers with a similar amount of formal education (see Table 6).[20] In fact, even white working-class women who have not completed high school have high-exposure scores nearly as often as women with more education in the Negro middle class. Differences in the constitution of the middle classes and the working classes in the two color groups, and their implications for acculturation to middle-class modes of

[20] The sample contains four cases of Negro middle-class mothers who have had some college education. Only one of them has a high-exposure score compared to 58 per cent among *white* middle-class respondents who have attended college.

behavior, may help to explain the differences noted above.

Reliance on experts' writings is part of a larger complex of orientations and modes of behavior that differentiate the child-rearing patterns of middle-class mothers from those in the working class in white society.[21] We would therefore expect to find this pattern more prevalent among women of middle-class origin than among those of working-class origin who have moved into the middle class.[22] Table 7 shows that high exposure

[21] That this practice is in fact more prevalent in the white middle than working class has been shown by a number of studies besides this one. See, e.g., White, "Social Class, Child Rearing Practices, and Child Behavior," and Kohn, "Social Class and Parent-Child Relationships." The latter study also contains a suggestive interpretation of these observed patterns of differences as reflections of differences in the value systems that prevail among the two strata.

[22] Class origin is defined by father's occupation when the respondent was sixteen years old. Respondents are classified as stationary members of the middle class if their fathers and husbands are in non-manual occupations, and as upwardly mobile members if their father did manual work but their husband does non-manual work. In the working class, downwardly mobile respondents are those whose fathers did non-manual work but whose husbands are manual workers, and stationary respondents are those whose fathers and husbands are manual workers. There is some variation in the age composition of these groups. Thus, the proportion over twenty-five years old in the white middle class

TABLE 6 Percentage Distribution of Exposure Scores, by Class, Education, and Color

Education and Color	Exposure			Total N
	High	Medium	Low	
	Middle Class			
Grades 8–11:				
White	29	29	42	7
Negro	0	43	57	7
High-school graduate or higher:				
White	50	40	10	76
Negro	33	50	17	12
	Working Class			
Grades 8–11:				
White	29	19	52	31
Negro	6	30	64	36
High-school graduate or higher:				
White	36	44	20	25
Negro	6	47	47	30

is in fact considerably more frequent among the stationary members of the white middle class (59 per cent) than among the upwardly mobile (32 per cent). Her newly won middle-class status does not automatically lead a woman to emulate the less visible forms of behavior that prevail among her established class peers. The acculturation process in this realm of behavior, as in others, requires opportunities for association with established members of the middle class in the course of which social pressure can be exerted upon the new members to adopt middle-class ways. Since the stationary members constitute the majority in the white middle class, such social opportunities would seem to be readily available to the upwardly mobile woman. And the fact that the tenure of the stationary members in the middle class has been of longer duration and that they are apt to be

is 58 per cent among stationary respondents and 45 per cent among the upward mobiles; in the white working class this proportion is 30 per cent among stationary respondents and 27 per cent among downward mobiles; and among Negroes it is 24 per cent among the upward mobiles and 44 per cent among stationary working-class respondents. However, the pattern of differences in exposure shown in Table 7 persists even when age is controlled (except that there are too few cases of older upwardly mobile Negroes to make meaningful comparisons).

better educated further enhances their ability to influence the incoming members of their group. Thus, the pattern of reliance on experts could be expected to spread by degrees among the upwardly mobile as they acquire longer tenure in their new position, resulting in closer conformity to the behavior of their stationary peers.

A comparison of the exposure scores of upwardly mobile white women with those of similar origin who have remained in the working class constitutes a crude test of this hypothesis. Although there is little difference in high exposure, the proportion with some exposure (high or medium) is considerably greater among the upwardly mobile (89 per cent) than among stationary members of the working class (55 per cent), which indicates that the former have assimilated the middle-class pattern to some degree—although not to the full extent, since *high* exposure is less widespread among them than among the stationary members of the middle class. Thus, the data lend support to our hypothesis concerning the acculturation effects that accompany upward mobility into the white middle class.

The constitution of the Negro middle class differs sharply from that of the white middle class, and therein may lie the explanation, at least to some degree, of the differences in the extent to which their members expose them-

TABLE 7　Percentage Distribution of Exposure Scores, by Class, Color, and Mobility

Class Position and Origin	Per Cent	Exposure				Total N*
		High	Medium	Low	Total	
White						
Middle class:						
Stationary	65	59	28	13	100	53
Upward mobile	35	32	57	11	100	28
Working class:						
Stationary	79	29	26	45	100	42
Downward mobile	21	36	55	9	100	11
Negro						
Middle class:						
Stationary	10		†		†	2
Upward mobile	90	24	41	35	100	17
Working class:						
Stationary	98	7	38	55	100	60
Downward mobile	2		†		†	1

* The class origin of ten respondents could not be ascertained, and these cases are excluded from the analysis.

† Among the Negro respondents are only two cases of stationary middle-class members and one case of a downwardly mobile member. All three of these respondents have medium exposure.

selves to child-rearing literature. Owing to the long history of pervasive economic and social discrimination against Negroes in our society the size of the established Negro middle class has traditionally been much smaller than its white counterpart, both in absolute and in relative terms. Since World War II, however, employment opportunities for Negroes in non-manual occupations have increased with a corresponding increase in the numbers who have recently moved from the working class into the middle class.[23] Indeed, in our sample fully 90 per cent of the middle-class Negro women come from working-class backgrounds, in contrast to 35 per cent in the white middle class. Owing to their insignificant number,[24] the stationary members of the Negro middle class are not in a position to exert any appreciable effect on the behavior of the upwardly mobile members of their class. And since the barriers of segregation allow for little, if any, informal association between members of the two color groups the upwardly mobile Negro woman is also cut off from the influence exerted by stationary members of the white middle class.

As a result, the acculturation of Negro upwardly mobile women to the modes of behavior that prevail in the middle class is likely to proceed at a slower pace than in the case of upwardly mobile whites, and this is exemplified by the differences between them in the extent of their exposure to the writings of child-rearing experts (see Table 7). In contrast to only one-tenth of the upwardly mobile whites, over one-third of the upwardly mobile Negroes have low exposure to this kind of literature.[25]

[23] This is not meant to imply, of course, that the size of the Negro middle class approaches that of the white middle class, even relative to the total Negro population, but only that the proportion of the Negro middle class with working-class origins is larger than the corresponding proportion in the white middle class. The analysis assumes that this is true for the Chicago population at large as well as for our sample, which is admittedly small and not representative.

[24] The tiny number of stationary middle-class Negroes (2) and of downwardly mobile working-class Negroes (1) in our sample makes impos-

sible some comparisons corresponding to those in the white group and results in some unavoidable gaps in the analysis.

[25] When age is controlled this difference becomes even more pronounced among younger women (under twenty-six): only 27 per cent of the upwardly mobile whites compared to 77 per cent of the upwardly mobile Negroes have low-exposure scores.

Analysis of the composition of the white working class also helps explain why even in this stratum exposure to experts' writings is more widespread than in the Negro middle class, despite the fact that the latter contains a larger proportion of better educated women. Although the large majority (79 per cent) of the white working-class respondents are stationary members of their stratum, the rest (21 per cent) were reared in the middle class and subsequently moved down into the working class. A comparison of the exposure scores of the downwardly mobile and stationary members of the white working class (see Table 7) shows that a higher proportion (91 per cent) of the former have high or medium scores than of the latter (55 per cent). And it is the presence of this down-wardly mobile contingent that largely accounts for the greater prevalence of high exposure in the white working class than in the Negro middle-class. For in the latter group the proportion with low-exposure scores (35 per cent) is less than among the stationary members of the white working class (45 per cent). But downwardly mobile white working-class mothers expose themselves considerably more to experts' writings than upwardly mobile Negro middle-class women, an indication that former social ties with her middle-class family and friends are maintained to some extent by the downwardly mobile woman who thereby remains subject to middle-class influences to a greater degree than the upwardly mobile Negro middle-class woman. But the data also suggest that the impact of middle-class influence on down-wardly mobile women has waned, since only 36 per cent of them have high exposure to child-rearing literature in contrast to 59 per cent of their former class peers, those who have retained their middle-class status.

However, although the downwardly mobile white mother shows evidence of being nega-tively influenced by her association with her new class peers, she may also act, to some degree, as a carrier of middle-class patterns of behavior to the stationary members of the working class with whom she develops social ties. For the stationary members of the white working class expose themselves more to child-rearing literature than stationary mem-bers of the Negro working class, despite the fact that the educational level of the mem-bers of the two strata is similar. But in the Negro working class in our sample there are virtually no downwardly mobile respondents (2 per cent) and consequently here the chances of exposure to middle-class social influences are most limited.

SUMMARY AND CONCLUSIONS

Exposure to informational sources in the realm of child-rearing was shown to be more widespread among white than among Negro mothers, regardless of class position. This pattern of Negro-white differences persists even when respondents' educational level is taken into account. But Negro women tend to express favorable sentiments toward child-rearing experts more often than white women, despite the fact that they expose themselves less to their writings. Simultaneous analysis of these two variables revealed that in all four class-color groups women with high or medium exposure were more prone to express ambivalence toward experts than those with little or no exposure. But an interesting pat-tern of differences was observed in the in-cidence of negative attitudes between the two color groups: among women with low ex-posure, whites were more often negative to-ward experts than Negroes, but no such differences were noted among women with higher exposure. This suggests that the preva-lence of a pattern of behavior in a group conditions the relationship between behavior and attitudes among its individual members. Where reading child-rearing literature is a widespread practice, as it is among white mothers, the very prevalence of this pattern within the group operates as a pressure to-ward conformity upon the individual. In *this* social context, *not* to read the experts consti-tutes a deviant act, and women who do not conform to the pattern of exposure feel con-strained to justify their deviance by denigrat-ing experts. But in a group where this practice is rare, as is the case among Negro mothers, the woman who does not read the experts is under no social or psychological pressure to provide rationalizations for her abstinence.

Analysis of the differences in the propor-tions of stationary and upwardly mobile members in the two middle classes helps to explain why the pattern of reading child-rearing literature is less widespread among Negro women, even the better educated

Negroes, than among whites. The existence of a stationary majority in the white stratum creates numerous opportunities for upwardly mobile women to become exposed to middle-class modes of behavior such as "reading the experts." And association with these better educated, more prestigeful members in their stratum constitutes the source of social pressure through which new members become acculturated to these middle-class ways. In contrast, the Negro middle class contains an overwhelming majority of upwardly mobile members. Thus the new member has fewer opportunities than her white counterpart for exposure to, and assimilation of, middle-class modes of behavior within her own color group, and the barriers of segregation forestall her exposure to these influences through association with the stationary members of the white middle class. Indeed, even white working-class mothers may have a better chance of exposure to middle-class influences through their association with the downwardly mobile members of their stratum. But the Negro working-class mother is removed from even this source of influence, since there are virtually no downwardly mobile women in her stratum.

That economic discrimination and social segregation are major impediments to the acculturation of the Negro masses to urban middle-class culture is well known. Our analysis helps to specify *how* these practices operate to delay this process even among middle-class, better educated Negroes. Cogni-

zant as we all are of the existence of a dual stratification system, we tend to think of the Negro and white class systems as similar though separate. Our findings suggest that there may be a number of structural differences between them that differentiate not only the rate with which middle-class norms diffuse among their members but also the amount of strain that accompanies the acculturation process. These differences in social structure mediate the effects that upward mobility and higher education exert on the attitudes and behavior of their individual members, not only in the realm of child-rearing, but probably in other realms of behavior as well. In other words, although the existence of a dual stratification system constitutes a grave social liability to a society that espouses democratic values, it constitutes an opportunity, while it persists, for the social scientist to make systematic comparisons between two class systems within a common cultural framework and thereby to gain a better understanding of how specific structural variables, present to a different degree in the two class systems, condition the diffusion of various kinds of norms, practices, and innovations among the members similarly situated within them. By the same token, it would undoubtedly prove fruitful to study the impact of desegregation on these processes by comparing their effects on Negroes who have gained opportunities for informal association with their white counterparts and on those similarly located in their class system for whom such opportunities still do not exist.

13

*Early experience and the socialization of cognitive modes in children**

ROBERT D. HESS AND VIRGINIA C. SHIPMAN

THE PROBLEM

One of the questions arising from the contemporary concern with the education of culturally disadvantaged children is how we should conceptualize the effects of such deprivation upon the cognitive faculties of the child. The outcome is well known: children from deprived backgrounds score well below middle-class children on standard individual and group measures of intelligence (a gap that increases with age); they come to school without the skills necessary for coping with first grade curricula; their language development, both written and spoken, is relatively poor; auditory and visual discrimination skills are not well developed; in scholastic achievement they are retarded an average of 2 years by grade 6 and almost 3 years by grade 8; they are more likely to drop out of school before completing a secondary education; and even when they have adequate ability are less likely to go to college (Deutsch, 1963;

Reprinted from *Child Development,* 1965, **36,** 869–886, by permission of the authors and the Society for Research in Child Development, Inc.

* This research is supported by the Research Division of the Children's Bureau, Social Security Administration; Department of Health, Education, and Welfare; Ford Foundation for the Advancement of Learning; and grants-in-aid from the Social Science Research Committee of the Division of Social Sciences, University of Chicago. Project staff members who made specific contributions to the analysis of data are Jere Brophy, Dina Feitelson, Roberta Meyer, and Ellis Olim.

Deutsch & Brown, 1964; Eells, Davis, Havighurst, Herriels, & Tyler, 1951; John, 1963; Kennedy, Van de Riet, & White, 1963; Lesser, 1964).

For many years the central theoretical issues in this field dealt with the origin of these effects, argued in terms of the relative contribution of genetic as compared with environmental factors. Current interest in the effects of cultural deprivation ignores this classic debate; the more basic problem is to understand how cultural experience is translated into cognitive behavior and academic achievement (Bernstein, 1961; Hess, 1964).

The focus of concern is no longer upon the question of whether social and cultural disadvantage depress academic ability, but has shifted to a study of the mechanisms of exchange that mediate between the individual and his environment. The thrust of research and theory is toward conceptualizing social class as a discrete array of experiences and patterns of experience that can be examined in relation to the effects they have upon the emerging cognitive equipment of the young child. In short, the question this paper presents is this: what *is* cultural deprivation, and how does it act to shape and depress the resources of the human mind?

The arguments we wish to present here are these: first, that the behavior which leads to social, educational, and economic poverty is socialized in early childhood—that is, it is learned; second, that the central quality involved in the effects of cultural deprivation is a lack of cognitive meaning in the mother-child communication system; and, third, that

125

the growth of cognitive processes is fostered in family control systems which offer and permit a wide range of alternatives of action and thought and that such growth is constricted by systems of control which offer predetermined solutions and few alternatives for consideration and choice.

In this paper we will argue that the structure of the social system and the structure of the family shape communication and language and that language shapes thought and cognitive styles of problem-solving. In the deprived-family context this means that the nature of the control system which relates parent to child restricts the number and kind of alternatives for action and thought that are opened to the child; such constriction precludes a tendency for the child to reflect, to consider and choose among alternatives for speech and action. It develops modes for dealing with stimuli and with problems which are impulsive rather than reflective, which deal with the immediate rather than the future, and which are disconnected rather than sequential.

This position draws from the work of Basil Bernstein (1961) of the University of London. In his view, language structures and conditions what the child learns and how he learns, setting limits within which future learning may take place. He identifies two forms of communication codes or styles of verbal behavior: *restricted* and *elaborated*. Restricted codes are stereotyped, limited, and condensed, lacking in specificity and the exactness needed for precise conceptualization and differentiation. Sentences are short, simple, often unfinished; there is little use of subordinate clauses for elaborating the content of the sentence; it is a language of implicit meaning, easily understood and commonly shared. It is the language form often used in impersonal situations when the intent is to promote solidarity or reduce tension. Restricted codes are nonspecific clichés, statements, or observations about events made in general terms that will be readily understood. The basic quality of this mode is to limit the range and detail of concept and information involved.

Elaborated codes, however, are those in which communication is individualized and the message is specific to a particular situation, topic, and person. It is more particular, more differentiated, and more precise. It permits expression of a wider and more complex range of thought, tending toward discrimination among cognitive and affective content.

The effects of early experience with these codes are not only upon the communication modes and cognitive structure—they also establish potential patterns of relation with the external world. It is one of the dynamic features of Bernstein's work that he views language as social behavior. As such, language is used by participants of a social network to elaborate and express social and other interpersonal relations and, in turn, is shaped and determined by these relations.

The interlacing of social interaction and language is illustrated by the distinction between two types of family control. One is oriented toward control by *status* appeal or ascribed role norms. The second is oriented toward *persons*. Families differ in the degree to which they utilize each of these types of regulatory appeal. In status- (position-) oriented families, behavior tends to be regulated in terms of role expectations. There is little opportunity for the unique characteristics of the child to influence the decision-making process or the interaction between parent and child. In these families, the internal or personal states of the children are not influential as a basis for decision. Norms of behavior are stressed with such imperatives as, "You must do this because I say so," or "Girls don't act like that," or other statements which rely on the status of the participants or a behavior norm for justification (Bernstein, 1964).

In the family, as in other social structures, control is exercised in part through status appeals. The feature that distinguishes among families is the extent to which the status-based control manoeuvers are modified by orientation toward persons. In a person-oriented appeal system, the unique characteristics of the child modify status demands and are taken into account in interaction. The decisions of this type of family are individualized and less frequently related to status or role ascriptions. Behavior is justified in terms of feelings, preference, personal and unique reactions, and subjective states. This philosophy not only permits but demands an elaborated linguistic code and a wide range of linguistic and behavioral alternatives in interpersonal interaction. Status-oriented families may be regulated by less individuated commands, messages, and responses. Indeed, by its nature, the status-oriented family will rely more heavily on a restricted code. The verbal exchange is inherent in the structure —regulates it and is regulated by it.

These distinctions may be clarified by two examples of mother-child communication using these two types of codes. Assume that the emotional climate of two homes is approximately the same; the significant difference between them is in style of communication employed. A child is playing noisily in the kitchen with an assortment of pots and pans when the telephone rings. In one home the mother says, "Be quiet," or "Shut up," or issues any one of several other short, preemptory commands. In the other home the mother says, "Would you keep quiet a minute? I want to talk on the phone." The question our study poses is this: what inner response is elicited in the child, what is the effect upon his developing cognitive network of concepts and meaning in each of these two situations? In one instance the child is asked for a simple mental response. He is asked to attend to an uncomplicated message and to make a conditioned response (to comply); he is not called upon to reflect or to make mental discriminations. In the other example the child is required to follow two or three ideas. He is asked to relate his behavior to a time dimension; he must think of his behavior in relation to its effect upon another person. He must perform a more complicated task to follow the communication of his mother in that his relationship to her is mediated in part through concepts and shared ideas; his mind is stimulated or exercised (in an elementary fashion) by a more elaborate and complex verbal communication initiated by the mother. As objects of these two divergent communication styles, repeated in various ways, in similar situations and circumstances during the preschool years, these two imaginary children would be expected to develop significantly different verbal facility and cognitive equipment by the time they enter the public-school system.

A person-oriented family allows the child to achieve the behavior rules (role requirements) by presenting them in a specific context for the child and by emphasizing the consequences of alternative actions. Status-oriented families present the rules in an assigned manner, where compliance is the *only* rule-following possibility. In these situations the role of power in the interaction is more obvious, and, indeed, coercion and defiance are likely interactional possibilities. From another perspective, status-oriented families use a more rigid learning and teaching model in which compliance, rather than rationale, is stressed.

A central dimension through which we look at maternal behavior is to inquire what responses are elicited and permitted by styles of communication and interaction. There are two axes of the child's behavior in which we have a particular interest. One of these is represented by an *assertive, initiatory* approach to learning, as contrasted with a *passive, compliant* mode of engagement; the other deals with the tendency to reach solutions impulsively or hastily as distinguished from a tendency to *reflect*, to compare alternatives, and to choose among available options.

These styles of cognitive behavior are related, in our hypotheses, to the dimensions of maternal linguistic codes and types of family control systems. A status-oriented statement, for example, tends to offer a set of regulations and rules for conduct and interaction that is based on arbitrary decisions rather than upon logical consequences which result from selection of one or another alternative. Elaborated and person-oriented statements lend themselves more easily to styles of cognitive approach that involve reflection and reflective comparison. Status-oriented statements tend to be restrictive of thought. Take our simple example of the two children and the telephone. The verbal categoric command to "Be quiet" cuts off thought and offers little opportunity to relate the information conveyed in the command to the context in which it occurred. The more elaborated message, "Would you be quiet a minute? I want to talk on the phone" gives the child a rationale for relating his behavior to a wider set of considerations. In effect, he has been given a *why* for his mother's request and, by this example, possibly becomes more likely to *ask* why in another situation. It may be through this type of verbal interaction that the child learns to look for action sequences in his own and others' behavior. Perhaps through these more intent-oriented statements the child comes to see the world as others see it and learns to take the role of others in viewing himself and his actions. The child comes to see the world as a set of possibilities from which he can make a personal selection. He learns to role play with an element of personal flexibility, not by role-conforming rigidity.

RESEARCH PLAN

For our project a research group of 163 Negro mothers and their 4-year-old children was selected from four different social status levels: Group A came from college-educated professional, executive, and managerial occupational levels; Group B came from skilled blue-collar occupational levels, with not more than high-school education; Group C came from unskilled or semiskilled occupational levels, with predominantly elementary-school education; Group D from unskilled or semi-skilled occupational levels, with fathers absent and families supported by public assistance.

These mothers were interviewed twice in their homes and brought to the university for testing and for an interaction session between mother and child in which the mother was taught three simple tasks by the staff member

(Brophy, Hess, & Shipman, 1965; Jackson, Hess, & Shipman, 1965; Meyer, Shipman, & Hess, 1964; Olim, Hess, & Shipman, 1965; Shipman & Hess, 1965).

RESULTS

The data in this paper are organized to show social-status differences among the four groups in the dimensions of behavior described above to indicate something of the maternal teaching styles that are emerging and to offer examples of relations between maternal and child behavior that are congruent with the general lines of argument we have laid out.

Social-Status Differences

VERBAL CODES: RESTRICTED VERSUS ELABORATED

One of the most striking and obvious differences between the environments provided by the mothers of the research group was in their patterns of language use. In our testing sessions, the most obvious social-class variations were in the total amount of verbal output in response to questions and tasks asking for verbal response. For example, as Table 1

TABLE 1   Mean Number of Typed Lines in Three Data-Gathering Situations

	Upper Middle N = 40	Upper Lower N = 40	Lower Lower N = 36	ADC N = 36
School situations	34.68	22.80	18.86	18.64
Mastery situations	28.45	18.70	15.94	17.75
CAT card	18.72	9.62	12.39	12.24
Total	81.85	51.12	47.19	48.63

and then asked to teach these tasks to the child.

One of these tasks was to sort or group a number of plastic toys by color and by function; a second task was to sort eight blocks by two characteristics simultaneously; the third task required the mother and child to work together to copy five designs on a toy called an Etch-a-Sketch. A description of various aspects of the project and some preliminary results have been presented in several papers

shows, mothers from the middle-class gave protocols that were consistently longer in language productivity than did mothers from the other three groups.

Taking three different types of questions that called for free response on the part of the mothers and counting the number of lines of typescript of the protocols, the tally for middle-class mothers was approximately 82 contrasted with an average of roughly 49 for mothers from the three other groups.

These differences in verbal products indicate the extent to which the maternal environments of children in different social-class groups tend to be mediated by verbal cue and thus offer (or fail to offer) opportunities for labeling, for identifying objects and feelings and adult models who can demonstrate the usefulness of language as a tool for dealing with interpersonal interaction and for ordering stimuli in the environment.

In addition to this gross disparity in verbal output there were differences in the quality of language used by mothers in the various status groups. One approach to the analysis of language used by these mothers was an examination of their responses to the following task: They were shown the Lion Card of the Children's Apperception Test and asked to tell their child a story relating to the card. This card is a picture of a lion sitting on a chair holding a pipe in his hand. Beside him is a cane. In the corner is a mouse peering out of a hole. The lion appears to be deep in thought. These protocols were the source of language samples which were summarized in nine scales (Table 2), two of which we wish to describe here.

The first scale dealt with the mother's tendency to use abstract words. The index derived was a proportion of abstract noun and verb types to total number of noun and verb types. Words were defined as abstract when the name of the object is thought of apart from the cases in which it is actually realized. For example, in the sentence, "The lion is an *animal*," "animal" is an abstract word. However, in the sentence, "This animal in the picture is sitting on his throne," "animal" is not an abstract noun.

In our research group, middle-class mothers achieved an abstraction score of 5.6; the score for skilled work levels was 4.9; the score for the unskilled group was 3.7; for recipients of Aid to Dependent Children (ADC), 1.8.

The second scale dealt with the mother's tendency to use complex syntactic structures such as coordinate and subordinate clauses, unusual infinitive phrases (e.g., "To drive well, you must be alert"), infinitive clauses (e.g., "What to do next was the lion's problem"), and participial phrases (e.g., "Continuing the story, the lion . . ."). The index of structural elaboration derived was a proportion of these complex syntactic structures, weighted in accordance with their complexity and with the degree to which they are strung together to form still more complicated structures (e.g., clauses within clauses), to the total number of sentences.

In the research group, mothers from the

TABLE 2 Social Status Differences in Language Usage (Scores are the means for each group)

	Social Status			
Scale	*Upper Middle* $N = 40$	*Upper Lower* $N = 42$	*Lower Lower* $N = 40$	*ADC* $N = 41$
Mean sentence length[a]	11.39	8.74	9.66	8.23
Adjective range[b]	31.99	28.32	28.37	30.49
Adverb range[c]	11.14	9.40	8.70	8.20
Verb elaboration[d]	.59	.52	.47	.44
Complex verb preference[e]	63.25	59.12	50.85	51.73
Syntactic structure elaboration[f]	8.89	6.90	8.07	6.46
Stimulus utilization	5.82	4.81	4.87	5.36
Introduced content	3.75	2.62	2.45	2.34
Abstraction[g]	5.60	4.89	3.71	1.75

[a] Average number of words per sentence.
[b] Proportion of uncommon adjective types to total nouns, expressed as a percentage.
[c] Proportion of uncommon adverb types to total verbs, adjectives, and adverbs, expressed as a percentage.
[d] Average number of complex verb types per sentence.
[e] Proportion of complex verb types to all verb types, simple and complex.
[f] Average number of weighted complex syntactic structures per 100 words.
[g] Proportion of abstract nouns and verbs (excluding repetitions) to total nouns and verbs (excluding repetitions), expressed as a percentage.

middle class had a structure elaboration index of 8.89; the score for ADC mothers was 6.46. The use of complex grammatical forms and elaboration of these forms into complex clauses and sentences provides a highly elaborated code with which to manipulate the environment symbolically. This type of code encourages the child to recognize the possibilities and subtleties inherent in language not only for communication but also for carrying on high-level cognitive procedures.

CONTROL SYSTEMS: PERSON VERSUS
STATUS ORIENTATION

Our data on the mothers' use of status- as contrasted with person-oriented statements comes from maternal responses to questions inquiring what the mother would do in order to deal with several different hypothetical situations at school in which the child had broken the rules of the school, had failed to achieve, or had been wronged by a teacher or classmate. The results of this tally are shown in Table 3.

ing them for new experiences. The data on this point come from answers to the question: "Suppose your child were starting to school tomorrow for the first time. What would you tell him? How would you prepare him for school?"

One mother, who was person-oriented and used elaborated verbal codes, replied as follows:

"First of all, I would remind her that she was going to school to learn, that her teacher would take my place, and that she would be expected to follow instructions. Also that her time was to be spent mostly in the classroom with other children, and that any questions or any problems that she might have she could consult with her teacher for assistance."

"Anything else?"

"No, anything else would probably be confusing for her at her particular age."

In terms of promoting educability, what did this mother do in her response? First, she was informative; she presented the school situation as comparable to one already fa-

TABLE 3   Person-Oriented and Status-Oriented Units on School Situation Protocols (Mothers)

		A. Mean Number			
Social Class	*Person-Oriented*		*Status-Oriented*		*P/S Ratio*	*N*
Upper middle	9.52	(1–19)	7.50	(0–19)	1.27	40
Upper lower	6.20	(0–20)	7.32	(2–17)	0.85	40
Lower lower	4.66	(0–15)	7.34	(2–17)	0.63	35
ADC	3.59	(0–16)	8.15	(3–29)	0.44	34

	B. Mean Per Cent		
Social Class	*Person-Oriented*	*Status-Oriented*	*N*
Upper middle	36.92	27.78	40
Upper lower	31.65	36.92	40
Lower lower	26.43	40.69	35
ADC	20.85	51.09	34

As is clear from these means, the greatest differences between status groups is in the tendency to utilize person-oriented statements. These differences are even greater if seen as a ratio of person-to-status type responses.

The orientation of the mothers to these different types of control is seen not only in prohibitive or reparative situations but in their instructions to their children in preparing them for new experiences.

miliar to the child; second, she offered reassurance and support to help the child deal with anxiety; third, she described the school situation as one that involves a personal relationship between the child and the teacher; and, fourth, she presented the classroom situation as one in which the child was to learn.

A second mother responded as follows to this question:

"Well, John, it's time to go to school now. You must know how to behave. The first day at school you should be a good boy and should do just what the teacher tells you to do."

In contrast to the first mother, what did this mother do? First, she defined the role of the child as passive and compliant; second, the central issues she presented were those dealing with authority and the institution, rather than with learning; third, the relationship and roles she portrayed were sketched in terms of status and role expectations rather than in personal terms; and, fourth, her message was general, restricted, and vague, lacking information about how to deal with the problems of school except by passive compliance.

A more detailed analysis of the mothers' responses to this question grouped their statements as *imperative* or *instructive* (Table 4).

STATUS DIFFERENCES IN CONCEPT UTILIZATION

One of the measures of cognitive style used with both mothers and children in the research group was the *S*'s mode of classificatory behavior. For the adult version, (Kagan, Moss & Sigel, 1963) *S* is required to make 12 consecutive sorts of MAPS figures placed in a prearranged random order on a large cardboard. After each sort she was asked to give her reason for putting certain figures together. This task was intended to reveal her typical or preferred manner of grouping stimuli and the level of abstraction that she uses in perceiving and ordering objects in the environment. Responses fell into four categories: descriptive part-whole, descriptive global, relational-contextual, and categorical-inferential. A descriptive response is a direct reference to physical attributes present in the stimuli, such as size, shape, or posture. Examples: "They're all children,"

TABLE 4 Information Mothers Would Give to Child on His First Day at School

Social Status	Imperative	Instructive	Support	Preparation	Other	N
			% of Total Statements			
Upper middle	14.9	8.7	30.2	8.6	37.6	39
Upper lower	48.2	4.6	13.8	3.8	29.6	41
Lower lower	44.4	1.7	13.1	1.2	39.6	36
ADC	46.6	3.2	17.1	1.3	31.8	37
			% of Mothers Using Category			
Upper middle	48.7	38.5	76.9	33.3	87.2	
Upper lower	85.4	17.1	39.0	19.5	70.7	
Lower lower	75.0	5.6	36.1	8.3	77.8	
ADC	86.5	16.2	43.2	8.1	86.5	

An imperative statement was defined as an unqualified injunction or command, such as, "Mind the teacher and do what she tells you to do," or "The first thing you have to do is be on time," or "Be nice and do not fight." An instructive statement offers information or commands which carry a rationale or justification for the rule to be observed. Examples: "If you are tardy or if you stay away from school, your marks will go down"; or "I would tell him about the importance of minding the teacher. The teacher needs his full cooperation. She will have so many children that she won't be able to pamper any youngster."

or "They are all lying down," or "They are all men." The subject may also choose to use only a part of the figure—"They both have hats on." In a relational-contextual response, any one stimulus gets its meaning from a relation with other stimuli. Examples: "Doctor and nurse," or "Wife is cooking dinner for her husband," or "This guy looks like he shot this other guy." In categorical-inferential responses, sorts are based on nonobservable characteristics of the stimulus for which each stimulus is an independent representative of the total class. Examples: "All of these people work for a living" or "These are all handicapped people."

TABLE 5   Mean Responses to Adult Sigel Sorting Task (Maps)

	Social Status			
Category	Upper Middle N = 40	Upper Lower N = 42	Lower Lower N = 39	ADC N = 41
Total descriptive	3.18	2.19	2.18	2.59
Descriptive part-whole	1.65	1.33	1.31	1.49
Descriptive global	1.52	0.86	0.87	1.10
Relational-contextual	5.52	6.79	7.38	6.73
Categorical-inferential	3.30	3.00	2.23	2.66

As may be seen in Table 5, relational responses were most frequently offered; categorical-inferential were next most common, and descriptive most infrequent. The distribution of responses of our status groups showed that the middle-class group was higher on descriptive and categorical; low-status groups were higher on relational. The greater use of relational categories by the working-class mothers is especially significant. Response times for relational sorts are usually shorter, indicating less reflection and evaluating of alternative hypotheses. Such responses also indicate relatively low attention to external stimuli details (Kagan, 1964). Relational responses are often subjective, reflecting a tendency to relate objects to personal concerns in contrast with the descriptive and categorical responses which tend to be objective and detached, more general, and more abstract. Categorical responses, in particular, represent thought processes that are more orderly and complex in organizing stimuli, suggesting more efficient strategies of information processing.

The most striking finding from the data obtained from the children's Sigel Sorting Task was the decreasing use of the cognitive style dimensions and increasing nonverbal responses with decrease in social-status level. As may be seen in the tables showing children's performance on the Sigel Sorting Task (Tables 6 and 7), although most upper middle-class children and a majority of the upper lower-class children use relational and descriptive global responses, there is no extensive use of any of the other cognitive style dimensions by the two lower lower-class groups. In looking at particular categories one may note the relative absence of descriptive part-whole responses for other than the middle-class group and the large rise in nonverbal responses below the middle-class level. These results would seem to reflect the relatively undeveloped verbal and conceptual ability of children from homes with restricted range of verbal and conceptual content.

Relational and descriptive global responses have been considered the most immature and would be hypothesized to occur most frequently in preschool children. Relational responses are often subjective, using idiosyncratic and irrelevant cues; descriptive global responses, often referring to sex and occupa-

TABLE 6   Children's Responses to Sigel Sorting Task (Means)

	Social Status			
Category	Upper Middle N = 40	Upper Lower N = 42	Lower Lower N = 39	ADC N = 41
Descriptive part-whole	2.25	0.71	0.20	0.34
Descriptive global	2.80	2.29	1.51	0.98
Relational-contextual	3.18	2.31	1.18	1.02
Categorical-inferential	2.02	1.36	1.18	0.61
Nonscorable verbal responses	5.75	6.31	6.64	7.24
Nonverbal	3.00	6.41	7.08	8.76
No sort	1.00	0.62	2.21	1.05

TABLE 7 Percentage of Four-Year-Old Children Responding in Each of the Categories

| | Social Status | | | |
| | Upper Middle $N = 40$ | Upper Lower $N = 42$ | Lower Lower $N = 39$ | ADC $N = 41$ |
Category				
Descriptive part-whole	40.0	28.6	18.0	14.6
Descriptive global	70.0	54.8	53.8	31.7
Total descriptive	80.0	66.7	59.0	39.0
Relational-contextual	77.5	66.7	41.0	43.9
Categorical-inferential	52.5	45.2	30.8	24.4
Nonscorable verbal	85.0	88.1	92.3	85.4
Nonverbal	52.5	66.7	82.0	87.8
No sort	12.5	7.1	25.6	19.5

tional roles, are somewhat more dependent upon experience. On the other hand, descriptive part-whole responses have been shown to increase with age and would be expected to be used less frequently. However, these descriptive part-whole responses, which are correlated with favorable prognostic signs for educability (such as attentiveness, control and learning ability), were almost totally absent from all but the upper middle-class group. Kagan (1964) has described two fundamental cognitive dispositions involved in producing such analytic concepts: the tendency to reflect over alternative solutions that are simultaneously available and the tendency to analyze a visual stimulus into component parts. Both behaviors require a delayed discrimination response. One may describe the impairment noted for culturally disadvantaged children as arising from differences in opportunities for developing these reflective attitudes.

The mothers' use of relational responses was significantly correlated with their children's use of nonscorable and nonverbal responses on the Sigel task and with poor performance on the 8-Block and Etch-a-Sketch tasks. The mothers' inability or disinclination to take an abstract attitude on the Sigel task was correlated with ineffectual teaching on the 8-Block task and inability to plan and control the Etch-a-Sketch situation. Since relational responses have been found (Kagan, Moss, & Sigel, 1963) to be correlated with impulsivity, tendencies for nonverbal rather than verbal teaching, mother-domination, and limited sequencing and discrimination might be expected and would be predicted to result in limited categorizing ability and impaired verbal skills in the child.

Analysis of Maternal Teaching Styles

These differences among the status groups and among mothers within the groups appear in slightly different form in the teaching sessions in which the mothers and children engaged. There were large differences among the status groups in the ability of the mothers to teach and the children to learn. This is illustrated by the performance scores on the sorting tasks.

Let us describe the interaction between the mother and child in one of the structured teaching situations. The wide range of individual differences in linguistic and interactional styles of these mothers may be illustrated by excerpts from recordings. The task of the mother is to teach the child how to group or sort a small number of toys.

The first mother outlines the task for the child, gives sufficient help and explanation to permit the child to proceed on her own. She says:

"All right, Susan, this board is the place where we put the little toys; first of all you're supposed to learn how to place them according to color. Can you do that? The things that are all the same color you put in one section; in the second section you put another group of colors, and in the third section you put the last group of colors. Can you do that? Or would you like to see me do it first?"

Child: "I want to do it."

This mother has given explicit information about the task and what is expected of the child; she has offered support and help of various kinds; and she has made it clear that she impelled the child to perform.

A second mother's style offers less clarity

and precision. She says in introducing the same task:

"Now, I'll take them all off the board; now you put them all back on the board. What are these?"

Child: "A truck."

"All right, just put them right here; put the other one right here; all right put the other one there."

This mother must rely more on nonverbal communication in her commands; she does not define the task for the child; the child is not provided with ideas or information that she can grasp in attempting to solve the problem; neither is she told what to expect or what the task is, even in general terms.

A third mother is even less explicit. She introduces the task as follows:

"I've got some chairs and cars, do you want to play the game?" Child does not respond. Mother continues: "O.K. What's this?"

Child: "A wagon?"

Mother: "Hm?"

Child: "A wagon?"

Mother: "This is not a wagon. What's this?"

The conversation continues with this sort of exchange for several pages. Here again, the child is not provided with the essential information he needs to solve or to understand the problem. There is clearly some impelling on the part of the mother for the child to perform, but the child has not been told what he is to do. There were marked social-class differences in the ability of the children to learn from their mothers in the teaching sessions.

Each teaching session was concluded with an assessment by a staff member of the extent to which the child had learned the concepts taught by the mother. His achievement was scored in two ways: first, the ability to correctly place or sort the objects and, second, the ability to verbalize the principle on which the sorting or grouping was made.

Children from middle-class homes were well above children from working-class homes in performance on these sorting tasks, particularly in offering verbal explanations as to the basis for making the sort (Tables 8 and 9). Over 60 per cent of middle-class children placed the objects correctly on all tasks; the performance of working-class children ranged as low as 29 per cent correct. Approximately 40 per cent of these middle-class children

who were successful were able to verbalize the sorting principle; working-class children were less able to explain the sorting principle, ranging downward from the middle-class level to one task on which no child was able to verbalize correctly the basis of his sorting behavior. These differences clearly paralleled the relative abilities and teaching skills of the mothers from differing social-status groups.

TABLE 8 Differences among Status Groups in Children's Performance in Teaching Situations (Toy Sort Task)

Social Status	Placed Correctly (%)	Verbalized Correctly (%)		N
A. Identity sort (cars, spoons, chairs):				
Upper middle	61.5	28.2	45.8[a]	39
Upper lower	65.0	20.0	30.8	40
Lower lower	68.4	29.0	42.3	38
ADC	66.7	30.8	46.2	39
B. Color sort (red, green, yellow):				
Upper middle	69.2	28.2	40.7[a]	39
Upper lower	67.5	15.0	22.2	40
Lower lower	57.9	13.2	22.7	38
ADC	33.3	5.1	15.4	39

[a] Per cent of those who placed object correctly.

The difference among the four status levels was apparent not only on these sorting and verbal skills but also in the mother's ability to regulate her own behavior and her child's in performing tasks which require planning or care rather than verbal or conceptual skill. These differences were revealed by the mother-child performance on the Etch-a-Sketch task. An Etch-a-Sketch toy is a small, flat box with a screen on which lines can be drawn by a device within the box. The marker is controlled by two knobs: one for horizontal movement, one for vertical. The mother is assigned one knob, the child the other. The mother is shown several designs which are to be reproduced. Together they attempt to copy the design models. The mother decides when their product is a satisfactory copy of the original. The products are scored by measuring deviations from the original designs.

TABLE 9 Differences among Status Groups in Children's Performance in Teaching Situations (8-Block Task)

Social Status	Placed Correctly (%)	One-Dimension Verbalized (%)		Both Verbalized (%)		N
A. Short O:						
Upper middle	75.0	57.5	57.5[a]	25.0	33.3[a]	40
Upper lower	51.2	39.0	43.2	2.4	4.8	41
Lower lower	50.0	29.0	33.3	15.8	31.6	38
ADC	43.6	20.5	22.2	2.6	5.9	39
B. Tall X:						
Upper middle	60.0	62.5	64.1[a]	27.5	45.8[a]	40
Upper lower	48.8	39.0	42.1	17.1	35.0	41
Lower lower	34.2	23.7	26.5	7.9	23.1	38
ADC	28.2	18.0	20.0	0.0	0.0	39

[a] Per cent of those who placed object correctly.

These sessions were recorded, and the non-verbal interaction was described by an observer. Some of the most relevant results were these: middle-class mothers and children performed better on the task (14.6 points) than mother and children from the other groups (9.2; 8.3; 9.5; [Table 10]). Mothers of the three lower-status groups were relatively persistent, rejecting more complete figures than the middle-class mothers; mothers from the middle class praised the child's efforts more than did other mothers but gave just as much criticism; the child's cooperation as rated by the observer was as good or better in low-status groups as in middle-class pairs (Table 11), there was little difference

TABLE 10 Performance on Etch-a-Sketch Task (Means)

	Social Status			
	Upper Middle N = 40	Upper Lower N = 42	Lower Lower N = 40	ADC N = 41
Total score (range 0–40)	14.6	9.2	8.3	9.5
Average number of attempts	12.7	17.2	12.2	15.1
Complete figures rejected	2.3	3.6	3.5	3.4
Child's total score	5.9	4.0	3.4	4.0
Child's contribution to total score (per cent)	40.4	43.5	41.0	42.1

TABLE 11[a] Mother-Child Interaction on Etch-a-Sketch Task (Means)

	Social Status			
	Upper Middle N = 40	Upper Lower N = 41	Lower Lower N = 39	ADC N = 39
Praises child	4.6	6.9	7.2	7.5
Criticizes child	6.4	5.5	6.4	5.9
Overall acceptance of child	2.2	3.2	3.4	3.6
Child's cooperation	5.6	5.3	4.5	5.1
Level of affection shown to child	4.8	5.4	5.2	5.8

[a] Ratings made by observer; low number indicates more of the quality rated.

between the groups in affect expressed to the child by the mother (Brophy et al., 1965).

In these data, as in other not presented here, the mothers of the four status groups differed relatively little, on the average, in the affective elements of their interaction with their children. The gross differences appeared in the verbal and cognitive environments that they presented.

Against this background I would like to return for a moment to the problem of the meaning, or, perhaps more correctly, the lack of meaning in cultural deprivation. One of the features of the behavior of the working-class mothers and children is a tendency to act without taking sufficient time for reflection and planning. In a sense one might call this impulsive behavior—not by acting out unconscious or forbidden impulses, but in a type of activity in which a particular act seems not to be related to the act that preceded it or to its consequences. In this sense it lacks meaning; it is not sufficiently related to the context in which it occurs, to the motivations of the participants, or to the goals of the task. This behavior may be verbal or motor; it shows itself in several ways. On the Etch-a-Sketch task, for example, the mother may silently watch a child make an error and then punish him. Another mother will anticipate the error, will warn the child that he is about to reach a decision point; she will prepare him by verbal and nonverbal cues to be careful, to look ahead, and to avoid the mistake. He is encouraged to reflect, to anticipate the consequences of his action, and in this way to avoid error. A problem-solving approach requires reflection and the ability to weigh decisions, to choose among alternatives. The effect of restricted speech and of status orientation is to foreclose the need for reflective weighing of alternatives and consequences; the use of an elaborated code, with its orientation to persons and to consequences (including future), tends to produce cognitive styles more easily adapted to problem-solving and reflection.

The objective of our study is to discover how teaching styles of the mothers induce and shape learning styles and information-processing strategies in the children. The picture that is beginning to emerge is that the meaning of deprivation is a deprivation of meaning—a cognitive environment in which behavior is controlled by status rules rather than by attention to the individual characteristics of a specific situation and one in which behavior is not mediated by verbal cues or by teaching that relates events to one another and the present to the future. This environment produces a child who relates to authority rather than to rationale, who, although often compliant, is not reflective in his behavior, and for whom the consequences of an act are largely considered in terms of immediate punishment or reward rather than future effects and long-range goals.

When the data are more complete, a more detailed analysis of the findings will enable us to examine the effect of maternal cognitive environments in terms of individual mother-child transactions, rather than in the gross categories of social class. This analysis will not only help us to understand how social-class environment is mediated through the interaction between mother and child but will give more precise information about the effects of individual maternal environments on the cognitive growth of the young child.

REFERENCES

Bernstein, B. Social class and linguistic development: a theory of social learning. In A. H. Halsey, Jean Floud, & C. A. Anderson (Eds.), *Education, economy, and society.* Glencoe, Ill.: Free Pr., 1961.

Bernstein, B. Family role systems, communication, and socialization. Paper presented at Conf. on Develpm. of Cross-National Res. on the Education of Children and Adolescents, Univer. of Chicago, February, 1964.

Brophy, J., Hess, R. D., & Shipman, Virginia. Effects of social class and level of aspiration on performance in a structured mother-child interaction. Paper presented at Biennial Meeting of Soc. Res. Child Develpm., Minneapolis, Minn., March, 1965.

Deutsch, M. The disadvantaged child and the learning process. In A. H. Passow (Ed.), *Education in depressed areas.* New York: Columbia Univer. T.C., 1963. Pp. 163–180.

Deutsch, M., & Brown, B. Social influences in Negro-white intelligence differences. *J. Soc. Issues,* 1964, **20** (2), 24–35.

Eells, K., Davis, Allison, Havighurst, R. J., Herrick, V. E., & Tyler, R. W. *Intelligence and cultural differences*. Chicago: Univer. of Chicago Pr., 1951.

Hess, R. D. Educability and rehabilitation: the future of the welfare class. *Marr. fam. Lvg*, 1964, **26,** 422–429.

Jackson, J. D., Hess, R. D., & Shipman, Virginia. Communication styles in teachers: an experiment. Paper presented at Amer. Educ. and Res. Ass., Chicago, February, 1965.

John, Vera. The intellectual development of slum children: some preliminary findings. *Amer. J. Orthopsychiat.*, 1963, **33,** 813–822.

Kagan, J. Information processing in the child: significance of analytic and reflective attitudes. *Psychol. Monogr.*, 1964, **78,** No. 1 (Whole No. 578).

Kagan, J., Moss, H. A., & Sigel, I. E. Psychological significance of styles of conceptualization. *Monogr. Soc. Res. Child Develpm.*, 1963, **28,** No. 2.

Kennedy, W. A., Van de Riet, V., & White, J. C., Jr. A normative sample of intelligence and achievement of Negro elementary school children in the southeastern United States. *Monogr. Soc. Res. Child Develpm.*, 1963, **28,** No. 6.

Lesser, G. Mental abilities of children in different social and cultural groups. New York: Cooperative Research Project No. 1635, 1964.

Meyer, Roberta, Shipman, Virginia, & Hess, R. D. Family structure and social class in the socialization of curiosity in urban preschool children. Paper presented at APA meeting in Los Angeles, Calif., September, 1964.

Olim, E. G., Hess, R. D., & Shipman, Virginia. Relationship between mothers' language styles and cognitive styles of urban preschool children. Paper presented at Biennial Meeting of Soc. Res. Child Develpm., Minneapolis, Minn., March, 1965.

Shipman, Virginia, & Hess, R. D. Social class and sex differences in the utilization of language and the consequences for cognitive development. Paper presented at Midwest. Psychol. Ass., Chicago, April, 1965.

4

Racial Differences and Intellectual Performance

To what extent are the contemporary social deprivation theories merely substituting notions of environmental immutability and fatalism for earlier notions of biologically determined educational unmodifiability? To what extent do these theories obscure more basic reasons for the educational retardation of lower-status children? To what extent do they offer acceptable and desired alibis for the educational default: the fact that these children, by and large, do not learn because they are not being taught effectively, they are not being taught because those who are charged with the responsibility of teaching them do not believe that they can learn, do not expect that they can learn, and do not act toward them in ways which help them to learn.

KENNETH B. CLARK, *Dark Ghetto*

INTRODUCTION

Many studies have found that black Americans score lower than whites on various indicators of intelligence. The reasons for these differences have been intensively debated. The major controversy centers on questions pertaining to whether the differences reflect genetically determined inferiority; the results of prolonged and continued deprivation; or inadequate measurement, curricula, and teaching methods.[1] Pettigrew's [14] exhaustive review of issues and re-

[1] Since this was written this debate has been renewed or intensified as a result of Jensen's (1969) support for the genetic hypothesis. A number of social scientists have challenged or discussed Jensen's assertions (Baratz & Baratz, 1969; Bereiter, 1969; Brazziel, 1969; Cronbach, 1969; Crow, 1969; Elkind, 1969; Hunt, 1969; Kagan, 1969).

search bearing on these questions is presented here. Additional theoretical considerations and more recent studies complement and update Pettigrew's analysis.

ADDITIONAL CONSIDERATIONS AND RESEARCH

Shuey (1966), who expanded her 1958 volume *The Testing of Negro Intelligence,* continues to favor a hereditarian position. Dreger (1967) is impressed with her painstaking efforts, but he concludes that "the vast accumulation of data in Shuey does not speak univocally for genetic determination of racial differences" (p. 50), because of a number of unresolved methodological issues (Dreger & Miller, 1960; in press). These include the fact that race has not been adequately defined as an experimental variable; comparisons are often made between groups which are primarily sociologically rather than genetically determined; and cultural factors are by no means all accounted for by matching Negroes and whites on socioeconomic status (see Chapter 1). Klineberg (1963), who also updated his earlier reviews, and Bronfenbrenner (1967), have come to much the same conclusions as Pettigrew and Dreger and Miller.

Evidence of the detrimental effects of deprivation, malnutrition, teachers' low expectations, irrelevant curricula, and poor teaching methods on the intellectual performance of black children continues to accumulate (see Bronfenbrenner, 1967; Dreger & Miller, in press). John (1963) found social class differences in language skills (labeling, relating, categorizing) between different groups of black children. Vane, Weitzman, and Applebaum (1966) and Carlson (1966) have emphasized cultural and environmental aspects in Negro performance on intelligence tests and visual-motor tasks. In a study of responses of white children and black children on intelligence, projective, and behavior tests, Ames and Ilg (1967) found that the sequence of development was similar for the two groups, but black children developed at a slower rate. Vosk (1966) indicates that black children who were identified as slow learners were handicapped in learning by their particular vulnerability to failure and lack of self-confidence in their own capabilities. This relationship between self-concept and achievement, which has already been referred to in Chapter 2, is further stressed by Green and Farquhar's (1965) study. They compared Negro and white high school students on measures of verbal aptitude, academic achievement (GPA), and academic motivation. Academic achievement and motivation were correlated in all subjects. Grade Point Average was highly correlated with aptitude for white males, but not at all for black males. Grade Point Average was most highly correlated with self-concept, as measured by a subscale of the achievement test, for both black males and females.

It has been well established that traditional intelligence tests fairly accurately predict future academic achievement in a standard middle-class educational environment. It is questionable, however, whether these I.Q. measures tap the same abilities in black and in white Americans. It seems reasonable to suspect, for example, in view of the ghetto's special subculture, that we might find an emphasis on skills different from those typically reinforced by middle-class society (Baratz & Baratz, 1969; Scott, 1965). Semler and Iscoe (1966), in fact, found no significant differences between black children and white children on the Raven Progressive Matrices at the eight- and nine-year levels, despite the lower WISC I.Q.'s of the black children. The Progressive Matrices involve new learning within the testing situation, and may thus be less susceptible to differences in prior training and experience. On the other hand, it has been argued that since in school Negro and white children typically have to perform according to the expectations and norms of middle-class society, instruments designed to assess an individual's ability to perform in this context are appropriate (Muzekari, 1967). Boney (1966), for example, has demonstrated that aptitude and mental ability tests predict academic achievement just as successfully for black as for white high school students. His results are in conflict, however, with those of Green and Farquhar already referred to. Further research is required to determine to what extent conventional aptitude tests can serve as valid and reliable predictors of academic achievement in black students. In any case, in comparing test results of black with those of white subjects, we need to be ever mindful of the experimenter effect (Kintz, Delprato, Mettee, Persons, & Schappe, 1965) on intelligence test performance. A number of studies (for example, Forrester & Klaus, 1964; Smith & May, 1967) have demonstrated that the examiner's race may influence the test results. (See also Chapters 1, 5, and 6.)

As Pettigrew [14] and Hunt (1961, 1964b) have noted, early experience plays a crucial role in the intellectual development of the child. Thus, the degree and type of stimulation available to children from lower-class and slum environments may, as already mentioned in Chapter 3, account for many of the racial differences in intellectual performance.

In the context of the foregoing one might expect that preschool education could play a crucial role in generally providing appropriate intellectual stimulation for all children and, more specifically, overcoming environmental deficits in culturally deprived children (Hunt, 1964a). How does the available empirical evidence on preschool effectiveness measure up to this expectation?[2]

Weikart (1967) suggests that the results of preschool education be evaluated in terms of the teaching methods emphasized. He distinguishes between three preschool teaching methods: the *traditional* nursery school method emphasizing social, emotional and motor development; the *structural* method focusing on cognitive and language development; and the *task-oriented* method aiming at specific predetermined abilities such as reading, arithmetic, or logical thinking (p. 122). On the basis of his review of the research literature, Weikart concludes that the traditional nursery schools are successful in promoting social and emotional development but are generally ineffective in producing intellectual gains. The structural and task-oriented programs, on the other hand, tend to enhance *both* affective and cognitive growth, particularly in disadvantaged children. In fact, some of the intellectual gains were rather spectacular. Dawe (1942), for example, obtained an increase in I.Q. scores of over 14 points in the experimental group after only 50 hours of specific reading instruction, in contrast to a slight loss in the control group. Weikart (1967) reports an increase of up to 20 I.Q. points in children who were enrolled in his preschool project for eight months. Bereiter and Engelman (1966), whose detailed and task-oriented curriculum focuses on language development, arithmetic, and reading, have also reported gains. Deutsch (1963, 1964), Kirk (1958) and Klaus and Gray (1968) have demonstrated significant improvement in the intellectual performance of preschoolers as a result of carefully structured programs. A number of investigators (Fournier, 1967; Goldschmid, 1967, 1968a, b; Goldschmid & Bentler, 1968a, b; Lasry, 1968), operating from a theoretical framework developed by Piaget (1952),

---

[2] Jensen (1969) has concluded that "compensatory education has been tried and it apparently failed" (p. 2). His assessment has been challenged by a number of writers (for references see fn. 1).

have shown that the acquisition of logical principles, such as conservation or inclusion, can be accelerated by special training methods.

But how stable are these early gains? Unfortunately, there are not yet enough longitudinal data to answer this question with any certainty. Preliminary impressions (Weikart, 1967) suggest that increases in intellectual achievement as a result of preschool education are particularly noticeable in the first year and then seem to taper off. Weikart (1967) proposes a three-stage evolution of preschool programs. The first stage would be geared essentially toward establishing rapport with the disadvantaged child, much as is done in traditional nursery schools. After contact has occurred, the second stage, involving structured problem solving and language development, would be initiated. The third stage would be directed at "long-term and systematic educational programming" (p. 156–157). It is the implementation of this last stage that Weikart feels is most difficult and yet most crucial in maintaining early gains and securing further acceleration. More research is necessary to pinpoint variables that enhance or impede long-term progress. Klaus and Gray (1968) have found that the effects of their two- or three-summer intervention programs have lasted to some extent through two years of public schooling. But they point out that "if no massive changes are made in the home conditions of a child, the situation which created the original deficit will continue to take its toll. . . . Nor have the public schools in general yet reached the point where it is possible for them to sustain adequately the kinds of gains that may have been made in an early intensive intervention program" (p. 63).

Weikart (1967) also raises the question of optimal timing for preschool intervention. Although, as noted before, there appear to be no social class or ethnic differences in mental growth during the first year of life, Pasamanick and Knoblock (1961) report significant differences between black children and white children at the age of three. Both groups had similar developmental quotients (D.Q.) at 40 weeks of age, but two years later, the D.Q. of the white children had risen by over 5 points, while that of the black children had decreased by more than 7 points. These findings suggest that "cultural deprivation" may occur before the age of four, when preschool programs are typically initiated. Pines (1967) has described a number of projects that are directed at infants before they enter nursery school. Schaefer (Pines, 1967), for example, has found that an hour of daily home tutoring of 15-month-old black babies from poor neighborhoods can be very effective. He reports I.Q. gains of over 10 points after one year. Moore (Pines, 1967; Moore & Anderson, 1968) has constructed a "talking typewriter" and "responsive environment," which help children develop their language skills early. Caldwell (1968) has also initiated programs for infants, in the age range from six months to three years. Hunt (1964b) has suggested that if such early intervention and preschool programs were available to deprived children on a much larger scale than is presently the case, social class and ethnic differences in intellectual performance might be significantly reduced.

In order to optimize the effectiveness of early training and, of course, education in general, future research must be directed at identifying the specific variables involved in the lower-class black child's intellectual progress. Lesser and his associates (Lesser, Fifer, & Clark, 1965; Stodolsky & Lesser, [15]) have attempted to determine the learning styles of different groups of disadvantaged children. As can be seen from the excerpt of their study that is included in this chapter, they examined patterns among various mental abilities (verbal ability, reasoning, number facility, and space conceptualization) in first graders from different social class (middle and lower) and ethnic background (Chinese, Jewish, Negro, and Puerto Rican) in New York City. The results indicate that both social class and ethnicity affect the *level* of performance differentially on each mental ability. In contrast, social class differences within each ethnic group do *not* modify the distinct *patterns* that emerge for each ethnic group. A replication study on Chinese and Negro children in Boston duplicated their earlier data almost exactly. Stodolsky and Lesser discuss the implications these striking results may have for school instruction and our understanding of cultural deprivation.

Other important areas to consider are motivation and expectations (of others and oneself) and their role in producing racial differences in intellectual performance. It has been surmised that lower I.Q.'s of black groups may be partially due to an absence of inherent motivation in the test situation itself. Tiber and Kennedy (1964), on the basis of their experimentation with different incentives, however, conclude that "explanations of I.Q. differences between cultural groups must be based on causes other than lack of intrinsic motivation provided by the intelligence test itself" (p. 187). Zigler and Butterfield (1968), on the other hand, attribute the increase in I.Q. in culturally deprived children who had attended nursery schools to motivational factors, rather than to an increased rate of intellectual development. Their results support their argument that preschool programs "should be assessed in terms of their success in fostering greater general competence among deprived children rather than their success in developing particular cognitive abilities alone" (p. 12). Terrell, Durkin, and Wiesley (1959) found material incentives more powerful in eliciting behaviors from lower-class children, whereas nonmaterial rewards were more effective for middle-class children. Lower-class status was also associated with a preference for immediate gratification and a small reward as opposed to delayed gratification and larger reward (Mischel, 1961).

Rosenthal and Jacobson (1968a, b) have suggested that disadvantaged children fall behind in school because their teachers expect them to. In their study, teachers were led to believe that a psychologist had identified "late starters" whose academic performance could be expected to improve considerably during the school year, on the basis of psychological test results. Actually, these children were chosen at random without regard to their I.Q. The results indicated the dramatic effects of the "self-fulfilling prophecy." Those children from whom the teachers expected improvement did in fact show a very significant gain in I.Q. scores at the end of the year.[3] Katz's [16] paper, which is included here provides a review of the issues and research related to expectations and motivational determinants in intellectual achievement. (For a considerable elaboration of this paper, see Katz, 1967.)

Finally, many authors (for example, Brown, 1965; Clark, 1965; Coles, 1967; Kohl, 1967; Kozol, 1967) have presented dramatic accounts of the deplorable and chaotic conditions in black ghettoes and slum schools where the cruel effects of deprivation mix with administrative and teacher apathy, incompetence, low expectations, and racism to the detriment of the black child's intellectual development.

To conclude, racial differences are strongly affected by environmental and cultural differences. The identification of specific variables that on the one hand limit or retard, and on the other, enhance a child's intellectual growth will greatly contribute to the development of optimally effective preschool programs, as well as improve public school education.

---

[3] Some of Rosenthal's work has been challenged by Barber (1969); Barber and Silver (1968a, b); Barber et al. (1969); and Silver (1968). For replies see Rosenthal (1968; 1969).

REFERENCES

Ames, L. B., & Ilg, F. L. Search for children showing academic promise in a predominantly Negro school. *The Journal of Genetic Psychology*, 1967, **110**, 217–231.

Baratz, S. S., & Baratz, J. G. Early childhood intervention: The social science base of institutionalized racism. Paper presented to the Society for Research in Child Development, Santa Monica, California, March, 1969.

Barber, T. X. Invalid arguments, postmortem analyses and the experimenter effect. *Journal of Consulting and Clinical Psychology*, 1969, **33**, 11–14.

Barber, T. X., & Silver, M. J. Fact, fiction, and the experimenter bias effect. *Psychological Bulletin Monograph Supplement*, 1968, **70**, 1–29. (a)

Barber, T. X., & Silver, M. J. Pitfalls in data analysis and interpretation: A reply to Rosenthal. *Psychological Bulletin Monograph Supplement*, 1968, **70**, 48–62. (b)

Barber, T. X., et al. Five attempts to replicate the experimenter bias effect. *Journal of Consulting and Clinical Psychology*, 1969, **33**, 1–6.

Bereiter, C. The future of individual differences. *Harvard Educational Review*, 1969, **39**, 310–318.

Bereiter, C., & Engleman S. *Teaching disadvantaged children in the preschool.* Englewood Cliffs, N.J.: Prentice-Hall, 1966.

Boney, J. D. Predicting the academic achievement of secondary school Negro students. *Personnel and Guidance Journal*, 1966, **44**, 700–703.

Brazziel, W. F. A letter from the South. *Harvard Educational Review*, 1969, **39**, 348–356.

Bronfenbrenner, U. The psychological costs of quality and equality in education. *Child Development*, 1967, **38**, 909–925.

Brown, C. *Manchild in the promised land.* New York: Macmillan, 1965.

Caldwell, B. H. The fourth dimension in early childhood education. In R. D. Hess & R. M. Baer (Eds.), *Early Education.* Chicago: Aldine, 1968.

Carlson, L. D. A comparison of Negro and Caucasian performances on the Bender-Gestalt test. *Journal of Clinical Psychology*, 1966, **22**, 96–98.

Clark, K. B. *Dark Ghetto: Dilemmas of social power.* New York: Harper & Row, 1965.

Coles, R. *Children of Crisis.* Boston: Little, Brown, 1967.

Cronbach, L. J. Heredity, environment, and educational policy. *Harvard Educational Review*, 1969, **39**, 338–347.

Crow, J. F. Genetic theories and influences: Comments on the value of diversity. *Harvard Educational Review*, 1969, **39**, 301–309.

Dawe, H. C. A study of the effect of an educational program upon language development and related mental functions in young children. *Journal of Experimental Education*, 1942, **11**, 200–209.

Deutsch, M. The disadvantaged child and the learning process: Some social, psychological and developmental considerations. In A. H. Passow (Ed.), *Education in depressed areas.* Part II. New York: Bureau of Publications, Teachers College, Columbia University, 1963.

Deutsch, M. Facilitating development in the preschool child: Social and psychological perspectives. *Merrill Palmer Quarterly of Behavior and Development*, 1964, **10**, 249–263.

Dreger, R. M. Hard-hitting hereditarianism. *Contemporary Psychology*, 1967, **12**, 49–51.

Dreger, R. M., & Miller, K. S. Comparative psychological studies of Negroes and whites in the United States. *Psychological Bulletin*, 1960, **57**, 361–402.

Dreger, R. M., & Miller, K. S. Comparative psychological studies Negroes and whites in the United States: 1959–1965. *Psychological Bulletin,* in press.

Elkind, D. Piagetian and psychometric conceptions of intelligence. *Harvard Educational Review,* 1969, **39,** 319–337.

Forrester, B. J., & Klaus, R. A. The effect of race of the examiner on intelligence test scores of Negro kindergarten children. *Peabody Papers in Human Development,* 1964, **2,** 1–7.

Fournier, E. Un apprentissage de la conservation des quantités continues par une technique d'exercises opératoires. Unpublished doctoral dissertation, Université de Montréal, Montréal, 1967.

Goldschmid, M. L. Different types of conservation and nonconservation and their relation to age, sex, IQ, MA, and vocabulary. *Child Development,* 1967, **38,** 1229–1246.

Goldschmid, M. L. The relation of conservation to emotional and environmental aspects of development. *Child Development,* 1968, **39,** 579–589. (a)

Goldschmid, M. L. The role of experience in the acquisition of conservation. *Proceedings,* 76th Annual Convention, APA, 1968, 361–362. (b)

Goldschmid, M. L., & Bentler, P. M. *Concept assessment kit—Conservation.* San Diego, California: Educational and Industrial Testing Service, 1968. (a)

Goldschmid, M. L., & Bentler, P. M. The dimensions and measurement of conservation, *Child Development,* 1968, **39,** 787–802. (b)

Green, R. L., & Farquhar, W. W. Negro academic motivation and scholastic achievement. *Journal of Educational Psychology,* 1965, **56,** 241–243.

Hunt, J. McV. *Intelligence and experience.* New York: Ronald, 1961.

Hunt, J. McV. The psychological basis for using preschool enrichment as an antidote for cultural deprivation. *Merrill-Palmer Quarterly of Behavior and Development,* 1964, **10,** 209–248. (a)

Hunt, J. McV. Introduction. In Montessori, Maria, *The Montessori method.* New York, Schocken Books, 1964. (b)

Hunt, J. McV. Has compensatory education failed? Has it been attempted? *Harvard Educational Review,* 1969, **39,** 278–300.

Jensen, A. R. How much can we boost IQ and scholastic achievement? *Harvard Educational Review,* 1969, **39,** 1–123.

John, U. P. The intellectual development of slum children: Some preliminary findings. *The American Journal of Orthopsychiatry,* 1963, **33,** 813–822.

Kagan, J. S. Inadequate evidence and illogical conclusions. *Harvard Educational Review,* 1969, **39,** 274–277.

Katz, I. The socialization of academic motivation in minority children. *Nebraska Symposium on Motivation,* 1967, **15,** 133–191.

Kintz, B. L., Delprato, D. J., Mettee, D. R., Persons, C. E., & Schappe, R. H. The experimenter effect. *Psychological Bulletin,* 1965, **63,** 223–232.

Kirk, S. A. *Early education of the mentally retarded.* Urbana, Ill.: University of Illinois Press, 1958.

Klaus, R. A., & Gray, S. W. The early training project for disadvantaged children: a report after five years. *Monographs of the Society for Research in Child Development,* 1968, **33,** No. 4.

Klineberg, O. Negro-white differences in intelligence test performance: New look at an old problem. *American Psychologist,* 1963, **18,** 198–203.

Kohl, H. R. *36 children.* New York: New American Library, 1967.

Kozol, J. *Death at an early age.* Boston: Houghton Mifflin, 1967.

Lasry, J. C. Enseignement opératoire de la notion d'inclusion. Unpublished doctoral dissertation. Université de Montréal, Montréal, 1968.

Lesser, G. S., Fifer, G., & Clark, D. H. Mental abilities of children from different social class and cultural groups. *Monographs of the Society for Research in Child Development,* 1965, **30** (No. 4).

Mischel, W. Delay of gratification, need for achievement and acquiesence in another culture. *Journal of Abnormal and Social Psychology,* 1961, **62,** 543–552.

Moore, O. K., & Anderson, A. R. The responsive environment project. In R. D. Hess & R. M. Baer (Eds.), *Early Education.* Chicago: Aldine, 1968.

Muzekari, L. H. Relationships between the Goodenough DAM and the Stanford-Binet in Negro and white public school children. *Journal of Clinical Psychology,* 1967, **23,** 86–87.

Pasamanick, B., & Knoblock, H. Epidemiologic studies on the complications of pregnancy and the birth process. In Caplan, C. (Ed.), *Prevention of Mental Disorders in Children.* New York: Basic Books, 1961.

Piaget, J. *The origins of intelligence in children.* New York: International Universities, 1952.

Pines, M. *Revolution in learning.* New York: Harper & Row, 1967.

Rosenthal, R. Experimenter expectancy and the reassuring nature of the null hypothesis decision procedure. *Psychological Bulletin,* 1968, **70,** 30–47.

Rosenthal, R. On not so replicated experiments and not so null results. *Journal of Consulting and Clinical Psychology,* 1969, **33,** 7–10.

Rosenthal, R., & Jacobson, L. F. Teacher expectations for the disadvantaged. *Scientific American,* 1968, **218,** 19–23. (a)

Rosenthal, R., & Jacobson, L. F. *Pygmalion in the classroom.* New York: Holt, Rinehart and Winston, 1968. (b)

Scott, R. Social-class correlates of selected cognitive functions. *Psychological Reports,* 1965, **18,** 63–68.

Semler, I. J., & Iscoe, I. Structure of intelligence in Negro and white children. *Journal of Educational Psychology,* 1966, **57,** 326–336.

Shuey, A. M. The testing of Negro intelligence (2nd ed.). New York: Social Science Press, 1966.

Silver, M. J. Experimenter modelling: A critique. *Journal of Experimental Research in Personality,* 1968, **3,** 172–178.

Smith, H. W., & May, W. T. Influence of the examiner on the ITPA scores of Negro children. *Psychological Reports,* 1967, **20,** 499–502.

Terrell, G., Durkin, K., & Wiesley, M. Social class and the nature of the incentive in discrimination learning. *Journal of Abnormal and Social Psychology,* 1959, **59,** 270–272.

Tiber, N., & Kennedy, W. A. The effects of incentives on the intelligence test performance of different social groups. *Journal of Consulting Psychology,* 1964, **28,** 187.

Vane, J. R., Weitzman, J., & Applebaum, A. P. Performance of Negro and white children and problem and non-problem children on the Stanford-Binet scale. *Journal of Clinical Psychology,* 1966, **22,** 431–435.

Vosk, J. S. Study of Negro children with learning difficulties at the outset of their school careers. *American Journal of Orthopsychiatry,* 1966, **36,** 32–40.

Weikart, D. P. (Ed.) *Preschool intervention: A preliminary report of the Perry preschool projects.* Ann Arbor, Michigan: Campus Publishers, 1967.

Zigler, E., & Butterfield, E. C. Motivational aspects of changes in IQ test performance of culturally deprived nursery school children. *Child Development,* 1968, **39,** 1–14.

14

Negro American intelligence

T. F. PETTIGREW

Extending beyond health, white supremacists maintain that Negroes are innately less intelligent than Caucasians. In a statement remarkably comparable to those made two centuries ago by advocates of the theory of American degeneration (Introduction), one modern-day racist phrases the claim in these words:

> Any man with two eyes in his head can observe a Negro settlement in the Congo, can study the pure-blooded African in his native habitat as he exists when left on his own resources, can compare this settlement with London or Paris, and can draw his own conclusions regarding relative levels of character and intelligence. . . . Finally, he can inquire as to the number of pure-blooded blacks who have made their contributions to great literature or engineering or medicine or philosophy or abstract science (Putnam, 1961, p. 7).

Such claims assumed special importance among the opponents of the Supreme Court's school desegregation ruling in 1954. Interracial education simply will not work, contended many segregationists; Negro children are too retarded innately to benefit and will only act to drag down the standards of the white children.

Americans are far less receptive to such reasoning now than they were a generation ago. Public opinion poll data reveal that, while only two out of five white Americans regarded Negroes as their intellectual equals in 1942, almost four out of five did by 1956 —including a substantial majority of white Southerners (Hyman & Sheatsley, 1956). Much of this change is due to the thorough repudiation of racist assertions by the vast majority of modern psychologists and other behavioral scientists. Indeed, the latest research in this area lends the strongest evidence yet available for this repudiation. This chapter takes a new look at this old controversy and presents a summary of the relevant research.[1]

THE "SCIENTIFIC RACIST" POSITION

The dominant scientific position on this subject has been termed an "equalitarian dogma" and described as "the scientific hoax of the century" by one psychologist, Professor-Emeritus Henry Garrett, (1962). He charges that other psychologists have prematurely closed the issue for ideological, not scientific, reasons.

Garrett is publicly joined by two other psychologists, out of the roughly twenty-one thousand who belong to the American Psychological Association. Frank McGurk, of Villanova University, has conducted research with an unvalidated intelligence test of his own design and concluded that "Negroes as a group do not possess as much [capacity for education] as whites as a group"[2] (1956). In 1956 this work gained wide attention when

Reprinted from *A Profile of the Negro American.* Princeton, New Jersey; Van Nostrand, 1964, Chapter 5, pp. 100–135, by permission of the author T. F. Pettigrew and D. Van Nostrand Company, Ltd.

[1] An earlier draft of this chapter by the author appeared in 1964 in the *Journal of Negro Education,* under the title of "Negro American Intelligence: A New Look at an Old Controversy."

[2] For a critical discussion of McGurk's work, see Anastasi (1958, pp. 557–558 and 562–563).

146

the *U.S. News and World Report* featured an article under the imposing title of "A Scientist's Report on Race Differences," in which McGurk surveyed six investigations that he claimed to be "the only existing studies that relate to the problem" (1956).

The crowning production of this small band is Audrey Shuey's *The Testing of Negro Intelligence* (1958). Shuey, a psychologist at Randolph-Macon Woman's College in Lynchburg, Virginia, provides a large, though carefully selected, review of over two hundred studies bearing on racial differences in intelligence.[3] She ignores the newer conceptions of intelligence and instead relies heavily upon the earlier, less sophisticated investigations, with over half of her references dated prior to World War II. She also concentrates on research performed in the South, with three-fourths of her studies on students coming from tightly segregated Southern and border communities. The great bulk of this research found most Negroes scoring lower on I.Q. tests than most whites. Shuey unhesitatingly interprets this fact as pointing "to the presence of some native differences between Negroes and whites as determined by intelligence tests" (1958, p. 318).

In addition to this "sheer weight of uncontrolled data" argument, these three psychologists attempt to show that the impoverished environment of the typical Negro cannot account for the observed test differences. One favorite example, prominently cited by all three, is H. A. Tanser's 1939 investigation of intelligence among the Negro and white children of Kent County, Ontario, Canada (1939). Tanser found that his white sample obtained a higher average I.Q. than his Negro sample; and the "scientific racists" maintain

---

[3] Garrett claims that Shuey's book examined "*all* of the comparative studies of Negro-white performance on mental tests over the past 40 years" (1962a, p. 1). This is not the case. Even papers by Garrett and McGurk are missing (1945; 1953a). But more critical is the exclusion of numerous and important publications which appeared prior to Shuey's work and run directly counter to its conclusion (Clark, 1956; DeStephens, 1953; Gilliland, 1951; Harrell, Woodyard, & Gates, 1956; Jenkins, 1958; Knoblock & Pasamanick, 1953; Pasamanick, 1946; Pasamanick & Knoblock, 1955; Roberts, 1948; Stalnaker, 1948; Theman & Witty, 1943; Witty & Jenkins, 1936).

that this is convincing evidence for their position, since in Kent County "the social and economic conditions of the whites and Negroes were substantially the same" (1962b).

THE MODERN PSYCHOLOGICAL POSITION

These arguments have not altered the dominant opinion of modern psychology on this topic. In the first place, the studies repeatedly cited by the "scientific racists" in defense of their position are not, upon closer scrutiny, critical tests of their contentions. Consider the Tanser work in Canada.[4] As in investigations in the United States, the "social and economic conditions" of the two groups were *not* equal. One psychologist, Mollie Smart, was born and raised in Kent County at approximately the time Tanser conducted his study there. She candidly describes the condition of the Negroes in this period:

> . . . Nearly all of [the Negroes'] houses were small wood buildings, often lacking paint and tending towards delapidation. The theaters had a policy of seating Negroes in certain areas. The all-Negro school had been abandoned by my day. My elementary school classes always included Negro children, but I remember none during the last 3 years of high school. My Negro classmates were usually poorly clothed and badly groomed. Negroes held the low-status jobs. They were the servants, garbage collectors, and odd-job men. People called them "Nigger" more often than "Negro." I did not know until I grew up that a Negro could be a doctor, lawyer, teacher, member of Parliament, or even a clerk in a store. . . . I cannot conceive of any social advantages which Negroes enjoyed in Kent County at the time of the Tanser study (Smart, 1963, p. 621).

Tanser himself admitted that his sample of Negro children had not attended school as regularly as the white children. Moreover, it cannot be said that Southern Ontario is free of racial prejudice and discrimination. Ever since the close of the American Civil War, the position of the Negro Canadian has steadily declined, with violent outbursts against Negroes occurring in Kent County itself (Chant

---

[4] For similar analyses of other investigations of so-called "equal groups" commonly cited by white supremacists see Anastasi (1958, pp. 556–558).

& Freedman, 1934; Franklin, 1961; McGurk, 1953b). The racial differences in I.Q. observed by Tanser, then, cannot be interpreted apart from the area's racial situation.

These difficulties point up the severely limiting methodological problems which confront this research realm. Any test of native intelligence must of necessity assume equivalent backgrounds of the individuals and groups under study. But until conditions entirely free from segregation and discrimination are achieved and the floor of Negro poverty is raised to the level of whites, the definitive research on racial differences in intelligence cannot be performed. Meanwhile, psychologists must conduct their work in a culture where training and opportunity for the two groups are never completely equal.

Other fundamental problems raised in Chapter 3 complicate the issue. The very concept of "race" injects special issues. Since Negro Americans do not even approach the status of a genetically pure "race," they are a singularly inappropriate group upon whom to test racist theories of inherent intellectual inferiority of the Negroid subspecies. In addition, confusion is introduced by the ambiguity of the phrase "race differences." To find that many descriptive investigations using intelligence tests elicit differences between the "races" does not necessarily mean that these differences *result* from race.

Empirical efforts are also hampered by the operation of selective factors in sampling. That is, Negroes and whites in the same situation—such as those inducted into the armed forces—may have been selected differently on intelligence, thus biasing the comparison of test scores between the two groups. For instance, Hunt found that the Navy during World War II did not employ the same screening and selection standards for the two groups, permitting a far higher proportion of mental defectives among Negro than among white acceptances (1947). Such a finding renders any comparisons in test scores between Negro and white sailors of dubious value. Much has been made of the intelligence test performances of the two "races" in both World Wars I and II, but such selective factors make these data difficult to interpret.

Despite these limitations, however, modern psychology has managed to achieve significant theoretical and empirical advances in this realm. These advances strongly favor a non-genetic interpretation of the typically lower intelligence test score averages of Negro groups. This work can be conveniently summarized under four general rubrics: (1) new theoretical conceptions; (2) the mediators of intellectual underdevelopment; (3) varying opportunities and group results; and (4) the individual versus the group.

NEW THEORETICAL CONCEPTIONS

Since World War II, psychologists and other scientists have seriously reviewed earlier notions about such basic concepts as "the environment," "heredity," and "intelligence." Instead of the older nature versus nurture conception, the emphasis is placed on nature and nurture.[5] Rather than asking which set of factors—environmental or hereditary—contributes more to a particular trait or ability like intelligence, investigators ask how the environment and heredity combine to form the observed characteristic. Genes not only set broad limits on the range of development, but also enter into highly complex interactions with the environment, interactions which have not been emphasized enough in the past.

An ingenious animal experiment by Cooper and Zubek illustrates this genetic-environmental interaction (1958). These investigators employed two genetically distinct strains of rats, carefully bred for 13 generations as either "bright" or "dull." Separate groups of the two strains grew up after weaning in three contrasting environments: a restricted environment, consisting of only a food box, water pan, and otherwise barren cage; a natural environment, consisting of the usual habitat of a laboratory rat; and an enriched environment, consisting of such objects as ramps, swings, slides, polished balls, tunnels, and teeter-totters plus a decorated wall beside their cages. Figure 1 shows the maze learning performances of the six groups of rats (the fewer the errors, the more "intelligent" the behavior). Note that the two genetically diverse groups did almost equally well in the enriched and restricted environments, sharply differing only in the natural situation. In fact,

---

[5] Much of the following discussion is based on Gottesman's review (1963).

the environment masks genetic potential to the point where it is impossible to distinguish the enriched dulls from the natural brights or the natural dulls from the restricted brights.

The data of Figure 1 bear important implications. "Genotypes," the true genetic potential, often do not coincide with "phenotypes," the actual, expressed trait. Similar genotypes may have different phenotypes

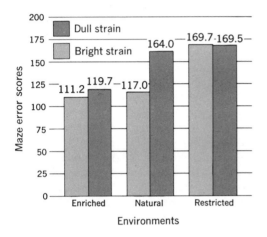

FIGURE 1 Maze error scores for genetically bright and dull rats reared in three contrasting environments. (Data from: R. M. Cooper and J. P. Zubek, "Effects of enriched and restricted early environments on the learning ability of bright and dull rats," *Canadian Journal of Psychology,* 1958, **12,** 159–164.)

(e.g., the bright rats in the restricted and enriched environments), and similar phenotypes may have different genotypes (e.g., the restricted bright and dull rats). Any phenotype is the composite product of the genotype and the environment in which the genetic potential must be realized. Relevant nature-nurture questions thus become: how environmentally modifiable is the phenotypic intelligence of each genotype? And what is the contribution of heredity to the intelligence score differences among a group of individuals on a specific test in a specified environment?

This newer view of the nature-nurture controversy and a mounting accumulation of new developmental evidence has resulted in a revised conception of the nature of intelligence. J. McV. Hunt presents this modern thinking in his volume, *Intelligence and Experience* (1961). Taking his cue from the strategies for information-processing that are currently programmed for electronic computers, Hunt defines intelligence as central neural processes which develop in the brain to mediate between the information coming into the individual via the senses and the return signals for motor reaction. Moreover, he maintains that the initial establishment and subsequent capacity of these processes are probably rooted in the child's earliest encounters with the world around him. Intelligence, then, is not merely an inherited capacity, genetically fixed and destined to unfold in a biologically predetermined manner. It is a dynamic, on-going set of processes that within wide hereditary limits is subject to innumerable experiential factors.

Hunt's view upsets two long-unquestioned dogmas about intelligence, dogmas critical in the area of race differences. He terms them the assumptions of "fixed intelligence" and "predetermined development." The first of these has its roots in Darwin's theory of natural selection. It accepts intelligence as a static, innately-given quantity, and it long influenced psychological thought and the design of I.Q. tests. Indeed, the assumption of fixed intelligence became so established before World War II that many psychologists regarded all evidence of substantial shifts in I.Q. as merely the product of poor testing procedures. But, objected Stoddard in 1943, "to regard all changes in mental status as an artifact is to shut one's eyes to the most significant and dramatic phenomenon in human growth" (1943, p. 281).

The second assumption of "predetermined development" refers to the idea that, barring extreme interference from the environment, intelligence will unfold "naturally" with gene-determined anatomical maturation. Classic work on salamanders and Hopi Indian children was cited to demonstrate this maturational effect and that prior experience was unnecessary for normal development (Carmichael, 1927; Coghill, 1929; Dennis, 1940). In this era, mothers were told to avoid overstimulating their children, to allow their children simply to grow "on their own." Hunt considers such advice "highly unfortunate," for it now appears that a proper matching of a child's develoment with challenging encounters with his environment is a critical requisite for increasing ability.

Notice this new outlook in no way denies an hereditary influence on intelligence, an influence well established by twin studies (Gottesman, 1963). Rather, it views intelligence in much the same way longevity is now regarded. A strong hereditary component is recognized in longevity; consistently long or short life spans typify many families. Yet, despite this component, the life expectancies at birth of Americans have almost doubled in the past century (Metropolitan Life Insurance Company, 1963). Better medical care, better diets, and a host of other environmental factors converge to enable Americans to make fuller use of their longevity potential. Likewise, the modern view of intelligence holds that we have not begun to expand our phenotypic intelligences even close to our genotypic potentials. From this vantage point, it appears our society has placed too much emphasis on personnel selection and eugenics at the expense of effective training programs and euthenics.

Some of the most imaginative experimentation behind this new thinking is that of the eminent Swiss psychologist, Jean Piaget (Hunt, 1951; Piaget, 1947). His ingenious and detailed studies with children of all ages provide abundant evidence that intelligence is the very antithesis of a fixed, predetermined capacity. And a wide range of other types of investigations amply bears out this conclusion. Even animal intelligence seems to be importantly affected by environmental opportunities. The previously-cited rat work of Cooper and Zubek shows how diverse cage environments affect later learning. In addition, pet-reared rats and dogs, with backgrounds of richly variegated experience, later evidence considerably more intelligent behavior than their cage-reared counterparts (Thompson & Heron, 1954; Thompson & Melzack, 1956). And Harlow has demonstrated that monkeys can "learn to learn"; that is, they can develop learning sets which enable them to solve general classes of problems almost at a glance (1949).

Similar effects of early environmental enrichment on the intelligence of young children have been noted. Kirk has shown that early educational procedures can often produce sharp increments in intellectual functioning among mentally retarded children, sometimes even among those diagnosed as organically impaired (1958). Other studies on normal children, both white and Negro, suggest that preschool training in nursery and kindergarten classes may act to raise I.Q.'s (Deutsch and Brown, 1964; Anastasi, 1958, pp. 200–205; Hunt, 1951, pp. 27–34; Lee, 1951). Among criticisms of this research is the contention that a selection factor could be operating. The natively brighter children may be those who tend to have preschool education. But among deprived children in an orphanage, the beneficial results of early schooling have been noted in a situation where selection factors did not operate (Wellman & Pegram, 1944). Also relevant is the tendency for orphans to gain in I.Q. after adoption into superior foster homes, the gain being greatest for those adopted youngest (Freeman, Holzinger, & Mitchell, 1928).

After reviewing research on cognitive learning in these early years, Fowler concludes that this is the period of human "apprenticeship" (1962). The infant is acquiring the most elementary and basic discriminations needed for later learning; like Harlow's monkeys, the infant is "learning to learn." Fowler speculates that conceptual learning sets, interest areas, and habit patterns may be more favorably established at these early stages than at later stages of the developmental cycle. Indeed, emphasis on "practical," concrete, gross motor learning in these early years may even inhibit later abstract learning.

In any event, research has documented the intellectually damaging consequences of deprived environments. An English study found that the children of such isolated groups as canal-boat and gypsy families achieved exceptionally low intelligence test scores, scores considerably below those typically found among Negro American children (Gordon, 1923). Interesting, too, is the fact that as these children grow older their I.Q.'s generally decline, though this is not the case for children of more privileged groups. In a similar fashion, children in orphanages and other institutions tend to have lower I.Q.'s and more retarded motor and linguistic development than children in stimulating home environments. Once again selection factors may operate, with the brighter, more developed children being more often chosen for adoption. However, studies which overcome much of this difficulty still note this institutional retardation (Brodbeck & Irwin, 1946; Dennis, 1960; Gilliland, 1949; Goldfarb, 1955).

A related finding concerns the trend toward lower I.Q.'s of children raised in large families (Anastasi, 1956). One common explanation of this phenomenon is simply that parents who have large families are natively less intelligent. Yet, as Hunt points out, other findings strongly suggest that it is partly because parents of large families have less time to spend with each child (Hunt, 1951). Thus, twins and doubles born close together in otherwise small families reveal a similar tendency toward lower I.Q.'s. And the negative relationship between family size and intelligence does not appear among wealthy families who can afford servants to provide stimulating attention for each child.

Finally, the extreme effects that can ensue from an impoverished environment are dramatically illustrated in a series of sensory-deprivation experiments (Bexton, Heron, & Scott, 1954). These investigations reveal that normal people respond with marked psychological disturbances when severely restricted in activity and stimulation. They typically experience temporal and spatial distortions and pronounced hallucinations; and they evidence sharply impaired thinking and reasoning both during and after their isolation.

THE MEDIATORS OF INTELLECTUAL UNDERDEVELOPMENT

Within this new perspective on intelligence as a relatively plastic quality, a series of environmental mediators of the individual Negro child's intellectual underdevelopment has been determined. In fact, these mediators exert their effects even upon the Negro fetus. One study found that dietary supplementation by vitamins supplied during the last half of pregnancy had directly beneficial effects on I.Q. scores of the children later (Harrell, Woodyard, & Gates, 1956). In a sample of mothers from the lowest socio-economic level, 80 per cent of whom were Negro, the group fortified with iron and vitamin B complex had children whose mean I.Q. at three years of age average five full points above the children of the unfortified control group, 103.4 to 98.4. One year later, the mean difference had enlarged to eight points, 101.7 to 93.6. The same researchers failed to find a similar effect among white mothers and their children from a mountain area. Presumably, the largely Negro sample was even poorer and more malnourished than the white sample from the mountains. Dire poverty, through the mother's inadequate diet, can thus impair intelligence before the lower-class Negro child is born.

Economic problems also hamper intelligence through the mediation of premature births (Knoblock & Pasamanick, 1962; Pasamanick & Knoblock, 1958). Premature children of all races reveal not only a heightened incidence of neurologic abnormalities and greater susceptibility to disease, but also a considerably larger percentage of mental defectives (Harper, Fischer & Rider, 1959; Knoblock, Rider, Harper & Pasamanick, 1959). A further organic factor in intelligence is brain injury in the newborn. And both of these conditions have higher incidences among Negroes because of their greater frequency in the most economically depressed sectors of the population (Chapter 4).

Later complications are introduced by the impoverished environments in which most Negro children grow up. At the youngest, preschool ages, race differences in I.Q. means are minimal. Repeated research shows that in the first two years of life there are no significant racial differences in either psychomotor development or intelligence (Gilliland, 1951; Knoblock & Pasamanick, 1953; Pasamanick, 1946). Racist theorists discount these findings on two conflicting grounds (Garrett, 1960; Shuey, 1958). They either claim that infant tests have no predictive value whatsoever for later I.Q. scores, or cite an older study by McGraw that found Negro infants retarded in comparison with white infants. Neither argument is adequate. Three recent investigations provide convincing evidence that properly administered infant tests *do* predict later scores (Drillien, 1959; Hurst, 1963; Knoblock & Pasamanick, 1960). And the 1931 McGraw study is no longer regarded as a decisive experiment—not even by Myrtle McGraw herself (1931; 1964; Pasamanick & Knapp, 1958). It was a pioneer effort that compared white infants with Negro infants of markedly smaller stature on an unvalidated adaptation of a European test. Furthermore, later Northern investigations show little or no Negro lag in intellectual development through kindergarten and five years of age when thorough socioeconomic controls are applied (Anastasi & D'Angelo, 1952; Brown, 1944).

It is only after a few years of inferior schooling have passed that many Negro children drop noticeably in measured I.Q. (Osborn, 1960; Tomlinson, 1944). Part of this drop is due to the heavier reliance placed by intelligence tests at these ages upon verbal skills, skills that are particularly influenced by a constricted environment. One Southern study of "verbal destitution" discovered that those Negro college students most retarded in a reading clinic came from small, segregated high schools and exhibited language patterns typical of the only adult models they had encountered—poorly educated parents, teachers, and ministers (Newton, 1960).

Another factor in the declining test averages over the school years is simply the nature of the schools themselves. Deutsch gives the example of an assignment to write a page on 'The Trip I Took,' given to lower-class youngsters in a ghetto school who had never been more than twenty-five city blocks from home. Psychologist Deutsch maintains: "The school represents a foreign outpost in an encapsulated community which is surrounded by what, for the child, is unknown and foreign" (1960, p. 3).

This tendency of the measured I.Q.'s of Negro children to diminish with increasing age is interpreted by racists not as evidence of the eroding effects of ghetto living, but as proof that Negroes mature more rapidly and begin to decline earlier than whites (Garrett, 1960; Shuey, 1958; Putnam, 1961). Such an idea, based on the belief that Negroes as a "race" are less evolved, is seriously challenged by the often demonstrated fact that environmentally-deprived Caucasian groups reveal precisely the same phenomenon—mountain and other rural children in America and the canal-boat and gypsy children in England (Anastasi, 1958). Furthermore, the positive relationship between socio-economic status and tested I.Q. among Negroes increases with age, again suggesting that environmental factors become evermore vital as the child matures (Tomlinson, 1944).

The nature of the disrupted family life of many lower-status Negro youths decreases further the slum's environmental stimulation. Most of these youngsters are reared in large families, with reduced parental contact. And, as noted in Chapter 1, many of them are in fatherless homes. Deutsch and Stetler have both demonstrated that Negro children raised in such broken homes score significantly below comparable Negro children from intact homes on intelligence measures (Deutsch, 1960; Deutsch & Brown, 1964; Stetler, 1959).

Other research pinpoints the tasks tested by intelligence tests which are most impaired by this restriction of stimulation. Woods and Toal (1957) matched two groups of Negro and white adolescents on I.Q. and noted subtest differences. While superior to the whites on some tests, the Negroes were noticeably deficient on tasks such as detection of errors and drawing pictorial completions which required spatial visualization. And other similar studies reach the same conclusion (Bean, 1942; Clarke, 1941; Davidson, Gibby, McNeil, Segal, & Silverman, 1950; DeStephens, 1953; Franklin, 1945; Hammer, 1954; Higgins & Sivers, 1958; Machover, 1943; Newland & Lawrence, 1953). One demonstrated that this difficulty with perceptual and spatial relations was considerably more marked in a Southern-reared Negro sample than in an I.Q.-matched Northern-reared Negro sample (Machover, 1943). This breakdown of spatial performance among otherwise intelligent Negro children, especially in the more restrictive South, offers a suggestive parallel with the comparable spatial breakdown noted in the sensory-deprivation research. In any event, two additional studies provide evidence that this disability is correctable (Boger, 1952; Eagleson, 1937). Both studies gave groups of Negro and white children special training in spatial perception and found that the Negro subjects benefited more from the practice I.Q. test scores were markedly higher for the Negro subjects five months after the training (Boger, 1952). Test authority Anne Anastasi believes this work supports the idea that the Negroes tested suffered from an unusually barren perceptual experience in early life (1958).

Organic complications and environmental impoverishment are not the only mediators depressing Negro American intelligence. Both the "functioning intelligence" and the measured I.Q. of an individual are inseparably intertwined with his personality (Gough, 1953; Kagan, Sontag, Baker, & Nelson, 1958; Sontag, Baker & Nelson, 1955; Stringer, 1959; Trumbull, 1953; Weisskopf, 1951). Edith Weisskopf has given case evidence of the great variety of ways personality problems can deter normal intellectual development (1951). A child may do poorly in learning situations in a conscious or unconscious desire to punish his parents, to inflict self-punishment, or to avoid self-evaluation. And Roen has demonstrated that such personality problems are more highly related to intelligence test scores among Negroes than among whites (1960). He equated two racial groups of soldiers on a wide range of social variables and found that a series of personality measures were more closely correlated with intelligence for the Negroes than for the whites. In particular, he noted that Negro soldiers who had low intelligence scores rated especially low on a self-confidence questionnaire.

Racist claims of Caucasian superiority contribute to the Negro's lack of intellectual self-confidence. This insecurity is especially provoked by any direct comparison with white performance. One investigation administered a task to Southern Negro college students with two different sets of instructions (Katz, Epps, & Axelson, unpublished paper). One set told how other students at their college did on the task, while the second told how whites throughout the nation did. Those subjects who anticipated white comparison performed significantly more poorly on the task and indicated stronger concern and anxiety about their performance.

The role of "Negro" is again a critical factor (Chapter 1). Put simply, the Negro is not expected to be bright. To reveal high intelligence is to risk seeming "uppity" to a white supremacist. And once more the self-fulfilling prophecy begins to operate, for the Negro who assumes a façade of stupidity as a defense mechanism against oppression is very likely to grow into the role. He will not be eager to learn, and he will not strive to do well in the testing situation. After all, an intelligence test is a middle-class white man's instrument; it is a device whites use to prove their capacities and get ahead in the white world. Achieving a high test score does not have the same meaning for a lower-status Negro child, and it may even carry a definite connotation of personal threat. In this sense, scoring low on intelligence measures may for some talented Negro children be a rational response to perceived danger.

In addition to stupidity, the role of "Negro" prescribes both passivity and lack of ambition as central traits. And these traits are crucial personality correlates of I.Q. changes in white children. The Fels Research Institute found that aggressiveness and intense need for achievement differentiate those children whose scores rise between six and ten years of age from those whose scores recede (Kagan, Sontag, Baker, & Nelson, 1958).

Another protective device is slowness. This trait assumes major importance in the speed instruments typically employed to estimate intelligence. In the Negro lower class there is no premium on speed, for work is generally paid by the hour and there are realistically few goals that fast, hard endeavor can attain. One experiment noted that differences in speed of response are primarily responsible for racial differences in I.Q. estimated by timed performance tests (Davidson, Gibby, McNeil, Segal & Silverman, 1950).

Playing "Negro" is made especially critical when the examiner is white. Even two-year-old Negroes, as mentioned in Chapter 2, seem verbally inhibited when tested by a white [6] (Pasamanick & Knoblock, 1955). In fact, this verbal inhibition may be the principal factor underlying the common observation that Negro children generally evidence verbal comprehension superior to their verbal communication (Carson & Rabin). One investigation had students of both races tested alternately by Negro and white examiners (Canady, 1936). For both groups, the mean I.Q. was approximately six points higher when the test was administered by an examiner of their own race.

Adult Negroes evidence a similar reaction. A public opinion poll in North Carolina asked Negro respondents for the names of the men who had just run for governor in a primary election (Price & Searles, 1961). Three out of five Negroes questioned by Negro interviewers knew at least two correct names and gave no incorrect names, compared with only two out of five of a similar sample questioned by whites. A Boston survey replicated these results with two measures tapping intelligence (Pettigrew, unpublished paper). The first consisted of six informa-

[6] Shuey (1958, p. 316) concludes that race of examiner is not important by omitting this key investigation (Pasamanick & Knoblock, 1955) and not mentioning the full results of another (Canady, 1936).

tional items; each respondent was asked to identify six famous men: two Africans (Kwame Nkrumah and Haile Selassie) and the rest Negro Americans (Louis Armstrong, Martin Luther King, Adam Clayton Powell, and Elijah Muhammad). The other test required synonyms for ten words, ranging in difficulty from "space" to "emanate." Negro interviewers questioned half of the respondents, and white interviewers the other half. The two samples were equivalent in income, age, education, and region of birth. Figure 2 presents the results. Note that on both tests the Boston Negro adults rendered more correct answers when interviewed by a Negro.

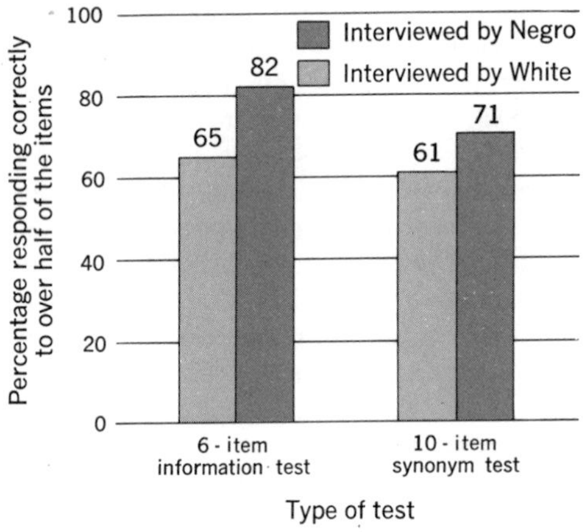

FIGURE 2   Race of interviewer and Negro test performance. (Data from: T. F. Pettigrew, "The Negro Respondent: New data on old problems," unpublished paper.)

Apart from the role of "Negro," the middle-class bias of intelligence testing situations operates to hinder a disproportionate share of Negro examinees. Children perform best in situations familiar to them, but the conditions best suited for lower-status children are seldom attained. Most I.Q. tests are strictly urban middle-class instruments, with numerous references to objects and situations unfamiliar to rural and lower-class people. Haggard showed that a less middle-class-oriented test led to significant increases in the performances of lower-class children (1954).

Tests are only one aspect of class bias, however. Middle-class students have generally internalized their need to excel at such tasks; a high test score is itself a reward.

Moreover, they perform most competently in silent testing atmospheres that place heavy reliance upon reading skills. By contrast, lower-class students frequently require tangible, external rewards for motivation. And their typically restricted home environments are overwhelmingly dominated by the spoken, rather than the written, word. It is not surprising, then, that Haggard discovered notable increments in intelligence test scores of lower-class children when there was extra motivation for doing well (e.g., a prize of movie tickets) and when the questions were read aloud as well as written (1954). Sophisticated testing in ghetto schools should follow such guidelines for more adequate estimates of the abilities of disadvantaged children (Society for the Psychological Study of Social Issues).

VARYING OPPORTUNITIES AND GROUP RESULTS

If all of these mechanisms are operating to mediate the influence of a lean, hostile, and constricted environment upon the individual Negro's tested intelligence, certain group trends under conditions of varying opportunities can be predicted. These testable hypotheses are: (a) in environments which approach being equally restrictive for children of both races, the intelligence test means of both will be low and will approach equality; (b) in environments which approach being equally stimulating for children of both races, the intelligence test means of both will be high and will approach equality; and (c) when any racial group moves from a restrictive to a comparatively stimulating environment, its measured I.Q. mean will rise.

The first of these hypotheses was tested on an isolated Caribbean island, offering little stimulation to its youth. It had:

> no regular steamship service, no railroad, motion picture theater, or newspaper. There were very few automobiles and very few telephones. The roads were generally poor. There were no government schools above the elementary level and no private schools above the secondary level. . . . People of all colors, then, were restricted to a rather narrow range of occupational opportunity (Curti, 1960, p. 14).

Even here, however, complete equality of status between whites and Negroes was not achieved. White skin was "highly respected," whites typically held the better jobs, and, while almost half of the white students attended private schools, nine-tenths of the Negroes attended government schools. Nevertheless, there were no significant color differences on nine of the fourteen intelligence measures. The Negroes did best on tests which were less class-linked, less threatening, and less dependent on uncommon words. Thus, socio-economic status was a more important factor than race on four of the five instruments which did yield racial discrepancies, and "lack of confidence," as rated independently by teachers, was highly related to three of them. In general, the island youngsters scored rather low on the tests, with race a relatively insignificant consideration. And the selective migration possibility that the brighter whites were leaving the island is not an explanation for these findings, since there was apparently little emigration or immigration. These data, gathered in a locality which approached being equally restrictive for both races, do "not lend support to the conclusion that colored inferiority in intelligence tests has a racial basis" (Curti, p. 26).

The second hypothesis has also received support from a number of studies. Three investigations, testing young children in Minneapolis, grade-school students in a Nevada city, and adolescents in the Boston area, revealed that, once social-class factors are rigorously controlled, there are only minor black-white mean I.Q. differences (Brown, 1944; McCord and Demerath, 1958; McQueen and Churn, 1960). In these relatively stimulating, educationally-desegregated urban communities, both racial groups secured test averages equal to the national norms.

An additional study was conducted in West Germany (Eyferth, 1959). A representative sample of 51 *neger-mischlingskinder*—the mulatto children of Negro American soldiers and German women—was administered a number of intelligence tests and their performance contrasted with a comparable group of 25 white German children. There were no significant differences. Two counterbalancing factors complicate the interpretation of this research. The Negro fathers of these children are undoubtedly an intelligent, highly selected group, selected not only in terms of being chosen to serve in the United States Army in Germany but also in terms

of having become acculturated enough to establish an intimate relationship with a German woman. But this factor is balanced by the fact that the children are mostly illegitimate and viewed as such in the German culture, almost by virtue of their color. Furthermore, most of their mothers are probably of lower-status backgrounds and as such have not been able to provide them with the cultural enrichment of the typical German home. And, finally, German culture, even in this post-Hitler era, can hardly be described as totally free of racist thinking. All in all, the satisfactory test performance of these mulatto Germans appears quite remarkable.

Thus, I.Q. means of groups are retarded where there are constrictive environmental conditions and elevated where there are at least average conditions. Three ecological projects provide further evidence for this generalization. One project correlated home rentals with the I.Q. averages of the school children in 300 New York City neighborhoods (Maller, 1933). Moderately high and positive relationships were found; the more expensive the neighborhood, the higher the test scores. Another noted very close and positive associations between such variables as per capita income and the mean I.Q. level of sixth-grade pupils in 30 American cities (Thorndike & Woodyard, 1942). The third project discovered that these ecological correlations tend to be higher for intelligence scores than for scholastic achievement, demonstrating again the extreme sensitivity of the measured I.Q. to the total social environment (Thorndike, 1951).

This research is confirmed by further investigations conducted exclusively among Negroes (Deutsch & Brown, 1964; Murray, 1949; Roberts, 1948; Robinson & Meenes, 1947). Especially since World War II and its attendant expansion of social class differentiation among Negro Americans, socioeconomic variables correlate highly and positively with I.Q. means in Negro samples. For example, the I.Q. means of groups of Negro third-graders in Washington, D.C. tended to be highest in areas where radios were most often present in the homes and where rents were highest.

These results suggest the third hypothesis: when any group moves from a restrictive to a comparatively stimulating environment, its measured I.Q. mean will rise. Dramatic evidence for this proposition comes from the unique situation of the Osage Indians. Like many other Indian groups, the Osage were granted land for the establishment of a reservation. Oil was later discovered on their land, and the Osage became relatively prosperous. Since the Osage had not chosen their land, the oil discovery was not an indication of native ingenuity beyond that of Indian groups in general. But now they could afford living standards vastly superior to other Indians, and on both performance and language tests they were found to meet the national norms and to have achieved the level of comparable whites in the area (Rohrer, 1942). This finding is all the more impressive when it is remembered that Indian children generally perform considerably below Negro children in I.Q. tests.

Similar improvements are recorded among white mountain children in East Tennessee, public school students in Honolulu, and white enlisted men in World War II. Wheeler gave tests to over three thousand mountain children in 1940, and compared their performance to that of children in the same areas and from virtually the same families in 1930 (1942). This ten-year span had witnessed broad economic, social, and educational changes in East Tennessee, and the median I.Q.'s reflected these changes in an increment of 11 points, from 82 to 93. Equally remarkable gains are reported for children of many racial groups in Honolulu after a 14-year period of steady improvement in the city's schools (Smith, 1942). And, finally, 768 soldiers, representative of white enlisted men in World War II, took the old Army Alpha verbal test of World War I and provided striking evidence of the nation's rising intelligence between the two wars. Tuddenham shows that the typical white World War II enlisted man did better on the test than 83 per cent of the enlisted men of the first war (1948).

This last study, incidentally, refutes reasoning put forward by Frank McGurk concerning the intelligence test performances of Negroes in the two world wars. He has argued that if environmental factors are responsible for racial differences in intelligence scores, then Negro scores should have steadily approached the white scores between the two wars; yet "the various differences in socioeconomic

environments of the Negroes, between 1918 and 1950, have not altered the Negro-white test score relationship" (1959). Such "logic" assumes that the socioeconomic standards of whites have not changed over the same years. But in fact the prosperity of whites throughout the nation has been increasing in many ways faster than that of Negro Americans (Chapter 8). If the old Alpha test had been administered to World War II Negroes, they would have most certainly done significantly better than World War I Negroes. "The Negro-white test score relationship," McGurk refers to, has only remained constant because Negroes have made giant strides in intellectual growth where environmental improvements allowed it. Meanwhile, as the Tuddenham data demonstrate, the white median intelligence has also been climbing with environmental improvements. Intelligence, like longevity, is not a fixed capacity for either Negroes or whites.

Another curious assumption made by racist theorists arises from interpreting regional as well as racial results on the World War I Alpha. A number of social scientists noted that Negro recruits in World War I from such states as Ohio and Illinois had higher median scores than white recruits from such states as Arkansas and Mississippi (Montagu, 1945). These extreme comparisons revealed that the environmental deprivations of some Southern whites clearly exceeded even those of some Northern Negroes. Garrett hesitated to apply his usual explanation for low scores; namely, to conclude that whites in these Southern states were innately inferior intellectually (1945). Instead, he emphasized that Negroes scored below whites within each state; he argued that the low white scores in the South were environmentally induced, but that the even lower Negro scores in the South were a combination of environmental factors and genetic inferiority. To advance this argument, Garrett had to assume that Negroes and whites in the South were *equally* deprived —even before World War I. This assumption, of course, is absurd. The period between 1890 and the First World War was the lowest ebb of Negro fortunes since slavery. Today the last traces of that era insure that Negro Southerners as a group are the most environmentally impoverished of all Southerners. And while there were often no public schools at all for Negroes in some rural areas of the South before World War I, the belatedly-improved facilities of today still lag behind those of the whites (Ashmore, 1954; Mc-Cauley & Ball, 1959; Southern School News, February, 1961).

Once the Negro American escapes from these inferior conditions, however, his improved performance parallels that of the Osage Indians and the East Tennessee mountain children. Service in the armed forces is one of the most important sources of wider experience and opportunities for Negroes, including those who are illiterate. The Army in the Second World War operated Special Training Units and provided a basic fourth-. grade education in eight weeks for 254,000 previously illiterate soldiers—roughly half of them Negroes and the great majority Southerners. A slightly higher percentage of the Negroes than whites successfully completed the intensive course, though how this bears on larger questions of Negro intelligence is a matter of debate, since the men given this special training were selected. There is no debate, however, over the fact that the success of these units proves the educability of many apparently retarded men of both races (Aptheker, 1946; Bradley, 1949; Erickson, 1946; Witty, 1945, 1946).

Another mode of improvement for many Negroes is migrating North. Negro Northerners routinely achieve higher test medians than comparable Negro Southerners (Alper & Boring, 1944; Davenport, 1946; Peterson & Lanier, 1929; Reitzes, 1958; Roberts, 1948). And Negro children born in the North achieve higher medians than those who come to the North from the South[7] (Klineberg, 1935; Lee, 1951; Long, 1934; Nancy St. John, 1962; Stetler, 1959). But do the Negro children who migrate improve their group performance as they remain in the North? This was the central question the eminent psychologist, Otto Klineberg, set out to answer in 1935; and it led to perhaps the best known research in the field of race differences (1935). Over three thousand ten-to-twelve-year-old Harlem Negroes took an array of

[7] In a re-analysis of her New Haven I.Q. data (1962), Nancy St. John found that the presence of at least one Northern-born parent was an even more critical variable than the region of birth of the child. (Private communication)

individual and group intelligence instruments. These data clearly indicate that the longer the Southern-born children had resided in New York City, the higher their intelligence scores. Those who had been in the North for a number of years approached the levels attained by the Northern-born Negroes. Smaller studies with less elaborate designs obtained parallel results in Cleveland and Washington, D.C. (Dombey, 1933; Long, 1934).

More recently, Lee replicated these findings in Philadelphia with the most rigorous research on the topic to date (Lee, 1951). Employing large samples in a variety of different schools, Lee analyzed the test scores of the same children as they progressed through the city's school system. Though never quite catching up with the Philadelphia-born Negro students, the Southern Negro migrants as a group regularly gained in I.Q. with each grade completed in Northern schools. And the younger they were when they entered the Philadelphia school system, the greater their mean increase and final I.Q. The effects of the more stimulating and somewhat less discriminatory North, then, are directly reflected in the measured intelligence of the youngest of Negro migrants.

The major complication in interpreting the Klineberg and Lee work is again introduced by possible selection biases. Those Negro Southerners who migrate North in search of a better life may be selectively brighter and rear brighter children. Such a possibility is emphasized by the "scientific racists," though Shuey concedes this factor could reasonably account for only one-third to one-half of the I.Q. increases observed (1958). But other possibilities also exist. Many of the more intelligent Negroes in the South gain some measure of success and establish roots that are more difficult to break than those of the less intelligent. This phenomenon would operate to make the Klineberg and Lee data all the more impressive. Or, perhaps, intelligence has little or nothing to do with the decision to migrate; personality traits, such as aggressiveness or inability to control hostility over racial frustrations, may be more decisive. In any event, Klineberg found the Southern school grades of 562 Negro youths who had since gone North were typical of the entire Negro school populations from which they migrated (1935). More research is needed, but it seems that selective migration cannot begin to account for the dramatic improvement in test performance demonstrated by Negro children who move to the North.

Further evidence that Negro ability goes up when environmental opportunities expand derives from the many diverse educational-enrichment programs current in our major cities. The best known of these is New York City's "Higher Horizons" project (Mayer, 1961). This effort provides a selected and largely Negro student body with an expensive saturation of skilled specialists: remedial-reading teachers, guidance counselors, psychologists, and social workers. Its results have been striking; in the first year, the program cut third graders' retardation in reading from six months down to a single month. Backed by major foundation grants, other cities have also begun to experiment. Detroit and Philadelphia tried sending "school-community agents" into ghetto schools in an attempt to win parental support for education. Kansas City's Central High School and Tucson's Pueblo High School initiated imaginative new programs (Mayer, 1961). And Washington, D.C., launched in 1959 a "talent search" project for 200 deprived seventh graders, 92 per cent of whom were Negro *(Southern School News*, June, 1960). Similar to Higher Horizons in its concentration of staff and exposure of students to new cultural experiences, the "talent search" was soon declared a success. Contrasted with a matched control group, the students of the program showed a sharply reduced scholastic failure rate and notable instances of I.Q. increments.

Perhaps, the most remarkable demonstration of all is Samuel Shepard's "Banneker Group" work in St. Louis (Baron, 1963; Silberman, 1962; *Southern School News*, January, 1959; August, 1959; April, 1960; May, 1960; November, 1960; February, 1961; September, 1961). A forceful educator, Shepard performs his "miracles" on the most underprivileged school children in the city without the vast expenditures of other efforts. The Banneker group consists of 23 elementary schools with over sixteen thousand slum and public housing children, more than 95 per cent of them Negro. A Negro who overcame serious economic disadvantages himself, Shepard adamantly rejects the old dogma that sub-standard school work is all you can realistically expect from ghetto children. He bluntly challenges the pupils, parents, principals, and teachers of the district to perform up to national standards; he appeals to race pride and resorts to continuous exhortations, rallies, contests, posters, and meetings with teachers and parents. Students who make good grades are asked to stand in assemblies for the applause of their classmates. Teachers are asked to visit the homes of their charges. And parents are asked to provide their offspring with encouragement, study space, a library card, a dictionary, and other books as gifts. As a concrete incentive, Shepard points out the new and better jobs now open to Negroes in St. Louis and the lack of qualified Negroes to fill them.

The results of the Banneker effort speak for themselves. Despite an unending stream of poorly educated migrants into the area from the South, all test indicators have risen. In the first four years of the program, the median I.Q. increased from the middle 80's to the 90's; median reading, language, and arithmetic levels all climbed; and the percentage of Banneker graduates accepted for the top-ability program in St. Louis's desegregated high schools tripled.

The striking results of these imaginative demonstrations may not be due directly to the exact procedures introduced. Given their vast variety of techniques and their uniform success, the demonstrations probably achieve most of their gains because of the sheer fact of intervention—any kind of thoughtful intervention. Often the rate of initial progress slows once the beginning enthusiasm cools. But this is irrelevant to the larger issue of Negro American intelligence. Dramatic improvement in Negro performance for whatever reason is evidence of the underlying potential for learning heretofore stifled by lack of opportunity and attention. This potential for learning is also evident in the findings of a recent experiment at the University of Texas (Semler & Iscoe, 1963). Negro children learned series of paired material as rapidly and well as white children, even though they came from lower socioeconomic backgrounds and had significantly lower I.Q.'s.

Such demonstrations arouse speculation concerning the effects of desegregation of public school systems. Segregationists have long voiced the unsubstantiated opinion that "school mixing" would mean educational chaos, with the Negroes dragging down the higher white standards. But the experience of a great diversity of communities indicates that these fears are unjustified. Administrators of 17 desegregated school systems appeared before the United States Civil Rights Commission in March, 1959, and candidly discussed their problems (Southern Regional Council, 1960). Twelve of the educators dealt with the question of academic standards. Ranging from Logan County, Kentucky, and Muskogee, Oklahoma, to Baltimore and Nashville, all twelve reported unequivocally that their academic standards had not been lowered—in fact, many maintained that their standards had improved for both races.

Washington, D.C. provided the acid test. It embarked upon a sweeping process of educational desegregation in 1954 with Negroes comprising three-fifths of the students, many of them from the South with limited backgrounds. The *U. S. News and World Report* soon published articles claiming that the District of Columbia's public school system was well on its way to ruin, and these tracts were widely quoted by segregationists (*United States News and World Report*: September, 1956; October 5, 1956; October 12, 1956; January, 1957). But such dire consequences never materialized. A four-track system of ability grouping and other innovations were adopted. Five years later, in 1959, a factual assessment of the changes was made (Hansen, 1960; *Southern School News*: May, 1959; July, 1959; December, 1959; January, 1960; July, 1960; August, 1960; Stallings, 1960). Though Negro students, swelled by migrants, now comprised three-fourths of the student body, achievement test scores had risen significantly for each grade level sampled and each subject area tested approached or equaled national norms. Furthermore, both Negro and white students shared in these increments.[8] Such results are not unique to Washington. Louisville reported substantial

gains in Negro performance and slight gains in white performance after only one year of desegregation (Southern Regional Council, 1960; Stallings, 1959).

Clearly, desegregation *per se* does not accomplish these feats. The Banneker demonstration in St. Louis took place in virtually all-Negro schools; Washington and Louisville witnessed sharply improved test medians among their Negro students, whether in biracial or uniracial schools. The principal factor seems to be the new and healthier self-image Negroes acquire in the process. The act of community desegregation bolsters and encourages Negro pupils, parents, and teachers alike. Combining with this heightening of morale is the entrenched Negro desire for education (Chapter 8). *Newsweek's* 1963 national poll revealed that 97 per cent of the nation's Negroes want their children at least to graduate from high school (July 23, 1963).

Also important is the sudden interest Negro education finally wins from the whole community. As long as Negro education is a racially separate system, dominant white interests can and do forget it. But once desegregation forces the community to handle the education of its youth in one package, to consider Negro education as an integral part of the whole process, new attention is given to the schools. Indeed, the rise in white test scores after desegregation suggests that public education as a whole benefits from the greater public interest. Washington offers an illustration. Prior to desegregation, survey testing was only done with the white pupils; Negroes were ignored (Southern Regional Council, 1960). But immediately after desegregation, testing throughout the system was instituted, and the same standards were applied at last to both races. Certainly, desegregation is no panacea for the immense problems faced by public school systems with large percentages of environmentally impoverished children, but it does prepare the way for tackling the *real* problems of modern education.

Thus, an array of stimulating circumstances —service in the armed forces, migration to the North, and participation in revitalized school systems—all act to lift substantially the intelligence and achievement levels of Negroes. Often these improvements still do not bring the average Negro performance completely up to white norms, but this can-

---

[8] This is not to say that school difficulties no longer exist in Washington. They continue not because of desegregation, however, but because certain Southern members of the House of Representatives insist on treating the District's "children as pawns in a wicked game designed to prove that desegregation cannot succeed." (*Washington Post* editorial, March 2, 1963)

not be considered as evidence for genetic racial differences until *all* racial discrimination is abolished.

THE INDIVIDUAL VERSUS THE GROUP

The discussion so far has concentrated on group results, yet many of the most important considerations involving Negro American intelligence concern the individual. Not even racists deny the existence of outstanding Negro Americans. Usually, however, the same individuals are cited—Marian Anderson, Ralph Bunche, George Washington Carver—and are considered "exceptions" and special "credits to their race." The truth is that a surprising number of such "exceptional" Negroes have somehow managed to overcome the formidable obstacles of discrimination. Many have naturally entered the struggle for equal rights. But others achieve such stature in non-stereotyped work that they are no longer thought of as Negro. For instance, the originator of the Hinton test for syphilis, the late Professor William A. Hinton, was well known as a bacteriologist and immunologist at Harvard Medical School but not as a Negro.

Superior intelligence comes in all skin colors. While the intelligence test means of the two races are still divergent, the range of performance—from the most retarded idiot to the most brilliant genius—is much the same in the two groups. Some Negro children score I.Q.'s into the gifted range (130 or over) and right up to the testable limit of 200 (Jenkins, 1948, 1950; Theman & Witty, 1943; Witty & Jenkins, 1936). To be sure, the frequency of such bright Negroes is less than that of whites, but this, too, can be explained by differential environmental factors. The great majority of these superior Negroes are located in biracial schools in the urban North and West, which suggests that many potentially gifted Negroes go either undiscovered or undeveloped in the segregated schools of the South (Jenkins, 1948; Jenkins & Randall, 1948). Proof that such children do exist in the South comes from programs which intensively seek talented Negro Southerners (Clark, 1963; Stalnaker, 1948). Once found, they receive scholarships and attend a variety of desegregated high schools and colleges in the North, and the great majority of them accommodate well to their new and challenging situations. Indeed, a recent study of Negro scholarship applicants from the South who have attended integrated colleges reveals that they have a far smaller drop-out rate than white students at the same colleges (Clark & Plotkin, 1963).

A further embarrassment to racist theories is created by the fact that the degree of white ancestry does not relate to Negro I.Q. scores (Herskovits, 1926; Klineberg, 1928; Peterson & Lanier, 1929; Witty & Jenkins, 1936). Among intellectually superior Negroes, for example, the proportions of those with varying degrees of white ancestry correspond closely with those of the total Negro American population (Witty & Jenkins, 1936). Indeed, the brightest Negro child yet reported —with a tested I.Q. of 200—had no traceable Caucasian heritage whatsoever (Theman & Witty, 1943; Witty & Jenkins, 1936). "Race *per se*," concludes Martin Jenkins, "is not a limiting factor in psychometric intelligence" (1948, p. 401).

There exists, then, a considerable overlap in the I.Q. distributions of the two groups. A few Negroes will score higher than almost all Caucasians, and many Negroes will score higher than most Caucasians. Figure 3 shows

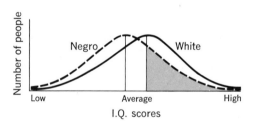

FIGURE 3   Typical test distributions with "25 per cent overlap."

two typical intelligence test distributions with an overlap of 25 per cent, that is, 25 per cent of the Negroes tested (shaded area) surpass the performance of half of the whites tested. Notice how the ranges of the two distributions are virtually the same, even though the means are somewhat different. This figure illustrates one of the most important facts about "race" and measured intelligence: individual differences in I.Q. *within* any one race greatly exceed differences *between* races.

There are two practical consequences of

this phenomenon for desegregated education. First, when a school system institutes a track program of ability grouping, there will be Negroes and whites at all levels. Second, some gifted Negroes will actually lead their biracial classes even during the initial stages of desegregation. Thus, Janice Bell, a seventeen-year-old Negro girl, led the first graduating class of superior students at Beaumount High in St. Louis (*Southern School News*: February, 1962); Julius Chambers, a twenty-four-year-old Negro Southerner, became the 1961–1962 editor of the University of North Carolina's *Law Review* in recognition of his leadership of his law school class (*Southern School News*: June, 1961); and Charles Christian, a thirty-seven-year-old Negro Virginian, led his Medical College of Virginia senior class academically in 1962 (*Southern School News*: June, 1962). "In the study of individuals," summarizes Anastasi, "the only proper unit is the individual" (1958, p. 50).

THE CURRENT CONCLUSION

Intelligence is a plastic product of inherited structure developed by environmental stimulation and opportunity, an alloy of endowment and experience. It can be measured and studied only by inference, through observing behavior defined as "intelligent" in terms of particular cultural content and values. Thus, the severely deprived surroundings of the average Negro child can lower his measured I.Q. in two basic ways. First, it can act to deter his actual intellectual development by presenting him with such a constricted encounter with the world that his innate potential is barely tapped. And, second, it can act to mask his actual functioning intelligence in the test situation by not preparing him culturally and motivationally for such a middle-class task. "Only a very uncritical psychologist would offer sweeping generalizations about the intellectual superiority or inferiority of particular racial or ethnic groups," comments Tuddenham, "despite the not very surprising fact that members of the dominant racial and cultural group in our society ordinarily score higher than others on tests of socially relevant accomplishments invented by and for members of that group" (Tuddenham, 1962, pp. 499–500).

The principal mechanisms for mediating these environmental effects vary from the poor nutrition of the pregnant mother to meeting the expectations of the social role of "Negro." Some of these mechanisms, like fetal brain injuries, can leave permanent intellectual impairments. Consequently, the permanency and irreversibility of these effects are not, as some claim, certain indicators of genetically low capacity. Fortunately, many of these effects are correctable. Moving North to better schools, taking part in special programs of environmental enrichment, and benefiting from challenging new situations of educational desegregation can all stimulate Negro children to raise their I.Q. levels dramatically.

From this array of data, the overwhelming opinion of modern psychology concludes that the mean differences often observed between Negro and white children are largely the result of environmental, rather than genetic, factors. This is *not* to assert that psychologists deny altogether the possibility of inherited racial differences in intellectual structure. There may be a small residual mean difference—small not only because of the demonstrably sweeping influence of experience, but also because the two "races" are by no means genetically "pure" and separate (Chapter 3).

Psychology is joined in this conclusion by its sister behavioral sciences: sociology and anthropology. Witness the following professional statements.

The Society for the Psychological Study of Social Issues, a division of the American Psychological Association, concluded in 1961:

There are differences in intelligence test scores when one compares a random sample of whites and Negroes. What is equally clear is that no evidence exists that leads to the conclusion that such differences are innate. Quite to the contrary, the evidence points overwhelmingly to the fact that when one compares Negroes and whites of comparable cultural and educational background, differences in intelligence diminish markedly; the more comparable the background, the less the difference. There is no direct evidence that supports the view that there is an innate difference between members of different racial groups. . . . We regret that Professor Garrett feels that his colleagues are foisting an "equalitarian dogma" on the public. There is no question of dogma involved. Evidence speaks for itself and it casts serious doubt on the conclusion that there is any innate inequality in intelligence in different racial groups . . .

The Society for the Study of Social Problems, a section of the American Sociological Association, concurred in the same year:

> . . . the great preponderance of scientific opinion has favored the conclusion that there is little or no ground on which to assume that the racial groups in question are innately different in any important human capacity . . . the conclusion of scientists is that the differences in test performance by members of so-called racial groups are due not to racial but to environmental factors. This is the operating assumption today of the vast majority of the competent scientists in the field . . .

The American Anthropological Association passed a resolution by an unanimous vote (192 to 0) in 1961:

> The American Anthropological Association repudiates statements now appearing in the United States that Negroes are biologically and in innate mental ability inferior to whites, and reaffirms the fact that there is no scientifically established evidence to justify the exclusion of any race from the rights guaranteed by the Constitution of the United States. The basic principles of equality of opportunity and equality before the law are compatible with all that is known about human biology. All races possess the abilities needed to participate fully in the democratic way of life and in modern technological civilization.

The final, definitive research must await a racially integrated America in which opportunities are the same for both races. But, ironically, by that future time the question of racial differences in intelligence will have lost its salience; scholars will wonder why we generated so much heat over such an irrelevant topic. Yet the results of this belated research should prove interesting. Even if small inherent differences are found, their direction cannot be taken for granted. Racists have never considered the possibility that the "true" Negro capacity might actually average somewhat above that of the white. Certainly, there are enough environmental barriers operating in the present situation to mask any such Negro superiority. If this possibility should actually be demonstrated, one wonders if white racists would be thoroughly consistent and insist that white children be given separate and inferior education.

The important conclusion for the present, however, is that if there are any inherent distinctions they are inconsequential. Even now, differences in I.Q. within any one race greatly exceed differences between races. Race as such is simply not an accurate way to judge an individual's intelligence. The *real* problems in this area concern ways to overcome the many serious environmental deprivations that handicap Negro youth. To return to the analogy with longevity, the problem is akin to that which faced medicine in the nineteenth century. Automatized America needs to expand the intelligence level of its underprivileged citizens in much the same way it has expanded the life potential of its citizens in the past one hundred years. The success of such programs as "the Banneker group" in St. Louis demonstrates this job can be accomplished when American society decides to put enough of its resources into it. "The U. S. must learn," writes Charles Silberman in *Fortune*, "to look upon the Negro community as if it were an undeveloped country" (1962, p. 151).

REFERENCES

Alper, Thelma G., & Boring, E. G. "Intelligence Test Scores of Northern and Southern White and Negro Recruits in 1918," *Journal of Abnormal and Social Psychology*, 1944, **39**, 471–474.

Anastasi, Anne. "Intelligence and Family Size," *Psychological Bulletin*, 1956, **53**, 187–209.

Anastasi, Anne. *Differential Psychology*. Third edition. New York: Macmillan, 1958.

Anastasi, Anne, & D'Angelo, Rita. "A Comparison of Negro and White Pre-School Children in Language Development and Goodenough Draw-a-Man I.Q.," *Journal of Genetic Psychology*, 1952, **81**, 147–165.

Aptheker, H. "Literacy, and the Negro and World War II," *Journal of Negro Education*, 1946, **15**, 595–602.

Ashmore, H. S. *The Negro and the Schools.* Chapel Hill: University of North Carolina Press, 1954.

Baron, H. "Samuel Shepard and the Banneker Project," *Integrated Education*, April, 1963, **1**, 25–27.

Bean, K. L. "Negro Responses to Verbal and Non-verbal Test Material," *Journal of Psychology*, 1942, **13**, 343–353.

Bexton, W. H., Heron, W., & Scott, T. H.

"Effects of Decreased Variation in the Sensory Environment," *Canadian Journal of Psychology*, 1954, **8,** 70–76.

Boger, J. H. "An Experimental Study of the Effects of Perceptual Training on Group I.Q. Test Scores of Elementary Pupils in Rural Ungraded Schools," *Journal of Educational Research*, 1952, **46,** 43–52.

Brodbeck, A. J., & Irwin, O. C. "The Speech Behavior of Infants without Families," *Child Development*, 1946, **17,** 145–156.

Brown, F. "An Experimental and Critical Study of the Intelligence of Negro and White Kindergarten Children," *Journal of Genetic Psychology*, 1944, **65,** 161–175.

Canady, H. G. "The Effect of 'Rapport' on the I.Q.: A New Approach to the Problem of Racial Psychology," *Journal of Negro Education*, 1936, **5,** 209–219.

Carmichael, L. "A Further Study of the Development of Behavior in Vertebrates Experimentally Removed from the Influence of Environment Stimulation," *Psychological Review*, 1927, **34,** 34–47.

Carson, A. S., & Rabin, A. I. "Verbal Comprehension and Communication in Negro and White Children," *Journal of Educational Psychology*, 1960, **51,** 47–51.

Chant, S. N. F., & Freedman, S. S. "A Quantitative Comparison of the Nationality Preferences of two Groups," *Journal of Social Psychology*, 1934, **5,** 116–120.

Clark, K. B. "The Most Valuable Hidden Resource," *College Board Review*, 1956, **29,** 23–26.

Clark, K. B., & Plotkin, L. *The Negro Student at Integrated Colleges.* New York: National Scholarship Service and Fund for Negro Students, 1963.

Clarke, D. P. "Stanford-Binet Scale L Response Patterns in Matched Racial Groups," *Journal of Negro Education*, 1941, **10,** 230–238.

Coghill, G. E. *Anatomy and the Problem of Behavior.* New York: Macmillan, 1929.

Cooper, R. M., & Zubek, J. M. "Effects of Enriched and Constricted Early Environments on the Learning Ability of Bright and Dull Rats," *Canadian Journal of Psychology*, 1958, **12,** 159–164.

Curti, Margaret W. "Intelligence Tests of White and Colored School Children in Grand Cayman," *Journal of Psychology*, 1960, **49,** 13–27.

Davenport, R. K. "Implications of Military Selection and Classification in Relation to Universal Military Training," *Journal of Negro Education*, 1946, **15,** 585–594.

Davidson, K. S., Gibby, R. G., McNeil, E. B., Segal, S. J., & Silverman, H. "A Preliminary Study of Negro and White Differences in Form I of the Wechsler-Bellevue Scale," *Journal of Consulting Psychology*, 1950, **14,** 489–492.

Dennis, W. "The Effect of Cradling Practices upon the Onset of Walking in Hopi Children," *Journal of Genetic Psychology*, 1940, **56,** 77–86.

Dennis, W. "Causes of Retardation among Institutional Children: Iran," *Journal of Genetic Psychology*, 1960, **96,** 47–59.

DeStephens, W. P. "Are Criminals Morons?" *Journal of Social Psychology*, 1953, **38,** 187–199.

Deutsch, M. "Minority Group and Class Status as Related to Social and Personality Factors in Scholastic Achievement," *Monograph of the Society for Applied Anthropology*, 1960, **2,** 1–32.

Deutsch, M., & Brown, B. "Social Influences in Negro-white intelligence differences. *Journal of Social Issues*, **20,** 1964, 24–35.

Dombey, E. H. "A Comparison of the Intelligence Test Scores of Southern and Northern Born Negroes Residing in Cleveland." Unpublished Master's thesis, Western Reserve University, 1933.

Drillien, C. M. "Physical and Mental Handicap in Prematurely Born," *Journal of Obstetrics and Gynaecology* [British], 1959, **66,** 721–728.

Eagleson, O. W. "Comparative Studies of White and Negro Subjects in Learning to Discriminate Visual Magnitude," *Journal of Psychology*, 1937, **4,** 167–197.

Erickson, R. W. "On Special-Training-Unit Performance as an Index of Negro Ability," *Journal of Abnormal and Social Psychology*, 1946, **41,** 481.

Eyferth, K. "Eine Untersuchung der Neger-Mischlingskinder in Westdeutschland," *Vita Humana*, 1959, **2,** 102–114.

Fowler, W. "Cognitive Learning in Infancy and Early Childhood," *Psychological Bulletin*, 1962, **59,** 116–152.

Franklin, J. C. "Discriminative Value and Patterns of the Wechsler-Bellevue Scales in the Examination of Delinquent Negro Boys," *Educational and Psychological Measurement*, 1945, **5,** 71–85.

Franklin, J. H. *The Militant South: 1800–1861.* Cambridge, Mass.: Harvard University Press, 1956.

Franklin, J. H. *From Slavery to Freedom.* Second edition. New York: Knopf, 1961.

Freeman, F. N., Holzinger, K. J., & Mitchell, B. C. "The Influence of Environment on the Intelligence, School Achievement, and Conduct of Foster Children," *27th Yearbook, National Society of Social Science Education,* 1928, Part I, 103–217.

Garrett, H. E. "Psychological Differences as Among Races," *Science,* 1945, **101,** 16–17.

Garrett, H. E. "A Note on the Intelligence Scores of Negroes and Whites in 1918," *Journal of Abnormal and Social Psychology,* 1945, **40,** 344–346.

Garrett, H. E. "Klineberg's Chapter on Race and Psychology: A Review," *Mankind Quarterly,* 1960, **1,** 15–22.

Garrett, H. E. "The Equalitarian Dogma," *Mankind Quarterly,* 1961, **1,** 253–257.

Garrett, H. E. "Rejoinder by Garrett," *Newsletter of the Society for the Psychological Study of Social Issues,* May, 1962a, 1–2.

Garrett, H. E. "The SPSSI and Racial Differences," *American Psychologist,* 1962b, **17,** 260–263.

George, W. C. *The Biology of the Race Problem.* New York: National Putnam Letters Committee, 1962.

Gilliland, A. R. "Environmental Influences on Infant Intelligence Test Scores," *Harvard Educational Review,* 1949, **19,** 142–146.

Gilliland, A. R. "Socioeconomic Status and Race as Factors in Infant Intelligence Test Scores," *Child Development,* 1951, **22,** 271–273.

Gordon, H. *Mental and Scholastic Tests Among Retarded Children.* London: Board of Education (Educational Pamphlet no. 44), 1923.

Goldfarb, W. "Emotional and Intellectual Consequences of Psychologic Deprivation in Infancy: A Revaluation." In P. H. Hoch and J. Zubin (Eds.), *Psychopathology of Childhood.* New York: Grune, 1955.

Gottesman, I. I. "Genetic Aspects of Intelligent Behavior." In N. Ellis (Ed.), *The Handbook of Mental Deficiency.* New York: McGraw-Hill, 1963, 253–296.

Gough, H. G. "A Nonintellectual Intelligence Test," *Journal of Consulting Psychology,* 1953, **17,** 242–246.

Gray, J. S., & Thompson, A. J. "Ethnic Prejudices of White and Negro College Students," *Journal of Abnormal and Social Psychology,* 1953, **48,** 311–313.

Haggard, E. A. "Social Status and Intelligence: An Experimental Study of Certain Cultural Determinants of Measured Intelligence," *Genetic Psychology Monographs,* 1954, **49,** 141–186.

Hansen, C. F. *Addendum: A Five-Year Report on Desegregation in the Washington, D. C. Schools.* New York: Anti-Defamation League of B'nai B'rith, 1960.

Harlow, H. F. "The Formation of Learning Sets," *Psychological Review,* 1949, **56,** 51–65.

Harper, P. A., Fischer, L. K., & Rider, R. V. "Neurological and Intellectual Status of Prematures at Three to Five Years of Age," *Journal of Pediatrics,* 1959, **55,** 679–690.

Harrell, R. F., Woodyard, E. R., & Gates, A. I. "Influence of Vitamin Supplementation of Diets of Pregnant and Lactating Women on Intelligence of Their Offspring," *Metabolism,* 1956, **5,** 555–562.

Herskovits, M. J. "On the Relation between Negro-White Mixture and Standing in Intelligence Tests," *Pediatrics Sem.,* 1926, **33,** 30–42.

Higgins, C., & Sivers, Cathryne. "A Comparison of Stanford-Binet and Colored Raven Progressive Matrices I.Q.'s for Children with Low Socioeconomic Status," *Journal of Consulting Psychology,* 1958, **22,** 465–468.

Hunt, J. McV. *Intelligence and Experience.* New York: Ronald, 1961.

Hunt, W. A. "Negro-White Differences in Intelligence in World War II—a Note of Caution," *Journal of Abnormal and Social Psychology,* 1947, **42,** 254–255.

Hurst, J. G. "Relationships between Performance on Preschool and Adult Intelligence Measures." Paper presented at the Annual Meeting of the American Psychological Association, Philadelphia, August, 1963.

Hyman, H. H., & Sheatsley, P. B. "Attitudes toward Desegregation," *Scientific American,* 1956, **195,** 35–39.

Ireland, R. R. "An Exploratory Study of Minority Group Membership," *Journal of Negro Education,* 1951, **20,** 164–168.

Jenkins, M. D. "The Upper Limit of Ability among American Negroes," *Scientific Monthly,* 1948, **66,** 399–401.

Jenkins, M. D., & Randall, Constance M.

"Differential Characteristics of Superior and Unselected Negro College Students," *Journal of Social Psychology*, 1948, **27**, 187–202.

Kagan, J., Sontag, L. W., Baker, C. T. & Nelson, Virginia. "Personality and I.Q. Change," *Journal of Abnormal and Social Psychology*, 1958, **56**, 261–266.

Katz, I., Epps, E. G., & Axelson, L. J. "The Effects of Anticipated Comparison with Whites and with Other Negroes upon the Digit-Symbol Performance of Negro College Students." Unpublished paper.

Kirk, S. A. *Early Education of the Mentally Retarded*. Urbana, Ill.: University of Illinois Press, 1958.

Klineberg, O. "An Experimental Study of Speed and Other Factors in 'Racial' Differences," *Archives of Psychology*, 1928, **15**, no. 93.

Klineberg, O. *Negro Intelligence and Selective Migration*. New York: Columbia University Press, 1935.

Knoblock, Hilda, & Pasamanick, B. "Further Observations on the Behavioral Development of Negro Children," *Journal of Genetic Psychology*, 1953, **83**, 137–157.

Knoblock, Hilda, & Pasamanick, B. "Environmental Factors Affecting Human Development before and after Birth," *Pediatrics*, 1960, **26**, 210–218.

Knoblock, Hilda, & Pasamanick, B. "Mental Subnormality," *New England Journal of Medicine*, 1962, **266**, 1092–1097.

Knoblock, Hilda, Rider, R., Harper, P., & Pasamanick, B. "Effect of Prematurity on Health and Growth," *American Journal of Public Health*, 1959, **49**, 1164–1173.

Lee, E. S. "Negro Intelligence and Selective Migration: A Philadelphia Test of the Klineberg Hypothesis," *American Sociological Review*, 1951, **16**, 227–233.

Long, H. H. "The Intelligence of Colored Elementary Pupils in Washington, D.C.," *Journal of Negro Education*, 1934, **3**, 205–222.

Machover, S. "Cultural and Racial Variations in Patterns of Intellect," *Teachers College Contributions to Education*, 1943, no. 875.

MacKenzie, Barbara. "The Importance of Contact in Determining Attitudes toward Negroes," *Journal of Abnormal and Social Psychology*, 1948, **43**, 417–441.

Maller, J. B. "Mental Ability and Its Relation to Physical Health and Social Economic Status," *Psychological Clinic*, 1933, **22**, 101–107.

Mayer, M. "The Good Slum Schools," *Harpers*, April, 1961, **222**, 46–52.

McCauley, P., & Ball, E. D. (Eds.). *Southern Schools: Progress and Problems*. Nashville, Tenn.: Southern Education Reporting Service, 1959.

McCord, W. M., & Demerath, III, N. J. "Negro Versus White Intelligence: A Continuing Controversy," *Harvard Educational Review*, 1958, **28**, 120–135.

McGurk, F. "Socio-Economic Status and Culturally-Weighted Test Scores of Negro Subjects," *Journal of Applied Psychology*, 1953a, **37**, 276–277.

McGurk, F. "On White and Negro Test Performance and Socio-Economic Factors," *Journal of Abnormal and Social Psychology*, 1953b, **48**, 448–450.

McGurk, F. "Psychological Tests: A Scientist's Report on Race Differences," *U. S. News and World Report*, September 21, 1956, 92–96.

McGurk, F. "Negro vs. White Intelligence— an Answer," *Harvard Educational Review*, 1959, **29**, 54–62.

McQueen, R., & Churn, B. "The Intelligence and Educational Achievement of a Matched Sample of White and Negro Students," *School and Society*, 1960, **88**, 327–329.

Metropolitan Life Insurance Company, "Progress in Longevity since 1850," *Statistical Bulletin*, July, 1963, **44**, 1–3.

Montagu, M. F. A. "Intelligence of Northern Negroes and Southern Whites in the First World War," *American Journal of Psychology*, 1945, **58**, 161–188.

Murray, W. I. "The I. Q. and Social Class in the Negro Caste," *Southwestern Journal of Anthropology*, 1949, **4**, 187–201.

Newland, T. E., & Lawrence, W. C. "Chicago Non-Verbal Examination Results on an East Tennessee Negro Population," *Journal of Clinical Psychology*, 1953, **9**, 44–46.

Newsweek editors. "The Negro in America," *Newsweek*, July 29, 1963, **62**, 15–34.

Newsweek editors. "How Whites Feel about Negroes: A Painful American Dilemma," *Newsweek*, October 21, 1963, **62**, 44–57.

Osborn, R. T. "Racial Differences in Mental Growth and School Achievement: A Longitudinal Study," *Psychological Reports*, 1960, **7**, 233–239.

Pasamanick, B. "A Comparative Study of the

Behavioral Development of Negro Infants," *Journal of Genetic Psychology*, 1946, **69**, 3–44.

Pasamanick, B., & Knapp, P. H. (Eds.). *Social Aspects of Psychiatry*, Washington, D.C.: American Psychiatric Association, 1958.

Pasamanick, B., & Knoblock, Hilda. "Early Language Behavior in Negro Children and the Testing of Intelligence," *Journal of Abnormal and Social Psychology*, 1955, **50**, 401–402.

Pasamanick, B., & Knoblock, Hilda. "The Contribution of Some Organic Factors to School Retardation in Negro Children," *Journal of Negro Education*, 1958, **27**, 4–9.

Peterson, J., & Lanier, L. H. "Studies in the Comparative Abilities of Whites and Negroes," *Mental Measurement Monograph*, 1929, no. 5.

Pettigrew, T. F. "The Negro Respondent: New Data on Old Problems," Unpublished paper.

Piaget, J. *The Psychology of Intelligence.* Translated by M. Piercy & D. E. Berlyne. London: Routledge and Kegan Paul, 1947.

Price, D. O., & Searles, Ruth. "Some Effects of Interviewer-Respondent Interaction on Responses in a Survey Situation." Paper presented at the Annual Meeting of the American Statistical Association, held in New York, December 30, 1961.

Putnam, C. *Race and Reason: A Yankee View.* Washington, D.C.: Public Affairs Press, 1961.

Reitzes, D. C. *Negroes and Medicine.* Cambridge, Mass.: Harvard University Press, 1958.

Roberts, S. O. "Socioeconomic Status and Performance on the ACE of Negro Freshmen College Veterans and Non-Veterans, from the North and South," *American Psychologist*, 1948, **3**, 266.

Robinson, Mary L., & Meenes, M. "The Relationship between Test Intelligence of Third Grade Negro Children and the Occupations of Their Parents," *Journal of Negro Education*, 1947, **16**, 136–141.

Roen, S. R. "Personality and Negro-White Intelligence," *Journal of Abnormal and Social Psychology*, 1960, **61**, 148–150.

Rohrer, J. H. "The Test Intelligence of Osage Indians," *Journal of Social Psychology*, 1942, **16**, 99–105.

St. John, Nancy. "The Relation of Racial Segregation in Early Schooling to the Level of Aspiration and Academic Achievement of Negro Students in a Northern High School." Unpublished doctoral thesis, Harvard University, 1962.

Semler, I. J., & Iscoe, I. "Comparative and Developmental Study of the Learning Abilities of Negro and White Children under Four Conditions," *Journal of Educational Psychology*, 1963, **54**, 38–44.

Shuey, Audrey. *The Testing of Negro Intelligence.* Lynchburg, Va.: Bell, 1958.

Silberman, C. E. "The City and the Negro," *Fortune*, March, 1962, **65**, 89–91, 139–154.

Smart, Mollie S. "Confirming Klineberg's Suspicion," *American Psychologist*, 1963, **18**, 621.

Society for the Psychological Study of Social Issues. "Guidelines for Testing Minority Group Children." Pamphlet in press.

Sontag, L. W., Baker, C. T., & Nelson, Virginia. "Personality as a Determinant of Performance," *American Journal of Orthopsychiatry*, 1955, **25**, 555–562.

Southern Regional Council. "Did You Find That There Was Much Difference in the Ability of Negro Children to Receive and Profit by Instruction?" *Report No. L-13*, December 15, 1959.

Southern Regional Council. "Desegregation and Academic Achievement," *Report No. L-17*, March 14, 1960.

Southern School News: (a) May, 1958, **4** (11); (b) January, 1959, **5**(7); (c) May, 1959, **5**(11); (d) July, 1959, **6**(1); (e) August, 1959, **6**(2); (f) December, 1959, **6**(6); (g) January, 1960, **6**(7); (h) April, 1960, **6**(10); (i) May, 1960, **6**(11); (j) June, 1960, **6**(12); (k) July, 1960, **7**(1); (l) August, 1960, **7**(2); (m) November, 1960, **7**(5); (n) February, 1961, **7**(8); (o) June, 1961, **7**(12); (p) September, 1961, **8**(3); (q) February, 1962, **8**(8); and (r) June, 1962, **8**(12).

Stallings, F. H. "A Study of the Immediate Effects of Integration on Scholastic Achievement in the Louisville Public Schools," *Journal of Negro Education*, 1959, **28**, 439–444.

Stallings, F. H. "Racial Differences and Academic Achievement," *Southern Regional Council's Report No. L-16*, February 26, 1960.

Stalnaker, J. M. "Identification of the Best Southern Negro High School Seniors," *Scientific Monthly*, 1948, **67**, 237–239.

Stetler, H. G. *Comparative Study of Negro and White Dropouts in Selected Connecticut High Schools*. Hartford: Connecticut Commission on Civil Rights, 1959.

Stoddard, G. D. *The Meaning of Intelligence*. New York: Macmillan, 1943.

Stringer, Lorene A. "Academic Progress as an Index of Mental Health," *Journal of Social Issues*, 1959, **15**, 16–29.

Tanser, H. A. *The Settlement of Negroes in Kent County, Ontario, and a Study of the Mental Capacity of Their Descendants*. Chatham, Ontario: Shephard, 1939.

Theman, V., & Witty, P. A. "Case Studies and Genetic Records of Two Gifted Negroes," *Journal of Psychology*, 1943, **15**, 165–181.

Thompson, W. R., & Heron, W. "The Effects of Restricting Early Experience on the Problem-Solving Capacity of dogs," *Canadian Journal of Psychology*, 1954, **8**, 17–31.

Thompson, W. R., & Melzack, R. "Early Environment," *Scientific American*, 1956, **194**(1), 38–42.

Thorndike, E. L., & Woodyard, Ella. "Differences within and between Communities in the Intelligence of Children," *Journal of Educational Psychology*, 1942, **33**, 641–656.

Thorndike, R. L. "Community Variables as Predictors of Intelligence and Academic Achievement," *Journal of Educational Psychology*, 1951, **42**, 321–338.

Tomlinson, H. "Differences between Pre-school Negro Children and Their Older Siblings on the Stanford-Binet Scales," *Journal of Negro Education*, 1944, **13**, 474–479.

Trumbull, R. "A Study in Relationships between Factors of Personality and Intelligence," *Journal of Social Psychology*, 1953, **38**, 161–173.

Tuddenham, R. D. "Soldier Intelligence in World Wars I and II," *American Psychologist*, 1948, **3**, 54–56.

United States News and World Report: (a) September 28, 1956, **41**, 98–107; (b) October 5, 1956, **41**, 68–69; (c) October 12, 1956, **41**, 82–88; and (d) January 4, 1957, **42**, 92–100.

Weisskopf, Edith. "Intellectual Malfunctioning and Personality," *Journal of Abnormal and Social Psychology*, 1951, **46**, 410–423.

Wellman, Beth L, & Pegram, Edna L. "Benet I.Q. Changes of Orphanage Preschool Children: A Re-analysis," *Journal of Genetic Psychology*, 1944, **65**, 239–263.

Witty, P. "New Evidence on the Learning Ability of the Negro," *Journal of Abnormal and Social Psychology*, 1945, **40**, 401–404.

Witty, P. "Reply to Mr. Erickson," *Journal of Abnormal and Social Psychology*, 1946, **41**, 482–485.

Witty, P., & Jenkins, M. D. "Intra-Race Testing and Negro Intelligence," *Journal of Psychology*, 1936, **1**, 179–192.

Woods, W. A., & Toal, R. "Subtest Disparity of Negro and White Groups Matched for I.Q.'s on the Revised Beta Test," *Journal of Consulting Psychology*, 1957, **21**, 136–138.

15

Learning patterns in the disadvantaged

SUSAN STODOLSKY AND GERALD S. LESSER

THE ORIGINAL STUDY

Aims

Our goal was to examine the patterns among various mental abilities in six- and seven-year-old children from different social-class and ethnic backgrounds. We accepted the definition of intelligence which postulates diverse mental abilities and proposes that intelligent behavior can be manifested in a wide variety of forms, with each individual displaying certain areas of intellectual strength and other forms of intellectual weakness. A basic premise of this study is that social-class and ethnic influences differ not only in degree

Design

Hypotheses were tested regarding the effects of social-class and ethnic-group affiliation (and their interactions) upon both the level of each mental ability considered singly and the pattern among mental abilities considered in combination. Four mental abilities (Verbal ability, Reasoning, Number facility, and Space Conceptualization) were studied in first-grade children from four ethnic groups (Chinese, Jewish, Negro, and Puerto Rican). Each ethnic group was divided into two social-class components (middle and lower), each in turn being divided into equal numbers of boys and girls.

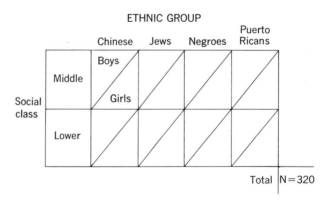

but in kind, with the consequence that different kinds of intellectual skills are fostered or hindered in different environments.

Excerpt (pp. 562–578) reprinted from *Harvard Educational Review*, **37**, Fall 1967, 546–593. Copyright © 1967 by President and Fellows of Harvard College. Reprinted by permission of the authors and *Harvard Educational Review*.

Thus, a 4 × 2 × 2 analysis-of-covariance design included a total of sixteen subgroups, each composed of twenty children. A total sample of 320 first-grade children was drawn from forty-five different elementary schools in New York City and its environs. Three test influences were controlled statistically: effort, responsiveness to the tester, and age of the subject.

The selection of four mental abilities (Verbal ability, Reasoning, Number facility, and Space Conceptualization) is described in detail elsewhere (Lesser, Fifer, & Clark, 1965, pp. 32–43). To obtain a first approximation to the assessment of intra-individual profiles of scores for the various mental abilities of children, these skills were assessed:

VERBAL

The skill is defined as memory for verbal labels in which reasoning elements, such as those required by verbal analogies, are reduced to a minimum. Verbal ability has long been regarded as the best single predictor of success in academic courses, especially in the language and social-science fields. It is involved to a marked degree in the work of all professions and in most semiprofessional areas.

REASONING

Reasoning involves the ability to formulate concepts, to weave together ideas and concepts, and to draw conclusions and inferences from them. It is, almost by definition, the central element of aptitude for intellectual activities and, therefore, is of primary importance in all academic fields and in most vocations.

NUMBER

The ability is defined as skill in enumeration and in memory and use of the fundamental combinations in addition, subtraction, multiplication, and division. It is of great importance in arithmetic in elementary schools and in mathematics in secondary schools.

SPACE CONCEPTUALIZATION

The ability refers to a cluster of skills related to spatial relations and sizes of objects and to visualizing their movements in space. It is involved in geometry, trigonometry, mechanics, and drafting; in elementary-school activities, such as practical arts and drawing; and in occupations such as mechanics, engineering, and architecture.

Procedural Issues

In this brief report, it is impossible to describe all the details of the procedures employed. Yet since research on the intellectual performance of "disadvantaged" children does impose some unique demands upon the investigator, at least the following procedural issues should be outlined.

A. GAINING ACCESS TO THE SCHOOLS

Perhaps the most formidable problem was that of gaining the cooperation of school boards and school authorities for research on such a supposedly controversial issue. An honest approach by the researcher to the school authorities must contain the words "ethnic," "Negro," "Jewish," and "lower-class," and yet it is precisely these loaded words which arouse immediate anxiety and resistance in those who are authorized to permit or reject research in the schools. We believed that our objective of supplying information and understanding about the intellectual strengths and weaknesses of the children being taught in school would be a strong inducement to participation. Not so. Only enormous persistence and lengthy negotiation—during which the researcher must agree to a succession of incapacitating constraints—permits such research at all.

Surely there are serious problems of ethics in educational research. Researchers should be (and most often are) as scrupulous as school authorities in maintaining the conditions of consent and confidentiality which protect subjects from unwarranted intrusions of privacy. But the legitimate ethical issues of privacy and free inquiry are not those that block access to the schools—the fear of controversy over racial issues seems to immobilize school authorities.

Beyond our own experiences in gaining access to the schools, numerous examples exist of how research on the disadvantaged is prevented or distorted by the decisions of school authorities. For example, in Coleman's (Coleman et al., 1966) study of *Equality of Educational Opportunity*, requested by the President and Congress of the United States, many major cities refused to participate, often because comparisons among racial groups were being made (although reasons for refusal were rarely stated).

Later in this paper, we shall discuss several new directions for future research comparing "disadvantaged" and "non-disadvantaged" children. These suggestions will remain the mental exercises of the academics unless some reasonable policies can be developed by researchers and school authorities to provide honest access to the school children, their parents, and their teachers.

B. LOCATING SOCIAL-CLASS AND ETHNIC-GROUP SAMPLES

An associated problem was to achieve an unambiguous definition and assessment of social-class and ethnic-group placement. (The detailed procedures used for sample selection are described in Lesser, Fifer, & Clark, 1965, pp. 21–32.) Both variables are clearly multidimensional in character, and to define and measure the necessary components in each is a formidable task. Since members of each ethnic group were to be located in both lower- and middle-class categories, additional problems arose in attempting to maintain an equal degree of separation between the two social-class categories for each ethnic group.

In addition, obtaining the data necessary to identify the social-class and ethnic-group placement of each child presented many practical problems. There are strong legal restrictions in New York State upon collecting the data necessary for social-class and ethnic identification—and these restrictions are perhaps quite justified—but since we were not allowed to ask parents or school authorities directly about education, or religion, or even occupation, we were forced to use information gathered indirectly through twenty-three different community agencies and four sources of census and housing statistics. Among sources such as the New York City Regional Planning Association, the Commonwealth of Puerto Rico, the China Institute in America, the Demographic Study Commission of the Federation of Jewish Philanthropies, and the *New York Daily News* Advertising Department, our best single source of information was one of the largest advertising agencies in New York City, which has within its "Component Advertising Division" (which develops special marketing appeals for different ethnic groups) enormous deposits of information on the locations of the many cultural groups in New York City. There was little willingness, of course, to allow us to use these data. But after endless sitting-in and sheer pestering, we were given access to this information. We could not possibly have completed this study without it.

C. DEVELOPING "CULTURE-FAIR" TEST MATERIALS

Perhaps the major technical problem was to insure the fact that observed differences among social-class and ethnic groups are in the children and not in the test materials themselves (or in the definitions upon which the tests are based). Therefore, tests were constructed which presuppose only experiences that are common and familiar within all of the different social-class and ethnic groups in an urban area. We had no intention to "free" the test materials from cultural influence, but rather to utilize elements which appear commonly in all cultural groups in New York City. If, for example, other Picture Vocabulary tests use pictures of xylophones or giraffes (which a middle-class child is more likely than a lower-class child to encounter in a picture book or in a zoo), we used pictures of buses, fire hydrants, lamp posts, garbage trucks, and police cars—objects to which all urban children are exposed.

D. CONTROLLING "EXAMINER BIAS"

Each child was tested by an examiner who shared the child's ethnic identity in order to maintain chances of establishing good rapport and to permit test administration in the child's primary language, or in English, or, more often, in the most effective combination of languages for the particular child. Thus, we had a Negro tester, a Spanish-speaking Puerto Rican tester, a Yiddish-speaking Jewish tester, and three Chinese-speaking Chinese testers to accommodate the eight different Chinese dialects encountered among our Chinese children. Each tester had been trained beyond the Master's degree level, and each had extensive experience administering psychological tests; but the tendency of the testers to empathize with the children from their own cultural groups demanded careful control of the testing procedures to insure uniform test administration. This standardization was accomplished through extensive video-tape training in which each examiner observed other testers and himself administer the test materials.

Some Findings

Hypotheses were tested regarding the influence of social class and ethnicity (and their interactions) upon the levels of the four mental-ability scores and upon the patterns among them. The results are summarized in Table 1.

TABLE 1   Summary of Results

Source of Influence	Effect upon Mental Abilities	
	Level	Pattern
Ethnicity	Highly Significant*	Highly Significant*
Social Class	Highly Significant*	Nonsignificant
Social Class x Ethnicity	Significant**	Nonsignificant

* p < .001.
** p < .05.

a. Distinctive ethnic-group differences: Ethnic groups are markedly different (p<.001) *both* in the absolute *level* of each mental ability and in the *pattern* among these abilities. For example, with regard to the effects of ethnicity upon the *level* of each ability, Figure 1 shows that

(1) on Verbal ability, Jewish children ranked first (being significantly better than all other ethnic groups), Negroes second, Chinese third (both being significantly better than Puerto Ricans), and Puerto Ricans fourth.

(2) on Space Conceptualization, Chinese ranked first (being significantly better than Puerto Ricans and Negroes), Jews second, Puerto Ricans third, and Negroes fourth.

But the most striking results of this study concern the effects of ethnicity upon the *patterns* among the mental abilities. Figure 1 (and the associated analyses-of-variance for group patterns) shows that these *patterns* are different for each ethnic group. More important is the finding depicted in Figures 2–5. Ethnicity does affect the pattern of mental abilities *and, once the pattern specific to the ethnic group emerges, social-class variations within the ethnic group do not alter this basic organization.* For example, Figure 2 shows the mental-ability pattern peculiar to the Chinese children—with the pattern displayed by the middle-class Chinese children duplicated at a lower level of performance by the lower-class Chinese children. Figure 3 shows the mental-ability pattern specific to the

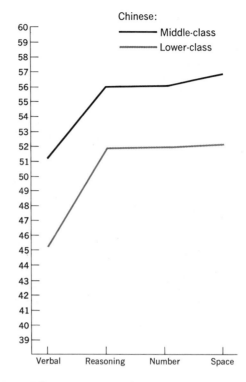

FIGURE 1 Patterns of normalized mental-ability scores for each ethnic group.

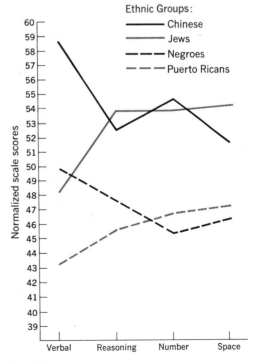

FIGURE 2 Patterns of normalized mental-ability scores for middle- and lower-class Chinese children.

Jewish children—with the pattern displayed by the middle-class Jewish children duplicated at a lower level of performance by the lower-class Jewish children. Parallel statements can be made for each ethnic group.

The failure of social-class conditions to transcend patterns of mental ability associated with ethnic influences was unexpected. Social-class influences have been described as superseding ethnic-group effects for such diverse phenomena as child-rearing practices, educational and occupational aspirations, achievement motivation, and anomie. The greater salience of social class over ethnic membership is reversed in the present findings on patterns of mental ability. Ethnicity has the primary effect upon the organization of mental abilities, and the organization is not modified further by social-class influences.

Many other findings are described in our full report of this original study (Lesser, Fifer, & Clark, 1965). Only a few additional findings will be mentioned here, either because they are prominent in our recent

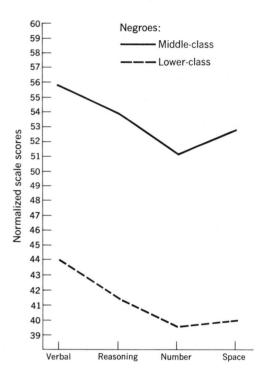

FIGURE 4 Patterns of normalized mental-ability scores for middle- and lower-class Negro children.

replication study or in our plans for future research.

b. Interactions between social-class and ethnicity: Table 1, summarizing our earlier findings, indicates significant interactions ($p < .05$) between social class and ethnicity on the level of each mental ability. Table 2 shows the mean level of each mental ability for Chinese and Negro children from each social-class group; the same interaction effects appear when Jewish and Puerto Rican children are included, but the present table has been reduced to the Chinese and Negro children to simplify the present discussion. Two effects combine to produce the interaction effect between social class and ethnicity:

(1) On each mental-ability scale, social-class position produces more of a difference in the mental abilities of the Negro children than for the other groups. That is, the middle-class Negro children are more different in level of mental abilities from the lower-class Negroes than, for example, the middle-class Chinese are from the lower-class Chinese.

(2) On each mental-ability scale, the scores

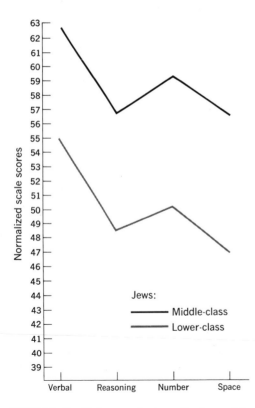

FIGURE 3 Patterns of normalized mental-ability scores for middle- and lower-class Jewish children.

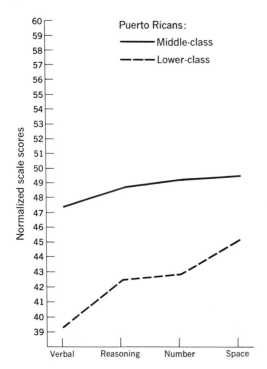

FIGURE 5 Patterns of normalized mental-ability scores for middle- and lower-class Puerto Rican children.

of the middle-class children from the various ethnic groups resemble each other to a greater extent than do the scores of the lower-class children from the various ethnic groups. That is, the middle-class Chinese, Jewish, Negro, and Puerto Rican children are more alike in their mental ability scores than are the lower-class Chinese, Jewish, Negro, and Puerto Rican children.

Some earlier research (see Anastasi, 1958, Chapter 15) suggested that social-class influences upon intelligence are greater in white than in Negro groups. No distinct contrast with white children was available in our study, but the evidence indicates that social-class influences upon the mental abilities of Negro children are very great compared with the other ethnic groups represented. One explanation for the apparent contrast between the earlier and present findings is that the earlier research, perhaps, did not include middle- and lower-class Negro groups that were distinctively different. In any event; our findings show that the influence of social class on the level of abilities is more powerful for the Negro group than for the other ethnic groups.

c. Group data vs. individual data: The data analyses described to this point refer to differences in the performance of groups and not to the performance of individuals. These analyses do not indicate how an individual will perform, but they suggest how he is likely to perform if he belongs to one of these eight groups. One technique we have used to proceed from group analyses to identifying particular patterns for individuals is called a "classification analysis" (see Table 3). This analysis allows the researcher to compare the pattern of mental-ability scores for each individual subject with the pattern profiles

TABLE 2 Mean Mental-Ability Scores for Chinese and Negro Children for Each Social-Class Group

	Verbal				Reasoning		
	Chinese	Negro			Chinese	Negro	
Middle	76.8	85.7	81.3	Middle	27.7	26.0	26.9
Lower	65.3	62.9	64.1	Lower	24.2	14.8	19.5
	71.1	74.3	72.7		25.9	20.4	23.2

Class x ethnicity, $F = 7.69$, $p < .01$ Class x ethnicity, $F = 11.32$, $p. < .01$

	Number				Space		
	Chinese	Negro			Chinese	Negro	
Middle	30.0	24.7	27.4	Middle	44.9	41.8	43.4
Lower	26.2	12.1	19.2	Lower	40.4	27.1	33.8
	28.1	18.4	23.3		42.7	34.4	38.6

Class x ethnicity, $F = 8.91$, $p < .01$ Class x ethnicity, $F = 10.83$, $p < .01$

TABLE 3 Classification Analysis

Group N = 40, each Group	Group Patterns							
	M Ch	L Ch	M J	L J	M N	L N	M PR	L PR
Middle Chinese	13*	10	6	1	5	1	2	2
Lower Chinese	6	14	2	4	3	1	1	9
Middle Jewish	4	0	32	4	0	0	0	0
Lower Jewish	0	1	9	18	7	4	0	1
Middle Negro	5	1	11	10	11	0	0	2
Lower Negro	1	3	0	3	0	28	0	5
Middle Puerto Rican	6	6	3	6	4	0	3	12
Lower Puerto Rican	0	7	1	1	0	8	3	20

* Figures to read across as follows: The scores of 13 middle-class Chinese subjects fit the middle-class Chinese pattern and level on the four mental ability scales; 10 middle-class Chinese look more like lower-class Chinese; 6 look more like middle-class Jews, 1 more like a lower-class Jew, etc.

of his group and other groups. It yields data on the degree to which a subject's profile resembles the profile of his or the other groups (Tatsuoka, 1957). If mental-ability scores were not associated significantly with social class and ethnicity and hence a chance frequency of correct placement of individuals occurred, random cell assignment in Table 3 would be approximately five cases per cell. Thus, if the forty middle-class Chinese children showed no distinctive pattern of their own, they would be expected to be distributed equally among all eight group patterns. The deviation of the actual frequencies in the underlined diagonal cells from the chance frequency of five indicates the degree of correct classification beyond chance obtained through knowledge of the individual's mental-ability scores. Thus, thirty-two middle-class Jewish children and twenty-eight lower-class Negro children fit their group patterns. In contrast, only three middle-class Puerto Rican children (two less than chance) were classified correctly. It is clear that the middle-class Puerto Rican children were the most heterogeneous of the eight groups. Overall, the number of cases classified correctly through knowledge of the mental-ability pattern surpassed chance classification at a probability value associated with thirty-six zeroes; i.e., the probability value for correct classifications was less than one in ten to the thirty-fifth exponent. In short, knowledge of the child's pattern of mental abilities allows the correct identification of

his social-class and ethnic-group membership to a degree far exceeding chance expectations.

We note this analysis for two reasons. Methodologically, it provides a useful device for moving from group data to the analysis of the individual case. Substantively, it has allowed us to identify the children who fit closely the profile of their group and those who are exceptions in their group but resemble the profile of some other group. This capability allows us to pinpoint cases in exploring questions about the origins of patterns of mental ability and about the fitting of school practices to these patterns.

Some Conclusions

The study demonstrated that several mental abilities are organized in ways that are determined culturally. Referring to social-class and ethnic groups, Anastasi (1958) proposed that "groups differ in their relative standing on different functions. Each . . . fosters the development of a different pattern of abilities." Our data lend selective support to this position. Both social-class and ethnic groups do "differ in their relative standing on different functions"; i.e., both social class and ethnicity affect the *level* of intellectual performance. However, only ethnicity "fosters the development of a different *pattern* of abilities," while social-class differences within the ethnic groups do not modify these basic patterns associated with ethnicity.

To return to our continuing discussion of

defining and delimiting the term "disadvantaged." Defining the "disadvantaged" as belonging to a particular ethnic group has one set of consequences for the development of intellectual skills—ethnic groups differ in both level and pattern of mental abilities. Defining the term using the social-class criteria of occupation, education, and neighborhood leads to quite different consequences—social-class affects level of ability, with middle class being uniformly superior; but does not alter the basic patterns of mental ability associated with ethnicity. Still other definitions—for example, unavailability of English language models, presence of a threatening and chaotic environment, matriarchal family structure, high family mobility, parental absence or apathy, poor nutrition—probably generate still other consequences, although we really know very little empirically about these relationships.

A REPLICATION STUDY [1]

Since our early results were both surprising and striking in magnitude, our next step was to conduct a replication and extension with first-graders in Boston. The replication was conducted with middle-class and lower-class Chinese and Negro children (the samples of Jewish and Puerto Rican children who fit our social-class criteria, were not available); the extension included an additional ethnic group—children from middle- and lower-class Irish-Catholic families.

Once again, the results were both striking and surprising. The replication data on Chinese and Negro children in Boston duplicated almost exactly our earlier data on similar samples in New York City. The striking, almost identical test performances in the original and replication study are shown in Figures 6–10. The raw mean scores of the Chinese children in Boston and in New York were different by an average of one-third of one standard deviation (Figure 6), and the Negro children in Boston and in New York were one-fifth of one standard deviation different from each other (Figure 7). Only one mean difference (numerical scores of Boston

[1] This replication study was conducted under the direction of Dr. Jane Fort, Laboratory of Human Development, Harvard University.

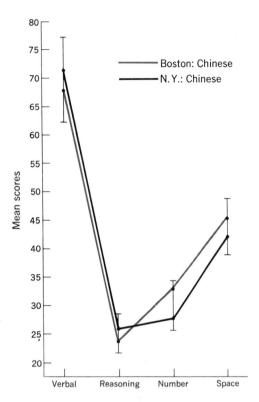

FIGURE 6 Mean mental-ability scores for Chinese children in Boston ($N = 20$) and New York ($N = 80$).

and New York Chinese) slightly exceeded one-half of one standard deviation.

The resemblance of the original and replication samples in patterns of mental ability is shown in Figure 8 (which contrasts the ethnic groups in the two cities with middle- and lower-class samples combined), Figure 9 (which displays the Chinese patterns in Boston and New York for each social-class group), Figure 10 (which displays the Negro patterns in Boston and New York for each social-class group). With very few exceptions (number skills, especially multiplication and division, of the middle-class Chinese in Boston are slightly superior to the middle-class Chinese in New York), both the levels and patterns of mental ability in the Boston data almost duplicate the New York City data for Chinese and Negro children.

This replication study also included an ethnic group not previously studied in New York City: middle- and lower-class Irish-Catholic children. These first-grade Irish-Catholic children, in contrast to all the other ethnic groups tested, displayed neither a distinctive ethnic-group pattern nor similarity of patterns for middle- and lower-class segments of the Irish-Catholic sample. Although we have no definitive explanation of this finding as yet, the absence of a distinctive ethnic-group pattern may be related to our failure to locate homogeneous concentrations of middle- and lower-class Irish-Catholic families in Boston. The Irish-Catholic families are less confined to limited geographic areas than the other ethnic groups. We could not locate either middle- or lower-class Irish-Catholic families who fit clearly the occupational, educational, and neighborhood criteria for social-class placement. In short, there are at least two plausible explanations for the failure to replicate our results on other ethnic groups with the Irish-Catholic children: poor sampling of middle-class and lower-class Irish-Catholic families (due to their unexpected unavailability in Boston) or a real difference between Irish-Catholic children and those from other ethnic groups tested.

In the report of our original study, we noted an interaction effect between social class and ethnicity in which the social-class difference produces more of a difference in

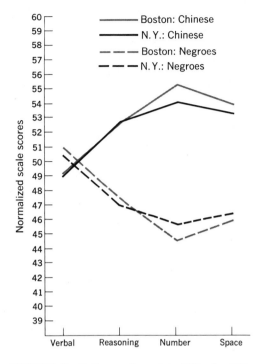

FIGURE 8 Patterns of mental ability for Chinese and Negro children: NY vs. Boston.

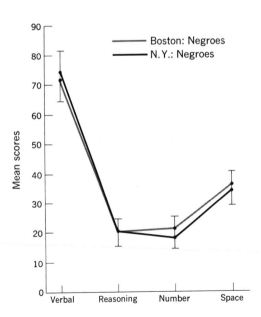

FIGURE 7 Mean mental-ability scores for Negro children in Boston ($N = 20$) and New York ($N = 80$).

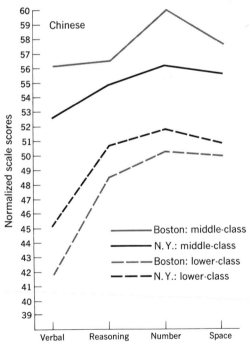

FIGURE 9 Patterns of mental ability for Chinese children; middle- and lower-class, NY vs. Boston.

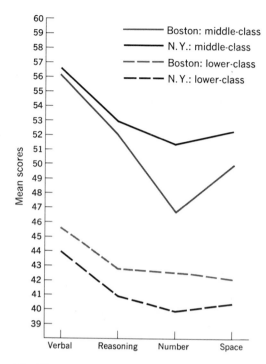

FIGURE 10 Patterns of mental ability for Negro children; middle- and lower-class; NY vs. Boston.

the mental abilities of the Negro children than for the other ethnic groups. In the replication study, this finding reappeared: the middle-class Negro children are more different in level of mental abilities from the lower-class Negro children than the middle-class Chinese or Irish-Catholic children are from the lower-class Chinese or Irish-Catholic children. It was also true in the replication, as in the original data, that the scores of the middle-class children from the various ethnic groups resembled each other more than the scores of the lower-class children from these ethnic groups. That is, the middle-class Chinese, Irish-Catholic, and Negro children are more alike in their mental ability scores (with the one exception of the middle-class Chinese in numerical ability) than are the lower-class Chinese, Irish-Catholic, and Negro children.

One further specific analysis should be noted before proceeding to a discussion of future research and the implications for educational policy. We have assessed the relative contributions of the five ethnic groups tested to the distinctiveness of ethnic-group patterning. The percentage of total ethnicity variance contributed by each ethnic group appears in Table 4. While the groups differ markedly in their relative contributions to the distinctiveness of ethnic-group patterns, all except the Irish-Catholic contribute to a statistically significant degree.

TABLE 4 Percentage of Variance Contributed by Each Ethnic Group to the Group x Tests Interaction Term

Ethnic Group	% of Variance
Chinese	39
Irish-Catholic	1
Jewish	38
Negro	13
Puerto Rican	9

Some results of Coleman's recent study, *Equality of Educational Opportunity*, are compatible with these findings. The study included children from Oriental-American, Negro, Puerto Rican, Mexican-American, Indian-American, and white groups. This study does not include all our mental-ability variables nor does it provide a good assessment of social-class for the younger children, but Coleman's data for Chinese, Negro, and Puerto Rican children on Verbal and Reasoning tests show patterns very similar to ours.

We have some confidence, then, in our earlier findings on the effects of social-class and ethnic-group influence on the development of patterns of mental abilities in young children: at least several mental abilities are organized in ways that are determined culturally, social class producing differences in the *level* of mental abilities (the middle-class being higher) and ethnic groups producing differences in both *level* and *pattern* of mental abilities.

16

Some motivational determinants of racial differences in intellectual achievement[1]

IRWIN KATZ

It is of considerable scientific and practical significance that in all regions of the United States the scholastic performance of Negro youth is, on the average, inferior to that of whites. The achievement gap has always existed, yet psychologists and educators lack precise understanding of its causes. Until recently there was little research done on the problem, and most of it was narrowly concerned with the measurement of racial differences in IQ scores. There is now emerging a more promising trend toward studies of cognitive and motivational processes in the development of children from different social backgrounds. This paper will examine the academic achievement of Negro students from the standpoint of some general concepts of motivational processes underlying the development of intellectual achievement behavior.

The basic facts about the public education of Negro Americans were recently assessed by Coleman *et al.* (1966) in a nationwide survey involving 645,000 pupils in over 4,000 elementary and high schools. This report describes conditions that have long been known to educators from informal observations. (a) On objective tests of scholastic achievement and ability, the average scores of Negroes at every grade level that was studied are about one standard deviation below white norms. This means that about 85 per cent of the Negro school population test below white averages for their grade levels. The racial gap, when expressed in terms of Negro and white score distributions remains fairly constant in the North throughout the school years, while in the South it grows progressively larger from grade 1 to grade 12. (b) In the North as well as the South most Negro students (about 66 percent for the entire nation) attend public schools with predominantly nonwhite enrollments. (c) Throughout the country the quality of educational services, including school curriculums and facilities, and the verbal ability of teachers, that are available to minority group members are usually inferior to those enjoyed by whites in the same communities. These facts provide the background against which to examine motivational aspects of Negro performance in the classroom. A number of general concepts for analyzing achievement striving have been advanced during the last few years.

THE ATKINSON MODEL OF ACHIEVEMENT MOTIVATION

Atkinson (1964) has proposed a conceptual model of achievement motivation in which the strength of the impulse to strive for success on a given task is regarded as a joint function of the person's motive to achieve (measured as a personality characteristic), the subjective probability of success,

Reprinted from *International Journal of Psychology*, 1967, **2**, 1–12, by permission of the author and the publishers.

[1] The preparation of this paper was supported under research contract N00014-67-A-0181-0004 between the Office of Naval Research and the University of Michigan.

and the incentive value of success. The notion of a motive to achieve, which grew out of McClelland's work on *n* Achievement (McClelland *et al.*, 1953), stresses a predisposition to experience gratification or its opposite in connection with self-evaluations of the quality of own performance. The incentive value of success is assumed by Atkinson to be equal to the apparent difficulty of the task, that is, to be an inverse function of the subjective probability of success. According to the model, on a task that has evaluative significance, *e.g.*, a classroom test, motivation is maximal when the perceived probability of success is intermediate, *i.e.*, is at the .50 level. One way in which the model has relevance for the study of minority group students is with respect to the effect of variations in the race of teachers and classmates on the expectancy of success, and the incentive value of success.

In a number of experiments the present author and associates found that Negro male college students tended to underperform on intellectual tasks when whites were present. These studies were reviewed in an article (Katz, 1964) which also speculated that for Negroes who find themselves in predominantly white academic achievement situations, the incentive value of success is high but the expectancy of success is low. This is because white standards of achievement are perceived as higher than own-race standards. By the same token, the perceived value of favorable evaluation by a white adult authority is high, but the expectancy of receiving it is low. Therefore, by experimentally controlling Negro subjects' expectancy of success on cognitive tasks it should be possible to produce the same, if not higher, levels of performance in white situations as in all-Negro situations.

Experiments have recently been carried out to test this line of reasoning. One study was done at a southern Negro college that has no admission criteria other than high school graduation. Most of the students had attended southern segregated public schools. Only a part of the experimental procedure and results need be described. Male freshmen were administered a digit-symbol task that was described as being part of a scholastic aptitude test. Their scores, they were told in advance, would be evaluated by comparison with the norms of certain other colleges,

which they knew to have predominantly white student bodies. By means of false feedback about their scores on a previous practice trial of the same test, one third of the men were led to believe they had little chance of equalling the norm for their age group, one third were informed they had about an even chance, and one third were told they had a very good chance. Then half of the men in each probability-of-success condition were tested by a white person, and half were tested by a Negro person. The results showed that in the low and intermediate probability conditions, performance on the digit-symbol task was better with a Negro tester, but when the stated probability of achieving the white norm was high the performance gap between the two tester groups closed. Another finding of interest was that, in accordance with Atkinson's theory, highest performance with both Negro and white testers occurred in the intermediate probability condition.

Another experiment, very similar to the previous one, except that the task consisted of a series of simple arithmetic problems, was replicated on male undergraduates at two southern Negro colleges. One college has relatively high standards of admission which exclude the lower 50 percent of the state's Negro high school graduates, while the other college admits all high school graduates, regardless of their academic standing. At both colleges, most students had attended southern segregated public schools. In Table 1 the results are presented.

It can be seen that at the nonselective

TABLE 1 Effect of Race of Tester and Probability of Success on Arithmetic Gain Scores (Post-Pre) of Male Students at Two Southern Negro Colleges*

	Probability of Success		
	Low	*Medium*	*High*
College A (Selective):			
White Tester	1.4	1.7	2.4
Negro Tester	.8	1.1	1.3
College B (Nonselective):			
White Tester	.4	.3	1.9
Negro Tester	2.1	2.5	1.9

* Significant main effects: College A, Race of Tester, $p < .05$; College B, Race of Tester, $p < .005$. Significant interaction: College B, Race $\times$ Probability of Success, $p = .05$.

college the effect of varying the race of tester was essentially the same as in the previous study, which used a different task. When the probability of success was low or intermediate, higher scores were obtained by the Negro tester groups, but in the high probability condition there was no tester difference. Turning now to the data from the selective college, scores were higher when the tester was white, regardless of the probability of success. At neither college was there a significant tendency for scores to peak in the intermediate probability condition. Summarizing, it appears that Negro students who had been average achievers in high school (the nonselective college sample) were discouraged at the prospect of being evaluated by a white person, except when they were made to believe that their chances of success were very good. But Negro students with a history of high academic achievement (the selective college sample) seemed to be stimulated by the challenge of white evaluation, regardless of the objective probability of success.

As yet, no studies of the type just described have been done on minority group students below the college level. It would be worthwhile to investigate in actual classroom settings the dynamics of expectancy of success and incentive value of success as they are related to the race of the teacher and the race of the minority pupil's classmates. Indirect evidence from the Coleman survey tends to support this writer's assumptions that in predominantly white situations, the value of achievement is relatively high for the typical Negro student, while the expectancy of achievement tends to be low. The survey found that in predominantly white, as compared with segregated Negro, schools in the North, the Negro pupils have a stronger sense of opportunity for meaningful achievement, but less confidence in their own ability.

INTERNAL VERSUS EXTERNAL SOURCES OF EVALUATION AND REWARD

Crandall (1960) has focused on the development of achieving behavior in young children. Unlike Atkinson, who is primarily concerned with that component of the incentive value of success that arises internally, from the feeling of pride of accomplishment,

Crandall attaches major importance to an external source of incentive value, the approval of significant other persons. Corresponding to internal and external sources of incentive value, in Crandall's formulation, are two types of achievement standard. Children and adults who are primarily motivated in achievement areas by the desire for approval, characteristically look to others to define the competence of their performance. Hence their standards mirror or reflect the standards or reactions of other persons and are designated *reflective achievement standards*. On the other hand, persons who are internally motivated to achieve are apt to evaluate their own efforts almost exclusively on the basis of their own subjective achievement standards, tending to ignore the standards of others. Such individuals are said by Crandall to hold *autonomous achievement standards*.

While Crandall does not elaborate this point, it is useful to think of the development of achieving behavior as a two-stage process. During the first stage, which begins as early as the second year of life in the white middle class home, the child's efforts to acquire language and solve problems are reinforced by strong expressions of approval from parents or parent surrogates. If the approval is given frequently yet selectively in response to reasonable efforts at mastery in a variety of verbal and cognitive areas, the child will eventually develop strong habits of striving for proficiency. To be maintained, these habits must continue to be reinforced in a consistent manner. The second stage of development is reached when parents' standards and values of achievement are internalized by the child. The process may be described as one in which the child's own implicit verbal responses acquire through repeated association with the overt responses of the parents, the same power to guide and reinforce the child's own achievement behaviors. That such verbal mediation processes occur in young children has been experimentally demonstrated by Russian psychologists in a series of ingenious conditioning experiments (reported by Razran, 1959). In all likelihood, internalization does not take place until strong, externally reinforced, achieving habits have developed. But there may be a considerable amount of overlap of the two stages, so that older children, and even adults may be impelled to achieve both by the desire for favorable self-evaluation, and the desire for the approval of others, the relative strength of each motive varying among individuals and also, perhaps, depending upon the type of achievement situation. Thus boys who are high achievers in high school have been found in a number of studies to be high on internal drive (*n* Achievement) and also docile, conforming and anxious (reviewed by Crandall, 1963).

Unfortunately the evidence bearing on the role of social reinforcement in the early acquisition of achievement behaviors is both sparse and contradictory (reviewed by Crandall, 1963). The inconsistency in results is probably due to the research methods employed, most of the findings being based upon interviews, often retrospective, with parents and children, rather than direct observation of parent-child interaction. Even interviews with mothers of young children would not necessarily provide the relevant information about child behavior-maternal reinforcement contingencies, since the mother may not be fully aware of the extent to which her own responses and those of the child have mutually "shaped" one another. The few studies that have employed direct observation of parent-child interaction generally show a relationship between maternal approval and children's achievement striving. Crandall *et al.* (1960) observed the behavior of white middle class mothers and their preschool children in the home. Mothers who usually rewarded approval-seeking and achievement efforts had children who displayed more achieving behavior both in the home and in a nursery school free-play situation where the mother was not present. Other types of maternal behavior, such as reactions to children's help-seeking and emotional support-seeking, were not predictive of children's performance. Rosen and D'Andrade (1959) took achievement tasks into the homes of boys who had very high or very low *n* Achievement scores, as measured projectively. Mothers of boys with strong *n* Achievement were more inclined to give approval when performance was good and to criticize incompetent efforts. Although these mothers, according to the investigators, were more likely to give their sons more option as to exactly what to do, they gave less option about doing something and doing it well.

One may reasonably expect to find class and race differences in the extent to which parents reinforce language and problem solving behavior. In low income homes, where families tend to be large, and mothers often work during the day, each child generally gets less individual attention from adults than do children in middle class households. Also, because of their own educational deficiencies it is often difficult for lower class parents to know how to encourage intellectual behavior in their children, or even how to recognize it when it occurs. The study of class and race differences in maternal behavior by means of direct observation has hardly been attempted as yet, except by Hess and associates at the University of Chicago. In a pioneering study (Hess and Shipman, 1965) they gave cognitive tasks to Negro mother-child pairs of different class backgrounds. Lower class mothers gave their children less praise for problem-solving attempts, and were less able to evaluate the quality of the child's responses.

The present assumption is that lower class children, and this would include most Negro children, because they have received less parental approval for early intellectual efforts, remain more dependent than middle class children on social reinforcement when performing academic tasks. Middle class children, who are likely to receive consistent social reinforcement of cognitive behavior in the home, have begun to internalize approval for success and standards of success by the time they enter elementary school. Children who have not been rewarded for intellectual efforts should tend to avoid intellectual achievement situations when they can, and to seek out more promising situations. But when constrained from avoiding intellectual activity, as in the classroom, they should display a high need for approval, and performance standards that are highly reflective of the immediate social environment. Crandall and others (1965a) found that northern Negro elementary school pupils scored higher than white pupils on a test of the need for approval, patterned on the Crowne-Marlow Social Desirability Scale. Moreover, high scorers were likely to be shy, withdrawn, inhibited, and lacking in self-confidence. There is also some evidence from other studies, for example, one by Rosen (1959) that lower class Negro boys are very low on *n* Achievement, which is here conceived as the capacity for self-praise and autonomous standard setting. Mingione (1965) found lower class Negro children to be lower on *n* Achievement than white children of low socio-economic status.

The empirical evidence dealing with race and class differences in children's responses to social reinforcement is meager and inconsistent. Zigler and Kanzer (1962) did an experiment in which two types of verbal reinforcers, those emphasizing praise and those emphasizing correctness, were dispensed to white seven-year-old boys working at a simple game-like task. Words connoting praise ("good" and "fine") were more effective reinforcers for lower class children than words connoting correctness ("right" and "correct"). The reverse was true for middle class children. However, a similar study by Rosenhan and Greenwald (1965) did not bear out the findings. Neither class nor race differences were observed in the relative effect of praise and correctness feedback on children's performance of a simple conditioning task. More recently, Rosenhan (1966) obtained results which seem to contradict both of the earlier experiments. White and Negro lower class boys, as compared with white middle class boys, showed greater facilitation when told "right" for correct responses, and greater decrements when told "wrong" for incorrect responses on a simple probability learning task. Perhaps the inconclusiveness of the social reinforcement experiments can be attributed to a failure to control and manipulate certain critical variables, and to use appropriate tasks. None of the studies used verbal-symbolic tasks of the sort that reveal race and class differences in academic achievement, and none varied either the child's need for approval or the class-ethnic characteristics of the experimenter. The adult experimenter who dispensed rewards was always recognizably white middle class. It is entirely possible that the visible social status of an adult authority strongly influences the socially disadvantaged child's interpretation of the adult's behavior.

Relating to this point is evidence that Negro and lower class children perceive their teachers as rejectant, and that the perceptions are to some extent veridical. Davidson and Lang (1960) found that, regardless of pupils' achievement level in school, those from blue-collar homes attributed to their teachers less favorable feelings toward them than did children from more advantaged homes. In another study, Negro students in northern integrated high schools described their white teachers as disinterested and insincere (Gottlieb, 1964). White middle class teachers, it has been reported, do in fact tend to underestimate the ability of minority children, misinterpret their goals, and express a preference for teaching white pupils (Gottlieb, 1963; Haryou, 1964).

In a recent unpublished experiment the present writer and associates undertook to assess the extent to which the verbal learning of minority group children from blue-collar homes is influenced by praise or blame from a Negro or white adult in interaction with their need for approval. Northern urban Negro boys of elementary school age were individually administered a list of paired associates for 10 trials. Subjects were assured at the outset that their performance would not affect their school grades. Half of the boys were tested by a Negro and half were tested by a white person. Also, half of them received periodic approval from the experimenter ("I'm pleased with the way you're doing," etc.) and half received periodic disapproval ("I'm disappointed in the way you're doing," etc.). Finally the sample was dichotomized into high and low on need for approval, measured before the learning task was introduced by means of a modified version of the Crowne-Marlow scale. Each boy's learning score was expressed as an average deviation (positive or negative) from the median learning scores of the total sample on three blocks of trials.

There were two main effects: More learning occurred with Negro testers than white testers, and more learning occurred when the tester gave approval than when he gave disapproval. But of greatest interest was an interaction of all three variables, the nature of which is revealed in Table 2. In order to account for the results, two types of assumptions will be made: (a) that the scale used to measure the need for approval actually tapped the subject's generalized predisposition to seek approval and avoid disapproval; and (b) that the Negro tester was perceived as predisposed to like the child and to react objectively to his performance, while the white tester was seen as inclined to dislike the child and to withhold genuine approval. The results

TABLE 2 Cell Means for Interaction Effect of Need for Approval, Race of Tester, and Tester Response on Learning Scores (Expressed as Deviations From Mean of Total Sample) of Negro Boys*

	Negro Tester		White Tester	
	Ap-proval	Disap-proval	Ap-proval	Disap-proval
High Need	2.41	1.42	1.24	−3.80
Low Need	2.51	−1.33	−1.82	− .79

* All differences between cell means of 2.04 and greater are significant at the .05 level of probability by the Duncan Test.

shown in Table 2 can now be interpreted in the following manner: When the Negro tester was approving, all boys, regardless of need level, were adequately motivated for the task. When the Negro tester was disapproving, high-need boys were somewhat disheartened, but continued to seek approval. Their learning was somewhat poorer than in the Negro tester-approval condition, but not significantly so. Low-need boys, on the other hand, tended to lose interest in the task, since it was defined at the outset as having no academic significance. When the tester was white and gave approval, high-need boys did not work quite as hard as boys who received approval from the Negro tester (difference nonsignificant). Though the white person's approval was seen as less genuine, their high need generated a moderate impulse to work, perhaps, in part, to avoid disapproval. Low-need boys were relatively unmotivated by white approval. When the white tester was disapproving, high-need children experienced debilitating anxiety, because the disapproval was taken as an overt expression of dislike; it was as though they could not hope to elicit a favorable response through greater expenditure of effort. The boys were virtually unable to learn at all. When low-need subjects were disapproved of by the white adult their performance did not deteriorate further. The slight nonsignificant improvement in scores over the white tester-approval condition is inexplicable except as a sampling error.

The experiment shows that in order to understand the effects of positive and negative social reinforcement on Negro children it is necessary to take into account the need state of the individual child and the racial identity

of the adult dispenser of reinforcement. Why the race of the tester influenced the verbal learning of northern urban Negro boys is not immediately apparent. While the assumption that the subjects felt less rapport with white experimenters is a reasonable one, there is no direct evidence to support it. Indeed, even if the assumption is valid, it is entirely possible that a relatively brief experience of friendly interaction with the adult would have changed the Negro child's responses in the learning situation. Therefore, the results may have implications not for biracial teacher-pupil pairs per se, but only for situations in which the Negro child perceives the white person as hostile, unfriendly, or disinterested.

Summarizing, it has been suggested as being of some significance that lower class Negro children tend to be externally oriented in situations that demand performance. That is, they are likely to be highly dependent on the immediate environment for the setting of standards and dispensing of rewards. Some of the implications for educational practices are immediately apparent. First, teacher attitudes toward Negro children will be highly important for their classroom behavior. It has already been noted that attitudes of white teachers toward Negro pupils may generally be less than optimal. The evidence on this point is very sparse. Even the Coleman survey (Coleman et al., 1966) did not adequately assess teacher attitudes toward minority group pupils. Second, Negro students should be highly sensitive to the educational quality of both teacher and classmates, so that variations in these qualities should produce larger differences in the academic achievement of Negroes than of whites.

The Coleman report has data bearing upon the last point. It was found that the achievement of both Negro and white pupils, when their family background characteristics were partialled out, was more closely related to the educational proficiency of their classmates than to all objective school characteristics together (*i.e.*, curriculum, expenditure per pupil, physical facilities, size of class, etc.), and to all teacher characteristics together. In the upper grades the apparent influence of the quality of the student body on individual achievement was two to three times greater for Negro pupils than for white pupils. The Coleman data represent correlations between variables, and causality must be inferred with utmost caution. Yet it seems a reasonable conclusion that a major part of the effect of the student body on individual achievement can be attributed to the high standards of performance set in the classroom. Teacher characteristics were almost as closely related to the Negro pupil's test scores as were student body characteristics. Teacher quality was much more important for Negro pupils than for white pupils. Beyond grade 1 Negroes were several times more sensitive to teacher variables than were whites. The most important characteristics of teachers were educational background and verbal ability.

Given the relatively high proficiency of white students and their teachers it is not surprising that as the proportion of white in a school increased, Negro achievement rose. The apparent impact of desegregation can be illustrated by comparing percentile scores on reading comprehension for northern Negro high school students who never had a white classmate with scores of northern Negroes with similar family backgrounds who attended integrated schools from the early grades. When figures from Table 3.3.2 of the Coleman report are consolidated, it is revealed that Negro ninth graders with the longest experience of integrated schooling had an average score of 48.2. This is about five points below the white norm for the same region, but less than two points below the national norm of 50. In contrast, ninth-grade minority group children who never had white classmates averaged 43.8. Thus it seems has desegregation reduced the racial achievement gap by almost half. The Coleman report also gives scores of twelfth graders, which were excluded from the present comparisons because the high rate of Negro dropouts makes them unrepresentative. Actually, the picture would not have been changed materially by their inclusion. When the influence of the student body's educational background and aspirations is controlled, the relationship between racial composition of schools and Negro test scores is sharply reduced. Thus the apparent beneficial effect of having a high proportion of white classmates comes not from racial composition per se, but from the high educational quality that is, on the average, found among white students.

Desegregation also appeared to have the effect of increasing the variability of Negro test scores. The differences in variance were small but consistent, and accord with notions advanced earlier in this paper regarding the complex determination of Negro motivation in predominantly white settings: because of the high prestige of white teachers and age peers, rejection by them is more disturbing to the Negro pupil, and their acceptance more facilitative, than similar responses from Negro teachers and peers. In addition, expectancy of success and value of success should tend to be affected in opposite ways by an increase in the proportion of white classmates, because of the elevation of achievement standards. Further unpublished analyses of the Coleman data by James McPartland (personal communication) reveal the expected difference between truly *integrated* and merely *desegregated* schools. Those schools with more than half white student bodies whose Negroes score well, when compared with similar schools whose Negroes score poorly, are characterized by greater cross-racial acceptance as predicted. Their students were much more likely to report close friends among members of the other race than students in the merely desegregated schools.

SENSE OF CONTROL OF REWARDS

Another valuable concept for understanding the educational achievement of children from different social backgrounds is Rotter's (Rotter *et al.*, 1962) sense of personal control of the environment. Individuals differ in the extent to which they feel they can extract material and social benefits from the environment through their own efforts. In its broadest meaning, this construct refers to the degree to which people accept personal responsibility for what happens to them. It has been applied more specifically to children in intellectual achievement situations by means of a questionnaire which assesses the extent to which favorable reactions from parents, teachers and peers are believed by the child to depend either upon the quality of his own efforts or upon extraneous factors (such as luck, or the personal bias or whim of the evaluator) (Crandall *et al.*, 1965b). A child's feelings about whether his own efforts determine his external rewards clearly will affect his perception of the attractiveness, or *value* of a given achievement goal, and his *expectancy* of success. The greater his need for approval in achievement situations, and the more his standards tend to be reflective, the closer will be these relationships. Crandall and others (1965b) found a tendency for sense of control and need for approval to be inversely related in white children. A reciprocal causal relationship should exist between beliefs about locus of control and achievement, since the beliefs will affect task motivation, and the level of performance will in turn affect the rate at which the environment dispenses rewards. Thus Crandall and others (1962) found that grade school boys who felt they controlled their reinforcements got high scores on intellectual tests and engaged in much intellectual free-play behavior. Similar results were obtained by Coleman and his coworkers. In this connection it is interesting to note that perception of internal control appears to be related to both white and middle class status (Battle and Rotter, 1963; Crandall *et al.*, 1965b; Coleman *et al.*, 1966).

In the Coleman survey, three expressions of student attitude were measured: interest in school work, self concept as regards ability, and sense of control of own fate. Of all the variables that were evaluated, including eight features of family background taken together, and a much greater number of objective school characteristics taken together, these attitudes showed the strongest relation to performance at all grade levels studied. For Negroes, perception of fate control was clearly the most important of the three attitudes. (To assess it, students were asked to respond to three statements—that "good luck is more important than hard work for success," that "every time I try to get ahead something or somebody stops me," and that "people like me don't have much of a chance to be successful in life.") With or without family background characteristics partialled out, sense of fate control accounted for about three times as much variance in the test scores of Negroes as of whites at the higher grade levels, both in the North and South. White proficiency was more closely related to self concept than to control of environment. In the words of the Coleman report, "it appears that children from advantaged groups assume that the environment will respond if they are able to affect it; children from dis-

advantaged groups do not make this assumption, but in many cases assume that nothing they will do can affect the environment—it will give benefits or withhold them but not as a consequence of their own action." (p. 321). The crucial role of this factor in determining level of performance is suggested by the finding that Negro pupils who answered "hard work" scored higher on a test of verbal ability than did white pupils who chose the "good luck" response. Only a small fraction of the variance in fate control was accounted for by family background factors, and almost none of it by objective school characteristics. However, one variable is consistently related both to this attitude and to self concept. As the proportion white in the school increased, the Negro child's sense of internal control increased, but his self concept declined. It would appear that in integrated classrooms minority group children were less confident of their ability to compete, but were more aware of opportunity.

SUMMARY

Several motivational concepts have relevance to the problem of racial differences in intellectual achievement in the United States. Among these are Atkinson's model of achievement motivation, Crandall's distinctions between external and internal sources of achievement standards and achievement value, and Rotter's notion of the locus of control. The purpose of this paper has been to suggest how these formulations can be integrated to account for many of the known facts about the performance of minority group students, and to suggest fruitful directions for future research. Among the broad research topics mentioned were race and class differences in the process whereby early social reinforcement of verbal-symbolic behaviors becomes internalized, race and class differences in external and internal dependency as related to academic motivation, and the role of expectancy of success and value of success on academic motivation. All of these factors need to be considered in the context of uniracial and biracial performance situations, with particular attention being given to the distinction between the racially integrated classroom, in which the minority child experiences genuine acceptance, and the merely desegregated classroom, where the minority child feels unwelcome.

REFERENCES

Atkinson, J. W. *An introduction to motivation.* New York: Van Nostrand, 1964.

Battle, E., & Rotter, J. Children's feeling of personal control as related to social class and ethnic group. *Journal of Personality,* 1963, **31,** 482–490.

Coleman, J. S. *et al. Equality of educational opportunity.* U.S. Dept. Health, Educ. & Welfare, Wash.: U.S. Govt. Printing Office, 1966.

Crandall, V. C., Crandall, V. J., & Katkovsky, W. A. A children's social desirability questionnaire. *Journal of Consulting Psychology,* 1965a, **29,** 27–36.

Crandall, V. C., Katkovsky, W., & Crandall, V. J. Children's beliefs in their own control of reinforcements in intellectual-academic achievement situations. *Child Development,* 1965b, **36,** 92–109.

Crandall, V. J. Achievement. In *Yearbook of national society for the study of education.* Chicago: The National Society for Study Education, 1963.

Crandall, V. J., Katkovsky, W., & Preston, A. Conceptual formulation for some research on children's achievement development. *Child Development,* 1960, **31,** 787, 797.

Crandall, V. J., Katkovsky, W., & Preston, A. Motivational and ability determinants of young children's intellectual achievement behaviors. *Child Development,* 1962, **33,** 643–661.

Crandall, V. J., Preston, A., & Rabson, A. Maternal reactions and the development of independence and achievement behavior in young children. *Child Development,* 1960, **31,** 243–251.

Davidson, H. H., & Lang, G. Children's perceptions of their teachers' feelings toward them related to self-perception, school achievement and behavior. *Journal of Experimental Education,* 1960, **29,** 107–118.

Gottlieb, D. Goal aspirations and goal fulfillments: Differences between deprived and affluent American adolescents. Unpublished paper, 1964.

Gottlieb, D. Teaching and students: The views of Negro and white teachers. Unpublished paper, 1963.

Harlem Youth Opportunities Unlimited, Inc. *Youth in the ghetto,* New York, 1964.

Hess, R. D., & Shipman, V. Early experience and the socialization of cognitive modes in children. *Child Development,* 1965, **36,** 869–886.

Katz, I. Review of evidence relating to effects of desegregation on the intellectual performance of Negroes. *American Psychologist,* 1964, **19,** 381–399.

McClelland, D. C., Atkinson, J. W., Clark, R. W., & Lowell, E. L. *The achievement motive.* New York: Appleton-Century, 1953.

Mingione, A. Need for achievement in Negro and white children. *Journal of Consulting Psychology,* 1965, **29,** 108–111.

Razran, G. Soviet psychology and psychophysiology. *Behavioral Science,* 1959, **4,** 35–48.

Rosen, B. Race, ethnicity and the achievement syndrome. *American Sociological Review,* 1959, **24,** 417–460.

Rosen, B., & D'Andrade, R. C. The psychological origins of achievement motivation. *Sociometry,* 1959, **22,** 185–218.

Rosenhan, D., & Greenwald, J. A. The effects of age, sex, and socioeconomic class on responsiveness to two classes of verbal reinforcement. *Journal of Personality,* 1965, **33,** 108–121.

Rosenhan, D. Effects of social class and race on responsiveness to approval and disapproval. *Journal of Personality and Social Psychology,* 1966, **4,** 253–259.

Rotter, J., Seeman, M., & Liverant, S. Internal *vs* external control of reinforcement: A major variable in behavior theory. In N. F. Washburne (Ed.), *Decisions, values and groups.* Vol. 2. London: Pergamon Press, 1962.

Zigler, E., & Kanzer, P. The effectiveness of two classes of verbal reinforcers on the performance of middle-class and lower-class children. *Journal of Personality,* 1962, **30,** 157–163.

5

Black Achievement in Integrated and Segregated Environments

The Negro revolt is evolving into more than a quest for desegregation and equality. It is a challenge to a system that has created miracles of production and technology to create justice. If humanism is locked outside of the system, Negroes will have revealed its inner core of despotism and a far greater struggle for liberation will unfold.

MARTIN LUTHER KING, JR., *Conscience for Change*

INTRODUCTION

Civil rights leaders have for a long time been pressing for complete integration. Progress, however, has been slow and now has "abruptly stalled and hope withered under bitter backlashing" (King, 1967, p. 2). The 1954 Supreme Court decision, based partly on social science documentation such as that by Kenneth Clark (1953), marked a cornerstone in American race relations. It was aimed primarily at bringing about the desegregation of public schools. Early optimism resulting from this court decision has recently given way to the shattering realization that de jure segregation, especially in the North, has been replaced by de facto segregation. Hopes for improving educational opportunities for black children have not been fulfilled (Scott, 1966; Silberman, 1964). Whites moving to the suburbs, as well as over-crowding and deteriorating living conditions in the inner city, have created new black ghettoes (Clark, 1965). Although many black leaders and an overwhelming majority of black Americans continue to demand integration,

187

black nationalists not only believe at present that white racism does not and will not permit true integration, but also that racial separation is indeed preferable for maintaining black pride and integrity and avoiding corruption by white American values. They insist that their schools be improved and run by blacks (Carmichael & Hamilton, 1967). Community control of schools through local school boards has in fact become a most controversial issue in New York and other cities.

There is evidence that black Americans attach more prestige to education than do whites because they differ more in educational attainment and because education is of greater occupational utility to them (Glenn, 1963). This is further demonstrated in the study by Luchterhand and Weller (1965), who found that lower-class black mothers with little education, despite strong white resistance, were determined to transfer their children out of segregated ghetto schools into integrated schools.

Pettigrew (1965a) discussed the possibility that desegregation may evolve faster in the South than in the North, but he pointed to socio-political variables, white resistance, and lack of black insistence as strong barriers which must first be overcome. An example of white resistance was the closing of public schools by the board of supervisors in Prince Edward County, Virginia, in defiance of a court order requiring school desegregation. Black students were severely affected by this educational deprivation, and were still performing at a much lower level after school had reopened (Green & Hofmann, 1965).

Negro colleges in the South have played an important role in providing higher education to large numbers of black people. Gurin and Epps (1966) examined the motivation for academic achievement and environmental influences on over 3,000 black students who, despite severe obstacles, were attending Negro colleges in the South. Although there were marked differences in family structure between very poor and economically more secure students, they all attached great importance to educational goals. The lower income group, however, had lower expectations of success (reflected in their choice of colleges with lower academic standards), despite the fact that they had the same academic potential as the upper income group. Jencks and Riesman (1967) have discussed the role of Negro colleges both in the past and the future. They indicate that these colleges have had and will continue to have difficulties in attracting good black students (who generally prefer integrated schools), as well as white students. They suggest that these colleges will probably remain academically inferior, but will continue to educate the majority of black students.

Many questions arise with respect to the relative merits of integrated and segregated schools. Will black pupils and students in an integrated school thrive intellectually, or will competition with white students who are favored by past and/or present discrimination impede their growth? What about the fears of some whites that integration may lower existing standards and affect their children's achievement? Is it possible to truly integrate schools when most housing is still segregated? If not, can the level of achievement in segregated schools be brought up to the level of that in white or integrated schools? What about achieving a racial balance by bussing children to schools outside their residential district? These and other problems will be discussed in this chapter.

EXPERIMENTAL STUDIES OF BIRACIAL SITUATIONS

Considerable empirical evidence has accumulated that has helped to pinpoint a number of important variables that facilitate or impede black achievement in different biracial situations. In the first paper, Katz [17] reviews the experimental literature that bears on the performance of black pupils in racially mixed classrooms. He identifies low expectancy of success, social threat, and failure threat as three factors that may detrimentally affect black pupils in a desegregated school; acceptance by white peers and adults as well as anticipation of white approval, on the other hand, may well prove beneficial to their performance.

Most of the research by Katz and his associates involved college students. A series of more recent studies was directed at elementary school children. Kennedy and Vega (1965) found that under white examiners the black children's response patterns to blame and praise were the same as those of the white subjects; they reacted with improvement to praise and with a decrement in performance to blame. Under black examiners, however, black children responded to blame with an increment in performance. In contrast to these results, Katz, Henchy, and Allen (1968) found that black children generally performed better with black examiners than with white examiners; specifically, when approval was given by black examiners. In addition, they discovered that the strength of the child's need for approval may modify his performance. It is difficult to reconcile the results of these two studies. It may be that regional differences, differences in the experimental paradigm, the learning task (a perceptual discrimination task was used in the former study, a paired-associate learning task in the latter), and the socioeconomic status of the subjects led to the different results.

In line with the results of Katz et al., Baratz (1967) found that black college students who were tested by black examiners scored lower on a test anxiety questionnaire than those tested by a white examiner. Rosenhan (1966), using only a white examiner, found that on a simple probability learning task, both black and white lower-class boys performed better under conditions of approval than did middle-class whites. Under conditions of disapproval they did worse than middle-class subjects. Rosenhan suggests that because of their alienation from middle-class values and surroundings, lower-class children are particularly sensitive to external reinforcements of approval and disapproval.

A number of studies have focused on Negro-white interactions in competitive situations. Lefcourt and Ladwig (1965), for example, found that in Negro-white competition, the high failure avoidance of Negroes is related to low expectancy of success. In a competitive achievement task (a two-person zero-sum game) involving a continuously winning white confederate of *E*, the degree of persistence of black subjects was associated with prior experience in obtaining positive reinforcement. Hatton (1967) placed black high school students who perceived whites as highly prejudiced against Negroes in a bargaining situation with Negro and white confederates who assumed either a yielding or demanding posture. With demanding whites, blacks became passive; with yielding whites they became demanding; whereas their bargaining response with black confederates was determined by the structure of the situation.

It is obvious that all these studies have implications for the black child's intellectual performance. Painstaking research efforts should enable us to determine the relative influence of the race and social class of the child, his peers and his teachers, situational stress, reinforcements, and the differential verbal reinforcement on his achievement in desegregated schools. The structuring of the school environment and teaching methods can then be adopted to the child's needs in order to maximize his chance of success in school.

THE COLEMAN REPORT

The Civil Rights Act of 1964 directed the U.S. Commissioner of Education to conduct a survey of "the lack of availability of equal educational opportunities by reason of race, color, religion, or national origin in public educational institutions at all levels." The studies carried out in response to this legislative request were presented in what has become known as the "Coleman report" (Coleman et al., 1966). The survey assessed the academic achievement, background and attitudes of over 600,000 pupils in grades 1, 3, 6, 9, and 12 in over 400 schools throughout the United States. In addition, the teachers in these schools took a verbal-ability test, and together with the principals and superintendents they responded to questionnaires. The study, one of the largest educational surveys ever undertaken, attempted to answer the following four principal questions.

1. *To what extent are racial minorities segregated in public schools?*

The data revealed that the overwhelming majority of American children attend racially segregated schools. Black pupils are by far the most segregated minority; more than 65 percent are in schools whose enrollment is 90 to 100 percent black. In the South most black students attend schools that are 100 percent black. White pupils are even more segregated; close to 80 percent in the first and twelfth grades attend schools that are from 90 to 100 percent white. Mexican Americans, Indians, Puerto Ricans, and Orientals are also segregated, but to a lesser extent than are blacks and whites.

The same pattern of segregation holds for teachers. Black children attend schools where on the average 65 percent of the teachers are black. The average white child is taught almost exclusively by white teachers (97 percent).

The 1954 Supreme Court decision, mentioned before, declared that separate schools for black children and white children are inherently unequal. According to this criterion, the huge majority of American children still received an inferior education, more than ten years later.

2. *Do the schools offer equal educational opportunities in terms of existing facilities and students', teachers', and principals' background?*

Here too, black children are at a disadvantage with respect to class size, teachers' qualifications, physical facilities (laboratories, libraries, textbooks, and so forth), and extracurricular programs, but ethnic differences are not consistent and are generally smaller than regional differences. The latter were often striking. For example, the report found that "100 percent of Negro high school students and 97 percent of whites in the metropolitan Far West attend schools having a remedial teacher compared with 46 percent and 65 percent, respectively, in the metropolitan South, and 4 percent and 9 percent in the nonmetropolitan Southwest" (p. 12). Or as Nichols (1966) has put it, "In terms of these indicators the educationally deprived groups in the U.S. are not racial or ethnic minorities, but children—regardless of race—living in the South and in the nonmetropolitan North" (p. 1312).

Clear differences were found on student body characteristics. Black children, for example, have fewer classmates whose mothers graduated from high school, more classmates who come from large families, and fewer who are enrolled in a college preparatory curriculum.

3. *Are there differences in intellectual achievement among minority and white children?*

As so many studies before it, the Coleman report reveals large racial differences on reading, writing, arithmetic, and problem-solving tests. In all grades, the average American Indian, Puerto Rican, and Negro (in this descending order) performs significantly below the level of the average white or Oriental American. The highest regional average score for blacks, furthermore, was below the lowest for whites. The gap appears to widen from first to twelfth grade; that is, "the deficiency in achievement is progressively greater for the minority pupils at progressively higher grade levels" (p. 21). In the metropolitan Northeast, for example, black pupils in the twelfth grade are 3.3 years behind whites in verbal achievement, whereas in the sixth grade they were only 1.6 years behind. (On standard deviation scores, however, the racial gap in achievement does not grow larger from early to late grades, except in the South.)

> For most minority groups, then, and most particularly the Negro, schools provide little opportunity for them to overcome this initial deficiency; in fact, they fall farther behind the white majority in the development of several skills which are critical to making a living and participating fully in modern society. Whatever may be the combination of nonschool factors—poverty, community attitudes, low educational level of parents, disadvantage in verbal and non-verbal skills, when they enter the first grade, the fact is the schools have not overcome it. (Coleman et al., 1966, p. 21.)

Nichols (1966) has argued that the increase in deficiency from first to twelfth grade is an artifact of the unequal intervals of an age scale. Since mental growth follows a negatively accelerating curve, he feels that "the role of the schools in increasing or decreasing differences between racial and ethnic groups is quite small" (p. 1313). It should further be added, as pointed out by Coleman himself and by Nichols, that the test scores at grade 12 are not entirely accurate. A higher percentage of black students drop out in the metropolitan North and West than in the South. It is conceivable, therefore, assuming that those who dropped out would have performed more poorly, that black achievement in the North may have been artificially elevated.

4. *What are the relationships between students' achievement and school characteristics?*

Individual differences in achievement within any one school will always exist, but the question that remains to be answered is why the average achievement is so much higher in some schools than in others. The data bearing on Coleman's first three questions brought few surprises, except perhaps with respect to the *magnitude* of racial segregation and racial differences in achievement; but the findings stemming from the fourth question were completely unexpected. Over-all, when socioeconomic factors are statistically controlled, the differences between schools (regarding teachers' ability and training, curriculum, libraries, laboratories, and so forth) "account for only a small fraction of differences in pupil achievement" (p. 22).

On the other hand, it appears that minority children are more affected by the quality of the school than are white children. One might therefore infer that improving the schools of minority pupils would have greater effects on achievement than improving those of whites. Among the school variables that are related to achievement, the teachers' verbal ability and educational background are the most important. The factors, however, which bear most significantly on a child's achievement are his own socioeconomic status and the educational background, aspirations, and socioeconomic status of his fellow students. The latter relationship holds particularly for minority children. Thus, the authors suggest that

> . . . if a white pupil from a home that is strongly and effectively supportive of education is put in a school where most pupils do not come from such homes, his achievement will be little different than if he were in a school composed of others like himself. But if a minority pupil from a home without much educational strength is put with school mates with strong educational background, his achievement is likely to increase (p. 22).

One might infer from this statement that school integration is likely to enhance the achievement of black children without impeding that of whites. (We shall return to this point in the last section of this introduction.) Nichols (1966) has challenged this conclusion. He declares Coleman guilty of interpreting a correlation as suggesting a cause and effect relationship and states that experimental studies with appropriate manipulations of different variables are necessary before such relationships can be ascertained. "Moreover, the findings on which it [Coleman's conclusion] is based might also be attributed to inadequate control for the preschool characteristics of students" (p. 1313). It is difficult to differentiate the effects of the child's initial ability (before entering school) and the effects of the school on his academic achievement. Longitudinal studies that control for "input" variables (abilities before schooling has begun) will be necessary to properly assess the role of schools with respect to "output" variables (achievement scores after some schooling).

It should be emphasized that while the survey was primarily directed at variability between schools, variability within the same school was four times as large. "For example, a pupil attitude factor, which appears to have a stronger relationship to achievement than do all the 'school' factors together, is the extent to which an individual feels that he has some control over his own destiny" (p. 23). Minority pupils, except for Orientals, demonstrate far less confidence than whites that they can affect their own fate by their own action. Those who do have such confidence, however, achieve higher scores than whites who lack that conviction. (See Chapter 2.)

To very briefly summarize the major findings of the Coleman report, racial school segregation is widespread indeed; racial differences on achievement tests are large; differences between minority and white schools do exist, but regional differences are more predominant; and finally, there appears to be little relationship between achievement and school characteristics. The implications of these findings can hardly be exaggerated. The survey has certain methodological flaws (some of which have been pointed out); but nevertheless it is just, in Nichol's words, "the best that has ever been done" (p. 1314) on the effects of education on minority group achievement.

> Until these findings are clarified by further research they stand like a spear pointed at the heart of the cherished American belief that equality of educational opportunity will increase the equality of intellectual achievement (Nichols, 1966, p. 1314).

What about other reactions to the Coleman report? Little notice seemed to have been taken by the educational establishment, the news media, and the general public of what Nichols referred to as of "literally revolutionary significance," namely the finding that "schools with widely varying characteristics differ very little in their effects" (p. 1314). Or as Moynihan (1967) put it, that "the American educational system as it now operates is turning out seriously unequal citizens" (p. 3). Academicians, however, did react to Coleman's report. An entire issue of the *Harvard Educational Review* (Winter,

1968), for example, was devoted to the subject of "Equal Educational Opportunity."

Although it would go beyond the scope of this introduction to go into the details of all the proposals made to bring about equal educational opportunity, it is nevertheless worthwhile to look at a few of them. As Moynihan (1967) has stated, "given unequal opportunity thereafter will produce unequal results . . . the problem of racial inequality is imprinted in the very nerve system of American society. Anyone who supposes it is going to fade gently away like the Vietnam war or the Soviet state is out of his mind" (p. 4). And he adds that "given the mounting extremism of American politics, to fail to deliver on the promises made to the Negro Americans in the first half of this decade will be to trifle with the stability of the American republic" (p. 13). Coleman (1966) has made several proposals:

(a) For those children whose family and neighborhood are educationally disadvantaged, it is important to replace this family environment as much as possible with an educational environment—by starting school at an earlier age, and by having a school which begins very early in the day and ends very late.

(b) It is important to reduce the social and racial homogeneity of the school environment, so that those agents of education that do show some effectiveness—teachers and other students—are not mere replicas of the student himself.

(c) The educational program of the school should be made more effective than it is at present (p. 74).

He also warns of the danger of "simple" school integration. Tracking (the clustering of pupils with similar abilities in one classroom) can easily lead to de facto segregation within the school. In a more recent article (Coleman, 1967), he suggests that "the teaching of elementary-level reading and arithmetic be opened up to entrepreneurs outside the schools, under contract with the school system to teach only reading or only arithmetic, and paid on the basis of increased performance by the children on standardized tests" (p. 25). This would in effect open up competition between the public schools and an alternative "free" school and would put the parents in a position to choose where they wanted their youngsters to be schooled.

Whatever one decides is the merit and feasibility of this specific approach, it should be obvious that only the most far-reaching, radically new, and dramatically more efficient programs will improve blacks' chances to compete effectively in American society. Unless they are able to learn the most basic skills, so-called equal opportunity, even where it appears to exist, remains an illusion.

Many favor integrated schools as an ultimate goal; but let there be no mistake—given the widespread segregation that, if anything, is increasing, we must make enormous financial resources, competence, and creativity available to exclusively black schools now. We just cannot wait for integration before we tackle the job of educating black children, who will soon be 20 percent of America's pupils. In the summer of 1968 there was an announcement in the press to the effect that the Berkeley school system was the first (and only one) to have become fully integrated in the United States. This, 14 years after the Supreme Court decision and involving only a small population, which includes a large university community!

Vane [**18**], in a longitudinal study included in this chapter, found much supporting evidence for Coleman's conclusions. Her results indicated that early achievement forecasts later performance in school. The majority of pupils who performed poorly in third grade were still performing below grade level in high school despite remedial help and tutoring. Social class was significantly related to both I.Q. and achievement. The degree of school integration independent of socioeconomic status did not affect the black children's achievement. The effects of integration in the classroom will be discussed in more detail in the next section.

RACIAL COMPOSITION IN SCHOOLS

The U.S. Commission on Civil Rights (1967), as required by President Johnson in November, 1965, investigated the extent and consequences of racial isolation in the public schools. The Commission appointed an advisory committee consisting of outstanding social scientists and educators and commissioned several empirical studies and position papers, and held hearings in a number of cities. Its fact-finding mission was directed at the four following areas: (1) the extent of racial isolation and the level of achievement of white and black school children; (2) the factors that contribute to and maintain school segregation; (3) the consequences of racial isolation on achievement and attitudes of blacks and whites; and (4) the effectiveness of programs aimed at remedying educational disadvantage or relieving racial isolation in the schools.

Most of the findings were based on reanalyses of Coleman's data, but they were presented within the context of the four questions referred to above. Chapter 3 of the Commission's report [**19**] is reprinted here, since it deals specifically with the effects of the classroom's racial composition and presents more detailed analyses of the Coleman data. The latter will serve to supplement the summary provided in the previous section of this introduction. The major conclusion reached in that chapter is that racial isolation in the schools adversely affects black pupils. Specifically, black children in integrated schools tend to demonstrate higher achievement, aspirations, and confidence in their ability to control their own destinies. More generally, integrated schooling appears to be related to more positive interracial attitudes of both whites and blacks and better job opportunities for blacks. These relationships become more positive and stronger as a direct function of how early school integration takes place. The Commission further concluded that there is no evidence that the achievement of white children in an integrated school is lowered by the presence of minority group children. Finally, it was found that compensatory education programs failed to improve black children's performance significantly.

The Commission's findings were not received with unanimous acclaim. Nichols (1968), for example, has serious reservations about the adequacy of the Commission's control over selective factors in the placement of black pupils in integrated schools. He refers to Wilson's longitudinal study (briefly discussed in the chapter reprinted here), which failed to demonstrate an independent effect of the racial composition of the school on achievement at any of the grade levels. Just like Coleman, however, Wilson did find that the social class composition of the school was related to achievement. Elliott and Badal (1965) found that with respect to reading and writing, educational progress is essentially the same in the schools with different racial composition, but for mathematics there was some indication that students progressed somewhat faster in schools with a relatively low percentage of black pupils.

The Commission recommended total integration of schools on the classroom level to counteract the failure of most black children to obtain even average achievement scores. In view of the equivocal evidence, however, Nichols warns that "desirable as integration may be for social and political reasons, the Commission may be setting the Negro up for yet another disillusionment by promoting school integration as a means of achieving equality of performance" (p. 9). Gregor (1968) also argued that the available evidence does not support the claim that minority children would be better off academically in integrated schools. More research, especially longitudinal and controlling social and educational background, is of vital importance to clarify the potential impact of integration on intellectual achievement. Gerard, Miller, and Singer (1967) have begun such a long-term study of Mexican American, black, and white children who are now attending recently desegregated schools.

Green (1966) urges that schools be integrated in the early grades to minimize prior educational handicaps and facilitate adjustment to the biracial situation, and suggests that competent teachers be assigned to these classes. He distinguishes between interracial and integrated schools. Interracial schools include both black and white children, but segregation may occur in the classroom as a result of assignments on the basis of achievement tests. The truly integrated school would not only have integrated classrooms but also would permit and encourage an open system of total interracial interactions on all levels, academic and social, students and staff. The latter is crucial when one realizes that integrated schools may not only offer better education, but also provide a convenient structure or institution supportive of interracial communication and understanding. As has been pointed out earlier, contact generally generates greater tolerance and reduces prejudice and discrimination (Pettigrew, 1969). Schools, in addition, offer the advantage of enhancing such contacts relatively early in the child's life (preschools should be integrated too!), thereby perhaps reaching an individual before his racial attitudes have hardened. Gottlieb and Ten Houten (1965) have found that a variety of social systems, such as school activities and leadership, popularity, and peer groups, in three different high schools were significantly affected by the racial composition of the schools.

Pettigrew (1967) has proposed a social evaluation theory to account for the dynamics of interracial classrooms. Such classrooms offer opportunities for cross-racial self-evaluation, "and it also follows that those children for whom peers of the other race become referent should evince the largest changes" (p. 287). Pettigrew suggests that Katz's, Coleman's, and the Commission's data confirm his hypotheses and argues that integration in the early elementary grades represents the best way to make quality education available to black children (Pettigrew, 1965). Riley (1968) compared several strategies for reducing the educational disadvantage of lower-class Negroes. Using findings based on reanalyses of Coleman's data and from other studies, Riley concludes that social class integration, coupled with classroom racial integration, is more promising than compensatory education programs. Teele, Jackson, and Mayo (1967) and Teele and Mayo (1969) have investigated black parents' reaction to the bussing of their children to white schools. They report that their respondents are primarily seeking quality education wherever it is available, either in integrated or in community controlled neighborhood schools. John H. Fisher (1966), the president of Columbia Teachers College, also objects to integration as the only solution:

> The contention that no school of Negro pupils can under any circumstances be satisfactory unless white students enter it is absurd. The argument insults every Negro child and credits white children with virtues they do not possess. But the effort to establish genuinely first-rate schools in Negro communities has been so long delayed that anyone undertaking to demonstrate that an insti-

tution known as a "Negro" school can produce first-rate results must be prepared to accept a substantial burden of proof (p. 493).

Hamilton (1968), on the other hand, maintains that black people are no longer exclusively interested in improving the effectiveness of the present school system, but are beginning to question its very legitimacy. He insists that in order to implement viable programs, more attention be paid to black demands than to the findings of experts. He proposes an alternative educational plan:

> This is a model which views the ghetto school as the focal point of community life. The educational system should be concerned with the entire family not simply with the children. We should think in terms of a Comprehensive Family-Community-School Plan with black parents attending classes, taking an active, day-to-day part in the operation of the school. Parents could be students, teachers, and legitimate members of the local governing board (p. 682).

Lewis (1969) also believes in self-determination for black communities, but he attacks the self-segregation of black students in colleges and universities. He suggests, furthermore, that black studies be pursued primarily by white students, while black students focus on the sciences and the professions so they will be able to compete for the top jobs in research, government, and industry.

> The struggle for community power in the neighborhood is not an alternative to the struggle for a better share of the integrated world outside the neighborhood, in which inevitably most of our people must earn their living. The way to a better share of this integrated economy is through the integrated colleges; but they can help us only if we take from them the same things that they give to our white competitors. If we enter them merely to segregate ourselves in blackness, we shall lose the opportunity of our lives (p. 54).

The controversy over the effects of integrated versus segregated environments on black achievement continues. No single approach, acceptable to all, is likely to emerge, but we must take the first step and, recognizing the disadvantaged position of black students in the present educational system, make a commitment to search for more viable alternatives.

REFERENCES

Baratz, S. S. Effect of race of experimenter, instructions, and comparison population upon level of reported anxiety in Negro subjects. *Journal of Personality and Social Psychology*, 1967, **7**, 194–196.

Carmichael, S., & Hamilton, C. V. *Black power.* New York: Random House, 1967.

Clark, K. B. Desegregation: An appraisal of the evidence. *Journal of Social Issues*, 1953, **9**, 2–76.

Clark, K. B. *Dark ghetto: Dilemmas of social power.* New York: Harper & Row, 1965.

Coleman, J. S. Equal schools or equal students? *The Public Interest*, 1966, 70–75.

Coleman, J. S. Toward open schools. *The Public Interest*, 1967, (9), 20–27.

Coleman, J. S., et al. *Equality of educational opportunity.* Washington, D.C.: Government Printing Office, 1966.

Elliott, M. H., & Badal, A. W. Achievement and racial composition of schools. *California Journal of Educational Research*, 1965, **16**, 158–166.

Fisher, J. H. Race and reconciliation: The role of the school. In T. Parsons and K. B. Clark (Eds.), *The Negro American.* Boston: Houghton Mifflin, 1966.

Gerard, H. B., Miller, N., & Singer, H. Factors contributing to adjustment and achievement in racially desegregated public schools. Grant application to U.S. Office of Education, 1967.

Glenn, N. D. Negro prestige criteria: A case study in the bases of prestige. *The American Journal of Sociology*, 1963, **68**, 645–657.

Gottlieb, D., & Ten Houten, W. D. Racial composition and the social systems of three high schools. *Journal of Marriage and the Family*, 1965, **27**, 204–212.

Green, R. L. After school integration—what? Problems in social learning. *Personnel and Guidance Journal*, 1966, **45**, 704–710.

Green, R. L., & Hofmann, L. J. A case study of the effects of educational deprivation on Southern rural Negro children, *Journal of Negro Education*, 1965, **34**, 327–341.

Gregor, A. J. Social science research and the education of the minority-group child. *Pediatrics Digest*, May, 1968.

Gurin, P., & Epps, E. Some characteristics of students from poverty backgrounds attending predominantly Negro colleges in the deep South. *Social Forces*, 1966, **45**, 27–40.

Hamilton, C. V. Race and education: A search for legitimacy. *Harvard Educational Review*, 1968, **38**, 669–684.

Harvard Educational Review. A special issue: Equal educational opportunity. *Harvard Educational Review*, 1968, **38**, 3–184.

Hatton, J. M. Reactions of Negroes in a biracial bargaining situation. *Journal of Personality and Social Psychology*, 1967, **7**, 301–306.

Jencks, C., & Riesman, D. The American Negro college. *Harvard Educational Review*, 1967, **37**, 3–60.

Katz, I., Henchy, T. & Allen, H. Effects of race of tester, approval-disapproval, and need on Negro children's learning. *Journal of Personality and Social Psychology*, 1968, **8**, 38–42.

Kennedy, W. A., & Vega, M. Negro children's performance on a discrimination task as a function of examiner race and verbal incentive. *Journal of Personality and Social Psychology*, 1965, **2**, 839–843.

King, M. L. *Conscience for change*. Toronto: CBC Publications, 1967.

Lefcourt, M. H., & Ladwig, G. W. The effect of reference group upon Negroes' task persistence in a biracial competitive game. *Journal of Personality and Social Psychology*, 1965, **1**, 668–671.

Lewis, W. A. The road to the top is through higher education—not black studies. *The New York Times Magazine*, May 11, 1969. (Reprinted from *University: A Princeton Quarterly*, 1969.)

Luchterhand, E., & Weller, L. Social class and the desegregation movement: A study of parents' decisions in a Negro ghetto. *Social Problems*, 1965, **13**, 83–88.

Moynihan, D. P. Education of the urban poor. *The Harvard Graduate School of Education Association Bulletin*, 1967, **12**, 1–13.

Nichols, R. C. Schools and the disadvantaged. *Science*, 1966, **154**, 1312–1314.

Nichols, R. C. A review of U.S. Commission on Civil Rights, racial isolation in the public schools. *American Educational Research Journal*, 1968, **5**, 700–707.

Pettigrew, T. F. Continuing barriers to desegregated education in the South. *Sociology of Education*, 1965, **38**, 99–111. (a)

Pettigrew, T. F. Social psychology and desegregation research. In I. Steiner and M. Fishbein (Eds.), *Current studies in social psychology*. New York: Holt, Rinehart and Winston, 1965. (b)

Pettigrew, T. F. Social evaluation theory: Convergences and applications. *Nebraska Symposium on Motivation*, 1967, **15**, 241–311.

Pettigrew, T. F. Racially separate or together? *Journal of Social Issues*, 1969, **25**, 43–69.

Riley, R. T. Strategies for the reduction of educational disadvantage. Paper presented at the New York State Psychological Association, May, 1968.

Rosenhan, D. L. Effects of social class and race on responsiveness to approval and disapproval. *Journal of Personality and Social Psychology*, 1966, **4**, 253–259.

Scott, R. First to ninth grade IQ change of Northern Negro students. *Psychology in the Schools*, 1966, **3**, 159–160.

Silberman, C. E. *Crisis in black and white*. New York: Random House, 1964.

Teele, J. E., Jackson, E., & Mayo, C. Family experiences in operations exodus. The bussing of Negro children. *Community Mental Health Journal*, Monograph Series, Number 3, 1967.

Teele, J. E., & Mayo, C. School racial integration: Tumult and shame. *Journal of Social Issues*, 1969, **25**, 137–156.

U.S. Commission on Civil Rights. *Racial isolation in the public schools*. Washington, D.C.: Government Printing Office, 1967.

17

Factors influencing Negro performance in the desegregated school[1]

IRWIN KATZ

This chapter focuses on the problem of identifying the important motivational determinants of Negro performance in the racially mixed classroom. Only a few studies have dealt directly with this problem, so that much of the evidence to be surveyed is only inferential. Included are the following: reports on the academic progress of Negro children attending integrated schools, evidence on as-

pects of the minority child's experience of desegregation that presumably affects his motivation to learn, relevant research on the behavioral effects of psychological stress, and, finally, a series of experiments on the intellectual performance and social reactions of Negro youths in biracial settings.

NEGRO AMERICANS

In this paper the term *Negro Americans* refers to a minority segment of the national population that is more or less distinguishable on the basis of skin color, hair texture, and so on, and that occupies a subordinate position in American culture. The extent of subordination varies in different regions and localities, but usually includes some degree of restriction on educational and economic opportunities, as well as social exclusion by whites and an attribution by whites of intellectual inferiority. While the term *race* will be used for convenience, no meaning is in-

Reprinted from *Social Class, Race, and Psychological Development*. M. Deutsch, I. Katz, & A. R. Jensen (Eds.). New York: Holt, Rinehart and Winston, 1967, Chapter 7, pp. 254–289, by permission of the authors and the publishers.

[1] This chapter is a revised version of a paper that appeared in the *American Psychologist*, 1964, **19**, 381–399. All the research on Negro performance by the author and his associates that is described was conducted under Contract Nonr 285(24) between the Office of Naval Research and New York University.

tended other than that of distinctiveness of appearance and commonality of experience; the issue of whether there are consequential differences in the genetic endowment of Negroes and whites will not be considered. Thus the present discussion should be more or less applicable to any American minority group whose status is similar to that of Negroes (for example, people with Puerto Rican or Mexican backgrounds).

DESEGREGATION

Educational desegregation is a politico-legal concept referring to the elimination of racial separation within school systems. As such it embraces a great variety of transitional situations having diverse effects upon the scholastic performance of Negro children. The meaning of desegregation has been broadened in recent years to include the reduction of racial clustering due to factors other than legal discrimination—that is, *de facto* segregation. A number of recent court decisions in the North have ruled that racial imbalance in a school (a preponderance of minority-group children) constitutes *de facto* segregation (The United States Commission on Civil Rights, 1962*a* and 1962*b*). Also described as *de facto* segregation by various social scientists are the racially homogeneous classes often found in schools where children are grouped according to ability (Dodson, 1962; Deutsch, 1963; Tumin, 1963).

The present concern is mainly with instances of desegregation that are marked by a substantial increase in the proportion of white peers, or both white peers and adult authorities, in the immediate environment of the Negro student. (In the South integration with white classmates is usually also the occasion of initial contacts with white teachers, while in the North the proportion of white teachers may be high even in schools where Negro students predominate.) Almost invariably in this type of desegregation experience the minority-group child is confronted with higher educational standards than prevail in segregated Negro schools (The United States Commission on Civil Rights, 1962*a* and 1962*b*). Both aspects of the Negro's experience—change in the racial environment and exposure to relatively high academic standards—are likely to have important influences on his scholastic motivation.

POSTULATED SITUATIONAL DETERMINANTS OF NEGRO PERFORMANCE IN DESEGREGATION

SOCIAL THREAT

Social threat refers to a class of social-stimulus events that tend to elicit anxious expectations that others will inflict harm or pain. One may assume that novel types of contact with white strangers possess a social-threat component for members of a subordinated minority group. The degree of threat should be a direct function of (a) the amount of evidence of white hostility (or the extent to which evidence of white friendliness is lacking), and (b) the amount of power possessed by whites in the contact situation, as shown by their numerical predominance, control of authority positions, and so forth. It seems likely that Negro children would be under some degree of social threat in a newly integrated classroom. Mere indifference on the part of white peers may frustrate their needs for companionship and approval, resulting in lowered self-esteem and the arousal of impulses to escape or aggress. In more extreme instances, verbal harassment and even physical hazing may elicit strong fear responses. These external threats are likely to distract the minority child from the task at hand, to the detriment of performance.

In addition, various psychological theories suggest that the Negro's own covert reactions to social threat would constitute an important source of intellectual impairment. In discussing the effect of psychological stress on the learning of skills, Deese (1962) mentions distraction by the internal stimuli of autonomic activation, as well as disruption of task responses by neuromuscular and other components of the stress reaction. Mandler and Sarason (1952) and others call attention to the disruptive role of task-irrelevant defensive responses against anxiety. Spence (1958) and Taylor (1963) propose that anxiety, conceptualized as drive, increases intratask response competition. And according to Easterbrook (1959), emotion lowers efficiency on complex tasks by narrowing the range of cue utilization. Also relevant is Bovard's (1959) hypothesis of a specific physiological mechanism to account for the apparent lowering of the stress threshold under conditions of social isolation.

Another way in which social threat may impair performance is by causing Negro children to abandon efforts to excel in order not to arouse further resentment and hostility in white competitors. That is, the latter may possess what French and Raven (1960) refer to as "coercive power." When academic success is expected to instigate white reprisals, then any stimulus which arouses the motive to achieve should also generate anxiety, and defensive avoidance of such stimuli should be learned. This response pattern would not be wholly nonadaptive in a situation where a small number of Negro students stood relatively powerless against a prejudiced white majority—if one assumes that evidence of Negro intellectual competence might have an ego-deflating effect on these white students. The Group for the Advancement of Psychiatry (1957, p. 10) has put the matter this way: ". . . A feeling of superior worth may be gained merely from the existence of a downgraded group. This leads to an unrealistic and unadaptive kind of self-appraisal based on invidious comparison rather than on solid personal growth and achievement. . . ."

Finally with regard to possible social threat emanating from a white teacher—given the prestige of the adult authority, any expression by a white teacher of dislike or devaluation, whether through harsh, indifferent, or patronizing behavior, should tend to have unfavorable effects on Negro performance similar to those just described, and perhaps of even greater intensity.

SOCIAL FACILITATION

When the minority newcomer in a desegregated school is accepted socially by his white classmates, his scholastic motivation should be influenced favorably. It was noted earlier that achievement standards tend to be higher in previously all-white schools than in Negro schools. From studies based on white subjects it is apparent that individuals are responsive to the standards of those with whom they desire to associate (reviewed by French and Raven, 1960; Bass, 1961; and Thibaut and Kelley, 1959). That Negro children want friendship with white age-mates was shown by Horowitz (1936); Radke *et al.* (1950); and Yarrow (1958). Another study, by Criswell (1939), suggests that Negro children in

racially mixed classrooms accept white prestige but increasingly withdraw into their own group as a response to white rejection. Thus, if their desire for acceptance is not inhibited or destroyed by sustained unfriendliness from white children, Negro pupils should tend to adopt the scholastic norms of the high-status majority group. Experimental support for this supposition comes from Dittes and Kelley (1956), who found with white college students that private as well as public adherence to the attitudinal standards of a group were highest among persons who had experienced a fairly high degree of acceptance from the group, with a possibility of gaining even fuller acceptance, while those who received a low degree of acceptance showed little genuine adherence to group norms.

Friendliness and approval on the part of white teachers should be beneficial to Negro motivation by increasing the incentive strength of scholastic success. Assuming that white teachers have more prestige for the minority child than do Negro teachers, the prospect of winning their approval should be more attractive. Hence, when such approval can be expected as a reward for good performance, motivation should be favorably influenced.

PROBABILITY OF SUCCESS

When the minority child is placed in a school that has substantially higher scholastic standards than he knew previously, he may become discouraged and not try to succeed. This common sense proposition is derivable from Atkinson's (1958a) theory of the motivational determinants of risk-taking and performance. For individuals in whom the tendency to approach success is stronger than the tendency to avoid failure, task motivation is assumed to be a joint function of the subjective probability of achieving success and the incentive value of success. From a postulated inverse relationship between the latter two variables (assuming external influences on incentive strength are held constant) he derives an hypothesis that the strength of motivation is at a maximum when the probability of success is 0.50, and diminishes as this probability approaches zero or unity. The hypothesis is supported by findings on arithmetic performance of white college students (Atkinson, 1958b), and white elementary school children (Murstein and

Collier, 1962), as well as on digit-symbol performance of white high school students (Rosen, 1961). (In these studies, the effect occurred regardless of whether subjects had scored relatively high or low on a projective personality measure of the motive to approach success.) It follows that if the Negro newcomer perceives the standards of excellence in a desegregated school as being substantially higher than those he encountered previously, so that the likelihood of his attaining them seems low, his scholastic motivation will decline.

FAILURE THREAT

Failure threat is a class of stimulus events in an achievement situation which tend to elicit anxious expectations of harm or pain as a consequence of failure. High probability of failure does not by itself constitute failure threat—it is necessary also that the failure have a social meaning. But in Atkinson's formulation, the negative incentive strength of failure varies inversely with the subjective probability of failure, so that fear of failure is most strongly aroused when the probability of failure is at an intermediate level. This leads to the paradoxical prediction that as the probability of failure increases beyond 0.50, fear of failure declines. The paradox is resolved when one recognizes that Atkinson's model deals only with that component of incentive strength that is determined by the apparent difficulty of the task. Sarason *et al.* (1960) call attention to the important influence of anticipated disapproval by parents and teachers on the negative valence of failure. (While their primary interest is in test anxiety as a personality variable, their discussion seems applicable to the present problem of identifying situational determinants of fear of failure.) Presumably, the child's belief that his failure to meet prevailing standards of achievement will bring adult disapproval is relatively unaffected by his own perception of the difficulty of a given task. Hence, fear of disapproval should increase as it becomes more probable—that is, as the subjective probability of failure increases. Sarason and his associates suggest that a high expectancy of failure arouses strong unconscious hostility against the adults from whom negative evaluation is foreseen. The hostility is turned inward against the self in the form of self-derogatory attitudes,

which strengthen the expectation of failure and the desire to escape the situation. Distraction by these and other components of emotional conflict may cause a decrement in the child's performance.

REPORTS ON ACADEMIC ACHIEVEMENT OF NEGROES IN DESEGREGATED SCHOOLS

There is a dearth of unequivocal information about Negro performance in desegregated schools. A number of factors have contributed to this situation. (1) Many desegregated school systems have a policy of racial nonclassification, so that separate data for Negroes and whites are not available. (2) Where total elimination of legal segregation has occurred it has usually been accompanied by vigorous efforts to raise educational standards in *all* schools; hence the effects of desegregation per se are confounded with the effects of improved teaching and facilities. (3) In several southern states only small numbers of highly selected Negro pupils have been admitted to previously all-white schools, and since before–after comparisons of achievement are not usually presented, reports of "satisfactory" adjustment by these Negro children shed little light on the question of relative performance.

Taking the published information for what it is worth, we find that most of it presents a favorable picture of Negro academic adjustment in racially mixed settings. Stallings (1959) has reported on the results of achievement testing in the Louisville school system in 1955–1956, the year prior to total elimination of legal segregation, and again two years later. Gains were found in the median scores of all pupils for the grades tested, with Negroes showing greater improvement than whites. The report gave no indication of whether the gains for Negroes were related to amount of actual change in the racial composition of schools. Indeed, Stallings stated, "The gains were greater where Negro pupils remained by choice with Negro teachers." A later survey on Louisville by Knowles (1962) indicated that Negro teachers had not been assigned to classrooms having white students during the period covered by Stallings' research. This means that the best Negro gains observed by Stallings were made by children who *remained in segregated classrooms,* and can only be attributed to factors *other* than desegregation, such as a general improvement in educational standards.

In both Washington, D.C., and Baltimore, where legal segregation was totally abolished in 1954, The United States Commission on Civil Rights found "some evidence that the scholastic achievement of Negroes in such schools has improved, and no evidence of a resultant reduction in the achievement of white students" (*Southern School News,* 1960). A detailed account of academic progress in the Washington schools since 1954 has been given by Hansen (1960). The results of a city-wide testing program begun in 1955 indicated year-to-year gains in achievement on every academic subject tested at every grade level where the tests were given. The data were not broken down by race. As in the case of Louisville, it seems reasonable to attribute these gains primarily to an ambitious program of educational improvement rather than to racial mixing. For several years, the Washington schools have had a steadily increasing predominance of Negro pupils (over 76 percent in 1960); this, combined with a four-track system of homogeneous ability-grouping which has the effect of concentrating Negroes in the lower tracks, has resulted in a minimal desegregation experience for the majority of Negro children.

Little relevant data have been published on other southern states where desegregation has been initiated. In 1960, twelve administrators of desegregated school systems testified at a federal hearing on whether integration had damaged academic standards (The United States Commission on Civil Rights, 1960). They unanimously replied in the negative, but only one official (from Louisville) mentioned gains in the achievement of Negro pupils. Reports of widespread academic failure on the part of desegregated Negro children are rare. Among those that have appeared recently is one by Day (1962) on Chapel Hill, N.C. Referring to a total of about forty-five Negroes in predominantly white schools, he stated that the experience of two years of desegregation has shown ". . . a disturbing portion of Negro children attending desegregated schools have failed to keep pace with their white classmates. . . .

The question remains as to how to raise the achievement of Negro pupils disadvantaged by their home background and lack of motivation" (p. 78). Wyatt (1962) quoted the Superintendent of Schools in Nashville, Tenn., as stating there was substantially more difficulty with Negro students entering desegregated situations in the upper grades. The official ascribed most of the difficulties to problems of social adjustment, although the cumulative effect of the generally lower achievement in the Negro schools was credited with some responsibility for the situation.

The most adequate data on the relationship between Negro academic achievement and racial balance in northern schools are contained in the report by Coleman *et al.* (1966) on American public education. An extensive sampling of metropolitan and rural communities revealed that as the proportion of white pupils in schools increased, Negro scores on achievement tests tended to rise. The apparent impact of desegregation can be illustrated by comparing percentile scores on reading comprehension for northern Negro high school students who never had a white classmate with scores of northern Negroes who attended integrated schools from the early grades. When figures from Table 3.3.2 of the Coleman report are consolidated, it is revealed that Negro ninth-graders with the longest experience of integrated schooling had an average point score of 48.2. This is about five points below the white norm for the same region, but less than two percentiles below the national norm of 50. In contrast, ninth-grade minority-group children who never had white classmates averaged 43.8. Thus it seems that desegregation reduced the racial achievement gap by almost half. (The Coleman report also gives scores of twelfth-graders, which were excluded from the present comparisons because the high rate of Negro dropouts makes them unrepresentative. Actually, the picture would not have been changed materially by their inclusion. The possibility exists that superior performance of Negroes in desegregated schools was due at least in part to having come from superior family or neighborhood backgrounds. However, the report does state that "cross tabulations on indicators of socioeconomic status showed that the differences [in achievement] are not accounted for by family background" (p. 331).)

When the influence of the student body's educational background and aspirations was controlled, the relationship between racial composition of schools and Negro test scores was sharply reduced. Thus much of the apparent beneficial effect of having a high proportion of white classmates comes not from racial composition per se, but from the high educational quality that is, on the average, found among white students.

Desegregation also appeared to have the effect of increasing the variability of Negro test scores. The differences in variance were small but consistent, and accorded with notions advanced earlier in this paper regarding the complex determination of Negro motivation in predominantly white settings: because of the high prestige of white teachers and age peers, rejection by them is more disturbing to the Negro pupil, and their acceptance more facilitative, than similar responses from Negro teachers and peers.

Further unpublished analyses of the Coleman data by James McPartland reveal the unexpected differences between truly *integrated* and merely *desegregated* schools. Those schools with more than half white-student bodies whose Negroes score well, when compared with similar schools whose Negroes score poorly, are characterized by greater cross-racial acceptance as predicted. Their students were much more likely to report close friends among members of the other race than were students in the merely desegregated schools.

The academic achievement of Negro graduates of segregated southern high schools who attended integrated colleges has been reviewed by the National Scholarship Service and Fund for Negro Students (1963). In a period of fifteen years, NSSFNS helped over 9000 Negro students to enroll in interracial colleges, situated mostly in the North. The report stated (p. 9) that "5.6 percent of these students had a scholastic average of A or A−; 50.3 percent B+, B, or B−; 32.4 percent C+, C, or C−; and 0.7 percent D or below. Not listing grades were 11 percent. Fewer than 5 percent withdrew from college for any reason. This record of college success . . . is far above the national average, which shows an over 40 percent incidence of dropouts from all causes."

It should be noted that these students were carefully selected by NSSFNS for their academic qualifications. Nonetheless, the NSSFNS experience demonstrates that qualified southern Negro youth can function effectively in predominantly white colleges of good quality. Later, there will be mention of additional material on these students which suggests that academic success was associated with social acceptance on the campus.

EVIDENCE OF DESEGREGATION CONDITIONS THAT MAY BE DETRIMENTAL TO THE PERFORMANCE OF NEGROES

It was proposed that the achievement motivation of Negro children in desegregation may be strongly influenced by the social behavior of their white classmates and teachers (social threat and facilitation), by their level of expectancy with regard to academic success (probability of success), and by their perception of the social consequences of failure (failure threat). In this section, evidence about conditions of desegregation that are assumed to have unfavorable effects will be considered. The focusing on negative factors is not meant to suggest that conditions favorable to Negro performance are lacking in present-day situations of desegregation, but rather that the former have received more attention from social scientists—apparently because they are more salient.

Social Rejection and Isolation

The rationale for assuming that social rejection is detrimental to the minority child's academic behavior has already been discussed. To what extent are Negroes rejected by white classmates? It is clear that this varies greatly from one community to another. The bulk of early studies on the racial attitudes of white school children in the North indicated that from an early age they expressed strong preference for their own racial group (for example, Horowitz, 1936; Criswell, 1939; Radke et al., 1949; and Radke et al., (1950). Two examples of desegregation that were highly stressful for Negro children have been described by a psychiatrist, Coles (1963). He writes of the first Negroes to enter white schools in Atlanta and New Orleans:

> . . . When they are in school they may experience rejection, isolation, or insult.

They live under what physicians would consider to be highly stressful circumstances . . . (p. 4).

During a school year one can see among these children all of the medical and psychiatric responses to fear and anxiety. One child may lose his appetite, another may become sarcastic and have nightmares. Lethargy may develop, or excessive studying may mark the apprehension common to both. At the same time one sees responses of earnest and effective work. . . . Each child's case history would describe a balance of defenses against emotional pain, and some exhaustion under it, as well as behavior which shows an attempt to challenge and surmount it (p. 5).

Out of thirteen original students who were studied during the first two years of integration, and forty-seven who became involved in integration one year later and were studied during the second year, "only one child has really succumbed to emotional illness." Coles does not present a systematic analysis of the various specific sources of fear and anxiety, but he suggests that worries about schoolwork were of less importance than reactions to the prejudice of white children. Nor does he present adequate information about academic success, merely noting that very few learning difficulties "were insurmountable."

Severe stress due to social rejection has been experienced also by Negro students at various newly desegregated colleges and universities in the South. For example, several months after entering the University of Mississippi as its first Negro student, during which time he was often in considerable physical danger, James Meredith emphasized that rejection and social isolation were the most difficult features of his experience. He referred to himself as "the most segregated Negro in the world," despite his enrollment at the University. "Through it all," he said, "the most intolerable thing has been the campaign of ostracizing me" (*Southern School News*, 1963).

Two Negro students who initiated integration at the University of Georgia experienced rejection and isolation during their entire two-year enrollment. Trillin wrote (1964, p. 83): "As Hamilton (Holmes) began his final ten-week quarter at Georgia, he had never eaten in a University dining hall, studied in the library, used the gymnasium, or entered the snack bar. He had no white friends outside the classroom. No white student had ever visited him and he had never visited one of them."

The other student, Charlayne Hunter, eventually entered into friendly relationships with several white classmates, and was generally in the company of other students when walking to and from classes or eating on campus. However, she remained totally ostracized in the dormitory where she occupied a room by herself. Both Negroes have since graduated, Holmes with a distinguished academic record. Miss Hunter is now married to a white southerner who was a fellow student at the university.

Desegregation under more favorable conditions has been investigated by Yarrow (1958). Comparable groups of Negro and white children of both sexes were observed in segregated and desegregated summer camps during two-week sessions. The campers were from low-income families in southern and border states. The biracial camps had integrated adult staffs that were highly motivated to "make desegregation work." It was found that the behavior of children in segregated and integrated groups was quite similar. An initial tendency for both white and Negro children to prefer white friends lessened during the two-week period studied. Satisfaction with the camp experience, as indicated by the percentage of children who expressed a desire that the camp session be extended, was somewhat higher in the desegregated camps. However, there were also indications of social conflict and emotional tension associated with the integration process. In older groups (ages twelve and thirteen) white children initially directed almost twice as much aggression toward Negro cabin mates as toward white age peers. At the beginning of contact 29 percent of all actions by white campers toward Negroes were hostile. On the other hand, Negro children of all ages aggressed more against one another than against whites. Overt manifestations of white prejudice tended to diminish during the two-week period. Nonetheless, tension symptoms appeared in almost twice as many children in desegregated as in segregated groups (71 percent compared with 38 percent). Frequencies were the same for Negroes and whites. But Negro children in desegregation were more likely to manifest covert or internalized signs of distress (enuresis, fears, nightmares, withdrawal, physical symptoms) than those that were more overt (fighting, generally disruptive behavior, obscene language, complaining). Of the Negro campers showing tension, 85 percent showed reactions of the covert type. For the white children showing tension, neither covert nor overt responses predominated. That Negroes were particularly fearful of white disapproval is suggested by their oversensitiveness in desegregation to aggressive and dominative behavior in other Negroes, and their denial of such impulses in themselves. Both reactions are further evidence of a tendency to conceal tensions in the presence of whites.

Regarding the relevance of this study to school integration, it should be noted that the total period of interracial contacts was brief, but peer interactions were probably more intimate and intense than the usual classroom contacts. A generally favorable picture of race relations in southern integrated schools was presented in an article by a journalist, Tanner (1964). He found that "younger white and Negro children attending desegregated classes seem to accept each other better than the older ones. Negro and white youngsters can be seen playing together on the slides and swings of almost any desegregated southern elementary school's playground."

One investigation has shown that experiences of social acceptance are associated with academic success. In the earlier-mentioned NSSFNS program of placing qualified Negro graduates of southern high schools in northern integrated colleges, it was found that those who participated in extracurricular activities, dated, and had a satisfactory number of friends got better marks than those who did not (National Scholarship Service and Fund for Negro Students, 1960). Though this finding is merely correlational, it is consistent with the proposition that acceptance by white peers is beneficial to the achievement motivation of Negro students.

Fear of Competition with Whites

It was suggested that low expectation of success is an important detrimental factor in the performance of minority children attending integrated schools. The evidence is strong that Negro students have feelings of intellectual inferiority which arise from an awareness of actual differences in racial achieve-

ment, or from irrational acceptance of the white group's stereotype of Negroes.

INADEQUACY OF PREVIOUS TRAINING

The low quality of segregated Negro education is well documented. Plaut (1957) has summarized the over-all situation:

> Negroes, furthermore, have long been aware that most of their schools in the South, and often the *de facto* segregated schools in the North, are rundown, poorly staffed, and shorthanded. Second- and third-rate schooling for Negroes leaves them without the ability to compete with white students and robs them of the initiative to compete. Even the 1955 Speaker of the Georgia House of Representatives admitted recently that "Negro education in Georgia is a disgrace. What the Negro child gets in the sixth grade, the white child gets in the third" (p. 5).

A few specific instances of educational disparity at the grade-school level will be cited. Findley (1957) found in testing for achievement in the Atlanta schools that from 40 percent to 60 percent of white pupils met the standards set by the top 50 percent of a national sample on the different tests; but only 2 percent to 10 percent of Negro pupils met this standard on the various tests. In Tennessee, according to Wyatt (1962), Negro students averaged one and one half to two years behind grade level when transferred to biracial schools in the upper grades. In earlier grades, transfers performed satisfactorily. The same report described the status of Negro and white teachers in a Tennessee urban area. Only 49 percent of 901 academically qualified Negro teachers passed the National Teachers Examination; among white teachers, more than 97 percent of 783 qualified teachers passed the test. The Tennessee survey showed that the academic retardation of the segregated Negro elementary school pupil is progressive.

The situation in northern Virginia was summarized by Mearns (1962) in a report written for The United States Commission on Civil Rights:

> The Negroes themselves have recognized that the achievement gap exists, but the only obvious reaction among most Negroes is reluctance to transfer to white schools. The question is raised as to whether Negroes really obtain a better education in desegregated schools where they must compete with better prepared, highly motivated

white students. Frustration and failure engulf the ill-prepared Negro pupils. . . . (pp. 209–210)

Other data indicate that the racial gap in achievement continues to widen through high school and college. Roberts (1963) pointed out that less than 3 percent of Negro graduates of segregated high schools would meet the standards of nonsegregated colleges. Roberts estimated that not more than 10 to 15 percent of Negro American college youth were capable of exceeding the threshold level score on the ACE that was recommended by the President's Commission (100 on the 1947 edition).

Even in the urban North, where schools are legally integrated, the education afforded Negroes tends to be inadequate. Deutsch (1960), for example, found that in time-samples of classroom activity, from 50 to 80 percent of all classroom time in New York City elementary schools with predominantly Negro lower-class children was "devoted to disciplining and various essentially nonacademic tasks." By comparison, only 30 percent of classroom time was given over to such activities in elementary schools attended mainly by white children of roughly similar economic status.

The foregoing material indicates that when grade-a-year plans of desegregation are adopted, it is obviously desirable from an educational standpoint to begin integration at the lowest grade and work upward. However, many southern school systems are on grade-a-year plans of reverse order, with integration starting in the twelfth grade and proceeding down.

UNREALISTIC INFERIORITY FEELINGS

Apparently, the Negro child's feeling of intellectual inferiority is based not only on reality experience, but reflects an emotional accommodation to the demeaning role in American culture that has been imposed upon his racial group by the dominant white majority. The Group for the Advancement of Psychiatry (1957) has summarized the observations of numerous investigators of Negro personality:

Wherever segregation occurs, one group, in this instance the Negroes, always suffers from inferior social status. The damaging effects of this are reflected in unrealistic inferiority feelings, a sense of humiliation, and constriction of potentialities for self-development. This often results in a pattern of self-hatred and rejection of one's own group, sometimes expressed by anti-social behavior toward one's own group or the dominant group. These attitudes seriously affect the levels of aspiration, the capacity to learn, and the capacity to relate in interpersonal situations (p. 10).

Two experiments with Negro male college students suggest the marked extent to which loss of confidence when competing with whites can override reality. Preston and Bayton (1941) found that when students at a Negro college were told that their own scores on intellectual tasks were the same as the average scores of white students, they tended to set their goal levels lower on the next few trials than they did when told that their scores equaled those of other Negro students. The results can be interpreted on the basis of Atkinson's (1958a) theory of goal-setting behavior. Assuming that his motive to succeed tended to be stronger than his motive to avoid failure, the Negro subject should have set his goal where the probability of success was 0.50. When a given level of performance was said to represent the white norm its apparent difficulty became greater than when it was supposed to represent the Negro norm, hence the goal level at which the expectancy of success was 0.50 tended to be lower immediately following the announcement of these norms. In an investigation of small biracial workteams at a northern university, Katz and Benjamin (1960) observed that Negro students who had actually scored as well as their white teammates on various intellectual tasks, afterwards rated their own performance as inferior. Here knowledge of white performance levels apparently influenced the Negro subjects' cognitions of their own *actual* performance, rather than just their estimations of *future* performances.

In an experiment suggested by Whyte's (1943) observations of status influence in a white street-corner gang, Harvey (1953) had members of white high-school cliques take turns on a dart-throwing task. After several practice trials, the boys openly estimated their own and their companions' future performance. Guesses were directly related to social rank in the group. Only boys of lowest rank showed a tendency to *under*estimate their own performance. Moreover, they were expected by those of middle and high status to perform more poorly than they actually did. It should be noted that it is unclear from Harvey's results whether rank influenced perception of own ability or merely what one was willing to say in front of higher-ranking clique-mates who had coercive power (French and Raven, 1960) to keep those of lesser rank "in their place."

EXPERIMENTS ON STRESS AND PERFORMANCE

Earlier some situational factors were described that presumably are detrimental to Negro academic achievement: social threat, low expectancy of success, and failure threat. Also, evidence was presented (some of it inferential) of their occurrence in actual situations of racial integration. A good deal of experimentation having to do with the influence of these factors on verbal and motor performance has been stimulated by the concept of psychological stress. Applezweig and Moeller (1957) proposed a definition of stress which focuses on the condition of the individual: stress occurs when a motive or need is strongly aroused and the organism is unable to respond in such a way as to reduce its motivation. Deese (1962) finds it more useful to define stress as a class of stimulus events that elicit a set of correlated responses, among which are feelings of discomfort. He points out that the effects of stress on performance are specific to particular components of the performance under consideration—that is, responses to stress may be either compatible or incompatible with the responses required in a given task.

Early studies of stress and performance did not employ the type of analytic comparison of stress responses and dimensions of ability in specific skills that Deese suggests. The general trend of findings on verbal performance (reviewed by Lazarus *et al.*, 1952) has been that stress impairs efficiency on relatively complex and difficult tasks, while on simple tasks stress has sometimes been shown to improve performance. The types of stress that have been used in experiments include failure feedback or threat of failure, exposure to highly difficult tasks (often under time pressure), annoying or painful stimulation such as electric shock, distraction such

as flashing lights or noises, disapproval or disparagement.

Many investigations have employed stress inductions that apparently aroused fear of failure. For example, using nine-year-old boys, Lantz (1945) observed an impairment of Stanford-Binet scores following a failure experience, but no such effect after a successful experience. An examination by Lantz of the differential effects of this failure experience upon the various subtests indicated that tasks requiring visual or rote memory were not affected, while those involving reasoning or thinking suffered a decrement. In other studies that were reviewed by Lazarus *et al.*, failure stress produced decrements in scores on the following verbal-symbolic tasks: learning and recall of nonsense syllables, digit-symbol substitution, arithmetic, recognition of briefly exposed sentences, sentence-formation, and digit-span. Similar effects were obtained on various types of perceptual-motor performance (for example, card-sorting, reaction time).

Turning to some representative studies of stress not directly involving failure, Barker *et al.* (1941) observed regression in the mental age of nursery-school children, as measured by the constructiveness of their play, when the children were frustrated by being denied access to attractive toys. Stress associated with the blocking of hostile impulses against an instigating agent (a teacher who arbitrarily disregarded the expressed desire of students) was found by Goldman *et al.* (1954) to impair performance on three tasks: retention of learned material, digit-span, and problem solving. Laird (1923) reported loss of body steadiness in college students who were "razzed" by future fraternity brothers while working on simple motor tasks. Klein (1957) found that a strong task-irrelevant drive (thirst) cause a reduction in the accuracy of visual-size judgments; and Callaway and Thompson (1953) obtained a similar effect when their subjects were required to hold one foot in a bucket of ice water.

During the past decade much research has been done on the role of personality factors in reactions to stress, with particular focus on the role of individual differences in chronic anxiety as measured by Taylor's Manifest Anxiety Scale and Mandler and Sarason's Test Anxiety Questionnaire. A lengthy review of this work would fall outside the scope of this paper, inasmuch as the primary concern here is with *situational* factors that affect Negro performance. Yet it is of interest to note the general pattern of experimental results. Greater decrements due to stress are found in the performance of highly-anxious individuals than in the performance of subjects lower in the anxiety-score distribution. These studies have been reviewed by Sarason (1960) and Taylor (1963).

Speculating about underlying physiological processes in stress, Bovard (1959) places the organizing center of bodily-emotional responses to stress in the posterior and medial hypothalamus. Of particular interest are his hypotheses that (a) activity in the anterior hypothalamus tends to inhibit or dampen posterior activity, and (b) excitation in the anterior hypothalamus is produced by certain types of social stimuli. *Thus an organism's vulnerability to stress depends upon the nature of its social environment.* Bovard reviewed studies which suggest that the presence of companions or members of the same species has a supportive effect under stress. At the human level it has been observed that separation from the family and evacuation from London was more stressful for London children than enduring the bombings with their families (Titmuss, 1950). Mandlebaum (1952) and Marshall (1951) dealt with the importance of social contact among soldiers in resisting battle stress. Research at Boston Psychopathic Hospital (1955) has shown that lysergic acid diethylamide (*LSD*) taken in a group situation results in less anxiety and inappropriate behavior than when taken individually. Schachter (1959) reported that fear, as well as hunger, increased the affiliative tendency in college students; and Wrightsman (1960) found that being with others in a similar plight was anxiety-reducing for students who were first-born or only children.

Similar phenomena have been observed at the animal level. Liddel (1950) found that the presence or absence of the mother goat determined whether young goats would develop an experimental neurosis in a conditioning situation. In experiments with rats, animals tested together under stressful conditions gave less fear-response (Davitz and Mason, 1955) and had less resultant ulceration (Conger *et al.*, 1957) than animals tested alone. Similarly, monkeys showed fewer fear-responses in a strange situation when another monkey was present (Mason, 1960). Monkeys raised in total isolation from age peers were deficient in normal defensive responses to environmental threat (Harlow and Harlow, 1962).

If Bovard's theory is correct, the extreme social isolation that is often experienced by Negroes in predominantly white environments would weaken their resistance to other stress conditions, such as might arise from the inherent difficulty of academic work, time pressure, financial problems, and so on.

Various theories have been invoked to account for the tendency of stress to reduce efficiency on complex tasks, but to facilitate performance, or have no effect, on simple tasks. Sarason and others (Mandler and Sarason, 1952; Child, 1954; Sarason *et al.*, 1960) have dealt primarily with the effects of individual differences in vulnerability to failure stress. They emphasize the interference that occurs when expectation of failure generates anxiety which, in turn, acts as an internal stimulus for defensive, task-irrelevant responses. Similarly, Deese (1962) mentions task interference from responses to the internal stimuli of stress-induced autonomic activity.

Some writers have concerned themselves with the effect of drive on specific characteristics of task-relevant behavior. Thus Easterbrook (1959) postulates an inverse relationship between drive level and the range of cue utilization. Complex tasks require a relatively broad awareness of cues for optimal efficiency, whereas simple tasks by definition require apprehension of only a few cues for successful responding. Hence, when drive is very high (as in stress), relevant cues will be missed on hard tasks, but more closely attended to on easy tasks. Hullian theory, as developed with respect to anxiety drive and learning by Spence *et al.*, deals with the energizing effect of drive on task responses. As strength of drive increases the number of habitual response tendencies that can be elicited in a given task increases also. When activation is strong (as in stress) intratask response competition is heightened. The theory is supported by the results of experiments in which high and low scorers on Taylor's Manifest Anxiety Scale were required to learn competitional and noncompetitional paired-word lists (reviewed by Spence, 1958;

and Taylor, 1963). Thus Easterbrook and the Hullians have each dealt with a particular component of a great number of tasks, and have tried to predict either favorable or detrimental effects of stress from the presence or absence of this component.

Discussing the effects of stress on perceptual motor skills, Deese (1962) points out the need for systematic analysis of (a) the characteristics of motor arousal under stress, in relation to (b) the dimensions of psychomotor abilities that are requisite for various task performances. Both Deese and Spence (1958) mention that a fundamental weakness of present thinking about the effects of stress on *verbal* learning is that not enough dimensions of verbal skills have yet been explored to know what kinds of effects to look for.

Summarizing this section, there is a considerable amount of experimental evidence that types of stress which may be present in desegregation (as varieties of social threat and failure threat) impair certain kinds of verbal and perceptual-motor learning. However, there does not exist at present any comprehensive system of variables for predicting the specific effects of different conditions of stress on the Negro child's performance of various academic tasks.

EXPERIMENTS ON NEGRO PERFORMANCE IN BIRACIAL SITUATIONS

In recent years this author and his associates have been engaged in a series of experiments on the intellectual productivity of Negro male college students in situations involving white peers and/or white authority figures. The general aim of the research is the identification of underlying psychological factors that have either favorable or detrimental effects on Negro efficiency. In connection with the interpretation of the results that are now to be presented, there evolved the set of postulated situational determinants of performance that were discussed earlier in this chapter.

BIRACIAL TEAMS

In two exploratory studies, conducted at a northern university (Katz *et al.*, 1958; and Katz and Benjamin, 1960), various cognitive and motor tasks were assigned to groups composed of two Negro students and two white students. Initially the men were total strangers. They worked together in several sessions for a total of 12½ hours. In general, it was found that Negroes displayed marked social inhibition and subordination to white partners. When teams were engaged in cooperative problem solving, Negro subjects made fewer proposals than did whites, and tended to accept the latter's contributions uncritically. On all tasks combined, Negroes made fewer remarks than did whites, and spoke more to whites, proportionately, than to one another. White men, on the other hand, spoke more to one another, proportionately, than to Negro men. These behaviors occurred even when group members could expect a monetary bonus for good teamwork, and were informed that their abilities were higher than those of subjects in other teams. Moreover, in the second experiment Negro and white partners were matched on intelligence, and were even made to display equal ability on certain group tasks (by means of secret manipulation of tasks). Yet on a terminal questionnaire Negroes ranked whites higher on intellectual performance, preferred one another as future work companions, and expressed less satisfaction with the group experience than did whites.

The findings on Negro behavior may have been a result of (a) social threat (that is, Negroes were fearful of instigating white hostility through greater assertiveness); (b) low-motivation in confrontation with white achievement standards (as derived earlier from Atkinson's model); or (c) failure threat (high expectancy of failure combined with anxious anticipation of disapproval and rejection by white peers and the white experimenter). The experimental data provide no basis on which to reject any of these factors as irrelevant.

In the next experiment, Katz and Cohen (1962) attempted to modify Negro behavior toward white partners in the direction of greater assertiveness and autonomy. It was predicted that (a) when Negroes were compelled to achieve on a task that was performed cooperatively with a white peer, they would subsequently display an increased amount of achieving behavior on another shared task of different content, and (b) Negro subjects who were not compelled to achieve on the first task would show an opposite tendency. Negro-white student dyads at a northern university engaged in cooperative solving of problems adapted from the Raven Progressive Matrices. Some of the problems were made easy, to ensure that both participants would perceive the correct answer. On other problems the subjects unknowingly received different information, so that one person had an easy version, while the other person had an insoluble version. Each subject had the easy version half the time. On every problem partners had to agree on a single team-answer, after which the experimenter announced the correct solution. Before and after the problem-solving experience a disguised measure of social influence between the two men was obtained on a task which required group estimates of certain quantitative characteristics of briefly exposed photographs (for example, the number of paratroopers in the sky).

In a control condition, the rules of the problem-solving situation did not require that each person openly propose an answer to every problem. It was found that Negroes tended to accept passively the suggestions of their white companions *even when they held the easy version and the teammate had to be in error*. With respect to intellectual efficiency, the private responses of Negroes, which they wrote down before each discussion began, showed *more errors than were made on the same problems at an earlier, individual testing session*. White subjects, on the other hand, made *fewer* private errors than they had made previously. As a consequence of the problem-solving experience in the control condition, Negroes showed increased social compliance on the picture estimations.

In an "assertion-training" condition the men were given their answer sheets from the previous session when they had worked alone. On every problem the two partners were required to read aloud their previous answers before negotiating a team reply. Thus, Negro subjects had the experience of openly announcing correct solutions in about half of all instances of disagreement (both men read off approximately the same number of correct answers). In the subsequent interactions over picture estimation there was an *increase* in the amount of influence Negroes had over the white partner. Further, Negro subjects were now inclined to accept the other person's influence only to the extent that he had displayed superior accuracy on previous pictures.

Thus, unless *forced* to express opinions at variance with those of a white peer, Negro students tended to suppress their own ideas in deference to the other person, and to show increased compliance on another task. But when they were *forced* to act independently on one task, they achieved greater autonomy in the second situation. The responses of white subjects on a postexperimental questionnaire indicate there may have been some hostility aroused against Negro partners who displayed intellectual competence. After working in the assertion-training condition whites tended to downgrade the Negro's performance and to accept him less as a future coworker. However, since there were no all-white control groups, it is not known whether these reactions of white subjects were specifically interracial.

The results suggest that Negro submissiveness with the white companion was an effect primarily of social threat, and that probability of success was a relatively unimportant factor. As already mentioned, in both the "assertion-training" and control conditions, disagreement was experimentally arranged on almost all problems, with random alternation between partners in the assignment of easy and insoluble versions (on a few items *both* men had either easy or hard versions). Also, after each team decision the experimenter announced the correct answer (fictitious when both men had hard items) so that subjects could check the accuracy of their own private response and of the solution the partner had openly proposed. While there was a stable tendency in control teams of whites to make slightly fewer private errors than Negroes (all partners had been matched on pretest scores), it is doubtful that the average race difference of about two private errors on forty-nine items could have been discriminated by the average Negro subject. Hence, the relative accuracy of own and partner's solutions was much the same for Negro subjects in the two experimental conditions, and the only difference between conditions was that in "assertion training" the Negro subject was forced to *disagree openly* with the partner. The disinhibiting effect of this experience on the Negro subject's behavior on another task seems attributable to a reduction in anxiety about instigating white hostility.

THE EFFECT OF INDUCED THREAT IN
DIFFERENT RACIAL ENVIRONMENTS

In the next experiment, Katz and Greenbaum (1963) examined more directly the influence of threat on Negro verbal performance by systematically varying the level of threat in different racial environments. Individual Negro students at a predominantly Negro college in the South were given a digit-symbol substitution task in the presence of two strangers who were both either white or Negro—an adult administrator and a confederate who pretended to be another student working on the same task. In order to minimize the amount of uncontrolled threat implicit in the white condition, there was no social interaction between the Negro subject and his white peer, and the task was described as a research instrument of no evaluative significance.

In addition to the variation of racial environment, the students were exposed to a condition of either high or low threat. Since the purpose of the threat variation was to determine whether individual Negroes were more vulnerable to debilitative effects of stress when they were alone with whites than when they were with other Negroes, it seemed desirable to use a threat stimulus that would not lead to intentional suppression of responses by changing the social meaning of the task situation. The experimenters used an announcement that severe electric shock (high-threat condition) or mild electric shock (low-threat condition) would be administered to the subject and the coworker at random times during the task. No shocks were actually delivered.

The results indicated that Negro students' scores on the digit-symbol task depended upon the particular combination of stress and racial-environment conditions under which they worked. When only mild shock was threatened they performed better in the presence of whites than of other Negroes. But when told to expect strong shock their efficiency in the Negro condition improved, while in the white condition it went down. Apparently, the prospect of successful competition against a white peer, and of approval from a white authority figure, had greater incentive strength than the corresponding prospect in the all-Negro situation. This is reasonable on the assumption that the whites (particularly the experimenter) had higher prestige for the subject than their Negro counterparts. Since in all experimental conditions the instructions for the task played down its intellectual significance, Negro subjects in the white environment, low shock-threat condition would not have experienced strong failure threat. Hence, they could respond to the stronger incentive strength of success in the white condition.

There are a number of ways of looking at the effects of shock threat. First, if Negro subjects cared more about performing well in the white condition they would have been more fearful lest the strong shock disrupt their task responses (failure threat). The expected stimulus would thus become more salient and distracting. An upward spiral of debilitation could then be set in motion as distraction and fear made the task seem more difficult, and this in turn aroused further emotion. Subjects in the Negro environment, on the other hand, had a relatively relaxed attitude toward the task in the low-threat condition (*too* relaxed for good performance). Hence they would not have been fearful of possible decrements due to shock, but perhaps just enough concerned to work harder than before. Also relevant to these data is Bovard's earlier mentioned notion that the ability to withstand stress is strengthened by the presence of familiar social stimuli that have nurturant associations (in this case other Negroes).

The Hullian conception of the energizing effect of drive is also applicable: efficiency declined in the white condition because the subject's initial stimulation in this racial environment, in combination with the additional stimulation of the strong shock threat, produced a total drive strength that exceeded the optimum for the assigned task. In the Negro condition initial stimulation was relatively low, so that the increment in arousal due to strong threat brought the total drive level closer to the optimum than it had been under mild threat.

One practical implication of Katz and Greenbaum's findings is that *in desegregation the performance of Negroes may show a wider range of variation in both upward and downward directions than in segregated situations, depending upon specific features of the situation.*

EFFECTS OF IQ VERSUS NON-IQ INSTRUCTIONS

In a follow-up on the preceding experiment, Katz *et al.* (1965) investigated the effects on Negro students' efficiency of three factors: the race of the task administrator, the difficulty of the task, and the evaluative significance of the task. All subjects were students at a southern Negro college. Half of them were tested individually by a Negro adult and the other half were tested by a white adult. In addition, one third of the total sample worked on a relatively easy digit-symbol code, one third were given a code of medium difficulty, and one third had to do a relatively hard code. In order to attach a relatively nonthreatening significance to the situation, the task was described as a research instrument for studying eye-hand coordination, a nonintellectual characteristic. Unlike the Katz and Greenbaum experiment, there was no experimental confederate who posed as a second subject. The findings were consistent with results obtained in the low-threat condition of the earlier study—Negro subjects worked more efficiently when tested by a white adult than when tested by a Negro adult. However, the favorable influence of the white administrator was apparent only on the most difficult of the three tasks. On the two easier codes there was no statistically reliable differences in achievement associated with the skin color of the experimenters. Apparently the easier tasks were too simple to reflect the differences in motivation.

Then two additional groups of Negro students were tested by the same Negro and white administrators on the most difficult task only. But instead of being told that the task measured eye-hand coordination, it was presented to these subjects as a test of intelligence. Now the subjects did not attain higher scores in the presence of a white experimenter; rather, the effect of the IQ instructions was to elevate, slightly, performance with a Negro tester, and to lower scores markedly in the white-tester group, so that the means for both testers were at about the same level. Thus, in this experiment, making the most difficult task relevant to intellectual ability had effects not unlike those of strong-shock threat in the previous study (by Katz and Greenbaum). On the assumption that intellectual instructions were more highly motivating than the motor-test instructions, one can again apply the Hullian interpretation that motivation in the IQ test with white-administrator treatment was excessive.

More directly relevant is Atkinson's (1958a) conception of motivation as a joint function of the subjective probability and incentive value of success, which was discussed earlier. Assuming again that a white experimenter has higher prestige for the Negro student than does a Negro experimenter, the prospect of eliciting the white person's approval would be more attractive. It follows that when the likelihood of winning approval by scoring well is equally high, whether the tester is Negro or white, the subject will work harder for the white person. Thus in this experiment Negro students performed better with a white adult than with a Negro adult when the task was supposed to assess an ability which Negroes are not stereotyped as lacking (eye-hand coordination). Presenting the task as an intelligence test ought to have raised the incentive value of achievement in both racial conditions, with perhaps an even greater increment occurring when the experimenter was white (since *intellectual* approval by a white adult might be uniquely gratifying to the Negro student's self-esteem).

But suppose that on the intellectual task the Negro subject saw very little likelihood of meeting the white experimenter's standard of excellence. Unless the incentive strength of success increased enough to counterbalance the drop in subjective probability, Atkinson's model would predict a reduction in task motivation. As an additional source of impairment in this situation, low expectancy of success could have aroused fear of earning the white tester's disapproval (failure threat).

Turning now to the situation where the tester is Negro, there is no reason to assume that the subject's expectation of success would be markedly lower when the task was described as intellectual than when it was presented as a motor test. In both instances the racial identity of the tester would tend to suggest to the subject that he was to be compared with other Negroes. Accordingly, performance with the Negro tester ought to go up under IQ instructions. The fact that it rose only slightly in our experiment may be ascribed to the subject's lack of clarity about the tester's frame of reference for evaluating his score. That is, he was not actually informed whether he would be compared with norms for Negro students only, or with norms for *all* college students. The next study deals directly with this issue.

EFFECTS OF VARIATIONS IN ANTICIPATED COMPARISON

Katz *et al.* (1964) investigated the effects on Negro students' digit-symbol performance of being told that they would be compared intellectually with other Negro students, or with white students. Hard and easy versions of the digit-symbol task were administered by a Negro to different groups of students at a southern Negro college under three different instructions: no test, scholastic aptitude test with own-college norms, and scholastic aptitude test with national- (that is, predominantly white-) college norms. Scores in all three conditions were reliably different from one another, with highest achievement occurring in the Negro-norms condition, intermediate achievement in the white-norms condition, and lowest achievement when no comparison was expected. These differences tended to be larger on the hard task than on the easy one.

Again referring to Atkinson's model, Negro performance was lowest in the no-test condition because of low incentive, while the difference between the two test conditions was due to higher subjective probability of success (closer to 0.50) when Negro subjects believed they were competing with members of their own race than when they expected to be compared with whites.

White students from a nearby state university were tested by a white person under comparable instructions on the hard task only. It was found that scores of the two norms groups—that is, own college and national—did not differ, and *both* groups were more efficient than subjects in the no-comparison condition.

Future research can determine the usefulness of this application of Atkinson's theory for understanding Negro behavior in integrated schools. For example, the present formulation predicts that if the subjective probability of success were held constant, Negro subjects would perform *better* on certain types of intellectual test when the administrator was white than when he was Negro, or when they were competing with white peers rather than with Negro peers.

AN EXPERIMENT ON THE EFFECT OF PROBABILITY-OF-SUCCESS FEEDBACK

In a recent unpublished study, the race of the tester, the race of the comparison group, and the probability of success were all manipulated independently. Freshmen at a southern Negro college were first administered, en masse, a digit-symbol task by a Negro experimenter, with neutral instructions. A few days later subjects were again tested, this time in small groups. The tester, who was now either white or Negro, introduced himself as a psychologist from the "Southern Educational Testing Service," a fictitious organization. Subjects were informed that the earlier session had really been a practice tryout for the scholastic-aptitude test which they were about to take, and that test norms were available. For the white-norms condition they were told that their scores would be compared with the average scores of students in all colleges and universities of the state, and for the Negro-norms condition the story was that that they would be compared with the freshmen average at their own college. The men were also told that immediately following the testing, the administrator would see each person individually, score the test immediately, and render an evaluation to the individual of his intelligence and his aptitude for college work. This was done to create a strong expectation of face-to-face evaluation by the adult authority.

Then for the probability-of-success manipulation each subject was handed a printed form letter in an envelope bearing his name. Ostensibly from the "Testing Service," the letter explained that from the subject's score on the practice trial of the digit-symbol test, it was possible to state the statistical probability of his achieving a score on the actual test that was at least equal to the average of his age group. The typed-in probability was either 10 percent, 60 percent, or 90 percent. It had no relation to the individual's true score on the pretest. (In a control condition no letters were distributed.) Finally, the digit-symbol test was administered.

The effect on performance of the three

independent variables is shown in Figure 1. Each square or circle represents the average digit-symbol score gain (posttest minus pretest) of about thirty Negro undergraduates. As Figure 1 suggests, the feedback of probabilities had a statistically significant effect on performance. The nature of the feedback effect is shown by the shape of the curves: for every combination of tester and norm the 60 percent feedback was superior to the 10

feedback, performance improved considerably. It would seem that variations in probability of success have especially marked effect when the tester is white and the comparison group is also white. By way of contrast, in the Negro-tester–Negro-norm condition, the 10 percent feedback, appears to have stimulated the subject to greater effort, as though he were determined to redeem himself.

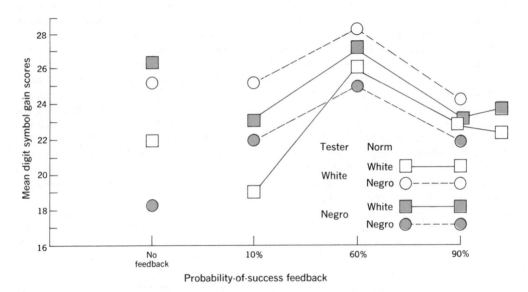

FIGURE 1   Effect of race of tester, race of norms, and probability feedback on digit-symbol scores of southern-Negro-male college students.

percent and 90 percent feedbacks, and also superior to no feedback. Each of these comparisons was statistically significant. Clearly the best motivation and performance occurred, regardless of racial conditions, when the subject was told he had a slightly better-than-even chance of succeeding. If his chances seemed very low or very high he apparently lost interest. This fits well with findings from a variety of other studies of achievement and risk-taking behavior.

One may speculate about possible relationships that are suggested by the shape of the curves, though they are not satistically significant. In the white-tester–white-norm treatment, scores dropped sharply from no feedback to 10 percent feedback, as though subjects were discouraged and perhaps made anxious by the feedback. With 60 percent

Another finding in this experiment was a significant interaction effect of race of tester and race of norm. When the tester was white, the Negro norm occasioned better performance than did the white norm. But when the tester was Negro the relationship reversed— the white norm elicited higher scores than the Negro norm. These differences were significant. A full interpretation of the experimental findings must await analysis of subjects' replies to a postexperimental questionnaire.

The alert reader may have detected a striking discrepancy between the findings of the last experiment and those of the preceding one by Katz *et al.* In the earlier investigation a Negro tester was used and the race of the comparison group was varied. Digit-symbol scores were higher in the Negro-norm condition than in the white-norm condition. In the last study the results when the tester was Negro were in the opposite direction, regardless of the kind of feedback used. There may be a simple regional explanation for these contradictory findings, since the earlier experiment was done in Florida, and the later one in Tennessee. Perhaps the Negro student in the Deep South is more fearful of competition with white peers than is the Negro student in the Upper South.

EMOTIONAL REACTIONS TO TEST SITUATIONS

Another line of investigation has to do with the appraisal of Negro subjects' emotional reactions to various test situations. In connection with the earlier discussion of failure threat, reference was made to the research of Sarason and his associates (1960) on emotional factors in the test-taking behavior of white school children. In their view, the child who chronically experiences anxiety when tested is reacting with strong unconscious hostility to the adult tester, who he believes will in some way pass judgment on his adequacy. The hostility is not openly expressed, but instead is turned inward against the self in the form of self-derogatory attitudes, which strengthen the child's expectation of failure and his desire to escape the situation. Thus he is distracted from the task before him by his fear of failure and his impulse to escape.

Sarason has not as yet presented direct evidence that situations of adult evaluation arouse hostility in highly test-anxious children. However, in clinical studies by Lit (1956), Kimball (1952), and Harris (1961), difficulty in expressing aggression openly was found to be associated with scholastic underachievement. Rosenwald (1961) found that students who were relatively unwilling to give aggressive responses on a projective test showed greater impairment in solving anagrams after a hostility induction than did students who showed less inhibition of aggression on the projective test. Mention has been made of a study by Goldman *et al.* (1954), which demonstrated an association between the degree to which strong hostility against an instigator was denied expression and the amount of disruption of intellectual functioning.

These studies are pertinent to the problem of Negro children's learning efficiency in in-

tegrated classrooms, because these children often have to suppress strong hostility. It was seen that Yarrow (1958) found a much higher incidence of covert symptoms of emotional disturbance in Negro children than in white children at a desegregated summer camp. White children, it will be recalled, aggressed openly against their Negro cabinmates, but the latter did not respond in kind. Rather, they tended to deny aggressive impulses in themselves and to show heightened alertness to aggressive behavior in other Negro children. Another investigator who has reported stronger trends toward denial of hostile impulses in Negro children than in white children is Karon (1958), who examined individual personality by means of a projective technique, the Picture Arrangement Test.

It was suggested earlier that when the administrator of an intellectual test is white, or when comparison with white peers is anticipated, Negro subjects tend to become fearful of failure. Anticipation of failure would tend to generate feelings of victimization and covert hostility against the white tester. Since hostility against white authorities is dangerous, the hostile impulse would be strongly inhibited. Katz *et al.* (1964) undertook to find out whether suppression of hostile responses occurs when a white adult makes Negro students take an intelligence test. Negro male students at a segregated high school in the South were given a test of aggression disguised as a concept-formation test. It consisted of fifty-eight four-word items, with instructions to "circle the word that does not belong with the others." In half of the items one word had aggressive meaning, one word was nonaggressive, and two words were ambiguous. Hence the subject could choose either a hostile or a neutral concept. Two equivalent forms of the test were administered on successive days. On the first day it was given informally to all subjects by a Negro teacher. The following day the entire sample was divided into four groups, each of which was tested by either a white or a Negro adult stranger, with instructions that described the task as either an intelligence test or a research instrument.

The results show that when neutral instructions were used on the second day, average scores in both the white-tester and Negro-tester groups were the same as on the pretest.

But in the intelligence-test condition, hostility scores *increased* over the previous day when the experimenter was a Negro, and they *decreased* when the experimenter was white. The authors' interpretation is that both administrators instigated hostile impulses in the subjects when they announced that the task would be used to evaluate intelligence; when the adult authority was a Negro person, students revealed their annoyance by responding to the aggressive connotations of ambiguous words, but when the adult was a white person the need to deny hostile feelings resulted in avoidance of aggressive word meanings. (The "denial" interpretation is, of course, inferential, since the results merely show that the hostility scores in the white-adult–IQ-test condition went down; there was no *direct* evidence of increased emotional conflict in this condition.)

If we assume that these findings actually reflect variations in ability to express hostile impulses under different testing conditions, they furnish an interesting clue as to the nature of emotional processes attendant upon the disruption of Negro students' performance in the white-adult–IQ-test condition of an earlier experiment (Katz *et al.*).

SUMMARY

This chapter brings together evidence relating to the effect of school desegregation on the academic performance of young Negroes. Negro Americans are defined as a subordinated minority group, and the focus of attention is on their adjustment in schools where white age peers and teachers predominate. In situations of this type there appear to be a variety of favorable and detrimental influences on Negro performance.

Low probability of success—where there is marked discrepancy in the educational standards of Negro and white schools, or where feelings of inferiority are acquired by Negro children outside the school, minority-group newcomers in integrated classrooms are likely to have a low expectancy of academic success; consequently, their achievement motivation should be low. *Social threat*—given the prestige and power of the white-majority group, rejection of Negro students by white classmates or teachers should tend to elicit emotional responses (fear, anger, and humiliation) that are detrimental to intellectual functioning. *Failure threat*—when academic failure entails disapproval by significant others (parents, teachers, and perhaps also classmates), low expectancy of success should elicit emotional responses that are detrimental to performance.

On the other hand, *acceptance* of Negroes by white peers and adults should have a *social facilitation* effect upon their ability to learn, by motivating them to adhere to white standards of academic performance; anticipation that high performance will win white approval should endow scholastic success with *high incentive value.*

Reports on the academic progress of Negro children in desegregated schools are on the whole inadequate for drawing any conclusions about the effects of biracial environments upon Negro performance. However, other types of evidence indicate that any or all of the situational factors mentioned above may be operative in specific instances. Research on psychological stress generally supports the assumption that social threat and failure threat are detrimental to complex learning.

Experiments on Negro male college students by the author and his associates have shown that in workteams composed of Negro and white students of similar intellectual ability, Negroes are passively compliant, rate their own performance as inferior even when it is not, and express less satisfaction with the team experience than do their white companions. These results are seen as due to social threat and/or failure threat. Later studies have sought to identify specific situational determinants of Negro behavior in biracial settings.

Forcing Negro subjects into attempts to influence nonhostile white partners in problem solving had the effect of increasing their influence over the same white partner on another task, apparently mainly through reduction of their fear of instigating hostility.

Experimentally creating a verbal task situation that was low in both social threat and failure threat resulted in better performance by Negroes in the presence of whites than in the presence of other Negroes, suggesting that the incentive value of success was greater in the white environment. But when threat of strong electric shock was introduced, the white setting became less favorable to performance than the Negro one. Thus vulnerability to stress was greater in the white condition, even though it was not apparent until a strong explicit threat was introduced.

The evaluative significance of a verbal task (that is, whether it was described as a perceptual motor test or an intellectual test) interacted with race of the tester in determining Negro performance, in a manner consistent with the notions that (a) the incentive value of success was higher with a white tester than with a Negro tester, and (b) the probability of success was lower with a white tester than with a Negro tester only when the task was defined intellectually.

Among Florida Negro college students, anticipated intellectual comparison with Negro peers was found to produce a higher level of verbal performance than anticipated comparison with white peers, in accordance with the assumption that the subjective probability of success was lower when the expected comparison was with whites. In Tennessee, Negro undergraduates responded more favorably to white norms than to Negro norms when the tester was Negro, but showed a reverse tendency when the tester was white. Information about the probability of success had marked effect on performance in all tester-norm treatments.

Finally, suppression of hostile impulses appeared to occur in Negro boys who were tested by a white adult, but not in those who were tested by a Negro adult.

Further research is needed to clarify the effects of the various situational factors mentioned above on the cognitive functioning of Negroes in biracial settings. However, it is possible even now to point out some implications for educational practice of the findings that have been reviewed.

IMPLICATIONS FOR EDUCATIONAL PRACTICE

The experiments on Negro performance have implications for understanding the problems of adjustment that face minority children in the integrated classroom. If the Negro student comes from a background that has oriented him toward scholastic achievement, the presence of a white teacher and white age peers may have strong emotional and motivational impact. The integrated situation is likely to be double-edged in the sense that failure will be more devastating and success more rewarding than similar experiences in the segregated school. Moreover, whether the Negro child succeeds or fails will depend to a great extent not only on his actual ability but on his expectations. If he expects to fail his actual chances of failing will be greater than they would be in an all-Negro setting, because his fear of failure will be more intense. On the other hand, if he has a high expectation of success in the integrated school he should be aroused to greater effort than he would be by a similar expectation of success in the segregated school. These generalizations must remain highly tentative, pending research on a wider variety of mental tasks than have as yet been studied.

The material that has been presented in this chapter is relevant also to a number of recent suggestions by social scientists on ways to foster movement toward equal education for all children (for example, Klopf and Laster, 1963):

1. Educational standards of Negro schools should be raised to the level of white schools, so that minority group children who transfer to previously all-white schools will have a reasonable chance of succeeding academically. This means, among other things, that the quality of training received by Negro teachers and the criteria used in selecting them for jobs must be raised to white levels, and racial integration of school faculties must be carried out.

2. Programs should be instituted for contacting parents and helping them to understand what they can do to prepare children for schooling, and to foster achievement once children are in school.

3. There should be in-service training of teachers and other personnel in newly integrated schools to develop awareness of the emotional needs of children in biracial situations. The training should include the imparting of techniques for helping children get acquainted with one another.

4. The widely accepted practice of assigning children to homogeneous ability groups (the "track" system) should be modified to afford maximum opportunity for periodic

reevaluations of potentiality. Ability grouping tends inevitably to freeze teachers' expectations as well as children's own self-images, hence it is particularly dangerous to intellectual development in the early grades.

5. Where grade-a-year plans of desegregation are adopted, the process should begin at the lowest grades, where Negro children have the smallest educational handicap and where unfavorable racial attitudes are least strongly learned.

REFERENCES

Applezweig, M. H., & Moeller, G. The role of motivation in psychological stress. *Office of Naval Research Technical Report*, 1957, No. 3.

Atkinson, J. W. "Motivational determinants of risk taking behavior." In J. W. Atkinson (Ed.), *Motives in fantasy, action, and society.* Princeton, N.J.: Van Nostrand, 1958*a*, 322–340.

Atkinson, J. W. "Towards experimental analysis of human motives in terms of motives, expectancies, and incentives." In J. W. Atkinson (Ed.), *Motives in fantasy, action, and society.* Princeton, N.J.: Van Nostrand, 1958*b*, 288–305.

Barker, R., Dembo, Tamara, & Lewin, K. Frustration and regression: An experiment with young children. *University of Iowa Studies of Child Welfare*, 1941, **18** (1).

Bass, B. M. "Conformity, deviation, and a general theory of interpersonal behavior." In I. A. Berg & B. M. Bass (Eds.), *Conformity and deviation.* New York: Harper & Row, 1961, 38–100.

Boston Psychopathic Hospital. Experimental psychoses. *Scientific American*, 1955, **192** (6), 34–39.

Bovard, E. W. The effects of social stimuli on the response to stress. *Psychological Review*, 1959, **66**, 267–277.

Callaway, E., & Thompson, S. V. Sympathetic activity and perception. *Psychosomatic Medicine*, 1953, **15**, 443–455.

Child, I. L. "Personality." In C. P. Stone & Q. McNemar (Eds.), *Annual Review of Psychology.* Stanford, Calif.: Annual Reviews, 1954, 149–170.

Coleman, J. S., & staff. *Equality of Educational Opportunity.* United States Department of Health, Education and Welfare.

Washington, D.C.: United States Government Printing Office, 1966.

Coles, R. *The desegregation of southern schools: A psychiatric study.* New York: Anti-Defamation League, 1963.

Conger, J. J., Sawrey, W. L., & Turrell, E. S. An experimental investigation of the role of social experience in the production of gastric ulcers in hooded rats. *American Psychologist*, 1957, **12**, 410. (Abstract)

Criswell, Joan H. A sociometric study of race cleavage in the classroom. *Archives of Psychology, New York*, 1939, (235).

Davitz, J. R., & Mason, D. J. Socially facilitated reduction of a fear response in rats. *Journal of Comparative Physiology and Psychology*, 1955, **48**, 149–151.

Day, R. E. "Part 2, North Carolina." In the United States Commission on Civil Rights, *Civil Rights U.S.A.—public schools, Southern states.* Washington, D.C.: United States Government Printing Office, 1962, 57–104.

Deese, J. "Skilled performance and conditions of stress." In R. Glaser (Ed.), *Training research and education.* Pittsburgh: University of Pittsburgh Press, 1962, 199–222.

Deutsch, M. Minority group and class status as related to social and personality factors in scholastic achievement. *Society of Applied Anthropology Monographs*, 1960 (2).

Deutsch, M. "Dimensions of the school's role in the problems of integration." In G. J. Klopf & I. A. Laster (Eds.), *Integrating the urban school.* New York: Teachers College, Columbia University, Bureau of Publications, 1963, 29–44.

Dittes, J. E., & Kelley, H. H. Effects of different conditions of acceptance upon conformity to group norms. *Journal of Abnormal and Social Psychology*, 1956, **53**, 100–107.

Dodson, D. Statement read at *Conference before the United States Commission on Civil Rights: Fourth annual education conference on problems of segregation and desegregation of public schools.* Washington, D.C.: The United States Commission on Civil Rights, 1962, 137–141.

Easterbrook, J. A. The effect of emotion on cue utilization and the organization of behavior. *Psychological Review*, 1959, **66**, 183–201.

Findley, W. G. *Learning and teaching in At-*

lanta public schools. Princeton, N.J.: Educational Testing Service, 1956.

French, J. R. P., Jr., & Raven, B. "The bases of social power." In D. Cartwright & A. Zander (Eds.), *Group dynamics.* Ed. 2. Evanston, Ill.: Row, Peterson, 1960, 607–623.

Goldman, M., Horwitz, M., & Lee, F. J. Alternative classroom standards concerning management of hostility and effects on student learning. *Office of Naval Research Technical Report*, 1954.

Group for the Advancement of Psychiatry. *Psychiatric aspects of school desegregation.* New York: GAP, 1957.

Hansen, C. F. The scholastic performances of Negro and white pupils in the integrated public schools of the District of Columbia. *Harvard Educational Review*, 1960, **30**, 216–236.

Harlow, H. F., & Harlow, Margaret K. Social deprivation in monkeys. *Scientific American*, 1962, **207** (5), 136–146.

Harris, I. *Emotional blocks to learning.* New York: Free Press, 1961.

Harvey, O. J. An experimental approach to the study of status relations in informal groups. *American Sociological Review*, 1953, **18**, 357–367.

Horowitz, E. The development of attitudes toward the Negro. *Archives of Psychology, New York*, 1936 (194).

Karon, B. P. *The Negro personality: A rigorous investigation of the effects of culture.* New York: Springer, 1958.

Katz, I., & Benjamin, L. Effects of white authoritarianism in biracial work groups. *Journal of Abnormal and Social Psychology*, 1960, **61**, 448–456.

Katz, I., & Cohen, M. The effects of training Negroes upon cooperative problem solving in biracial teams. *Journal of Abnormal and Social Psychology*, 1962, **64**, 319–325.

Katz, I., Epps, E. G., & Axelson, L. J. Effect upon Negro digit-symbol performance of anticipated comparison with whites and with other Negroes. *Journal of Abnormal and Social Psychology*, 1964, **69**, 77–83.

Katz, I., Goldston, Judith, & Benjamin, L. Behavior and productivity in biracial work groups. *Human Relations*, 1958, **11**, 123–141.

Katz, I., & Greenbaum, C. Effects of anxiety, threat, and racial environment on task performance of Negro college students. *Jour-*

nal of Abnormal Social Psychology, 1963, **66**, 562–567.

Katz, I., Roberts, S. O., & Robinson, J. M. Effects of difficulty, race of administrator, and instructions on Negro digit-symbol performance. *Journal of Personality and Social Psychology*, 1965, **70**, 53–59.

Katz, I., Robinson, J. M., Epps, E. G., & Waly, Patricia. Effects of race of experimenter and test vs. neutral instructions on expression of hostility in Negro boys. *Journal of Social Issues*, 1964, **20**, 54–59.

Kimball, Barbara. Sentence-completion technique in a study of scholastic underachievement. *Journal of Consulting Psychology*, 1952, **16**, 353–358.

Klein, G. S. "Need and regulation." In M. R. Jones (Ed.), *Nebraska symposium on motivation: 1957.* Lincoln: University of Nebraska Press, 1957, 224–274.

Klopf, G. J., & Laster, I. A. (Eds.). *Integrating the urban school.* New York: Teachers College, Columbia University, Bureau of Publications, 1963.

Knowles, L. W. "Part 1, Kentucky." In the United States Commission on Civil Rights, *Civil Rights U.S.A.—public schools, Southern states.* Washington, D.C.: United States Government Printing Office, 1962, 19–56.

Laird, D. A. Changes in motor control and individual variations under the influence of "razzing." *Journal of Experimental Psychology*, 1923, **6**, 236–246.

Lantz, Beatrice. Some dynamic aspects of success and failure. *Psychological Monographs*, 1945, 59 (1, Whole No. 271).

Lazarus, R. S., Deese, J., & Osler, Sonia F. The effects of psychological stress upon performance. *Psychological Bulletin*, 1952, **49**, 293–317.

Liddell, H. "Some specific factors that modify tolerance for environmental stress." In H. G. Wolff, S. G. Wolf, Jr., & C. C. Hare (Eds.), *Life stress and bodily disease.* Baltimore: Williams and Wilkins, 1950, 155–171.

Lit, J. Formal and content factors of projective tests in relation to academic achievement. *Dissertation Abstracts*, 1956, **16**, 1505–1506 (Order No. 16,311).

Mandlebaum, D. G. *Soldier groups and Negro soldiers.* Berkeley: University of California Press, 1952.

Mandler, G., & Sarason, S. B. A study of

anxiety and learning. *Journal of Abnormal and Social Psychology*, 1952, **47**, 166–173.

Marshall, S. L. A. *Men against fire.* Washington, D.C.: Combat Forces Press, 1951.

Mason, W. A. Socially mediated reduction in emotional responses of young rhesus monkeys. *Journal of Abnormal and Social Psychology*, 1960, **60**, 100–104.

Mearns, E. A., Jr. "Part 4, Virginia." In The United States Commission on Civil Rights, *Civil Rights U.S.A.—public schools, Southern states.* Washington, D.C.: United States Government Printing Office, 1962, 155–217.

Murstein, B. I., & Collier, H. L. The role of the TAT in the measurement of achievement as a function of expectancy. *Journal of Projective Techniques*, 1962, **26**, 96–101.

National Scholarship Service and Fund for Negro Students. *Annual report 1959–1960.* New York: NSSFNS, 1960.

National Scholarship Service and Fund for Negro Students. *Annual report 1962–1963.* New York: NSSFNS, 1963.

Plaut, R. L. *Blueprint for talent searching.* New York: National Scholarship Service and Fund for Negro Students, 1957.

Preston, M. G., & Bayton, J. A. Differential effect of a social variable upon three levels of aspiration. *Journal of Experimental Psychology*, 1941, **29**, 351–369.

Radke, Marian, Sutherland, Jean, & Rosenberg, Pearl. Racial attitudes of children. *Sociometry*, 1950, **13**, 154–171.

Radke, Marian, Trager, Helen G., & Davis, Hadassah. Social perceptions and attitudes of children. *Genetic Psychology Monograph*, 1949, **40**, 327–447.

Roberts, S. O. Test performance in relation to ethnic group and social class. Report, 1963, Fisk University, Nashville (mimeo).

Rosen, M. Valence, expectancy, and dissonance reduction in the prediction of goal striving. *Dissertation Abstracts*, 1961, **21**, 3846 (Order No. 61–2062).

Rosenwald, G. The assessment of anxiety in psychological experiments. *Journal of Abnormal and Social Psychology*, 1961, **63**, 666–673.

Sarason, I. G. Empirical findings and theoretical problems in the use of anxiety scales. *Psychological Bulletin*, 1960, **57**, 403–415.

Sarason, S. E., Davidson, K. S., Lighthall, F. F., Waite, R. R., & Ruebush, B. K. *Anxi-ety in elementary school children.* New York: Wiley, 1960.

Schachter, S. *The psychology of affiliation.* Stanford: Stanford University Press, 1959.

Southern School News. Untitled. *Sth. Sch. News*, 1960 (August), **7**, 6 Cols. 1–29.

Southern School News. Untitled. *Sth. Sch. News*, 1963 (April), **9**, 11 (Col. 2).

Spence, K. W. A theory of emotionally based drive (D) and its relation to performance in simple learning situations. *American Psychologist*, 1958, **13**, 131–141.

Stallings, F. H. A study of the immediate effects of integration on scholastic achievement in the Louisville Public Schools. *Journal of Negro Education*, 1959, **28**, 439–444.

Tanner, J. C. Integration in action. *Wall Street Journal*, January 26, 1964, **64** (1).

Taylor, Janet A. "Drive theory and manifest anxiety." In Martha T. Mednick & S. A. Mednick (Eds.), *Research in personality.* New York: Holt, Rinehart and Winston, 1963, 205–222.

Thibaut, J., & Kelley, H. H. *The social psychology of groups.* New York: Wiley, 1959.

Titmuss, R. M. *Problems of social policy.* London, England: His Majesty's Stationery Office and Longmans, Green, 1950.

Trillin, C. *An education in Georgia.* New York: Viking Press, 1964.

Tumin, M. "The process of integration." In G. J. Klopf & I. A. Laster (Eds.), *Integrating the urban school.* New York: Teachers College, Columbia University, Bureau of Publications, 1963, 13–28.

United States Commission on Civil Rights. *Second annual conference on education, Gatlinburg, Tenn.* Washington, D.C.: United States Government Printing Office, 1960.

United States Commission on Civil Rights. *Civil Rights U.S.A.—public schools, cities in the North and West.* Washington, D.C.: United States Government Printing Office, 1962*a*.

United States Commission on Civil Rights. *Civil Rights U.S.A.—public schools, Southern states.* Washington, D.C.: United States Government Printing Office, 1962*b*.

Whyte, W. F. *Street corner society; the social structure of an Italian slum.* Chicago: University of Chicago Press, 1943.

Wrightsman, L. S., Jr. Effects of waiting with others on changes in level of felt anxiety.

Journal of Abnormal and Social Psychology, 1960, **61**, 216–222.

Wyatt, E. "Part 3, Tennessee." In The United States Commission on Civil Rights, *Civil Rights U.S.A.—public schools, Southern states*. Washington, D.C.: United States Government Printing Office, 1962, 105–130.

Yarrow, Marian R. (Issue Ed.) Interpersonal dynamics in a desegregation process. *Journal of Social Issues*, 1958, **14** (1, entire issue).

18

Relation of early school achievement to high school achievement when race, intelligence, and socioeconomic factors are equated

JULIA R. VANE

This is a study of the achievement of 272 Negro and white students attending an integrated high school in a suburban school district. The relation of achievement to intelligence, socioeconomic level, and race are considered, as well as the achievement of Negro children in integrated and nonintegrated schools in the suburban district and in a large city school system.

The records of all children who had attended the six elementary schools in a suburban school district continuously from third through eighth grade and who continued in the central four-year high school were evaluated. The student body of two elementary schools was approximately 95% white and 5% Negro; one school was 11% white and 89% Negro; three schools ranged from 62% to 87% white when the students entered the

Reprinted from *Psychology in the Schools*, 1966, **3**, 124–129, by permission of the author and Psychology Press Inc.

kindergarten to 48% to 76% white when the students graduated from eighth grade. The high school enrollment was 71% white and 29% Negro.

This study was done in retrospect and no artificial conditions were introduced that might have influenced the outcome. During the time when the children were attending the elementary school the relationship between the Negro and white children seemed amiable in all schools. Evaluation of achievement and intelligence was made possible because the district administered standardized achievement and intelligence tests each year to all children in grades three through eight.

RESULTS

Table 1 shows that correlations between all achievement scores were high and positive and that the majority of students were consistent in their achievement. When in third

TABLE 1   Means, Standard Deviations and Correlations of Intelligence Achievement Test Scores and Socioeconomic Index

	Mean	SD	Correlations							
			3rd	4th	5th	6th	7th	8th	HS	SEI[a]
IQ	111.2	12.2	.65	.65	.68	.71	.71	.67	.56	.46
3rd	.41[b]	1.0		.85	.82	.81	.79	.76	.66	.51
4th	.68	1.1			.86	.83	.80	.80	.65	.48
5th	.77	1.4				.89	.84	.82	.69	.49
6th	1.04	1.5					.89	.86	.70	.51
7th	.86	1.6						.90	.71	.47
8th	1.00	1.6							.72	.46
HS	.78[c]	9.6								.46

[a] Socioeconomic index based upon U. S. Census categories and classified as follows: 1. professional and technical; 2. managers, owners; 3. clerical, sales; 4. craftsmen, foremen; 5. operatives; 6. service workers; 7. laborers.

[b] Achievement reported in deviation from grade expectation. All deviations are positive indicating mean achievement was above grade expectation.

[c] Achievement reported in grade average.

grade 185 children were achieving above grade level. By the time they had reached eighth grade, 174 of these children were still achieving above grade level. This same consistency was shown by the underachievers. Of the 87 children who had been achieving below grade level in the third grade, 57 of these were still achieving below grade in the eighth. The fact that 85% of the 272 children maintained the same level of performance from third grade through eighth suggests that early school achievement foreshadows later school achievement to a marked degree. What makes the situation even more serious with regard to the underachievers is that these children had been given special help in the form of remedial reading, psychological counseling, and parent-teacher intervention in order to bring them up to grade level.

Evaluation of comparative achievement in high school was difficult because students were enrolled in different courses and were not given standardized achievement tests. Averages of marks in English, Mathematics, Science, and Social Science were used. The results showed that 65% of the students who had achieved above grade level in elementary school received marks of 80 or above in high school. Only 7% of the students who had achieved above grade level in elementary school received marks below 70. Conversely, only 5% of the students who were below grade level in elementary school received marks of 80 or above, and 60% of these students received marks below 70 in high school. The correlation between third grade achievement and marks in first and second year high school was +.66.

The results in Table 1 also show that there were fairly high positive correlations between intelligence and achievement, and between achievement and socioeconomic status as measured by the occupation of the parents. Table 2 shows that the mean intelligence of the "above achieving" group was considerably higher than the mean intelligence of the "below achieving" group. As might be expected occupational status of the "above achieving" group was also higher, with 63% of the parents in the white collar class, whereas only

TABLE 2   Mean Intelligence, Achievement and Socioeconomic Index of "Above Achieving" and "Below Achieving" Groups and Matched Groups

	N	SEI	Mean IQ	SD	3rd	8th
Above achieving group	174	2.9	118.9	9.5	+.92	+1.84
Below achieving group	57	4.8	100.0	9.2	−.66	−1.30
Matched above achieving	27	5.5	103.7	7.8	+.49	+1.19
Matched below achieving	27	5.5	105.8	8.1	−.64	−1.15

TABLE 3 Mean Socioeconomic Index, Intelligence, and Achievement of Negro Children in Integrated and Nonintegrated Schools

			Means			
	N	*SEI*	*IQ*	*3rd*	*8th*	*HS*
Total integrated	52	5.0	102.4	−.23	−.32	71
Total nonintegrated	19	5.9	103.0	−.46	−.35	71
Matched integrated	17	5.9	100.1	−.24	−.56	71
Matched nonintegrated	17	5.9	100.2	−.56	−.52	71

19% of the "below achieving" children had parents who were in the white collar class.

In order to control for the difference in intelligence and socioeconomic status of these two groups, 27 children in the "below achieving" group were matched with 27 from the same socioeconomic background and same intelligence level in the "above achieving" group. The number of Negroes and whites was equal. Despite the control of intelligence and socioeconomic status the difference in achievement between the matched groups grew larger every year. The difference was one year in grade three and two years in grade eight.

In order to evaluate the effect of integrated and nonintegrated schooling on achievement, comparisons were made between the records of the 52 Negro children who had attended the five schools in which the white population predominated, called integrated schools, and the 19 Negro children who had attended the one school with a Negro population of 89%. It was possible to equate socioeconomic status and intelligence of 17 of the Negro children from the nonintegrated school with 17 Negro children from the integrated schools. Table 3 indicates that there were no significant differences in achievement at any level. There was a nonsignificant trend for Negro students in the integrated schools to achieve slightly better in the third grade, but this advantage had disappeared in eighth grade and in high school.

Further evidence of the influence of socioeconomic level on achievement was found when the mean achievement in each of the six elementary schools was compared with the percentage of children in each school whose parents were in the white collar class. Table 4 shows that the schools with the highest mean achievement also had the highest mean IQ scores and the greatest propor-tion of children with parents in the white collar class.

Table 4 also shows that the suburban school district contained no school in which the majority of students were Negro with parents in the white collar class. It contained only one school in which the majority of students were white with parents in the non-white collar class.

In order to evaluate schools of this type, letters were sent to 50 districts in the United States that might have schools with such populations. Two large city districts replied. The schools listed by one of the districts did not meet the criteria because they were of the type already under study, namely, schools in which the population was predominantly Negro from the nonwhite collar class, or schools predominantly white from the white collar class. The other city district did have several schools that met the criteria and this district supplied mean achievment figures and

TABLE 4 Relation of Achievement to Parent Occupational Status and Race in Six Elementary Schools in a Suburban School District

School	Mean Achvt.	Mean IQ	% in white collar class	% of Negro students[a]
1	+1.45	114.0	67%	5%
2	+ .91	112.6	59%	5%
3	+ .40	107.7	38%	66%
4	+ .22	103.9	32%	88%
5	+ .34	106.5	30%	37%
6	− .40	99.7	12%	90%

[a] These percentages apply to the elementary schools at the time the study was being completed and not at the time the 272 students in this study were attending the schools. As can be noted there had been a rapid increase in the Negro enrollment in Schools 3 and 4 during the period following the graduation of the 272 students from eighth grade.

the occupation of the parents of the children in these schools. Table 5 indicates that the achievement and intelligence of the students of these schools was independent of race. A strong relationship was shown between achievement and socioeconomic level. School A with the largest percentage of students with parents in the white collar class also had the highest mean achievement record and the

TABLE 5 Relation of Achievement to Parent Occupational Status and Race in Seven Large City Schools

School	Mean Achvt.[a]	Mean IQ	% in white collar class	% of Negro students
A	+1.4	107	49%	69%
B	+ .8	104	41%	74%
C	+ .7	104	38%	78%
D	+ .9	104	30%	81%
E	+ .7	103	21%	61%
F	− .6	98	11%	0
G	0	98	10%	0

[a] The mean achievement of the schools in the suburban district cannot be directly compared with the mean achievement of the schools in the city district because different standardized tests were used in each district.

majority of students were Negro. School D, which might be considered a nonintegrated school because it contained 81% Negro students, also had a high mean achievement level. School F and School G, containing 100% white native-born students whose parents were largely from the nonwhite collar class, had the lowest mean achievement level.

DISCUSSION

The results of the present study indicate that with regard to achievement in general the pattern of educational progress is set early and few children improve once they make a poor start. Two other long term studies of achievement support this conclusion. Shaw and McCuen (1960) studied achievers and underachievers in a single California school district and showed that male underachievers tended to receive lower grades than achievers beginning in grade one. The underachievers showed a decrease in academic work every

year through to the high school level. Scannell (1960) found that a correlation of +.60 between fourth grade achievement and college success among 1500 Iowa students attending two Iowa colleges. The necessity of developing new approaches to help underachievers is highlighted by the fact that most of the children in the suburban school district in this present study, who were achieving below grade level, had average intelligence and attended schools with small classes, excellent programs, well trained staff, and ample remedial and psychological services. The importance of concentrating on the early school years seems evident.

The results also indicate that consideration must be given to socioeconomic level when comparisons are made between groups with regard to achievement. Despite the fact that in the present study only a simple method of evaluating the socioeconomic level was used, namely the occupation of the parent, the results are consistent in showing the relationship of this factor to achievement and intelligence. It is felt had it been possible to utilize a more complete measure of socioeconomic level, the relationship would have been more marked.

The tendency for children from low socioeconomic strata to achieve below grade level was also shown in a study by Deutsch (1960) in which he compared the achievement of fourth, fifth and sixth grade Negro and white students from low socioeconomic homes. Deutsch found that both groups were achieving below grade level, although the Negro group was achieving below the white. This latter finding is not unusual, for most studies have shown that even when Negro and white groups are equated for socioeconomic level, the white groups usually perform better. The difficulty of equating socioeconomic levels of the two groups is usually given as a reason and appears to be a valid one in view of the limitations placed upon the life of the American Negro in terms of education, social mobility and social acceptance. The various factors mentioned by Katz (1964) such as the unrealistic inferiority feelings of Negro children, their social rejection and isolation and their fear of competition with whites, all undoubtedly cause their achievement to be below that of whites of similar socioeconomic level.

The allegation that Negroes will achieve

better in an integrated school setting was not supported by the data in this study. The achievement of the Negro children in the suburban integrated and nonintegrated schools was shown to be equal when socioeconomic level was held constant. The mean achievement of the students in the five predominantly Negro city schools was all above grade level.

Hansen's study (1960) also supports the fact that Negroes can show an improvement in achievement even though they are not in integrated schools, although Hansen did not set out to demonstrate this. His study indicates that there was a small but steady improvement in achievement following integration in the District of Columbia schools, but his figures also show that as achievement improved there was an increase in the percentage of Negroes attending the schools studied, from 63% in 1956 to 71% in 1959. In this situation the improvement in achievement cannot be attributed to integration, since there was less integration in 1959 than in 1956. Actually schools with a Negro population of 71% would be considered segregated by most standards. The improvement in achievement seems to have been related to the effective efforts to raise the educational standards throughout the schools and occurred in schools that would usually be considered segregated.

The results of the studies mentioned indicate that Negro and white children tend to achieve on a level commensurate with their socioeconomic standing and that integration by itself is not likely to bring about significant improvement in achievement. This should not be construed as an excuse to maintain segregation, but hopefully may alter the popular belief that the Negro child cannot achieve well unless he is in the company of white children. Although it has been expedient to use this belief, as well as figures showing extremely poor achievement levels in segregated schools in order to demonstrate the need for integration, the belief is hardly flattering to the Negro. While it continues to have widespread acceptance it will undoubtedly continue to contribute to the unrealistic lack of confidence of the Negro in himself mentioned by Katz (1964). The abandonment of this belief should not lessen the desire to achieve integration with its many values, but in situations where immediate desegregation is not possible, improved educational methods and facilities, as well as increased opportunities for the Negro to move up the socioeconomic scale should be followed by an overall improvement in Negro achievement.

REFERENCES

Deutsch, M. Minority group and class status as related to social and personality factors in scholastic achievement. *Society for Applied Anthropology Monographs*, 1960, No. 2.

Hansen, C. F. The scholastic performances of Negro and white pupils in the integrated public schools of the District of Columbia, *Harvard Educational Review*, 1960, **80,** 216–236.

Katz, I. Review of evidence relating to effects of desegregation on the intellectual performance of Negroes. *American Psychologist*, 1964, **19,** 381–399.

Scannell, Dale P. Prediction of college success from elementary and secondary performance. *Journal of Educational Psychology*, 1960, **51,** 130–135.

Shaw, M. C., & McCuen, J. R. The onset of academic underachievement in bright children. *Journal of Educational Psychology*, 1960, **51,** 103–109.

19

Racial isolation and the outcomes of education

Since 1954, when the Supreme Court ruled that segregation in public schools sanctioned by law violated the Constitution, increasing attention has been given to the effects of school segregation not based on law. Does such segregation have a negative effect upon the performance and attitudes of Negro students?

The question is difficult to answer, for it requires that the influence of one aspect of a child's education—the racial composition of his school—be determined apart from all other relevant factors. The question is further complicated by the fact that the intellectual and emotional development of children is related not only to their schools but to a much broader social and educational context. Apart from the possible effects of a school's racial composition, the results of schooling also are affected by the social and economic circumstances in which children grow up, the quality of education provided in their schools, and the achievement and aspirations of their classmates. It is not a simple matter to separate elements which in reality are so closely interwoven. And the outcomes of education cannot be measured solely by children's grades in school—they extend also to their attitudes and experiences as adults.

There are a number of tested standards by which the effects of education can be assessed. Although none is absolutely accurate, each is a useful indicator of the outcomes of education. Most familiar is students' performance on achievement tests. Since achievement in other subjects depends strongly upon reading, tests of reading or verbal achievement are the usual measure of academic progress. The

Reprinted from U.S. Commission of Civil Rights *Racial Isolation in Public Schools,* Washington, D.C.: Government Printing Office, 1967.

effects of education also include children's attitudes and aspirations. Thus measures have been devised to assess the schools' influence upon these factors.

The main purpose of education in America is to prepare students for future careers and lives as citizens. Occupational success now requires highly developed knowledge and technical skills, and public schools increasingly are expected to provide preparation for later education. One measure of their long-range effect, therefore, is a student's success in further education. Another is his relative occupational and economic attainment as an adult.

Marked differences exist between Negro and white Americans when measured by each of these standards. The disparities appear early in school. The verbal achievement of the average third grade Negro student in the Northeastern United States is about a year behind the average white in the same region.[1] Differences of the same magnitude exist in all other regions of the Nation.[2]

This disparity typically is greater in higher grades. The average third grade Negro student in the Midwest has a verbal achievement level approximately one year behind the average white student, but in the 12th grade the difference is nearly 3 years.[3] Commission studies in individual cities revealed that this pattern is general.[4]

Differences in achievement also are apparent on other standard tests. The U.S.

[1] *OE Survey 223,* table 3.11.3. All data from the *OE Survey* cited in this chapter are for metropolitan areas.

[2] *OE Survey 223,* table 3.11.3.

[3] *OE Survey 223,* table 3.11.3.

[4] In Boston, predominantly Negro schools made consistently lower median scores in read-

Army administers tests to all inductees, the results of which depend upon ". . . the level of . . . educational attainment [and] . . . the quality of . . . education . . .".[5] The most recent test was given in 1965; it shows that while 18 percent of all whites failed, more than half of all Negroes failed.[6]

In spite of these differences in academic performance, Negro students generally ex-

ing achievement at every grade level tested than the predominantly white schools. In the higher levels, the difference in the achievement increased steadily. *Boston Study,* Section F–1, tables 2 and 3.

In Philadelphia differences in average reading achievement (expressed in grade level equivalents) between predominantly Negro and white schools increased from 0.8 in the second grade to 3.3 in the tenth grade. Scores from the School and College Aptitude Test for the eleventh grade, 1965–66, revealed a similar disparity: All schools over 90 percent Negro obtained school percentiles in the lowest quarter. Generally, the scores for predominantly white schools were consistently higher than those for the predominantly Negro schools; the highest Negro school ranked considerably below the white schools. (Test scores from Department of Research and Development, School District of Philadelphia.)

In Cleveland, a similar pattern was found. Nearly all-Negro schools start off at approximately one half of a grade level below white schools according to scores made in kindergarten on the Lee Clark Reading Readiness Test; at the ninth grade level medians for Negro schools typically were nearly two years behind white schools; grade equivalents for Negro schools ranged from 7.7 to 8.3, while for white schools the range was 8.3 to 10.1. By the twelfth grade, Negro schools were *all* below the city median, the white schools were all above the city median, and the lowest white school scored substantially higher than the highest score for the nearly all-Negro schools. (Scores obtained from Bureau of Educational Research, Cleveland Board of Education.)

In Atlanta, in 1965, in the Negro schools the median grade equivalent of the eighth grade in reading achievement was 3.9; in predominantly white schools it was almost 5 grades higher, 8.7 (Scores obtained from the Department of Research, Atlanta Public Schools). Similar disparities were noticed in test scores received from the public schools in Oakland, Milwaukee, and St. Louis.

[5] Office of the Surgeon General, U. S. Army, 21 *Supplement to Health of the Army* 2 (1966).
[6] *Supplement to Health of the Army* 2, p. 8.

press a desire for academic success.[7] Nevertheless they are less likely to have definite plans to attend college.[8] Moreover, Negro students more often feel that they will be unsuccessful later in life.[9]

There also are dissimilarities when further education is considered. Negroes less often are enrolled in college than whites and they are much more likely to be enrolled in high schools which send a relatively small proportion of their graduates to college.[10] Indeed, Negro students finish public school less often than whites and they are much more likely to attend schools with high dropout rates.[11]

Differentials also exist in the distribution of income and occupations in later life. Negroes with college education earn less on the average than high school-educated whites.[12] Negroes with some college education are less likely than similarly educated whites to be employed in white collar trades.[13]

These disparities arise from a variety of sources. In many respects they are related to factors which do not affect all children, such as racial discrimination in employment. Yet the outcomes of education for all students are shaped by a number of common factors.

One, the importance of which long has been recognized, is the educational and economic circumstances of a child's family. Students from differing circumstances, i.e. different social class backgrounds, bring to school differently developed attitudes and verbal skills. Both have a strong influence upon their performance in school and later in life.[14]

Similarly, the social class level of a given student's classmates usually has a strong

[7] *OE Survey,* p. 196, table 2.43.2.
[8] *OE Survey,* p. 195, table 2.43.2.
[9] *OE Survey,* p. 199, table 2.43.3.
[10] *OE Survey,* p. 193, table 2.43.1.
[11] *OE Survey,* p. 196, table 2.43.2.
[12] U. S. Dept. of Labor, *The Negroes in the United States: Their Economic and Social Situation* 208, table IV B–13 (June, 1966). In 1963 nonwhite males with one or more years of college had a median annual income of slightly more than $4,000. In the same year the median annual income of white males with four years of high school was $5,000.
[13] *The Negroes in the United States,* p. 204, table IV B–10.
[14] Goldberg, "Factors Affecting Educational Attainment in Depressed Urban Areas" in *Education in Depressed Areas* 68, 87 (Passow ed. 1963).

bearing upon his performance and aspirations. A student who attends school with other youngsters who intend to go to college is more likely to desire this himself than if most of his schoolmates do not plan to attend college or even finish public school.[15]

Students also are influenced by the quality of education they receive in school. The elements of school quality generally thought to be important can be gauged in part by those factors which educators typically emphasize when they seek to improve the schools. One is reduced class size, permitting more attention to individual students. Another is the recruitment of more highly qualified teachers, which often requires improved salaries and teaching conditions. It also has been recognized that an important aspect of a teacher's qualifications is his attitudes and the level of performance he expects of his students. A fourth is the development of more advanced educational curricula and facilities, particularly in such areas as language and science.[16]

Finally, increasing numbers of educators believe that the racial composition of schools can affect the performance and attitudes of students. There is some evidence that the academic achievement of Negro students is lower in majority-Negro than in majority-white schools, and many educators have said that attending school almost exclusively with children of the same race has a negative effect upon the attitudes of both Negro and white students.[17]

[15] A study of high school seniors of the San Francisco Bay Area indicated that working class youth who aspired to attend college were more likely to be attending predominantly middle class schools. Kraus, "Sources of Educational Aspirations Among Working Class Youth," **29** *American Sociological Review* 867, 875, 877 (1964).

[16] See, e.g., The Educational Policies Commission of the National Education Association and the American Association of School Administrators, *American Education and the Search for Equal Opportunity* (1965).

[17] *American Education and the Search for Equal Opportunity*, p. 30. See also: Clark, "Educational Stimulation of Racially Disadvantaged Children" in *Education in Depressed Areas* 156 (Passow ed. 1963); Testimony of Miss M. Tillman, Boston public school teacher, *Hearing Before the U.S. Commission on Civil Rights, Boston, Massachusetts, October 4–5, 1966* (original transcript) at 88. [Hereinafter cited as *Boston Hearing*.]

In this chapter we consider the influence of these factors on the outcomes of education for Negro students. In attempting to make judgments there are three problems which must be borne in mind. First, it is difficult to compare a given characteristic of schools or students apart from other factors. The best teachers most often are found in schools whose students come from fairly affluent homes. These schools also tend to have the most advanced educational programs and the best educational facilities. Their students almost always are white. This makes it difficult to measure the effect of very high levels of school quality upon student bodies of other social or racial backgrounds. Similarly, the fact that most Negroes attend school almost exclusively with Negroes makes it difficult to assess the relationship between the racial composition of schools and student performance.

Second, the process of education is very complex, and simple causal connections cannot be drawn. It may seem reasonable, for example, to say that a student's motivation to learn directly affects his academic performance. Thus when it is found that students with strong motivation have high grades, it might be concluded that the motivation caused the performance. Undoubtedly, however, there is a complicated causal relationship in which levels of motivation and academic performance interact, each reinforcing the other.

Finally, the standards for measuring the outcomes of education have clear limitations. Although tests of verbal achievement do assess the basic skills needed for academic and occupational success, they are only a limited measure of a child's potential. Within these limitations, this chapter represents an effort to provide some new insight in an important area. If appropriate remedies for unequal educational opportunity are to be devised, it is important and perhaps crucial to know whether the racial composition of schools influences educational outcomes.

SOCIAL CLASS AND THE OUTCOMES OF EDUCATION

The outcomes of education are strongly related to the social class origin of students. This relationship holds for both Negroes and whites. The educational attainment of an individual student is related both to his own social class and to the social class level of his classmates.

Individual Social Class

In a few years which separate their infancy from entry into school, children are exposed to profound formative influences. During those years verbal skills and styles of speech and thought are shaped, a child's view of himself develops, and his aspirations begin to form.

Most social scientists have rejected the proposition that "innate" ability is related to the race or social class of individual children.[18] Nor is there in America a well-defined culture of poverty, or a single life style associated with affluence. There are, however, some general characteristics associated with lives of relative poverty or affluence which are closely related to success or failure in school.[19]

Compare, for example, a child growing up in an economically deprived environment with another in a well-to-do neighborhood. The first is more likely to be poorly fed and clothed, and his family to be constantly concerned with meeting immediate material needs. In contrast to the advantaged child, the children of poverty often come to school undernourished and sometimes with serious, often undetected, medical problems.[20] Children from advantaged homes do not ordinarily suffer material deprivation or inadequate health care.

Poor children also must contend with their immediate neighborhood environment. Typically, their contacts and associations are much more restricted than those of more advantaged children. Disadvantaged children do not go outside their neighborhood as often as youngsters from more advantaged homes— whether it is to visit a museum, to travel beyond the city, or to go shopping.[21] Their neighborhoods also are typically disadvantaged. Calvin Brooks, a recent high school graduate, said of his neighborhood when he testified at the Commission hearing in Cleveland, Ohio:

> [It] is a slum . . . a very depreciated area, and you find all kinds of people . . . alcoholics . . . along the streets. . . .[22]

The chief vehicle of formal education is verbal and written communication. Children who have grown up in homes where reading is encouraged and books are commonplace come to school well prepared. They typically have a style of speech and habits of thought similar to those of their teachers.[23] Progress in school often is easy and they are likely to have facility with the tests used to measure their achievement, on the basis of which students often are placed in grades or ability groups. In contrast, children who grow up in poor neighborhoods often have styles of speech markedly different from those used in the schools or in written English, and are less likely to read before they enter school. Thus their early school experiences are with less familiar modes of communication, and they typically have greater difficulty with the tests used to measure achievement. The tendency for teachers to regard these children as deficient makes their adjustment to school more difficult.[24]

The differences between poverty and affluence extend beyond formal learning. In more affluent communities, schooling often is a basic concern of parents, who frequently are deeply involved in school affairs. Parents in poor neighborhoods are not usually any less concerned with education; indeed, they typi-

[18] See generally: Hunt, *Intelligence and Experience* (1961); Pettigrew, *A Profile of the Negro American* 133–135 (1964).

[19] Miller, "The American Lower Classes: A Typological Approach" in *Mental Health of the Poor* 139 (Pressman ed. 1964); Deutsch, "The Disadvantaged Child and the Learning Process" in *Education in Depressed Areas* (Passow ed. 1963).

[20] See, e.g., Jeffers, *Three Generations*, Case Materials for the Child Rearing Study Sponsored by the Health and Welfare Council of the National Capital Area (Sept.–Oct. 1966); Jackson, *Poverty's Children*, Case Materials for the Child Rearing Study sponsored by the Health and Welfare Council of the National Capital Area (Sept.–Oct. 1966).

[21] Deutsch, *Minority Group and Class Status As Related to Social and Personality Factors in Scholastic Achievement* 4 (1960).

[22] *Cleveland Hearing* 280.

[23] Deutsch, *The Disadvantaged Child and the Learning Process*, p. 174.

[24] Ravitz, "The Role of the School in the Urban Setting" in *Education in Depressed Areas* 15–21 (Passow ed. 1963).

cally regard it as the chief avenue out of poverty.[25] Yet, it is often more difficult to find time to become involved in school affairs when the problems of material existence are pressing. Many parents do not participate because they do not believe that they can have much influence in school affairs. Indeed, some students of education have said that schools often are less responsive to poorly educated parents. Patricia Sexton, professor of sociology at New York University, points out in her study of social class and education that:

> . . . upper income groups have usually been in control of school boards and thereby in control of what goes on in the schools and the methods of distributing rewards. In addition there is the fact that very little pressure is applied to the schools by lower-income individuals or groups representing them while upper-income groups tend to have great influence in the schools and to be active in school affairs.[26]

Finally, a child from an affluent neighborhood learns early that education is the chief vehicle of success in later life. He is likely to assume that he will attend college and may even define his goals less in terms of college than in terms of the professional education he desires after college. Such children are not likely to have serious financial barriers to their further education. They find it easy to entertain longer-range aspirations, for there is less pressure to earn money immediately.

Growing up in poverty, on the other hand, lends urgency to a child's ambitions and aspirations. He is more likely to want to find work as soon as possible, and infrequently has the independent means to pay for a college education. In a recent study of poverty one mother described a son who left school:

> Donald stopped school in the 8th grade because we didn't have food in the house and he also wanted a little money to spend. He said he wanted to stop school and go to work and help the family and that's what he did.[27]

In addition, although they may aspire to attend college, these children have few everyday contacts with college-educated adults. Thus while aspirations may be high, financial

means are limited and models of achievement are few. As a recent study of families in poverty pointed out, the concrete plans of the poor often are at variance with their expressed aspirations:

> Many, if not most, low-income families find themselves straddling two ways of life as they try, or express the wish to be able to meet selected middle-class goals but find themselves bogged down and pulled back to "basics" by the demands of daily life.[28]

INDIVIDUAL SOCIAL CLASS AND PERFORMANCE

These differences have a close relationship to performance in school. The *Equality of Educational Opportunity* survey—one of the most extensive studies of student attitudes and performance ever made—found that the greatest proportion of the achievement differences among students are accounted for by the differences in their social class.[29]

Figure 1 depicts the average verbal achievement in grade levels of 12th-grade Negro and white students, ranked by a measure of the student's social class.[30] In this case the indicator of social class used is the level of the parents' education.[31] It shows that students of lower social class have distinctly lower average verbal achievement than those from more privileged backgrounds.

In a study of Richmond, Calif., performed for the Commission by Alan Wilson, Pro-

[25] Jackson, *Poverty's Children*, p. 19.

[26] Sexton, *Education and Income*, pp. 7–8 (1961).

[27] Jeffers, *Three Generations*, p. 20.

[28] Jeffers, *Three Generations*, pp. 1–2.

[29] *OE Survey*, pp. 298–300.

[30] It should be noted that Fig. 1 is only an approximate measure of the achievement differences between children. None of the students' other experiences, such as the character of their schooling, have been taken into account. These same data, with appropriate adjustments for the sample design, are described in further detail in the *OE Survey* where the large regional differences and the degree of overlap in the distributions of Negro and white student test scores are shown. (*OE Survey*, pp. 219–275).

[31] With the exception of Alan Wilson's study, all text references to social class which follow are based upon the average educational attainment of a student's parents. The tables refer to "Low," "Medium," and "High": these headings refer respectively to less than high school, high school graduate, and more than high school graduate. Where the text refers to disadvantaged students, this designates the "Low" category. "Social class" is used in the text as a convenient designation for measures of relative educational disadvantage.

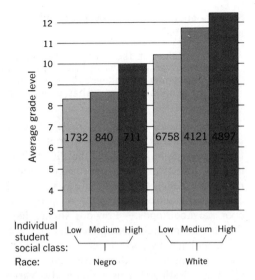

FIGURE 1 Average grade level performance, of twelfth grade Negro and white students by individual student social class; Metropolitan Northeast

fessor of Education at the University of California at Berkeley, the relationship between a student's social class and his school achievement was assessed. In this case the index of social class was parents' occupational levels. Wilson found that social class was the single factor most closely related to the academic achievement of children in the early grades.[32] This relationship was closer for white than Negro students, a result also found in the Office of Education survey.[33]

The attitudes and aspirations of students also are strongly related to their social class. One useful indicator of aspirations is the ambition for further education. Children from poorer backgrounds are less likely than children from well-to-do backgrounds to have concrete and definite plans for college. They also are less likely to have followed through on their aspirations by contacting a college official or reading a college catalogue.[34] Wil-

son also found a strong association between aspirations and individual students' social class.[35]

These differences do not suggest that to be poor in America automatically implies failure in school. They do suggest that, on the average, the social class of a student has a strong relationship to his academic success and aspirations. This is of particular significance for Negro students. In America a greater proportion of Negro than white children are poor, and thus the educational damage that stems from poverty is proportionately greater for the Negro than for the white population.

The Social Class Composition of Schools

The social class level of a student's classmates also has an important relationship to the outcomes of his education. From the early grades through senior high school, children increasingly are open to the direct influence of their peers. Both the Commission's Richmond study and the *Equality of Educational Opportunity* survey conclude that while family status is of great importance for early school achievement, in the later grades the influence of family gives way more and more to the influence of students' peers.[36] Dr. Charles Pinderhughes, a psychiatrist who testified at the Commission's Boston hearing, described the importance of the environment created by the student body:

> . . . [W]hat the pupils are learning from one another is probably just as important as what they are learning from the teachers. This is what I refer to as the hidden curriculum. It involves such things as how to think about themselves, how to think about other people, and how to get along with them. It involves such things as values, codes, and styles of behavior. . . .[37]

SOCIAL CLASS SEGREGATION AMONG SCHOOLS

A poor child is not only likely to have lower verbal achievement and aspirations himself, but he is very likely to attend school where most of the students have similar achievement and aspirations.[38]

[32] Wilson, *Educational Consequences of Segregation in a California Community*, in *app. C–3* (vol. II) on this Report. [Hereinafter cited as *Wilson app. C–3.*]

[33] *OE Survey*, pp. 300, 301, table 3.221.3, 6.

[34] *App. C–1*, tables 3.3 and 3.4.

[35] See *Wilson app. C–3*, pp. 193–199.

[36] *OE Survey*, p. 304; See *Wilson app. C–3*, p. 174.

[37] *Boston Hearing*, p. 138.

[38] For white students see *app. C–1* tables 8.6 and 8.7, pp. 137–138. For Negro students see *app. C–1* table 4.1, p. 66; table 3.2, p. 59.

An example of these differences in student environment is depicted in Figure 2. It summarizes the average verbal achievement of the 12th grade Negro and white students in schools of different social class compositions.[39] The figure shows that the average 12th grader's achievement in schools with lower social class levels is well below the average achievement level in more advantaged schools.

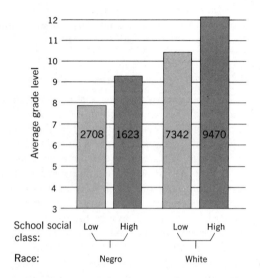

Note. The numbers in the bars represent the number of cases.

Source. USCCR analysis of *OE Survey* data. See App. C–1.

FIGURE 2 Average grade level performance of twelfth grade Negro and white students in schools of different social class compositions; Metropolitan Northeast

The distribution of student attitudes follows a similar pattern. Children raised in poverty are more likely than privileged children to attend school with students who feel that they will not be successful in life, and are less likely to have classmates with definite college plans.[40]

Norman Gross, a Rochester, N.Y., high school teacher who testified at the Commission's hearing there, described the differences in students' aspirations between Madison High

School—attended mostly by poor children—and a suburban school:

> . . . [O]ne of the Madison youngsters said: "[A]t Madison we asked a question, 'are you going to college?' " At Brighton the question always is "what college are you going to." [41]

One particularly sensitive indicator of a student's attitudes is whether or not he has the sense that he can affect the direction of his own life. It has been said that powerlessness—the feeling that one's life is not under one's own control—is typical of people in poor neighborhoods.[42] Previous studies have shown a definite relationship between the level of an individual's performance and the presence or absence of the sense that he can affect his destiny.[43] This attitude also varies with the social class level of the school.[44] Students in school with a majority of disadvantaged students more often are exposed to other students who feel they cannot affect their own destiny.

SCHOOL SOCIAL CLASS AND PERFORMANCE

The effect of the social class composition of schools upon student performance can best be seen if the average social class of the en-

---

[39] *App. C–1,* table 4.1, p. 66; table 3.2, p. 59.

[40] For Negroes see *app. C–1* table 4.2, p. 67; for whites see *app. C–1* table 8.6, p. 137.

[41] *Rochester Hearing,* p. 130.

[42] See, e.g., Harlem Youth Opportunities Unlimited, Inc., *Youth in the Ghetto,* pp. 10–11 (1964).

[43] Some studies have been undertaken to inquire into the relationship between feelings of powerlessness and the acquisition of knowledge and information. See, e.g., Seeman and Evans, "Alienation and Learning in a Hospital Setting," 27 *American Sociological Review* 772 (1962). In a hospital study of tuberculosis patients, Seeman and Evans found that those with the strongest feelings of powerlessness had less knowledge about tuberculosis than those who were not so alienated. Seeman, "Alienation and Social Learning in a Reformatory," 59 *American Journal of Sociology,* p. 270 (1963). In a reformatory setting, inmates with greater feelings of powerlessness learned relatively little when given information about parole, even though it might have helped shorten their confinement. All had over 100 IQ and at least 9th grade education. There was no correlation between IQ and alienation.

[44] *App. C–1,* table 3.5, p. 62; *OE Survey* 200, table 2.43.4; see also Havighurst, "Urban Development and the Educational System" in *Education in Depressed Areas* 24 (Passow ed. 1963).

tire student body is distinguished from the social class of individual students. Thus the performance of individual students of a given social class can be examined in schools with different social class compositions.

These relationships are examined in Figure 3 where the social class level and race of

with similarly low levels of education, and (2) those where a majority of the students have parents with at least a high school education. When the two bars are compared it is seen that the average performance of disadvantaged Negro students is better when the social class level of the student body is higher.

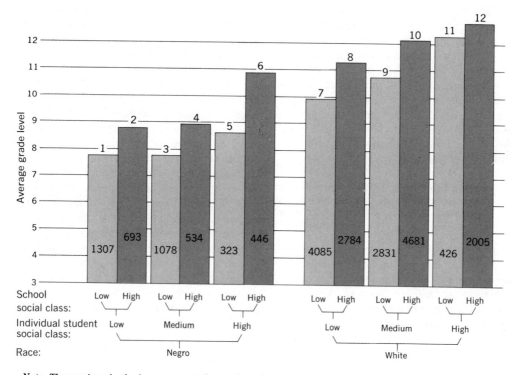

Note. The numbers in the bars represent the number of cases.
Source. USCCR analysis of *OE Survey* data. See App. C–1.

FIGURE 3 Average grade level performance of Negro and white twelfth grade students by social class level of the school and the social class origin of the student; Metropolitan Northeast

individual students, and the social class composition of the schools they attend are shown.[45] The first set of bars (1 and 2) compares the average grade level performance of Negro students from homes where parents have less than a high school education, in two different types of schools: (1) those in which a majority of the students have parents

[45] The social class level of the school is measured by the average parents' education of all students in the school. This measure is used in all figures and tables dealing with school social class. For a discussion, see *app. C–1,* pp. 37–39; 40–41.

As the figure also shows (7 and 8), this relationship is true for disadvantaged white students as well.

The performance of Negro students from more advantaged backgrounds in schools of different social class compositions also is compared. The third set of bars (5 and 6) depicts the average verbal achievement level of more advantaged students in schools of the same social class levels just described. These bars show that the performance of more advantaged students also varies with the social class level of the student body. This tendency holds for white students as well (11 and 12).

In Wilson's study of Richmond students, a marked relationship also was found between the social class composition of schools and student performance. Richmond students—regardless of their own social class—were more likely to perform well in predominantly middle class than in predominantly lower class schools.[46]

The Richmond study also measured the relative importance of individual and school social class for white and Negro students separately. It was found that the student environment had a stronger relationship to the performance of Negro than white students. White students' performance—although still strongly related to the social class level of their fellow students—was even more closely related to family background than that of Negroes. Wilson concluded:

. . . the family has much more influence on the achievement of white students than Negro students; the latter are more sensitive to variation in the school milieu.[47]

This relationship was assessed on a national scale by the *Equality of Educational Opportunity* survey. Its findings were the same as those in the Richmond study. The survey concluded that the "environment provided by the student body . . . has its greatest effect on those [students] from educationally deficient backgrounds."[48]

Wilson's study also weighed the effects of the social class composition of schools upon the same students over their entire school careers. It was found that the influence of individual social class is of great importance for student performance in the early elementary grades, and the social class composition of schools was of little significance. Over the course of the first eight school years, however, the cumulative effect of the social class composition of the elementary schools these children attended increased sharply. In the eighth grade it was as significant for student performance as individual social class.[49]

This pattern generally is the same when student attitudes are considered. The most striking comparison appears when college aspirations and plans are examined. Figure 4 compares the relationship between students' definite plans to attend college and the social class composition of their schools.[50] The first set of bars (1 and 2) compares the proportion of disadvantaged Negro students with definite plans to attend college in schools with either low or high social class compositions. This comparison shows that their college plans are more frequent in schools with a higher social class level. Relatively advantaged Negro students in schools of lower social class levels (5 and 6), are seen to be less likely to plan to attend college than similar students who are in school with a majority of more advantaged students. Regardless of their individual social class or race, students are more likely to have definite plans to attend college when they are in schools of higher social class compositions.

There is, then, a strong relationship between the attitudes and achievements of students and the social class composition of their schools. Disadvantaged students—especially Negroes—are more strongly influenced by the student environment than advantaged students. This relationship grows stronger over time. Although family and school social class factors vary in their individual importance at different grade levels, their combined influence always is great.

The Question of Selection

The data examined above suggest that the student environment has a connection with student performance. They tend to confirm the maxim that students learn as much from each other as from their teachers. Robert J. Havighurst, Professor of Sociology at the University of Chicago, in reviewing existing research on this question, recognized the problems of attributing cause. He concluded:

. . . [T]he consensus of students of the sociology and psychology of education is that the fact of attending a lower class school does have something to do with the lower academic achievement of the pupils from that school.[51]

Havighurst and others have noted that the relation between school social class and student performance may be the result of a

---

[46] *Wilson app. C–3*, pp. 182–84.

[47] *App. C–3*, p. 187.

[48] *OE Survey*, p. 304.

[49] *Wilson app. C–3*, table 21, p. 184.

[50] See *app. C–1*, table 3.2, p. 59.

[51] Havighurst, *Urban Development and the Educational System*, p. 32.

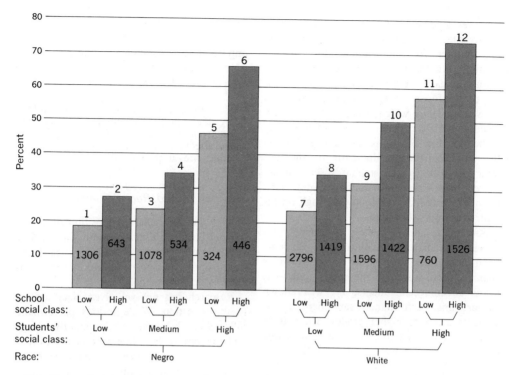

Note. The numbers in the bars represent the number of cases.
Source. USCCR analysis of *OE Survey* data. See App. C–1.

FIGURE 4 Proportion twelfth grade Negro and white students with definite college plans by students' social class origin and social class level of the school; Metropolitan Northeast

selective factor.[52] That is, lower class students in predominantly middle class schools may be there because their parents, viewing certain schools as better, deliberately enrolled their children in those schools. These students would be likely to be more highly motivated and to have appreciably higher verbal achievement when they entered school. If this were true, the connection between student performance and school social class would be put in doubt.

Wilson's study examined this question. Because his research dealt with the same students over time, it was possible to consider the problem of self-selection. To consider the selective factor, differences in the students' first-grade verbal achievement were taken into account when inspecting the effects of school social class upon later school achievement.[53] The study found that there was still a strong

effect of school social class, apart from the students' early achievement. Wilson concluded that:

> . . . allowing for variation in primary-grade mental maturity, the social class composition of the primary school has the largest independent effect upon the sixth grade reading level.[54]

Factors other than selection—in the student's school experience and environment—must be involved.

It is difficult to specify precisely the ways in which the student environment affects performance and attitudes. There is a complicated relationship between the standards set by the performance and attitudes of a student's schoolmates and his own performance and attitudes. It seems reasonable to suggest, however, that at least two elements are present.

First, different backgrounds influence what students see as attainable goals. A disad-

[52] Havighurst, *Urban Development and the Educational System*, p. 32.

[53] See *Wilson app. C–3*, table 17, p. 187.

[54] *App. C–3*, table 17, p. 187.

vantaged student in school mostly with other disadvantaged students is exposed primarily to youngsters for whom immediate work and earnings are the most concrete need. While it may be easy for a given student to express his desire for a college education, there is little around him which suggests that his own friends and social equals regard such a thing to be possible. Since, as they move through the grades, students increasingly measure their behavior by the standards set and accepted by their friends and associates, such a student is unlikely to follow through on his aspirations for college.[55]

Second, a similar process is probably involved in academic achievement. Students from poor backgrounds do not perform as well in school—even in the early grades—as more advantaged students. As was shown earlier, this performance gap increases as students move to higher grades. Students in schools where early and continuing academic difficulty are typical are likely to suffer from the cumulative disadvantage of their classmates. The students provide each other both with academic standards and with varying degrees of academic interchange. Where the majority of students have low achievement, others will be likely to follow suit.

This was illustrated in testimony by David Jaquith, President of the Syracuse Board of Education, at the Commission hearing in Rochester. Explaining the positive effects of a transfer of disadvantaged students from Madison Junior High School to Levi, a junior high school which had a more advantaged student body, he said:

> . . . at Madison Junior High School, if you cooperated with the teacher and did your homework, you were a "kook."
> At Levi Junior High School, if you don't cooperate with the teacher and don't do your homework, you are a "kook." Peer pressure has tremendous effect on the motivation and motivation has a tremendous effect on achievement.[56]

* * *

In summary, there is a strong relationship between student and school social class, and performance and attitudes. The social class composition of schools is the single most important school factor affecting student performance and attitudes. As the *Equality of Educational Opportunity* survey concluded:

> . . . the inequalities imposed on children by their home, neighborhood, and peer environment are carried along to become the inequalities with which they confront adult life at the end of school.[57]

Social Class and Racial Composition

Thus far the racial composition of schools has not been taken into account. Does it have a relationship to performance which is distinct from that associated with the social class composition of schools?

Research has not yet given clear answers to this question. While serious performance differences between predominantly Negro and predominantly white schools are evident, there has been disagreement on whether the differences are due entirely to factors associated with the social class level of schools or whether racial composition is an important additional factor.[58]

Figure 5 depicts all three dimensions of the relationship in question. Two—the social class level of individual Negro students and the social class level of their schools—already have been discussed. The third, which is depicted here for the first time, is the racial composition of classrooms.[59]

Comparisons among the first four bars show that when relatively disadvantaged Negro students are in class with a majority of similarly disadvantaged white students (4), their performance is higher than when they are in class with a majority of equally disadvantaged Negroes (1). A similar relationship obtains for more advantaged Negro students, when those in school with similarly advantaged Negroes (13) are compared with those in school with similarly advantaged whites (16).

When disadvantaged Negro students in

[55] See note 36, *supra;* Alexander and Campbell, "Peer Influences on Adolescent Aspirations and Attainments," **29** *American Sociological Review,* p. 568 (1964). See also *Wilson app. C–3,* p. 181.

[56] *Rochester Hearing,* pp. 473–474.

[57] *OE Survey,* p. 325.

[58] *OE Survey,* pp. 307–312. See *Wilson app. C–3,* pp. 182–187.

[59] With the exception of the section on school quality, all tabulations involving racial composition refer to the racial composition of classrooms. For a fuller discussion, see *app. C–1,* pp. 40–42.

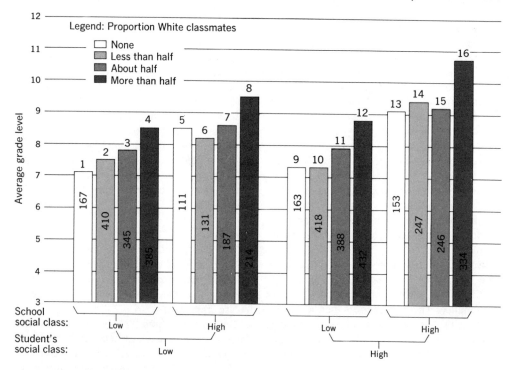

Note. The numbers in the bars represent the number of cases.
Source. USCCR analysis of *OE Survey* data. See App. C–1.

FIGURE 5 Average grade level performance of twelfth grade Negro students by individual social class origin, social class level of school and proportion white classmates last year; Metropolitan Northeast

school with more advantaged Negroes are considered (5), there also is a performance improvement. Yet only a small proportion of the Negro population is middle class, and disadvantaged Negroes generally must attend school with whites if they are to be in school with a majority of more advantaged students. The combined effects of social class integration and racial desegregation are substantial. When disadvantaged Negro students are in class with similarly situated whites (4), their average performance is improved by more than a full grade level. When they are in class with more advantaged white students (8), their performance is improved by more than two grade levels.

These comparisons suggest a relationship between the performance of Negro students and the racial composition of classrooms. They do not, however, explain it. There are a number of possible explanations.

First, there may be differences in the quality of education offered in majority-Negro and majority-white schools which account for the higher average Negro performance in majority-white schools.

Second, it may be that there is a process of selection involved, whereby only initially more able Negro students attend majority-white schools.

Finally, there may be student environment factors directly connected with racial composition which relate to the attitudes and performance of Negro students. These possibilities, which are not mutually exclusive, will be discussed in succeeding pages.

SCHOOL QUALITY AND STUDENT PERFORMANCE

Performance differences between schools with predominantly Negro and predominantly white enrollments often have been attributed to disparities in the quality of education between such schools. It is certainly true that the quality of a school's curriculum, the character of its facilities, and the attitudes and qualifications of its teaching and administrative staff can affect the attitudes, morale, and performance of students.

This section, however, is addressed to a more specific problem. Differences in the performance of Negro students have been shown which relate to the social class composition of their schools and—additionally—to their racial composition. Certain differences in accepted measures of school quality also exist between predominantly Negro and predominantly white schools. Do existing differences in school quality account completely for the performance differences which relate to the social and racial composition of schools?

This section first presents a discussion of those differences in school quality which appear to have some relationship to student performance. These differences then are compared with the achievement and attitude differences which appear to relate to the social class and racial composition of schools. In this way it can be determined whether the differences in school quality explain the relationship between achievement and the racial composition of schools.

The Extent of Disparities

Three aspects of the quality of education were mentioned earlier: educational facilities, including language and science laboratories; curriculum, including the presence or absence of specialized study in particular subjects; and the attitudes and qualifications of teachers.

FACILITIES

There are some noticeable differences in the quality of school facilities available to Negro and white students in the Nation's metropolitan areas. The *Equality of Educational Opportunity* survey reported that although Negro and white children were equally likely to attend schools with libraries, whites more often attended schools with more library volumes per student.[60] White students also were more likely to attend schools which had science laboratories.[61]

EDUCATIONAL PROGRAM

Similar disparities existed in the educational offerings available to Negro and white

[60] *OE Survey*, p. 78, table 2.21.13.
[61] *OE Survey*, p. 73, table 2.21.8

students. The survey reported that whites more often were in schools which had advanced courses in particular subjects, such as science and language. They also were more likely to be in schools with fewer pupils per teacher.[62] In most cities studied by the Commission it was found that schools with nearly all-Negro enrollments were overcrowded more often than nearly all-white schools. This often resulted in the establishment of classes in temporary structures—sometimes in the basements of churches or other public buildings.[63]

TEACHERS

Teachers are the most important element in the quality of education schools offer. The extent of their experience, the quality of their training, and their attitudes toward students all are important.

The survey found no significant national differences in the educational attainment, as measured by years of school completed, of teachers in majority-Negro and majority-white schools. Negro students, however, were exposed less often than white students to teachers whose college major was in an academic subject—mathematics, science, or literature.[64]

Negro students also were more likely than whites to have teachers with lower verbal achievement levels. Part of the survey involved a vocabulary test administered to teachers. The results of the test in the Metropolitan Northeast, for example, show that in those majority-Negro classrooms included

[62] *OE Survey*, p. 70, table 2.21.4; 100, table 2.24.2.
[63] For example, nearly half of the majority-Negro schools in Philadelphia in the 1965–66 school year were overcrowded (i.e., the average percentage enrollment of capacity exceeded 109%). Approximately one third of Philadelphia's nearly all-white schools were similarly overcrowded. (*Philadelphia Study*, app. A–3); in Cleveland, Ohio, between 1957 and 1964, 95 percent of all units rented to relieve overcrowding were at nearly all-Negro schools. (*Cleveland Study*, Section Ba). In the 1965–66 school year a greater proportion of mobile units in Chicago were in use in Negro schools. Of all mobile units used in that school year, 68% were at nearly all-Negro schools while only 20% were at nearly all-white schools. (Information obtained from the U. S. Office of Education.)
[64] *OE Survey*, p. 140, table 2.33.8.

in the sample almost none of the 12th grade students had faculties which scored in the highest range of this test.[65] Commission studies in various cities resulted in an analogous finding. In those cities which administered teacher examinations, such as St. Louis, Atlanta, and Philadelphia, the faculties of nearly all-Negro schools had lower average test scores than faculties in all-white schools.[66]

Nationally the survey found that Negro and white students had equally experienced teachers. Differences were revealed, however, in Commission investigations in specific cities. In Oakland, for example, more probationary teachers were found in nearly all-Negro schools than in nearly all-white schools.[67] In Philadelphia, a greater proportion of substitute teachers was found in nearly all-Negro schools.[68] In some cities—such as Boston and Milwaukee—there has been higher teacher turnover in schools with increasing Negro enrollment than in nearly all-white schools.[69]

Marked national differences in teachers' attitudes about remaining in their present schools were found in the survey. Negro students were more likely than whites to have teachers who preferred not to remain in their present school.[70] One writer has commented: ". . . in many cities across the country the depressed areas have been the 'Siberias' of the local school system . . ."[71]

On the other hand, Negro students more often than whites had teachers who said they preferred to teach children from a variety of social backgrounds and their teachers more often expressed liberal racial attitudes.[72]

School Quality and Social Class Composition of Schools

Do such differences in the quality of education available to Negro and white children explain the relationship reported earlier between the social class composition of schools and student performance?

Two composite measures of educational quality were devised to examine this question. The use of composite measures makes it possible to take into account simultaneously those school quality differences which show some general relation to achievement. Each composite measure permits comparison of student achievement and attitudes in schools which have high or low levels of the educational quality being measured. One relates to school facilities and educational program and the other deals only with teacher qualifications and attitudes.[73]

FACILITIES AND CURRICULUM

Table 1 depicts the achievement of disadvantaged Negro students, the social class level of their schools, and variations in the quality of educational program and facilities in their schools.[74] It thus permits an assessment of the relationship between differences in school quality and student achievement. When column I is read down, it is seen that there are some variations in students achievement which relate to variations in the quality of educational facilities and programs.

The table also shows that improvements in the achievement of disadvantaged Negro stu-

[65] See *app. C–1*, table 7.18, p. 121.

[66] *Atlanta Study*, p. 66, table 18; 41; *Philadelphia Study*, Part III B; Reisner, *Equality of Education Opportunity in St. Louis*, pp. 48, 54 (unpublished report to the U.S. Office of Education, July, 1965).

[67] About one third of all Oakland teachers are probationary—i.e., have taught less than three years. There is a higher proportion of probationary teachers in elementary schools with higher Negro enrollment. *Oakland Study*, p. 70.

[68] *Philadelphia Study*, Part III B.2.b., table 13.

[69] ". . . As the percentage of non-white pupils increases, there is a general increase in teacher turnover rates." *Milwaukee Study* Part III.b., pp. 2–3.

". . . There is a high degree of relatedness between the frequency of staff change and the degree to which a school has a high non-white enrollment." *Boston Study*, "Staff Quality and School Quality: Selected Characteristics," p. 2.

[70] *OE Survey*, p. 156, table 2.34.8.

[71] Ravitz, *The Role of the School in the Urban Setting*, p. 19.

[72] *OE Survey*, p. 168, table 2.35.2.

[73] The index of school facilities and curriculum is composed of the following measures: science laboratories, comprehensiveness of curriculum, and extracurricular activities. For further details see *app. C–1*, sec. 1.5, pp. 43–44.

The index of teacher qualifications is composed of the following teacher measures: educational level, type of college major, desire to continue teaching in current school, and years teaching experience. For further details see *app. C–1*, sec. 1.5, pp. 44–46.

[74] See *app. C–1*, table 7.4, p. 107.

TABLE 1   School Quality, Student Performance, and the Social Class Composition of Schools. (Average verbal achievement test scores, 12th grade, by school quality index, parents' education, and school average of parents' education, expressed in grade level equivalents; Metropolitan Northeast)

Individual's Parents' Education (social class of students)	School Average: Parents' Education (social class level of school)	School Quality Index	Achievement Level I
Less than high school. (low)	Less than high school graduate. (low)	Low Medium High	7.4 7.8 8.2
	High school graduate or more. (medium or high)	Low Medium High	8.5 8.6 9.2

Source: USCCR analysis of *OE Survey* data. See App. C-1.

dents when in school with a majority of advantaged students was not explained by variations in school facilities and curriculum. This suggests that performance variations associated with differences in the social class composition of schools are distinct from variations in school facilities and curriculum. Yet the magnitude of the differences must be remembered. Present differences in school curriculum and facilities in metropolitan areas are noticeable, but not massive. This analysis only weighs existing differences in school quality.

TEACHERS

Consistent differences also appear when the social class background, qualifications, and attitudes of teachers are considered. Table 2 weighs the relationship between differences in teacher quality and student achievement. It also permits comparison of these differences with those associated with variations in the social class composition of schools.

The table shows that differences in the qualifications and attitudes of teachers have a regular relationship to student performance. Consider, for example, the first row (A) which depicts disadvantaged Negro students in schools with a majority of other disadvantaged students. When such students have less qualified teachers (1), they do less well than when their teachers are more qualified (2). The same relationship holds when disadvantaged Negro students are in schools with a majority of advantaged students (B). At each school social class level, students with more qualified teachers perform at higher levels than those with less qualified teachers.

When the variations in teacher quality are held constant, however, differences associated with school social class still appear. Compare, for example, disadvantaged Negro students with equally well qualified teachers, in school either with a majority of disadvantaged students (A2), or a majority of more advantaged students (B2). Those with a more

TABLE 2   Teacher Quality, Student Performance, and the Social Class Composition of Schools. (Average grade level performance of low-social-class 12th grade Negroes, social-class level of the school and teacher quality; Metropolitan Northeast)

Individual's Parents' Education (social class of students)	School Average: Parents' Education (social class level of school)	Teacher Average: Index	Grade Level Performance
Less than high school graduate. (low)	(A) Less than high school graduate. (low)	(1) Low (2) High	7.7 8.1
	(B) High school graduate or more. (medium to high)	(1) Low (2) High	8.6 8.9

Source: USCCR analysis of *OE Survey* data. See App. C-1.

advantaged student body perform at a higher level.

An even more severe comparison of teacher quality and school social class is possible. A comparison of rows A2 and B1 weighs improved teacher quality in majority-disadvantaged schools against improved social class in schools with poorer teachers. The effects of school social class outweigh those of teacher quality.

There is, then, a pronounced relationship between the qualifications of teachers and the performance of students. It appears to be consistent for Negro students of all social class levels in schools of different social class compositions. The relationship between teacher qualifications and student performance, however, is not as consistently strong as the relationship between student performance and the social class composition of schools. Although teacher quality is important, when taken into account it does not alter the significance of the relationship between the social class composition of schools and the achievement of Negro students.

quality is considered, however, there are relationships with student performance which vary with the racial composition of classrooms.

The performance of disadvantaged Negro children in majority-Negro classrooms is analyzed in Table 3.[76] When column I is read down it is possible to compare the relationship between different levels of teacher quality and the verbal achievement of disadvantaged Negro students. In row A they are in classes with a majority of similarly disadvantaged Negro students and in row B with a majority of more advantaged Negro students. The comparison in row A shows that higher teacher quality is associated with improvements in student performance in classes with a majority of disadvantaged Negro students.

A comparison of row A2 with B1 indicates that having highly qualified teachers or attending school with more advantaged Negroes may be of about equal importance to disadvantaged children. Children lag severely when both factors are missing. When either factor

TABLE 3   Teacher Quality and Student Performance in Majority-Negro Schools. (Average achievement in grade levels of lower social class 12th grade Negro students in majority-Negro schools, by teacher quality and school social class; Metropolitan Northeast)

Individual's Parents' Education (social class of students)	School Average: Parents' Education (social class level of school)	Teacher Average: Index	Achievement Level I
Less than high school. (low)	(A) Less than high school graduate. (low)	(1) Low	7.3
		(2) High	7.7
	(B) High school graduate or more. (medium to high)	(1) Low	7.8
		(2) High	8.6

Source: USCCR analysis of *OE Survey* data. See App. C–1.

School Quality and Racial Composition

The remaining question is whether, when the racial composition of schools is taken into account, the results differ from those related to social class.

When facilities and curriculum were considered, they showed a limited association with student achievement in schools of differing racial compositions.[75] When teacher

is present, children perform better. When both factors are present, children perform at an even higher level. The distinct effects of teacher quality and social class compositions reported in the earlier consideration of social class, then, hold in majority-Negro schools.

When more advantaged Negro students are considered, there also is a relationship between teacher quality and student performance. Yet for these students the effect of

[75] *App. C–1*, table 7.4, p. 107.   [76] See *App. C–1*, table 7.16, p. 119.

social class composition is even greater than the effect of teacher quality.[77]

Do similar results exist in majority-white schools? Table 4 presents the same comparisons, except that the schools in this case are majority-white.[78] Reading down column I reveals that the student achievement differences associated with variations in teacher quality are virtually nonexistent in four of the six comparisons (A, B, C, and D). This suggests that improvements in teacher quality have less relation to the performance of Negro students in majority-white schools than they do in majority-Negro schools.[79]

vantaged Negro students.[80] Reading across rows A1 and 2 and B1 and 2 reveals that at each level of teacher quality and school social class, the performance of Negro students is substantially higher in majority-white (column II) than majority-Negro (column I) schools.

A more refined comparison of the relative importance of teacher quality and racial composition is possible. Consider disadvantaged Negro students in schools with poorer teachers and a majority of equally disadvantaged white students (row A1, column II). They perform at a higher level than similarly dis-

TABLE 4   Teacher Quality and Student Performance in Majority-White Schools. (Average achievement in grade levels of 12th grade Negro students in majority-white schools, by teacher quality, individual social class, and school social class; Metropolitan Northeast)

Individual's Parents' Education (social class of students)	*School Average: Parents' Education (social class level of school)*	*Teacher Average: Index*	*Achievement Level I*
Less than high school. (low)	(A) Less than high school graduate. (low)	(1) Low	8.5
		(2) High	8.6
	(B) High school graduate or more. (medium to high)	(1) Low	9.5
		(2) High	9.5
High school graduate. (medium)	(C) Less than high school graduate. (low)	(1) Low	8.5
		(2) High	8.6
	(D) High school graduate or more. (medium to high)	(1) Low	10.0
		(2) High	9.7
More than high school graduate. (high)	(E) Less than high school graduate. (low)	(1) Low	9.1
		(2) High	10.7
	(F) High school graduate or more. (medium to high)	(1) Low	11.4
		(2) High	11.9

Source: USCCR analysis of *OE Survey* data. See App. C-1.

The effect of differences in the social class level of schools does not change when the racial composition of schools varies. The effect of differences in teacher quality varies, however, and is smaller for Negro students in majority-white than majority-Negro schools.

What is the relative importance of teacher quality and racial composition? Table 5 provides direct comparison of these for disad-

advantaged Negro students in school with better teachers and a majority of equally disadvantaged Negroes (row A2, column I). The same comparison holds (row B) when the disadvantaged Negro students are in schools with more advantaged children.

The relative strength of racial composition also was found to be at least as great for more advantaged Negro students.[80a] Although teacher quality has a consistent relationship to student achievement in majority-Negro schools, it is equally consistently outweighed

[77] *App. C-1*, table 7.16, p. 119.

[78] See App. *C-1*, Table 7.16, p. 119.

[79] It might be suggested that this is related to Negro students' greater sensitivity to student body characteristics, as opposed to teacher characteristics. See *OE Survey*, p. 302.

[80] See *App. C-1*, table 7.16, p. 119.

[80a] *App. C-1*, table 7.16, p. 119.

by the effect of being in majority-white schools.

Teachers affect more than their students' verbal achievement. Their attitudes, and the standards they set for students also are likely to be related to their students' attitudes and aspirations. Other studies have highlighted the effect of teacher expectations on student performance. In one study, teachers were told that certain students, who actually had been selected at random, had especially high ability. As a result, their own expectations for these students rose and the students' performance improved markedly.[81] It seems

obtained in the analysis of student achievement were found.[83] The clearest relationships were found between teachers' education and students' college plans.[84] Negro students in majority-Negro schools who have more highly educated teachers more frequently have definite plans to attend college.

This association, however, is weakened in majority-white schools. Differences in teacher qualifications are not as closely related to the frequency with which Negro students in such schools report definite college plans. Yet Negro students in these schools are more likely to have definite college plans than sim-

TABLE 5   Teacher Quality and Student Performance in Majority-White and Majority-Negro Schools. (Average achievement in grade levels of low social class 12th grade Negroes by school social class, teacher quality, and racial composition of schools; Metropolitan Northeast)

Individual's Parents' Education (social class of students)	School Average: Parents' Education (social class level of school)	Teacher Average: Index	Proportion White Classmates	
			Less than half I	More than half II
Less than high school. (low)	(A) Less than high school graduate. (low)	(1) Low	7.3	8.5
		(2) High	7.7	8.6
	(B) High school graduate. (medium to high)	(1) Low	7.8	9.5
		(2) High	8.6	9.5

Source: USCCR analysis of *OE Survey* data. See App. C-1.

likely that a similar relationship exists for student attitudes. Indeed, some studies suggest that students tend to adjust to what they perceive their teachers' expectations to be and to aspire and perform accordingly.[82]

Similar relationships were found in the Commission's further analysis of data from the *Equality of Educational Opportunity* survey. When the relationship between teacher qualifications and attitudes was tested against student aspirations, results similar to those

ilar situated students in majority-Negro schools, regardless of the quality of their teachers. Thus the advantages of having more highly qualified teachers seem to be outweighed by the advantage of attending majority-white schools.

It must be noted again that this analysis deals only with existing variations in teacher quality. It cannot assess the potential effects upon Negro students of improved teacher quality and teaching techniques.

It seems clear, however, that the performance of Negro students is distinctly less related to differences in the quality of schools and teachers than the social class and racial composition of their schools. This further reinforces the conclusion that the quality of

[81] Rosenthal, *Experimenter Effects in Behavioral Research*, p. 411 (1966). This effect was clear only in primary grades.

[82] Davidson and Lang, "Children's Perceptions of Their Teachers' Feelings Toward Them Related to Self-Perception, School Achievement, and Behavior," **29** *Journal of Experimental Education*, p. 107 (1960); See also: *Boston Hearing*, p. 98 (Testimony of Mrs. Joyce Johnson).

[83] See *App. C-1*, table 7.23–7.30, pp. 126–33.

[84] *App. C-1*, tables 7.23 and 7.24, pp. 126–127.

education presently provided in schools does little to reverse the inequalities imposed upon children by factors within and outside the schools. The analysis thus suggests that changes in the social class or racial composition of schools would have a greater effect upon student achievement and attitudes than changes in school quality.[84a]

RACIAL COMPOSITION AND STUDENT PERFORMANCE

In the preceding sections it has been shown that there is a relationship between the social class composition of schools and student performance which is distinct from the relationship between school quality and student performance. A relationship has been shown, too, between student performance and the racial composition of schools which also apparently is distinct from considerations either of school social class or school quality.

Two questions remain. First, does the higher performance of Negro children in majority-white schools result from a process of selection—the fact that they initially were more able students?

Second, if this is not the case, what does account for the performance differences between Negro students in majority-white and majority-Negro schools?

Selection

Wilson examined the question of selection in his study of Richmond students. Since the students' early elementary achievement was known, it was possible to determine whether the Negro students in majority-white schools initially were more able. When Wilson examined this question he found that:

> The Negro students who attended integrated schools had higher mental maturity test scores in their primary grades, and came from homes better provided with educative materials.[85]

A related question, then, was whether the racial composition of the majority-white schools had an effect on the academic performance of the Negro children, in addition to their initial greater ability. When the early

elementary achievement of these students was held constant, Wilson found that "the racial composition of schools, while tending to favor Negro students in integrated schools, does not have a substantial effect."[86] There was, however, still a strong effect of the social class composition of their schools.[87]

Yet if the Richmond Negro students who were in majority-white schools were initially more able, this still leaves open the question of the effects of majority-white schools on the performance of a broader range of Negro students, many of whom probably were not initially more able. Because of the small size of the sample, Wilson could not examine this question fully.

The Commission did examine the question —in further analysis of the survey data— with a larger sample of students. To determine whether the racial composition of schools had an effect upon the performance of a range of students, the achievement of *less able* Negro students in schools of different racial compositions was analyzed.

First, the performance of Negro students in different ability groups was studied. It is unlikely that Negro students in low ability groups uniformly would have been more able students earlier in school.[88]

The results of this analysis are summarized in Table 6.[89] It shows the verbal achievement levels of disadvantaged ninth grade Negro students, in low ability groups, in majority-white schools, in classrooms of different racial compositions. When row 1 is read across it is seen that there is relationship between verbal achievement and having a majority of white classmates. When row 2 is read, a similar but more pronounced relationship exists. When the columns are read down a marked relationship to social class composition is seen.

The achievement of a broad range of Negro students also can be examined by holding the average verbal achievement of their schools constant, while the relationship between student achievement and racial composition is assessed. The social class of individual students also is taken into account. Table 7 depicts the results for disadvantaged

[84a] *OE Survey*, p. 325.
[85] See *Wilson app. C–3*, p. 185.

[86] Wilson *app. C–3*, p. 185.
[87] Wilson, *app. C–3*, p. 185.
[88] For a full discussion, see *App. C–1*, sec. 1.2, p. 37.
[89] *App. C–1*, table 5.6, p. 91.

TABLE 6   Achievement of Negro Students in Low and Medium Ability Groups. (Average verbal achievement in grade levels of 9th grade Negro students, in majority-white schools in low and medium ability groups; Metropolitan Northeast)

Individual's Parents' Education (social class of students)	School Average Parents' Education (social class level of school)	Percent White in Classroom	
		Less than half	More than half
Less than high school graduate. (low)	(1) Less than high school. (low)	5.8	6.2
	(2) High school or more. (medium to high)	6.3	7.0

Source: USCCR analysis of *OE Survey* data. See App. C1.

Negro students.[90] When row 1 is read across, it is seen that the achievement of disadvantaged Negro students in the lowest achieving schools increases in majority-white classrooms. The trend grows stronger as the average achievement level of the school rises.

Another approach to the problem was taken in a study prepared for the Commission by David J. Armor, Assistant Professor of Sociology at Harvard University. Armor further analyzed the Office of Education survey data to examine more closely the relationship be-

of the school, but their achievement which influenced the aspiration differences.

Armor thus dealt separately with the most academically able Negro male students, and weighed the relationship between racial composition of their classrooms and their college plans. The study focused on students whose verbal achievement was above the median for the region and who had "A" and "B" grades in school.

Armor found no consistent relationship between student aspirations and the racial

TABLE 7   Negro Students' Achievement Controlling for School Average Achievement. (Average verbal achievement in grade levels for 9th grade Negro students by parents' education, average of school's verbal achievement scores, and proportion white classmates; for Metropolitan Northeast)

Individual's Parents' Education (social class of students)	School Environment: School average verbal achievement	Proportion White Classmates		
		None	Less than half	About half or more
Less than high school. (low)	(1) 8.0– 9.3	5.5	6.1	5.9
	(2) 9.4–10.8	6.3	6.6	6.7
	(3) 11.0	6.3	6.1	7.4

Source: USCCR analysis of *OE Survey* data. See App. C1.

tween college aspirations and the racial composition of schools. His study sought to determine whether the higher college aspirations of Negro students in majority-white schools could be accounted for solely by their higher academic achievement. If they uniformly were more able then it might be argued that it was not the racial composition

composition of schools for advantaged Negro students. When he considered disadvantaged students of high ability, however, Armor concluded:

> . . . [I]t is the qualified, bright student from a lower class background . . . who is most aided by integration (or, conversely, hurt most by segregation). In a sense, he is the one for whom the most help is required. . . . For the able middle class Negro in a better school, there is not as much effect due to integration. But do these students

[90] *App. C–1*, table 4.13, p. 82. The school average achievement includes all students.

need the help? . . . 85 percent are already planning college . . . how much improvement do they need?

Clearly, the effects of integration have been shown to help those with the greatest need for a boost. . . .[91]

The analysis suggests that selectivity does not entirely account for the relationship between the racial composition of schools and the achievement and aspirations of Negro students.

The Racially Isolated School

What is it, then, about the racially isolated school which seems to result in the poorer achievement of many Negro students? And conversely, what factors in the majority-white school account for the more positive attitudes and higher achievement of Negro students?

Negro students often come to school with attitudes and experiences which bear upon their performance in school. Like all children they become aware of racial differences at an early age. Young Negro children, however, often tend to reject their own skin color, and to have problems of self-esteem.[92] Kenneth Morland, Chairman of the Department of Sociology and Anthropology at Randolph-Macon College, has written:

In a sense, American society educates for prejudice. Studies in both Northern and Southern communities . . . show that Negro as well as white children develop a bias for the white race at an early age. This bias is indicated by both a preference for and an identification with whites rather than with Negroes.[93]

There is reason to believe that the racial composition of schools can serve either to overcome or to compound these problems

of low self-esteem.[94] For example, Calvin Brooks, during his testimony at the Cleveland hearing, described the environment at his school and its effects upon the students:

. . . it had an effect because they were there and all they saw were Negroes and they were raised in an environment of poverty and the building was old and it had an effect I don't know of—of hopelessness. They didn't think that they could do anything because their fathers had common labor jobs and they didn't think they could ever get any higher and they didn't work, some of them.[95]

In part, the relationship between racially isolated schools and poor performance and low self-esteem is based upon the fact that predominantly Negro schools are generally regarded as inferior by the community. James Allen, Commissioner of Education for the State of New York, pointed out at the Commission hearing in Rochester that:

. . . the all-Negro schools . . . are looked upon by the community as being poor schools. . . . No matter what you do to try to make them better, in the minds of most white people in these communities, they are poor schools.[96]

At other Commission hearings parents and teachers often testified that predominantly Negro schools are stigmatized institutions. Dr. Charles Pinderhughes, a psychiatrist who testified at the Boston hearing, said that "the Negro school carries with it a stigma that influences the attitudes both on the part of out-

---

[91] See *Armor app. C–2*, p. 146.

[92] For summaries and interpretation of studies and literature on low self-esteem among Negroes see: Vontress, "The Negro Personality Reconsidered," **35** *Journal of Negro Education*, p. 210 (1966); Ausubel and Ausubel, "Ego Development Among Segregated Negro Children" in *Education in Depressed Areas* 109 (Passow ed. 1963); Karon, *The Negro Personality* (1958); **20** *Journal of Social Issues* [*The Negro American Personality*, spec. issue] (Pettigrew and Thompson ed. April, 1964).

[93] Morland, "The Development of Racial Bias in Young Children," **2** *Theory Into Practice*, p. 120 (1963). In another study, Morland found

that Negro nursery school children attending segregated schools in Lynchburg, Virginia, tended to identify themselves as white rather than Negro. "Racial Self-Identification: A Study of Nursery School Children," **24** *The American Catholic Sociological Review*, p. 231 (Fall, 1963). In a later study, Morland compared two groups of children, one from Lynchburg, Virginia, and the other from Boston, Massachusetts. He found that both groups of Negroes manifested a bias for whites. Morland, "A Comparison of Race Awareness in Northern and Southern Children," **36** *American Journal of Orthopsychiatry*, p. 22 (January, 1966). This bias toward whites does not appear to be a regional phenomenon.

[94] Clark, "Educational Stimulation of Racially Disadvantaged Children" in *Education in Depressed Areas* (Passow ed. 1963).

[95] *Cleveland Hearing*, p. 283.

[96] *Rochester Hearing*, p. 420.

siders and on the part of parents, students, and teachers . . .".[97] Dr. John Fischer, President of Teachers College at Columbia University, has written of the

> . . . unfortunate psychological effect upon a child of membership in a school where every pupil knows that, regardless of his personal attainments, the group with which he is identified is viewed as less able, less successful, and less acceptable than the majority of the community.[98]

The impact of negative community attitudes upon children was illustrated at the Commission hearing in Cleveland where a teacher at an all-Negro high school was asked about a student exchange between his school and an all-white suburban high school. He explained how his students felt about themselves and the school after the exchange:

> . . . I think the reaction is somewhat illuminating as one of my students in one of my classes said last year, "Well, it was nice of them to come down to the zoo to see us." [99]

Community attitudes toward schools which identify them as inferior also are recognized by their teaching and administrative staff. Testimony at Commission hearings tended to confirm the conclusions of some researchers that teachers in racially isolated schools recognize the stigma of inferiority which is attached to their schools. At the Cleveland hearing, one teacher, asked how he felt when he was informed that he had been assigned to a school that was 95 percent Negro, replied:

> Well, I think I was a little bit disappointed personally. I knew . . . that any time a school is predominantly Negro . . . that there is a stigma that goes with it, that it just can't be first class. I not only feel that this is true in the minds of Negroes, but also in the minds of most whites.[100]

There is evidence that this affects the attitudes and performance of many teachers in majority-Negro schools. At the Commission hearing in Rochester, Franklyn Barry, Superintendent of Schools in Syracuse, N.Y., testified that in such schools teachers often "average down" their expectations of the students.[101] A study of schools in Harlem discussed the low teacher expectations there, and concluded that:

> The atmosphere stemming from such expectations cannot be conducive to good teaching, and is manifest in friction between teachers, abdication of teaching responsibilities . . . [and] a concern with discipline rather than learning . . .[102]

This is consistent with data from the *Equality of Educational Opportunity* survey which noted that Negro students were more likely to have teachers who did not want to remain in their present school. Their teachers also were more likely to feel that other teachers regarded their school as a poor one.[103]

Conversely the student environment in desegregated schools can offer substantial support for high achievement and aspirations.[104] The majority of the children in such schools do not have problems of self-confidence due to race and the schools are not stigmatized as inferior. The students are likely to assume that they will succeed in school and in their future careers, for the school reflects the mainstream of American society. The environment in such schools is well endowed with models of academic and occupational success. For Negro childen, desegregated schools may pose problems of racial identification.[105] But they also offer association with other students who see a clear connection between their education and later careers with no contradictions or serious doubts. High aspirations held by Negro students in such schools are

[97] *Boston Hearing*, p. 139.

[98] John H. Fischer, "Race and Reconciliation: The Role of the School," **95** *Daedalus*, p. 26 (Winter, 1966).

[99] *Cleveland Hearing*, p. 308 (Testimony of Charles Bohi).

[100] *Cleveland Hearing*, p. 302 (Testimony of Ulysses Van Spiva).

[101] *Rochester Hearing*, p. 468.

[102] Harlem Youth Opportunities Unlimited, Inc., *Youth in the Ghetto*, p. 239.

[103] *OE Survey*, p. 154, table 2.34.6.

[104] This discussion includes influence of desegregated schools in which there is a relative absence of tension. For further discussion, see *app. C–1*, p. 42–43.

[105] For a general discussion of problems of identity, see, e.g., Erikson, "A Memorandum on Identity and Negro Youth," **20** *Journal of Social Issues*, p. 29 (October, 1964); Lesser et. al., "Some Effects of Segregation and Desegregation in the Schools," *Integrated Education*, p. 20 (June–July, 1964).

more likely to be supported by the similar aspirations of their schoolmates.[105a]

School personnel in predominantly white schools more often feel that their students have the potential and the desire for high attainment. The *Equality of Educational Opportunity* survey found that white students are more likely to have teachers with high morale, who want to remain in their present school, and who regard their students as capable.[106]

The environment of schools with a substantial majority of Negro students, then, offers serious obstacles to learning. The schools are stigmatized as inferior in the community. The students often doubt their own worth, and their teachers frequently corroborate these doubts. The academic performance of their classmates is usually characterized by continuing difficulty. The children often have doubts about their chances of succeeding in a predominantly white society and they typically are in school with other students who have similar doubts. They are in schools which, by virtue both of their racial and social class composition, are isolated from models of success in school.

Cumulative Effects

The time spent in a setting of racial isolation or desegregation has an impact on student attitudes and achievement. The longer Negro students are in racially isolated schools, the greater the negative impact is likely to be. The cumulative effects of isolation also extend to income and occupation.

SCHOOL EFFECTS

A number of witnesses at Commission hearings testified to this effect. Amanda Houston, a Boston high school student, related the difficulties she encountered when she first entered a predominantly white high school from a racially isolated elementary school where her grades always had been very high. Asked if she had difficulty adjusting to the high school, she replied:

> Yes. Very much. Psychologically and academically. I had a very hard time keep-

ing up with the other girls. . . . I just wasn't prepared to keep up with the standard of Girls Latin School. I wasn't prepared at the time I entered the school. . . . [and] I had never been really involved with white children before.[107]

Asked about Negro students in her high school who had attended desegregated schools earlier, Miss Houston said:

> They have done much better. There were two girls and both of them were recommended for their "National Merit" and . . . they seem to have adjusted very well. . . .[108]

The cumulative effect of desegregation was reflected in data from the *Equality of Educational Opportunity* survey. Figure 6 depicts the academic performance of Negro students in majority-white schools in relation to the time spent in racially isolated and desegregated schools.[109] It shows a consistent trend toward higher academic performance for Negro students the longer they are in school with whites. By contrast, there is a growing deficit for Negroes who remain in racially isolated schools. The trend in most cases is maintained whatever the students' family background or the social class level of their classmates. Disadvantaged Negro children generally perform at higher levels if they have been in school with whites for some time, regardless of the present social class level of their classmates. They perform at even higher levels if, instead of simply being in schools with whites whose family background is the same as theirs, they are in schools where the students are from families of higher educational background.

The cumulative effect on attitudes is similar. Negro students who have had contact with whites since the early elementary grades are more likely to feel able to affect their own destiny than those who have not had that experience.[110]

Both the academic performance and attitudes of Negro students, then, are affected by the duration of their school contact with whites. Students whose first contact with whites was late in elementary or early in secondary schools are at a distinct disadvantage when compared with Negroes who have

---

[105a] It may also be that there is a greater challenge to Negro students in desegregated schools.

[106] *OE Survey*, p. 156, table 2.34.8.

[107] *Boston Hearing*, pp. 202–203.

[108] *Boston Hearing*, p. 207.

[109] See *app. C–1*, table 2.1, p. 48.

[110] *App. C–1*, table 3.5, p. 62.

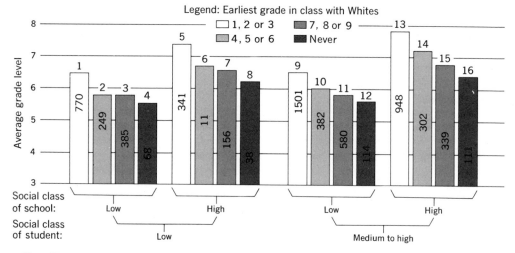

Legend: Earliest grade in class with Whites
□ 1, 2 or 3   ■ 7, 8 or 9
▨ 4, 5 or 6   ■ Never

Note. The numbers in the bars represent the number of cases.
Source. USCCR analysis of *OE Survey* data. See App. C–1.

FIGURE 6   Average grade level performance for ninth grade Negro students, by social class origin of student, social class level of school and earliest grade in class with whites; Metropolitan Northeast

had school contact with whites since the early grades.

INCOME AND OCCUPATION

The cumulative effects of education extend in later life to differences in income and occupation. Negroes with levels of education similar to whites do not earn similar amounts of money or hold similar jobs. These differences have been attributed both to employment discrimination and the quality of education.[111] The racial composition of schools, however, has not been taken into account in these comparisons. When they are, important differences appear.

A national survey of Negro and white adults conducted for the Commission shows that for both Negroes and whites, levels of personal income rise with levels of education.[112] As Table 8 shows, Negro adults

TABLE 8   Income Levels: Percent of Negroes Earning over $6,500 Per Year (Median Income of the Sample)

Education	Desegregated School	Isolated School
Some high school	42.3	36.6
High school graduate	62.8	52.8
College	75.5	77.3

Source: NORC Survey.

who attended desegregated schools are more likely to be earning more than $6,500 a year than otherwise similarly situated Negroes who attended racially isolated schools.[113] Only when Negroes with college education are considered does racial isolation appear not to affect one's chances of earning more than $6,500 a year.

Simillar differences appear in occupations. As Table 9 shows, the proportion of Negroes in white-collar jobs increases as their level of education rises, but Negroes who attended desegregated schools are more likely to be in

---

[111] See, e.g., Council of Economic Advisors, "Annual Report" in *Economic Report of the President,* p. 107 (1966); U.S. Dept. of Labor, *Report on Manpower Requirements, Resources, Utilization and Training,* p. 36 (1965); Harrington, *The Other America,* pp. 61–81 (1963).

[112] For a description of this survey see *app. C–5,* p. 211. The survey was conducted by the National Opinion Research Center, at the University of Chicago, and the data analysis performed at Harvard University under the super-

vision of Dr. Thomas F. Pettigrew. The survey sample included some 1,600 Negroes and some 1,300 whites. [Hereinafter referred to as *NORC Survey.*]

[113] *App. C–5,* table 2, p. 215.

TABLE 9   Percent of Negroes Where Main Family Earner Holds a White-Collar Job

Education	Type of School Attended	
	Desegregated	Isolated
Some high school	18.5	11.8
High school graduate	28.6	19.6
College	53.5	59.5

Source: NORC Survey.

white collar occupations than Negroes who attended racially isolated schools.[114] Again, this does not hold for Negroes who have a college education.

These differences in income are not accounted for by economic or social disparities in family background.[115] The source of the difference probably arises from both the academic advantages Negroes derive from desegregated schools, the increased associations they have with whites, and an ability to function better in desegregated situations.

* * *

Racially isolated schools, then, generally are regarded by the community as inferior institutions. The stigma attached to such schools affects the attitudes of both students and teachers. Students sense the community attitudes and the fact that their teachers often expect little of them. The combination of poor performance and low expectations reinforces their sense of futility and their image in teachers' minds as children who cannot learn. The negative attitudes and poor performance of Negro children in isolated schools accumulate over time, making a successful interruption of the process increasingly difficult. They carry over into adult life and are reflected there in levels of income and occupation.

The Perpetuation of Racial Isolation

The damaging consequences of racially isolated schools extend beyond the academic performance and attitudes of Negro school-children and the subsequent impairment of their ability to compete economically and

[114] *App. C–5*, table 1, p. 215.

[115] *App. C–5*, table 1, p. 215. When the economic and social characteristics of the respondents' parents were controlled the relationship still existed.

occupationally with whites. Racial isolation in the schools also fosters attitudes and behavior that perpetuate isolation in other important areas of American life. Negro adults who attended racially isolated schools are more likely to have developed attitudes that alienate them from whites. White adults with similarly isolated backgrounds tend to resist desegregation in many areas—housing, jobs, and schools.

At the same time, attendance at racially isolated schools tends to reinforce the very attitudes that assign inferior status to Negroes. White adults who attended schools in racial isolation are more apt than other whites to regard Negro institutions as inferior and to resist measures designed to overcome discrimination against Negroes. Negro adults who attended such schools are likely to have lower self-esteem and to accept the assignment of inferior status.

Conversely, Negroes who have attended desegregated schools tend to have a higher self-esteem, higher aspirations and are more likely to seek desegregated situations. Whites who have had desegregated education are more likely to report a willingness to accept Negroes in desegregated situations and to support measures that will afford equal opportunity.

Racial Attitudes

The racial attitudes and preferences of both Negroes and whites are influenced by the racial composition of the schools they attend. The process begins early.

For example, a 1962 study was made of student preferences in Louisville, Ky., where students are allowed to choose the high school they will attend. The city had six high schools, all but one of which was predominantly white. That school, Central High, had been segregated by law before 1954, and but for one white student, was still all-Negro in 1962.[116]

The study found that most of the Negro students who chose the majority white high schools previously had attended desegregated elementary or junior high schools, while most of the Negroes who chose Central High had

[116] U.S. Commission on Civil Rights, *Civil Rights, U.S.A. Public Schools Southern States, 1962*, p. 30.

not. It concluded: "The inference is strong that Negro high school students prefer biracial education only if they have experienced it before. If a Negro student has not received his formative education in biracial schools, the chances are he will not choose to enter one in his more mature years."[117]

Data from the Office of Education's survey bear out the inference that Negro students are much more likely to prefer racially isolated schools if they have attended only isolated schools and are more likely to prefer desegregated schools if they have attended such schools.[118]

The same relationship holds for white students. Those who have not attended class with Negroes are likely to express a preference for segregated classrooms, while those who have been in desegregated classrooms are more likely to prefer desegregated classrooms. Moreover, white students whose interracial education began in the early grades are even more likely to prefer desegregated schools than whites whose first association with Negroes in school was in the upper elementary or secondary grades.[119]

The survey data also suggest that school desegregation has its greatest impact upon student attitudes and preferences through the mediating influence of friendship with students of the other race. Negro and white students who attend school with each other, but have no friends of the other race, are less likely to prefer desegregated situations than students in desegregated schools who have such friends. Having attended schools with students of the other race and having friends of the other race contribute to preferences for desegregation. The effect is strongest for students who have had both experiences.[120]

By the time students graduate from high school, they generally have formed racial attitudes and preferences that carry over into later life. A study of recent high school graduates in Oakland, Calif., revealed that 89 percent of the Negroes who attended desegregated schools, but only 72 percent of those who attended segregated schools, have white friends.[121] Negroes who attended desegregated schools in Oakland are more at ease with whites than those who attended segregated schools.[122] They are far more likely to disagree with the statement: "If a Negro is wise he will think twice before he trusts the white man as much as he would another Negro."[123] This is true whether they come from middle-class or working-class homes.[124]

Sharp dissimilarities emerge when the attitudes of these recent graduates toward school desegregation are compared. Almost all are in favor of school desegregation, but the Negroes who attended desegregated schools appear more interested in having their children attend desegregated schools. Seventy-six percent of the Negroes with desegregated education, but only 52 percent of the Negroes with segregated education responded affirmatively to the question: "Would you be willing to send your child out of the neighborhood to go to an integrated school?" The dissimilarity extends to neighborhood preferences as well. Seventy percent of the high school graduates who attended desegregated schools indicate that they would go out of their way to obtain housing in a desegregated neighborhood, compared to only 50 percent of those who attended racially isolated schools.[125] Thus, the racial attitudes, preferences, and future plans of recent high school graduates are strongly influenced by the racial composition of the schools they attended.

Negro adults show a pattern of attitudes and preferences similar to that found for recent high school graduates. In a national survey of Negro adults it was found that those Negroes who had attended majority-white schools were more likely than those who attended racially isolated schools to reject the statement about not trusting ". . . a white as much as . . . another Negro." This was true no matter what their age, sex, or educational levels, or whether they were born in the South or the North. As in the survey of recent graduates, the Negro adults who attended desegregated schools also expressed greater willingness to live in an interracial neighbor-

---

[117] U.S. Commission on Civil Rights, *Civil Rights*, pp. 30–31.

[118] See *app. C–1*, tables 6.7 and 6.8, pp. 98–99.

[119] See *app. C–1*, tables 8.8–8.11, pp. 138–41 and sec. 1.6 at 46; *OE Survey*, p. 333, table 3.3.5.

[120] See *app. C–1*, tables 6.7, 6.8, and 8.10, pp. 98, 99, 141.

[121] See *Oakland app. C–4*, table 3, p. 209.

[122] *App. C–4*, table 5–7, pp. 209–10.

[123] *App. C–4*, table 4, p. 209.

[124] *App. C–4*, table 4, p. 209.

[125] *App. C–4*, tables 1 and 2, p. 208.

hood, even if they would have to pioneer to do so.[126] Negro adults who had attended racially isolated schools were less likely to express a desire for their children to be in desegregated schools and they more often expressed the view that Negro children would have a difficult time in desegregated schools.[127]

Further, respondents in the adult Negro survey who are products of predominantly Negro schools revealed a lower sense of self-esteem. This trend persisted even when other types of interracial association—such as white friends and interracial neighborhoods—were accounted for. And it also held for both sexes and for different social class and age groups. Differences were most pronounced for those who never had been to college.[128]

The attitudes of whites—sampled in another national survey of adults—also were related to the racial composition of the schools they attended. Whites who attended desegregated schools expressed greater willingness to reside in an interracial neighborhood, to have their children attend desegregated schools, and to have Negro friends.[129] They consistently were more favorable toward the elimination of discrimination in employment against Negroes.[130] They more often favored fair employment laws and agreed that "Negroes should have as good a chance as white people to get any kind of job."[131]

Racial Association

These attitudes are associated with behavior. When actual patterns of residence, schooling, and association are examined for Negro and white adults, sharp differences again emerge between those who attended segregated and desegregated schools. Negroes who once attended desegregated schools are more likely to have children in desegregated schools today than those who had not.[132] As Table 10 shows, the chances of having children in desegregated schools increased as education levels rose. Negroes of higher edu-

TABLE 10 Percent of Negro Parents with Children in Majority-White Schools

Education	Type of Schools Attended	
	Majority-White	Majority-Negro
Less than high school graduate	44.8	35.4
High school graduate	43.1	37.5
College	63.4	56.2

Source: NORC Survey.

cational status—and thus higher income—in general were less likely to have children in majority-Negro schools. But, irrespective of levels of education and income, Negroes are more likely to have children in majority-white schools if they attended such schools themselves.[133]

Negroes who attended desegregated schools also were more likely than those who attended racially isolated schools to reside presently in interracial neighborhoods. As Table 11 shows,

TABLE 11 Percent of Negro Adults Living in Mostly White Neighborhoods

Education	Type of Schools Attended	
	Majority-White	Majority-Negro
Less than high school graduate	27.3	20.7
High school graduate	35.5	17.0
College	36.3	28.9

Source: NORC Survey.

the racial composition of schools attended has a consistent relationship to later residential isolation independent of educational and economic limitations. This is true at every level of education.[134]

These comparisons suggest that the effects of racial isolation and desegregation carry over from early life into later life. The more time spent in racially mixed schools, the greater is the probability of living in integrated neighborhoods, of having children who attend desegregated schools, and of having close white friends.

[126] *App. C–5*, table 5, p. 227.
[127] *App. C–5*, table 7, p. 229.
[128] *App. C–5*, tables 11–15, pp. 223–37.
[129] *App. C–5*, tables 5–15, pp. 227–37.
[130] *App. C–5*, tables 13–15, pp. 235–37.
[131] *App. C–5*, tables 12–15, pp. 234–37.
[132] *App. C–5*, tables 6 and 6a, p. 216.
[133] *App. C–5*, tables 6 and 6a, p. 216.
[134] *App. C–5*, table 3, p. 215.

6

Racism: Prejudice and Discrimination

White people cannot, in the generality, be taken as models of how to live. Rather, the white man is himself in sore need of new standards, which will release him from his confusion and place him once again in fruitful communion with the depth of his own being. And I repeat: The price of the liberation of the white people is the liberation of the blacks—the total liberation, in the cities, in the towns, before the law, and in the mind.

JAMES BALDWIN, *The Fire Next Time*

INTRODUCTION

Most of the research discussed thus far has directly or indirectly pointed to the destructive effects of white racism on the identity, family, emotional and intellectual growth, and achievement of black Americans. The Kerner Commission concluded that white racism is the principal cause of the many civil disorders in recent years. Thus, it is crucial to try to understand the antecedents and manifestations of racism, as well as the mechanisms that maintain it. This chapter, therefore, includes research primarily on whites rather than blacks.

"Prejudice," in the present context, refers to a negative bias or distortion in an individual's perceptions of and beliefs about a *particular group* and its members (Allport, 1954). "Discrimination" here refers to an overt act that places a particular group and its members at a disadvantage. "Racism" may be viewed as consisting of prejudice, its attitudinal component, and discrimination, its behavioral component; a person may be prejudiced but not discriminatory and vice versa, depending on environmental demands at a given moment. Consequently, we shall first explore prejudice, then discuss discrimination in housing and employment, and finally analyze experimental studies of prejudice and discrimination. (See also Chapter 1 for further definitions.)

253

WHITE BELIEFS AND PREJUDICE

The assessment of prejudice has taken a variety of forms. Different measures of prejudice are not necessarily equivalent in content, validity, or reliability. The surveys reviewed here have focussed primarily on white beliefs or attitudes about blacks. Other studies discussed in this chapter have investigated cognitive, affective, and behavioral dimensions of prejudice, or have attempted to derive indices of prejudice by means of social distance scales or measures of stereotypes.

The first paper included in this chapter, by Campbell and Schuman [20], surveyed racial attitudes in 15 major American cities.[1] Over 2,500 white and 2,800 black respondents representing a cross-section of the population of each race in the age range from 18 to 69 were interviewed in 1968. Campbell and Schuman's findings with respect to the black population will be reviewed in the next chapter. Here we are primarily concerned with white views.

Whites were almost as aware of discriminatory housing practices as were blacks, but they felt there is less discrimination in employment than blacks did. Two-thirds of the white sample felt that many whites dislike Negroes. A greater number of white respondents felt that blacks dislike whites. In contrast to the view of most social scientists who have repeatedly pointed to historical and environmental factors in explaining the blacks' disadvantaged position in the United States, most whites blamed Negroes themselves for their inferior status. Although whites indicated relatively strong support for the *principle* of nondiscrimination in housing, employment, and education, they were more reluctant to support *laws* that would help prevent such discrimination, particularly in housing. Interestingly enough, however, a sizeable portion of the sample agreed that the government should act to improve housing and employment and particularly education, even at the cost of higher taxes. A majority of whites in these cities did not believe that more oppressive measures, such as rigid police control, are adequate to prevent future riots.

Given the present racial tension, the respondents' attitudes are perhaps not as hostile as one might expect. Although a sizeable minority consistently holds clearly racist views, the majority of whites recognize the need for action to ameliorate the living conditions of blacks. It should be kept in mind, however, that we are dealing here with the attitudes rather than actual behavior. Furthermore, the survey excluded Southern cities, thereby most likely biasing the results in a "pro-Negro" direction.

Surveys and opinion polls pertaining to racial views have only recently gained widespread attention. National polls by Gallup and Harris (Brink & Harris, 1964; 1967) as well as smaller surveys on race relations have been reviewed periodically by Erskine (1962, 1967, 1968).

In a series of articles, Hyman and Sheatsley (1956, 1964; Sheatsley, 1966) have analyzed white attitudes toward Negroes. In a nationwide sample, they found a steadily increasing number of whites who favor school integration. For example, 30 percent in 1942 as compared to 49 percent in 1956 and 62 percent in 1963 favored such action. The corresponding figures for the white South were 2 percent, 14 percent, and 31 percent, and for the white North 40 percent, 61 percent and 73 percent respectively. Thirty-five percent of the white national total in 1942, 51 percent in 1956, and 64 percent in December, 1963 approved of residential integration. The corresponding figures for

---

[1] Baltimore, Boston, Chicago, Cincinnati, Cleveland, Detroit, Gary, Milwaukee, Newark, New York (Brooklyn only), Philadelphia, Pittsburgh, San Francisco, St. Louis, and Washington, D.C.

southern whites were 12 percent, 38 percent, and 51 percent and for northern whites 42 percent, 58 percent, and 70 percent respectively.

In 1963 (Sheatsley, 1966) a national sample of whites was asked how each felt about a number of issues related to the civil rights movement. From their responses it was possible to form a Guttman scale of pro-integration attitudes based on the eight items shown in Table 1.

TABLE 1 Guttman Scale of Pro-Integration Sentiments

Item	Per Cent Giving Pro-Integration Response (December 1963)
1. "Do you think Negroes should have as good a chance as white people to get any kind of job, or do you think white people should have the first chance at any kind of job?" ("As good a chance.")	82
2. "Generally speaking, do you think there should be separate sections for Negroes in street cars and buses?" ("No.")	77
3. "Do you think Negroes should have the right to use the same parks, restaurants and hotels as white people?" ("Yes.")	71
4. "Do you think white students and Negro students should go to the same schools, or to separate schools?" ("Same schools.")	63
5. "How strongly would you object if a member of your family wanted to bring a Negro friend home to dinner?" ("Not at all.")	49
6. "White people have a right to keep Negroes out of their neighborhoods if they want to, and Negroes should respect that right." ("Disagree slightly" or "Disagree strongly.")	44
7. "Do you think there should be laws against marriages between Negroes and whites?" ("No.")	36
8. "Negroes shouldn't push themselves where they're not wanted." ("Disagree slightly" or "Disagree strongly.")	27

Reprinted with permission from the author and *Daedalus*. (Paul B. Sheatsley, "White attitudes toward the Negro." In T. Parsons and K. B. Clark (Eds.), *The Negro American*, Table 2, p. 310.)

Chances are at least 9 in 10 that a person who rejects one item in the scale will also reject the item immediately following it. The table indicates that most support for blacks comes in the areas of integration in employment, public transportation and accommodation, and schools. There is still enormous white prejudice with respect to interracial marriage, interracial social contact, and integrated housing.

Each respondent was assigned a score on the Pro-Integration Scale ranging from 0 to 8 depending on how many pro-integration responses he made. Sheatsley then computed the average score for a number of subgroups in his sample. These figures are presented in Table 2.

Marked differences emerged, especially between different regional, educational and occupational groups. Southern whites, with few exceptions, did not endorse more than the first three statements in the scale. Jewish respondents, followed by northern professionals, achieved the highest scores on the Pro-Integration Scale. Poorly educated southern whites in urban counties are most opposed to integration. Attitudes toward the Negro protest movement in the North and South followed the same trend (we shall return to this issue in the next chapter).

Sheatsley (1966) points to the remarkable over-all consistency in these

TABLE 2   Mean Scores on Pro-Integration Scale (White Population, U.S.A., December 1963)

	North	South		North	South
TOTAL	4.97	2.54			
A. By region:			**F. By age group:**		
New England	5.03	—	Under 25	5.70	2.76
Middle Atlantic	5.47	—	25–44	5.34	2.86
East North Central	4.61	—	45–64	4.71	2.33
West North Central	4.37	—	65–up	4.07	2.10
South Atlantic	—	2.53			
East South Central	—	1.89	**G. By religion:**		
West South Central	—	2.70	Protestant	4.75	2.38
Mountain	4.33	—	Catholic	5.18	3.41
Pacific	5.43	—	Jewish	6.44	a
B. By population size:			**H. By strength of**		
10 largest M.A.'s	5.33	a	**religious belief:**		
All other M.A.'s	4.97	2.65	Very strong	5.00	2.34
Urban counties	5.04	1.36	Strong	5.15	2.86
Rural counties	4.23	2.70	Moderate	4.87	2.53
			Not strong	4.30	2.37
C. By number of Negroes					
in public schools:			**I. By educational level:**		
No Negroes	4.62	2.29	8 years or less	3.88	1.70
A few Negroes	5.01	2.80	9–12 years (H.S.)	5.01	2.71
Considerable number	5.49	a	Attended college	5.96	3.54
D. By prior residence:			**J. By family income:**		
Formerly lived in			Under $5,000	4.36	2.20
South	4.80	—	$5,000–7,499	5.24	2.75
Never lived in South	5.05	—	$7,500–9,999	5.26	2.78
Formerly lived in			$10,000 or over	5.56	3.41
North	—	3.22			
Never lived in North	—	1.97	**K. By occupation:**		
			Professional	6.08	4.32
E. By sex:			Proprietors, managers	5.09	2.79
Male	4.91	2.57	Clerical, sales	4.96	2.98
Female	5.03	2.51	Skilled	4.90	2.04
			Semi-skilled	4.77	1.63
			Unskilled	4.73	1.82
			Farm	3.86	2.87

a Insufficient cases to justify reliable answers.

Reprinted with permission from the author and *Daedalus*. (Paul B. Sheatsley, "White attitudes toward the Negro." In T. Parsons and K. B. Clark (Eds.), *The Negro American*, Table 3, p. 312.)

survey results, which, in his view, indicate that positive attitudes toward integration are growing steadily. He adds:

> Certainly there is no evidence that the majority of Americans eagerly look forward to integration. Most are more comfortable in a segregated society and they would prefer that the demonstrations slow down or go away while things are worked out more gradually. But most of them know also that racial discrimination is morally wrong and recognize the legitimacy of the Negro protest (pp. 322–323).

Noel and Pinkney (1964) also analyzed survey data collected between 1948 and 1952 in four smaller American cities representing the four geographical regions. Their measure of prejudice was a modified social distance scale, which assessed the respondents' reaction to a number of social and interpersonal interactions with (a) member(s) of the other race (sitting at the same table, dancing, going to a party, and marriage). As in the previously discussed surveys, they found a negative correlation between education and prejudice for both races. The same was true for whites with respect to occupational status. For the black respondents, however, both high and low occupational status were associated with high prejudice, and the medium group was least prejudiced. Both white and black single persons were more prejudiced than married respondents. In contrast to more recent surveys that have found younger whites to be less prejudiced than older whites, they found no relationship between age and prejudice. Both black and white women were more prejudiced than men, even when a number of factors, such as education, interracial contact, and marital status were controlled. Supporting Sheatsley's finding with respect to religion, they found that whites who attend church fairly regularly were less prejudiced than those who attend infrequently. The same holds true for whites who belong to social organizations as opposed to those who do not. Again, as reported in other studies, Noel and Pinkney found that whites who have social contacts with Negroes were less prejudiced than those who do not. Smith and Prothro (1957) had found that Negroes scored higher than whites on authoritarianism as measured by the *F* (Fascism) scale. Noel and Pinkney found confirmation of this trend in their own data, although when they controlled for SES the differences were negligible. As expected they also found a positive relationship between authoritarianism and prejudice among both whites and Negroes. They conclude that "the similarities in the correlates of anti-Negro and anti-white prejudice far outweigh the differences" (p. 622).

BLACK BELIEFS AND PREJUDICE

The empirical evidence indicates by and large that black Americans have been far less prejudiced towards whites than vice versa. For example, Noel and Pinkney (1964) found that 41 percent of their black respondents "received the lowest possible prejudice score (i.e., answered all of the index items negatively) and only 17 percent received the highest possible score (i.e., answered all of the index items positively" (p. 610). The corresponding figures for whites were 5 percent and 48 percent respectively! Moreover, this highly significant difference was obtained for all socioeconomic levels. Proenza and Strickland (1965) found that black college students exhibited significantly less social distance toward whites than white students exhibited toward blacks. Black students were also more favorable toward the concept "white" than were whites toward the concept "Negro." Bogardus (1958), Bryant, Gardner, and Goldman (1966), and Webster (1961) found similar results. Thus, it is clear that black prejudice toward whites, although much more easily justifiable in view of centuries of white oppression of blacks, is much less common than white prejudice toward blacks. We shall discuss black attitudes toward whites more fully in the next chapter.

DISCRIMINATION IN HOUSING AND EMPLOYMENT

To this point we have focussed primarily on prejudice or the attitudinal aspect of racism. Now we shall turn to the behavioral component of racism, discrimination. One of the areas where discrimination is practiced, namely the schools, was discussed in the last chapter. Quite likely, discrimination in employment and housing has an even more devastating effect on the lives of black Americans.

Residential segregation as presently constituted has been viewed by some as the most critical cause of racial inequality. However, cause and effect relationships between segregation and the black's inferior status in America are not very obvious nor easy to prove empirically. In fact, there are those who would attribute segregation to the Negro's inferior economic and political position as well as to historical factors. Some black leaders, on the other hand, perceive the large black communities in the inner cities to be the real or potential black strength from which equality may emerge.

What is the extent of racial segregation in the United States today? Taeuber and his associates (e.g., Taeuber, 1965; Taeuber & Taeuber, 1965; Farley & Taeuber, 1968) and Hauser (1966) have analyzed the scope, the underlying factors, and the historical trends in residential segregation. In 1790 (first census year) over 90 percent of black Americans lived in the South, mostly in rural areas. This distribution had changed little before World War I. During the last 50 years, however, marked population shifts have occurred. Negroes have moved to the North and West, particularly to the cities and more specifically to the inner core of the cities, while large numbers of whites have moved to the periphery or suburbs of the cities. By 1960, 73 percent of the black population resided in urban centers and over 40 percent lived in the North and West. "Thus, within a period of fifty years, less than a lifetime, the Negro has been transformed from a predominantly rural to a predominantly urban resident" (Hauser, 1966, p. 75). Throughout this period, however, the segregation of blacks was much greater than that of any foreign ethnic group. This was documented by means of the segregation index, "a strictly objective measure, based on census data, of the general unevenness in the distribution of white and Negro households among residential neighborhoods" (Taeuber, 1965, p. 14). A segregation index of zero would indicate that the numbers of black and white residents who live in a particular city block are representative of the city population as a whole. An index of 100, on the other hand, would reflect complete residential segregation. Based on the 1960 census, Taeuber calculated the segregation index for 207 American cities, all of which contained at least 1,000 nonwhite households. The results reflect the widespread and marked degree of segregation. For these cities the index ranged from 60.4 to 98.1, the median being 87.8. Negroes were by far the most segregated minority. Not only were they segregated from whites, but also from Mexican Americans, Puerto Ricans, and Orientals. Segregation between blacks and whites remained high between 1940 and 1960, while it declined between American whites and European immigrants and other minority groups. The figures suggest that by 1960 southern cities were reaching the condition of complete segregation and that the nation as a whole would require many decades before it would reflect even the semblance of integration. Myrdal (1944) sought to explain segregation as being attributable to the Negro's preference for living in black neighborhoods, white discrimination against blacks, and the poverty of large numbers of black Americans. Taeuber (1965) concludes on the basis of his data that

> . . . neither free choice nor poverty is a sufficient explanation for the universally high degree of segregation in American cities. *Discrimination* is the principal cause of Negro residential segregation, and there is no basis for anticipating major changes in the segregated character of American cities until patterns of housing discrimination can be altered (p. 19, emphasis added).

A follow-up study by Farley and Taeuber (1968), based on special censuses in the mid-1960's for 13 cities, indicates a relative decline in the number of white city dwellers, and a relative increase in the number of black city dwellers. Emigration from the South has diminished, but the higher black birth rate has further added to the density of the black population in the inner city. On the whole, the data reflect a continued prevalence of racial segregation, which, if anything, is increasing rather than declining. (For further analyses see also Clark, 1965; Drake & Cayton, 1962.)

Discrimination in employment against Negroes is also well documented. There is a considerable income gap between blacks and whites. In 1960, for example, white family heads with four or more years of college earned a median income of $9,315, as compared with $7,875 for nonwhites with the same education. The figures for less than seven years of elementary school were $3,656 and $2,294 and for one to three years of high school, $5,882 and $3,449, respectively (Drake, 1966). Unemployment rates are more than twice as high for blacks as for whites (Moynihan, 1966). Thirty-five percent of blacks (8.3 million) as opposed to 10 percent of whites (17.6 million) live below the poverty level, which the U.S. Department of Labor in 1966 considered to be $3,335 for a nonfarm family of four. Despite the fact that the present black generation is economically better off than previous ones, the *gap* between whites and blacks has not been narrowed. On the contrary, it appears to be widening in many areas (Drake, 1966; Fein, 1966; Moynihan, 1966). Black Americans are indeed separate, but they are certainly not equal.

Black people made their greatest strides during and shortly after World War II, a period marked by high employment (Silberman, 1964), but they continued to be disproportionately vulnerable to economic fluctuation (Glenn, 1963). Negroes who feel a "job threat," furthermore, appear less likely to join civil rights organizations because they fear retaliation from fellow white employees or white employers (Ross & Wheeler, 1967). Glenn (1967) has suggested that desegregation by itself would not significantly improve the Negro's economic status. He also maintains (1964) that the size of the Negro population and Negro occupational status are not necessarily inversely related. On the other hand, an increasing number of Negroes who are moving into intermediate level occupations may offset a strong degree of discrimination in those communities where the proportion of the black population is large. In a more recent paper Glenn (1966) presents data indicating that a large number of whites in urbanized areas of the South benefit both economically and occupationally from the inferior economic status of the Negro. Contrary to popular belief, his evidence suggests that it is not the lower-class white who benefits most, but the middle-class white.

In a paper included in this chapter, Lieberson and Fuguitt [21] attempt to project Negro-white occupational differences in the absence of discrimination. Their analysis suggests that occupational equality will not come about for another sixty to eighty years, even if discrimination ceases immediately. Past discrimination reflected in lower educational levels and inferior job training may handicap Negro mobility for years to come. Lieberson and Fuguitt conclude that occupational disadvantage is a function of both present discrimination and nonracial social factors.

It should not be forgotten that discrimination and the concomitant inferior position of blacks represent a heavy burden for *all* citizens. Depressed Negro buying power, low Negro tax contributions, and government expenditures for welfare, sickness, unemployment, and so forth, affect all Americans. Glenn (1966) suggests, however, that although the detrimental consequences of the black's subordinate status are more diffuse and therefore less noticed and worrisome to the relatively large number of whites affected, a few whites who profit from the Negro's inferior economic position are therefore more aware of it and are likely to fight for the status quo.

Another paper in this chapter sounds a more optimistic note. Moskos [22] suggests that there has been marked progress in racial integration in the armed forces. But here again, there are indications that past discrimination in both civilian and military life is taking its toll. Because of inferior education and training, many black soldiers do not receive favored assignments and advancement to officer status. It must be stressed that Moskos' data also reveal severe off-base and off-duty segregation and discrimination both in the United States and foreign assignments, including Vietnam. Nevertheless desegregation of army units has led to better performance by Negroes and more favorable white attitudes toward black Americans and integration. In fact, the more contact white soldiers have with blacks, the more favorably disposed they become toward them. It is not surprising, then, that most black soldiers feel that there is less prejudice and more opportunity in the military than in civilian life and that twice as many blacks as whites reenlist. Moskos concludes by suggesting that military integration offers some clues to what might happen if American society became integrated.

Before turning to the experimental literature on prejudice and discrimination, the potential role of industrial psychologists in helping to bring about racial equality in the selection and promotion of employees should briefly be mentioned. In 1964, industrial psychologists held a special symposium (Parrish, 1966) to discuss selection and assessment devices to insure equal employment opportunity. Lopez (1966) found that selection instruments operate differentially within certain subgroups of job applicants. Negroes, although inferior to whites on aptitude tests that are high in verbal content, score as well as whites on special job sample tests (Lopez, 1967). Special oral tests, furthermore, may actually be fairer to minority group members than the more "objective" written tests. Lopez suggests that psychologists use a larger number of selection instruments, including situational and performance tests, and employ them with the particular applicant in mind.

To conclude, the evidence discussed here presents a rather gloomy picture. Results from surveys and polls seem to suggest a decrease in white prejudice; but data on black employment and housing indicate that residential segregation and the economic gap between blacks and whites has remained stable or is increasing. Clearly, the latter are the more critical statistics, since they reflect the actual living conditions of black Americans. The seeming contradiction between the two sets of evidence is not easily explained. On the one hand, it may be argued that inequality between the races is not only a function of present white discrimination, but also of a mixture of larger political, economic, educational, and social factors, as well as past discrimination. On the other hand, it may well be that the expression of white beliefs in opinion polls and surveys does not represent a true measure of the whites' prejudice toward blacks. We shall return to the question of the relationship between attitude and behavior in the next section.

EXPERIMENTAL STUDIES OF PREJUDICE AND DISCRIMINATION

Social scientists have for a long time attempted to discover the etiology of prejudice and discrimination (Allport, 1954; Harding, Kutner, Proshansky, & Chein, 1954; Marx, 1967; Proshansky, 1966). There are no final answers, but a number of theories have been proposed and a considerable number of experimental studies have been carried out. This section will highlight some of the major dimensions that have emerged.

Development of Racism

As we have seen in Chapter 2, racial awareness develops early in an individual's life. The study by Renninger and Williams [23] included in this chapter demonstrates that white children's awareness of color connotations develops between the ages of three and five. These children from North Carolina demonstrated a bias against black color and black playmates, and favored the color white and playmates of their own race. Renninger and Williams' hypothesis that color connotations may develop earlier than racial connotations was refuted by a more recent study (Williams & Roberson, 1967), which suggested that racial awareness develops concurrently with color meanings, the latter possibly reinforcing the former. The extent of bias that already existed in these white preschoolers was rather striking. Over 86 percent of the five-year-olds scored in the prejudiced direction 11 or 12 times out of 12 opportunities. A control procedure using a measure of sexual identification demonstrated that they "knew their prejudice about as well as they knew their sex role" (p. 686). Apparently there are strong and early pressures in the whites' environment to reject the color black and black Americans.

The strong pressure to conform to societal norms has been pointed out by Pettigrew (1961) as a crucial factor in the attitudes of white Southerners towards Negroes:

> It is the path of least resistance in most Southern circles to favor white supremacy. When an individual's parents and his peers are racially prejudiced, when his limited world accepts racial discrimination as a given way of life, when his deviance means certain ostracism, then his anti-Negro attitudes are not so much expressive as they are socially adjusting (p. 109).

Pettigrew advocates research that pays more attention to sociocultural or normative factors, as distinct from personality variables, involved in interracial situations. Viewing discrimination in the context of conformity to prevalent norms, one may well conceive of racism as sociopathology rather than individual psychopathology. In fact, as we have seen in Chapter 1, Martin Luther King suggested an "association of maladjusted people," people who refuse to adjust to racist norms.

Areas of interracial contact, as well as competitive or cooperative task situations, may also influence the degree of prejudice expressed (Goldman, Warshay, & Biddle, 1962; Meer & Freedman, 1966; Rice & White, 1964).

Stereotypes may play a role in the environmental transmission of prejudice (Ehrlich, 1963; Ehrlich, 1964; Ehrlich & Rinehart, 1965). Widespread acceptance of negative stereotypes about Negroes increases the likelihood that diffusion of racist attitudes will take place even among whites who had never had any personal contact with blacks. It also encourages the transmission of prejudice to each generation at successively earlier ages before positive attitudes based on real experiences with blacks can be established.

Social class membership is yet another factor in the development of interracial attitudes. Gordon (1964) has proposed the concept of "ethclass," a combined membership in a particular ethnic group and social class. Such membership, he maintains, directly affects one's group identity and social and cultural behavior. However, of the two components of the ethclass, social class is seen as dominant to ethnic group membership. Landis, Datwyler, & Dorn (1966) found confirmation for Gordon's thesis. Their findings indicate that regardless of race the social distance scores of middle-class respondents were lower than those of lower-class respondents, indicating their relatively stronger inclination to relate socially to other groups. Whites, however, had higher social distance scores than blacks.

Prejudice and Personality

The authoritarian personality studies of the late 1940's and early 1950's constitute one of the earlier attempts to explain the roots of prejudice in terms of a specific constellation of personality attributes (Adorno et al., 1950; Christie & Jahoda, 1954). The authoritarian personality may be described as consisting of such characteristics as respect for force, submission to superiors, dominance of subordinates, intolerance of deviance. Presumably such characteristics are acquired early in life and result from extreme frustration and deprivation in parent-child relationships, coupled with lack of genuine acceptance, and parental demands for obedience and impulse control. Individuals who exhibit these traits usually score high on the *F* Scale and are predisposed to racist attitudes, as reflected by high scores on the *E* (Ethnocentrism) Scale. Epstein [24], in a paper included in this chapter, studied the white subjects' imitation of aggression toward a black "victim" as a function of their score on the *F* Scale and the aggressive model's race and socioeconomic status. He found that high *F* scorers were more likely to imitate the Negro than the white model. The results suggest an interaction between personality characteristics and a particular interracial situation.

The frustration-aggression hypothesis (Dollard et al., 1939) has also been invoked to explain prejudice. The theory postulates that frustration results in aggressive tendencies, which are displaced from a less assailable or less accessible target to a more vulnerable or more accessible one. A scapegoat thus becomes the object of aggressive behavior. Society may designate certain groups (such as ethnic minorities) as "legitimate" scapegoats, rationalizing this action by pointing out "undesirable" characteristics of these "outgroups" (Allport, 1954).

Explanations of prejudice in terms of personality dynamics are of limited usefulness without consideration of environmental and social variations (van den Berghe, 1967). It may be, however, that in the case of extreme authoritarianism, valid prediction of a person's degree of prejudice can be made relatively independent of the situation.

Kitano (1966) has also called attention to the limitations in ascribing psychopathology to all who practice discrimination. He hypothesized that a person with a "normal" personality discriminates in a passive way "through limiting interaction and 'input' from other groups, but when queried might express nondiscriminatory attitudes. He might verbalize the equalness of all groups, but in the critical area of behavioral interaction he would prefer that his friends and friends of his children be of his own reference group" (p. 23). Kitano assumed that the individual who has fully identified with and is integrated into his subculture—the normal personality—is more likely to discriminate than the marginal person who is alienated from his subculture. His comparison between delinquent and nondelinquent Japanese youths on a variety of interpersonal indices supports his thesis. We may thus be faced with the dilemma that "ethnic or religious subcultural integration can turn into parochialism and isolation as easily as it can turn to a process that aids individuals and groups through the difficult problems of socialization and acculturation" (p. 31).

Belief versus Race

A new theory to account for prejudice was offered by Rokeach, Smith, & Evans (1960). They argued that prejudice may be determined to a large extent by perceived discrepancies in belief systems rather than by different ethnic membership. An example of the promising line of research stimulated by Rokeach's thesis is the study by Smith, Williams, & Willis [25] included in this chapter. Their findings, supporting those of Rokeach et al., indicated that belief similarity was more salient in friendship choice than race and sex for both black and white respondents. Only the deep-South white sample tended to view a person as a potential friend on the basis of race. Since much of the related literature is reviewed by Smith et al., it will suffice here to briefly discuss more recent studies.

A large-scale study by Stein (1966) demonstrated that when the beliefs of a person to be selected or rejected as a friend are made known, these beliefs become the primary determinant of hypothetical friendship choice. The more similar the beliefs, the more likely is the stimulus-person to be chosen as a friend regardless of his race, religion, or socioeconomic status. These results held both for the white gentiles' attitudes towards Negroes and Jews, and for the Jews' and Negroes' attitudes towards the white majority. In situations involving more intimate interracial contacts (where societal taboos and pressures are likely to exist), however, "gentile subjects are much more prone to react in racial terms, frequently rejecting contact with Negroes" (Stein, 1966, p. 27). The latter finding supported Triandis' (1961) claim that race is a more powerful variable in white rejection of Negroes as neighbors than belief. Stein attempted to reconcile Rokeach's and Triandis' interpretations by stating that

> . . . knowledge of belief systems, if they reflect belief congruence, leads many more gentile subjects to evaluate their feelings and potential behaviors towards Negroes in a positive manner. Without that knowledge, Negroes are assumed to have dissimilar beliefs and values and are consequently rejected. Even when information about belief systems is supplied, there are still some subjects who either feel bound by societal pressures or genuinely harbor hostile feelings towards Negroes and refuse to interact with them particularly in the areas of intimate contact (p. 28).

As indicated by Smith et al. [25] and by the present discussion, most studies have so far supported but have qualified Rokeach's theory. Insko and Robinson (1967) found both belief and race to be critical variables in white Southern adolescents' reactions to Negroes although belief had a somewhat greater effect than race. The data revealed the same trends as Stein's; differences in race are more critical in those situations where "institutionalized norms may override individual psychological propensities to respond in terms of belief similarity" (p. 221). Triandis, Loh and Levin (1966) propose that research on prejudice reorient itself according to interactions between specific stimulus person's characteristics (race, sex, age, nationality, religion, and so forth) and specific behaviors (marriage, friendship, residential integration, and so forth). They found, for example, that the level of spoken English was more important than race for social acceptance (for example, admiration), whereas race was more important for social distance (for example, integrated housing). Contact theory (Pettigrew, 1969) lends further support to Rokeach's theory. When Negroes and whites interact, particularly on an equal-status basis, as in integrated neighborhoods, the military, and in schools, prejudice and discrimination tend to decrease. Such prolonged contact, one might assume, serves to reduce or eliminate stereotypes and make known each other's true belief system and values, thereby diminishing the salience of race.

ATTITUDES AND BEHAVIORS

A number of experimental studies have related attitudinal judgments to behaviors in concrete situations (Cook & Selltiz, 1964; DeFleur & Westie, 1963; Himmelstrand, 1960; Katz & Stotland, 1959; Merton, 1940). In a classic study, DeFleur and Westie (1958), for example, found that the behavior of 30 percent of their subjects was not predictable from their attitudes. Linn (1965) patterned his study after DeFleur and Westie's but constructed a questionnaire directly related to the assessed behavior (posing for a photograph with a Negro of the opposite sex). Despite the fact that the items in the questionnaire were identical to the observed behavior, he found discrepancies between attitudes and overt behavior in 59 percent of the cases. In both these studies, the attitudes expressed were more liberal (less discriminatory) than actual behavior (negative discrepancy). Earlier studies, however, demonstrated that the reverse discrepancy may also occur. The famous study by LaPierre (1934) revealed that over 90 percent of the hotels and restaurants contacted by mail said that they would refuse to serve and offer accommodation to Chinese tourists, even though a Chinese couple had in actual fact been refused service only once. It is highly probable that the presence of the white LaPierre, who accompanied the Chinese couple, biased the results, but the differences were enormous and, furthermore, it should be noted that Kutner, Wilkins, and Yarrow (1952), in a better-controlled study, found essentially the same results with a Negro tourist.

Bray (1950) and Berg (1966), in studies involving autokinetic judgments, also found significant discrepancies between verbal measures of attitudes and behaviors in an interracial social situation. Campbell, Kruskal and Wallace (1966) dealt with this problem by developing a method of quantifying overt behavior as an index of interracial attitudes. They computed the departure from randomness in the number of Negro-white seating adjacencies in four different college samples and found a significant aggregation by race in the direction expected from a prior ranking of anti-Negro attitudes that prevailed in these colleges. The authors suggest that this aggregation index, as well as others that could be constructed (on the playground, in waiting lines, in stores, in theaters, and so forth) might serve as indicators of interracial attitudes in a variety of situations.

A number of investigators have attempted to measure the emotional component they presumed present in prejudice by physiological indices. Westie and DeFleur (1959), for example, obtained higher galvanic skin responses (GSR) for prejudiced than for nonprejudiced whites when all were viewing color slides of Negroes in various social situations. Similarly, Cooper (1959) reported higher GSR for prejudiced subjects. Porier and Lott (1967), in an experimental interracial face-to-face interaction, demonstrated a low but significant correlation between GSR scores and E Scale scores. Cook and Selltiz (1964) also attempted to deal with the often-found discrepancy between attitude and behavior. They pointed out that past research efforts have often been directed at very different aspects of attitudes and behavior. They define an attitude as

. . . an underlying disposition which enters, along with other influences, into the determination of a variety of behaviors toward an object or class of objects, including statements of beliefs and feelings about the object and approach avoidance actions with respect to it (p. 36).

They emphasize that in addition to the influence of one's attitudes on one's behavior, other individual characteristics (values, motivation, expressive style, and so forth) and attributes of the situation (for example, norms of behavior, expectations, consequences of behavior) may affect behavior. Woodmansee and Cook (1967) did not find the typically assumed cognitive, affective, and conative components of attitudes in their large-scale assessment of verbal racial attitudes. Instead some 11 dimensions of racial attitudes having to do with "public policy in race relations, social relationships with Negroes, empathy with their emotional reaction to derogatory treatment," and so on, emerged.

Finally, it should be pointed out that the race of the investigator may affect the respondents' expression of prejudice. In general, when the interviewer or test administrator belongs to a minority group, white respondents tend to show less prejudice towards minority group members (Athey et al., 1960; Bryant, Gardner, & Goldman, 1966; Summers & Hammonds, 1966).

To conclude, researchers on prejudice and discrimination are confronted with two major problems. First, social scientists have been relatively unsuccessful in developing intrapsychic or attitudinal measures of prejudice that would accurately forecast discriminatory behaviors. The difficulties appear to be primarily related to the complexity and inconsistency of attitudes as well as to social or situational determinants that significantly alter one's expression of prejudice and racial discrimination. Second, little research evidence from the laboratory and even less from experimental field investigations exists that would pinpoint the major dimensions involved in the manifestations of discrimination. Survey data, anecdotal descriptions, and case studies documenting discrimination abound. In this connection it should be pointed out that black Americans are most affected by overt responses of whites. In this sense prejudice is less crucial than discrimination. A white person who feels an inner resentment toward black people but still accords them equal treatment in his overt behavior (for example, because of laws or social norms) obviously inflicts less harm on blacks than a white individual who harbors no personal hostility toward blacks, but nevertheless discriminates against them for the same reasons. Scientific investigations of actual day-to-day behavior are exceedingly difficult to carry out, but they are absolutely essential to our understanding of the roots and expression of white racism and particularly to its modification.

MODIFICATION OF WHITE RACISM

The Kerner Commission Report was explicit in blaming white racism for the black rebellion, but it did not adequately articulate the elements of white racism. It appeared (as indicated by a recent Gallup poll) that most whites had absolved themselves from all guilt since they did not identify themselves as being racist. Though mass media have publicized more blatant forms of white racism, such as the use of cattle prods, police dogs, and murder in the South, they have generally overlooked the more subtle forms, such as de facto discrimination in classrooms and block-busting to prevent residential integration. It should be obvious, though, that massive reduction and eventually total elimination of all forms of racism must be brought about, if justice is to be achieved in America.

As Tomlinson (1968) has put it, we should not only be concerned with what can be done for Negroes but also with what should be done about whites. Education undoubtedly could serve a major role. From preschool on, children must be told about the blacks' accomplishments and contributions. Black history, and particularly white racism, must be made explicit to all children. There are surely ways to make these issues comprehensible to children. Miel and Kiester (1967) have described the need to include these aspects of American life in the curriculum of suburban schools where white children rarely have any contact with black children. Mass media, particularly TV, would be ideally suited to educate white adults.

Little research evidence is available to suggest efficient means for combating racism (Proshansky, 1966). This would be an extremely useful area for social scientists to explore, to complement the existing research on blacks and white prejudice. In fact such studies could be incorporated into "white studies" programs as a complement to black studies programs being established at many universities and colleges. As Hauser (1966) has put it:

> A saturation program of corrective education for whites is without question as important as compensatory education for Negroes to pave the way for an integrated society (p. 97).

and

> . . . to continue to deny the Negro any of the choices which are available to whites is to threaten the very premises, and to undermine the foundations, of our democratic society (p. 100).

REFERENCES

Adorno, T. W., et al. *The authoritarian personality*. New York: Harper & Row, 1950.

Allport, G. W. *The nature of prejudice*. Cambridge, Mass.: Addison-Wesley, 1954.

Athey, K. R., et al. Two experiments showing the effect of the interviewer's background on response to questionnaires concerning racial issues. *Journal of Applied Psychology*, 1960, **44**, 244–246.

Berg, K. R. Ethnic attitudes and agreement with a Negro person. *Journal of Personality and Social Psychology*, 1966, **4**, 215–220.

Bogardus, E. S. Racial distance changes in the United States during the past thirty years. *Sociology and Sociological Research*, 1958, **43**, 127–135.

Bray, D. W. The prediction of behaviour from two attitude scales. *Journal of Abnormal and Social Psychology*, 1950, **45**, 64–84.

Brink, W., & Harris, L. *The Negro revolution in America*. New York: Simon and Schuster, 1964.

Brink, W., & Harris, L. *Black and white: A study of U.S. racial attitudes today*. New York: Simon and Schuster, 1967.

Bryant, E. G., Gardner, I., Jr., & Goldman, M. Responses on racial attitudes as affected by interviewers of different ethnic groups. *The Journal of Social Psychology*, 1966, **70**, 95–100.

Campbell, D. T., Kruskal, W. H., & Wallace, W. P. Seating aggregation as an index of attitude. *Sociometry*, 1966, **29**, 1–15.

Christie, R., & Jahoda, M. (Eds.) *Studies in the scope and method of "The Authoritarian Personality."* New York: Free Press, 1954.

Clark, K. B. *Dark ghetto: Dilemmas of social power*. New York: Harper & Row, 1965.

Cook, S. W., & Selltiz, C. A multiple-indicator approach to attitude measurement. *Psychological Bulletin*, 1964, **62**, 36–55.

Cooper, J. B. Emotion in prejudice. *Science*, 1959, **130**, 314–318.

DeFleur, M. L., & Westie, F. R. Verbal attitudes and overt acts: An experiment on the salience of attitudes. *American Sociological Review*, 1958, **23**, 667–673.

DeFleur, M. L., & Westie, F. R. Attitude as a scientific concept. *Social Forces*, 1963, **42**, 17–31.

Dollard, J., et al. *Frustration and aggression*. New Haven, Conn.: Yale University Press, 1939.

Drake, St. C. The social and economic status of the Negro in the United States. In T. Parsons and K. B. Clark (Eds.), *The Negro American*. Boston: Houghton Mifflin, 1966, pp. 3–46.

Drake, St. C., & Cayton, H. R. *Black metropolis*. New York: Harcourt, Brace, 1962.

Ehrlich, H. J. Stereotyping and Negro-Jewish stereotypes. *Social Forces*, 1963, **41**, 171–176.

Ehrlich, H. J. Instrument error and the study of prejudice. *Social Forces*, 1964, **43**, 197–206.

Ehrlich, H. J., & Rinehart, J. W. A brief report on the methodology of stereotype research. *Social Forces*, 1965, **43**, 564–575.

Erskine, H. G. The polls: Race relations. *Public Opinion Quarterly*, 1962, **26**, 137–148.

Erskine, H. G. The polls: Negro housing. *Public Opinion Quarterly*, 1967, **31**, 482–498.

Erskine, H. G. The polls: Demonstrations and race riots. *Public Opinion Quarterly*, 1967–1968, **31**, 655–677.

Erskine, H. G. The polls: Negro employment. *Public Opinion Quarterly*, 1968, **32**, 132–153.

Farley, R., & Taeuber, K. E. Population trends and residential segregation. *Science*, 1968, **159**, 953–956.

Fein, R. An economic and social profile of the Negro American. In T. Parsons and K. B. Clark (Eds.), *The Negro American*. Boston: Houghton Mifflin, 1966, pp. 102–133.

Glenn, N. D. Some changes in the relative status of American non-whites, 1940–1960. *Phylon*, 1963, **24**, 109–122.

Glenn, N. D. The relative size of the Negro population and Negro occupational status. *Social Forces*, 1964, **43**, 42–49.

Glenn, N. D. White gains from Negro subordination. *Social Problems*, 1966, **14**, 159–178.

Glenn, N. D. Negro population concentration and Negro status. *Journal of Negro Education*, 1967, **36**, 353–361.

Goldman, M., Warshay, L. H., & Biddle, E. H. Residential and personal social distance toward Negroes and non-Negroes. *Psychological Reports*, 1962, **10**, 421–422.

Gordon, M. M. *Assimilation in American life*. New York: Oxford, 1964.

Harding, J., Kutner, B., Proshansky, H., & Chein, I. Prejudice and ethnic relations. In G. Lindzey (Ed.), *Handbook of social psychology*. Reading, Mass.: Addison-Wesley, 1954, pp. 1021–1061.

Hauser, P. M. Demographic factors in the integration of the Negro. In T. Parsons and K. B. Clark (Eds.), *The Negro American*. Boston: Houghton Mifflin, 1966, pp. 71–101.

Himmelstrand, U. Verbal attitudes and behavior. *Public Opinion Quarterly*, 1960, **24**, 224–250.

Hyman, H. H., & Sheatsley, P. B. Attitudes toward desegregation. *Scientific American*, 1956, **195,** 35–39.

Hyman, H. H., & Sheatsley, P. B. Attitudes toward desegregation. *Scientific American*, 1964, **211,** 16–23.

Insko, C. A., & Robinson, J. E. Belief similarity versus race as determinants of reactions to Negroes by Southern white adolescents: A further test of Rokeach's theory. *Journal of Personality and Social Psychology*, 1967, **7,** 211–216.

Katz, D., & Stotland, E. A preliminary statement to a theory of attitude structure and change. In S. Koch (Ed.), *Psychology: A study of a science. Vol. 3. Formulations of the person and the social context.* New York: McGraw-Hill, 1959, pp. 423–475.

Kitano, H. L. Passive discrimination: The normal person. *The Journal of Social Psychology*, 1966, **70,** 23–31.

Kutner, B., Wilkins, C., & Yarrow, P. R. Verbal attitudes and overt behavior involving racial prejudice. *Journal of Abnormal and Social Psychology*, 1952, **47,** 649–652.

Landis, J. R., Datwyler, D., & Dorn, D. S. Race and social class as determinants of social distance. *Sociology and Social Research*, 1966, **51,** 78–86.

La Pierre, R. T. Attitudes versus actions. *Social Forces*, 1934, **13,** 230–237.

Linn, L. S. Verbal attitudes and overt behavior: A study of racial discrimination. *Social Forces*, 1965, **43,** 353–364.

Lopez, F. M. Current problems in test performance of job applicants. *Personnel Psychology*, 1966, **19,** 10–18.

Lopez, F. M. Personal communication, 1967.

Marx, G. T. *Protest and prejudice.* New York: Harper & Row, 1967.

Meer, B., & Freedman, E. The impact of Negro neighbors on white home owners. *Social Forces*, 1966, **45,** 11–19.

Merton, R. K. Fact and factitiousness in ethnic opinionaires. *American Sociological Review*, 1940, **5,** 353–364.

Miel, A., & Kiester, E., Jr. *The shortchanged children of suburbia.* New York: Institute of Human Relations Press, 1967.

Moynihan, D. P. Employment, income and the ordeal of the Negro family. In T. Parsons and K. B. Clark (Eds.), *The Negro American.* Boston: Houghton Mifflin, 1966, pp. 102–133.

Myrdal, G. *An American dilemma.* New York: Harper & Row, 1944.

Noel, D. L., & Pinkney, A. Correlates of prejudice: Some racial differences and similarities. *The American Journal of Sociology*, 1964, **69,** 609–622.

Parrish, J. A. (Ed.), The industrial psychologist: Selection and equal employment opportunity (a symposium). *Personnel Psychology*, 1966, **19,** 1–39.

Pettigrew, T. F. Racially separate or together? *Journal of Social Issues*, 1969, **25,** chologist, 1961, **16,** 105–112.

Pettigrew, T. F. Racially separate or together. *Journal of Social Issues*, 1969, **25,** 43–69.

Porier, G. W., & Lott, A. J. Galvanic skin responses and prejudice. *Journal of Personality and Social Psychology*, 1967, **5,** 253–259.

Proenza, L., & Strickland, B. R. A study of prejudice in Negro and white college students. *The Journal of Social Psychology*, 1965, **67,** 273–281.

Proshansky, H. M. The development of intergroup attitudes. In L. W. and M. Hoffman (Eds.), *Review of Child Development Research*, Vol. II. New York: Russell Sage, 1966, pp. 311–371.

Rice, G. E., Jr., & White, K. R. The effects of education on prejudice as revealed in a game situation. *The Psychological Record*, 1964, **14,** 341–348.

Rokeach, M., Smith, P. W., & Evans, R. I. Two kinds of prejudice or one? In

M. Rokeach (Ed.), *The open and closed mind.* New York: Basic Books, 1960, pp. 132–168.

Ross, J. C., & Wheeler, R. Structural sources of threat to Negro membership in militant voluntary association in a Southern city. *Social Forces,* 1967, **45,** 583–586.

Sheatsley, P. B. White attitudes toward the Negro. In T. Parsons and K. B. Clark (Eds.), *The Negro American.* Boston: Houghton Mifflin, 1966, pp. 303–324.

Silberman, C. E. *Crisis in black and white.* New York: Random House, 1964.

Smith, C. U., & Prothro, J. W. Ethnic differences in authoritarian personality. *Social Forces,* 1957, **35,** 334–338.

Stein, D. D. The influence of belief systems on interpersonal preference: A validation study of Rokeach's theory of prejudice. *Psychological Monographs,* 1966, **80** (Whole No. 616), 1–29.

Summers, G. F., & Hammonds, A. D. Effect of racial characteristics of investigator on self-enumerated responses to a Negro prejudice scale. *Social Forces,* 1966, **44,** 515–518.

Taeuber, K. E. Residential segregation. *Scientific American,* 1965, **213,** 12–19.

Taeuber, K. E., & Taeuber, A. F. *Negroes in cities.* Chicago: Aldine, 1965.

Tomlinson, T. M. White racism and the common man: An extension of the Kerner Commission's report on American racism. Unpublished paper. Washington, D.C.: Office of Economic Opportunity, 1968.

Triandis, H. C. A note on Rokeach's theory of prejudice. *Journal of Abnormal and Social Psychology,* 1961, **62,** 184–186.

Triandis, H. C., Loh, W. D., & Levin, L. A. Race, status, quality of spoken English, and opinions about civil rights as determinants of interpersonal attitudes. *Journal of Personality and Social Psychology,* 1966, **3,** 568–572.

Van den Berghe, P. L. *Race and racism.* New York: Wiley, 1967.

Webster, S. W. The influence of interracial contact on social acceptance in a newly integrated school. *Journal of Educational Psychology,* 1961, **52,** 292–296.

Westie, F. R., & DeFleur, M. L. Autonomic responses and their relationship to race attitudes. *Journal of Abnormal and Social Psychology,* 1959, **58,** 340–347.

Williams, J. E., & Roberson, K. A method for assessing racial attitudes in preschool children. *Educational and Psychological Measurement,* 1967, **27,** 671–689.

Woodmansee, J. J., & Cook, S. W. Dimensions of verbal racial attitudes: Their identifiications and measurement. *Journal of Personality and Social Psychology,* 1967, **7,** 240–250.

20

White beliefs about Negroes

A. CAMPBELL AND H. SCHUMAN

Although the National Advisory Commission on Civil Disorders observes in its opening paragraphs that "our nation is moving toward two societies, one black, one white," the fact is, of course, that these two societies have existed, separate and unequal, in this country for over three hundred years. The long period of slavery set a pattern of division which remains in modified form a century later.

One of the results of this separation is a barrier of psychological distance between the races which makes it difficult for either race to form an accurate picture of the other and makes it easy for each to develop misunderstanding, apprehension, and mistrust. The preceding chapter has reviewed the perceptions and attitudes of Negroes regarding whites; we now examine the beliefs and attitudes the white population holds toward Negroes.

WHITE BELIEFS REGARDING NEGROES

Although the relative disadvantage of Negroes in virtually every economic, educational, social, and political aspect of American life has been documented many times over it cannot be assumed that these facts are fully comprehended by the white population. Several questions were asked of the white respondents of our survey specifically intended to reveal their perceptions of the status of Negroes and their appreciation of

Reprinted from *Racial attitudes in fifteen American cities,* Supplemental Studies for the National Advisory Commission on Civil Disorders, Washington, D.C.: U.S. Government Printing Office, Chapter 3, pp. 29–38.

the presence of racial discrimination. The first of these had to do with job opportunities; do white people believe discrimination against Negroes in the work situation is prevalent or relatively infrequent (Table 1)?

TABLE 1 "Do you think that in (Central City) many, some, or only a few Negroes miss out on jobs and promotions because of racial discrimination?"

(In percent)

	White		
	Men	*Women*	*Total*
Many	23	20	22
Some	33	35	34
Only a few	25	26	26
None	12	13	12
Don't know or not ascertained	7	6	6
	100	100	100

As we see, about one-fifth of the white sample expressed the belief that many Negroes suffer from discrimination in the job situation and an additional third agreed that this was the case for "some" Negroes. Perhaps more impressive is the fact that nearly four out of ten white people apparently believe that few if any Negroes are subject to discrimination in hiring or promotions. One white respondent in eight specifically denied the presence of any such discrimination even though this option was not given in the alternatives presented in the question.

A somewhat stronger sense of the special problems Negroes face was found when we directed our question toward discrimination in housing. In this case two-thirds of the white sample agreed that "many" or "some" Negroes have difficulties in renting or buying houses from white owners (Table 2).

TABLE 2   "Do you think that in (Central City) many, some, or only a few Negroes miss out on good housing because white owners won't rent or sell to them?"

(In percent)

	White		
	Men	Women	Total
Many	38	38	38
Some	30	29	30
Only a few	21	22	22
None	4	5	4
Don't know	7	6	6
	100	100	100

A rather different distribution appeared when we asked our white respondents about the treatment they thought Negroes received from the police. Only a small fraction of our white sample accepted without reservation the suggestion that Negroes might be more subject to rough treatment and disrespect from the police than white people and over half of them rejected it as probably or unqualifiedly untrue (Table 3). As we will see later, when we asked our white and Negro

TABLE 3   "It is sometimes said that the things we have just been talking about, such as unnecessary roughness and disrespect by the police, happen more to Negroes in (Central City) than to white people. Do you think this is definitely so, probably so, probably not so, or definitely not so?"

(In percent)

	White		
	Men	Women	Total
Definitely so	11	7	9
Probably so	29	28	29
Probably not so	27	33	30
Definitely not so	27	25	26
Don't know	6	7	6
	100	100	100

samples whether they had actually experienced disrespect or rough treatment from police, Negroes were far more likely to report such incidents. It is apparent, however, that many of our white respondents do not want to accept this implied reflection on the even-handedness of American justice.

In order to assess the perception white people have of the relative status of Negroes in contrast to themselves, we asked our white respondents to compare their income to what they thought Negroes of the same educational achievement as themselves would have. It may have been difficult for some of our respondents to abstract from the total Negro population just those whose educational level was comparable to their own; however, most of them answered the question (Table 4).

TABLE 4   "I would like you to think of Negroes who have the same education you have. As far as the present income of your family goes, do you think you are better off, worse off, or in about the same position as the average Negro with the same education?"

(In percent)

	White		
	Men	Women	Total
Better off	43	41	42
About the same	45	46	46
Worse off	6	5	5
Don't know	6	8	7
	100	100	100

Nearly half of these saw themselves as better off than Negroes of comparable education; only five percent classed themselves as worse off. Since these figures would be equal if there were no difference in white perceptions of the comparative economic status of whites and Negroes of equal training, this discrepancy again reflects recognition within a part of the white population of the effects of discrimination.

Finally, we confronted our white respondents with the fact that Negroes as a whole in their city have poorer jobs, education, and housing than they themselves do and asked them whether they thought these differences were primarily the result of racial discrimination or mainly due to some failure in Negroes themselves. As we see in Table 5, the majority of our white respondents felt that Negroes themselves were responsible for their disadvantaged situation and an additional fraction believed that both discrimination and Negro inadequacies contributed to their circumstances.

TABLE 5 "On the average, Negroes in (Central City) have worse jobs, education and housing than white people. Do you think this is due mainly to Negroes having been discriminated against, or mainly due to something about Negroes themselves?"

(In percent)

	White		
	Men	Women	Total
Mainly due to discrimination	18	19	19
Mainly due to Negroes themselves	56	57	56
A mixture of both	20	17	19
Don't know	6	7	6
	100	100	100

We asked those respondents who told us they thought the deprived conditions of Negroes in their city were due mainly to failures among Negroes themselves or to a combination of such failures and racial discrimination, "What is it about Negroes themselves that makes them have worse jobs, education, and housing?" While it is not possible to present the full detail of answers which this open question evoked, it is clear that those white people who placed some or all of the responsibility for the deficiencies of Negro life on Negroes themselves (approximately three-quarters of the total white sample) tended to think in terms of failures of motivation among Negroes. Nearly half of them spoke of the Negro's presumed laziness, lack of ambition, or unwillingness to take advantage of opportunities. Very few made any reference to supposed innate inferiority or other inherited racial differences.

In order to pursue this latter consideration specifically we asked these same people whether they thought the inadequacies they saw in Negroes were the consequence of some inborn trait, or were characteristics

which were subject to change (Table 6). We find that only a very small proportion (six percent of the total white sample) were prepared to accept the belief common in earlier years that Negroes are subject to some inherent defect which is beyond the possibility of change.

TABLE 6 "Do you think Negroes are just born that way and can't be changed, or that changes in the Negro are possible?"

(In percent)

	White		
	Men	Women	Total
Those who felt Negro conditions are mainly or partly due to Negroes themselves:			
Negroes are born that way	7	4	6
Changes are possible	66	66	66
Don't know	3	4	3
Those who felt Negro conditions are due to discrimination or did not know what they are due to	24	26	25
	100	100	100

In responding to the question "what is it about Negroes" that explains their deprived situation and to various other questions in the interview which invited a full answer, a certain proportion of the white respondents revealed overtly hostile attitudes toward Negroes. These ranged from full-blown expressions of racial bigotry to more moderate statements of exasperation with the insistence of Negro demands for change. We cannot summarize these comments in this report; we mention them here to remind the reader that many of the opinions which are brought together in the tables of this report are held with great intensity.

Some indication of the impression white people themselves have of white attitudes toward Negroes may be obtained from the question from the interview which reads "Do you think that only a few white people in the (City) area dislike Negroes, many dislike Negroes, or almost all dislike Negroes?"

About a quarter of our white respondents said they thought only a few white people dislike Negroes, nearly six in ten thought many do, and one in ten thought almost all do. The rest would not offer an opinion. We offset this question with a corresponding question regarding Negro attitudes toward whites, "How about the reverse: Do you think only a few Negroes dislike white people, many dislike white people, or almost all dislike white people?" In this case the proportion of the white sample who thought nearly all Negroes dislike white people is about one in five, twice as large as the corresponding estimate of white opinion, and the other categories are somewhat smaller.

We cannot say precisely how these people interpreted the word "dislike" and we cannot assume that the actual distribution of white dislike of Negroes or of Negro dislike of whites corresponds to our sample's perception of them. However, it is evident from the answers to our questions that two-thirds of our white respondents sense some degree of negative feeling toward Negroes as widespread among the white population and their sense of Negro dislike of whites is if anything even stronger.

A simple cross-tabulation of the answers to the two questions reveals a substantial association between white perception of widespread dislike of Negroes among whites and their perception of widespread dislike of whites among Negroes. The relationship can be seen in the following comparisons:

Of those whites who think few white people dislike Negroes:
53 percent believe few Negroes dislike whites.
8 percent believe almost all Negroes dislike whites.
Of those whites who think almost all white people dislike Negroes:
8 percent believe few Negroes dislike whites.
67 percent believe almost all Negroes dislike whites.

It seems evident that our white respondents tend strongly to hold a rather general view of racial hostility; what they see on one side they also see on the other side. We did not ask these people to report their own degree of liking or dislike of Negroes; it seems very probable that their perceptions of much or little dislike among others reflect their own feelings in some part.

In order to assess the extent to which generational differences exist within the white population in the way they perceive and respond to these issues of race relations we have divided the men and women of the sample according to the decade of their age. The youngest age category in Table 7 contains those respondents less than 20 years old and the succeeding categories represent the succeeding decades.

The general pattern of Table 7 is clear. There is a consistent tendency for the younger age cohorts to express a stronger appreciation of the discrimination to which Negroes are subject and to accept the presumption that Negro disadvantages in jobs, education and housing are primarily the result of this discrimination. The folk belief that Negroes "are born that way and can't be changed" is accepted by very few people but by a much larger proportion of older people than younger.

From these seven tables we may draw the following conclusions regarding prevailing white beliefs concerning the prevalence and consequences of discrimination against Negroes:

1. Although a majority of white people are prepared to admit that Negroes are handicapped by discriminatory practices in employment and housing, there is a minority of significant size which denies the existence of such practices or regards them as infrequent.

2. Most white people do not accept the suggestion that Negroes are subjected to rougher treatment by the police than are whites themselves. A quarter of the white sample specifically deny this charge.

3. While admitting the presence of discrimination white people show a strong tendency to blame the disadvantaged circumstances of Negro life on Negroes themselves. Although they do not subscribe to genetic theories of racial inferiority, they find much to criticize in the attitudes and behavior patterns they see as characteristic of Negroes and apparently feel that it is within the power of Negroes to improve their own situation.

4. These beliefs regarding racial discrimination vary systematically by age among white people. The overall distribution of beliefs is similar in the different

TABLE 7   White Beliefs Regarding Negroes among Age Categories

(*In percent*)

	Men by Age					
	16–19	*20–29*	*30–39*	*40–49*	*50–59*	*60–69*
Think many Negroes miss out on jobs because of discrimination	36	28	24	14	18	19
Think many Negroes miss out on housing because of discrimination	47	45	41	32	31	33
Think Negroes are definitely or probably more subject to police roughness than white people	55	48	48	27	36	25
Think Negro disadvantages are due mainly to discrimination	30	22	20	10	15	15
Think Negroes are born that way and can't be changed	1	1	4	8	12	13

	Women by Age					
Think many Negroes miss out on jobs because of discrimination	26	29	21	21	11	15
Think many Negroes miss out on housing because of discrimination	49	47	45	36	31	27
Think Negroes are definitely or probably more subject to police roughness than white people	40	45	36	33	26	30
Think Negro disadvantages are due mainly to discrimination	30	28	20	11	11	22
Think Negroes are born that way and can't be changed	2	1	3	6	7	5

generations but younger people are clearly more willing to agree that discrimination exists and that it has deleterious effects on Negroes. The direction of the generational differences we see in our data strongly suggests that a long-term shift is occurring in the white population away from the traditional racial attitudes of an earlier time in this country. While this appears to be a significant movement, it cannot be said that a dramatic reversal of the pattern of racial attitudes has occurred even among the youngest age group.

INTEGRATION AND SEGREGATION

The pattern of interracial relations in a society depends for the most part on the willingness of individual citizens to enter into personal contact of one kind or another with members of the other race. The patterns which have evolved in this country over the past generations are very complex and we cannot hope to represent them fully in this survey. We have limited our inquiry to a series of questions regarding white attitudes toward racial integration in housing, work, children's play, and related situations.

The issue of open housing is at present the focus of legislative attention throughout the country. The Civil Rights Act of 1968 laid down federal regulations on the sale of homes, and various states and municipalities have recently passed, rejected, or considered ordinances of a similar vein. Although it is not likely that any of these legislative acts will have any immediate effect on the housing pattern in American cities, the issue has taken on a certain symbolic importance. When we asked our white respondents their opinions on the "rights" of whites and Negroes regarding housing we found a strong majority who supported the basic principle of open housing (Table 8).

It is certainly not surprising that when confronted with a question implying equal rights a majority of white Americans give their verbal support. Many earlier inquiries have

TABLE 8 "Which of these statements would you agree with: First, white people have a right to keep Negroes out of their neighborhoods if they want to, or Second, Negroes have a right to live wherever they can afford to just like white people?"

(In percent)

| | White | | |
	Men	Women	Total
Whites have a right to keep Negroes out	27	32	30
Negroes have a right to live anywhere	64	59	62
Negroes have a right to live anywhere if they are the "right kind"	3	2	2
Other	3	3	3
Don't know	3	4	3
	100	100	100

demonstrated the willingness of large majorities of the American public to approve statements of democratic principle of this sort.

Those respondents who expressed some degree of approval of the right of Negroes to live wherever they wish were asked a subsequent question intended to measure their willingness to convert this sentiment into a specific legal requirement (Table 9). We now discover that a significant fraction of those who support the principle of open housing are opposed to specific legislation to prevent discrimination in housing. If we combine

TABLE 9 "How about laws to prevent discrimination against Negroes in buying or renting houses and apartments? Do you favor or oppose such laws?"

(In percent)

| | White | | |
	Men	Women	Total
Favor such laws	42	38	40
Oppose such laws	23	19	21
Undecided, don't know	8	11	9
Feel whites have a right to keep Negroes out	27	32	30
	100	100	100

those who are forthrightly opposed to neighborhood integration with those who are not ready to accept laws to bring it about we find that they outnumber those who favor such laws.

On the assumption that some of these whites who favored open occupancy in principle but rejected the suggestion of laws to enforce it might have felt such laws were unnecessary, we asked this fraction of the sample (slightly over one-fifth of the total white sample) if they would favor such legislation if there were "no way for Negroes to get enough good housing without such laws." Although the majority of this group maintained their opposition in the face of this contingency, a substantial number accepted the necessity of a law under these terms and their change of vote brought the division of attitude of the total sample to virtually an even balance of those favoring and opposing legislation in support of open housing.

In order to approach this complicated issue in a more specific way we asked our respondents to visualize a situation in which the first Negro family had moved into an otherwise white neighborhood. Would they favor setting a limit on the number of Negro families who might move into the neighborhood—a quota of some sort to prevent the neighborhood from changing from all white to all black. This proposal divided our white respondents very closely (Table 10).

Nearly half of those who expressed an opinion felt there should be some limit; of

TABLE 10 "Suppose there are 100 white families living in a neighborhood. One white family moves out and a Negro family moves in. Do you think it would be a good idea to have some limit on the number of Negro families that move there, or to let as many move there as want to?"

(In percent)

| | White | | |
	Men	Women	Total
There should be some limit	45	52	48
Let as many move there as want	44	36	40
Don't know	11	12	12
	100	100	100

these one in five specified that no additional families should be admitted and half of the remainder would limit the addition to no more than 10 percent. Of those people who felt there should be a limit but set their quota at some point higher than zero, about half felt that a limit of the kind they proposed would make them more willing to have Negro families in the neighborhood. The other half (about 16 percent of the total sample) did not feel such a quota would make any significant difference to them.

Our final inquiry in this series on housing brought the issue down to the more specific question of how the respondent would feel about having a Negro "with about the same education and income" as himself living next door. Approximately half of the sample felt this would cause them no concern at all; about one in five seemed seriously disturbed by the prospect (Table 11). It is of interest

TABLE 11   "If a Negro family with about the same income and education as you moved next door to you, would you mind it a lot, a little, or not at all?"

(In percent)

	White		
	Men	Women	Total
Mind a lot	17	21	19
Mind a little	25	26	25
Not at all	53	44	49
There is already a Negro family next door	3	5	4
Don't know	2	4	3
	100	100	100

that of the small number of white respondents who were in fact living next door to a Negro family at the time of the interview most said this caused them no concern and about one in ten said they "minded it a lot."[1]

From the problem of housing, our questions moved to the area of employment. We

[1] About one in seven of the white respondents reported in answer to another question that they or someone in their families had at one time moved from a neighborhood because Negroes were moving in.

first asked whether our white respondents felt there should be preference given to white applicants in filling desirable jobs. This blunt statement of discrimination went too far for most of our sample; 95 percent of them chose the alternative that "race should not make any difference one way or the other." We then asked these people how they would feel about laws to prevent discrimination on the job. A substantial majority declared themselves in favor of such legislation, perhaps realizing that fair employment practice laws have been in force for some years (Table 12). None-

TABLE 12   "Do you favor or oppose laws to prevent discrimination against Negroes in job hiring and promotion?"

(In percent)

	White		
	Men	Women	Total
Favor	68	66	67
Oppose	20	18	19
Don't know	8	12	10
Favor preference for whites	4	4	4
	100	100	100

theless, one respondent in five declared himself opposed to such laws, a much larger number than had earlier accepted the proposal of outright discrimination in favor of hiring white job applicants.

Again bringing the issue to a question of direct personal contact we asked the white respondents how they would feel about having a "qualified Negro" as their supervisor on a job. Although there was a very small minority who thought they would find this situation difficult, the great majority of the sample classified themselves as being not at all concerned with this prospect (Table 13).

In order to assess white opinion regarding a proposal which has been put forward by some leaders of the Negro community we asked the sample of white respondents how they would feel about reserving the various kinds of service jobs in Negro neighborhoods exclusively for Negroes. This proposal drew a divided response. Although a third of the respondents were ready to agree with this

TABLE 13 "Suppose you had a job where your supervisor was a qualified Negro. Would you mind that a lot, a little, or not at all?"

(In percent)

| | White | | |
	Men	Women	Total
Mind a lot	4	4	4
Mind a little	7	9	8
Mind not at all	87	84	86
Don't know	2	3	2
	100	100	100

suggestion, over half, especially of the men, were not (Table 14). Apparently they saw this suggestion as a violation of the principle of equal treatment in job placement which they had earlier supported so overwhelmingly.

One further question was asked regarding attitudes toward personal contact between the races, in this case contact among young children. Although, as we see in Table 15, well over half of the white respondents say either that they would prefer for their children to have Negro friends or that they don't care one way or the other, there is a solid one-third of the white sample who say they would prefer for their children to have exclusively white friends. We cannot say as yet whether these people who object to interracial contact among "small children" are simply expressing a general rejection of any form of integration or whether the prospect

TABLE 14 "Some Negro leaders think all the teachers, bus drivers, store clerks, and other employees in Negro neighborhoods should be Negroes. Would you agree with that idea or would you disagree?"

(In percent)

| | White | | |
	Men	Women	Total
Agree	30	39	34
Disagree	66	55	60
Other	0	1	1
Don't know	4	5	5
	100	100	100

of contact among children holds some special threat. Our question did not specify Negro children of comparable class background and it may be that our white respondents thought in terms of a stereotype of lower-class children with rough language and manners. Or the suggestion of Negro friends may have implied the presence of Negro families in the neighborhood, a prospect which we know to be disturbing to many white people. Our survey did not inquire into the rationale behind this specific attitude although subsequent analysis of our data may help us understand it.

In order to assess attitudes in one additional area of urban life, an area which is becoming more significant as the Negro population of the cities increases, we asked our white respondents how they would feel about voting for a Negro for mayor in their city.

TABLE 15 "If you had small children would you rather they had only white friends, or would you like to see them have Negro friends too, or wouldn't you care one way or the other?"

(In percent)

| | White | | |
	Men	Women	Total
Only white friends	30	37	33
Negro friends too	19	19	19
Don't care one way or the other	48	43	46
Don't know	3	1	2
	100	100	100

This question requires the assumption that the Negro candidate is of the respondent's party and that he be a capable man and under these conditions most of the respondents felt that they would support him. There was a visible minority, however, who found this prospect unacceptable (Table 16). When we asked the respondents in Cleveland and Gary how they had actually voted in their recently held mayorality elections a large majority reported that they had supported the white candidates, especially in Gary. These reports coincide with the evidence of racial voting in these cities obtained from precinct records.

TABLE 16 "If a capable Negro of your own party preference was running for Mayor of (Central City), would you vote for him or not?"

(In percent)

	White		
	Men	Women	Total
Yes; if he were the better man	61	58	60
No	20	21	20
Not eligible to vote	10	10	10
Don't know	4	6	5
Live in Cleveland or Gary	5	5	5
	100	100	100

When we again divide our sample by age categories we find that integrationist attitudes are stronger in the younger cohorts than they are in the older. This is particularly true in the question posing the principle of open housing. Differences between age groups in response to some of the other questions were not as great and there are some inconsistencies, especially among the men, but the overall pattern of Table 17 is unmistakable.

If we carry this analysis one step further by dividing our sample by both age and education simultaneously, we find a pattern which was not apparent in the simple comparison of age groups. We see that years of formal education exert an influence on racial perceptions and attitudes but it is not a simple

TABLE 17 White Attitudes toward Integration and Segregation among Age Categories
(In percent)

	Men by Age					
	16–19	20–29	30–39	40–49	50–59	60–69
Believe Negroes have a right to live where they choose	70	67	68	60	65	55
Favor laws preventing discrimination in housing	49	47	45	36	38	38
Favor letting as many Negroes as want move into a neighborhood	50	48	45	37	42	41
Would not mind at all having Negro family next door	55	59	55	42	45	60
Favor laws preventing discrimination against Negroes in jobs	68	78	73	65	60	64
Would not mind at all having a Negro supervisor	89	89	85	83	88	86
Oppose idea of all-Negro employment in Negro neighborhoods	70	62	72	61	63	74
Would like to see their children have Negro friends	27	24	24	16	14	14
Would vote for a qualified Negro mayor		70	74	58	59	66

	Women by Age					
Believe Negroes have a right to live where they choose	80	69	57	52	50	57
Favor laws preventing discrimination in housing	60	42	40	32	33	30
Favor letting as many Negroes as want move into a neighborhood	58	45	33	31	27	33
Would not mind at all having Negro family next door	54	46	40	42	40	48
Favor laws preventing discrimination against Negroes in jobs	78	68	70	58	66	64
Would not mind at all having a Negro supervisor	91	86	85	83	76	87
Oppose idea of all-Negro employment in Negro neighborhoods	59	58	59	49	56	53
Would like to see their children have Negro friends	30	24	18	13	18	15
Would vote for a qualified Negro mayor		67	66	65	55	57

cumulative effect and it is much stronger among younger people than among older people. We present in Figure 1 the data from two of the questions we have reviewed in this chapter; it may be seen that the pattern of findings is very similar in Parts 1 and 2 of Figure 1.

Among people over 40 years of age, those with higher levels of education are no more or less likely to support an open housing law or to express lack of concern at having a Negro family next door than people of lower educational attainment. The picture is quite different among people age 20 through 39. Here we see that the attitudes expressed by young people whose formal education has not gone beyond high school do not differ from older people of similar educational level. But those who have gone on to college differ substantially both from less educated people of their own generation and from college-educated people of the older generation. More of them believe that there should be a law guaranteeing open housing and more of them say they are not at all disturbed at the prospect of a Negro neighbor.

The general pattern of these two figures recurs when we plot the answers to a wide variety of questions regarding perceptions, attitudes, and opinions. There are many irregularities, due in part to the small number

of respondents in some of these educational categories. The educational contrasts are not always as sharp as those shown in Parts 1 and 2 of Figure 1. In some cases the college graduates of the older generation show something of the same movement away from the prevailing attitudes of their age group as the younger college people do. But there is a persistent configuration in the data: (1) In the older generation educational level has a consistently weaker relationship to racial attitudes than it has in the younger generation, and (2) in the younger generation attitudes of people of various educational levels below college do not vary greatly but there is a strong swing among college people toward clearer recognition of racial discrimination, greater acceptance of racial integration, and stronger support of Negro civil rights.

These findings raise questions regarding the nature of social change which we will not be able to consider fully here. It appears from the data that prior to about 1945, the educational experience of white Americans in the schools had relatively little effect on their perceptions and attitudes regarding race. Great individual differences were present, of course, but these apparently developed out of family background, community norms, or personal experience and were not systematically deflected one way or the other by what

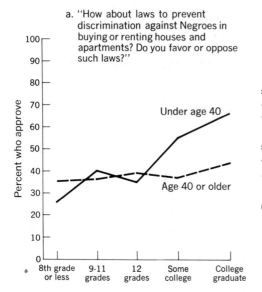

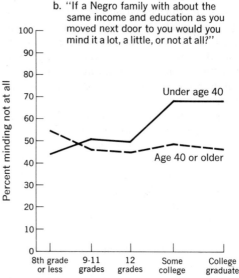

FIGURE 1 Relation of racial attitudes to educational levels among white men

these people were exposed to in school. The schools appear to have accepted without question the prevailing culture of race relations. Since World War II those white students who have gone on to college have evidently been exposed to influences which have moved their attitudes away from the traditional pattern in the directions we have observed. We cannot say whether this resulted from specific instruction regarding questions of race or from a general atmosphere of opinion in the college community but it is clear that a sizable proportion of these postwar generation college students were affected. In contrast, the high schools which our respondents attended during the postwar years seem to have been little more involved in the nation's racial problems than they were in the prewar period. Or, to be more precise, their involvement has been so peripheral that it has had relatively little influence on the racial attitudes of their graduates.

We have explored the possibilities of long-term changes in racial attitudes in the preceding chapter and we do not propose to repeat that discussion here. Our survey has shown a significant deflection in the points of view of young white college people from the prevailing attitudes of their parents' generation. As these younger cohorts move through the life cycle, replacing their elders and being followed by generations with even larger proportions of college-exposed people, the potential for massive change in the traditional pattern of white racial attitudes in this country seems great. However, this is a projection based on simple assumptions of persistence and takes no account of events which may intervene to bring about unforeseeable alteration in the pace and even the direction of this change.

The conclusions which we may draw from these questions regarding white attitudes toward these various aspects of racial integration or segregation are necessarily rather general, but they give some sense of the willingness of white people in these northern cities to accept specific patterns of racial contact.

1. When white people are asked to respond to the concept of the right of Negroes to equal treatment they come down strongly against discrimination. This is especially true in the job situation and it is true in lesser degree in the apparently more sensitive area of neighborhood integration.

2. The prospect of passing laws to protect Negro rights to equal treatment is less warmly supported by white people than the abstract right itself. Even so, a substantial majority approve of laws to ensure fair employment practices. Opinion on the desirability of an open housing law seems about evenly divided.

3. The prospect of close personal contact with Negroes in a job situation seems to disturb relatively few white people, even when a subordinate relationship to a "qualified Negro" is proposed. Living arrangements are clearly more sensitive; although half of the white sample declared themselves free of any concern about having a Negro neighbor of their own income and educational class, there were almost as many who expressed some degree of opposition to this prospect.

4. Attitudes toward various aspects of racial integration are clearly more favorable among young people than among the older generations. The differences are not extreme; they do not approach a reversal of attitudes from one generation to the next. But they indicate a movement over time away from the traditional pattern of racial segregation. An important component of this movement is contributed by those members of the below-40 generation who have attended college.

PROPOSALS FOR ACTION

Our survey attempted not only to assess white attitudes toward various aspects of interracial contact but also to measure white reaction to proposals to improve the circumstances of life in the urban centers. Several questions were asked in our interviews, some suggesting general governmental programs dealing with unemployment, schools and housing, and others concerned with specific actions intended to alleviate the conditions which may have led to the urban riots.

The first of these questions dealt with the issue of full employment; do white people in the northern cities accept the proposition that the federal government has some responsibility to see to it that everyone who seeks a job should have one? The answer is that well over half of the sample accept this proposal (Table 18). Although no reference is made to Negro unemployment in the question and we cannot assume that our respondents had Negroes in mind in answering the question, there is no doubt that such a policy would have special meaning to the urban Negro.

TABLE 18   "Some people say that if there are not enough jobs for everyone who wants one, the government should somehow provide the extra jobs needed. Others say that the government should not do this. What is your opinion?"

(In percent)

	White		
	Men	Women	Total
Government should do this	58	60	59
Government should not do this	38	35	37
Don't know	4	5	4
	100	100	100

A second question proposing governmental action to improve the quality of the public schools in depressed areas of the cities attracted even stronger support (Table 19). The implication of the question that all schools in the city should come up to an

TABLE 19   "Some neighborhoods in and around (Central City) have public schools with better buildings and more trained teachers than others. Do you think the government should provide money to bring the poorer schools up to the standard of the better schools, or that the government shouldn't do this?"

(In percent)

	White		
	Men	Women	Total
Government should do this	75	81	78
Government should not do this	19	12	15
Don't know	6	7	7
	100	100	100

equal standard apparently had particular appeal to our respondents.

The third question in this series dealt with housing and here again a majority of the white respondents accepted the proposal that the federal government take an active role in the urban problem (Table 20).

TABLE 20   "There are areas in cities like (Central City) where the housing is rundown and overcrowded. Some say the government should provide money to help improve the housing in such places. Others don't think the government should do this. What is your opinion?"

(In percent)

	White		
	Men	Women	Total
Government should do this	58	60	59
Government should not do this	38	35	36
Don't know	4	5	5
	100	100	100

In each of these instances the white respondents favored the intervention of the federal government to help solve the difficulties of the cities. We later asked a question which summarized the content of the previous questions and specifically related the proposed governmental programs to the improvement of the conditions of urban Negroes in order "to prevent riots" (Table 21). Two-thirds of

TABLE 21   "If top government officials in Washington said that a program of spending more money for jobs, schools, and housing for Negroes is necessary to prevent riots, would you go along with such a program or would you oppose it?"

(In percent)

	White		
	Men	Women	Total
Go along with it	64	67	66
Oppose it	32	25	28
Don't know	4	8	6
	100	100	100

the respondents answered this omnibus proposal favorably, a proportion very comparable to those found for the individual questions.

We followed this question with a probe intended to compel the respondents to face the financial implications of a program of governmental assistance. Even when threatened with a tax increase of ten percent to finance the proposed program, slightly over half of the sample still were willing to support the proposal (Table 22). This is no doubt an unrealistically high estimate of the support such a tax would actually receive in any of these cities; we intend the question merely as a measure of concern with the problem involved.

TABLE 22 "Suppose the program increased your own taxes by ten percent—that is, if you were paying $300 last year, you would pay $330 this year, and so forth. Would you be willing in that case?"

(In percent)

	White		
	Men	Women	Total
Yes, would be willing	53	53	53
No, would not be willing	10	16	13
Don't know	5	6	6
Oppose such a program	32	25	28
	100	100	100

Finally we asked the respondents to face the problem of what to do about the urban riots and to choose between the alternative of tighter police control or a greater effort to improve the condition of Negroes in the cities. The responses to this question are generally consistent with those given to the more generally phrased questions. Relatively few white respondents saw the answer to the urban problem exclusively in terms of more effective police control. For the most part the respondents felt the solution was more likely to be found in "trying harder" to improve the conditions of urban Negroes (Table 23).

Comparison of the reactions of the younger and older age groups to these proposals for action reveals the same pattern we have seen in the earlier tables. There is a consistent but

TABLE 23 "Thinking about the next five to ten years, what do you think would be the best thing to do about the problem of riots—build up tighter police control in the Negro areas, or try harder to improve the condition of Negroes?"

(In percent)

	White		
	Men	Women	Total
Tighter police control	17	15	16
Improve Negro conditions	53	56	54
Do both	28	27	28
Don't know	2	2	2
	100	100	100

not remarkable tendency among the younger white people to give stronger support to these proposals to improve the conditions of the urban Negro than among the older generations (Table 24).

These questions in our survey have in effect asked our sample of white citizens to respond to a plebiscite on several proposals regarding public action to be taken on the urban problem. We cannot be sure, of course, that the distributions of opinions we have reported would be precisely the same as those that might be obtained in a referendum vote in these cities with all the attendant political pressures that might be involved. However, two conclusions from the data we have reviewed seem firm and important.

1. There is a willingness among the white population of these northern cities to see government play a strong hand in helping bring about improvement in the conditions of the cities. This opinion is not unanimous; there is a substantial minority who oppose the suggestion of such programs. But there is a consistent majority on all these proposals who accept the necessity of governmental assistance and this approval is not reduced when the purpose of the assistance is specifically related to the needs of the Negro population and the prevention of riots.

2. The superficially simple solution to the problem of urban riots—more rigid police control of the Negro areas—is not generally seen by white urban residents as

TABLE 24 White Attitudes toward Proposals for Action among Age Categories
(In percent)

	Men by Age					
	16–19	*20–29*	*30–39*	*40–49*	*50–59*	*60–69*
Agree that government should provide needed jobs	63	62	60	55	55	54
Agree that government should improve schools	89	83	71	72	70	69
Agree that government should improve slum housing	69	66	58	53	63	51
Would go along with program of spending to help Negroes	72	71	64	56	64	59
Willing to pay more taxes for program to help Negroes	59	55	50	42	56	54
Prefer to try harder to improve condition of Negroes	58	57	54	57	44	49
	Women by Age					
Agree that government should provide needed jobs	79	59	50	55	62	68
Agree that government should improve schools	95	91	77	81	73	73
Agree that government should improve slum housing	78	65	51	57	59	53
Would go along with program of spending to help Negroes	77	74	61	66	61	63
Willing to pay more taxes for program to help Negroes	61	57	48	54	49	48
Prefer to try harder to improve condition of Negroes	71	68	55	49	46	54

an adequate answer. The large majority of these people accept the proposition that there must be an improvement in the conditions of Negro life.

THE WHITE SUBURBS

When we compare the beliefs of white suburbanites concerning the prevalence of racial discrimination to those we have just reviewed we find no differences of any consequence. White people in the suburbs are somewhat more likely to feel they are better off economically than Negroes of similar educational status and this probably reflects the fact that their own economic situation is on the average better than that of white people within the cities. Suburban white people also differ very little from whites within the city limits in their attitudes on most aspects of racial integration and in their acceptance of the desirability of governmental programs to improve conditions within the cities. The one point at which suburban people show a special sensitivity is in the area of segregated housing. They are more likely to support the proposition that white people may properly keep Negroes out of their neighborhood if they wish and they show more resistance to the prospect of having a Negro family living next door. These differences are small, less than ten percentage points, but they are not chance.

21

Negro-white occupational differences in the absence of discrimination[1]

STANLEY LIEBERSON AND GLENN V. FUGUITT

The disadvantages faced by racial and ethnic groups are one of the central concerns in the study of intergroup relations, but insufficient attention has been paid to the two basic types of handicaps. First, there is the disadvantage that occurs when members of a group are rejected or discriminated against solely because of their race or ethnic origin. The difficulties faced by Negroes with sufficient funds in the housing market are an obvious instance of discrimination based on racial or ethnic membership. A second basic disadvantage faced by a group is not the product of immediate discrimination, although it may reflect earlier discriminatory acts. This situation occurs when members of a group occupy a position in the social structure which puts them at a disadvantage by lowering their opportunities even under the operation of non-racial or universalistic criteria. For example, if discrimination against Negroes on the job market were to disappear, they would still hold jobs inferior to whites because of lower education, poorer training, and the like. Suppose an employer wishes to hire only applicants with a high school education. Assuming that he indiscriminately chooses whites and Negroes at random, fewer Negroes will be hired on a proportional basis simply because the segment of the Negro labor force with a high school education is smaller than that for whites. Thus the net effect of racially neutral employment practices may still favor one group over another.

The analytical distinction between the disadvantages derived from discrimination and those based on universalistic social processes is applied in this paper to the occupations held by Negro men. Even if the present disadvantaged status of Negroes in the United States is entirely a consequence of discrimination, a complete end to discrimination would not mean an immediate end to their social and economic liabilities. The difficulties faced because of job training and education requirements, work experience, and similar factors suggest taking an intergenerational approach, since it is across generations that most major shifts in occupation may take place.[2] By means of a simple mathematical model, the Markov chain, the possible consequences an end to discrimination would have on Negro-white occupational differences are traced in terms of intergenerational occupational mobility. The results generated by the Markov model are used to describe the implications of current non-discriminatory disadvantages faced by Negroes rather than as a means of prediction, for we are aware that our assumptions do not fully describe what will realistically be expected to occur.

Reprinted from *The American Journal of Sociology*, 1967, **73**, 188–200, by permission of the authors and the University of Chicago Press. Copyright © 1967, the University of Chicago Press.

[1] The assistance of Lee J. Haggerty in the analysis of these data is gratefully acknowledged.

[2] See Otis Dudley Duncan, "Occupation Trends and Patterns of Net Mobility in the United States," *Demography*, **III**, No. 1 (1966), 15.

METHODS

The Markov model has had a variety of applications in the social sciences in recent years, particularly in the study of social mobility.[3] It assumes a set of observations that may be classified into a finite number of different states. A given observation may move from one state to another over a time period t, and there is a sequence of such time periods. The probability that an observation will move from state i to state j between t and $t + 1$ is given by P_{ij}. The basic assumption of the model is that the probability of moving from i to j depends only on the state at time t and that this probability is constant over the sequence of time intervals.

Consideration of the Markov-chain process can be greatly simplified by matrix algebra. If t is a row vector of the proportion of observations in each state at time zero, and P is the matrix of transitional probabilities, then $t_0 P = t_1$, where t_1 is the proportion in each state at time 1. Also, it can be shown that $t_0 P^n = t_n$, that is, by raising P to the nth power and premultiplying by

[3] These include S. J. Prais, "Measuring Social Mobility," *Journal of the Royal Statistical Society,* Ser. A, **CXVIII** (1955), 56–66; *idem,* "The Formal Theory of Social Mobility," *Population Studies,* **IX** (July, 1955), 72–81; Judah Matras, "Comparison of Intergenerational Occupational Mobility Patterns: An Application of the Formal Theory of Social Mobility," *Population Studies,* **XIV** (November, 1960), 163–69; and Robert W. Hodge, "Occupational Mobility as a Probability Process," *Demography,* III, No. 1 (1966), 19–34. Examples of other applications to social science are Irma G. Adelman, "A Stochastic Analysis of the Size Distribution of Firms," *Journal of the American Statistical Association,* **LIII** (December, 1958), 893–904; C. G. Judge and E. R. Swanson, "Markov Chains: Basic Concepts and Suggested Uses in Agricultural Economics" (research report AERR-49 [Urbana, Ill.: Department of Agricultural Economics, 1961]); Daniel I. Padberg, "The Use of Markov Processes in Measuring Changes in Marketing Structure," *Journal of Farm Economics,* **XLIV** (February, 1962), 189–99; and Glenn Fuguitt, "The Growth and Decline of Small Towns as a Probability Process," *American Sociological Review,* **XXX** (June, 1965), 403–11.

t_0, one obtains the proportion in each state at time n.[4]

An intergenerational-mobility table may be transformed into a matrix of transition probabilities necessary for the Markov model. The proportional distribution of the sons' occupations tabulated by the occupations of their fathers can be treated as rows of p_{ij} values, with each row adding to 1.000. In Table 1, which provides the basic set of p_{ij} values, we see, for example, that the probability of becoming a professional for the son of a professional is .410, whereas p_{ij} for the son of a craftsman becoming a professional is .130.

In this paper we have operationalized an end to discrimination by assuming that an intergenerational-mobility table for all men applies to Negroes as well as whites. This table is used because data were not available for whites alone. However, the matrix is heavily weighted by the white rates, since Negroes are a relatively small proportion of the total labor force. The matrix of transition probabilities obtained from this mobility table is successively multiplied by the appropriate occupational-distribution vector for Negro men as well as by the corresponding white vector, yielding expected occupational distributions for the two races under the Markov assumption. If this P is a regular stochastic matrix (and it is), we know that both Negro and white occupational distributions will approach convergence at equilibrium, which is determined by the values of P alone. What is of interest here is the changing pattern of Negro-white differences over time until they become negligible, which depends both upon the P matrix and the two initial vectors used. This process tells us about the joint effect of intergenerational mobility and racial differences within the social structure.

An alternate analysis was carried out using an educational-mobility table. Assuming that an end to discrimination would result in common intergenerational-educational-mobility patterns for Negroes and whites, expected educational distributions for the two races are projected across generations to convergence. These are then converted into another

[4] For a general elementary discussion of Markov chains see John G. Kemeny, J. Laurie Snell, and Gerald L. Thompson, *Introduction to Finite Mathematics* (Englewood Cliffs, N.J.: Prentice-Hall, Inc., 1956).

TABLE 1 Son's Occupation by Father's Occupation, 1962

Father's Occupation	Son's Occupation (See Stub)										All Sons
	1	2	3	4	5	6	7	8	9	10	
1. Professional, technical, and kindred	.410	.175	.090	.069	.087	.103	.031	.019	.012	.004	1.000
2. Managers, officials, and proprietors, except farm	.216	.341	.091	.071	.139	.085	.025	.019	.010	.003	1.000
3. Sales workers	.195	.300	.150	.062	.119	.104	.032	.020	.017	.001	1.000
4. Clerical and kindred	.281	.178	.078	.097	.169	.092	.061	.030	.014	.000	1.000
5. Craftsmen, foremen, and kindred	.130	.165	.047	.078	.294	.175	.051	.048	.008	.004	1.000
6. Operatives and kindred	.117	.122	.044	.066	.239	.259	.059	.076	.009	.009	1.000
7. Service workers, including private household	.101	.142	.057	.095	.210	.209	.111	.063	.010	.002	1.000
8. Laborers, except farm and mine	.059	.080	.036	.080	.226	.263	.091	.142	.012	.011	1.000
9. Farmers and farm managers	.053	.115	.025	.047	.197	.205	.052	.085	.178	.043	1.000
10. Farm laborers and foremen	.023	.075	.020	.038	.205	.260	.081	.134	.062	.102	1.000

Note. Persons not reporting their fathers' occupations are excluded.

set of occupational distributions by means of a cross-tabulation of education and occupation.

An end to discrimination is operationalized here by positing common intergenerational-mobility patterns for Negroes and whites. Factors other than discrimination, however, such as family structure and possible differences in level of aspiration, may make for differences between the mobility of Negroes and whites having the same occupational or educational background.[5] Thus this procedure may overstate the rate of upward mobility for Negroes under the assumption that racial differences not explained by structural characteristics are a function of discrimination.[6]

There are a number of aspects of the model which are unrealistic, in addition to the obvious one of an immediate end to discrimination. By applying occupational- or educational-mobility rates under Markov assumptions, we assume that the mobility pattern is unchanged over a series of generations. In point of fact, mobility matrixes have changed through the years in the United States.[7]

Fertility, mortality, and the length of generations differ between the races as well as across educational and occupational groups, but these facts are ignored since the data necessary for making such adjustments are not available. While these demographic forces are significant for explaining the patterns of social mobility in the United States or for policy decisions, it is convenient to assume

[5] Beverly Duncan observed, e.g., that growing up in a broken family means from 0.6 to 1 year less schooling for a boy. See her "Family Factors and School Dropout: 1920–1960" (Ann Arbor: University of Michigan, 1965), p. 8. For a discussion of Negro-white differences in family disorganization, see Office of Policy Planning and Research, U.S. Department of Labor, *The Negro Family* (Washington, 1965).

[6] See the discussion of problems in the measurement of discrimination in H. M. Blalock, Jr., "Theory, Measurement, and Replication in the Social Sciences," *American Journal of Sociology,* **LXVI** (January, 1961), 346–47.

[7] Otis Dudley Duncan, "The Trend of Occupational Mobility in the United States," *American Sociological Review,* **XXX** (August, 1965), 491–98; Natalie Rogoff, "Recent Trends in Urban Occupational Mobility," in Paul K. Hatt and Albert J. Reiss, Jr. (Eds.), *Cities and Society* (Glencoe, Ill.: Free Press, 1957), pp. 432–45.

the constancy of these vital processes for the problem tackled here. In effect, it is assumed that each father will have one son who will survive to take an occupation according to the mobility table and to have one male forebear, etc.

The unit of analysis here is the occupational (or educational) distribution of white or Negro males thirty-five to forty-four years of age. In the *Current Population Survey* from which the occupational-mobility table was obtained, respondents were asked their fathers' occupations when the former were sixteen. Since the mobility rates are applied over successive hypothetical generations, this age range was chosen because these men are the ones most likely to have sixteen-year-old sons.

We repeat that our objective is not to make predictions about what will happen or to compare data generated by our model with empirical data obtained now or in the future. Rather, the importance of universalistic disadvantages suffered by Negroes because of their structural position is demonstrated by projecting current patterns of intergenerational mobility under the hypothetical case where no future racial discrimination exists in employment.

FATHER'S OCCUPATION

Our basic source of intergenerational occupational mobility is a table cross-tabulating the current occupations of male respondents twenty-five to sixty-four years of age by their fathers' occupations when the respondents were sixteen (Table 1). These data were obtained by the U.S. Bureau of the Census in a 1962 *Current Population Survey.*[8] The table mixes together a wide variety of cohorts among both generations. A sixty-four-year-old respondent who was born when his father was forty would report his father's occupation for a year actually preceding the birth of some twenty-five-year-old respondent's father. It was necessary to substitute this for the appropriate table based on males thirty-five to forty-four since the latter was not pub-

[8] U.S. Bureau of the Census, "Lifetime Occupational Mobility of Adult Males, March, 1962," *Current Population Reports,* Ser. P-23, No. 11 (May, 1964).

lished in full. The two marginal distributions and the principal diagonal were given, however, and show low deviations from corresponding values in the complete table we used. The index of dissimilarity between the present distribution of the occupations of sons in the two tables is only 2.5 for ten occupational classes (excluding those not reporting their father's occupations), while the corresponding index for the occupational distribution of fathers is 1.7.

Negro-white differences in occupational composition in 1960 are shown under the first-generation heading in Table 2. The index of dissimilarity between the races is 40. In other words, 40 per cent of one or the other race would have to change occupational categories if the two races were to have identical occupational distributions. Markov-chain analysis enables us to compare the occupations of each race in the thirty-five to forty-four age group with those that would eventually occur in each generation and at

final equilibrium, under the assumption that current rates of intergenerational mobility persist indefinitely. This final equilibrium is much closer to first-generation whites than Negroes; the indexes for the two groups from the equilibrium stage are 16 and 48, respectively. (The equilibrium stage is defined in this paper as the point at which P, on being raised to successive powers, is equal to a matrix having rows identical to each other at two decimal places. At this point in the process both whites and Negroes have distributions equal to these rows and hence identical to each other to two decimal places. Since the true equilibrium stage is approached but not reached by P raised to any power, the white and Negro distributions are never exactly identical but rather converge asymptotically.)

If discrimination had disappeared by 1960, then the next generation of Negro and white men would have had the occupational composition shown under the second-generation

TABLE 2   Negro-White Occupational Composition: Frequency Distributions and Indexes of Dissimilarity

| Occupation | Percentage Distributions by Generation and Race | | | | | | | | | |
| | First (1960) | | Second | | Third | | Fourth | | Seventh | |
	White	Negro	White	Negro	White	Negro	White	Negro	White	Negro
Professional, technical, and kindred	13	4	18	12	20	18	21	20	22	22
Managers, officials, and proprietors, except farm	14	2	18	13	19	18	20	19	20	20
Sales workers	7	1	7	5	7	6	7	7	7	7
Clerical and kindred	7	6	7	7	7	7	7	7	7	7
Craftsmen, foremen, and kindred	24	13	20	22	19	20	18	19	18	18
Operatives and kindred	20	30	17	22	16	18	15	16	15	15
Service workers, including private household	4	13	5	8	5	5	5	5	5	5
Laborers, except farm and mine	5	22	5	8	5	6	5	5	4	4
Farmers and farm managers	5	4	2	2	1	1	1	1	1	1
Farm laborers and foremen	1	5	1	1	1	1	1	1	1	1
Total	100	100	100	100	100	100	100	100	100	100
Indexes of dissimilarity:										
White-Negro	40		13		4		2		0	
White-equilibrium	16		6		3		1		0	
Negro-equilibrium	48		19		7		3		0	

heading. If the current set of father-son patterns continue, Negroes and whites will be considerably closer in occupational composition in the next generation (the index of dissimilarity is only 13). The gains for Negroes in one generation without race-specific discrimination are very great. In the first generation, 13 per cent of whites and 4 per cent of Negroes are professionals. By contrast, the Negro percentage in professional occupations would increase in one generation to 12 per cent, while that of whites would increase to 18 per cent. The percentage of Negro professionals would triple in the course of a single generation without discrimination, although it would still be lower than that of whites. The percentage of Negroes employed as laborers (excluding farms and mines) would drop from 22 to 8 per cent in the same generation. It is evident that the second-generation occupational composition of both whites and Negroes is much closer than the first to the final or equilibrium occupational composition. There is a drop in the index from 16 to 6 for whites and from 48 to 19 for Negroes.

In the third and fourth generations the races would, of course, become increasingly alike in their job distributions. By the fourth generation, there would be virtually no difference in occupational composition between Negro and white men aged thirty-five to forty-four, although it would take seven generations for complete equality. In short, were racially based discrimination on the job market to have ended in 1960 in the United States, and if each twenty-year-old father had a son, then under the assumptions described earlier it would take about eighty years before racial occupational inequality would be virtually nil. However, very rapid progress would be made long before this, with a radical decline in racial differences in just one generation, resulting in differences of 6 percentage points or less for any one occupational group. After two generations, or about forty years, there would be differences of 2 percentage points or less.

EDUCATION

Based on a regression analysis of intergenerational occupational mobility in Chicago, Duncan and Hodge reported that the influ-

ence of education on a man's occupation is greater than that of his father's occupation. Moreover, they concluded that the latter factor "was influential in large part because of its association with education."[9] Nevertheless, ideally we would like to introduce both factors into a Markov process such as that presented by Carlsson for Sweden, in which he was able to consider the joint influence of father's occupation and son's education.[10] Unfortunately, we were unable to obtain such data for the United States. However, the October, 1960, *Current Population Survey* reports the educational status of men twenty to twenty-four years of age cross-tabulated by the education of their fathers.[11]

TABLE 3   Education of Sons Twenty to Twenty-four Years of Age by Father's Education, 1960

Father's Education	Son's Education		
	Less than High School	High School	More than High School
Less than high school	.43	.34	.23
High school	.10	.36	.54
More than high school	.05	.15	.80

Source: U.S. Bureau of the Census, *Current Population Reports, Populaiton Characteristics*, Ser. P-20, No. 110 (July, 1961), Table A.

Table 3 shows the transition matrix that can be developed on the basis of these data. The table slightly misstates final educational attainment since some of the sons may yet complete their education. Such a bias should not be great, however, and therefore this is a reasonably appropriate matrix for the unit of this study, males thirty-five to forty-four.

[9] Otis Dudley Duncan and Robert W. Hodge, "Educational and Occupational Mobility: A Regression Analysis," *American Journal of Sociology*, **LXVIII** (May, 1963), 644.

[10] Gosta Carlsson, *Social Mobility and Class Structure* (Lund: C. W. K. Gleerup, 1958), chap. vii.

[11] U.S. Bureau of the Census, "School Enrollment, and Education of Young Adults and Their Fathers: October 1960," *Current Population Reports*, Ser. P-20, No. 110 (July, 1961).

The table shows that father's education significantly influences his sons' education even in the current period of rising levels of attainment. For example, among fathers who failed to graduate from high school, nearly one-half of their sons likewise did not complete high school. This is far greater than the percentage failing to complete high school among the sons of more highly educated fathers. Likewise, there is an orderly and important increment in the percentage of sons attending college which reflects father's education. Fully 80 per cent of the sons of men with some college also went beyond high school, whereas college training was obtained by about one-half of the men whose fathers had only completed high school and one-fourth of those whose fathers did not finish high school.

The educational status of Negroes is lower

TABLE 4   Educational Composition by Race: Frequency Distributions and Indexes of Dissimilarity

Generation and Race	Percentage Distributions			Index of Dissimilarity
	Less than High School	High School	More than High School	
First:				
White	46	31	23	29
Non-white	75	16	9	
Second:				
White	24	30	46	13
Non-white	34	33	33	
Third:				
White	16	26	58	6
Non-white	20	28	52	
Fourth:				
White	12	23	64	4
Non-white	14	25	61	
Fifth:				
White	11	22	67	2
Non-white	11	23	66	
Sixth:				
White	10	22	68	1
Non-white	11	22	67	
Seventh:				
White	10	21	69	1
Non-white	10	22	68	
Eighth:				
White	10	21	69	0
Non-white	10	21	69	

than that of whites. About three-quarters of the non-white men thirty-five to forty-four years of age in the experienced civilian labor force had not completed high school in 1960, compared with slightly less than one-half of the white males.[12] If the educational-mobility rates for the total population were to operate for both non-whites and whites, the educational status of the two groups would come together over future generations.

In 1960, the index of dissimilarity in education between white and non-white employed men was 29 (see Table 4). This would drop to 13 in the second generation, 6 in the third generation, and would eventually reach 0 in the eighth generation. Thus, if the current relation between fathers' and sons' educations were to persist, educational equality would be fairly close after several generations, with white and non-white difference for each educational class within 3 percentage points at the end of about 60 years. Identical percentage distributions (to whole numbers) would not be attained, however, for about 140 years, allowing 20 years for each generation.

EDUCATION AND OCCUPATION

Examination of the occupational composition of the races in each generation, based solely on the cross-tabulation between occupation and education existing for white men thirty-five to forty-four years of age in 1960, allows us to convert the projected educational differences into a measure of the occupational differences that would result.

The relationships between fathers' education and sons' education, and then in turn between sons' education and occupations, are more complex than our data allow for. In particular, it is not possible to determine whether there is any statistical interaction between the variables. Rather, an additive model is assumed in which one can examine the influence of educational attainment on racial differences in occupational composition.

In 1960, as well as in earlier periods, whites and non-whites with the same level of education obtained different degrees of occupa-

[12] Due to data limitations, it is necessary to use information on non-whites rather than Negroes.

tional success.[13] Table 5 shows the relationship between education and occupation for men thirty-five to forty-four years of age separately by race. There are differences which are clearly unfavorable to non-whites. For example, a quarter of all non-whites with less than a high school education are laborers (except farm and mine), whereas less than 10 per cent of whites with a similar level of education are so employed. These racial dif-

Using the educational composition projected for future generations of whites and non-whites, we shall assume that there is no longer any discrimination between the races in quality of education under two different conditions: first, that there is no discrimination between job applicants with the same level of schooling and, second, that the influence of education on occupation remains different for the races. The first two columns

TABLE 5   Occupational Percentage Distributions by Education and Race for Males in the Experienced Civilian Labor Force Ages Thirty-five to Forty-four, 1960

Occupation	Less than High School		High School		More than High School	
	White	Non-white	White	Non-white	White	Non-white
Professional, technical, and kindred	2	1	7	3	41	36
Managers, officials, and proprietors, except farm	8	2	16	5	23	8
Sales workers	4	1	9	3	11	3
Clerical and kindred	4	3	10	14	7	15
Craftsmen, foremen, and kindred	29	13	28	18	9	10
Operatives and kindred	31	32	17	26	4	11
Service workers, including private household	5	12	4	15	2	10
Laborers, except farm and mine	8	26	3	13	1	5
Farmers and farm managers	6	4	5	2	2	1
Farm laborers and foremen	3	6	1	1	0	1
Total	100	100	100	100	100	100

Source: U.S. Bureau of the Census, *U.S. Census of Population: 1960. Subject Reports. Educational Attainment* (Final Report PC(2)-5B), Table 8.

ferences in occupational composition between men with the same educational achievement no doubt reflects discrimination against Negroes on the job market, lower-quality education for Negroes with the same formal levels of attainment as whites, and the technical fact that educational attainment has only been trichotomized.[14]

[13] See, e.g., Paul M. Siegel, "On the Cost of Being a Negro," *Sociological Inquiry,* **XXXV** (Winter, 1965), 41–57, and Nathan Hare, "Recent Trends in the Occupational Mobility of Negroes, 1930–1960: An Intracohort Analysis," *Social Forces,* **XLIV** (December, 1965), 166–73.

[14] For a description of the inferior educational opportunities for Negroes, see Leonard Broom and Norval Glenn, *Transformation of the Negro American* (New York: Harper & Row, 1965), pp. 90–96.

for each generation show, respectively, the occupational composition of whites and non-whites under the first condition. If the influence of education on occupation for non-white men in 1960 was the same as that found for white men, then in 1960 the index of dissimilarity between the races in occupations for men thirty-five to forty-four years of age would have been 14 rather than 38.[15]

The indexes of dissimilarity indicate that a rapid decline would occur in racial occupational differences if non-white educational

[15] The discrepancy between this index of 38 and the index of 40 reported in Table 2 is due to the fact these data are for non-whites rather than Negroes only and because the data for whites here are based on a 5 per cent sample.

mobility were the same as for the total population and if Negroes and whites with the same educational attainment were employed identically in the job market. In the second generation the index would be only 8; in the third generation it would be 4; and virtually complete identity would be reached in the eighth generation, with an index of 0. The progress of occupational equality found earlier by examining the influence of fathers' occupations on those of sons' is rather similar to that obtained by means of this approach to occupations based on the influence of education. The second-generation index of dissimilarity would be 13 under the first model and 8 under the second approach, but they would be identical in the third generation, and both reach exact equality one generation apart. In either case then, a sharp decline in racial differences would occur in the course of one generation if there were no longer discrimination in the United States.

By contrast, observe what happens to white–non-white occupational differences if it is assumed that the influence of education on occupation for non-white men in 1960 applies to future generations of non-whites (shown in the third column under each generation). The index of dissimilarity is actually 38 between the races in 1960. We again observe that racial dissimilarities in occupation decline in each succeeding generation, but at a rather slow rate. The index is 35 in the second generation, 31 in the third, and eventually flattens out at 29 in the eighth and later generations. Non-whites are still occupationally disadvantaged, despite the equality in formal educational attainment, because they do not obtain the same jobs as whites with identical education.

The equilibrium stage under assumption 2 provides important implications about the future status of Negro-white employment if their levels of formal education were the same but the current non-white relationship between education and occupation remained unaltered. Non-whites would still be overrepresented in the lower job levels even after educational parity with whites was achieved. Inspection of the results for the eighth generation in Table 6 indicates that Negroes would be far more likely to be employed as laborers, service workers, and operatives. Although they would also be overrepresented in the clerical occupations, Negro men would

be less likely to be employed as managers, officials, and proprietors, as well as sales workers. To a lesser degree they would remain underemployed as professionals and craftsmen.

Compare the actual occupations held by non-white men aged thirty-five to forty-four in 1960 with the occupational composition that would have occurred for non-white men in 1960 if their formal levels of education had yielded the same occupations as those of whites yielded (the second and third columns, respectively, under the first generation in Table 6). The index of dissimilarity in occupations between the races would have been 14 rather than 38. Thus the first index, which reflects only the lower formal education among Negroes, is little more than one-third the size of the actual difference in 1960.[16] The actual racial gap in 1960 reflects the additional influences of discrimination against non-whites of comparable achievement, inferior quality of education for Negroes, the possible masking of greater educational attainment of whites because of the broad categories used, and a wide array of other possible factors, such as access to opportunities.

These results indicate that if Negro formal educational attainment were to reach the same level as that of whites, the effect on Negro-white occupational equality would be limited if other factors remained unchanged. Moreover, if the educational matrixes were to continue to operate in the future, and if the current relationship between education and occupation for non-whites were to remain unaltered, the racial index of dissimilarity in occupations would decline from 38 to 29 after eight generations, but never get lower than that.

DISCUSSION

We have distinguished between two types of handicaps faced by Negroes. The first, discrimination, involves rejection of Negroes

[16] The differences between the two indexes cannot be used to determine the percentage of the actual 1960 index which is not explained by formal educational attainment. The indexes, taken pair-wise, are not simply additive. For formulas on the minimum and maximum restrictions, see Stanley Lieberson, *Ethnic Patterns in American Cities* (Glencoe, Ill.: Free Press, 1963), p. 39.

TABLE 6 Influence of Education on Occupation by Generation and Race: Percentage Distributions and Indexes of Dissimilarity

Occupation	Percentage Distributions by Generation and Race														
	First			Second			Third			Fourth			Eighth		
	W	NW*	NW†	W	NW*	NW†	W	NW*	NW†	W	NW*	NW†	W	NW*	NW†
Professional, technical, and kindred	12	6	4	21	16	13	26	24	20	28	27	23	30	30	26
Managers, officials, and proprietors, except farm	14	10	3	17	15	5	19	18	6	19	19	6	20	20	6
Sales workers	7	5	1	9	8	2	9	9	3	10	10	3	10	10	3
Clerical and kindred	7	5	6	7	7	10	8	7	12	8	7	13	8	8	14
Craftsmen, foremen, and kindred	24	27	13	20	22	13	17	18	12	16	17	12	15	15	12
Operatives and kindred	21	27	29	15	18	23	12	13	20	10	11	18	9	9	16
Service workers, including private household	4	5	13	3	4	13	3	3	12	3	3	12	3	3	11
Laborers, except farm and mine	5	7	22	3	4	15	2	3	11	2	2	10	2	2	9
Farmers and farm managers	5	6	4	4	5	3	3	4	2	3	3	2	3	3	2
Farm laborers and foremen	1	2	5	1	1	3	1	1	2	1	1	1	0	0	1
Total	100	100	100	100	100	100	100	100	100	100	100	100	100	100	100
Index of dissimilarity between whites and non-whites		14	38		8	35		4	31		2	30		0	29

* Based on white relationship between education and occupation.
† Based on non-white relationship between education and occupation.

simply because they are Negroes; the second occurs because the group occupies an inferior aggregate position on variables which, although racially neutral, operate to their disadvantage. Using an intergenerational approach, by means of the Markov-chain model, we operationalized the end to discrimination by assuming both races follow mobility patterns found to prevail for the total population. Starting with observed Negro and white occupational distributions for 1960, we then traced the changes that would take place over several generations. An alternative approach started with educational mobility, and we then employed the relation between education and occupation to produce comparable occupational distributions.

Using both approaches, Negro and white distributions converged rapidly, at least in terms of a generational time scale, so that differences were negligible after about sixty or eighty years. Whether this convergence is "fast" or "slow" is of course beyond the purview of the sociologist. These data do underscore the position that an end to discrimination will not result in occupational equality immediately. And for those in favor of this equality as quickly as possible, the results may provide some support for programs to speed up the processes of intra- and intergenerational occupational mobility among Negroes.

We wish to reiterate our cautions about the assumptions made, the crudeness of the data used, and the uncertainty about the long-run continuation of the transitional probabilities employed to project future occupational composition. Somewhat different conclusions could be obtained if different assumptions were made about the ongoing social processes. Based on changes in median education between 1940 and 1960, Broom and Glenn projected identical medians for men within forty-five years from 1960, a much shorter period than our approach indicates.[17] However, it appears unlikely, under any circumstances, that Negro-white occupational equality could be reached in a decade or two even if racial discrimination in the job market were completely eliminated.

But even if our data were more complete and included the entire range of working

years, occupational structure and changes in structure could not be deduced from intergenerational occupational mobility. We have traced the consequences of certain artificial assumptions on an intergenerational succession of fathers and sons thirty-five to forty-four years old, and any possible implications are so limited.[18]

Based on the gross influence of father's occupation on son's occupation, several generations would be required before racial parity in the labor force could be met, although we found that men thirty-five to forty-four years of age were much closer in occupational composition after one generation. In analyzing the education of men thirty-five to forty-four and its influence on both their occupations and the education of the next generation, it was not possible to consider the effect of occupation on the next generation's educational attainment. However, about a third of the racial difference in occupational composition in 1960 for the thirty-five- to forty-four-year-old generation could be attributed to differences in formal levels of educational attainment. Again, it would take several generations to overcome current educational disadvantages faced by non-whites even if all other factors, including the quality of Negro education and the relationship between education and occupation, were eliminated. Thus our simple projections into the future of current patterns indicate that disadvantages to a group·can continue, although not indefinitely, even when the initial thrust of discrimination is eliminated.

An important implication of Markov's theory is that the length of time necessary for occupational parity between the races is a function of the transitional matrixes but is in general not influenced by the initial vector (in this case, the current occupational or educational composition of the races).[19] As a consequence, the number of generations

---

[17] *Transformation of the Negro American,* p. 84.

[18] Duncan, "Occupation Trends and Patterns of Net Mobility in the United States."

[19] Thus the time required to reach equilibrium at a given level of precision (say to two decimal places) is determined by the lowest power of the P matrix which has rows with corresponding terms identical to this number of places. Then both the white and Negro distributions are the same as these rows. Except for possible effects of rounding, two initially different distributions should not be equivalent before this point.

necessary for the attainment of racial equality in the absence of discrimination is not at all influenced by the initial occupational or educational handicaps but is purely a function of the fluidity between generations in the society. On the other hand, although the time necessary for equality is not affected, the initial occupational or educational differences between the races determine the magnitude of the racial differences in each generation and therefore the severity of the social problem.

Race and ethnic relations nearly always involve one group enjoying an edge over another in the economic and social spheres. In determining the sources of these advantages, it is necessary to consider both the structural, non-racial factors and the discriminatory factors. Granted that the inferior position occupied by a group may often be a product of current and past discriminations, the effect of this position then becomes independent of its causes. In this sense, we have seen that Negro-white occupational differences would not be eliminated immediately after the demise of discrimination. Indeed, if the United States were a castelike society where all children took up the occupations of their fathers, then the absence of discrimination would *never* lead to occupational equality between the races. On the other hand, if occupational mobility were so open that neither fathers' education nor occupations had any influence on the occupations pursued by their offspring (in other words, the p_{ij} values for different i's were all identical for a given j), then discrimination would be the only means for maintaining occupational differences between the races, and the elimination of one would lead to disappearance of the other in one generation. Thus the differential positions occupied by racial and ethnic groups in society may be viewed as a function of the interaction between discriminatory practices and structural, non-racially based, social processes.

22

Racial integration in the armed forces[1]

CHARLES C. MOSKOS, JR.

On July 28, 1948, President Truman issued an executive order abolishing racial segregation in the armed forces of the United States. By the middle 1950's this policy was an accomplished fact. The lessons of the racial integration of the military are many.

Within a remarkably short period the makeup of a major American institution underwent a far-reaching transformation. At the same time, the desegregation of the military can be used to trace some of the mutual permeations between the internal organization of the mili-

Reprinted from *The American Journal of Sociology*, 1966, **72**, 132–148, by permission of the author and the University of Chicago Press. Copyright © 1967, the University of Chicago Press.

[1] Many persons have given the writer invaluable assistance during his collection and analysis of the materials for this paper. I would especially like to thank Lieutenant Colonel Roger W. Little, U.S. Military Academy, John B. Spore, editor of *Army* magazine, Philip M. Timpane, staff assistant for civil rights, Department of Defense, and Morris Janowitz, University of Chicago. Also, the writer's access to military personnel at all levels was made possible by the more than perfunctory co-operation of numerous

tary establishment and the racial and social cleavages found in the larger setting of American society. Further, because of the favorable contrast in the military performance of integrated Negro servicemen with that of all-Negro units, the integration of the armed services is a demonstration of how changes in social organization can bring about a marked and rapid improvement in individual and group achievement. The desegregated military, moreover, offers itself as a graphic example of the abilities of both whites and Negroes to adjust to egalitarian racial relations with surprisingly little strain. Also, an examination of the racial situation in the contemporary military establishment can serve as a partial guideline as to what one might expect in a racially integrated America. It is to these and related issues that this paper is addressed.[2]

military information officers, men who perform a difficult task with both efficiency and good humor. Financial support was given by the Inter-University Seminar on Armed Forces and Society sponsored by the Russell Sage Foundation. Additional funds for travel were made available by the University of Michigan, and the Council for Intersocietal Studies of Northwestern University. It must be stressed, however, that the usual caveat that the author alone accepts responsibility for the interpretations and conclusions is especially relevant here.

[2] The information on which the observations presented in this paper are based is of a varied sort. A primary source are Department of Defense statistics and those United States government reports dealing with racial relations in the armed forces: President's Committee on Equality of Treatment and Opportunity in the Armed Forces ("Fahy Committee"), *Freedom To Serve: Equality of Treatment and Opportunity in the Armed Forces* (Washington, D.C.: Government Printing Office, 1950); U.S. Commission on Civil Rights, "The Negro in the Armed Forces," *Civil Rights '63* (Washington, D.C.: Government Printing Office, 1963), pp. 169–224; President's Committee on Equal Opportunity in the Armed Forces ("Gesell Committee"), "Initial Report: Equality of Treatment and Opportunity for Negro Personnel Stationed within the United States" (mimeographed; June, 1963), and "Final Report: Military Personnel Stationed Overseas and Membership and Participation in the National Guard" (mimeographed; November, 1964). Also, participant observations were made by the writer while on active duty in the Army and during field trips to military installations in Ger-

DESEGREGATING THE MILITARY[3]

Negroes have taken part in all of this country's wars. An estimated 5,000 Negroes, some scattered as individuals and others in segregated units, fought on the American side in the War of Independence. Several thousand Negroes saw service in the War of 1812. During the Civil War 180,000 Ne-

many, Viet Nam, and Korea in the summer of 1965 and in the Dominican Republic in the spring of 1966. Additionally, during the field trip in Germany, sixty-seven formal interviews were conducted with soldiers who made up nearly all of the total Negro enlisted personnel in two Army companies. Another source of data is found in Operations Research Office ("ORO"), *Project Clear: The Utilization of Negro Manpower in the Army* (Chevy Chase, Md.: Operations Research Office, Johns Hopkins University, April, 1955). The ORO surveys queried several thousand servicemen during the Korean War on a variety of items relating to attitudes toward racial integration in the Army. The findings of Project Clear, heretofore classified, have now been made available for professional scrutiny. Some comparable data were obtained from the section dealing with Negro soldiers in Samuel A. Stouffer *et al.*, *The American Soldier: Adjustment during Army Life,* Vol. I (Princeton, N.J.: Princeton University Press, 1949), pp. 486–599.

[3] This background of the Negro's role in the American military is derived, in addition to the sources cited above, from Seymour J. Schoenfeld, *The Negro in the Armed Forces* (Washington, D.C.: Associated Publishers, 1945); Paul C. Davis, "The Negro in the Armed Services," *Virginia Quarterly,* **XXIV** (Autumn, 1948), 499–520; Herbert Aptheker, *Essays in the History of the American Negro* (New York: International Publishers, 1945); Arnold M. Rose, "Army Policies toward Negro Soldiers," *Annals of the American Academy of Political and Social Science,* **CCXLIV** (March, 1946), 90–94; Eli Ginzburg, "The Negro Soldier," in his *The Negro Potential* (New York: Columbia University Press, 1956), pp. 61–91; David G. Mandelbaum, *Soldiers Groups and Negro Soldiers* (Berkeley: University of California Press, 1952); and Benjamin Quarles, *The Negro in the Making of America* (New York: Collier Books, 1964), *passim*. A good account of the early days of military desegregation is Lee Nichols, *Breakthrough on the Color Front* (New York: Random House, 1954).

Though the last several years have seen little

groes were recruited into the Union army and served in segregated regiments.[4] Following the Civil War four Negro regiments were established and were active in the Indian wars on the Western frontier and later fought with distinction in Cuba during the Spanish-American War. In the early twentieth century, however, owing to a general rise in American racial tensions and specific outbreaks of violence between Negro troops and whites, opinion began to turn against the use of Negro soldiers. Evaluation of Negro soldiers was further lowered by events in World War I. The combat performance of the all-Negro 92nd Infantry, one of its regiments having fled in the German offensive at Meuse-Argonne, came under heavy criticism. Yet it was also observed that Negro units operating under French command, in a more racially tolerant situation, performed well.

---

social science research on racial relations in the armed forces, there has recently been a spate of novels dealing with this theme. See, e.g., John Oliver Killens, *And Then We Heard the Thunder* (New York: Alfred A. Knopf, Inc., 1963); James Drought, *Mover* (New York: Avon Books, 1963); Webb Beech, *Article 92* (Greenwich, Conn.: Gold Medal Books, 1964); Gene L. Coon, *The Short End* (New York: Dell Publishing Co., 1964); Hari Rhodes, *A Chosen Few* (New York: Bantam Books, 1965); and Jack Pearl, *Stockade* (New York: Pocket Books, 1965).

It should be noted that Negroes have not been the only ethnic or racial group to occupy a unique position in the American military. Indians served in separate battalions in the Civil War and were used as scouts in the frontier wars. Filipinos have long been a major source of recruitment for stewards in the Navy. The much decorated 442nd ("Go For Broke") Infantry Regiment of World War II was composed entirely of Japanese-Americans. Also in World War II, a separate battalion of Norwegian-Americans was drawn up for intended service in Scandinavia. The participation of Puerto Ricans in the American military deserves special attention. A recent case of large-scale use of non-American soldiers are the Korean fillers or "Katusas" (from Korean Augumentation to the U.S. Army) who make up roughly one-sixth of the current personnel of the Eighth Army.

[4] A particularly insightful contemporary report on Negro soldiers in the Civil War is Thomas Wentworth Higgins, *Army Life in a Black Regiment* (New York: Collier Books, 1962).

In the interval between the two world wars, the Army not only remained segregated but also adopted a policy of a Negro quota that was to keep the number of Negroes in the Army proportionate to the total population. Never in the pre-World War II period, however, did the number of Negroes approach this quota. On the eve of Pearl Harbor, Negroes constituted 5.9 per cent of the Army; and there were only five Negro officers, three of whom were chaplains. During World War II Negroes entered the Army in larger numbers, but at no time did they exceed 10 per cent of total personnel. Negro soldiers remained in segregated units, and approximately three-quarters served in the quartermaster, engineer, and transportation corps. To make matters worse from the viewpoint of "the right to fight," a slogan loudly echoed by Negro organizations in the United States, even Negro combat units were frequently used for heavy-duty labor. This was highlighted when the 2nd Cavalry was broken up into service units owing to command apprehension over the combat qualities, even though untested, of this all-Negro division. The record of those Negro units that did see combat in World War II was mixed. The performance of the 92nd Infantry Division again came under heavy criticism, this time for alleged unreliability in the Italian campaign.

An important exception to the general pattern of utilization of Negro troops in World War II occurred in the winter months of 1944–45 in the Ardennes battle. Desperate shortages of combat personnel resulted in the Army asking for Negro volunteers. The plan was to have platoons (approximately 40 men) of Negroes serve in companies (approximately 200 men) previously all-white. Some 2,500 Negroes volunteered for this assignment. Both in terms of Negro combat performance and white soldiers' reactions, the Ardennes experiment was an unqualified success. This incident would later be used to support arguments for integration.

After World War II, pressure from Negro and liberal groups coupled with an acknowledgment that Negro soldiers were being poorly utilized led the Army to reexamine its racial policies. A report by an Army board in 1945, while holding racial integration to be a desirable goal and while making recommendations to improve Negro opportunity in the Army, concluded that practical considerations required a maintenance of segregation and the quota system. In light of World War II experiences, the report further recommended that Negro personnel be exclusively assigned to support rather than combat units. Another Army board report came out in 1950 with essentially the same conclusions.[5] Both reports placed heavy stress on the supervisory and disciplinary problems resulting from the disproportionate number of Negroes, as established by Army examinations, found in the lower mental and aptitude classification levels. In 1950, for example, 60 per cent of the Negro personnel fell into the Army's lowest categories compared with 29 per cent of the white soldiers. From the standpoint of the performance requirements of the military, such facts could not be lightly dismissed.

After the Truman desegregation order of 1948, however, the die was cast. The President followed his edict by setting up a committee, chaired by Charles Fahy, to pursue the implementation of equal treatment and opportunity for armed forces personnel. Under the impetus of the Fahy committee, the Army abolished the quota system in 1950, and was beginning to integrate some training camps when the conflict in Korea broke out. The Korean War was the coup de grâce for segregation in the Army. Manpower requirements in the field for combat soldiers resulted in many instances of *ad hoc* integration. As was true in the Ardennes experience, Negro soldiers in previously all-white units performed well in combat. As integration in Korea became more standard, observers consistently noted that the fighting abilities of Negroes differed little from those of whites.[6] This contrasted with the blemished record of the all-Negro 24th Infantry Regiment.[7] Its performance in the Korean War was judged to be so poor

that its divisional commander recommended the unit be dissolved as quickly as possible. Concurrent with events in Korea, integration was introduced in the United States. By 1956, three years after the end of the Korean War, the remnants of Army Jim Crow disappeared at home and in overseas installations. At the time of the Truman order, Negroes constituted 8.8 per cent of Army personnel. In 1964 the figure was 12.3 per cent.

In each of the other services, the history of desegregation varied from the Army pattern. The Army Air Force, like its parent body, generally assigned Negroes to segregated support units. (However, a unique military venture taken during the war was the formation of three all-Negro, including officers, air combat units.) At the end of World War II the proportion of Negroes in the Army Air Force was only 4 per cent, less than half what it was in the Army. Upon its establishment as an independent service in 1947, the Air Force began to take steps toward integration even before the Truman order. By the time of the Fahy committee report in 1950, the Air Force was already largely integrated. Since integration there has been a substantial increase in the proportion of Negroes serving in the Air Force, from less than 5 per cent in 1949 to 8.6 per cent in 1964.

Although large numbers of Negroes had served in the Navy during the Civil War and for some period afterward, restrictive policies were introduced in the early 1900's, and by the end of World War I only about 1 per cent of Navy personnel were Negroes. In 1920 the Navy adopted a policy of total racial exclusion and barred all Negro enlistments. This policy was changed in 1932 when Negroes, along with Filipinos, were again allowed to join the Navy but only as stewards in the messman's branch. Further modifications were made in Navy policy in 1942 when some openings in general service for Negroes were created. Negro sailors in these positions, however, were limited to segregated harbor and shore assignments.[8]

---

[5] The 1945 and 1950 Army board reports are commonly referred to by the names of the officers who headed these boards: respectively, Lieutenant General Alvan C. Gillem, Jr., and Lieutenant General S. J. Chamberlin.

[6] These evaluations are summarized in ORO, *Project Clear,* pp. 16–19, 47–105, and 582–83.

[7] The notoriety of the 24th Infantry Regiment was aggravated by a song—"The Bug-Out Boogie"—attributed to it: "When them Chinese mortars begin to thud / The old Deuce-Four

begin to bug / When they started falling 'round the CP [command post] tent / Everybody wonder where the high brass went / They were buggin' out / Just movin' on."

[8] A lesson in the rewriting of history is gained from the movie *PT-109,* a dramatization of

In 1944, in the first effort toward desegregation in any of the armed services, a small number of Negro sailors in general service were integrated on ocean-going vessels. After the end of World War II the Navy, again ahead of the other services, began to take major steps toward elimination of racial barriers. Even in the integrated Navy of today, however, approximately a quarter of Negro personnel still serve as stewards. Also, despite the early steps toward integration taken by the Navy, the proportion of Negro sailors has remained fairly constant over the past two decades, averaging around 5 per cent.

The Marine Corps has gone from a policy of exclusion to segregation to integration. Before World War II there were no Negro marines. In 1942 Negroes were accepted into the Marine Corps but assigned to segregated units where they were heavy-duty laborers, ammunition handlers, and anti-aircraft gunners. After the war small-scale integration of Negro marines into white units was begun. In 1949 and 1950 Marine Corps training units were integrated, and by 1954 the color line was largely erased throughout the Corps. Since integration began, the proportion of Negroes has increased markedly. In 1949 less than 2 per cent of all marines were Negroes compared with 8.2 per cent in 1964.

Although the various military services are all similar in being integrated today, they differ in their proportion of Negroes. As shown in Table 1, the Negro distribution in

the total armed forces in 1962 and 1964, respectively, was 8.2 per cent and 9.0 per cent, lower than the 11–12 per cent constituting the Negro population in the total population. It is virtually certain, however, that among those *eligible*, a higher proportion of Negroes than whites enter the armed forces. That is, a much larger number of Negroes do not meet the entrance standards required by the military services. In 1962, for example, 56.1 per cent of Negroes did not pass the preinduction mental examinations given to draftees, almost four times the 15.4 per cent of whites who failed these same tests.[9] Because of the relatively low number of Negroes obtaining student or occupational deferments, however, it is the Army drawing upon the draft that is the only military service where the percentage of Negroes approximates the national proportion. Thus, despite the high number of Negroes who fail to meet induction standards, Army statistics for 1960–65 show Negroes constituted about 15 per cent of those drafted.

Even if one takes account of the Army's reliance on the selective service for much of its personnel, the most recent figures still show important differences in the number of Negroes in those services meeting their manpower requirements solely through voluntary enlistments; the 5.1 per cent Negro in the Navy is lower than the 8.2 per cent for the Marine Corps or the 8.6 per cent for the Air Force. Moreover, the Army, besides its drawing upon the draft, also has the highest Negro initial enlistment rate of any of the services. As reported in Table 2, we find in 1964 that the Army drew 14.1 per cent of its volunteer incoming personnel from Negroes

TABLE 1 Negroes in the Armed Forces and Each Service as a Percentage of Total Personnel, 1962 and 1964

Service	1962	1964
Army	11.1	12.3
Air Force	7.8	8.6
Navy	4.7	5.1
Marine Corps	7.0	8.2
Total armed forces	8.2	9.0

Source: U.S. Commission on Civil Rights, "The Negro in the Armed Forces," p. 218; Department of Defense statistics.

TABLE 2 Negroes in Each of the Armed Services as a Percentage of Initial Enlistments 1961, 1963, and 1965

Year	Army	Air Force	Navy	Marine Corps
1961	8.2	9.5	2.9	5.9
1963	11.2	10.5	4.3	5.5
1965	14.1	13.1	5.8	8.4

Source: Department of Defense statistics.

[9] Department of Labor ("Moynihan Report"), *The Negro Family: The Case for National Action* (Washington, D.C.: Government Printing Office, 1965), p. 75.

John Kennedy's war exploits. In this film, released in the early 1960's, the Navy is portrayed as racially integrated in World War II.

as compared with 13.1 per cent for the Air Force, 8.4 per cent for the Marine Corps, and 5.8 per cent for the Navy. As also shown in Table 2, there has been a very sizable increase in Negro enlistments from 1961 to 1965 in all four of the armed services.

There are also diverse patterns between the individual services as to the rank or grade distribution of Negroes. Looking at Table 3, we find the ratio of Negro to white officers is roughly 1 to 30 in the Army, 1 to 70 in the Air Force, 1 to 250 in the Marine Corps, and 1 to 300 in the Navy. Among enlisted men, Negroes are underrepresented in the top three enlisted ranks in the Army and the top four ranks in the other three services. We also find a disproportionate concentration of Negroes in the lower noncommissioned officer ranks in all of the armed forces, but especially so in the Army. An assessment of these data reveals that the Army, followed by the Air Force, has not only the largest proportion of Negroes in its total personnel, but also the most equitable distribution of Negroes throughout its ranks. Although the Navy was the first service to integrate and the Army the last, in a kind of tortoise and hare fashion, it is the Army that has become the most representative service for Negroes.

TABLE 3 Negroes as a Percentage of Total Personnel in Each Grade for Each Service, 1964

Grade	Army	Air Force	Navy	Marine Corps
Officers:				
Generals/ admirals		0.2		
Colonels/ captains	0.2	0.2		
Lt. cols./ commanders	1.1	0.5	0.6	
Majors/ lt.commanders	3.6	0.8	0.3	0.3
Captains/ lieutenants	5.4	2.0	0.5	0.4
1st lieutenants/ lts. (j.g.)	3.8	1.8	0.2	0.4
2d lieutenants/ ensigns	2.7	2.5	0.7	0.3
Total officers	3.4	1.5	0.3	0.4
Enlisted:*				
E-9 (sgt. major)	3.5	1.2	1.5	0.8
E-8 (master sgt.)	6.1	2.2	1.9	1.2
E-7 (sgt. 1st class)	8.5	3.2	2.9	2.3
E-6 (staff sgt.)	13.9	5.3	4.7	5.0
E-5 (sgt.)	17.4	10.8	6.6	11.2
E-4 (corp.)	14.2	12.7	5.9	10.4
E-3 (pvt. 1st class)	13.6	9.7	6.6	7.8
E-2 (private)	13.1	11.7	5.7	9.5
E-1 (recruit)	6.8	14.4	7.1	9.1
Total enlisted men	13.4	10.0	5.8	8.7

* Army and Marine Corps enlisted titles indicated in parentheses have equivalent pay grades in Navy and Air Force.
Source: Department of Defense statistics.

CHANGING MILITARY REQUIREMENTS AND NEGRO OPPORTUNITIES

A pervasive trend within the military establishment singled out by students of this institution is the long-term direction toward greater technical complexity and narrowing of civilian-military occupational skills.[10] An indicator, albeit a crude one, of this trend toward "professionalization" of military roles is the changing proportion of men assigned to combat arms. Given in Table 4, along with

TABLE 4 Total Negro Army Enlisted Personnel and White and Negro Enlisted Personnel in Combat Arms, 1945 and 1962

Category	1945*	1962
Negroes as percentage of total personnel	10.5	12.2
Percentage of total personnel in combat arms	44.5	26.0
Percentage of total white personnel in combat arms	48.2	24.9
Percentage of total Negro personnel in combat arms	12.1	33.4

* Excludes Army Air Force.
Source: ORO, *Project Clear,* pp. 563–64; U.S. Civil Rights Commission, "The Negro in the Armed Forces," pp. 219–22.

[10] Morris Janowitz with Roger Little, *Sociology and the Military Establishment* (New York: Russell Sage Foundation, 1965), pp. 17–49; and Kurt Lang, "Technology and Career Management in the Military Establishment," in Morris Janowitz (Ed.), *The New Military: Changing Patterns of Organization* (New York: Russell Sage Foundation, 1964), pp. 39–81.

concomitant white-Negro distributions, are figures comparing the percentage of Army enlisted personnel in combat arms (e.g., infantry, armor, artillery) for the years 1945 and 1962. We find that the proportion of men in combat arms—that is, traditional military specialties—dropped from 44.5 per cent in 1945 to 26.0 per cent in 1962. Also, the percentage of white personnel in traditional military specialties approximates the total proportional decrease in the combat arms over the seventeen-year period.

For Negro soldiers, however, a different picture emerges. While the percentage of Negro enlisted men in the Army increased only slightly between 1945 and 1962, the likelihood of a Negro serving in a combat arm is almost three times greater in 1962 than it was at the end of World War II. Further, when comparisons are made between military specialties *within* the combat arms, the Negro proportion is noticeably higher in line rather than staff assignments. This is especially the case in airborne and marine units. Put in another way, the direction in assignment of Negro soldiers in the desegregated military is testimony to the continuing consequences of differential Negro opportunity originating in the larger society. That is, even though integration of the military has led to great improvement in the performance of Negro servicemen, the social and particularly educational deprivations suffered by the Negro in American society can be mitigated but not entirely eliminated by the racial egalitarianism existing within the armed forces.[11] These findings need not be interpreted as a decline in the "status" of the Negro in the integrated military. Actually there is evidence that higher prestige—but not envy—is accorded combat personnel by those in non-combat activities within the military.[12] And taken within the historical

context of "the right to fight," the Negro's overrepresentation in the combat arms is a kind of ironic step forward.[13]

Moreover, the military at the enlisted ranks has become a major avenue of career mobility for many Negro men.[14] As shown earlier in Table 3, in all four services, and especially in the Army, there is some overrepresentation of Negroes at the junior NCO levels (pay grades E-4–E-6). The disproportionate concentration of Negroes at these levels implies a higher than average re-enlistment as these grades are not normally attained until after a second enlistment. This assumption is supported by the data given in Table 5. We find that in 1964 for all four services the Negro reenlistment rate is approximately twice that of white servicemen. Indeed, about half of all first-term Negro servicemen chose to remain in the armed

TABLE 5 First-Term Re-enlistment Rates in the Armed Forces and Each Service by Race, 1964 (Per Cent)

Race	Total Armed Forces	Army	Air Force	Navy	Marine Corps
White	21.6	18.5	27.4	21.6	12.9
Negro	46.6	49.3	50.3	41.3	25.3

Source: Department of Defense statistics.

---

[11] World War II evidence shows much of the incidence of psychoneurotic breakdown among Negro soldiers, compared to whites, was associated with psychological handicaps originating before entrance into military service (Arnold M. Rose, "Psychoneurotic Breakdown among Negro Soldiers," *Phylon*, **XVII**, No. 1 [1956] pp. 61–73).

[12] Stouffer *et al., The American Soldier,* **II,** 242–89; Raymond W. Mack, "The Prestige System of an Air Base: Squadron Rankings and Morale," *American Sociological Review,* **XIX**

(June, 1954), 281–87; Morris Janowitz, *The Professional Soldier* (Glencoe, Ill.: Free Press, 1960), pp. 31–36.

[13] There are, as should be expected, differences among Negro soldiers as to their desire to see combat. From data not shown here, interviews with Negro soldiers stationed in Germany revealed reluctance to go to Viet Nam was greatest among those with high-school or better education, and northern home residence. This is in direct contrast with the findings reported in *The American Soldier.* In the segregated Army of World War II, northern and more highly educated Negro soldiers were most likely to want to get into combat, an outcome of the onus of inferiority felt to accompany service in support units (Stouffer, *The American Soldier,* **I,** 523–24).

[14] The emphasis on academic education for officer careers effectively limits most Negro opportunity to the enlisted levels (Lang, "Technology and Career Management in the Military Establishment," p. 62).

forces for at least a second term. The greater likelihood of Negroes to select a service career suggests that the military establishment is undergoing a significant change in its NCO core. Such an outcome would reflect not only the "pull" of the appeals offered by a racially egalitarian institution, but also the "push" generated by the plight of the Negro in the American economy.[15] At the minimum, it is very probable that as the present cohort of Negro junior NCO's attains seniority there will be a greater representation of Negroes in the advanced NCO grades. The expansion of the armed forces arising from the war in Vietnam and the resulting opening up of "rank" will accelerate this development.

ATTITUDES OF SOLDIERS

So far the discussion has sought to document the degree of penetration and the kind of distribution characterizing Negro servicemen in the integrated military establishment. We now introduce certain survey and interview data dealing more directly with the question of soldiers' attitudes toward military desegregation. Commenting on the difficulties of social analysis, the authors of *The American Soldier* wrote that few problems are "more formidable than that of obtaining dependable records of attitudes toward racial separation in the Army."[16] Without underestimating the continuing difficulty of this problem, an opportunity exists to compare attitudes toward racial integration held by American soldiers in two different periods. This is done by contrasting responses to equivalent items given in World War II as reported in *The American Soldier* with those reported in Project Clear a study sponsored by the Defense Department during the Korean War.[17]

[15] Documentation shows the gap between Negro and white job opportunities has not diminished appreciably, if at all, in the past twenty years (Department of Labor, *The Negro Family*, pp. 19–21; Thomas F. Pettigrew, *A Profile of the Negro American* [Princeton, N.J.: D. Van Nostrand Co., 1964], pp. 168–74).

[16] Stouffer *et al., The American Soldier*, p. 566.

[17] What methodological bias exists is that the Korean War question was a stronger description of racial integration than the item used in

In both *The American Soldier* and Project Clear (the surveys under consideration were conducted in 1943 and 1951, respectively) large samples of Army personnel in segregated military settings were categorized as to whether they were favorable, indifferent, or opposed to racial integration in Army units. We find, as presented in Table 6, mas-

TABLE 6 Attitudes of White and Negro Soldiers toward Racial Integration in the Segregated Army, 1943 and 1951

Attitude toward Integration	White Soldiers (Per Cent)		Negro Soldiers (Per Cent)	
	1943	*1951*	*1943*	*1951*
Favorable	12	25	37	90
Indifferent	4	31	27	6
Oppose	84	44	36	4
Total	100	100	100	100
(No. of cases)	(4,800)	(1,983)	(3,000)	(1,384)

Source: Stouffer *et al., The American Soldier*, p. 568; ORO, *Project Clear*, pp. 322, 433.

sive shifts in soldiers' attitudes over the eight-year period, shifts showing a much more positive disposition toward racial integration among both whites and Negroes in the later year. A look at the distribution of attitudes held by white soldiers reveals opposition to integration goes from 84 per cent in 1943 to less than half in 1951. That such a change could occur in less than a decade counters viewpoints that see basic social attitudes in large populations being prone to glacial-like changes. Yet, an even more remarkable change is found among the Negro soldiers. Where in 1945, favorable, indifferent, or opposing attitudes were roughly equally distributed among the Negro soldiers,

World War II. Compare "What is your feeling about serving in a platoon containing both whites and colored soldiers, all working and training together, sleeping in the same barracks and eating in the same mess hall?" with "Do you think white and Negro soldiers should be in separate outfits or should they be together in the same outfits?" (respectively, ORO, *Project Clear*, p. 453, and Stouffer *et al., The American Soldier*, p. 568).

TABLE 7 Attitudes of Negro Soldiers in 1965 Comparing Racial Equality in Military and Civilian Life, Total and by Home Region

Where More Racial Equality	Per Cent		
		Home Region	
	Total	North	South
Military life	84	75	93
Civilian life	3	6	0
No difference	13	19	7
Total	100	100	100
(No. of cases)	(67)	(36)	(31)

by 1951 opposition or indifference to racial integration had become negligible. Such a finding is strongly indicative of a reformation in Negro public opinion from traditional acquiescence to Jim Crow to the ground swell that laid the basis for the subsequent civil rights movement.

ing deviations from military policy at the level of informal discrimination, the military establishment stands in sharp and favorable contrast to the racial relations prevalent in the larger American society.

One of the most celebrated findings of *The American Soldier* was the discovery that the more contact white soldiers had with Negro troops, the more favorable was their reaction toward racial integration.[18] This conclusion is consistently supported in the surveys conducted by Project Clear. Again and again, comparisons of white soldiers in integrated units with those in segregated units show the former to be more supportive of desegregation. Illustrative of this pattern are the data shown in Table 8. Among combat infantrymen in Korea, 51 per cent in all-white units say outfits are better segregated as compared to 31 per cent in integrated units. For enlisted personnel stationed in the United States, strong objection to integration characterizes 44 per cent serving in segregated

TABLE 8 Racial Attitudes of White Soldiers in Segregated and Integrated Settings, 1951

Racial Attitudes	All-White Units		Integrated Units	
	Per Cent	No.	Per Cent	No.
Combat infantrymen in Korea saying segregated outfits better	51	(195)	31	(1,024)
Enlisted personnel in the U.S. strongly objecting to racial integration	44	(1,983)	17	(1,683)
Officers rating Negroes worse than white soldiers	79	(233)	28	(385)

Source: ORO, *op. cit.*, pp. 141, 322, 333, 356.

While the data on Negro attitudes toward integration given in Table 6 were elicited during the segregated military of 1943 and 1951, we also have evidence on how Negro soldiers react to military integration in the contemporary setting. As reported in Table 7, the Army is overwhelmingly thought to be more racially egalitarian than civilian life. Only 16 per cent of sixty-seven Negro soldiers interviewed in 1965 said civilian life was more racially equal or no different than the Army. By region, as might be expected, we find southern Negroes more likely than northern Negroes to take a benign view of racial relations in the Army when these are compared to civilian life. The data in Table 7 support the proposition that, despite exist-

units while less than one-fifth of the men in integrated units feel the same way. Seventy-nine per cent of officers on segregated posts rate Negroes worse than white soldiers as compared with 28 per cent holding similar beliefs on integrated posts.

OFFICIAL POLICY AND ACTUAL PRACTICE

For the man newly entering the armed forces, it is hard to conceive that the military was one of America's most segregated institutions less than two decades ago. For today

[18] Stouffer *et al.*, p. 594.

color barriers at the formal level are absent throughout the military establishment. Equal treatment regardless of race is official policy in such non-duty facilities as swimming pools, chapels, barbershops, post exchanges, movie theaters, snack bars, and dependents' housing as well as in the more strictly military endeavors involved in the assignment, promotion, and living conditions of members of the armed services.[19] Moreover, white personnel are often commanded by Negro superiors, a situation rarely obtaining in civilian life. Recently the military has sought to implement its policy of equal opportunity by exerting pressure on local communities where segregated patterns affect military personnel. This policy deserves careful examination owing to its ramifications on the traditional separation of civilian and military spheres in American society. A measure of the extent and thoroughness of military desegregation is found in comparing the 1950 President's committee report dealing with racial integration and the 1963 and 1964 reports of a second President's committee. Where the earlier report dealt entirely with internal military organization, the recent reports address themselves primarily to the National Guard and off-base discrimination.[20] Along this same line, Congressman Adam Clayton Powell has said that up to the middle 1950's he used to receive 5,000 letters a year from Negro servicemen complaining of discrimination in the military. In recent years, he receives less than 1,500 such letters annually and these largely pertain to off-base problems.[21] In brief, military life is characterized by an interracial equalitarianism of a quantity and of a kind that is seldom found in the other major institutions of American society.

In their performance of military duties, whites and Negroes work together with little display of racial tension. This is not to say racial animosity is absent in the military. Racial incidents do occur, but these are reduced by the severe sanctions imposed by the military for such acts. Such confrontations are almost always off-duty, if not off-base. In no sense, however, is the military sitting on top of a racial volcano, a state of affairs differing from the frequent clashes between the races that were a feature of the military in the segregated era. Additionally, it must be stressed that conflict situations stemming from non-racial causes characterize most sources of friction in the military establishment, for example, enlisted men versus officers, lower-ranking enlisted men versus non-commissioned officers, soldiers of middle-class background versus those of the working-class, conscriptees versus volunteers, line units versus staff units, rear echelon versus front echelon, combat units versus non-combat units, newly arrived units versus earlier stationed units, etc.

Yet the fact remains that the general pattern of day-to-day relationships *off the job* is usually one of mutual racial exclusivism. As one Negro soldier put it, "A man can be my best buddy in the Army, but he won't ask me to go to town with him." Closest friendships normally develop within races between individuals of similar educational background. Beyond one's hard core of friends there exists a level of friendly acquaintances. Here the pattern seems to be one of educational similarities overriding racial differences. On the whole, racial integration at informal as well as formal levels works best on-duty vis-à-vis off-duty, on-base vis-à-vis off-base, basic training and maneuvers vis-à-vis garrison, sea vis-à-vis shore duty, and combat vis-à-vis non-combat. In other words, the behavior of servicemen resembles the racial (and class) separatism of the larger American society, the more they are removed from the military environment.

For nearly all white soldiers the military is a first experience with close and equal contact with a large group of Negroes. There has developed what has become practically a

---

[19] The comprehensive scope of military integration is found in the official guidelines set forth under "Equal Opportunity and Treatment of Military Personnel," in *Army Regulation 600-21, Air Force Regulation 35-78,* and *Secretary of the Navy Instruction 5350.6.*

[20] Cf. the Fahy committee report (1950), with the Gesell committee reports (1963 and 1964). The Moynihan Report comments, "Service in the United States Armed Forces is the only experience open to the Negro American in which he is truly treated as an equal. . . . If this is a statement of the ideal rather than reality, it is an ideal that is close to realization" (Department of Labor, *The Negro Family,* p. 42).

[21] In an interview with the *Overseas Weekly,* a newspaper published in Germany with a large readership among American servicemen. Personal communication with staff members.

military custom: the look over the shoulder, upon the telling of a racial joke, to see if there are any Negroes in hearing distance. Some racial animosity is reflected in accusations that Negro soldiers use the defense of racial discrimination to avoid disciplinary action. Many white soldiers claim they like Negroes as individuals but "can't stand them in bunches." In a few extreme cases, white married personnel may even live off the military base and pay higher rents rather than live in integrated military housing. On the whole, however, the segregationist-inclined white soldier regards racial integration as something to be accepted pragmatically, if not enthusiastically, as are so many situations in military life.

The most overt source of racial unrest in the military community centers in dancing situations. A commentary on American mores is a finding reported in Project Clear: three-quarters of a large sample of white soldiers said they would not mind Negro couples on the same dance floor, but approximately the same number disapproved of Negro soldiers dancing with white girls.[22] In many non-commissioned officer (NCO) clubs, the likelihood of interracial dancing partners is a constant producer of tension. In fact, the only major exception to integration within the military community is on a number of large posts where there are two or more NCO clubs. In such situations one of the clubs usually becomes tacitly designated as the Negro club.

Although there is almost universal support for racial integration by Negro soldiers, some strains are also evident among Negro personnel in the military. There seems to be a tendency among lower-ranking Negro enlisted men, especially conscriptees, to view Negro NCO's as "Uncle Toms" or "hand-kerchief heads." Negro NCO's are alleged to pick on Negroes when it comes time to assign men unpleasant duties. Negro officers are sometimes seen as being too strict or "chicken" when it comes to enforcing military discipline on Negro soldiers. As one Negro serviceman said, "I'm proud when I see a Negro officer, but not in my company."

One Negro writer, who served in the segregated Army and now has two sons in the integrated military, has proposed that

what was thought by soldiers in all-Negro units to be racial discrimination was sometimes nothing more than harassment of lower-ranking enlisted personnel.[23] In fact, the analogy between enlisted men vis-à-vis officers in the military and Negroes vis-à-vis whites in the larger society has often been noted.[24] It has been less frequently observed, however, that enlisted men's behavior is often similar to many of the stereotypes associated with Negroes, for example, laziness, boisterousness, emphasis on sexual prowess, consciously acting stupid, obsequiousness in front of superiors combined with ridicule of absent superiors, etc. Placement of white adult males in a subordinate position within a rigidly stratified system, that is, appears to produce behavior not all that different from the so-called personality traits commonly held to be an outcome of cultural or psychological patterns unique to Negro life. Indeed, it might be argued that relatively little adjustment on the part of the command structure was required when the infusion of Negroes into the enlisted ranks occurred as the military establishment was desegregated. It is suggested, in other words, one factor contributing to the generally smooth racial integration of the military might be due to the standard treatment—"like Negroes" in a sense—accorded to all lower-ranking enlisted personnel.

Looking at changes in Negro behavior in the integrated military we find other indications of the immediate effects of social organization on individual behavior. Even though I am fully cognizant of the almost insurmountable difficulties involved in comparing crime statistics, the fact remains that students of the problem agree Negro crime is far higher than white crime.[25] There is no con-

---

[23] James Anderson, "Fathers and Sons: An Evaluation of Military Racial Relations in Two Generations" (term paper, University of Michigan, December, 1965).

[24] Stouffer and his associates, for example, report enlisted men as compared to officers, as Negro soldiers to white soldiers, were more prone to have "low spirits," to be less desirous of entering combat, and to be more dissatisfied than perceived by others (Stouffer *et al., The American Soldier,* **II,** 345, and **I,** 392–94, 506, 521, and 538.

[25] Marvin E. Wolfgang, *Crime and Race* (New York: Institute of Human Relations Press, 1964); and Department of Labor, *The Negro Family,* pp. 38–40.

[22] ORO, *Project Clear,* p. 388.

sensus, however, on what amount of the difference is due, on the one hand, to Negro cultural or psychological conditions or, on the other, to structural and class variables. Presented here, in a very preliminary fashion, is some evidence bearing on the consequences arising from changes in social organization on Negro crime. Reported by Project Clear are Negro-white crime differentials for three segregated posts in 1950. Proportionately, Negro soldiers committed four times more crime than white soldiers.[26] In 1964, in the integrated military, statistics of a major Army Command in Europe show Negroes accounting for 21 per cent of the crime while constituting 16 per cent of the total personnel. In a large combat unit in Viet Nam, for a three-month period in the summer of 1965, Negroes received 19 per cent of the disciplinary reports but made up 22 per cent of the troop assignment. These are the only Negro-white crime ratios in the integrated military that the writer has seen.[27] Although these findings, of course, are incomplete, they do point to a marked drop in Negro crime as compared with both the earlier segregated military as well as contemporary civilian life.[28]

THE NEGRO SOLDIER OVERSEAS

Some special remarks are needed concerning Negro servicemen overseas. Suffice it to say for prefatory purposes, the American soldier, be he either white or Negro, is usually in a place where he does not understand the language, is received with mixed feelings by the local population, spends the greater

---

[26] ORO, *Project Clear*, p. 354.

[27] The data reported here are from offices of the Military Police, private communication.

[28] A caution to be introduced in assessing these findings is that the Army discharged many personnel of limited potential as determined by aptitude tests in 1957–58. Negroes were disproportionately represented in the released personnel (U.S. Commission on Civil Rights, "The Negro in the Armed Forces," pp. 176–77). Although Negroes are still overrepresented in the lower classification levels, there are probably proportionately fewer in these categories today than in 1950, and this most likely has some effect on the drop in Negro crime in the Army.

part of his time in a transplanted American environment, sometimes plays the role of tourist, is relatively affluent in relation to the local economy, takes advantage and is at the mercy of a *comprador* class, and in comparison with his counterpart at home is more heavily involved in military duties.

In general, the pattern of racial relations observed in the United States—integration in the military setting and racial exclusivism off-duty—prevails in overseas assignments as well. This norm is reflected in one of the most characteristic features of American military life overseas, a bifurcation of the vice structure into groups that pander almost exclusively (or assert they do) to only one of the races. A frequent claim of local bar owners is that they discourage racially mixed trade because of the demands of their G.I. clientele. And, indeed, many of the establishments catering to American personnel that ring most military installations are segregated in practice. To a similar degree this is true of shore towns where Navy personnel take liberty. Violation of these implicit taboos can lead to physical threat if not violence.

The pattern of off-duty racial separatism is most pronounced in Japan and Germany, and less so in Korea. A major exception to this norm is found in the Dominican Republic. There all troops are restricted and leaving the military compound necessitates soldiers collaborating if they are not to be detected; such ventures are often as not interracial. In certain off-duty areas on Okinawa, on the other hand, racial separatism is complicated by interservice rivalries and a fourfold ecological pattern shows up: white-Army, Negro-Army, white-Marine Corps, and Negro-Marine Corps. Combat conditions in Viet Nam make the issue of off-duty racial relations academic for those troops in the field. In the cities, however, racial separatism off-duty is already apparent. It is said that the riverfront district in Saigon, Kanh Hoi, frequented by American Negro soldiers was formerly patronized by Senegalese troops during the French occupation.

In Germany one impact of that country's economic boom has been to depress the relative position of the American soldier vis-à-vis the German working man. In the German of ten or fifteen years ago (or the Korea of today) all American military personnel were

affluent by local standards with all that implied. This was (and is in Korea) an especially novel experience for the Negro soldier.
The status drop of American soldiers stationed in Germany has particularly affected
the Negro serviceman, who has the additional
handicap of being black in a country where
there are no Negro girls. The old "good
duty" days for Negro soldiers in Germany
are now coming to an end as he finds his
previous access to girls other than prostitutes
severely reduced. The German economic
boom has affected Negro soldiers in another
way. In recent years there has been some
friction between foreign laborers (mostly
Mediterranean) and Negro soldiers. Both
groups of men apparently are competing for
the same girls. At the same time, the foreign
workers have little contact with white American soldiers who move in a different segment
of the vice structure.

Nonetheless, overseas duty for the Negro
serviceman, in Germany as well as the Far
East, gives him an opportunity, even if peripheral, to witness societies where racial
discrimination is less practiced than it is in
his home country. Although the level of
Negro acceptance in societies other than
America is usually exaggerated, the Negro
soldier is hard put not to make invidious
comparisons with the American scene.[29]
In interviews conducted with Negro servicemen in Germany, 64 per cent said there
was more racial equality in Germany than
America, 30 per cent saw little difference
between the two countries, and only 6 per
cent believed Negroes were treated better
in the United States.

Observers of overseas American personnel have told the writer that Negro soldiers
are more likely than whites to learn local
languages (though for both groups of servicemen this is a very small number). Evidence for this supposition is given in Table
9. Three German-national barbers, who
were permanently hired to cut the hair of
all the men in one battalion, were asked
by the writer to evaluate the German lan-

TABLE 9 Command of German Language by
White and Negro Soldiers in a German-Based
U.S. Army Battalion, 1965

	Per Cent	
*Command of German**	*White Soldiers*	*Negro Soldiers*
Conversational	1.4	7.4
Some	3.0	7.4
Little or none	95.6	85.2
Total	100.0	100.0
(No. of cases)	(629)	(98)

* Based on evaluations of German-national battalion
employees.

guage proficiency of the individual personnel in that battalion.[30] When these evaluations were correlated with race, it was
found that Negro soldiers were five times
more likely to know "conversational" German, and three times more likely to know
"some" German than were white soldiers.[31]
Actually, the likelihood of Negro soldiers
compared to whites in learning the language of the country in which they are
stationed may be even greater than indicated in Table 9. Several of the German-
speaking white soldiers were of German
ethnic background and acquired some
knowledge of the language in their home
environments back in the United States.
These data testify, then, that the Negro
soldiers overseas, perhaps because of the
more favorable racial climate, are more
willing to take advantage of participation
at informal levels with local populations.[32]

[29] A social-distance study conducted among
Korean college students found the following
placement, from near to far: Chinese, Europeans
and white Americans, Filipinos, Indians (from
India), and Negroes (Man Gap Lee, Seoul National University, personal communication).

[30] These barbers were focal points of much of
the battalion's gossip and between themselves
saw every man in the battalion on the average
of at least twice a month.

[31] The same data, in tables not shown here,
reveal that there is an *inverse* correlation between formal education (as ascertained from
battalion personnel records) and likelihood of
learning German! This reflects the greater likelihood of Negro soldiers, compared to whites,
to learn German while averaging fewer years of
formal education.

[32] In 1965 a widely seen German television
commercial portrayed two American soldiers,
one white and the other Negro. Only the Negro
soldier spoke German.

CIVIL RIGHTS AT HOME AND WAR ABROAD

It is important to remember that the military establishment was desegregated before the current civil rights drive gained momentum. In the segregated military, embroilments between Negro units and whites were an ever present problem. In the light of subsequent developments in the domestic racial picture, it is likely that severe disciplinary problems would have occurred had military integration not come about when it did. The timing of desegregation in the military defused an ingredient—all-Negro military units—that would have been potentially explosive in this nation's current racial strife.[33]

It is also probable, however, that military experience contributes to an activist posture on the part of Negro servicemen returning to civilian life. The Negro ex-serviceman, that is, may be less willing to accommodate himself to second-class citizenship after participation in the racially egalitarian military establishment. Further, especially in situations where Negroes are intimidated by physical threat or force, techniques of violence and organizational skill acquired in military service may be a new factor in the Negro's quest for equality. Robert F. Williams, the leading advocate of armed self-defense for Negroes, explicitly states that his Marine Corps experience led to his beliefs.[34] It also seems more than coincidence that the ten founders of the Deacons for Defense and Justice, a paramilitary group organized in 1964 to counter Ku Klux Klan terrorism, were all veterans of Korea or World War II.[35]

[33] Although non-violence is the hallmark of the main thrust of the modern civil rights movement, there is, nevertheless, the leitmotiv of a Negro insurrection in the thinking of such Negro figures as James Baldwin, Malcolm X, William Epton, Warren Miller, and LeRoi Jones. Congruent with the idea of armed conflict between the races are the gothic endings—whites and Negro soldiers engaging in a bloodbath—in recent Negro-authored novels (see Killens, *And Then We Heard the Thunder,* and Rhodes, *A Chosen Few*).

[34] Robert F. Williams, *Negroes with Guns* (New York: Marzani & Munsell, 1962).

[35] *The Militant,* November 22, 1965, p. 1.

One must also take into account the possible consequences of the civil rights movement on Negro military behavior. Much attention has been given to a convergence of an important segment of the civil rights movement with the movement against the was in Vietnam. The Student Nonviolent Coordinating Committee has formally denounced American action in Viet Nam as aggression. Civil rights organizers claim they find Negroes who do not want to fight "whitey's war." A Negro is barred from taking his seat in the Georgia legislature because he condones violations of the draft law. Rumors are heard of isolated incidents of Negro insubordination in the armed services. Despite this chain of events, however, the main stream of the civil rights drive has remained largely removed from those groups highly critical of this country's recent military policies. Indeed, the antiwar movement will likely aggravate an already existing cleavage between moderate and radical leaders—between those who accept versus those who reject the legitimacy of the American political system—in the civil rights movement itself. The more pertinent question at this time appears to be not what are the implications of the civil rights movement for the military establishment, but what will be the effects of the Vietnam war on the civil rights movement itself. Although it would be premature to offer a definitive statement on any future interpenetrations between the civil rights and antiwar movements, a major turning away of Negroes per se from military commitment is viewed as highly doubtful. Most likely, and somewhat paradoxically, we will witness more vocal antiwar sentiment within certain civil rights organizations at the same time that the military is becoming an avenue of career opportunity for many Negro men.

Nevertheless, there has usually been and is today a presumption on the part of America's military opponents that Negroes should be less committed soldiers than whites. Whether for tactical or ideological reasons, the Negro serviceman has been frequently defined as a special target for propaganda by forces opposing America in military conflicts. In World War II the Japanese directed radio appeals specifically to Negro servicemen in the Pacific theater. The Chinese in the Korean War used racial arguments on Negro prisoners of war. Yet a careful study of American POW behavior in Korea made no mention of differences in Negro and white behavior except to note that the segregation of Negro POW's by the Chinese had a boomerang effect on Communist indoctrination methods.[36]

The current military involvement of the United States on the international scene raises again the question of the motivation and performance of Negro soldiers in combat. A spokesman for the National Liberation Front of South Vietnam has recently asserted that "liberation forces have a special attitude toward American soldiers who happen to be Negroes."[37] Up to now at least, however, efforts to test the loyalty of Negro soldiers have not met with success. This writer, as well as others, detected no differences in white or Negro combat performance in Vietnam.[38] In the Dominican Republic, where the proportion of Negroes in line units runs as high as 40 per cent, a pamphlet was distributed to Negro soldiers exhorting them to "turn your guns on your white oppressors and join your Dominican brothers."[39] Again, personal observation buttressed by comments from Dominicans revealed no significant differences between white and Negro military performance.[40]

[36] Albert D. Biderman, *March to Calumny* (New York: Macmillan Co., 1964), p. 60.

[37] *The Minority of One,* October, 1965, p. 9.

[38] "Only One Color," *Newsweek,* December 6, 1965, pp. 42–43; Robin Moore, *The Green Berets* (New York: Avon Books, 1965), *passim;* and Herbert Mitgang, "Looking for a War," *New York Times Magazine,* May 22, 1966, pp. 114–15.

[39] A copy of the entire pamphlet is reproduced in the Dominican news magazine *Ahora* (No. 108, September 18, 1965). Although many whites were unaware of the pamphlet's existence, virtually every Negro soldier the writer talked to in Santo Domingo said he had seen the pamphlet. The effectiveness of the pamphlet on Negro soldiers was minimal, among other reasons, because it claimed Negro equality existed in the Dominican Republic, a statement belied by brief observation of the Dominican social scene.

[40] Similarly in an interview with a Negro reporter, the commandant of "constitutionalist rebel" forces in Santo Domingo stated that to his dismay Negro American soldiers fought no differently than whites (Laurence Harvey, "Report from the Dominican Republic," *Realist,* June, 1965, p. 18).

The writer's appraisal is that among officers and NCO's there is no discernible difference between the races concerning military commitment in either the Dominican Republic or Vietnam. Among Negro soldiers in the lower enlisted ranks, however, there is somewhat greater disenchantment compared to whites as to the merits of America's current military ventures. Such unease, however, has little effect on military performance, most especially in the actual combat situation. The evidence strongly suggests that the racial integration of the armed forces, coming about when it did, effectively precluded any potential success on the part of America's military opponents to differentiate Negro from white soldiers.

CONCLUSION

Although the military was until recent times one of America's most segregated institutions, it has leaped into the forefront of racial equality in the past decade. What features of the military establishment can account for this about-face? There is a combination of mutually supporting factors that operate in the successful racial integration of the armed forces. For one thing, the military —an institution revolving around techniques of violence—is to an important degree discontinuous from other areas of social life. And this apartness served to allow, once the course had been decided, a rapid and complete racial integration. The path of desegregation was further made easier by characteristics peculiar or at least more pronounced in the military compared to other institutions. With its hierarchical power structure, predicated on stable and patterned relationships, decisions need take relatively little account of the personal desires of service personnel. Additionally, because roles and activities are more defined and specific in the military than in most other social arenas, conflicts that might have ensued within a more diffuse and ambiguous setting were largely absent. Likewise, desegregation was facilitated by the pervasiveness in the military of a bureaucratic ethos, with its concomitant formality and high social distance, that mitigated tensions rising from individual or personal feelings.

At the same time it must also be remembered that the military establishment has means of coercion not readily available in most civilian pursuits. Violations of norms are both more visible and subject to quicker sanctions. The military is premised, moreover, on the accountability of its members for effective performance. Owing to the aptly termed "chain of command," failures in policy implementation can be pinpointed. This is turn means that satisfactory carrying out of stated policy advances one's own position. In other words, it is to each individual's personal interest, if he anticipates receiving the rewards of a military career, to insure that decisions going through him are executed with minimum difficulty. Or put in another way, whatever the internal policy decided upon, racial integration being a paramount but only one example, the military establishment is uniquely suited to realize its implementation.

What implications does the military integration experience have for civilian society? Although it is certainly true that the means by which desegregation was accomplished in the military establishment are not easily translated to the civilian community, the end result of integration in the contemporary armed forces can suggest some qualities of what—if it came about—an integrated American society would be *within the context of the prevailing structural and value system.* Equality of treatment would be the rule in formal and task-specific relationships. Racial animosity would diminish but not disappear. We would expect a sharp improvement in Negro mobility and performance in the occupational sphere, even taking into consideration on-going social and educational handicaps arising from existing inequities. Yet, because of these inequities, Negroes would still be overconcentrated in less skilled positions. We would also expect primary group ties and informal associations to remain largely within one's own racial group. But even at primary group levels, the integrated society would exhibit a much higher interracial intimacy than exists in the non-integrated society.

Such a description of the racially integrated society is, of course, what one finds in today's military establishment. Although the advent of the integrated society in this country is yet to occur, the desegregation of the armed forces has served to bring that day closer.

23

Black-white color connotations and racial awareness in preschool children[1]

CHERYL A. RENNINGER AND JOHN E. WILLIAMS

A popular way of referring to racial groups is by color-code: Caucasians are called "white," Negroes "black," Indians "red," and Orientals "yellow." American adults read in the press of problems between Black America and White America; and children in Sunday School sing, "Red and yellow, black and white, all are precious in His sight." While the color-coding of racial groups seems convenient, it is far from precise: the modal skin color of American Negroes is not black, but brown; while the skin color of Caucasians is not white, but pinkish-tan. It has been questioned (Williams, 1964) whether this inaccurate use of color names to designate groups of persons may influence the way these groups are perceived.

There is much anecdotal material suggesting that the words black and white carry rather specific evaluative connotations (Williams, 1964). Isaacs (1963) has noted that the use of black to symbolize evil and wickedness, and white to symbolize goodness and

Reprinted from *Perceptual and Motor Skills,* 1966, **22,** 771–785, by permission of the authors and Psychological Reports, Perceptual and Motor Skills.

[1] This paper is based upon an undergraduate honors thesis done by the first author under the supervision of the second author. The study was supported in part by a grant to the second author from the Wake Forest College Graduate Council. The authors are indebted to the administrators and teachers of the participating schools for their assistance.

purity, pervades our culture: the symbolism is to be found in our most influential works of literature from the Bible to Shakespeare (Isaacs, 1963), to Poe and Melville (Levin, 1960); the goodness of white and the badness of black fills our language with such terms as white lie and white-wash, and black list and black sheep; social custom clothes brides in white and mourners in black; and so on. In an objective study of the connotative meanings of color names, Williams (1964) used the semantic differential to obtain ratings by Caucasian and Negro Ss of 10 color names, among them black and white. For both groups, white was rated most positively among the 10 color names on the evaluation (good-bad) dimension, while black, along with gray, was rated most negatively. Thus, the names commonly used to designate Caucasian and Negro persons can be shown to differ in their general evaluative connotations of goodness and badness.

The regular association of color names with racial groups raises the question of whether the connotations of the color names may become conditioned to concepts representing the racial groups. Staats and Staats have demonstrated that the evaluative connotations of words are conditionable both to nonsense syllables (1957) and to the names of national groups (1958). In a study of the conditionability of color connotations, Harbin and Williams (1966) had Ss learn pairs of nonsense syllables and color names in a paired-associate learning task. When the nonsense syllables were subsequently rated on the semantic differential, the syllables paired with black and white were rated significantly differently on the evaluative dimension, the syllables associated with white being rated more "good" than the syllables associated with black. Williams (in press) hypothesized that, if the practice of color-coding were influencing the meaning of racial concepts, groups of concepts linked by the color-code (e.g., White—White Person—Caucasian, or Black—Black Person—Negro) should show a greater similarity in connotative meaning than concepts not so linked. For Caucasian *S*s, this hypothesis was clearly confirmed.

Taken together, the observations and research findings noted above suggest that the designation of racial groups by color names may be one determinant of the way in which racial groups are perceived and, hence, may be one factor influencing the complex phenomenon known as racial prejudice. An approach to the further clarification of the significance of color-coding in prejudice would be to study its possible role in the childhood origins of racial attitudes. A first step in this direction would be to determine the age period during which the concept of white as good and black as bad is being learned, and to relate this to the age period during which racial attitudes are forming. Numerous investigators have found that racial attitudes begin to develop in Caucasian children during the preschool years (e.g., Horowitz, 1939; Goodman, 1964, Morland, 1958, 1962). Morland (1958) found that the ability of Caucasian children to recognize individuals by race increased during the ages 3 to 5, with four-fifths of 5-yr.-olds being able to point out "colored" and "white" persons quite consistently. In a second study, Morland (1962) found a majority of Caucasian children, aged 3 to 5, expressing preference for light-skinned playmates and noted that the per cent showing this preference increased only slightly with age. Goodman (1964) reported varying degrees of racial awareness among Caucasian 4-yr.-olds: from vague recognition of color differences, to ability to name racial groups and express consistent preferences, to rather adultlike prejudices.

The principal purpose of this investigation was to study the degree of awareness of the connotative meanings of white as good and

black as bad among Caucasian preschool children. A secondary purpose of the investigation was to attempt to determine whether the awareness of color connotation develops prior to, concurrent with, or subsequent to the development of the child's awareness of racial differences between Caucasian and Negro persons.

METHOD

Subjects

*S*s were 129 Caucasian children from Winston-Salem, North Carolina: 13 male and 14 female 3-yr.-olds, 25 male and 30 female 4-yr.-olds, and 23 male and 24 female 5-yr.-olds. The age classification was based on *S*'s having passed the given birthday but not having attained the next. One hundred and twenty-three *S*s were attending day nurseries and preschools: 69 of these attended two half-day schools, serving children from average to better-than-average socio-economic backgrounds; 26 attended an all-day nursery, serving children primarily from average socio-economic backgrounds; and 28 attended an all-day nursery, serving children primarily from below-average backgrounds. The remaining 6 *S*s were obtained from nurseries of two suburban churches, serving better-than-average income groups.

Apparatus

Two sets of materials were designed by the first author for use in this study: a series of picture cards[2] for determining the degree of the child's awareness of the connotative meanings of black and white; and a picture puzzle for assessing the child's degree of racial awareness.

PICTURE CARD SERIES

The 8-card picture series consisted of 4 "test" cards occupying serial positions 1, 3, 5, and 7, and 4 "filler" cards occupying positions 2, 4, 6, and 8. On each of the four test cards were a black and a white figure, identical except for color, positioned side by side

---

[2] Card size varied from 5 in. × 8½ in. to 8½ in. × 11½ in. and 5 in. × 13 in. to 9 in. × 13½ in. in this study but now has been standardized.

on a background card of medium blue or bright yellow. The two figures occupied from one-half to two-thirds of the area of the card which varied unsystematically from 5 in. × 8½ in. to 8½ in. × 11½ in. The figures used were as follows: Card 1, a black and a white horse standing profile (blue background); Card 3, a small black dog and a small white dog standing semi-profile (yellow background); Card 5, a black kitten and a white kitten crouched in a "playful" position and wearing red bows (blue background); Card 7, a black teddy bear and a white teddy bear sitting face-forward and wearing red-and-white-checked bibs (yellow background). The four filler cards varied unsystematically in size from 5 in. × 13 in. to 9 in. × 13½ in. Each filler card pictured two figures, which were identical except for color and were presented in colors other than black and white: Card 2, a purple airplane and a green airplane with eyes, nose, and smiling mouth (yellow background); Card 4, a tan telephone and a red telephone (white background); Card 6, a red wagon and a blue wagon (white background); Card 8, a green top and a yellow top with cord for spinning (blue background). For filler cards 2 and 8, each of the colored objects was set on a small white background to minimize differential attractiveness against the blue and yellow cards. For these filler pictures, the colors of the figures and backgrounds were selected to introduce variety into the over-all task and were not chosen according to any prearranged system.

The four test cards were combined with the four filler cards by alternating them in the orders given above, i.e., horses, airplanes, dogs, telephones, kittens, wagons, teddy bears, tops. The filler cards were employed to minimize the chance of Ss merely perserverating in their initial responses to the first black-white card. On the black-white test cards, the black figure was on the left for Cards 1 and 5 and on the right for Cards 3 and 7 in order to minimize the effect of any right-left position preference.

PICTURE PUZZLE

A picture puzzle was employed in assessing S's degree of racial awareness. The puzzle (14 in. × 22 in.) was constructed of poster paper, backed by corrugated cardboard, with figures drawn on in ink and the entire puzzle colored with crayons. When assembled, the puzzle showed two families, each having a picnic. One family was in the top-left area of the picture (7 in. × 15 in.) and the other family was in the lower-right area (7 in. × 13 in.), with a rocky stream running between the two groups from upper-right to lower-left.

Respective members of the two families were identical except for skin and hair color: one family was pinkish-tan-skinned with blond or brown hair; the other family medium-brown-skinned with black hair. The pieces for respective family members were interchangeable, so that the families could be assembled in the puzzle with or without regard to "race." Each family consisted of five members, from right to left: a small boy running to the group, a mother kneeling with her back to the boy and taking a pie from the picnic basket, a baby sitting facing the mother and holding a flower, a father sitting facing the mother and eating a sandwich, a small girl standing behind the father and holding a bunch of flowers behind her.

The puzzle pieces—10 persons, each with a small background of grass—were all rounded and of distinctly different shapes for different members of the families, varying in size from about 3 in. × 3 in. for the babies, to 5 in. × 2½ in. for the children, and 5 in. × 4 in. for the seated parents. The puzzle frame consisted of green (i.e., "grassy") marginal space in the areas occupied by the families and had 2 large unoccupied areas—the upper-right corner (7 in. × 7 in.), picturing an area of flowers, and the lower-left corner (7 in. × 7 in.), picturing a large gray rock with flowers growing at its base.

Procedure

E was a female Caucasian college student and a stranger to the children. In each school, E was introduced to the entire class as "someone who has some pictures and a puzzle she'd like to show you and talk to you about." The teacher then told each child when it was his turn to go with E. The data were gathered in a 10-min. private interview with each S in an area somewhat removed from the general activity of the school, usually a separate room or corridor, and in one instance a secluded corner of the main schoolroom. S and E sat facing each other at a low table. After preliminary questions as to full name and age, both for information and rapport, the actual testing began.

PICTURE-CARD SERIES:
COLOR-MEANING AWARENESS TEST

S was given the following instructions: "What I have here are some pictures I'd like to show you and tell you stories about, and I'd like for you to help me by finishing every story the way you think it should end. I'll show you what I mean." *S* was then shown the series of 8 picture cards in the order horses, airplanes, dogs, telephones, kittens, wagons, teddy bears, tops. As *E* held each picture upright on the table midway between *E* and *S,* she told a story. A typical story for the black-white test cards was: "One of these horses is a very *good* horse. Whenever Johnny goes out to the farm to see him, the horse runs right up to the fence and lets Johnny pet his nose. What horse do you think is the *good* horse?" For the filler (non-black-white) cards, a typical story was "Johnny took his airplanes out in the yard to play with them, and he flew them way up in the sky. One of them flew so high that it got caught up in a tree. Which airplane do you think got caught?" When the 8 picture cards had been shown once through, *S* was told, "Now let's look at the pictures again with some different stories"; and *S* was then shown the pictures again in the same order. In all, then, *S* was exposed twice to each of the 4 test cards and thus had 8 opportunities to respond to the black and white figures.

Each of the stories for the black-white test cards stressed one of eight evaluative words as the basis for *S*'s choice. The words *good, clean, happy,* and *nice* were chosen to represent the positive end of the evaluative dimension, while *bad, dirty, sad* and *naughty* were chosen to reflect the negative end. The basis for grouping the words in this fashion was the earlier work with adults by Osgood and his associates (1957), who found that the semantic differential scales "good-bad," "clean-dirty," "happy-sad," and "nice-awful" were heavily weighted on the evaluation factor. The Williams studies (1964, in press) had employed "good-bad," "clean-dirty," and "nice-awful," in addition to other evaluative scales. In this study, the word naughty was considered more appropriate for preschool children than the word awful.

The test-card stories with their key evaluative words were presented in two orders. Order A began with the story using the word good, followed, in order, by stories using the words naughty, happy, dirty, sad, clean, bad, and nice. Order B began with a story using the word dirty, followed, in order, by stories using the words good, naughty, happy, nice, sad, clean, and bad. The orders were presented to alternate *S*s with 65 *S*s receiving Order A and 64 *S*s receiving Order B. The two orders were used to see whether there would be any difference in *S*s' responses to a series beginning with a more concrete expression, i.e., dirty, and *S*s' responses to a list beginning with a more abstract expression, i.e., good.

In responding to each picture, *S* was permitted to point to or to indicate verbally the figure he chose, e.g., the good horse. When *S* had responded, *E* removed the card and presented the next card in the series without commenting on *S*'s choice. *S*'s only "reinforcement" for his response was a new picture and story.

While showing the picture-card series, *E* noted whether *S* chose the black or the white figure for each of the stories involving a black-white choice. Scores on color awareness were obtained by totaling the number of answers *S* made in the "expected" direction, that is, how many times his answers indicated the black figure for stories stressing bad, dirty, sad, naughty, and the white figure for stories stressing good, clean, happy, nice. Since there were eight presentations of the black-white test cards, a score of 8 was the highest *S* could obtain, while a score of 4 would represent average random choice.

PUZZLE INTERVIEW: RACIAL AWARENESS TEST

E placed the puzzle frame flat on the table directly in front of *S* with the following instructions: "Here is a puzzle I'd like for you to put together. It tells a story about two families out on a picnic. Do you know what a family is? (If no definition was given: 'It's like all the people who live in your house.') See if you can put the families together in the puzzle. One family goes here and the other family goes here. (*E* indicated the two groups of spaces in the puzzle frame for the two families.) Here are the people. Put them where you think they should go."

The puzzle pieces were then placed in a scrambled pile at the lower left corner of the puzzle frame, and the child was allowed to work freely in assembling the puzzle. Although rates in assembling the puzzle varied among *S*s, almost all *S*s were able to work without assistance from *E*, who said nothing until the puzzle was completely assembled. Five of the 3-yr.-olds needed some direction in order to be kept from quitting; and, in these cases, *E* pointed to the two possible places for the puzzle piece *S* was holding and suggested that he try one of them.

When *S* had completed the puzzle, *E* said: "All right, now that you've finished the puzzle, look and see if you have all the people in the right places. Are they all where you want them to go?" After a pause to allow *S* to check the puzzle and to make any desired changes, *E* removed the two children of the same sex as *S* from the puzzle, held them upright in front of *S*, and said, "Let's look at these little girls (boys) for a minute. Suppose you were going outside to play. Which of these little girls would you like to go play with?" *E* then paused for *S*'s answer. Following this, *E* indicated the dark-skinned figure and asked, "Can you tell me what *kind* of a little girl this little girl is?" The question, "Which would you like to play with?" was asked to determine *S*'s preference for the light- or the dark-skinned figure. The question, "What *kind* of a little girl is this?" was asked to determine whether *S* had learned to apply any specific name to dark-skinned (i.e., Negro) persons. The terms "colored," "Negro" or its derivatives, and "black" were scored as racial labels. Brown was scored as a racial label if *S* designated the light-skinned figure racially (i.e., white), but brown was considered as a descriptive term and not scored if *S* designated the light-skinned figures descriptively (i.e., pink, yellow, tan).

A second set of questions was then asked to determine whether *S* could connect the racial labels "Negro," "colored," and "white" with the appropriate figure, when these labels were supplied by *E*. *S* was asked to find the Daddies and then to point to the Negro Daddy, to find the little boys and to point to the colored boy, to find the Mommies and point to the white Mommy, etc. Recognizing that, in a given choice, a correct response might be made by chance 50% of the time, *E* asked *S* to connect each of the three racial labels with appropriate figures twice in order to minimize the likelihood of *S*'s identifying

the figures correctly simply on a chance basis. If *S* connected the term "white" with the light-skinned figure twice and the term "colored" and/or "Negro" with the dark-skinned figure twice, he was scored as being able to connect racial labels with the appropriate figure.

During the entire puzzle interview, non-race-related questions were thoroughly interspersed with questions about race, so that no question about race directly followed another question about race. Such "filler" questions were centered around the activity depicted in the puzzle; e.g., "What do you think the little girl was doing just a minute ago? Who is she bringing the flowers to?" etc. At the close of the interview, *S* was asked to find all of the flowers in the picture, and, if he was a 4- or 5-yr.-old, to count the bunches of flowers. *S* was praised highly for this effort. (At no other time during the puzzle interview did *E* overtly indicate approval or disapproval of *S*'s answers.) *E* then requested *S* to put all the puzzle pieces in one pile; and, while this was being done, *E* noted *S*'s responses to the puzzle interview questions, his arrangement of the puzzle pieces, and any spontaneous remarks pertaining to race.[3]

RESULTS

Picture Card Series: Awareness of Color Meaning

The datum for analysis from the picture-card series was the color-meaning concept score for each *S*. This score was the number of times out of eight opportunities that he completed the stories by using black to indicate negative evaluation and using white to indicate positive evaluation. Table 1 presents frequency distributions of concept scores at each of the three age levels studied. Under each age heading, the column headed f_O contains the obtained frequency of scores at that age; the column headed f_E contains the frequency which would be expected if *S*s were responding by chance; and the third column expresses the obtained frequencies as a per

[3] Readers interested in the puzzle-interview procedure just described also should see Ammons' (1950) account of the doll-play interview as it has been used in the study of racial awareness in white males 2 to 6 yr. of age.

cent of the total number in the age group. In the bottom lines of Table 1 are given χ^2s computed for each age level separately, and for all Ss combined, which indicate that the color-meaning concept was present to a significant degree among children at each of the three age levels studied.

The data in Table 1 also indicate that awareness of the color-meaning concept was increasing as a function of age. This trend can be seen in Fig. 1 in which all Ss with scores of 5 or less are grouped into a "no awareness" group, with scores of 6 designated "low awareness," scores of 7 called "medium awareness," and scores of 8 called "high awareness." Using these designations, it can be seen that the per cent of highly aware Ss increased from 7 in the 3-yr. group to 43 in the 5-yr. group. If the three awareness groups are pooled (scores of 6, 7, 8), the per cent of Ss showing "some awareness" increased from 30 of the 3-yr.-olds, to 73 of the 4-yr.-olds, and to 81 of the 5-yr.-olds. Another observation from Fig. 1 is that the modal classification of Ss shifts from "no awareness" for 3-yr.-olds to "high awareness" in 5-yr.-olds. These data were interpreted as indicating that most of these Caucasian children were learning the color-meaning concept during the third, fourth, and fifth years.

In addition to the principal analysis just described, several subordinate analyses of the color-meaning data were made. The data were subdivided by sex of S but no significant

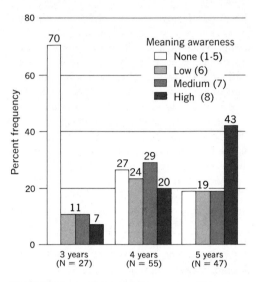

FIGURE 1   Per cent of Ss in each of three age groups classified by level of black-white color-meaning awareness.

differences were found. The scores were analyzed separately for Order A and Order B (see above); the mean color-meaning concept score for Order A (beginning with "good") was 5.90 while the mean score for Order B (beginning with "dirty") was 6.49, a difference significant at the .05 level. This result suggests that beginning the test series with the more concrete term dirty may have provided some reinforcement for the color-meaning concept. This order effect was not

TABLE 1   Expected (Chance) Frequencies, Obtained Frequencies, and Per Cent Frequencies of Black-White Color-Meaning Scores for Each of Three Age Groups

Score	3-Yr.-Olds (N = 27)			4-Yr.-Olds (N = 55)			5-Yr.-Olds (N = 47)			All Ss (N = 129)		
	f_E	f_o	%	f_E	f_o	%	f_E	f_o	%	f_E	f_o	%
0	0.1	0	0	0.2	0	0	0.2	0	0	0.5	0	0
1	0.8	0	0	1.7	1	1.8	1.5	1	2.1	4.0	2	1.5
2	2.9	1	3.7	6.0	0	0	5.2	0	0	14.1	1	0.8
3	5.9	2	7.4	12.0	3	5.5	10.3	1	2.1	28.2	6	4.6
4	7.4	7	25.9	15.0	2	3.6	12.9	3	6.4	35.3	10	7.8
5	5.9	9	33.3	12.0	9	16.4	10.3	4	8.5	28.2	24	18.6
6	2.9	3	11.1	6.0	13	23.6	5.2	9	19.1	14.1	24	18.6
7	0.8	3	11.1	1.7	16	29.1	1.5	9	19.1	4.0	28	21.7
8	0.1	2	7.4	0.2	11	20.0	0.2	20	42.6	0.5	33	25.6
	$x^2 = 10.14$, $df = 2$, $p < .01$			$x^2 = 155.22$, $df = 4$, $p < .01$			$x^2 = 165.05$, $df = 4$, $p < .01$			$x^2 = 286.35$, $df = 4$, $p < .01$		

Note. Horizontal rules divide categories used in computing χ^2s.

critical, however, since significant χ^2s were obtained within each order, considered separately. A final analysis of the color-meaning data concerned the question of whether the four words scored for positive evaluation and the four words scored for negative evaluation represented equally well their respective ends of the evaluation dimension. Among the negative words (bad, sad, naughty, and dirty), no significant differences were found in the frequency of expected usage, i.e., in association with black. Among the positive words, however, there appeared to be some difference: "clean" was associated with white by 111 of the 129 Ss; "nice" by 99; "happy" by 91; and "good" by only 85. This result, with a χ^2 significant at the .05 level, suggests that the more descripitve term clean was used in the expected way with greater frequency than the more abstract term good. In general, it appeared that Ss had learned the positive and negative ends of the evaluation dimension about equally well; the mean response in the expected direction for the 4 negative words was 102.0 (79%) while that for the 4 positive words was 96.5 (75%).

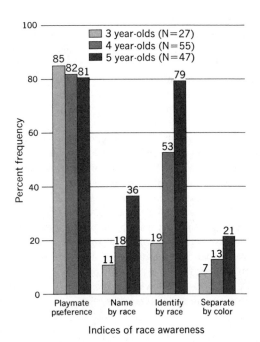

FIGURE 2　Per cent of Ss in each of three age groups scoring positively on each of four indices of race awareness.

Puzzle Interview: Awareness of Race

The puzzle-interview data were collected in order to make some judgments of degree of racial awareness in the children for whom the color-meaning data were being obtained. Through the interview, four key questions were explored: (1) whether S preferred the light-skinned or dark-skinned child of the same sex as a playmate; (2) whether S could apply a racial name to the dark-skinned child of the same sex; (3) whether S could connect the racial labels "Negro," "colored," and "white" with appropriate figures when the labels were supplied by E; (4) whether S "segregated" the families in the puzzle arrangement. The data dealing with these four questions are displayed in Fig. 2.

In considering the first question above, it can be seen at the left of Fig. 2 that there was a high preference (81% to 85%) for the light-skinned child as a playmate, a result significantly ($p < .01$) beyond the chance expectancy of 50%. It can also be observed that this preference did not change as a function of age. Thus, most Ss at all age levels discriminated among the children in the puzzle on the basis of skin and hair color

and expressed a preference for the lighter child.

Regarding the second question, the data second from the left in Fig. 2 shows the per cent of children who applied some common racial label to the darker-skinned child when asked "What *kind* of a little girl is this?" It can be seen that a minority of children at each age level (age 3, 11%; age 4, 18%; age 5, 36%) produced a racial label in response to this non-specific question. The observed trend for racial naming to increase with age was statistically significant ($p < .01$).

To the right of center in Fig. 2 are the data for racial identification, i.e., the child's ability to designate racial groups correctly when given the racial labels "white," "Negro," and "colored." In order to be scored positively here, the child had to be correct in both of his responses to "white" and in both responses to "Negro" and/or both responses to "colored." If Ss were responding by chance alone, 7/64 or 11% of them would have been scored positively; and this provided a baseline for consideration of the percentages displayed in Fig. 2. It can be seen that 18.5% of 3-yr.-olds were scored positively. This result suggested some racial awareness but was not significantly different from chance expectancy. The per cent of 4-yr.-olds displaying racial awareness by this index was 54.5, while the per cent for 5-yr.-olds was 78.7, both results being significantly ($p < .01$) greater than chance. A test of the trend for racial identification to increase by age was statistically significant ($p < .01$).

At the right of Fig. 2 is given the per cent of each age group which "segregated" the two families by "race." In evaluating these percentages, the probability of segregating the puzzle pieces on a chance basis (2/32 or 6%) served as a baseline. The apparent tendency for segregation of puzzle pieces to increase with age was not significant. However, when Ss from all three age groups were combined, the total per cent of Ss segregating by color (14.7%) was significantly ($p < .01$) above chance expectancy.

Awareness of Color Meaning and Race Considered Jointly

The purpose of this analysis was to evaluate individual differences in the development of the color-meaning and race concepts to

taining scores of 6, 7, or 8 on the color-meaning test were classified as "aware" of the connotative meaning of black as bad and white as good. The probability of S's obtaining a score of 6 or above by chance was 14.4%.

Table 2 presents the results of the joint classification of Ss by race awareness and color-meaning awareness. As would be expected from the separate analyses reported above, the data in Table 2 reflect the fact that the race and color concepts are being acquired by most children during ages 3 to 5: at age 3, 59% of Ss were unaware of either concept, while at age 5 only 2% were still unaware of either concept; at age 3 only 7% of Ss were aware of both concepts, while at age 5 64% were aware of both. (The chance probability of an S being classified as aware of both concepts was approximately 1.5%.) Of particular interest in Table 2 are the data concerning Ss who were aware of one concept but not the other, i.e., the question of priority of learning. It can be seen that at each age level the percent of Ss who were aware of color meaning but not of race was greater than the per cent of Ss who

TABLE 2   Percentages of Ss at Three Age Levels Classified by Awareness of Black-White Color-Meaning and Race

S Classification	Age 3 (N = 27)	Age 4 (N = 55)	Age 5 (N = 47)	All Ss (N = 129)
Unaware of Either Concept	59.3	16.4	2.1	20.2
Aware of Color, Not of Race	22.2	32.7	19.1	25.6
Aware of Race, Not of Color	11.1	16.4	14.9	14.7
Aware of Both Concepts	7.4	34.6	63.9	39.5

see what information could be found regarding the priority of development of the two concepts. It was recognized that the methods employed were not adequate to provide a precise test of the priority of concept development.

For this analysis, a child was said to be "aware" of race when he was scored positively on the racial identification aspect of the puzzle interview, i.e., when he correctly identified both "white" persons and both "Negro" persons and/or both "colored" persons. It was noted above that the probability of S's doing this by chance alone was 11%. Ss ob-

were aware of race but not of color meaning. At the 3- and 4-yr. levels, the ratio between the two percentages was about 2:1. This evidence of more frequent priority of the color-meaning concept must be discounted somewhat due to the difference in chance probabilities noted above, i.e., it was slightly more likely (14.4% vs 11%) that an S responding by chance alone would have been classified as aware of color meaning than as aware of race, and this may have led to a slight inflation of the number of color-meaning-aware Ss relative to the number of race-aware Ss.

DISCUSSION

The results of this study indicated that Caucasian children are learning the evaluative meanings of black as bad, and white as good, during their preschool years, the period in which awareness of race is also developing. One may speculate about the possible implication of the color-meaning concept in the childhood origins of anti-Negro prejudice. If the preschool child is learning that white things are good and black things are bad, it seems reasonable that these meanings could generalize to groups of persons designated by the color-code as "white" and "black." Thus, the "convenient" designation of racial groups by color names may provide the child with a general evaluative frame of reference, within which the more specific learnings of prejudice can be easily incorporated. Consistent with this notion are the findings of Blake and Dennis (1943) who reported that elementary school children tended to view Negroes as generally "bad," while high school students viewed Negroes in a more complex way which was similar to adult stereotypes.

It is interesting to speculate concerning the learning situations in which the preschool child acquires the concept of black as bad and white as good. Some of these situations may be almost universal, such as the frightening images and dreams which children experience in the darkness of night, or the "black" clouds associated with thunderstorms. A close link between darkness and blackness is suggested by the work of Palermo and Jenkins (1964), who found that among elementary school children "dark" was the word most commonly associated with black. Another potent reinforcement may result from the linkage of "dirtiness" and "blackness." The authors have heard mothers admonish their children to "go wash those dirty, black hands" and subsequently praise them for their "clean, white hands" (also see Goodman, 1964). The child's experiences with children's books and with television and the movies are also likely to reinforce the concept of white as good and black as bad, since all employ color symbolism in this way. In Sunday School or nursery school, the child is likely to be exposed to the black-white, dark-light symbolism of Judeo-Christian religion. A dramatic instance of this was encountered at a church-related nursery school visited during this study. At this school, a teacher showed *E* a commercially-printed teaching aid called "The Wordless Book." This was a booklet of five colored pages in which each color represented a particular religious concept, with the black page used to represent sin and the white page, the absence of sin. Thus, there are many avenues through which the connotative meanings of black as bad and white as good may be communicated to the young child.

The color-meaning data of the present study provided some indirect evidence regarding the "semantic space" of the preschool child. It was noted above that the positive and negative evaluation words used in the color-meaning test had been so classified on the basis of Osgood's research with adults, in which semantic differential scales composed of these words were found to be heavily weighted on a general evaluative factor. In view of this, it is interesting that the preschool children appeared to respond to the words much as did the adults, i.e., all four of the adults' positive words were used in a similar fashion by the children, with the same finding for the four negative words. This result suggests that the general evaluation factor, which is so prominent in the responses of adults, is already present in the responses of preschool children.

It was seen that when racial awareness was defined by racial identification, the black-white color-meaning concept appeared to be developing somewhat earlier, on the average, than awareness of race. However, the variability in results among the various indices of racial awareness points up a general methodological problem. The data suggest that racial awareness is a complex concept if, indeed, it can be considered a unitary concept at all. Although a strong preference for Caucasian playmates was already present in the 3-yr.-olds, little racial awareness was evident from the other indices. The degree of preference appeared to remain constant across the age groups studied, while the other measures of awareness were increasing. The racial identification measure showed the most dramatic gain during the ages studied, from less than one-fifth of 3-yr.-olds to four-fifths of 5-yr.-olds. The child's tendency to apply racial names to "kinds" of people and the child's tendency to segregate by race may develop more slowly, being found very rarely in the 3-yr. group and in only a small minority of the 5-yr. group. Thus, it seems clear that the degree of racial awareness which will be found in studies of children is determined, in part, by the specific measure of racial awareness which is employed. Further research is needed to clarify this problem (see Clark & Clark, 1952; Stevenson & Stewart, 1958).

The Williams (1964) study with adults indicated that the connotative meanings of the colors black and white are more "culturally" determined than "racially" determined, i.e., Negroes and Caucasians rated the color meanings in a highly similar fashion. This finding suggests that the Negro child may also be acquiring the black is bad, white is good concept in early childhood. A pilot study directed at this question has been conducted by the authors, with a Negro *E* administering the black-white picture-card series of the present study with slightly modified procedures to Negro preschoolers. While these data are not adequate for comparison with the data of the preesnt study, it is quite clear that a large percentage of Negro children are acquiring the black as bad, white as good concept during the preschool years. This finding may be related to the findings of Clark and Clark (1950), Morland (1962), and others, that a majority of Negro preschoolers express a preference for light-skinned over dark-skinned figures in various choice situations. The further exploration of this line of research might have significant implications for the understanding of self-concept development in Negro children. As James Baldwin has written (1962, p. 65), "Negroes . . . are taught to despise themselves from the minute they open their eyes on the world. This world is white and they are black."

REFERENCES

Ammons, R. B. Reactions in a projective doll-play interview of white males two to six years of age to differences in skin color and facial features. *J. genet. Psychol.*, 1950, **76**, 323–341.

Baldwin, J. Letter from a region in my mind. *New Yorker*, 1962, **38**, 59–60.

Blake, R., & Dennis, W. The development of stereotypes concerning the Negro. *J. abnorm. soc. Psychol.*, 1943, **38**, 525–531.

Clark, K. B., & Clark, M. P. Emotional factors in racial identification and preference in Negro children. *J. Negro Educ.*, 1950, **19**, 341–350.

Clark, K. B., & Clark, M. P. Racial identification and preference in Negro children. In G. E. Swanson, T. M. Newcomb, & E. L. Hartley (Eds.), *Readings in social psychology*. New York: Holt, 1952. Pp. 551–560.

Goodman, M. E. *Race awareness in young children*. New York: Collier Books, 1964.

Harbin, S. P., & Williams, J. E. Conditioning of color connotations. *Percept. mot. Skills*, 1966, **22**, 217–218.

Horowitz, R. E. Racial aspects of self-identification in nursery school children. *J. Psychol.*, 1939, **7**, 91–99.

Isaacs, H. R. *The new world of Negro Americans*. New York: John Day, 1963.

Levin, H. *The power of blackness*. New York: Vintage, 1960.

Morland, J. K. Racial recognition by nursery school children in Lynchburg, Virginia. *Soc. Forces*, 1958, **37**, 132–137.

Morland, J. K. Racial acceptance and preference of nursery school children in a southern city. *Merrill-Palmer Quart.*, 1962, **8**, 271–280.

Osgood, C. E., Suci, G. J., & Tannenbaum, P. H. *The measurement of meaning*. Urbana: Univer. of Illinois Press, 1957.

Palermo, D. S., & Jenkins, J. J. *Word association norms*. Minneapolis: Univer. of Minnesota Press, 1964.

Staats, C. K., & Staats, A. W. Meaning established by classical conditioning. *J. exp. Psychol.*, 1957, **54**, 74–80.

Staats, A. W., & Staats, C. K. Attitudes established by classical conditioning. *J. abnorm. soc. Psychol.*, 1958, **57**, 37–40.

Stevenson, H. W., & Stewart, E. C. A developmental study of racial awareness in young children. *Child Develpm.*, 1958, **29**, 399–409.

Williams, J. E. Connotations of color names among Negroes and Caucasians. *Percept. mot. Skills*, 1964, **18**, 721–731.

Williams, J. E. Connotations of racial concepts and color names. *J. pers. soc. Psychol.*, 1966.

24

Aggression toward outgroups as a function of authoritarianism and imitation of aggressive models

RALPH EPSTEIN

Although an increasing body of correlational evidence points to the role of imitation of ingroup attitudes as a determinant of prejudicial attitudes (Epstein & Komorita, 1966; Mosher & Scodel, 1960), experimental studies of imitatively derived hostility towards outgroups are virtually nonexistent. The potential fruitfulness of such studies is suggested by research demonstrating the imitative basis of diverse behavioral systems, for example, aggression (Bandura, Ross, & Ross, 1961), moral judgments (Bandura & McDonald, 1963), and autism (Eisenberg, 1957). The current study attempts to extend the range of investigated behaviors by focusing on imitation of overt aggression as manifested by the administration of shock to a victim. Furthermore, whereas previous investigations of imitation have focused upon either the observer's personality characteristics, that is, self-esteem (deCharms & Rosenbaum, 1960) or the model's characteristics, that is, status (Bandura & Kupers, 1964), social approval (Gelfand, 1962), the current study assumed that maximal prediction may be obtained by investigating the interaction between the observer's personality structure

Reprinted from *Journal of Personality and Social Psychology,* 1966, **3,** 574–579, by permission of the author and the American Psychological Association.

and the model's stimulus characteristics upon aggression towards outgroups.

Thus, the goal of this exploratory study was to investigate the personality characteristics of the observer and the stimulus characteristics of aggressive models, that is, race and social status, as determinants of imitative aggression towards a Negro victim. On the basis of theory derived from the *Authoritarian Personality* (Adorno, Frenkel-Brunswik, Levinson, & Sanford, 1950), as well as research by Hart (1957), it may be assumed that authoritarian attitudes are a function of parental punishment for independent, autonomous behavior and parental approval for conforming, imitative, and submissive behavior. Therefore, it was predicted that high authoritarians will be more imitative of an aggressive model relative to low authoritarians. Furthermore, insofar as authoritarian attitudes result from harsh and punitive discipline which lead to excessive sensitization to power relations of strong versus weak, superior versus inferior, as these dimensions are culturally defined by social status, it was predicted that whereas high authoritarians will be more imitative of a middle-class than a working-class model, the low authoritarian's aggressiveness will be relatively uninfluenced by the model's differential social status.

The final prediction related to the ethnic characteristics of the aggressive model. It was assumed that conflict may be aroused by the cognition that one is aggressing (administering shock) against an individual and justification for the aggression in terms of the victim's provocative behavior or the presence of negative cognitions regarding the victim is lacking. It may be assumed that college students' awareness of the Negro's underdog status in American society would contribute to their perception of a white model giving shocks to a Negro victim as an instance of unjustifiable aggression. On the other hand, it is plausible to assume that justification for aggressing towards a member of a minority group may be derived by the prior observation that his own group considers him to be a legitimate target for aggression. This reasoning leads to the prediction that aggression towards a Negro will be facilitated by the prior observation of a Negro rather than a white aggressive model. Furthermore, on the basis of previous research (Berkowitz & Holmes, 1959; Weatherley, 1961) regarding the generalized and undifferentiated nature of authoritarian hostility, it is predicted that high authoritarians will show less differentiation among ethnic models relative to non-authoritarian subjects.

METHOD

Subjects

Authoritarianism was measured by the 30-item F Scale which was group administered to 144 white, male, undergraduate students enrolled in introductory psychology courses at Wayne State University. One-third of the highest and one-third of the lowest scorers were randomly assigned to eight experimental conditions ($N = 8$ per cell) with the remaining 32 subjects assigned to a control group in which subjects were not exposed to an aggressive model. These experimental groups reflected a $2 \times 2 \times 2$ factorial design based on the following independent variables: authoritarianism, high versus low; socioeconomic status of the model, low versus middle; and race of the model, Negro versus white.

Behavioral Situation

Aggression was defined operationally as a response which delivers noxious stimuli to another person. A modified "aggression machine" (Buss, 1961) was employed so that five intensities of electric shock ranging from very low to very high could be administered to a victim.

In addition to the white, naive subject, other participants included two accomplices, a Negro who played the role of the victim, and a Negro or white accomplice who served as an aggressive model. Upon arriving at the experimental room, subjects were told that they were participating in a study to evaluate the effect of shock upon learning. Thus, one participant would play the role of a learner, whereas the other two would serve as experimenters. In order to determine who would play the victim or learner's role, the participants were asked to select a number from 1 to 10. Insofar as this procedure was rigged, the same Negro accomplice was selected as the learner for all subjects. The remaining participants, the subject and accomplice, were told that they would play the role of experimenters in a study on the effects of shock upon learning. This role would be played by shocking the learner for incorrectly anticipating stimulus words presented serially on a memory drum. It was emphasized that the experimenter could press any one of the five buttons clearly marked from very low to very high. At this point, the remaining accomplice (Negro or white) "spontaneously" requested to play the role of the experimenter first since his time was limited. In this manner, the accomplice always served as the aggressive model. The naive subject was requested to observe and record the accomplice's selection of shock so that level of shock could be related to rate of learning. In this manner, the subject was given an opportunity to observe the level of shock employed by the second accomplice, now serving as an aggressive model.

Depending on the appropriate condition, the model was either Negro or white, low or high status. In the low status condition, the model wore old, disheveled clothes and responded to an orally administered questionnaire so as to reveal the following information about himself within the hearing distance of the naive subject: family income, less than $3,000; parental occupation, unemployed. In the high status condition, the model appeared well dressed and responded in the following manner: family income, $15,000 per annum; parental occupation, executive in an advertising firm.

The Negro victim made a programed series of responses such that 32 shocks were administered by the model, and subsequently, by the naive subject in a seven-trial learning series. Unknown to the subject, however, a locked switch precluded the actual administration of shock to the victim. Furthermore, after an initial warm-up period in which the model delivered only weak shocks to the victim for errors during the first serial presentation, he delivered the highest level of shock; namely, "very high" shock, for subsequent errors. After the victim had learned the correct order of serially presented words, the subject was given the opportunity to play the role of the experimenter. This time the victim was asked to learn a new set of words. Recordings of the shock intensities were made by observing a series of differentially colored lights located in the experimenter's room and wired to the aggression machine.

Measure of the Dependent Variable

The dependent variable, aggression, was operationally defined in terms of the intensity of shock administered to the victim. In line with Buss' (1961) suggestion that the administration of weak or mild shock levels may be indicative of a motive to help the victim learn more effectively, whereas utilization of very strong shock intensities may be more directly indicative of aggression, it was decided to score each subject's protocol by counting only those shocks whose intensities were labeled as "very strong."

RESULTS

For the purpose of intergroup comparisons, Table 1 summarizes the means and standard deviations of the very strong shocks for the eight experimental groups.

An analysis of variance based on these scores indicated that whereas the effect of

TABLE 1   Means and Standard Deviations of Shocks of Experimental Groups

| Social Status | High Authoritarian | | Low Authoritarian | | M |
	Negro	White	Negro	White	
Middle class	36.11	32.78	32.22	15.00	29.03
	(11.28)[a]	(10.30)	(16.00)	(9.13)	
Working class	35.56	31.67	26.67	12.77	26.67
	(16.72)	(15.11)	(5.27)	(8.50)	

	Mean shock intensity
High authoritarian	34.03
Low authoritarian	21.67
Negro	32.64
White	23.06

[a] Standard deviations are enclosed in parentheses.

Several procedures were employed in order to convince the subject that the aggression machine was operative. Prior to the first trial, subjects were encouraged to touch the victim's electrodes and receive a sample shock. In addition, the subject observed the experimenter carefully place the electrodes on the victim's wrist and fingertips. Finally, the victim emitted appropriate groans subsequent to each shock.

the model's differential social status upon imitative aggression was not significant, the subject's authoritarianism and the model's ethnic characteristics were important determinants of imitative aggression. Thus, the main effects for authoritarianism ($F = 16.72$, $df = 1/64$), and race ($F = 10.05$, $df = 1/64$), both significant at the .01 level, indicate that high authoritarians were more aggressive than lows and the Negro model elicited greater aggression relative to the white model.

The predicted interaction between authoritarianism and race barely misses significance at the .05 level ($F = 3.90$, $df = 1/64$). It is likely that significance would have been achieved were it not for a mild heterogeneity of variance ($F = 10.60$, $df = 9$). However, this interaction does suggest an interesting trend whereby the Negro and white model elicited comparable levels of aggression from high authoritarians, whereas the low authoritarians' aggressiveness was differentiated according to the ethnic characteristics of the model. More specifically, low authoritarians, although administering generally less shock relative to high authoritarians, were more imitative of a Negro than a white model ($t = 8.20$, $p < .01$). Also, the white model was more imitated by high than low authoritarians ($t = 9.72$, $p < .01$). Insofar as the difference in shocks between the experimental groups ($M = 27.85$) and the control group ($M = 10.63$) is highly significant ($t = 8.52$, $p < .001$), it may be concluded that the observation of an aggressive model had a profound effect on levels of shock administered by the subjects. Finally, Table 1 indicates no support for the predicted interaction between authoritarianism and social status.

DISCUSSION

A primary finding in this study is that the imitation of anti-Negro aggression is a function of an interaction between the subject's level of authoritarianism and the model's racial characteristics. More specifically, these results support the prediction that whereas ethnic models will elicit comparable aggressiveness from high authoritarians, the low authoritarian's aggression is influenced differentially by the model's ethnic characteristics, that is, greater imitation of a Negro than a white model. Although these results are compatible with previous research (Anisfeld, Munoz, & Lambert, 1963; Berkowitz, 1962; Epstein, 1965; Epstein & Komorita, 1966) which demonstrated that authoritarian hostility is a generalized phenomenon across situations, they also suggest that this generality may be across models as well as targets. Thus, it would appear that the fre-

quently reported relationship between authoritarianism and ethnocentrism (Adorno et al., 1950; Pettigrew, 1959) may not only be a function of the authoritarian individual's vulnerability to frustration as manifested by scapegoating behavior, but also a tendency to be more imitative of hostile models.

Furthermore, the low authoritarian's tendency to be significantly more imitative of a Negro than a white model is congruent with recent research (Berkowitz, 1962; Weatherley, 1961) which demonstrates greater perceptual and cognitive differentiation among tolerant persons. Unlike these previous findings, however, the current results suggest that the greater discriminability among tolerant subjects may occur under nonstressful conditions, and in relation to aggressive models, as well as targets of aggression. It is interesting to note that whereas previous investigators have reported the greater responsiveness of low authoritarians to environmental or situational changes, that is, less childhood ethnocentrism as a result of an interracial experience (Mussen, 1950), lowered estimates of United States' superiority subsequent to the appearance of the sputniks (Mischel & Schopler, 1959), the current findings also demonstrate similar modifiability in overt aggressiveness as a function of external conditions.

There has been increasing recognition that a major limitation of traditional social-psychological conceptualizations of hostility towards outgroups is the neglect of outgroup characteristics which facilitate their selection as targets (Zawadzki, 1948). For example, the predictive efficiency of a specific conceptualization, for example, the "scapegoat" hypothesis, has been enhanced by attention to such characteristics, that is, "prior dislike" (Berkowitz, 1962), visibility (Williams, 1947), and social status (Epstein, 1965; Epstein & Komorita, 1966). The current study indicates the potential utility of further exploring the hypothesis that the perception of intragroup hostility may serve to justify and thereby contribute to the selection of a group as a target for aggression. This effect may be pronounced even for those individuals, that is, low authoritarians, who would ordinarily refrain from imitating an aggressive model. More specifically, these findings suggest that the low authoritarian's anxiety or inhibition regarding the expression of hostility towards outgroups may dissipate when these groups are viewed as victimized by their own member. The high authoritarian's greater imitativeness of the white model relative to low authoritarians is suggestive of the high Fs greater identification with the ingroup. This identification may result in a lower threshold for aggressive behavior when exposed to a white model.

An important reservation which may be placed on the conclusion that intragroup hostility within a minority group increases the aggressiveness of the majority is that this experiment has provided no information regarding the potential modeling effects of minority group members other than those from the victim's ethnic group. For example, it is conceivable that the use of an Oriental model may have elicited a comparable degree of aggression relative to the Negro model. In this case, one would conclude that aggression among minority group members, regardless of the degree of similarity between the model and the victim, increases the aggressiveness of the majority. Further research will be undertaken in which the ethnic affiliation of the subjects and victims as well as the models' will be varied in order to clarify these relationships.

An important implication of these results is that the development of attitudes of self-rejection and self-derogation among outgroups (Clark, 1963; Lewin, 1935), as these attitudes may be manifested by intragroup hostility within a minority group, may serve to increase the vulnerability of the group to rejection and hostility on the part of the majority. This interpretation is consistent with the naturalistic observation (Arendt, 1963), that the Nazis' aggression towards the Jews during World War II was made justifiable by the majority's perception of some Jews participating directly and indirectly in the liquidation of their own ethnic group.

Furthermore, this study may have important implications for current theory regarding the antecedents of hostility towards outgroups. The most prevalent formulation, the "scapegoat" hypothesis (Berkowitz, 1962) suggests that the anticipation of punishment for frustration-induced aggression directed towards the ingroup results in displacement from the original sources of frustration to outgroups. However, this hypothesis is not clearly compatible with the naturalistic ob-

servation of a striking dissimilarity between the ingroup frustraters and the victims of displaced aggression (Buss, 1961). Attempts to clarify this inconsistency between theory and observation have focused on the ethnocentric individual's "prior dislike" for outgroups (Berkowitz, 1959), as well as his poor discrimination under stressful conditions (Berkowitz, 1962). The current results suggest that the direction of hostility may be determined by an interaction between personality characteristics of the aggressor and the stimulus characteristic of the aggressive model.

Whereas previous research (Epstein, 1965; Epstein & Komorita, 1966) demonstrated that the social status of the victim relates to his vulnerability to displaced aggression, the current study indicates that the model's social status had minimal effect on the imitation of aggression. It would appear that the salient effects attributable to the ethnic characteristics of the model and the victim overshadowed the social status variable. Insofar as the social status of the victim was relatively undefined and somewhat ambiguous, further research might involve the manipulation of the status variable for both the model and the victim.

REFERENCES

Adorno, T. W., Frenkel-Brunswik, E., Levinson, D. J., & Sanford, R. N. *The authoritarian personality.* New York: Harper, 1950.

Anisfeld, M., Munoz, S. R., & Lambert, W. E. The structure and dynamics of ethnic attitudes of Jewish adolescents. *Journal of Abnormal and Social Psychology*, 1963, **66,** 31–36.

Arendt, H. *Eichmann in Jerusalem: A report on the banality of evil.* New York: Viking Press, 1963.

Bandura, A., & Kupers, C. J. Transmission of patterns of self-reinforcement through modeling. *Journal of Abnormal and Social Psychology*, 1964, **69,** 1–9.

Bandura, A., & McDonald, F. J. The influence of social reinforcement and the behavior of models in shaping children's moral judgments. *Journal of Abnormal and Social Psychology*, 1963, **67,** 274–281.

Bandura, A., Ross, D., & Ross, S. A. Transmission of aggression through imitation of aggressive models. *Journal of Abnormal and Social Psychology*, 1961, **63**, 575–582.

Berkowitz, L. *Aggression: A social psychological analysis.* New York: McGraw-Hill, 1962.

Berkowitz, L., & Holmes, D. S. The generalization of hostility to disliked objects. *Journal of Personality*, 1959, **27**, 565–577.

Buss, A. *The psychology of aggression.* New York: Wiley, 1961.

Clark, K. B. *Prejudice and your child.* Boston: Beacon Press, 1963.

deCharms, R., & Rosenbaum, M. E. Status variables and matching behavior. *Journal of Personality*, 1960, **28**, 492–502.

Eisenberg, L. The fathers of autistic children. *American Journal of Orthopsychiatry,* 1957, **27**, 715–724.

Epstein, R. Authoritarianism, displaced aggression, and social status of the target. *Journal of Personality and Social Psychology*, 1965, **2**, 585–589.

Epstein, R., & Komorita, S. S. Childhood prejudice as a function of parental ethnocentrism, punitiveness, and outgroup characteristics. *Journal of Personality and Social Psychology*, 1966, **3**, 259–264.

Gelfand, D. M. The influence of self-esteem on rate of verbal conditioning and social matching behavior. *Journal of Abnormal and Social Psychology*, 1962, **65**, 259–265.

Hart, I. Maternal child-rearing practices and authoritarian ideology. *Journal of Abnormal and Social Psychology*, 1957, **55**, 232–237.

Lewin, K. Psycho-sociological problems of minority groups. *Character and Personality*, 1935, **3**, 175–187.

Mischel, W., & Schopler, J. Authoritarianism and reactions to "sputniks." *Journal of Abnormal and Social Psychology*, 1959, **59**, 142–145.

Mosher, D. L., & Scodel, A. A study of the relationship between ethnocentrism in children and the ethnocentrism and authoritarian rearing practices of their mothers. *Child Development*, 1960, **31**, 369–376.

Mussen, P. H. Some personality and social factors related to changes in children's attitudes toward Negroes. *Journal of Abnormal and Social Psychology*, 1950, **45**, 423–446.

Pettigrew, T. F. Regional differences in anti-Negro prejudice. *Journal of Abnormal and Social Psychology*, 1959, **59**, 28–36.

Weatherley, D. Anti-Semitism and the expression of fantasy aggression. *Journal of Abnormal and Social Psychology*, 1961, **62**, 454–457.

Williams, R. M., Jr. The reduction of intergroup tensions: A survey of research on problems of ethnic, racial, and religious group relations. *Social Science Research Council Bulletin*, 1947, No. 57.

Zawadzki, B. Limitations of the scapegoat theory of prejudice. *Journal of Abnormal and Social Psychology*, 1948, **43**, 127–141.

25

Race, sex, and belief as determinants of friendship acceptance[1]

CAROLE R. SMITH, LEV WILLIAMS, AND RICHARD H. WILLIS

Rokeach, Smith, and Evans (1960) provided evidence supporting a belief-congruence theory of prejudice. According to this theory, similarity of belief about basic issues, rather than racial or ethnic similarity per se, is the primary determinant of social acceptance. When a person rejects a priori a member of another group, it is because he assumes that the outsider holds different views on basic issues. In this way the theory subsumes racial and ethnic prejudice as a special case under belief prejudice. This belief-congruence formulation is quite in the spirit of the structural balance notion of Heider (1958), the ABX model of Newcomb (1959), and the other related theories of cognitive consistency.

In the first of two studies, Rokeach et al. demonstrated that white subjects making

Reprinted from *Journal of Personality and Social Psychology*, 1967, **5**, 127–137, by permission of the authors and the American Psychological Association.

[1] This research is based on two master's theses directed by Richard H. Willis and submitted to the Graduate School, Washington University (Smith, 1966; Williams, 1964). Carole R. Smith's thesis formed the basis for Study I, while Study II is based on that of Lev Williams. We wish to thank the following persons for their much-appreciated assistance in the collection of the data: Vernon L. Allen (University of Wisconsin), C. O. Atchison (Tennessee State University), John Dickerson (Mississippi Vocational College), Vera Kanareff Presbie (Newcomb College), L. Nicholson and T. A. Weir (Harris Teachers College), and Eugene Runyon (Central State University).

hypothetical choices were more accepting of Negroes who agreed with them on important issues that they were of whites disagreeing with them. This was true both for a northern and a southern sample. In a second study, they showed that Jewish children accepted Gentiles agreeing with them to a greater extent than they did Jews disagreeing with them. Additional support for the theory comes from the research of Byrne and co-workers (Byrne, 1961; Byrne & McGraw, 1964; Byrne & Wong, 1962).

Subsequently Stein, Hardyck, and Smith (1965) demonstrated that both race and belief play significant roles, with race being important in the absence of information about beliefs, but with beliefs on basic issues being more important when both were presented.

In neither study reported by Rokeach et al. were stimulus persons identified as to sex, while in the investigation by Stein et al., male subjects responded to male stimulus persons and female subjects responded to female stimulus persons. All subjects in all three studies were white.

The two investigations reported in this paper represent direct extensions of the "North-South Study" by Rokeach et al. (1960), the one concerning Negro-white relations. In Study I, sex of stimulus persons was introduced as a third determinant of friendship acceptance, along with race and belief. Two of the three samples contained only white subjects, while the third included a Negro subsample. In Study II, three samples of Negro subjects were used. Both studies incorporated a north-south gradient by the use of one sample from the North, one from a border region, and one from the deep South.

The purpose of the present research is to assess further the validity of the belief-congruence theory of prejudice by (*a*) pitting belief congruence against both race and sex membership, and (*b*) utilizing Negro as well as white subjects from various parts of the country.

STUDY I

Except for the extensions indicated, the data-collection procedures and statistical analyses of Rokeach et al. (1960) were followed as closely as possible. Two personality scales, however, were omitted—an anti-Negro scale and Rokeach's Opinionation scale. Both had shown rather low correlations with discrimination responses.

Method

SUBJECTS

Subjects were 140 college students enrolled in an introductory psychology course, distributed by sex and region of residence at the time of the study as shown in Table 1. The Wisconsin sample was recruited from the University of Wisconsin, while the Missouri sample came from Harris Teachers College in St. Louis.[2] The Louisiana sample contained subjects from Newcomb College and Tulane University in New Orleans.

TASK

Subjects responded to stimulus items consisting of paired descriptions of hypothetical friendship candidates. Pairs of candidates differed with regard to race, sex, belief, or combinations of any two of these factors. It was the subject's task to rate each member of each pair on friendship potential along a 9-point scale. The low end of the scale was defined as indicating "I *can't* see myself being friends with such a person," while the high end was defined as indicating "I can *very*

---

[2] Although Missouri may possibly be considered a border state, it should be borne in mind that all subjects in the Missouri sample came from St. Louis, and St. Louis is more northern than border so far as relations between the races are concerned.

TABLE 1   Distribution of Subjects in Study I by Sex and Region of Residence at Time of Study

Sample	Sex		Residence			Total
	Male	Fe-male	North	St. Louis	South	
Wisconsin	23	19	42	—	—	42
Missouri (white)	9	13	—	22	—	22
Negro sub-sample[a]	5	16	—	21	—	21
Louisiana	26	29	10	—	45	55

[a] The Negro subsample was drawn from the entire Missouri sample.

easily see myself being friends with such a person."

EXPERIMENTAL DESIGN

Subjects were presented with a questionnaire containing 192 pairs of statements descriptive of hypothetical friendship candidates, or stimulus persons. Each stimulus person was assigned a race (white or Negro), a sex, and a belief on one of eight issues. Four of these issues were general in nature, while four concerned Negro-white relations. The general issues dealt with belief in God, socialized medicine, communism, and labor unions. The Negro-white issues concerned immediate versus gradual desegregation, fundamental equality of races, interracial fraternities and sororities, and freedom of Negroes to own homes wherever they wish.

The stimulus pairs were of six types. With eight issues and four pairs of a given type per issue (from combinations of sex and position on the issue), there were 32 pairs of each type. These types were:

Type R: Difference in race only.

Type B: Difference in belief only, on a specified issue.

Type S: Difference in sex only.

Type RB: Differences in both race and belief.

Type SB: Differences in both sex and belief.

Type RS: Differences in both race and sex.

One of the Type R pairs was

a) A Negro boy who believes in God.

b) A white boy who believes in God.

while an illustrative pair of Type RB was

    a) A Negro boy who believes in God.

    b) A white boy who is an atheist.

The pairs of all types were presented to subjects in a random order in a mimeographed questionnaire entitled, "Survey of Friendship Choices."

SCORING

Separate scores were computed, for each subject, for the four general beliefs taken together, and for the four Negro-white beliefs taken together. The scores were of two kinds. An *absolute score* was simply the rating from 1 to 9 circled by the subject. A *difference score* was the value obtained by subtracting one from the other of the ratings given to the two members of a stimulus pair.

Signs were attached to difference scores in accordance with information that had been obtained for each subject as to race, sex, and stand on each of the issues. A positive sign indicated a preference in the direction of own race, own sex, or own belief, while a negative sign signified a preference in the opposite direction.

Results

First we shall consider the 119 white subjects, and later we shall look at the Negro subsample. "The Missouri sample" will hereafter refer specifically to the 22 white subjects from Missouri, while "the Negro subsample" will be used later to refer to the 21 Negro subjects contained in the Missouri group.

Shown in Table 2 are the frequencies with which white subjects preferred *Negroes who agreed* more than, equal to, and less than *whites who disagreed*, for each issue separately. Each subject made two such discrimination responses per issue, one for each sex of stimulus persons in a pair. Because neither sex of subject nor sex of stimulus pairs had any appreciable effect, only the overall frequencies are presented.

For the Wisconsin and Missouri samples, the balance of ratings for each issue was clearly in favor of Negroes who agreed over whites who disagreed. For these two samples, agreement was considerably more important than similarity of race, as predicted by the belief congruence theory of prejudice.

For the Louisiana sample, however, a different pattern was observed. For six of the

TABLE 2 Number of White Subjects (Study I) Who Prefer Negroes Who Agree More than, Equal to, and Less than Whites Who Disagree

		Negro Is Rated		
Belief	Sample	Higher than White	Equal to White	Lower than White
General beliefs				
God vs. atheism	Wisconsin	63	9	12
	Missouri[a]	37	5	2
	Louisiana	58	8	44
Socialized medicine	Wisconsin	64	9	11
	Missouri[a]	19	13	12
	Louisiana	46	6	58
Communism vs. anti-communism	Wisconsin	84	0	0
	Missouri[a]	40	2	2
	Louisiana	91	6	13
Labor unions	Wisconsin	60	10	14
	Missouri[a]	19	10	15
	Louisiana	45	12	53
Negro-white beliefs	Wisconsin	65	4	15
	Missouri[a]	39	1	4
Immediate vs. gradual desegregation	Louisiana	52	2	56
Fundamental differences in races	Wisconsin	65	0	19
	Missouri[a]	38	2	4
	Louisiana	55	2	55
Interracial fraternities and sororities	Wisconsin	69	2	13
	Missouri[a]	22	4	18
	Louisiana	31	2	77
Segregated housing	Wisconsin	71	1	12
	Missouri[a]	31	5	8
	Louisiana	52	5	53

Note. Figures in each row sum to twice the sample size because two entries are tabulated for each subject, one for each sex of stimulus persons in a pair. No noteworthy differences were observed due to sex of stimulus pairs or sex of subjects.

[a] White subjects only.

eight issues, the majority of ratings were in favor of whites who disagreed over Negroes who agreed, although for five of these six issues the differences in frequencies were slight.

For the remaining issue, concerning interracial fraternities and sororities, well over twice as many unequal ratings favored whites who disagreed over Negroes who agreed. Race was somewhat more important than belief in this southernmost white sample, in contradiction to the belief-congruence theory. Rokeach et al., it will be recalled, found belief to outweigh race in both of their groups, including a southern (Houston, Texas) sample.

The same picture is revealed by the correlations in Table 3. If the discrimination re-

TABLE 3 Correlations between Discrimination Responses when Race and Belief are Varied (Type RB) with Race Discrimination (Type R) and Belief Discrimination (Type B) Responses: Study I

Correlation between Race-Belief Difference Scores and:	Sample	Negro-White Beliefs	General Beliefs
Race differ-ence scores	Wisconsin	.19	.21
	Missouri	.18	.21
	Louisiana	.58**	.59**
Belief differ-ence scores	Wisconsin	.91**	.95**
	Missouri	.93**	.96**
	Louisiana	.38*	.43*

$* p < .05.$
$** p < .01.$

sponses to Type RB pairs were due solely to race, then such responses should have correlated highly with responses to Type R pairs, but not with Type B pairs. If, on the other hand, responses to Type RB pairs were due solely to belief, they should have correlated highly with Type B pairs, but not with Type R pairs. The difference between $r_{RB.B}$ and $r_{RB.R}$ is thus an indicator of the relative influence of the belief and race factors. The correlations in Table 3 show that belief congruence was a much more important consideration than race for the Wisconsin and Missouri samples, but that race was somewhat more important than belief for the Louisiana sample.

Hotelling's test for differences between correlated correlations (Guilford, 1965, pp. 190–191) was used to compare corresponding values of $r_{RB.B}$ and $r_{RB.R}$. For the Wisconsin and Missouri samples, all four such pairs of

correlations were significantly ($p < .001$) different. For the Louisiana sample, however, neither pair differed significantly.[3]

Fisher's z transformation test (Guilford, 1965, pp. 189–190) was used to test the differences between correlations of the same kind between independent samples. Within either kind of belief, no pair of $r_{RB.R}$ differed significantly. Within either kind of belief, $r_{RB.B}$ for the Louisiana sample was significantly lower ($p < .001$) than that for either of the other samples.

We conclude: race was not significantly more important than belief for the Louisiana sample, but race was significantly more important in this sample—relative to belief—than it was for either of the other samples. Kind of belief, general or Negro-white, made very little difference in any sample.

Correlations analogous to those of Table 3 are used to compare the relative strength of sex and belief (Table 4), and race and sex

TABLE 4 Correlations between Discrimination Responses when Sex and Belief are Varied (Type SB) with Sex Discrimination (Type S) and Belief Discrimination (Type B) Responses: Study I

Correlation between Sex-Belief Difference Scores and:	Sample	Negro-White Beliefs	General Beliefs
Sex difference scores	Wisconsin	−.14	−.01
	Missouri	.20	.18
	Louisiana	.01	−.01
Belief differ-ence scores	Wisconsin	.94**	.95**
	Missouri	.94**	.90**
	Louisiana	.93**	.94**

$** p < .01.$

(Table 5). From Table 4 it can be seen that belief congruence was of overwhelmingly greater potency than was similarity of sex, for all three samples. From Table 5, it appears that race was substantially more important than sex, for all three samples. The Hotelling test was applied to appropriate pairs of correlations in both tables, as in

[3] Two-tailed tests of significance were employed throughout.

TABLE 5 Correlations between Discrimination Responses when Race and Sex are Varied (Type RS) with Race Discrimination (Type R) and Sex Discrimination (Type S) Responses: Study I

Correlation between Race-Sex Difference Scores and:	Sample	Negro-White Beliefs	General Beliefs
Race differ-ence scores	Wisconsin	.94**	.96**
	Missouri	.83**	.93**
	Louisiana	.93**	.95**
Sex difference scores	Wisconsin	.27*	.48**
	Missouri	.37*	.19
	Louisiana	.28*	.23

* $p < .05$.
** $p < .01$.

Table 3. All differences tested were highly significant ($p < .01$), for all samples, for both kinds of beliefs.

Belief congruence was clearly the most important of the three determinants of friendship acceptance for the Wisconsin and Missouri samples, with race second, and sex a poor third. For the Louisiana sample, race was the primary consideration, with belief not far behind, and sex again last.

Still another way of demonstrating the same results is through the mean differences in ratings for those who agreed versus those who disagreed, Negroes versus whites, and same versus opposite sex—as in Table 6. The higher

TABLE 6 Differences in Mean Acceptance of Those Who Agree and Disagree, Negroes and Whites, and Same and Opposite Sex: Study I

Comparison	Sample	Negro-White Beliefs	General Beliefs
Agreers vs. disagreers	Wisconsin	25.61	42.30
	Missouri	28.93	52.28
	Louisiana	11.55	37.71
Negroes vs. whites	Wisconsin	10.51	10.94
	Missouri	15.39	13.49
	Louisiana	53.79	49.75
Same vs. opposite sex	Wisconsin	.31	.82
	Missouri	2.05	−6.37
	Louisiana	4.13	2.84

mean rating always accompanied the same belief, race, or sex. For the Wisconsin and Missouri samples, the largest differences were due to belief, and the smallest due to sex. For the Louisiana sample, the largest differences were due to race, and the smallest again due to sex. The picture drawn from Tables 2–5 is reconfirmed in all details. It can also be seen from Table 6 that general beliefs were more important than Negro-white beliefs, insofar as they were associated with larger differences between those who agreed and those who disagreed.

Rokeach et al. (1960) argued that *true* racial discrimination implies that the outgroup is discriminated against, but that, at the same time, the ingroup is favored. This definition is in line with Levinson's (1949) conception of ethnocentrism, which implied vilification of the outgroup and overglorification of the ingroup. We should accordingly expect to find a *negative* correlation between acceptance of Negroes and acceptance of whites. Similar arguments could be drawn with regard to those who agree and those who disagree, or with regard to the same and the opposite sex, as ingroups and outgroups.

Instead, positive correlations were found. For the Wisconsin and Missouri samples, acceptance of Negroes and acceptance of whites were substantially correlated, the coefficients ranging between .56 and .77. Thus, for these samples, it is more accurate to speak of misanthropy (or philanthropy) than of discrimination or ethnocentrism. The correlations for the Louisiana sample—although still positive—were quite low, .11 and .20 for Negro-white and general beliefs, respectively. Both were significantly ($p < .01$) lower than the correlations in the other samples, by the z transformation test. Although a general misanthropy dimension was faintly present, since the correlations were not actually negative, the discrimination or ethnocentrism component of friendship acceptance was relatively prominent.

For Negro-white and general beliefs, respectively, Rokeach et al. obtained correlations of .81 and .79 for the Michigan sample, and correlations of .51 and .35 for the Texas sample. That is, they found slightly less true racial discrimination in the North, and moderately less true racial discrimination in the South, relative to present findings. The difference between the Louisiana and Texas samples was significant ($p < .01$) for the Negro-white beliefs, by the z transformation test. Other differences were not significant.

The correlations between agreers and disagreers were also found to be positive, for all three samples and both kinds of beliefs. The range was from .29 to .80, and no north-south gradient was observed. In each case, the correlation for general beliefs was lower than the corresponding coefficient for Negro-white beliefs, but only for the Missouri sample was the difference significant ($p < .01$).

Here again, the Louisiana sample differed from the Texas sample of Rokeach et al. Their sample yielded correlations between agreers and disagreers of .20 and −.14 for Negro-white and general beliefs, respectively. Their southern sample thus exhibited more true belief discrimination than did the present southern sample, and both differences were highly significant ($p < .002, p < .001$).

All three samples showed correlations in the middle and high .90s between acceptance of the two sexes. Acceptance of one sex was almost perfectly correlated with acceptance of the other. Discrimination, in the sense described above, was nonexistent, and individual differences in ratings were due entirely to a general misanthropy (or philanthropy) dimension.

In order to assess the interaction between each pair of variables, mean acceptance ratings were computed for race and belief stimulus subgroups, for belief and sex stimulus subgroups, and for race and sex stimulus subgroups. By and large, interaction effects were negligible. Sex of stimulus persons made little or no difference in the magnitude of preference for agreers over disagreers, for example. In addition, sex made very little difference in the extent of preference for whites over Negroes. For the Wisconsin and Missouri samples, Negroes of the opposite sex were rated lower than Negroes of the same sex, while for the Louisiana sample Negroes and whites of the opposite sex were rated higher than those of the corresponding race of the same sex—but all these differences were miniscule.

In the Missouri and Louisiana samples, for general beliefs there was a slight but noticeable tendency for belief congruence to make more difference in the case of whites, the ingroup, than Negroes. This tendency was not present in the Wisconsin sample, nor to any appreciable extent in the Negro-white beliefs for any sample. No conclusion appears warranted. With only occasional and minor exceptions, then, first-order interaction effects were absent.

THE NEGRO SUBSAMPLE

In addition to the 22 white subjects in the complete Missouri sample, there were 21 Negroes. Analysis of the data from this Negro subsample revealed that these subjects reacted very similarly to the white subjects in the Wisconsin and Missouri samples. For all eight issues, whites who agreed were preferred to Negroes who disagreed, by substantial margins, and the size of these margins was comparable to those observed in these two white samples. The belief-congruence theory of prejudice worked just as well for the Missouri Negroes as for the Wisconsin and Missouri whites.

Correlations similar to those presented in Tables 3, 4, and 5 were computed for the Negro subsample, as were mean differences in acceptance like those in Table 6. The general patterning was much the same as that found in the Wisconsin and Missouri samples. Belief congruence clearly had the greatest relative influence, while similarity of sex had the least. Race was still the intermediate factor. Application of the Hotelling test showed belief to be significantly ($p < .01$) more important than race, for both kinds of beliefs. Race was significantly ($p < .01$) more important than sex for Negro-white beliefs only. When belief and sex were compared, however, the correlations were significantly different ($p < .01$) only for the general beliefs. As with white subjects, first-order interaction effects were negligible.

The correlations between acceptance of Negroes and whites were .90 for the Negro-white beliefs and the same for the general beliefs. The corresponding correlations for agreers and disagreers were .78 and .46, while those for the same and the opposite sex were .99 and .99. These figures are comparable to those for white subjects, except for the correlations between races, which were somewhat higher than the Wisconsin and Missouri samples, and much higher than the Louisiana sample. The difference between the Negro subsample and the Wisconsin sample, for Negro-white beliefs, was significant at the .01 level, while that for general beliefs was significant at the .05 level. Both differences between the Negro subsample and the Louisiana sample were highly significant ($p < .001$). One interpretation of these findings is that these Negro subjects discriminated on a racial basis less than the white subjects—especially the southern white subjects—making a general misanthropy/philanthropy factor sufficient to account for individual differences in level of acceptance.

STUDY II

Method

The only essential difference between Study II and Study I was the nature of the samples. Whereas the large majority of subjects in Study I were white, all 167 subjects in Study II were Negro. These were distributed by sex and region of residence at the time of the study as shown in Table 7. The Ohio sample was drawn from Central State University in Wilberforce, while the Tennessee sample came from Tennessee Agricultural and Industrial State University in Nashville. Students in both samples were enrolled in psychology classes. The students from the Mississippi sample were recruited from physical education classes at Mississippi Vocational College in Itta Bena. All three institutions are attended primarily or exclusively by Negroes.

Results

Table 8 presents the frequencies with which Negro subjects preferred *whites who agreed* more than, equal to, and less than *Negroes who disagreed*, for each issue separately. Each subject made two such discriminations per issue, one for each sex of stimulus persons in a pair. For all three samples, and for all eight

TABLE 8 Number of Negro Subjects (Study II) Who Prefer Whites Who Agree More than, Equal to, and Less than Negroes Who Disagree

		White is Rated		
Belief	Sample	Higher than Negro	Equal to Negro	Lower than Negro
General beliefs	Ohio	105	13	4
God vs.	Tennessee	97	21	12
atheism	Mississippi	55	21	6
Socialized	Ohio	69	43	10
medicine	Tennessee	70	47	13
	Mississippi	57	15	10
Communism	Ohio	98	17	7
vs. anti-	Tennessee	87	29	14
commu-	Mississippi	39	30	13
nism				
Labor	Ohio	71	38	13
unions	Tennessee	65	55	10
	Mississippi	44	23	15
Negro-white	Ohio	76	29	17
beliefs	Tennessee	74	37	19
Immediate	Mississippi	37	21	24
vs. gradual				
desegre-				
gation				
Fundamental	Ohio	65	37	20
differences	Tennessee	73	31	26
in races	Mississippi	41	18	23
Interracial	Ohio	82	21	19
fraterni-	Tennessee	63	20	47
ties &	Mississippi	44	26	12
sororities				
Segregation	Ohio	97	17	8
in housing	Tennessee	97	20	13
	Mississippi	58	16	8

Note. Figures in each row sum to twice the sample size because two entries are tabulated for each subject, one for each sex of stimulus persons in a pair.

TABLE 7 Distribution of Subjects in Study II by Sex and Region of Residence at Time of Study

	Sex		Residence						Total
Sample	Male	Female	North	Border	South	East	Midwest	West	Total
Ohio	13	48	27	2	0	23	9	0	61
Tennessee	27	38	0	40	13	5	5	2	65
Mississippi	19	22	1	2	38	0	0	0	41

issues, a substantial majority of subjects preferred whites who agreed to Negroes who disagreed. These data are clearly and consistently in line with the belief-congruence theory of prejudice.

The correlations in Table 9 lead to the same conclusion. The correlations between responses to Type RB pairs and Type R pairs appear to cluster about zero, while those between responses to Type RB pairs and Type B pairs are all high, ranging between .71 and .93. Differences between corresponding RB-B and RB-R correlations were all highly significant ($p < .001$) by the Hotelling test. Again it is demonstrated that belief congruence was more important than race similarity for all three samples.

TABLE 9 Correlations between Discrimination Responses when Race and Belief are Varied (Type RB) with Race Discrimination (Type R) and Belief Discrimination (Type B) Responses: Study II

Correlation between Race-Belief Difference Scores and:	Sample	Negro-White Beliefs	General Beliefs
Race difference scores	Ohio	.13	.22
	Tennessee	−.10	−.09
	Mississippi	.02	−.09
Belief difference scores	Ohio	.93**	.90**
	Tennessee	.71**	.71**
	Mississippi	.77**	.82**

** $p < .01$.

In contrast to the data from the white subjects in Study I, there was no appreciable overall effect due to the north-south gradient. When the correlations of Table 9 were computed for male and female subjects separately, however, it was noted that the RB-B correlations were consistently lower for females than for males. Furthermore, while differences were small for the Ohio and Tennessee samples, they were appreciable for the Mississippi sample: .93 versus .72 for general beliefs, and .93 versus .53 for Negro-white beliefs. The first difference was significant at the .05 level, and the second at the .01 level, by the z transformation test. The female Negro subjects from Mississippi assigned a sig-

nificantly greater weight to race, relative to belief, than did their male counterparts. Still even the females gave most weight to belief.

Table 10 makes use of SB-B and SB-S correlations to show the relative influence of belief congruence and sex of stimulus persons. Correlations between responses to Type SB pairs and Type S pairs appear to cluster about zero, while those between Type SB and Type B pairs are all rather large, ranging from .55 to .83. Belief congruence was more important than similarity of sex in all three samples. Differences were all significant at the .05 level at least, and at the .01 level in most cases, according to the Hotelling test.

TABLE 10 Correlations between Discrimination Responses when Sex and Belief are Varied (Type SB) with Sex Discrimination (Type S) and Belief Discrimination (Type B) Responses: Study II

Correlation between Sex-Belief Difference Scores and:	Sample	Negro-White Beliefs	General Beliefs
Sex difference scores	Ohio	.26	−.10
	Tennessee	−.01	.10
	Mississippi	.17	−.10
Belief difference scores	Ohio	.83**	.80**
	Tennessee	.58**	.63**
	Mississippi	.55**	.53**

** $p < .01$.

The relative influence of race and sex is indicated in Table 11. In all cases but one, the correlation between Type RS pairs and Type R pairs was larger than that between Type RS pairs and Type S pairs. Race was, by and large, more important than sex, but the two factors were much more evenly matched for the three Negro samples of Study II than for the three white samples of Study I (Table 5). Two out of the three pairs of correlations for Negro-white beliefs were significant ($p < .05$, $p < .01$), while only that for Mississippi was significant ($p < .05$) for the general beliefs.

For all three samples of Study II, then, belief congruence was by far the most important determinant of friendship acceptance. Race was second, and sex again last, although

TABLE 11 Correlations between Discrimination Responses when Race and Sex are Varied (Type RS) with Race Discrimination (Type R) and Sex Discrimination (Type S) Responses: Study II

Correlation between Race-Sex Difference Scores and:	Sample	Negro-White Beliefs	General Beliefs
Race difference scores	Ohio	.69**	.10
	Tennessee	.40**	.37**
	Mississippi	.32	.65**
Sex difference scores	Ohio	.41**	.33**
	Tennessee	−.30**	.22
	Mississippi	.06	.22

** $p < .01$.

it came in a somewhat better last than it did in the case of the white samples.

A reaffirmation is obtained through the patterning of mean differences in ratings for agreers and disagreers, Negroes and whites, and the same and opposite sexes. These appear in Table 12. The belief factor produced the largest differences, while sex produced the smallest, in perfect agreement with the correlational analysis. In addition, a comparison of Tables 6 and 12 reveals that the more nearly even influence of race and sex in Study II was due primarily to the smaller influence of race in Study II, relative to its effect in Study I.

TABLE 12 Differences in Mean Acceptance of Those Who Agree and Disagree, Negroes and Whites, and Same and Opposite Sex: Study II

Item	Sample	Negro-White Beliefs	General Beliefs
Agreers vs. disagreers	Ohio	47.14	45.99
	Tennessee	45.07	43.66
	Mississippi	33.14	34.73
Negroes vs. whites	Ohio	4.97	2.92
	Tennessee	2.22	1.63
	Mississippi	4.91	6.56
Same vs. opposite sex	Ohio	.53	1.73
	Tennessee	.43	.05
	Mississippi	−.78	1.17

Correlations between acceptance of Negroes and whites, and between males and females, were all high and positive, ranging from .70 to .95. Correlations between responses to agreers and disagreers, on the other hand, ranged between −.09 and .13 and did not differ significantly in any case from zero. True discrimination, in the sense of vilification of the outgroup and overglorification of the ingroup, was approximated only with regard to belief. With regard to race and sex, a general misanthropy/philanthropy dimension was sufficient to account for individual variations.

The essentially zero correlations between agreers and disagreers in Study II stand in sharp contrast with the findings of Study I. The Negro subsample of Study I resembled closely the white samples in this regard. For some reason, the Negro subjects of Study II (but not the Negro subjects of Study I) bordered on indulging in true belief ethnocentrism. Since seven out of eight correlations in Study I were significant, and none even approached significance in Study II, the overall difference between studies can be taken as significant.

First-order interactions were investigated by computing mean ratings of acceptance for belief and race stimulus subgroups, belief and sex stimulus subgroups, and race and sex stimulus subgroups. Interactions between belief and sex, and between race and sex, were quite negligible.

There was, however, a clear-cut interaction between belief and race. For all three samples, and for both kinds of beliefs, mean differences in friendship acceptance of agreers and disagreers were larger for Negroes than for whites. This pattern held, without exception, when differences were computed separately for male and female subjects. The two-tailed sign test shows the consistency of this patterning to be significant beyond the .001 level. Furthermore, in 8 out of the 12 instances, Negroes who disagreed were actually rated lower than whites who disagreed. We can say that for the Negro subjects in Study II (but not for those in Study I, recall) there was a tendency to penalize excessively members of their own race who disagreed, as if such people were seen as turncoats or renegades. This *renegade effect*, somewhat surprisingly perhaps, was equally strong for general beliefs as for specifically Negro-white beliefs.

DISCUSSION

The results of both studies, taken together, provide extensive additional substantiation of the belief-congruence theory of prejudice. Not only most whites, but Negroes as well allot significantly greater weight to belief than to race in their ratings of friendship acceptance.[4] Furthermore, similarity of sex has been demonstrated to be no competition to belief congruence, or even to race in most instances.

At the same time, the belief-congruence theory sustains one major defeat. The New Orleans whites evidently considered race more important even than belief congruence, unlike the subjects in the Houston sample of Rokeach et al. (1960). There is a difference of perhaps 5 or 6 years in the collection of data between the two studies. It is quite possible that there had been during this time an increase in the salience of race as a result of the civil rights movement. If so, this increased salience may have been greater in the South, resulting in a greater relative importance of race.

It is also possible that place, not time, is the operative variable. Houston is some 300 miles west of New Orleans. Moreover, 70% of the students in the Houston sample were born in Texas, a large and culturally heterogeneous state. If substantial numbers of these university students were from western Texas, this could be expected to exert an attenuation of the effect of the institutionalized mores of the deep South. Additional research is needed to clarify the point.

It should be noted that, even if some groups do give most weight to racial and ethnic factors, this is not necessarily fatal for the belief-congruence theory of prejudice. People may often assume, a priori, that members of the outgroup hold basically different beliefs, making belief the underlying consideration after all. Subjects in the Louisiana sample, in particular, may have tended to assume belief incongruence as regards *other* beliefs in the case of Negroes who agreed.

Although this remains to be demonstrated, strong evidence can be cited (e.g., Willis, 1960) that group stereotyping processes need not depend upon motivational factors; cognitive factors can suffice.

A major weakness in the evidence supporting the theory stems from the fact that most of the directly relevant studies, including the present ones, have employed college students responding to hypothetical and contrived situations. It would not necessarily follow that the theory works equally well in cognitively real settings and/or with less educated subjects. Recent findings, however, indicate that perhaps it often does. Rokeach and Mezei (1966) conducted three experiments on sociometric choice from among real and present persons differing in belief and race. Two of these experiments again used college students, but the third included as subjects job applicants for positions of janitor, laundry worker, and attendant in mental hospitals. In all experiments the choices, which were made following a group discussion, were cognitively real for the subjects. The belief-congruence principle was consistently the best predictor of choices in all three experiments.

It would also appear that the theory is extendable to the area of interpersonal attraction. Several dimensions of similarity in personality have been found to correlate with actual friendship (e.g., Miller, Campbell, Twedt, & O'Connell, 1966) and with marriage choices (Tharp, 1963). More particularly, interpersonal attraction has been found by Newcomb (1961) to be substantially related to agreement on a variety of social issues. The fact that Newcomb's data can be cited in support of the belief-congruence theory, while his theoretical discussion is couched in terms of structural balance, strain towards symmetry, and the like, serves to emphasize the previously mentioned close relationship between the belief-congruence principle and theories of cognitive consistency.[5]

The only noteworthy interaction effect observed was the renegade effect among Negro

---

[4] Additional evidence that the belief-congruence formulation of acceptance works for Negro as well as white subjects is to be found in Stein (1966).

[5] Rokeach and Rothman (1965) have recently extended the belief-congruence principle to the area of cognitive interaction, and in doing so have made more explicit its relationship to another formulation of cognitive consistency, the congruity principle (Osgood & Tannenbaum, 1955).

subjects of Study II. Why do Negroes from de facto segregated colleges, but not those from integrated colleges, nor whites to any extent, penalize members of their own race more for disagreeing than they do members of a racial outgroup? Perhaps this can be understood as minority-group behavior. Consensus, a concerted pulling together, is more vital to a disadvantaged minority than to a large and relatively secure majority. The dominant group has less need for cohesiveness and can so afford to show more tolerance towards deviant opinion. Certainly Schachter's (1951) finding of greater rejection of deviates in more highly cohesive groups is consistent with this interpretation. A possible point against it, though, is the fact that the renegade effect was fully as pronounced in connection with general beliefs as with Negro-white beliefs.

The lack of interaction between race and sex came as a surprise. It had been anticipated that members of the opposite sex belonging to the other race would be rated as considerably less acceptable as friends than those of the same race, in some samples at least. It was also expected that this effect would be stronger for white than Negro subjects, because of the status differences between the races. These expectations assumed that friendship choices involving the opposite sex would be perceived, not necessarily as implying intimacy, but as implying a definite potential for such intimacy. As interracial sexual intimacy is in violation of the prevailing social norms in many quarters, such implied potential for intimacy might be expected to result in the specific rejection of members of the opposite sex of the other race.

That such an interaction did not occur is probably best explained by assuming that subjects of both races interpreted "being friends with" a member of the opposite sex in a purely platonic fashion. This explanation is made all the more tenable by the finding of Triandis and Davis (1965), especially Table 4 (p. 722), that belief is more important in the case of nonintimate behavioral intentions, while race is more important in the case of intimate behavioral intentions.[6]

Although no sample showed the negative

[6] See also the exchange between Triandis (1961) and Rokeach (1961).

correlations indicative of "true" discrimination in the sense of simultaneous vilification of the outgroup and overglorification of the ingroup, the southern whites bordered on such true *racial* discrimination, while all three Negro samples in Study II bordered on such true *belief* discrimination. One rather speculative but provocative conjecture is that de facto segregation encourages true discrimination, the specific type depending upon circumstances. The Wisconsin and Missouri samples, including the Negro subsample, were from integrated educational institutions and exhibited high mean correlations both between acceptance of Negroes and whites, and between agreers and disagreers. All three samples in Study II, as well as the Louisiana sample in Study I, were from de facto segregated institutions. The fact that only Negroes from de facto segregated institutions exhibited the renegade effect lends additional plausibility to this conjecture.

REFERENCES

Byrne, D. Interpersonal attraction and attitude similarity. *Journal of Abnormal and Social Psychology*, 1961, **62**, 713–715.

Byrne, D., & McGraw, C. Interpersonal attraction towards Negroes. *Human Relations*, 1964, **17**, 201–213.

Byrne, D., & Wong, T. J. Racial prejudice, interpersonal attraction, and assumed dissimilarity of attitudes. *Journal of Abnormal and Social Psychology*, 1962, **65**, 246–253.

Guilford, J. P. *Fundamental statistics in psychology and education.* (4th ed.) New York: McGraw-Hill, 1965.

Heider, F. *The psychology of interpersonal relations.* New York: Wiley, 1958.

Levinson, D. J. An approach to the theory and measurement of ethnocentric ideology. *Journal of Psychology*, 1949, **28**, 19–39.

Miller, N., Campbell, D. T., Twedt, H., & O'Connell, E. J. Similarity, contrast, and complementarity in friendship choice. *Journal of Personality and Social Psychology*, 1966, **3**, 3–12.

Newcomb, T. M. Individual systems of orientation. In S. Koch (Ed.), *Psychology: A study of a science.* Vol. 3. New York: McGraw-Hill, 1959. Pp. 384–422.

Newcomb, T. M. *The acquaintance process.*

New York: Holt, Rinehart & Winston, 1961.

Osgood, C. E., & Tannenbaum, P. H. The principle of congruity in the prediction of attitude change. *Psychological Review,* 1955, **62,** 42–55.

Rokeach, M. Belief versus race as determinants of social distance: Comments on Triandis' paper. *Journal of Abnormal and Social Psychology,* 1961, **62,** 187–188.

Rokeach, M., & Mezei, L. Race and shared belief as factors in social choice. *Science,* 1966, **151,** 167–172.

Rokeach, M., & Rothman, G. The principle of belief congruence and the congruity principle as models of cognitive interaction. *Psychological Review,* 1965, **72,** 128–142.

Rokeach, M., Smith, P. W., & Evans, R. I. Two kinds of prejudice or one? In M. Rokeach (Ed.), *The open and closed mind.* New York: Basic Books, 1960. Pp. 132–168.

Schachter, S. Deviation, rejection, and communication. *Journal of Abnormal and Social Psychology,* 1951, **46,** 190–207.

Smith, C. R. Friendship choice as a function of race, sex, and belief. Unpublished master's thesis, Washington University, 1966.

Stein, D. D. The influence of belief systems on interpersonal preference. *Psychological Monographs,* 1966, **80** (Whole No. 616).

Stein, D. D., Hardyck, J. A., & Smith, M. B. Race *and* belief: An open and shut case. *Journal of Personality and Social Psychology,* 1965, **1,** 281–290.

Tharp, R. G. Psychological patterning in marriage. *Psychological Bulletin,* 1963, **60,** 97–117.

Triandis, H. C. A note on Rokeach's theory of prejudice. *Journal of Abnormal and Social Psychology,* 1961, **62,** 184–186.

Triandis, H. C., & Davis, E. Race and belief as determinants of behavioral intentions. *Journal of Personality and Social Psychology,* 1965, **2,** 715–725.

Williams, L. Friendship as a function of race, sex, and belief. Unpublished master's thesis, Washington University, 1964.

Willis, R. H. Stimulus pooling and social perception. *Journal of Abnormal and Social Psychology,* 1960, **60,** 365–373.

7

Black Militancy and Violence

Take the man whom I almost killed: Who was responsible for that near murder—I? I don't think so, and I refuse it . . . He bumped me, he insulted me. Shouldn't he for his own personal safety, have recognized my hysteria, my "danger potential"? He, let us say, was lost in a dream world. But didn't he control that dream world—which alas, is only too real!—and didn't he rule me out of it? And if he had yelled for a policeman, wouldn't I have been taken for the offending one?

RALPH ELLISON, *Invisible Man*

Heretofore blackness has been a stigma, a curse with which we were born. Black Power means that this curse will henceforth be a badge of pride rather than scorn.

ROBERT S. BROWNE, *The Case for Black Separatism*

INTRODUCTION

As black consciousness and pride grew and as white racism continued to take its toll, the seething frustration and anger in the black ghettoes exploded. A stunned nation witnessed the unleashing of pent-up bitterness and rage as city after city was hit by massive civil disorders. The black rebellion had become violent and could no longer be ignored by the American public.

After the worst outbreaks in the summer of 1967, President Johnson appointed a commission (referred to previously as the Kerner Commission) to "answer three basic questions: What happened? Why did it happen? What can be done to prevent it from happening again?" (Report of the National Advisory Commission on Civil Disorders, 1968, p. 1.) A number of studies were carried out on behalf of and independently of the Commission. This chapter will deal with some of the issues raised by these studies. We shall

339

explore the views of black Americans, the facets of militancy and characteristics of militants, the immediate and distant causes of the rebellion, the reactions of black and white citizens, and some consequences of militancy.

It is hoped that this chapter will serve as an introduction to the rapidly growing literature on protest and change by social scientists (for example, Killian, 1968; Killian & Grigg, 1964; Marx, 1967; Waskow, 1966) and black writers (for example, Baldwin, 1963; Carmichael, 1966; Carmichael & Hamilton, 1967; Cleaver, 1968; Fannon, 1961).

BLACK VIEWS OF RACIAL ISSUES

Campbell and Schuman [26][1] found that the overwhelming majority of their black respondents prefer integration to racial separation in school, housing, stores, and friendship. Among over three million Negroes in the 15 cities they studied, there were nevertheless an estimated 200,000 who take an extreme separatist position and over half a million who sympathize "with the use of racial criteria in making specific institutionalized policy" (p. 5). The latter group, particularly, emphasizes black ownership of stores and black administration of schools in Negro neighborhoods. The emphasis on black culture and achievement, however, appears to be a much stronger trend than separation. Over 40 percent of the black sample, for example, endorsed the statement, "Negro school children should study an African language." Black consciousness is definitely growing, but *"a substantial number of Negroes want both integration and black identity"* (p. 6, emphasis added).

Racial discrimination, particularly in employment and housing, was the major complaint of the black respondents. In addition, about a third of the sample saw whites as hostile and repressive, another third viewed whites as indifferent to Negroes, and the final third saw most whites as well-intentioned. In comparison with the white respondents, the black sample expressed consistently more dissatisfaction with public services, governmental efforts to solve urban problems, police practices, and prices and treatment in local stores.

Contrary to widely held beliefs stemming from the recent upheavals in many cities, the picture that emerges from Campbell and Schuman's data is one of black moderation and compassion. Marx's (1967) nationwide survey in 1964 came to much the same conclusion. He found that, using a 1964 standard, only one third of the black community consistently expressed militant attitudes, and even fewer were strongly anti-white or anti-Jewish. Civil rights militants, furthermore, tended to be less anti-white than the more apathetic. The moderate civil rights groups, such as NAACP and SCLC, were the most popular, and the Black Muslims had relatively few supporters. Finally, the more deprived blacks, who would tend to benefit most from social change, were the least likely to be militants.

In a postscript to the recent edition of his book Marx (1969) presented a summary of 14 studies done since 1967, which he feels still support the conclusion he had reached earlier:

> Our data suggest that many people hold an overly sensational image of the Negro mood. To be sure, there is a deep anger and frustration, as well as varying degrees of suspicion and resentment of whites. Yet there is still optimism about the possibility of change within the system. Most Negroes favor integration in principle, are loyal to the United States, are opposed to indiscriminate violence and not consistently anti-white or anti-Semitic. (Marx, 1969, p. 216.)

[1] For a description of this study see Chapter 6.

Yet his warning in 1966 is still relevant:

> Such findings offer no grounds for complacency. The magnitude of moral injustice, the intensity of concern felt by many, and the ever-increasing potential for social disruption cannot be measured by a simple counting of the "Yeas" and "Nays." (Marx, 1967, p. 206.)

How prophetic this warning turned out to be was demonstrated by the massive disturbances which occurred the following summer.

BLACK ACTIVISM

While the focus here is on recent events, it should be kept in mind that the revolt of blacks is as old as their oppression. Time and time again, since slavery, blacks have fought in a variety of ways to be free (Bronz, 1964; Fishel & Quarles, 1967; Wish, 1964). But in the sixties black resistance against subordination has taken on a more organized, massive, and assertive form than ever before and is likely to involve a widening circle of active participants.

In the fifties and early sixties, mostly in the South, blacks (later supported by white activists) began organized but nonviolent demonstrations of protest. These activities were directed at the most obvious expressions of white racism, such as segregation in public facilities and police brutality. As long as the demonstrators were willing to take the brunt of white hate without physically fighting back, the nation on the whole sympathized with them and perhaps identified with their underdog role. As the protest movement spread to northern cities and became more violent, the public reacted with fear and resentment. Mass media became prone to focus on those who used the most violent revolutionary rhetoric (Rustin, 1967) and the reports on the "riots" and their aftermath were bound to create a distorted image of the mood in the black community. It is therefore, crucial that we carefully analyze the objective evidence on black activism and militants.

One of the stereotypes of black militants is that they are all consumed by profound hatred of whites. As we have already seen, Marx found little substance to this claim (with the exception of a small number of black nationalists). In line with Marx's results, Noel (1964), in a study referred to in Chapter 6, found that strong group identification was associated with low generalized prejudice. Black "identifiers" (those who manifested group pride) furthermore, expressed less frustration and authoritarianism than "disparagers" (those who agreed with disparaging comments about Negroes). Identifiers were also more likely than disparagers to be NAACP members, have a high educational level and occupational status, and engage in interracial social contacts. Noel concludes that "this challenges the belief that the rejection of outgroups (e.g., whites) is an almost inevitable concomitant of in-group (e.g., black) pride and suggests that an unequivocally positive group identification can be functional for societal integration" (p. 83). A later report (Noel, 1966), which revealed that identifiers are also more likely to identify with the total community (blacks and whites), approve of residential desegregation, and vote in a presidential election, substantiated his conclusion. Gore and Rotter (1963) found that black college students who were involved in social protest movements against segregation expressed more confidence in their ability to determine their own fate (internal control) than those who were less committed. On the other hand, Surace and Seeman (1967) found that whereas interracial contact, lack of status concern, and internal control were associated with civil rights activism for whites, no such relationships held for blacks.

Before turning to a discussion of "riot" participants, the more ordinary social and political participation of Negroes should briefly be discussed in order to provide a broader context and perspective for the black rebellion. It is a widely held belief that black Americans, in contrast to immigrants and other whites, lack sufficient organizational resources to express their concerns and fight for their demands. Orum (1965) however, found that black lower-class city residents were more likely to belong to and actively participate in political and church groups than their white counterparts. Middle-class and upper-class whites, on the other hand, tended to join organizations more often than their black counterparts. Orum also indicated that Negro voting in presidential elections (see also Middleton, 1962) has recently increased considerably and could have reached the white voter turnout were it not for their generally lower educational level and extralegal restrictions in the South.

Wilson (1966) has also analyzed the Negro's role in politics. He points to gains in voter strength, particularly in the South, but he is doubtful as to whether Negro politics will accomplish more than limited objectives. In the North, it is likely that blacks will concern themselves more with local elections under local leadership, whereas in the South they will involve themselves with state and national elections as well, for it is the latter that more directly affect the Negro. This political development appears paralleled by the evolution of black protest actions in the last year or two. Former national, state, or regional campaigns, often with massive white liberal support (for example, the march on Washington) and oriented towards global aims (equal opportunity, voting rights, and so forth), have recently been almost completely replaced by highly localized demonstrations. The latter (sometimes involving only a section or a few blocks of a city) are organized by militant indigenous leaders, often excluding whites, and concentrate on more specific local issues (control of the school board, integration of a particular store, rent control, and so forth). This does not mean that traditional national leaders have lost the allegiance of the black masses. On the contrary, as suggested before, such leaders as Roy Wilkins are still relatively very popular. Rather, it appears that black citizens now expect better results from local activism.

What about the role of religion in black activism? Marx's [27] study deals with the relationship between religion and participation in the civil rights struggle. His data suggest that involvement in conventional churches is generally associated with a lower degree of militancy. There is, however, a distinction between those who place emphasis on life beyond death and those who are more concerned with the here and now. An "otherwordly" orientation seems to inhibit active protest, and a temporal one may actually encourage it.

On the whole, it appears that traditional social, political, and religious organizations have been relatively unsuccessful, and in some instances have inhibited the forceful and productive expression of legitimate Negro grievances and demands. Williams (1968; see also Boesel, 1968) has pointed out that when legitimate channels are unavailable, immigrant groups attempt to enter into the mainstream of American society by forming power blocs or by illicit means. Negroes, however, have been unable either through legitimate or illegitimate means to break through the existing power structure. The appointment or elections of black mayors (for example, Washington, Stokes, Hatcher, and Evers), Williams suggests, represents a turning point, since they provide access to power and thereby entry into the social system by the group. By and large, though, second-generation blacks (whose parents migrated to urban centers from the rural South) have been socialized in ways that leave them inadequately equipped to handle current problems. Moreover, they are also faced with "discontinuities between a cultural system which encourages minority group expectations and a social system which operates to block their attainment" (p. 17). Under these circumstances violent explosions, even self-destructive impulses, are not surprising.

BLACK "RIOTERS" AND COMMUNITY RESPONSE

Following the massive civil disorders in Watts in 1965 and many other cities since then, a number of studies have attempted to pinpoint the extent of participation in the disturbances and the characteristics of the rioters. An excerpt of Fogelson and Hill's [28] report, based on riot arrestees' records from 10 cities and 1960 census figures, and a report on the Watts riot by Sears and Tomlinson [29] are included here.

Contrary to the widely held belief among most whites and some Negroes that rioters are mostly hoodlums, communists, outside agitators, and transients (that is, all "riffraff") these studies demonstrated that those who participated were not the most depressed segments of the black community nor recent arrivals—nor were their numbers as small as the public seemed to believe. The third myth—that all but a small fraction of the black community were opposed to the riots—was also shattered by these data. What emerges is a deep split in the interpretation of the events between the citizens at large and those most affected in the ghetto. The majority of whites have misunderstood the causes and meaning of the black rebellion and have underestimated the involvement of the black community. Rationalizing the riots as the doings of a small criminal element may bring temporary relief from the shock most people experienced in the wake of the massive violence, but the failure to grasp and deal with the root causes of black unrest and the failure to recognize the potentially large number of black "rebels" available has ominous implications.

The reactions to the riots by whites such as policemen, educators, social workers, merchants, and political party workers who came in frequent contact with ghetto residents were surveyed by Rossi et al. (1968) in 15 cities, which had all experienced some form of civil disturbance. Their findings revealed that even these whites had distorted views of ghetto life and the causes of the riots.

> Their views can be characterized as optimistic denials of the full seriousness of the position of urban Negroes in their cities. More than half felt that Negroes were being treated in their cities on a par with whites . . . .
>
> They gave a much more important role to militants and "agitations" than the Commission's Report was able to find was actually the case . . . .
>
> Police, merchants, and employers generally took positions on most issues which strongly denied that there was inequality for Negroes in their city, which tended to blame riots on agitators, and which held unfavorable images of the Negro population (pp. 74–75).

The differences between black and white reactions to the riots is also clearly demonstrated in the final excerpt from Campbell and Schuman's [30] study. For example, most blacks believe that better employment and improved communications between Negroes and whites as well as an end to discrimination would prevent future riots. Most whites, however, have more faith in repressive measures, such as increased police control. Most blacks point to discrimination and unsatisfactory living conditions as the cause of the riots. Many whites see the presence of radicals and undesirables as a more important reason for the riots. Campbell and Schuman also report that the number of potential white counter-rioters is nearly as great as that of the potential black rioters.

The Kerner Commission concluded:

> Our nation is moving toward two societies, one black, one white—separate and unequal. Reaction to last summer's disorders has quickened the movement and deepened the division. Discrimination and segregation have long permeated much of American life: they now threaten the future of every American (p. 1).

It is difficult to convey the deep despair and frustration one experiences in reading and analyzing the documentation on the riots. Kenneth Clark has said, "It is a kind of Alice in Wonderland—with the same moving picture re-shown over and over again, the same analysis, the same recommendations, and the same inaction" (p. 29). The massive commitment the Kerner Commission called for has not materialized. The white masses seemingly remain untouched and indifferent and the governments have not drastically altered their priorities. The richest country in the world refuses to recognize that its very survival or at least its democratic values are threatened. It refuses to shift its vast expenditures from Vietnam, defense contracts, and the race to the moon and elsewhere to resolving its greatest crisis. An eerie feeling of incredulity and unreality creeps in as one begins to realize this fact.

Pessimism has been expressed by many of the social scientists who have made a serious effort to document the crisis:

> [These interracial differences] indicate a profound lack of communication and the absence of understanding or compassion among a very large portion of the white public. (Marx, 1969, p. 226.)

> There is no reason to believe that aggressive ghetto rioting will cease of its own accord, or that new violent tendencies on the side of Negroes—such as terrorism—will not develop out of the present pattern of disorder. (Goldberg, 1968, p. 129.)

> There are no immediate responses within the repertoire of any agency or person which are sufficient to expunge the outrage that gives birth to Negro violence, except the Negro's own fear of the burning and killing, and that comes only after the riot has occurred. (Tomlinson, 1967, p. 71.)

> It is one measure of the depth and insidiousness of American racism that the nation ignores the rage of the rejected—until it explodes in Watts or Harlem. The wonder is that there have been so few riots, that Negroes generally are law-abiding in a world where the law itself has seemed an enemy. (Clark, 1966, p. 63.)

Proposals to move America out of her dilemma abound. Realistic short-term and long-term plans have been outlined by responsible blacks and whites, and potential resources exist. These efforts are to no avail, however, without the will and determination to commit energies and funds commensurate with the urgency of the crisis.

Yet a significant number of white radical youths, particularly in colleges and universities, have begun fighting along with blacks. Cleaver (1968) has paid them tribute:

> There is in America today a generation of white youth that is truly worthy of a black man's respect, and this is a rare event in the foul annals of American history . . . .

> If a man like Malcolm X could change and repudiate racism, if I myself and other former Muslims can change, then there is hope for America. It was certainly strange to find myself, while steeped in the doctrine that all whites were devils by nature, commanded by the heart to applaud and acknowledge

respect for these young whites—despite the fact that they are descendants of the masters and I the descendant of slaves. The sins of the fathers are visited upon the heads of the children—but only if the children continue in the evil deeds of the fathers (pp. 82–83).

REFERENCES

Baldwin, J. *The fire next time.* New York: Dell, 1963.

Boesel, D. P. Negro youth and the ghetto riots. Unpublished paper. Johns Hopkins University, 1968.

Bronz, S. H. *Roots of Negro racial consciousness.* New York: Libra, 1964.

Carmichael, S. Toward black liberation. *The Massachusetts Review,* Autumn, 1966.

Carmichael, S., & Hamilton, C. V. *Black power.* New York: Vintage, 1967.

Clark, K. B. The wonder is there have been so few riots. In L. E. Berson, *Case study of a riot.* New York: Institute of Human Relations Press, 1966.

Cleaver, E. *Soul on ice.* New York: Dell, 1968.

Fanon, F. *The wretched of the earth.* New York: Grove, 1961.

Fishel, L. H., Jr., & Quarles, B. *The Negro American: A documentary history.* Glenview, Ill.: Scott, Foresman, 1967.

Goldberg, L. C. Ghetto riots and others: The faces of civil disorder in 1967. *Journal of Peace Research,* 1968, **5,** 116–132.

Gore, P. M., & Rotter, J. B. A personality correlate of social action. *Journal of Personality,* 1963, **31,** 58–64.

Killian, L. M. *The impossible revolution?* New York: Random House, 1968.

Killian, L. M., & Grigg, C. *Racial crisis in America.* Englewood Cliffs, N.J.: Prentice-Hall, 1964.

Marx, G. T. *Protest and prejudice.* New York: Harper & Row, 1967.

Marx, G. T. Social movements and mass opinion. Postscript to G. T. Marx, *Protest and prejudice.* New York: Harper Torchbook, 1969.

Middleton, R. The civil rights issue and presidential voting among Southern Negroes and whites. *Social Forces,* 1962, **40,** 209–215.

Noel, D. L. Group identification among Negroes: An empirical analysis. *The Journal of Social Issues,* 1964, **20,** 71–84.

Noel, D. L. Minority group identification and societal integration. Paper read at the 1966 Meeting of the American Sociological Association, Miami Beach, Florida.

Orum, A. M. A reappraisal of the social and political participation of Negroes. *American Journal of Sociology,* 1965, **66,** 353–358.

Report of the National Advisory Commission on Civil Disorders. New York: Bantam, 1968.

Rossi, P. H., et al. Between white and black: The faces of American institutions in the ghetto. In *Supplemental studies for the National Advisory Commission on Civil Disorders.* Washington, D.C.: Government Printing Office, 1968.

Rustin, B. Foreword in G. T. Marx, *Protest and prejudice.* New York: Harper & Row, 1967.

Surace, S. J., & Seeman, M. Some correlates of civil rights activism. *Social Forces,* 1967, **46,** 197–207.

Tomlinson, T. M. Ideological foundations for Negro action: A comparative analysis of militant and non militant views of the Los Angeles riot. Unpublished paper. Institute of Government and Public Affairs, University of California, Los Angeles, 1967. To be published in *Journal of Social Issues,* 1970, **26** (1).

Waskow, A. *From race riot to sit-in.* Garden City, N.Y.: 1966.

Williams, B. Riots and the second generation. Unpublished paper. Office of Economic Opportunity, Washington, D.C., 1968.

Wilson, J. Q. The Negro in politics. In T. Parsons and K. B. Clark (Eds.), *The Negro American*. Boston: Houghton Mifflin, 1966.

Wish, H. (Ed.) *The Negro since emancipation*. Englewood Cliffs, N.J.: Prentice-Hall, 1964.

26

Black views of racial issues

A. CAMPBELL AND H. SCHUMAN

A group of Negro college students at a major northern university in May, 1968, demanded the provision of separate dormitory accommodations. To some ears it sounded like a call for segregation by race, another example of recent repudiations by some Negroes of the goal of integration. In the first section of this chapter we will describe the extent to which integration remains a goal of black Americans in the 15 cities we studied. We will also examine the *meaning* attached by Negroes to integration in such concrete contexts as schools. The second section attempts to look for possible signs of change in our data, so that we do not too quickly impose a static view on what is obviously a volatile period in American racial history. In the third section we present fragmentary but interesting evidence on a type of change in Negro aspirations that is not really located on a simple separatist-integrationist dimension. The fourth section turns to an account of the appeal militant leaders have to nonseparatist followers. Negro perceptions of discrimination and prejudice are described and a preliminary attempt is made to locate

Reprinted from *Racial attitudes in fifteen American cities,* Supplemental Studies for the National Advisory Commission on Civil Disorders, Washington, D.C.: U.S. Government Printing Office, Chapter 2, pp. 15–28.

these in terms of the dimensions of age and education. The chapter ends with a brief consideration of some of the main strategies adopted by Negroes in confronting obstacles perceived as due to white racial attitudes and practices.

RACIAL INTEGRATION AND BLACK SEPARATISM

We did not ask many general questions about the desirability of integration, but posed the issue concretely in terms of several specific areas of life. For example, the following table (Table 1) gives the results of a question concerned with residential integration.

Nearly half the Negro sample indicate a preference for a mixed neighborhood and another third claim that the racial character of the neighborhood makes no difference to them. Only one Negro respondent out of eight in our sample favors residential separation. The overwhelming majority prefer "integration" either in the positive sense of "racial balance" or in the nondiscriminatory sense of race being irrelevant to decisions about neighborhood.

These percentages must not be taken too literally: they are influenced not only by general attitudes toward integration or separation, but by the particular subject matter

TABLE 1* "Would you personally prefer to live in a neighborhood with all Negroes, mostly Negroes, mostly whites, or a neighborhood that is mixed half and half?"

(In percent)

	Negro		
	Men	Women	Total
All Negro	7	8	8
Mostly Negro	7	4	5
Mostly white	1	1	1
Mixed half and half	47	48	48
Makes no difference	37	37	37
Don't know	1	2	1
	100	100	100

* See Appendix B for notes on the format of this and other tables.

of the question, in this case, residence, and by peculiarities of wording. A better idea of the range of answers to questions on integration and separation is provided in Table 2, which lists all the questions we included within this area broadly defined. The questions are ordered in terms of the percentage giving an answer that seems in a "separatist" direction—that is, show some rejection of whites or some preference for racial exclusiveness.

The findings from this table are clear-cut. When Negro respondents are asked whether they wish their children to have only Negro friends, they reject this possibility by 19 to 1. When asked whether they favor "a separate black nation here" (the exact location unspecified), they again reject this by 19 to 1. Both in their personal lives and on issues concerning public institutions, Negroes in these 15 cities oppose black separatism by an overwhelming margin. The largest support for racial exclusiveness turns on the ownership by Negroes of stores in a Negro neighborhood, which is supported by nearly one out of five members of the sample; yet even on this highly publicized current issue, four out of five respondents refuse to introduce race as a criterion for ownership or control.

It may be argued that reponses implying integration are chosen largely for pragmatic reasons. As reported in Chapter IV, Negroes tend to perceive neighborhood services in white or mixed residential areas as better than those in largely Negro areas. White businessmen may be seen as having capital to maintain a wider range of merchandise. White schools may be regarded as having the benefit of better facilities or less crowded conditions. Because of such real social and economic differences, Negroes might lean toward "mixed" or "white" responses for purely practical reasons.

In order to explore this issue, we asked respondents to explain their answers to several of the questions given in Table 2. The results of two such follow-up inquiries are shown in Tables 3 and 4. They point in two directions. First, a sizable proportion of the Negro sample do, in fact, mention a "practical" reason for preferring mixed schools and mixed neighborhoods—24 percent in the former case and 14 percent in the latter. But second, as large or an even larger proportion give a more purely integrationist response (30

TABLE 2 Percentage of Negroes Favoring Separatist Response to Each of Ten Questions

	Men	Women	Total
Believe stores in "a Negro neighborhood should be owned and run by Negroes"	21	15	18
Believe school with mostly Negro children should have Negro principal	17	12	14
Prefer to live in all Negro or mostly Negro neighborhood	14	12	13
Believe school with mostly Negro children should have mostly Negro teachers	13	7	10
Agree that "Negroes should have nothing to do with whites if they can help it"	11	8	9
Believe whites should be discouraged from taking part in civil rights organizations	9	6	8
Prefer own child to go to all or mostly Negro school	7	6	6
Believe close friendship between Negroes and whites is impossible	6	5	6
Agree that "there should be a separate black nation here"	7	4	6
Prefer child to have only Negro friends, not white friends too	6	4	5

TABLE 3   "Why do you feel that way?" (Follow-up Question to Preference for Racial Composition of School)

(In percent)

	Negro		
	Men	Women	Total
Type of Explanation Given by Those Preferring "Mixed" Schools:			
Mixed schools have better facilities (e.g., "teachers take more time in a mixed school")	24	25	24
Learn to get along with each other (e.g., "kids should grow up together and learn to get along")	30	29	30
Other (e.g., "race shouldn't be that important")	6	6	6
Inapplicable—Already said race should not make any difference— not asked follow-up question	30	29	30
Prefer Negro school	7	6	6
Don't know	3	5	4
	100	100	100

percent for schools and 18 percent for neighborhoods) which emphasizes the desirability of Negroes and whites learning "to get along with each other." To these latter integrationist respondents, we should add the more than a third of the sample who claimed that race should not make any difference at all, since such people can hardly be seen as individuals who would favor racial exclusiveness. The results then indicate that a majority of Negro respondents not only favor integration, but that they do so because of either a commitment to racial harmony or a conviction that

racial considerations should be transcended entirely.

The desire for better school and neighborhood facilities and a belief in integration as an end in itself are, of course, not mutually exclusive. The higher percentage of Negroes (95 percent) in Table 2 who would like their children to have white as well as Negro friends suggests that many respondents who mention "practical facilities" to other questions are not intending to rule out an interest in integration for its own sake. On the other hand, results to be presented in Chapter IV

TABLE 4   "Why do you feel that way?" (Follow-up Question to Preference for Racial Composition of Neighborhood)

(In percent)

	Negro		
	Men	Women	Total
Type of Explanation Given by Those Preferring "Mixed" Neighborhood:			
Mixed neighborhood has better services (e.g., "schools are better")	5	4	4
Mixed neighborhood better place to live (e.g., "less crime," "quieter")	9	12	10
Learn to get along with each other (e.g., "we should learn to live together")	18	17	18
Other (e.g., "race should not make any difference in choosing a place to live")	9	8	9
Inapplicable—Already said race should not make any difference— not asked follow-up question	37	37	37
Prefer Negro neighborhood	14	12	13
Don't know	8	10	9
	100	100	100

indicate that Negroes in these 15 cities have many specific dissatisfactions about their cities that have little to do directly with issues of integration.

It is also worth noting that even responses which suggest an apparent desire for "black power" may in reality reflect a somewhat different concern. Although 14 percent of the Negro sample believe a mostly Negro school should have a Negro principal, only a tiny proportion explain this in terms of black control of black institutions. Most speak in terms of the better understanding Negro principals will have of Negro children, or their superior ability to work closely with the parents of their pupils. And, of course, despite these quite practical reasons for wanting Negro principals in all-Negro schools, *most* Negroes in our sample do *not* believe that race should enter into the selection process.

In summary, it is clear that in early 1968 the major commitment of the great majority of the Negro population in these 15 cities was not to racial exclusiveness insofar as this meant personal rejection of whites or an emphasis on racial considerations in running community institutions. Negroes hold strongly, perhaps more strongly than any other element in the American population, to a belief in nondiscrimination and racial harmony.

WINDS OF CHANGE?

The conclusions of the previous section do not provide much support for the sense of radical change that comes from listening to new and more militant voices from the black community. One possibility is that these new leaders have no following. However, another possibility is that our data reflect well enough the inertia of opinion in this large urban Negro population, but not at all well the potentiality for change growing rapidly within it. In this section we will attempt to look hard at the data both for signs of such growth and for the importance of what change may already have occurred. This will require a somewhat more speculative orientation than we follow in most other parts of this report.

First, it is reasonable to argue that the small percentage of separatist thinking that does appear in the preceding tables deserves to be taken seriously in its own right. Small

percents can represent large numbers of people. In this study, one percent of the Negro sample stands for approximately 33,000 people, ages 16 to 69, in the 15 cities in which we interviewed. A finding of 10 percent represents 330,000, or nearly one-third of a million persons. (This counts only Negroes in the 15 cities, there being an unknown but undoubtedly large number of individuals with similar beliefs in other American cities.) Thus when we say that six percent of the sample advocates the formation of a separate black nation, we are implying that some 200,000 Negroes in these 15 cities feel so little a part of American society that they favor withdrawing allegiance from the United States and in some sense establishing a separate national entity.

Unlike election polls where it is usually correct to focus on majority or at least plurality figures, "small" percentages in this study must not be disregarded as unimportant. In a formal election six percent of the vote means little, but in a campaign to change minds and influence policies, six percent of a population can represent a considerable force. This is particularly true when the six percent represents deviation from a traditional position, since it is likely that many of those who hold to the majorty position do so with little thought or commitment. To deviate from a very widely held norm probably requires more conviction than to hold to it, and if we could estimate this extra factor and weight it into the results we might well find the force behind black nationalism to be considerably greater than its numbers suggest. Finally, the high degree of residential and general social segregation in these cities promotes communication and association among such individuals, and provides them with easy access to just the audience they wish to reach.

In addition to appreciating the absolute size and strength of separatist opinion, there is the equally important question of how fast it is growing, if indeed it is growing at all. A single survey, however, is like a single photograph, and there is no direct way it can measure recent rates of change, let alone predict with precision future rates. There is no past survey of this 15-city population with which we can closely compare our present results, and we must rely on age as an indirect indication of change. We make the assumption that what change there is in the long-term goal of integration is likely to occur most rapidly among the young. It was a relatively young minister, Martin Luther King, who at the age of 27 led the Montgomery bus boycott in 1957. College students were the main participants in the "sit-ins" of the early 1960's. Today, as we near the end of the decade, it appears to be black youth in colleges and black youth on ghetto streets who are least satisfied with America as it is, or perhaps even as their parents wish it to be. This fits the common assumption that the young are less conservative in the generic sense of the word: satisfaction with the currently traditional ways of doing things. If the youth in our sample show more separatist thinking than the older men and women, one can interpret this as a sign of change, using the shape and steepness of the age curve as a rough measure of the rate of change.

The use of age as an indicator in this way has definite problems. One is the difficulty of separating the trend movement in which we are interested from youthful rebellions

that have no lasting effect but subside into middle-aged acceptance. Nor, on the other hand, can we be sure that the "rate of change" one estimates by comparing young and old is itself unchanging; if the rate accelerates, young children coming of "interview age" will differ more from their teenage fellows than the latter do from present adults. More generally, the projection of present trends to describe the future is full of risk, since unforeseen events—an assassination, a war, a major racial clash—following discussion must be read with these reservations in mind.

Five of the ten questions discussed earlier were selected as conceptually closest to "separatism," and the relation of each to age is shown in Table 5. The overall trend seems clear: younger people are somewhat more accepting of separatist beliefs than are older people. The trend is more consistent for men than for women, with the latter showing little perceptible change on the more extreme items (defined as those with the smallest percentage of separatist response for the sample as a whole). There is also one quite consistent

TABLE 5 Percentage in Each Age Category Showing Separatist Thinking on Five Questions

	Negro Men					
	16–19	*20–29*	*30–39*	*40–49*	*50–59*	*60–69*
Believe stores in "a Negro neighborhood should be owned and run by Negroes"	28	23	20	18	14	18
Believe school with mostly Negro children should have mostly Negro teachers	22	15	13	6	5	15
Agree that "Negroes should have nothing to do with whites if they can help it"	18	14	6	12	4	13
Believe whites should be discouraged from taking part in civil rights organizations	19	12	8	6	3	5
Agree that "there should be a separate black nation here"	11	10	5	5	4	10
	Negro Women					
Believe stores in "a Negro neighborhood should be owned and run by Negroes"	18	16	16	15	13	8
Believe school with mostly Negro children should have mostly Negro teachers	11	9	6	5	5	12
Agree that "Negroes should have nothing to do with whites if they can help it"	11	7	7	8	5	7
Believe whites should be discouraged from taking part in civil rights organizations	11	7	7	5	7	3
Agree that "there should be a separate black nation here"	9	3	2	6	4	3

reversal of the main trend: the oldest males "double-back" and are much more separatist than would be expected from the primary direction of change. We suspect this involves an irrelevant artifact, but cannot explore the problem in the present report.

Table 6 presents broad age trends in conjunction with educational groupings. The latter show little relation to separatist response, but the age differences continue to hold within almost all educational groups. There is a hint in the table, which will need further investigation, that institutional self-rule appeals to more educated Negroes, while wholesale rejection of whites appeals to the less educated.

In general, then, younger Negroes do assert separatist beliefs more strongly than do older Negroes. If one ignores the oldest age group (60–69) as artifactual, the change between the 50 to 59 group and the 16 to 19 represents at least a doubling of percent separatist thinking for women and a tripling for men. If the 60 to 69 cohort is included, as caution dictates, the increase is about .50 over the total age span contained in the table. The largest jump is from individuals in their 20s to the 16 to 19 category.

If we were to assume that the younger people will hold to their beliefs, then in a little more than a generation separatism would rise noticeably over the whole population. *Even then*, however, it would remain a distinctly minority position within the Negro community. Instead of being represented by five or ten percent of the Negro population, it would characterize 15 or at most 20 percent of the adult Negroes in these 15 cities. The majority would still have to be described as "integrationist" in goal and sentiment.

It would be possible to project more dramatic change in Negro opinion if one introduced one or both of two additional assumptions. For example, if we assumed that the rate of change for maturing age groups continued for those cohorts entering the adult population, rather than remaining at the level we have observed in this survey, there would obviously be a long-term increment in separatist thinking. Thus we would have to assume that the attitudes of the new generation entering the 16 to 19 year-old category departed even further from the general average of the total Negro population than the present 16 to 19 year-old group

does. Our data showing the rate of change from one age group to the next might be interpreted as suggesting some such increment but the evidence could only be taken as inferential and does not demonstrate the validity of the assumption in question.

A second assumption which might be considered would project an increase in separatist opinion in those age cohorts where such thought is now least popular, the older generations. If separatist thinking increases among the young and is "taken up" by popular leaders and the influential mass media, one might assume that it would diffuse in some degree into the larger Negro population.[1] To the extent that this diffusion was successful the separatist position might change from the clearly deviant one it is today to one of far greater influence.

We must emphasize again, however, that these speculations go far beyond what our data tell us. Even the age trends on which much of this speculation is based are not as steep or consistent as many readers might have expected. In fact, sharper age differences are reported in Chapter V on another subject (the use of violence) but evidence is also presented there that casts doubt on how much the differences represent long-term shifts in orientation; they seem at least as much to represent youthful boldness, much of which may not persist with maturation.[2]

At this point, then, it is useful to reiterate the main findings presented earlier in the

---

[1] There are some indications of such a shift in some sections of the Negro press. For example, the *Michigan Chronicle,* the major Negro newspaper for Detroit, has changed in tone since the 1967 riot. The word "black" has been substituted for "Negro," a regular column of commentary by a leading militant spokesman has been added, and more regular coverage is given to groups advocating separation. Much of the change, however, fits better the type of cultural shift discussed in our next section, rather than being fully separatist.

[2] It should be noted that our sample does not represent college students living on campuses and thus misses an important body of young, educated opinion. This may have some effect when we break the sample by age and education, but it is too small to influence major trends appreciably. We also do not represent current military personnel, whose thinking is probably a good deal closer to the modal character of the present results.

TABLE 6 Percentage in Each Age and Education Group Showing Separatist Thinking
(Results for Negro men and women averaged)

	Age 16–19*	Age 20–39					Age 40–69				
		8th grade or less	9–11 grades	12 grades	Some college	College graduate	8th grade or less	9–11 grades	12 grades	Some college	College graduate
Believe stores in "a Negro neighborhood should be owned and run by Negroes"	22	19	18	18	20	30	16	13	13	17	13
Believe school with mostly Negro children should have mostly Negro teachers	16	8	11	10	10	20	10	4	5	5	3
Agree that "Negroes should have nothing to do with whites if they can help it"	14	18	11	6	6	0	14	5	5	5	4
Believe whites should be discouraged from taking part in civil rights organizations	15	14	7	8	11	10	5	5	5	5	5
Agree that "there should be a separate black nation here"	10	8	5	6	2	4	8	3	2	5	0

* This group combines all educational categories.

chapter. Most Negroes of all age groups today reject separatist thinking both in the political and in the personal sense. Commitment to the values of nondiscrimination and racial harmony are paramount for Negroes in these 15 cities.

PLURALISM:
AN ALTERNATE PATH

"Black separatism," both as preached and as practiced, actually has two clearly distinguishable aspects. One side is largely political and social, calling for black control of institutions that serve the black population and for concentration of all informal social relationships within the black community. We have already seen that this program has relatively little support at present within the Negro population of these 15 cities. The other aspect of the program is cultural in the sociological sense of the term and attempts to encourage the growth of a positive black identity, a realization of the significance of black achievement, both in Africa and in America, and a desire to contribute to the development of the black community. We find in our data some important evidence that this cultural emphasis has wide appeal within the urban Negro population.[3]

The results of four questions that point in this direction are presented in Table 7.[4] It is perhaps no surprise to learn that 96 percent of the sample affirm that "Negroes should take more pride in Negro history," or that nearly as many agree "there should be more Negro business, banks, and stores." But it is striking indeed that 42 percent of this sample believe "Negro school children should study an African language." Unfortunately, we had no other question that so clearly taps positive identification with a black heritage without

[3] An excellent discussion of the distinction made here appears in Milton Gordon's *Assimilation in American Life,* New York: Oxford Press, 1964.

[4] Unfortunately all four items are of an agree/disagree type and worded in the same direction, thus allowing for "response set" effects. They are almost the only such items of this type in the questionnaire. It appears from internal evidence in the questionnaire that such effects may be raising marginal percentages here by about five percent.

TABLE 7 Percentage of Negroes Approving Each of Four Positive Cultural Identity Statements

	Men	Women	Total
"Negroes should take more pride in Negro history"	96	96	96
"There should be more Negro business, banks, and stores"	95	92	94
"Negroes should shop in Negro owned stores whenever possible"	70	69	70
"Negro school children should study an African language"	46	38	42

at the same time implying rejection of whites. But the support for this single proposition, which a few years ago was scarcely discussed by most Negroes and still seems exotic and impractical to most white ears, is so impressive that it suggests a considerable potential for the growth of black cultural identity in America. It also suggests that the more frequently voiced demand for more Negro history in public schools probably has very broad support in the Negro population.

The gap between the 42 percent agreement with this item and the 9 percent agreement reported earlier with the item "Negroes should not have anything to do with whites if they can help it" (Table 2) is a good indication of the difference in appeal between programs emphasizing positive cultural identity and programs espousing rigid social separation. The positive character of this interest in having children study African languages is further brought out by some of the explanations respondents gave for agreeing with the item:[5]

> "Since all races have a language of their own it would be good if we had one too. Italians, Germans, Jews have one, why not us?"

[5] For each closed question in the interview we obtained from a random subsample of about 50 interviewees an explanation of why their responses were chosen. The method used is described in H. Schuman, "The Random Probe: A Technique for Evaluating the Validity of Closed Questions," *American Sociological Review,* **31**, 2 (April, 1966), pp. 218–222.

The majority of the explanations are in fact universalistic, offering a reason that is very much in keeping with general American values:

> "I feel they should study all languages."

> "They teach every other language, an African language could be taught too."

And a few responses carry a negative edge:

> "In school you are only taught the white man's language. You are not taught the Negro native language."

The proposal thus has appeal to many segments of the Negro population.

Results of the African language item by age and education are shown in Table 8.

question in the interview; while not surprising, the exact meaning of this will have to be clarified through further analysis.

There is one other finding in Table 7 that is of interest but also somewhat puzzling. Over two-thirds of the sample agree with the statement that "Negroes should shop in Negro owned stores whenever possible." This was intended as an indicator of separatism and might well have been listed in Table 2. The percentage agreement, however, is so far out of line with any question in the separatism set that we feel it was understood by many people in a way different than intended. Note, for example, that in Table 2, 80 percent of the sample rejected giving Negroes the exclusive right to own stores in Negro areas.

TABLE 8   "Negro school children should study an African language"
(Percentages for men and women averaged)

		Age 20–39					Age 40–69				
	Age 16–19*	*8th grade or less*	*9–11 grades*	*12 grades*	*Some college*	*College graduate*	*8th grade or less*	*9–11 grades*	*12 grades*	*Some college*	*College graduate*
Approve	44	54	41	39	43	28	43	44	38	33	33
Disapprove	46	33	47	46	44	61	37	38	51	49	42
Don't know**	8	7	11	12	12	9	17	17	10	18	24
Other	2	6	1	3	1	2	3	1	1	0	1
	100	100	100	100	100	100	100	100	100	100	100

* This group combines all educational categories.
** The "don't know" category is quite large and probably of substantive importance in indicating uncertainty, hence it has been distinguished from other miscellaneous responses.

They indicate a slight trend for agreement to be associated with *lower* education, but no consistent relation to age. This is somewhat puzzling and suggests that the item represents not so much a new idea, but more an appeal to rather long-standing needs within the Negro community. Its greater attraction to the less-educated may also indicate that its importance is mostly symbolic, since those least able to add such an extra language burden to their education are most willing to approve a proposal to do so. It may also indicate that the item appeals especially to those in the Negro community who are furthest from having achieved a middle-class American way of life. The item also has one of the highest "don't know" percentages of any

Our assumption is borne out by explanations of those who indicated agreement. They talk for the most part in terms of offering positive support for the struggling Negro businessman who is trying to make a success of his business. They seldom relate this to not patronizing white-owned stores. Perhaps having just earlier indicated their agreement that "there should be more Negro business, banks, and stores," the need to patronize such stores to make them successful was especially salient to respondents. In any case, we interpret the result here as more an emphasis on promoting positive Negro achievement than on separatism or rejection of whites, though it obviously is a somewhat ambiguous item.

In summary, this section suggests strongly

the value of further study of the interest of urban Negroes in positive racial symbols of achievement and identity, without confounding this interest with more social or political issues involving separatism. As in the case of religious and ethnic groups in America, there seems to be wide support for cultural individuality *within* a larger interracial social structure. Such affirmation of black identity is in keeping with American pluralism and should not be termed "separatism." It does, however, contain a source from which leaders advocating separatism can draw, especially if there is wide disillusion with the possibility of making integration work in social and political contexts.

SOURCES OF DISSATISFACTION

The rise of angry and militant black leaders, like the outbursts of urban rioting, are not only disturbing to many white Americans, but puzzling as well. Considering the improvements for Negroes over the past 15 years—visible in Supreme Court decisions, in civil rights legislation, in appointments to high offices, and perhaps most of all in the appearance for the first time of black faces in restaurants and airplanes, on television and movie screens—why aren't black Americans more satisfied? Why, indeed, are they not gratified by the enormous progress that has occurred in race relations during and since what a distinguished author referred to as "a revolutionary decade, 1954 to 1964," one that the "most far-seeing of men standing at the beginning of the period, would have been quite unlikely to predict. . . ."[6]

The following that "black nationalist" spokesmen have can easily be exaggerated, of course. In our survey, as in all previous studies we know of, their popular support is much less than that for the NAACP or for the late Dr. Martin Luther King (Table 9). Nevertheless, the at least partial support they have is not small, particularly when one considers that the militant figures mentioned in Table 9 were hardly known at all several years ago. Stokely Carmichael's "stand" is approved or partly approved by 35 percent of

the sample, the same percentage that show clear disapproval. H. Rap Brown wins less support, but nevertheless more than a quar-

TABLE 9 "Now I want to read you a list of people active in civil rights. For each one, please tell me whether you approve or disapprove of what the person stands for, or don't know enough about him to say?"

(In percent)

	Negro		
	Men	Women	Total
Stokely Carmichael			
Approve	18	10	14
Partly approve and partly disapprove	24	17	21
Disapprove	34	36	35
Don't know	24	37	30
	100	100	100
Martin Luther King			
Approve	70	74	72
Partly approve and partly disapprove	22	16	19
Disapprove	5	4	5
Don't know	3	6	4
	100	100	100
Roy Wilkins			
Approve	54	46	50
Partly approve and partly disapprove	13	11	12
Disapprove	4	2	3
Don't know	29	41	35
	100	100	100
H. Rap Brown			
Approve	17	10	14
Partly approve and partly disapprove	14	12	13
Disapprove	46	44	45
Don't know	23	34	28
	100	100	100
How about the NAACP?			
Approve	77	74	75
Partly approve and partly disapprove	12	10	11
Disapprove	3	3	3
Don't know	8	13	11
	100	100	100

[6] Anthony Lewis and The New York Times, *Portrait of a Decade: The Second American Revolution*, New York, Bantam Books, 1965.

ter of the sample gives general or partial
approval to what he "stands for," and slightly
less than half the sample disapproves. The
names of both men seem to be slightly better
known than the name of Roy Wilkins, Executive Director of the NAACP.

Approval or partial approval for a man
does not necessarily mean approval for his
specific programs—the connections are frequently hazy to the average respondent. We
have already seen that there is little support
for black separatism as a political movement.
In Chapter V we will show that support for
violence is somewhat greater, but still quite
limited in percentage terms. The main attraction that men like H. Rap Brown and Stokely
Carmichael have to the wider Negro community is probably their emphasis on the serious
difficulties Negroes face and the vociferous
attribution of these difficulties to white
America.

Our interest here lies not so much in the
amount of support for any particular spokesman, but rather in the extent to which *racial*
conditions are seen by Negroes as cause for
profound and justified criticism. We will look
at this in terms of two general areas of possible criticism: first, the extent of overt discrimination that is perceived to exist today
in America, and second, Negro perceptions
of white racial attitudes of a more intangible
nature.

1. An End to Discrimination?

We began this chapter by noting that a
large proportion of the white population probably believe that much progress has been
made over the last 15 years in eliminating
overt racial discrimination in the United
States. No single question about such change
was asked of whites and we state this as an
assumption of what we would find.[7] We did
ask Negroes such a question, however, and
the results are illuminating. The question
(Table 10) concerns the amount of progress
that has been made over the past ten or
fifteen years "in getting rid of racial discrimination" in America. Although a majority of the Negro sample believes that
substantial progress has been made, the more

[7] In Chapter III we do discuss in some detail
white beliefs about *current* levels of discrimination.

TABLE 10 "Some people say that over the
past 10 or 15 years there has been a lot of progress in getting rid of racial discrimination. Others
say that there hasn't been much real change for
most Negroes over that time. Which do you agree
with most?"

(In percent)

	Negro		
	Men	Women	Total
A lot of progress	63	60	62
Hasn't been much real change	34	36	35
Don't know	3	4	3
	100	100	100

striking finding is that one out of every three
respondents agrees that there has not been
"much real change for most Negroes" over
a period that dates roughly from the 1954
Supreme Court decision on school desegregation. The basic assumption of major improvement, so seemingly obvious to many
white Americans, is not accepted by many
black Americans.

One might expect denial that progress has
occurred to come especially from younger
people. They did not experience the more
blatant forms of discrimination characteristic of America in 1950, nor did they see one
type of racial segregation after another out-
lawed over a relatively short time. The age
trends for the data provide some support for
this expectation. Of teenagers, 43 percent of
the males and 37 percent of the females dis-
claim progress, but in the 60 to 69 year old
groups the percentages drop to 28 and 26
percent, respectively. The age trend is smooth
for men, but somewhat irregular for women.
Among younger people (ages 20 to 39), the
more educated of both sexes recognize more
change; there is little relation of education
to perception of change for persons over 40.
Taken together these results suggest that those
who are older and those who have more education are better able to recognize the broad
movement of events of the last decade and
a half. Negroes too young to have personally
experienced the break-up of many traditional
racial patterns and those with less general
awareness of recent history (or perhaps simply lower incomes, a correlate of education

not yet explored) are more likely to deny that meaningful change has occurred.

But these effects are only moderate. Even among the oldest and among the best educated, a quarter still report that there has not been much real change for most Negroes. They do this apparently because from their perspective there has indeed been little visible change, whatever may have occurred elsewhere in the country. Respondents who said "no change" explained their responses in the following way:

"We can do the same job as whites but get unequal pay. Education is different in white and colored schools."

". . . We bought this nice furniture, thought we were going to buy a house. When they found out we were Negroes they wouldn't sell to us."

"There has been some but not much. There are still a lot of jobs that Negroes can't get and there are a lot of houses that Negroes can't rent or buy."

"On the whole the prejudice of people is still the same. They are just pretending today."

The question just discussed speaks of discrimination in the abstract. Most of our inquiries in this area were more specific. Table 11 presents the results of nine questions dealing with employment. The first two questions indicate that more than a third of the Negro males in the sample claim to have *personally* experienced racial discrimination in employment. The figure is somewhat smaller for women, probably because fewer have been in the labor force. To avoid confusing recent with ancient history, we asked how long ago

the last such incident had happened. For those mentioning any discrimination at all, the majority report an incident of discrimination within the past five years, and nearly three-quarters report an incident within the past ten years. We have no way, of course, to verify these reports. Even in a current situation it is often difficult to prove or disprove that job discrimination occurred. What is clear, however, is that a great many Negroes believe that discrimination not only happens, but that it has happened personally to them during the same "past ten or fifteen years" referred to in the earlier question on change.

When job discrimination is asked about in more general terms, Table 11 indicates that about 70 percent of the sample believe that "many" or "some" Negroes (as against "few") miss out on good jobs because of their race. (Only about 40 percent, however, choose the term "many," rather than the vague word "some.") Approximately 40 percent of the sample believe that Negroes are discriminated against in federal employment, and the figure rises to over 50 percent when city employment is considered. The claim by some large private companies that they are looking for all the capable Negroes they can find to put into good jobs has also not made a great impression in these 15 cities: nearly 80 percent of the sample believe that such hiring is only of a token nature. There is little difference by sex on any of these questions on perceptions of extent of discrimination, unlike the reports of personal experience mentioned above.

Discriminatory personal experience in the job area is reported most frequently by per-

TABLE 11 Percentage of Negroes Perceiving Discrimination in Employment

	Men	Women	Total
Report having been refused a job because of racial discrimination	34	25	30
Report having been refused promotion on a job because of racial discrimination	18	9	14
Believe many or some Negroes miss out on jobs today because of discrimination	72	70	71
Believe many or some Negroes miss out on promotions today because of race	68	67	68
Believe there is discrimination in hiring by the federal government	40	40	40
Believe there is discrimination in hiring by their city government	51	49	50
Believe there is discrimination in hiring in teaching	35	33	34
Believe big companies hire a few Negroes only for show purposes, to appear to be non-discriminatory	78	76	77
Believe discrimination in hiring and promotions is increasing or not changing	42	43	42

sons in their 20's and 30's, and less both by teenagers and by persons over 40 and especially over 50 (Table 12). The lower rate in the former group is presumably due to the large proportion still in school. The lack of reporting in the older groups is less easily accounted for; these people may never have attempted to get jobs in competition with whites, or may be settled in their jobs and have forgotten early instances of discrimination, or may have been less ready to define an ambiguous situation as discriminatory. However, exactly the same trends occur for all the questions on extent of job discrimination. (Age trends for two such general items are shown in Table 12, along with the personal experience questions.) The mild curvilinear relationship that is repeated over all four questions in the table is difficult to account for. Rephrasing the explanation given above, we might hypothesize that those who are in their prime working years have the most involvement with employment and promotion and therefore the most immediate opportunity to perceive discrimination. This explanation does not seem to us wholly satisfactory, and further analysis will be required to support it or to arrive at a more adequate interpretation of the data.

Most knowledgeable white Americans agree that job discrimination is still a problem in American cities, but some comfort is often taken in the belief that such discrimination is decreasing. Whatever the truth of the matter, this belief is shared by only half the Negro respondents in our sample (Table 11 above). In fact, 20 percent of the sample

believe job discrimination to be on the increase, the remaining 30 percent perceiving no change at all. Education makes some difference in this case for women—the more educated see a decrease in job discrimination —but there is no such relation for men. A better understanding of this difference will require analysis using employment status, and must be reserved for later reports.

Discrimination in housing is seen in dimensions that are roughly similar to those for employment (Table 13). We did not ask about *personal experience* in this area because much residential segregation is self-perpetuating: few Negroes seek housing in all-white areas which they think will prove inhospitable. Instead we asked whether there were "many, some, or just a few places" in the city where the respondent believed he "could *not* rent or buy a house because of racial discrimination." It should be noted that the question referred directly to the city itself and did not ask about the much more highly segregated suburban areas. Two out of five respondents believed there were many such places in their city, and another quarter felt there were "some" rather than few.

About the same proportion answered a more general question on whether Negroes "miss out on good housing" in their city because of race: 45 percent say "many" do and 30 percent that "some" do. Finally, a little over 50 percent of the sample see no decrease in residential discrimination underway at present. There are no differences by sex on any of these questions; age and education trends have not yet been studied.

TABLE 12   Age Trends among Negroes for Four Questions on Employment Discrimination

(Percentages for men and women averaged.*)

	Age					
	16–19	*20–29*	*30–39*	*40–49*	*50–59*	*60–69*
Have been personally discriminated against in employment	21	33	37	30	24	18
Have been personally discriminated against for promotions	4	12	17	18	12	13
Believe many Negroes miss out on good jobs because of discrimination	34	38	44	42	40	26
Believe many Negroes miss out on promotions because of discrimination	29	37	46	41	37	24

* Trends are very similar for men and women considered separately.

Our questionnaire did not deal in detail with other social areas, for example, education. But Table 13 does sample two quite different public spheres. Judicial behavior, in theory far removed from racial bias, is seen as discriminatory by 22 percent of the sample. A much larger proportion—three out of five—expect unequal treatment when they go as citizens to make a request to "city officials." Indeed, this question produces the most widespread perception of discrimination of any item of the questionnaire.[8] Both from it and from the earlier question on employment opportunities in city government, it seems that city hall does not ordinarily represent a model of social justice in the eyes of the majority of Negroes in our sample.

From a descriptive standpoint, these results may come as a surprise to readers of several viewpoints. To those who feel deeply the existence of racial discrimination in the United States, it will be surprising that half the Negro population in these 15 cities are somehow unable or unwilling to stress discrimination as an overwhelming factor in their lives. Yet clearly many Negroes either do not perceive much discrimination or deny it to be a serious problem. Indeed, had we presented our data from the opposite direction, we could have shown that about a quarter of the sample see job and housing discrimination as applying to only a few Negroes, not to "many" or even to "some." Not all black urban Americans see the world as

TABLE 13 Percentage of Negroes Perceiving Discrimination in Housing and Other Areas

	Men	*Women*	*Total*
Believe "many" or "some" Negroes (as against "few") in this city miss out on good housing because of racial discrimination	75	76	76
Believe there are "many" places (as against "some" or "none") in this city where they could not rent or buy a house because of discrimination	42	44	43
Believe that racial discrimination in housing is increasing or not changing	54	53	54
Believe judges in this city are harder on Negroes than on whites	25	19	22
Believe "city officials" pay less attention to a request from a Negro than a white person	62	59	60

Although the percentages vary depending on the particular question, in general about 40 percent to 50 percent of the Negroes interviewed emphasize the seriousness of current discrimination to as great an extent as a given question allows. (This range does not apply to questions about personal experience or about rate of change.) The other half do not by any means discount discrimination as a force acting upon Negroes, but they qualify their answers somewhat where qualification is provided. This is especially true for the quarter of the sample that take the *least* emphatic way of describing discrimination, e.g., say that there are *"few* places" in the city where they could not rent or buy a house because of race.

[8] The question on hiring of Negroes by "big companies" for high paying jobs (Table 11) shows a higher percentage, but it is not comparable in wording to most of the other questions discussed in this section.

does Stokely Carmichael, or indeed even as does a "moderate" civil rights organization such as the NAACP.

But white Americans who would like to believe that discrimination, at least in employment if not in housing, is an "out of date issue" in 1968, must face the fact that half the Negro population in 15 major cities see discriminatory treatment as a major obstacle to getting a good job, finding a good house, or even having complaints listened to by officials of one's own city. For a substantial proportion of the Negro sample, discontent can find a basis not only in economic deprivation and psychological dissatisfaction, but in the belief that basic improvement in one's condition of life is barred by overt white discrimination.

2. Black Perceptions of White Attitudes

Overt discrimination in such crucial areas as hiring is the side of racial tension in the

TABLE 14   "Do you think Negro customers who shop in the big downtown stores are treated as politely as white customers, or are they treated less politely?"

(Results for Negro men and women averaged. In percent)

	Age					
	16–19	*20–29*	*30–39*	*40–49*	*50–59*	*60–69*
As politely	60	56	60	67	66	64
Less politely	35	36	30	22	23	16
Don't know	5	8	10	11	11	20
	100	100	100	100	100	100

United States easiest to condemn, easiest to legislate against, and easiest to ask survey questions about. Yet it seems clear that beyond initial decisions to employ, promote, or rent to another person, more personal actions and expressed attitudes are fundamental to black-white relations in 1968. What Negroes think whites think about Negroes (and vice versa) may in the end be as important as more clearcut issues of discrimination and economic advancement.[9]

A good introduction to this complex issue is provided by a question that lies somewhere between explicit discrimination and the subtler expression of attitudes. We chose an area of social life where "integration" has been widespread for many years in most of the 15 cities, and where at least superficially pleasant relations between Negroes and whites are clearly called for by the official norms of the situation. The question concerns politeness to customers in downtown department stores, and is shown by age categories in Table 14. More than a quarter of the sample responded that Negro customers receive less courtesy than white customers in major stores. This feeling is a good deal stronger among younger people, where the percentage perceiving discourtesy is twice that of the oldest age category.

gory. More than one out of three Negroes in their teens and twenties expect to be the object of discourteous behavior when they shop in downtown stores. This applies equally to men and women and it applies at all educational levels.

A much more direct question about white attitudes is shown in Table 15, having to do with perceptions of the extent to which black Americans are disliked by white Americans. One out of eight Negroes in the sample per-

TABLE 15   "Do you think only a few white people in (City) dislike Negroes, many dislike Negroes or almost all white people dislike Negroes?"

(In percent)

	Negro		
	Men	*Women*	*Total*
Few white people dislike Negroes	38	37	38
Many dislike Negroes	44	46	45
Almost all dislike Negroes	13	11	12
Don't know	5	6	5
	100	100	100

ceive a world where almost all white people dislike Negroes. (This includes one and a half percent who volunteered that *all* white people, not just almost all, dislike Negroes.) Again it is worthwhile to remind ourselves that these percentages stand for a great many people—in the present instance some 400,000 adults who face what they think of as an almost totally hostile white America. Moreover they are supported in their beliefs by another 45 percent of the sample who an-

[9] "Dearborn Forces Out Black Residents" was a 1968 headline in the *Michigan Chronicle* (June 15, 1968), which is seen by some 65 percent of the adult Negro population in Detroit. (Number of readers estimated by the Detroit Area Study, The University of Michigan, from data collected May, 1968.) The "force" in this case was apparently not violence or even the threat of violence, but verbal hostility and social ostracism on the part of the neighbors of the only Negro family that had been living in the city of Dearborn, a large suburb of Detroit.

ticipate dislike from "many" whites, which in the context of the other alternatives probably means at least half the white population. Altogether in these 15 cities, nearly two million Negro adults from 16 to 69 see themselves as a widely disliked racial minority.

The word "dislike" was a compromise among several terms—distrust, fear, depreciate, hate—that might have been chosen in phrasing the above question. One specification of it may be seen in a question about whether most white people want to see Negroes get a better break, want to keep Negroes down, or don't care one way or the other (Table 16).

TABLE 16 "On the whole, do you think most white people in (City) want to see Negroes get a better break, or do they want to keep Negroes down, or don't they care one way or the other?"

(In percent)

	Negro		
	Men	Women	Total
Most whites want to see Negroes get a better break	30	28	29
Most whites want to keep Negroes down	28	26	27
Most whites don't care	34	34	34
Don't know	8	12	10
	100	100	100

The results of this question are more polarized than the previous one. Three Negro respondents out of ten believe most white people are basically sympathetic to Negro advancement, but nearly the same proportion believe that most whites want to keep Negroes down. Another third see whites as indifferent to the fate of Negro Americans. Note that the selection of the sympathetic response did not require a belief that whites were willing to *do* anything about improving conditions of Negroes, but only that whites "want" to see Negroes get a better break. The finding that seven out of ten Negroes reject such a statement points to a wide gulf, in Negro eyes, between black aspirations and white desire to support such aspirations.

Age and education trends for the two previous questions are somewhat complex, as

shown in Table 17. Putting together the results for both questions, we can summarize the trends as follows: Negro adults in their 20's and 30's—the generation that came of age in the years following World War II— perceive more hostility and less sympathy from whites than does the older prewar generation. The differences are not great, but they are consistent over most educational levels and for both questions. However, there is no evidence that the loss of faith in whites is increasing even more with the Negro adults of tomorrow: youth 16 to 19 answer these two questions in much the same way as does the 20 to 29 year old category. Whether they will remain at this level we have no way of knowing.[10]

There is a hint in the data that college-level education in earlier years was associated with a more optimistic view of white attitudes, but if this was indeed the case it is apparently not so with the post-World War II generation. Among the young adults college experience is not associated with a more positive view of whites. What college training does seem to do, and this is true of educational effects in the two tables more generally, is to modulate perceptions of whites, so that the respondent gives a less extreme response. More educated respondents are less likely to assert that all whites dislike Negroes or want to keep Negroes down, and more likely to see whites as indifferent or to recognize that there may be some genuine white support for Negroes. But education does not increase the proportion of Negroes who see *most* whites as sympathetic. These effects of education may be largely the result of greater sophistication, which makes a person less likely to choose an extreme response when a somewhat more qualified one is available.[11]

In summary, the three questions reviewed in this section provide evidence that the ma-

[10] The teenage group presented certain special interviewing problems and it is possible that it is less representative of that cohort than is true of our other age categories.

[11] Since younger Negroes are more educated, age and education tend to work against each other in this population. Youth is associated with greater perceived distance from whites, but greater education makes it more difficult to classify all whites as hostile. This suggests a "tension" which might be especially great for Negro college students in mixed university settings.

TABLE 17 Age and Education Trends in Negro Perception of White Attitudes
(Results for men and women averaged. In percent)

	Age 16–19*	Age 20–39					Age 40–69				
		8th grade or less	9–11 grades	12 grades	Some college	College graduate	8th grade or less	9–11 grades	12 grades	Some college	College graduate
Question on number of whites who dislike Negroes											
Few white people dislike Negroes	38	28	36	33	36	38	39	39	38	49	60
Many dislike Negroes	47	42	45	51	48	53	40	45	47	42	34
Almost all dislike Negroes	12	22	11	12	9	6	11	9	8	4	5
Don't know	3	8	8	4	7	3	10	7	7	5	1
	100	100	100	100	100	100	100	100	100	100	100
Question on white stance toward Negro advancement											
Most whites want to see Negroes get a better break	27	18	27	28	19	17	31	30	39	46	46
Most whites want to keep Negroes down	29	32	29	29	28	16	26	29	24	18	15
Most whites don't care	40	38	33	36	39	64	27	31	30	28	29
Don't know	4	12	11	7	14	3	16	10	7	8	10
	100	100	100	100	100	100	100	100	100	100	100

* This group combines all educational categories.

jority of Negroes expect little from whites other than hostility, opposition, or at best indifference. On the common-sense assumption that people who feel themselves the object of dislike will in turn feel dislike toward the perceived source, we would expect a great deal of black hostility toward whites. This return hostility might or might not be expressed openly, of course, depending upon a number of factors. We saw in the first section of this chapter that only some 10 percent of the Negro sample express open rejection of whites. At a more indirect attitudinal level we asked respondents whether they felt "they could trust Negroes more than white people, the same as white people, or less than white people." About a quarter of the sample (23 percent) indicated greater trust of Negroes than whites, while the rest reported no difference (68 percent) or claimed they trusted whites more than Negroes (7 percent). Age trends are quite similar to those just reported, but even sharper: the proportion (31 percent) of young people who trust Negroes more than whites is twice as great as the proportion (14 percent) among persons in their 60's. Figure 1

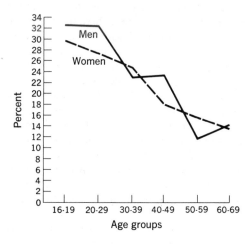

FIGURE 1 Percentages of Negroes trusting other Negroes more than whites.

shows the trend to be generally smooth, but it is interesting to note again that the teenage group is not more extreme than the age 20 to 29 cohort. There is also a slight trend for the more educated respondents to say they trust members of both races the same.

The question on trust and the questions dealt with at the beginning of this chapter

are the only ones that attempted to assess black antipathy toward whites. There is certainly evidence of such antagonism, but it is less great in these data than one would expect on the basis of the "mirror-image" assumption. It may be that our interview simply did not pick up such emotional hostility very well, but it is also possible that other factors serve to dilute the simple reciprocity implied by the assumption.

STRATEGIES FOR CHANGE

We have seen thus far that about half the Negro sample perceive serious problems with discrimination in areas such as employment. Roughly the same proportion expect hostility from whites at a more personal level. What then are the solutions Negroes see to racial problems in 1968?

Only a small minority, although not a trivial one in numbers, has moved very far toward separatist solutions. Most Negroes appear to have incorporated too strongly the values of equal opportunity regardless of race to change suddenly to criteria that make racial considerations a major factor in decisions. Indeed, most Negroes reject the imposition of black political control even in areas of life where Negroes clearly predominate and where other ethnic groups have often demanded and received at least informal control.

Perhaps a supporting factor here is the belief that the race of the person in control has not in itself always been of decisive importance. We asked several questions about the effects of race on treatment and discovered only limited support for the notion that replacement of whites by blacks will make any great difference to most Negroes. With regard to whether black policemen treat Negroes better than do white policemen, 73 percent of the sample could not see any difference; the rest were divided somewhat more in favor of white policemen than of Negro policemen.[12] With regard to stores in Negro

[12] The above results do not mean lack of support for more Negroes in the police force. In the "pretest" to this study we found almost unanimous support for the idea of there being more Negro policemen. But the reasons had to do largely with jobs—the more Negroes who can get jobs as police the better—and not with the

364 Black Militancy and Violence

neighborhoods, Negro and white owned stores are thought to be about the same in terms of fair pricing. Black storekeepers are seen as somewhat more respectful of Negro customers than are white storekeepers (15 percent to 7 percent), but nonetheless 70 percent of the sample feel there is no difference by race.

The one question that does suggest some faith in the benefits of substituting black for white control asked whether the election of Negro mayors in Cleveland and Gary would make things better, worse, or not make any difference. More than three-fifths of the sample expected an improvement in those two cities. There is some reason to wonder, however, whether this response does not reflect less than the race of the mayor and more the knowledge or suggestion that he is a crusader for Negro rights. A white political leader with such a reputation might well draw as large an indication of support. If this is the case, it indicates considerable backing for political action in traditional spheres, rather than a strong leaning toward black leadership as such.

Our study did uncover unexpectedly strong support for a kind of cultural pluralism, symbolized by the study of Negro history and of African languages. This seems to turn not so much on the rejection of whites as on the acceptance of things black. It involves a commitment to the development of Negro identity as a valid basis for cultural life within a larger interracial and if possible integrated society. Such a movement from race to ethnicity may help Negroes in a number of ways, but it does not promise quick relief to problems of perceived discrimination and unfair treatment.

There would seem to be two directions which point toward a solution, and Negroes appear to have a commitment to both. One is to work within the system through individual advancement, trusting that it is possible by effort to overcome all barriers. A question concerned with the validity of this approach —that a young Negro who works hard enough "can usually get ahead in this country in

spite of prejudice and discrimination"—finds nearly four out of five Negroes (78 percent) in agreement. Faith in the system then is very strong, being held even by many who perceive a great deal of discrimination.

An analysis by age and education reveals clear regularities which have, by now, familiar and contradictory implications. The results are presented separately by sex in Table 18, since they show some differences in clarity if not in trend. Education has a clear *positive* association with belief that a Negro can get ahead in America despite prejudice and discrimination. The relation is sharpest for men in their 20's and 30's, where the belief in individual accomplishment is held by 93 percent of the college graduates but only 68 percent of those with grade school education. We cannot, of course, tell what is cause and what is effect here—whether the more ambitious go on with their education, or whether those obtaining more education gain more confidence, or whether there is a third factor such as ability that underlies both, or finally whether some mix of all of these occurs.

The age trends are more complex and also less certain. But it appears that for men these age differences are concentrated largely among the less educated: there is little difference by age for those with 12 or more years of education, but among those who failed to complete high school, the younger men are more willing to attribute lack of success to prejudice and discrimination than are the older men. The teenage male group in this instance, unlike other cases discussed earlier, continues the general age trend—that is, is even more inclined to see failure to get ahead as caused by racial injustice. Among women, younger people at all levels of education are more inclined to blame the system for failure to get ahead.

The age and education trends taken together suggest that for males a belief in the value of individual initiative and in the possibility of individual achievement continues to reinforce the person who manages to go through school. The more he gets ahead, the more he thinks he should be able to get ahead. But what is often called the school drop-out lacks the possibility of achievement, and apparently in a growing proportion of cases he believes that it is society that is at fault, not he himself.

When a belief in individual accomplish-

___

effect of having Negro policemen on the fairness of law enforcement. Perhaps the explanations would have been different if we had asked the question about higher ranking police officers or about a Negro police commissioner.

TABLE 18 "If a young Negro works hard enough, do you think he or she can usually get ahead in this country in spite of prejudice and discrimination, or that he doesn't have much chance no matter how hard he works?"

(In percent)

	Age 16–19*	Age 20–39					Age 40–60				
		8th grade or less	9–11 grades	12 grades	Some college	College graduate	8th grade or less	9–11 grades	12 grades	Some college	College graduate
				Negro Men							
Can get ahead	72	68	75	82	81	93	79	83	81	85	91
Doesn't have much chance	26	27	24	15	16	7	19	16	14	15	6
Don't know	2	5	1	3	3	0	2	1	5	0	3
	100	100	100	100	100	100	100	100	100	100	100
				Negro Women							
Can get ahead	76	72	72	79	76	72	74	80	80	93	89
Doesn't have much chance	18	22	25	18	18	13	20	18	18	4	4
Don't know	6	6	3	3	6	15	6	2	2	3	7
	100	100	100	100	100	100	100	100	100	100	100

* This group combines all educational categories.

ment fails, to what can an individual turn? He can try to reform the system or he can try to destroy it. Reform actions were not well covered in our questionnaire, and we have at present little to report about types of individuals who attempt to change the system in important but specific ways. We did include substantial material on the urban riots, and we shall review much of it in Chapter V. This approach may seem to focus solely on attempts to destroy the American system, yet as we will see, the riot itself is viewed by most Negroes not as an attempt to destroy America, but as a loud protest, the culmination of many protests, calling for reform rather than revolution.

27

Religion: Opiate or inspiration of civil rights militancy among Negroes?*

GARY T. MARX

The relationship between religion and political radicalism is a confusing one. On the one hand, established religious institutions have generally had a stake in the status quo and hence have supported conservatism. Furthermore, with the masses having an otherworldly orientation, religious zeal, particularly as expressed in the more fundamentalist branches of Christianity, has been seen as an alternative to the development of political radicalism. On the other hand, as the source of universal humanistic values and the strength that can come from believing one is carrying out God's will in political matters, religion has occasionally played a strong positive role in movements for radical social change.

This dual role of religion is clearly indicated in the case of the American Negro and race protest. Slaves are said to have been first brought to this country on the "good ship Jesus Christ."[1] While there was occasional controversy over the effect that religion had on them it appears that most slave-owners eventually came to view supervised religion as an effective means of social control. Stampp, in commenting on the effect of religion notes:

> . . . through religious instruction the bondsmen learned that slavery had divine sanction, that insolence was as much an offense against God as against the temporal master. They received the Biblical command that servants should obey their masters, and they heard of the punishments awaiting the disobedient slave in the hereafter. They heard, too, that eternal salvation would be their reward for faithful service . . .[2]

In discussing the period after the Civil War, Myrdal states that ". . . under the pressure of political reaction, the Negro church in the South came to have much the same role as it did before the Civil War. Negro frustration was sublimated into emotionalism, and Negro hopes were fixed on the after world."[3] Many other analysts, in considering the consequences of Negro religion from the end of slavery until the early 1950's

Reprinted from *American Sociological Review,* 1967, **32,** 64–72, by permission of the author and the American Sociological Association. See also: Chapter 3 (pp. 94–105) in G. T. Marx, *Protest and Prejudice,* New York: Harper and Row, 1967.

* Revision of paper read at the annual meeting of the American Sociological Association, August, 1966. This paper may be identified as publication A-72 of the Survey Research Center, University of California, Berkeley. I am grateful to Gertrude J. Selznick and Stephen Steinberg for their work on the early phase of this project, and to the Anti-Defamation League for support.

[1] Louis Lomax, *When the Word is Given,* New York: New American Library, 1964, p. 34.
[2] Kenneth Stampp, *The Peculiar Institution,* New York: Alfred A. Knopf, 1956, p. 158.
[3] Gunnar Myrdal *et al., An American Dilemma,* New York: Harper, 1944, pp. 851–853. About the North he notes that the church remained far more independent "but on the whole

reached similar conclusions about the conservatizing effect of religion on race protest.[4]

However, the effect of religion on race protest throughout American history has by no means been exclusively in one direction. While many Negroes were no doubt seriously singing about chariots in the sky, Negro preachers such as Denmark Vesey and Nat Turner and the religiously inspired abolitionists were actively fighting slavery in their own way. All Negro churches first came into being as protest organizations and later some served as meeting places where protest strategy was planned, or as stations on the underground railroad. The richness of protest symbolism in Negro spirituals and sermons has often been noted. Beyond this symbolic role, as a totally Negro institution, the church brought together in privacy people with a shared problem. It was from the church experience that many leaders were exposed to a broad range of ideas legitimizing protest and obtained the savoir faire, self-confidence, and organizational experience needed to challenge an oppressive sys-

tem. A recent commentator states that the slave churches were "the nucleus of the Negro protest" and another that "in religion Negro leaders had begun to find sanction and support for their movements of protest more than 150 years ago."[5]

Differing perceptions of the varied consequences religion may have on protest have continued to the present time. While there has been very little in the way of empirical research on the effect of the Negro church on protest,[6] the literature of race relations is rich with impressionistic statements which generally contradict each other about how the church either encourages and is the source of race protest or inhibits and retards its development. For example, two observers note, "as primitive evangelism gave way to a more sophisticated social consciousness, the church became the spearhead of Negro protest in the deep South,"[7] while another indicates "the Negro church is a sleeping giant. In civil rights participation its feet are hardly wet."[8] A civil rights activist, himself a clergyman, states: ". . . the church

---

even the Northern Negro church has remained a conservative institution with its interests directly upon other-worldly matters and has largely ignored the practical problems of the Negro's fate in this world."

[4] For example Dollard reports that "religion can be seen as a mechanism for the social control of Negroes" and that planters have always welcomed the building of a Negro church on the plantation but looked with less favor upon the building of a school. John Dollard, *Caste and Class in a Southern Town,* Garden City: Doubleday Anchor, 1957, p. 248. A few of the many others reaching similar conclusions are, Benjamin E. Mays and J. W. Nicholson, *The Negro's Church,* New York: Institute of Social and Religious Research, 1933; Hortense Powdermaker, *After Freedom,* New York: Viking Press, 1939, p. 285; Charles Johnson, *Growing Up in the Black Belt,* Washington, D.C.: American Council of Education, 1941, pp. 135–136; Horace Cayton and St. Clair Drake, *Black Metropolis,* New York: Harper and Row, 1962, pp. 424–429; George Simpson and Milton Yinger, *Racial and Cultural Minorities,* New York: Harper, rev. ed., 1958, pp. 582–587. In a more general context this social control consequence of religion has of course been noted throughout history from Plato to Montesquieu to Marx to Nietzsche to Freud to contemporary social theorists.

[5] Daniel Thompson, "The Rise of Negro Protest," *Annals of the American Academy of Political and Social Science,* 357 (January, 1965).

[6] The empirical evidence is quite limited. The few studies that have been done have focused on the Negro minister. Thompson notes that in New Orleans Negro ministers constitute the largest segment of the Negro leadership class (a grouping which is not necessarily the same as "protest leaders") but that "The vast majority of ministers are primarily interested in their pastoral role . . . their sermons are essentially biblical, dealing only tangentially with social issues." Daniel Thompson, *The Negro Leadership Class,* Englewood Cliffs, New Jersey: Prentice-Hall, 1963, pp. 34–35. Studies of the Negro ministry in Detroit and Richmond, California also stress that only a small fraction of Negro clergymen show any active concern with the civil rights struggle. R. L. Johnstone, *Militant and Conservative Community Leadership Among Negro Clergymen,* Ph.D. dissertation, University of Michigan, Ann Arbor, 1963, and J. Bloom, *The Negro Church and the Movement for Equality,* M.A. thesis, University of California, Berkeley, Department of Sociology, 1966.

[7] Jane Record and Wilson Record, "Ideological Forces and the Negro Protest," *Annals, op. cit.,* p. 92.

[8] G. Booker, *Black Man's America,* Englewood Cliffs, N.J.: Prentice-Hall, 1964, p. 111.

today is central to the movement . . . if there had been no Negro church, there would have been no civil rights movement today."[9] On the other hand, a sociologist, commenting on the more involved higher status ministers, notes: ". . . middle class Negro clergymen in the cities of the South generally advocated cautious gradualism in race activities until the mid-1950's when there was an upsurge of protest sentiment among urban Negroes . . . but most of them [ministers] did not embrace the more vigorous techniques of protest until other leaders took the initiative and gained widespread support."[10] Another sociologist states, "Whatever their previous conservative stance has been, the churches have now become 'spearheads of reform.' "[11] Still another indicates: ". . . the Negro church is particularly culpable for its general lack of concern for the moral and social problems of the community . . . it has been accommodating. Fostering indulgence in religious sentimentality, and riveting the attention of the masses on the bounties of a hereafter, the Negro church remains a refuge, and escape from the cruel realities of the here and now."[12]

Thus one faces opposing views, or at best ambiguity, in contemplating the current effect of religion. The opiating consequences of religion are all too well known as is the fact that the segregated church is durable

and offers some advantages to clergy and members that might be denied them in a more integrated society. On the other hand, the prominent role of the Negro church in supplying much of the ideology of the movement, many of its foremost leaders, and an institution around which struggle might be organized—particularly in the South—can hardly be denied. It would appear from the bombings of churches and the writings of Martin Luther King and other religiously inspired activists that for many, religion and protest are closely linked.

Part of this dilemma may lie in the distinction between the church as an institution in its totality and particular individual churches within it, and the further distinctions among different types of individual religious concern. This paper is concerned with the latter subject; it is an inquiry into the relationship between religiosity and response to the civil rights struggle. It first considers how religious denomination affects militancy, and then how various measures of religiosity, taken separately and together, are related to civil rights concern. The question is then asked of those classified as "very religious" and "quite religious," how an "otherworldy orientation"—as opposed to a "temporal" one—affects militancy.

In a nationwide study of Negroes living in metropolitan areas of the United States, a number of questions were asked about religious behavior and beliefs as well as about the civil rights struggle.[13] Seven of the questions dealing with civil rights protest have been combined into an index of conventional militancy.[14] Built into this index are a num-

[9] Rev. W. T. Walker, as quoted in William Brink and Louis Harris, *The Negro Revolution in America,* New York: Simon and Schuster, 1964, p. 103.

[10] N. Glenn, "Negro Religion in the U.S." in L. Schneider, *Religion, Culture and Society,* New York: John Wiley, 1964.

[11] Joseph Fichter, "American Religion and the Negro," *Daedalus* (Fall, 1965), p. 1087.

[12] E. U. Essien-Udom, *Black Nationalism,* New York: Dell Publishing Co., 1962, p. 358.

Many other examples of contradictory statements could be offered, sometimes even in the same volume. For example, Carleton Lee stresses the importance of religion for protest while Rayford Logan sees the Negro pastor as an instrument of the white power structure (in a book published to commemorate 100 years of emancipation). Carleton Lee, "Religious Roots of Negro Protest," and Rayford Logan, "Educational Changes Affecting American Negroes," both in Arnold Rose, *Assuring Freedom to the Free,* Detroit: Wayne University Press, 1964.

[13] This survey was carried out in 1964 by the Survey Research Center, University of California, Berkeley. A non-Southern metropolitan area probability sample was drawn as well as special area samples of Negroes living in New York City, Chicago, Atlanta and Birmingham. Since the results reported here are essentially the same for each of these areas, they are treated together. More than 90% of the interviews were done with Negro interviewers. Additional methodological details may be found in Gary Marx, *Protest and Prejudice: A Study of Belief in the Black Community,* New York: Harper & Row, forthcoming.

[14] Attention is directed to conventional militancy rather than to that of the Black Nationalist variety because a very small percentage of

ber of dimensions of racial protest such as impatience over the speed of integration, opposition to discrimination in public facilities and the sale of property, perception of barriers to Negro advancement, support of civil rights demonstrations, and expressed willingness to take part in a demonstration. Those giving the militant response to five or more of the questions are considered militant, those giving such a response to three or four of the questions, moderate, and fewer than three, conservative.[15]

DENOMINATION

It has long been known that the more fundamentalist sects such as the Holiness groups and the Jehovah's Witnesses are relatively uninterested in movements for secular political change.[16] Such transvaluational movements with their otherworldly orientation and their promise that the last shall be first in the great beyond, are said to solace the individual for his lowly status in this world and to divert concern away from efforts at collective social change which might be brought about by man. While only a minority of Negroes actually belong to such groups, the proportion is higher than among whites. Negro literature is rich in descrip-

---

the sample offered strong and consistent support for Black Nationalism. As in studying support for the KKK, the Birch Society or the Communist Party, a representative sample of normal size is inadequate.

[15] Each of the items in the index was positively related to every other and the index showed a high degree of internal validity. The index also received external validation from a number of additional questions. For example, the percentage belonging to a civil rights organization went from zero among those lowest in militancy to 38 percent for those who were highest, and the percentage thinking that civil rights demonstrations had helped a great deal increased from 23 percent to 58 percent. Those thinking that the police treated Negroes very well decreased from 35 percent to only 2 percent among those highest in militancy.

[16] Liston Pope, *Millhands and Preachers,* New Haven: Yale University Press, 1942, p. 137. J. Milton Yinger, *Religion, Society, and the Individual,* New York: The Macmillan Company, 1957, pp. 170–173.

tions of these churches and their position on race protest.

In Table 1 it can be seen that those belonging to sects are the least likely to be militant; they are followed by those in predominantly Negro denominations. Ironically those individuals in largely white denominations (Episcopalian, Presbyterian, United Church of Christ, and Roman Catholic) are those most likely to be militant, in spite of the perhaps greater civil rights activism of the Negro denominations. This pattern emerged even when social class was held constant.

In their comments members of the less conventional religious groups clearly expressed the classical attitude of their sects toward participation in the politics of the secular world. For example, an Evangelist in the Midwest said, "I don't believe in participating in politics. My church don't vote—they just depends on the plans of God." And an automobile serviceman in Philadelphia, stated, "I, as a Jehovah's Witness, cannot express things involving the race issue." A housewife in the Far West ventured, "In my religion we do not approve of anything except living like it says in the Bible; demonstrations mean calling attention to you and it's sinful."

The finding that persons who belong to sects are less likely to be militant than the non-sect members is to be expected; clearly this type of religious involvement seems an alternative for most people to the development of radicalism. But what of the religious style of those in the more conventional churches which may put relatively less stress

TABLE 1 Proportion Militant (%) by Denomination*

Denomination	% Militant	
Episcopalian	46	(24)
United Church of Christ	42	(12)
Presbyterian	40	(25)
Catholic	40	(109)
Methodist	34	(142)
Baptist	32	(658)
Sects and Cults	20	(106)

* 25 respondents are not shown in this table because they did not specify a denomination, or belonged to a non-Christian religious group, or other small Christian group.

on the after-life and encourage various forms of secular participation? Are the more religiously inclined within these groups also less likely to be militant?

RELIGIOSITY

The present study measured several dimensions of religious involvement. Those interviewed were asked how important religion was to them, several questions about orthodoxy of belief, and how frequently they attended worship service.[17] Even with the sects excluded, irrespective of the dimension of religiosity considered, the greater the religiosity the lower the percentage militant. (See Tables 2, 3 and 4.) For example, mili-

TABLE 2 Militancy by Subjective Importance Assigned to Religion*

Importance	% Militant
Extremely important	29 (668)
Somewhat important	39 (195)
Fairly important	48 (96)
Not too important	56 (18)
Not at all important	62 (13)

* Sects are excluded here and in all subsequent tables.

TABLE 3 Militancy by Orthodoxy

Orthodoxy	% Militant
Very high	27 (414)
High	34 (333)
Medium	39 (144)
Low	47 (68)
Very low	54 (35)

TABLE 4 Militancy by Frequency of Attendance at Worship Services

Frequency	% Militant
More than once a week	27 (81)
Once a week	32 (311)
Once a month or more but less than once a week	34 (354)
Less than once a month	38 (240)

[17] These dimensions and several others are suggested by Charles Y. Glock in "On the Study of Religious Commitment," *Religious Education*

tancy increases consistently from a low of only 29 percent among those who said religion was "extremely important" to a high of 62 percent for those who indicated that religion was "not at all important" to them. For those very high in orthodoxy (having no doubt about the existence of God or the devil) 27 percent were militant while for those totally rejecting these ideas 54 percent indicated great concern over civil rights. Militancy also varies inversely with frequency of attendance at worship service.[18]

Each of these items was strongly related to every other; when taken together they help us to better characterize religiosity. Accordingly they have been combined into an overall measure of religiosity. Those scored as "very religious" in terms of this index attended church at least once a week, felt that religion was extremely important to them, and had no doubts about the existence of God and the devil. For progressively lower values of the index, frequency of church attendance, the importance of religion, and acceptance of the belief items de-

Research Supplement, **57** (July–August, 1962), pp. 98–100. For another measure of religious involvement, the number of church organizations belonged to, the same inverse relationship was noted.

[18] There is a popular stereotype that Negroes are a "religious people." Social science research has shown that they are "over-churched" relative to whites, i.e., the ratio of Negro churches to the size of the Negro population is greater than the same ratio for whites. Using data from a nationwide survey of whites, by Gertrude Selznick and Stephen Steinberg, some comparison of the religiosity of Negroes and whites was possible. When these various dimensions of religiosity were examined, with the effect of education and region held constant, Negroes appeared as significantly more religious *only* with respect to the subjective importance assigned to religion. In the North, whites were more likely to attend church at least once a week than were Negroes; while in the South rates of attendance were the same. About the same percentage of both groups had no doubts about the existence of God. While Negroes were more likely to be sure about the existence of a devil, whites, surprisingly, were more likely to be sure about a life beyond death. Clearly, then, any assertions about the greater religiosity of Negroes relative to whites are unwarranted unless one specifies the dimension of religiosity.

TABLE 5   Militancy by Religiosity

Religiosity	Very Religious	Somewhat Religious	Not Very Religious	Not at All Religious
% Militant	26	30	45	70
N	(230)	(523)	(195)	(36)

TABLE 6   Proportion Militant (%) by Religiosity, for Education, Age, Region, Sex, and Denomination

	Very Religious	Somewhat Religious	Not Very Religious	Not at All Religious
Education				
Grammar school	17 (108)	22 (201)	31 (42)	50 (2)
High school	34 (96)	32 (270)	45 (119)	58 (19)
College	38 (26)	48 (61)	59 (34)	87 (15)
Age				
18–29	33 (30)	37 (126)	44 (62)	62 (13)
30–44	30 (53)	34 (180)	48 (83)	74 (19)
45–59	25 (71)	27 (131)	45 (33)	50 (2)
60+	22 (76)	18 (95)	33 (15)	100 (2)
Region				
Non-South	30 (123)	34 (331)	47 (159)	70 (33)
South	22 (107)	23 (202)	33 (36)	66 (3)
Sex				
Men	28 (83)	33 (220)	44 (123)	72 (29)
Women	26 (147)	28 (313)	46 (72)	57 (7)
Denomination				
Episcopalian, Presbyterian, United Church of Christ	20 (15)	27 (26)	33 (15)	60 (5)
Catholic	13 (15)	39 (56)	36 (25)	77 (13)
Methodist	46 (24)	22 (83)	50 (32)	100 (2)
Baptist	25 (172)	29 (354)	45 (117)	53 (15)

cline consistently until, for those scored "not at all religious," church is rarely if ever attended, religion is not considered personally important and the belief items are rejected.

Using this measure for non-sect members, civil rights militancy increases from a low of 26 percent for those labeled "very religious" to 30 percent for the "somewhat religious" to 45 percent for those "not very religious" and up to a high of 70 percent for those "not at all religious."[19] (Table 5.)

[19] When the sects are included in these tables the results are the same. The sects have been excluded because they offer almost no variation to be analyzed with respect to the independent variable. Since virtually all of the sect members scored as either "very religious" or "somewhat religious," it is hardly possible to measure the

Religiosity and militancy are also related to age, sex, education, religious denomination and region of the country. The older, the less educated, women, Southerners and those in Negro denominations are more likely to be religious and to have lower percentages scoring as militant. Thus it is possible that the relationship observed is simply a consequence of the fact that both religiosity and militancy are related to some third factor. In Table 6 it can be seen however,

effect of their religious involvement on protest attitudes. In addition the import of the relationships shown in these tables is considerably strengthened when it is demonstrated that religious involvement inhibits militancy even when the most religious and least militant group, the sects, are excluded.

that, even when these variables are controlled the relationship is maintained. That is, even among those in the North, the younger, male, more educated and those affiliated with predominantly white denominations, the greater the religiosity the less the militancy.

The incompatibility between piety and protest shown in these data becomes even more evident when considered in light of comments offered by the respondents. Many religious people hold beliefs which clearly inhibit race protest. For a few there was the notion that segregation and a lowly status for Negroes was somehow God's will and not for man to question. Thus a housewife in South Bend, Indiana, in saying that civil rights demonstrations had hurt Negroes, added: "God is the Creator of everything. We don't know why we all dark-skinned. We should try to put forth the effort to do what God wants and not question."[20]

A Negro spiritual contains the lines "I'm gonna wait upon the Lord till my change comes." For our respondents a more frequently stated belief stressed that God as the absolute controller of the universe would bring about change in his own way and at his own time, rather than expressing segregation as God's will. In indicating her unwillingness to take part in a civil rights demonstration, a Detroit housewife said, "I don't go for demonstrations. I believe that God created all men equal and at His appointed time He will give every man his portion, no one can hinder it." And in response to a question about whether or not the government in Washington was pushing integration too slowly, a retired clerk in Atlanta said: "You can't hurry God. He has a certain time for this to take place. I don't know about Washington."

Others who desired integration more strongly and wanted immediate social change

[20] Albert Cardinal Meyer notes that the Catholic Bishops of the U.S. said in their statement of 1958: "The heart of the race question is moral and religious." "Interracial Justice and Love," in M. Ahmann, Ed., *Race Challenge to Religion,* Chicago: H. Regnery, 1963, p. 126. These data, viewed from the perspective of the activist seeking to motivate Negroes on behalf of the civil rights struggle, suggest that this statement has a meaning which Their Excellencies no doubt did not intend.

felt that (as Bob Dylan sings) God was on their side. Hence man need do nothing to help bring about change. Thus a worker in Cleveland, who was against having more civil rights demonstrations, said: "With God helping to fight our battle, I believe we can do with fewer demonstrations." And in response to a question about whether Negroes should spend more time praying and less time demonstrating, an Atlanta clergyman, who said "more time praying," added "praying is demonstrating."[21]

RELIGION AMONG THE MILITANTS

Although the net effect of religion is clearly to inhibit attitudes of protest it is interesting to consider this relationship in the opposite direction, i.e., observe religiosity among those characterized as militant, moderate, and conservative with respect to the civil rights struggle. As civil rights concern increases, religiosity decreases. (Table 7). Militants were twice as likely to be scored "not very religious" or "not at all religious" as were conservatives. This table is also of interest because it shows that, even

TABLE 7 Religiosity by Civil Rights Militancy

	Militants	Moderates	Conservatives
Very religious	18%	24%	28%
Somewhat religious	48	57	55
Not very religious	26	17	16
Not at all religious	8	2	1
Total	100	100	100
N	332	419	242

[21] A study of ministers in Richmond, California notes that, although almost all questioned were opposed to discrimination, very few had taken concrete action, in part because of their belief that God would take care of them. One minister noted, "I believe that if we all was as pure . . . as we ought to be, there would be no struggle. God will answer my prayer. If we just stay with God and have faith. *When Peter was up, did the people march to free him? No. He prayed, and God did something about it.*" (Bloom, *The Negro Church and the Movement for Equality,* italics added.)

for the militants, a majority were scored either "very religious" or "somewhat religious." Clearly, for many, a religious orientation and a concern with racial protest are not mutually exclusive.

Given the active involvement of some churches, the singing of protest spirituals, and the ideology of the movement as it relates to Christian principles of love, equality, passive suffering,[22] and the appeal to a higher moral law, it would be surprising if there were only a few religious people among the militants.

A relevant question accordingly is: Among the religious, what are the intervening links which determine whether religion is related to an active concern with racial matters or has an opiating effect?[23] From the comments reported above it seemed that, for some, belief in a highly deterministic God inhibited race protest. Unfortunately the study did not measure beliefs about the role of God as against the role of men in the structuring of human affairs. However, a related variable was measured which would seem to have much relevance—the extent to which these religious people were concerned with the here and now as opposed to the after-life.

The classical indictment of religion from the Marxist perspective is that by focusing concern on a glorious after-life the evils of this life are ignored. Of course there are important differences among religious institutions and among individuals with respect to the importance given to other worldly concerns. Christianity, as with most ideologies, contains within it, if not out-and-out contradictory themes, then certainly themes which are likely to be in tension with one another. In this fact, no doubt, lies part of the explanation of religion's varied consequences for protest. One important strand of Christianity stresses acceptance of one's

lot and glorifies the after-life;[24] another is more concerned with the realization of Judeo-Christian values in the current life. King and his followers clearly represent this latter "social gospel" tradition.[25] Those with the type of temporal concern that King represents would be expected to be higher in militancy. A measure of temporal vs. other-worldly concern has been constructed. On the basis of two questions, those interviewed have been classified as having either an other worldly or a temporal orientation.[26] The evi-

---

[22] Non-violent resistance as it relates to Christianity's emphasis on suffering, sacrifice, and privation, is discussed by James W. Vander Zanden, "The Non-Violent Resistance Movement Against Segregation." *American Journal of Sociology,* **68** (March, 1963), pp. 544–550.

[23] Of course, a most relevant factor here is the position of the particular church than an individual is involved in. Unfortunately, it was difficult to obtain such information in a nationwide survey.

[24] The Muslims have also made much of this theme within Christianity, and their militancy is certainly tied to a rejection of otherworldly religiosity. The Bible is referred to as a "poison book" and the leader of the Muslims states, "No one after death has ever gone any place but where they were carried. There is no heaven or hell other than on earth for you and me, and Jesus was no exception. His body is still . . . in Palestine and will remain there." (As quoted in C. Eric Lincoln, *The Black Muslims in America,* Boston: Beacon Press, 1961, p. 123.)

However, while they reject the otherworldly theme, they nevertheless rely heavily on a deterministic Allah; according to E. U. Essien-Udom, this fact leads to political inactivity. He notes, "The attainment of black power is relegated to the intervention of "Almighty Allah" sometime in the future . . . Not unlike other religionists, the Muslims too may wait for all eternity for the coming of the Messiah, the predicted apocalypse in 1970 notwithstanding." E. U. Essien-Udom, *Black Nationalism, op. cit.,* pp. 313–314.

[25] He states: "Any religion that professes to be concerned with the souls of men and is not concerned with the slums that damn them, the economic conditions that strangle them, and the social conditions that cripple them is a dry-as-dust religion." He further adds, perhaps in a concession, that "such a religion is the kind the Marxists like to see—an opiate of the people." Martin Luther King, *Stride Toward Freedom,* New York: Ballantine Books, 1958, pp. 28–29.

John Lewis, a former SNCC leader and once a Baptist Divinity student, is said to have peered through the bars of a Southern jail and said, "Think not that I am come to send peace on earth. I came not to send peace, but a sword." (Matthew 10:34.)

[26] The two items used in this index were: "How sure are you that there is a life beyond death?"; and "Negroes should spend more time praying and less time demonstrating." The latter item may seem somewhat circular when observed in relation to civil rights concern. However, this is precisely what militancy is all about. Still it

dence is that religiosity and otherworldly concern increase together. For example, almost 100 percent of the "not at all religious" group were considered to have a temporal orientation, but only 42 percent of the "very religious" (Table 8). Those in predominantly white denominations were more likely to have a temporal orientation than those in all-black denominations.

TABLE 8 Proportion (%) with Temporal (as Against Otherworldly) Concern, by Religiosity

Religiosity	% with Temporal Concern
Very religious	42 (225)
Somewhat religious	61 (531)
Not very religious	82 (193)
Not at all religious	98 (34)

Among the religious groups, if concern with the here and now is a relevant factor in overcoming the opiating effect of religion then it is to be anticipated that those considered to have a temporal religious orientation would be much higher in militancy than those scored as otherworldly. This is in fact the

TABLE 9 Proportion Militant (%) by Religiosity and Temporal or Otherworldly Concern

Concern	Very Religious	Somewhat Religious
Temporal	39 (95)	38 (325)
Otherworldly	15 (130)	17 (206)

case. Among the otherworldly religious, only 16 percent were militant; this proportion increases to almost 40 percent among those considered "very religious" and "somewhat religious" who have a temporal religious outlook (Table 9). Thus it would seem that an important factor in determining the effect of religion on protest attitudes is the nature

would have been better to measure otherworldly vs. temporal concern in a less direct fashion; unfortunately, no other items were available. Because of this the data shown here must be interpreted with caution. However it does seem almost self-evident that civil rights protest which is religiously inspired is related to a temporal religious outlook.

of an individual's religious commitment. It is quite possible, for those with a temporal religious orientation, that—rather than the effect of religion being somehow neutralized (as in the case of militancy among the "not religious" groups)—their religious concern serves to inspire and sustain race protest. This religious inspiration can, of course, be clearly noted among some active civil rights participants.

CONCLUSION

The effect of religiosity on race protest depends on the type of religiosity involved. Past literature is rich in suggestions that the religiosity of the fundamentalist sects is an alternative to the development of political radicalism. This seems true in the case of race protest as well. However, in an overall sense even for those who belong to the more conventional churches, the greater the religious involvement, whether measured in terms of ritual activity, orthodoxy of religious belief, subjective importance of religion, or the three taken together, the lower the degree of militancy.

Among sect members and religious people with an otherworldly orientation, religion and race protest appear to be, if not mutually exclusive, then certainly what one observer has referred to as "mutually corrosive kinds of commitments."[27] Until such time as religion loosens its hold over these people or comes to embody to a greater extent the belief that man as well as God can bring about secular change, and focuses more on the here and now, religious involvement may be seen as an important factor working against the widespread radicalization of the Negro public.

However, it has also been noted that many militant people are nevertheless religious. When a distinction is made among the religious between the "otherworldly" and the "temporal," for many of the latter group, religion seems to facilitate or at least not to inhibit protest. For these people religion and race protest may be mutually supportive.

Thirty years ago Donald Young wrote:

[27] Rodney Stark, "Class, Radicalism, and Religious Involvement," *American Sociological Review,* **29** (October, 1964), p. 703.

"One function which a minority religion may serve is that of reconciliation with inferior status and its discriminatory consequences . . . on the other hand, religious institutions may also develop in such a way as to be an incitement and support of revolt against inferior status."[28] The current civil rights

[28] Donald Young, *American Minority Peoples,* New York: Harper, 1937, p. 204.

These data are also consistent with Merton's statement that it is premature to conclude that "all religion everywhere has only the one consequence of making for mass apathy" and his

struggle and the data observed here certainly suggest that this is the case. These contradictory consequences of religion are somewhat reconciled when one distinguishes among different segments of the Negro church and types of religious concern among individuals.

insistence on recognizing the "multiple consequences" and "net balance of aggregate consequences" of a given institution such as religion. Robert Merton, *Social Theory and Social Structure,* Glencoe: Free Press, 1957, revised edition, p. 44.

28

Who riots? A study of participation in the 1967 riots

ROBERT M. FOGELSON AND ROBERT B. HILL

THE EXTENT OF PARTICIPATION

There is little hard evidence that supports the first point of the riffraff theory—that an infinitesimal fraction of the Negro population, no more than 1 or 2 per cent, actively participated in the 1960s riots. For, if only 1 or 2 per cent of the Negroes rioted in, say, Detroit or Newark, then, in view of the large number of persons arrested there, one would have to conclude that the police must have apprehended almost all of the rioters,[1] a con-

Reprinted from *Who riots? A study of participation in the 1967 riots.* Supplemental study for the National Advisory Commission on Civil Disorders, Washington, D.C.: Government Printing Office, 1968, Chapters 3, 4, and 5, pp. 229–240.

[1] The 5,637 Negro arrestees in Detroit, themselves constituted 1.2 per cent of the city-wide nonwhite population. Similarly, the 1,387 Negro arrestees in Newark were 1.0 per cent of the nonwhite population in the city.

clusion which, as noted above, is sharply contradicted by the eye-witness accounts of these riots. Also, as previously noted, surveys of riot areas have obtained much higher rates of participation. According to the University of Michigan's Survey Research Center, for example, 11 per cent of the Negroes 15 years and older rioted in Detroit, and 45 per cent of the Negro males between the ages of 15 and 35 rioted in Newark.[2] It is, however, much harder to reach a more precise estimate of how large a segment of the Negro population actively participated in the riots. For any estimate depends on the answers to two very difficult questions: How many Negroes in a community might have joined in the riots? and how many Negroes there did join

[2] Caplan and Paige in *Kerner Report,* fn. 112, p. 172. *Report of the National Advisory Commission on Civil Disorders* (N.Y.: Bantam Books, March, 1968), Chapter 5 (hereafter referred to as the Kerner Report).

in the riots? Nonetheless, the survey research and arrest data provide the basis for tentative, if highly speculative, answers to these questions and for rough estimates of riot participation.

To determine how many Negroes in a community might have joined in the riots, it is incorrect to use the total number of Negroes living there. The reason why is well illustrated by a brief discussion of the McCone Commission report, which based its estimate of riot participation on all of Los Angeles County's 650,000 Negroes.[3] Such a base figure was wrong for at least two reasons. First, the 1965 riots occurred principally in southcentral Los Angeles, and not in Los Angeles County's other small and dispersed black enclaves. Negroes from these other communities should not have been counted any more than Negroes from Chicago's South Side should be counted to determine how many might have joined in the West Side rioting of 1966. Second, southcentral Los Angeles—like any other community—contains a sizable number of residents who, for a variety of reasons, could not possibly have participated in the 1965 riots. Neither the infants and the elderly, the lame, the halt, and the blind, nor the residents in prisons, hospitals, and the armed forces should have been counted either. Thus to determine how many Negroes in a community might have joined in the riots, it is essential to compute the number of potential rioters living there.

Who, then, are the potential rioters? They are, to begin with, the Negro residents of the riot area—not the metropolis, nor the city, and not necessarily even the poverty area, but rather the neighborhood which experienced the rioting. To chart the riot area—or, in effect, to fix the boundaries of the rioting, looting, arson, and assault—is an overwhelming task, and one well beyond the scope of this brief report. Fortunately, the Kerner Commission mapped the riot areas for several

cities—among them, Detroit, Newark, Cincinnati, Grand Rapids, New Haven, and Dayton—in the course of its investigation.[4] And it was on the basis of the Commission's maps that we computed the number of Negroes living in the riot areas. Only some of the Negroes living in the riot areas—namely, the males and females between the ages of 10 and 59 inclusive—are defined by us as the potential rioters. This definition is a rather broad one. It excludes children under 10 and adults over 59 not only for reasons of common sense, but, more important, because together they constitute only one per cent of the arrestees. It includes, however, the handicapped and the institutionalized, who are admittedly few in number, and women, even though they were less likely than men to join in the riots.[5]

This definition of potential rioters as all Negroes living in the riot areas between the ages of 10 and 59 inclusive tends to maximize the base of the population and thereby minimize the extent of participation. It is, if anything, biased in favor of the riffraff theory. In any event, if this definition is applied to the six cities for which the Kerner Commission mapped the riot areas, the number of Negroes who might have joined in the riots is, as Table 1 indicates 149,000 in Detroit, 46,500 in Newark, 42,000 in Cincinnati, 5,700 in Grand Rapids, 5,200 in New Haven, and 3,100 in Dayton. It is important to point out, however, that since we are using 1960

[3] See, for example, Scoble, "The McCone Commission," p. 11. *Violence in the City—An End or a Beginning?* A Report by the Governor's Commission on Los Angeles Riots, 1965, 4–5 (hereafter referred to as the McCone Report); and Fogelson, "White on Black," p. 345. (Fogelson, R. M., "White on Black: A Critique of the McCone Commission Report on the Los Angeles Riots," *Political Science Quarterly,* 1967, **82,** p. 345.)

[4] *Kerner Report,* p. 113.

[5] In his survey of riot participation in the Rochester riots of 1964, Schulman defined the "riot eligible" population as persons from 11 to 50 years old. We have used a slightly wider age range to define "potential rioters" than he did. Our data reveal that only one-tenth of one per cent of riot arrestees are less than 10 years old and only one per cent are 60 years and older. The census data indicate that about 27 per cent of the nonwhite residents in the riot areas are under 10 years old, whereas about 8 per cent of these residents are over 59 years old. Thus, we are subtracting about 35 per cent of the total nonwhite population in the riot areas from the base figures in our computations. The remaining 65 per cent constitute the "potential rioters." See Jay Schulman, "Ghetto Residence, Political Alienation and Riot Orientation," *Urban Disorders, Violence and Urban Victimization,* L. Masotti, Ed. (Sage Publishers, July, 1968), fn. 10, p. 32.

TABLE 1 Age Distribution of Nonwhites in Riot Areas

City	Total non-white popu-lation	Under 10	Over 59	Total poten-tial rioters
Detroit	219,730	54,263	16,479	148,988
Newark	69,915	19,158	4,265	46,492
Cincinnati	65,676	17,809	5,845	42,022
Grand Rapids	9,068	2,814	512	5,742
New Haven	7,839	2,138	455	5,246
Dayton	4,700	1,028	575	3,097

census tract data, the total number of potential rioters presented in Table 1 for each city is much smaller than the total number of Negroes between the ages of 10–59 who resided in these areas when the riots occurred in 1967, because all of these cities have increased their Negro population since 1960. Thus, we will be sharply underestimating the actual number of rioters in our analysis.[6]

In order to derive estimates of the total number of Negro rioters in the above six cities we relied upon the three surveys of riot areas that were available to us—the 1967 Caplan surveys of Newark and Detroit and the 1965 Sears survey of southcentral Los Angeles.[7] Unfortunately, each of these surveys had either age or sex limitations for its

[6] U.S. Bureau of the Census. *U.S. Censuses of Population and Housing: 1960. Census Tracts.* U.S. Government Printing Office, Washington, D.C. 1962. All of the figures are based on 1960 U.S. Census statistics because these are the only figures available by census tracts. The census tracts that make up the riot area for the six cities are as follows: Cincinnati, Final Report PHC(1)–27, 19 tracts: 3, 8, 11, 14, 15, 21, 23, 34–39, 41, 66–68, 77, 86–B; Dayton, Final Report PHC(1)–36, one tract: 0008–1A; Detroit, Final Report PHC(1)–40 74 tracts: 11–16, 20, 24, 28, 31–33, 40, 42, 120, 121, 151–157, 161–165, 167–169, 176–A, 176–N, 176–C, 176–D, 177–189, 211, 212, 301–B, 519, 525, 530–533, 545, 551–559, 759–764, 793; Grand Rapids, Final Report PHC(1)–55, 3 tracts: 23–25; New Haven, Final Report PHC(1)–102, 4 tracts: 6, 7, 15, 22; and Newark, Final Report PHC(1)–105, 22 tracts: 29–32, 37–40, 53, 55–57, 59, 61–67, 81–82.

[7] Caplan and Paige in the *Kerner Reports,* fn. 115, p. 172.

respondents that hampered our efforts somewhat. The Newark survey, for example, was limited to Negro males between the ages of 15 and 35; the Detroit survey, while including both males and females, did not interview anyone under the age of 15. And, in the Los Angeles survey, which also included both males and females, the lowest age limit was never made explicit. Since each of these surveys contained only a segment of our potential riot population, we had to find a way by which we could calculate the rate of participation for all the Negro riot area residents between the ages of 10 and 59. We decided to select, wherever possible, an age category that was known to have a high proportion of arrestees (such as between 15 and 35 years old) and to use its reported rate of participation in our calculations.

The approach that we used to derive our estimates of riot participation (with the aid of survey, arrest and census data) requires two fairly simple, though not totally reliable, calculations. First, we obtain a "riot ratio" by dividing the number of potential rioters in a given age interval by the number of arrestees in the same age interval for each of the three cities (which are Detroit, Newark, and Los Angeles) where surveys had been taken. Second, we apply the average of the three ratios to the other cities (where no surveys had been conducted) by multiplying the ratio times the total number of arrestees in each city—and so derive our estimates of the total number of rioters in each city.

Using the above approach, we obtained the following results. Of the 33,600 or so Negroes in the Los Angeles ghetto between the ages of 25 and 34, approximately 1,200 were arrested in the 1965 riots, and (according to the Sears survey) roughly 22 per cent, or 7,200, were active in the riots. Hence the ratio of rioters to arrestees for Los Angeles was about six to one. Of the 9,800 or so Negro males in the Newark riot area between the ages of 15 and 35, approximately 900 were arrested in the 1967 riots, and (according to the Caplan survey) roughly 45 per cent, or 4,400 participated in the riots. Hence the ratio of rioters to arrestees for Newark was about five to one. Of the 147,000 or so Negroes in the Detroit riot area 15 years and older, approximately 5,400 were arrested in the 1967 riots, and (again, according to the Caplan survey) roughly 11 per cent, or

16,200, joined in the riots. Hence the ratio of rioters to arrestees for Detroit was about three to one. Whether the ratios which hold for Los Angeles, Newark, and Detroit would also hold for the other cities is impossible to say. But we can say that the ratios are fairly similar in the three cities and that they are extremely conservative.[8]

TABLE 2 Estimates of Rioters in Riot Areas for Six Cities

City	Riot Ratio[a]	Total Number of Negro Arrestees	Total Number of Negro Rioters[b]	Percent of Riot Area Residents Who Rioted[c]
Detroit	3:1	5,642	16,900	11
Newark	5:1	1,387	6,900	15
Cincinnati	5:1	350	1,800	4
Grand Rapids	5:1	189	900	16
New Haven	5:1	353	1,800	35
Dayton	5:1	160	800	26

[a] The "riot ratio" was derived by dividing the number of nonwhite residents within a particular age category by the number of Negro arrestees within the same age category.

[b] The total number of Negro rioters was derived by multiplying the total number of Negro arrestees by the riot ratio for each city.

[c] The percent of residents who rioted was derived by dividing the total number of Negro rioters by the total nonwhite residents of the riot area who were between the ages of 10 and 59 inclusive.

Since Newark's five to one ratio fell between Los Angeles' six to one ratio and Detroit's three to one ratio, it was arbitrarily applied to the remaining four cities. Consequently, the total number of Negroes who participated in the riots is, as Table 2 indicates, 16,900 in Detroit, 6,900 in Newark, 1,800 in Cincinnati, 900 in Grand Rapids, 1,800 in New Haven and 800 in Dayton. As these figures do not reflect the rise in the

Negro population of these cities since 1960, they are conservative estimates of the minimum number of rioters for each city. The Negro population in Newark, for example, increased from 34 per cent in 1960 to an estimated 47 per cent in 1965. Thus, our estimate of the total number of rioters in Newark is probably underestimating the true figure by at least 13 per cent. There is probably less of an underestimation with regard to Detroit and Cincinnati, each of which experienced only slight increases in its Negro population since 1960; Detroit's Negro population rose by 4 per cent from 1960 to 1965 and Cincinnati's by 2 per cent over the same period.[9]

These estimates, to repeat, are highly speculative: our figures are based on 1960 census data, riot areas are not precise boundaries, ghetto residents are constantly on the move, the reliability of self-reports about deviant behavior in surveys is questionable, and police arrest practices differ from one city to another. But these estimates are no more speculative than the personal impressions of courageous, but terribly harried, newspaper reporters or the official statements of concerned, but hardly dispassionate, public figures.[10] Furthermore, these estimates far exceed the riffraff theory's estimates, and, perhaps even more noteworthy, nowhere, except in Cincinnati, do they even remotely approximate 1 or 2 percent of the black population. Hence the rioters were a minority, but hardly a tiny minority—and, in view of the historic efficacy of the customary restraints on rioting in the United States, especially among Negroes, hardly an insignificant minority either. And to characterize them otherwise, as the first point of the riffraff theory does, is not only to distort the historical record, but, even worse, to mislead the American public.

[9] For 1965 estimates of the Negro population in various cities, see *Kerner Report*, p. 248.

[10] Because of their smaller Negro populations, the smaller communities have a higher per cent of residents who rioted than the larger communities; this result is partly due to the mathematical artifact of having a smaller base figure. The greater severity of the riot in the larger communities is undoubtedly due to the fact that although a small percentage of the populace rioted, the absolute number of rioters was extremely large.

[8] These ratios provide estimates of the proportions of the rioters not apprehended by the police. In Detroit, for example, two-thirds of the rioters escaped apprehension, whereas in Newark 80 per cent of the rioters were estimated to have avoided arrest. Caplan and Paige in the *Kerner Report*, fn. 112, p. 172.

THE COMPOSITION OF THE RIOTERS

The second component of the riffraff theory —that the rioters, far from being representative of the Negro community, were principally the riffraff and outside agitators—is perhaps the most difficult to test using arrest statistics because of their built-in biases in favor of this theory. For it is a fact that for similar offenses, lower-class persons (who tend to have most of the traits of the riffraff: unattached, uprooted, unskilled, unemployed and criminal) are much more likely to get arrested than middle-class persons.[11] Therefore, it is to be expected that the riffraff element would be overrepresented among riot arrestees.

At the same time, however, since most Negroes are either lower- or working-class persons, it is also to be expected that these so-called riffraff traits can be found among large segments of the Negro community. Many Negroes, whether rioters or not, are single, or otherwise unmarried; many are juveniles or young adults, many are recent immigrants from the South, many unemployed or unskilled, and many have criminal records.[12] Hence to test the second point of the riffraff theory, it is not enough just to ask whether many of the rioters have these traits; the answer, obviously, is they do. It is also necessary to ask whether a greater proportion of the actual rioters than of the potential rioters possess these traits. But even if we do find that a higher proportion of actual rioters than potential rioters have certain riffraff characteristics, our task is not yet complete. We must still assess the proportion of the actual rioters that these traits account for.

Therefore, despite the built-in biases of the arrest statistics in favor of the riffraff theory, we shall use these data in conjunction with census data—and, whenever possible, survey data—to assist us in determining the social composition of rioters.

Before we examine the so-called riffraff traits it seems instructive to begin with a discussion of the sex distribution of riot arrestees and the potential rioters.

Since 90 per cent of those arrested for nonriot offenses in the general population are males, it should come as no surprise that riot arrestees are also predominantly male—and, by the same proportion of nine to one.[13] According to arrest statistics, therefore, it seems safe to conclude that men are much more likely to participate in riots than females.

A different picture of sex involvement in riots is obtained, however, when one observes the findings of survey reports of riot participation. In the Detroit survey 39 per cent of the self-reported rioters were females, whereas only 10 per cent of the Detroit riot arrestees were females. Thus, assuming the survey findings are reliable, the Detroit arrest data are under-representing the participation of women in riots by almost 30 per cent. A similar under-representation of the extent of female participation in riots was found in the Los Angeles survey of 1965. Fully one-half of those who reported they were "active" in the riot were females, whereas only 13 per cent of the Los Angeles arrestees were females. If the survey data are reliable, the Los Angeles arrest data are grossly under-representing the participation of females in the 1965 riot by almost 40 per cent.[14]

Since about 50 per cent of the potential rioters in the riot area are males, the 90 per cent for males among riot arrestees would indicate that males are heavily over-represented in riots. Yet, if the 60 per cent figure for males from the Detroit survey or the 50 per cent figure for males from the Los Angeles survey is compared to the 50 per cent figure for the potential rioters, one would have to conclude that males are only slightly over-represented, if at all, in riots. Eye-witness accounts of the riots also indicate that a higher proportion of males participate in riots than

[11] Richard K. Korn and Lloyd W. McCorkle, *Criminology and Penology.* New York: Holt, Rinehart and Winston, 1959.

[12] Caplan and Paige in the *Kerner Report,* pp. 172–175.

[13] Korn and McCorkle, *Criminology and Penology,* pp. 23–24.

[14] Sears, "Riot Activity," Table 4. David O. Sears, "Riot Activity and Evaluation: An Overview of the Negro Survey," 1966, 1–2, unpublished paper written for the U.S. Office of Economic Opportunity; Governor's Commission on the Los Angeles Riots, Archives, II, in the University of California Library, Los Angeles (hereafter referred to as the McCone Archives).

females. In view of the above data, it appears that the safest conclusion that we can make about sex involvement in riots is that although males are more likely than females to participate in riots, their differential rates of participation are much closer than arrest statistics indicate. Policemen, for one reason or another, are permitting large numbers of female rioters to go unapprehended.

Although one may not ordinarily consider being young a riffraff characteristic, it is a trait that is commonly identified with the undesirable elements in riots. In fact, it is widely assumed in some quarters that teenagers are primarily responsible for most riots. In Table 3 we compare the relative proportions of juveniles (defined as youths between the ages of 10 and 17 inclusive) among the arrestees and the potential rioters (that is, the

TABLE 3 Proportion of Juveniles and Adults among Arrestees and Residents[a]

City	Total[b] Negro Arrestees	Arrestees (percent)		Residents[c] (percent)	
		Juveniles	Adults	Juveniles	Adults
Detroit	5,642	16.6	83.4	7.2	92.8
Newark	1,387	18.4	81.6	12.8	87.2
New Haven	353	8.1	91.9	12.0	88.0
Cincinnati	350	32.4	67.6	18.9	81.1
Buffalo	190	22.1	77.9	13.9	86.1
Grand Rapids	189	25.4	74.6	16.0	84.0
Plainfield	161	10.1	89.9		
Dayton	160	15.2	84.8	11.9	88.1
Phoenix	111				
Boston	62	11.3	88.7	15.0	85.0

[a] We define "juvenile" as those persons under the age of 18. This definition of juvenile is consistent with that employed by most police departments. For Detroit, however, juveniles refer to those persons 16 years and under. The arrestee data throughout this report will refer only to Negro arrestees.

[b] Although these base figures for Negro arrestees will not be presented in any of the succeeding tables, they should be used to compute the absolute frequencies of particular categories, when necessary.

[c] The residents (or the "potential rioters") refer only to the nonwhite persons between 10–59 years old residing in the riot area; whites residing in the area are excluded from our analysis. The juveniles among the residents are defined as those nonwhite youths between the ages of 10 and 17. The figures for the nonwhite residents were obtained from 1960 census tract data. See U.S. Bureau of the Census, "U.S. Censuses of Population and Housing: 1960. Census Tracts" U.S. Government Printing Office, Washington, D.C., 1962.

riot area residents between 10–59 inclusive) for each city. With the exception of two cities (New Haven and Boston), it is noteworthy that the proportion of juveniles is considerably higher among the arrestees than among the potential rioters. Yet it is also important to note that in no city is the proportion of juveniles a majority of the arrestees. In fact, the highest proportion of juvenile arrestees is 32 per cent (in Cincinnati) and the lowest proportion is 8 per cent (in New Haven). Thus, the riot arrestees are overwelmingly adults. It may very well be, however, that as with the case of female involvement in riots, higher proportions of juveniles are participating than are reflected by arrest statistics. Since we do not have survey data available on the rate of participation in riots of persons under the age of 15, we cannot draw upon that data to make generalizations about the participation of juveniles in riots. It would appear, however, that descriptions of the riots tend to indicate a higher degree of involvement by juveniles than is reflected in the arrest statistics. But even this degree of participation by juveniles appears to be much less than the involvement of adults in riots.

In Table 4 we are provided with a more detailed breakdown of the age distribution among the arrestees and potential rioters. It reveals that if any age-group is over-represented in the riots, it is not primarily the juveniles. It is rather the young adults between the ages of 15 and 24. Forty-five per cent to 73 per cent of the arrestees in the ten cities are between 15 and 24 years old. But only 13 per cent to 23 per cent of the potential rioters fall within that age category. Even among the arrestees, in only three of the ten cities (Cincinnati, Buffalo and Dayton) do those persons between the ages of 15 and 24 constitute a clear majority. However, the young people between the ages of 15 and 34 constitute an overwhelmingly majority of the arrestees; these proportions range from 70 per cent in Detroit to 93 per cent in Buffalo. Yet the similar proportions of those between 15 and 34 among the potential rioters—with the exception of one city (New Haven)—are all under 50 per cent. In all, those persons between 15–24 are highly over-represented among the arrestees, those between the ages of 25 and 34 are slightly over-represented, whereas the elderly (35–39) and the children (10–14) are under-represented in the riots.

TABLE 4   Age Distribution of Arrestees and Residents of Riot Areas
(In percent)

City	Arrestees				Residents			
	10–14	*15–24*	*25–34*	*35–39*	*10–14*	*15–24*	*25–34*	*35–39*
Detroit	3.6	49.7	27.1	19.6	12.4	17.1	22.7	47.8
Newark	5.3	45.2	29.0	20.5	29.4	13.4	17.2	40.0
New Haven	0	47.4	35.4	17.2	11.6	23.5	28.1	36.8
Cincinnati	7.0	73.4	15.6	4.0	14.2	20.1	22.1	43.6
Buffalo	0	71.7	21.0	7.3	13.7	19.8	25.0	41.5
Grand Rapids	19.7	51.8	19.0	9.5	15.8	22.0	23.7	38.5
Plainfield	1.2	45.2	35.1	18.9				
Dayton	0	58.6	24.3	17.1	12.2	16.3	20.5	51.0
Phoenix	0	53.1	30.7	16.2	16.7	23.0	20.6	39.7
Boston	1.6	51.6	29.1	17.7	13.3	21.0	24.4	41.3

Thus, we conclude that on the basis of the arrest data, individuals between the ages of 15 and 34 and especially those between the ages of 15 and 24 are most likely to participate in riots.

Since Table 4 revealed that the age category with the highest proportion of arrestees was young adults between the ages of 15 and 24, we would expect a large proportion of the arrestees to be single. And, if we can assume that single persons are more likely than married persons to participate in riots, then we would expect a higher proportion of the arrestees to be single than the potential rioters. And, indeed, Table 5 reveals this to be the case. In every city, there are at least twice as many arrestees who are single, as there are potential rioters who are single. In Detroit, for example, about one-fifth of the riot area residents are single, but almost half of the arrestees are single. On the other hand, between 56 to 60 per cent of the potential rioters are married, but only 23 to 48 per cent of the arrestees are married. Thus, arrestees are for the most part, more likely to be single, but less likely to be married, separated, widowed, or divorced than are the potential rioters. Yet it is also important to note that in only two out of the five cities (Cincinnati and Buffalo) do the single persons constitute a clear majority of the arrestees. In fact, when those two cities are excluded, the differences between the proportions of single arrestees and married arrestees vary from a low of 3 per cent to a high of 9 per cent. Consequently, there are almost as many arrestees who are married as there are those

who are single. Nevertheless, it is clear that single persons are over-represented among the arrestees, whereas married, separated, widowed, and divorced persons are under-represented among the arrestees. In short, one unattached group (the single persons) is over-represented, whereas the other unattached group (the formerly married) is under-represented among the arrestees.

One popular assumption about riot participation is that the rioters are primarily the

TABLE 5   Marital Status of Arrestees and Residents of Riot Areas[a]
(In percent)

City[b]	Arrestees			Residents		
	Sin-gle	*Mar-ried*	*Other*	*Sin-gle*	*Mar-ried*	*Other*
Detroit	48.4	38.4	13.2	19.2	60.1	20.7
Cincinnati	75.6	22.5	1.9	20.2	58.3	21.5
Buffalo	69.0	28.7	2.3	21.2	59.6	19.2
Grand Rapids	44.8	38.6	16.6	20.9	58.5	20.6
Boston	51.6	48.4	0	24.2	55.7	20.1

[a] The figures for marital status of both arrestees and residents are presented only for persons 14 years and over.

[b] Newark, Plainfield, Dayton, Phoenix and New Haven are omitted from the above table because marital status information on their arrestees were not available. It will be our practice to omit a city whenever we do not have arrest data information on the item in question. The Detroit figures were obtained from a study of 500 Detroit male Negro arrestees conducted for the U.S. Department of Labor. See Sheldon Lachman and Benjamin Singer, "The Detroit Riot of July 1967", Behavior Research Institute, Detroit, Michigan, 1968, p. 19.

uprooted—those immigrants from the rural South who have not been able to make a successful adjustment to the demands of urban life. According to this view we would expect the Southern-born to be over-represented among the arrestees. The data in Table 6, however, do not indicate this. In each of the three cities (Detroit, Cincinnati, and Boston) for which we have comparative information on both arrestees and residents, we find that the arrestees are somewhat less likely to be Southern-born than are the poten-

TABLE 6 Birthplace of Arrestees and Residents of Riot Areas[a]

(In percent)

City[b]	Arrestees			Residents		
	Born in State	Outside of State		Born in State	Outside of State	
		North	South		North	South
Detroit	35.5	5.7	58.9	26.9	8.2	64.9
New Haven	18.0	16.0	66.0			
Cincinnati	72.4	8.5	19.1	44.5	2.5	53.0
Grand Rapids	21.5	20.3	58.2			
Plainfield	53.2	8.2	38.6			
Boston	41.0	16.4	42.6	40.5	11.1	48.4

[a] Our definition of "South" includes the following eleven states: Alabama, Arkansas, Florida, Georgia, Louisiana, Mississippi, North Carolina, South Carolina, Tennessee, Texas and Virginia. All the remaining states constitute the "North."

[b] Newark, Buffalo, Dayton, and Phoenix have been omitted from the above table because of lack of birthplace information on its arrestees.

tial rioters. Among the arrestees, however, we find that in three cities (Detroit, New Haven, and Grand Rapids) a majority was born in the South and in the remaining three cities (Cincinnati, Plainfield, and Boston) a majority was born in the North. Thus, it appears that southerners may be just as likely to participate in riots as northerners. But arrestees are more likely to be born in the state where the riot occurred than are the potential rioters. In Cincinnati, for example, whereas less than half (45 per cent) of the potential rioters were born in the state of Ohio, almost three-fourths (72 per cent) of the arrestees were native-born.

Therefore, we conclude that the "uprooted" thesis of riot participation is not supported by our data. Northerners are just as likely as southerners to participate in riots; and, more important, native-born residents of the state are more likely than those born in other states to become involved in riots.

Another important theme of the riffraff theory is that the rioters are recruited primarily from those who are poorly-trained and who lack the skills to obtain good-paying jobs. Thus, it would be expected that the unskilled are over-represented among the riot arrestees. This expectation is confirmed by the figures presented in Table 7. For we find that the arrestees are much more likely to be unskilled than are the potential rioters. The smallest difference between the proportions of the two groups is 10 per cent (in Grand Rapids) and the largest difference is 29 per cent (in Newark). Among the arrestees, we find that in all cities, except Boston, the proportion of unskilled persons is over 49 per cent; it ranges from 47 per cent in Boston to 67 per cent in Cincinnati. Among the potential rioters, however, the proportion of the unskilled goes from 28 per cent in Detroit to 48 per cent in Cincinnati. Although the arrestees are over-represented on the lowest skill level, there are, nonetheless, strong similarities between the occupational distributions of the arrestees and the potential rioters. In both groups, for example, the proportion of these holding either semi-skilled or unskilled jobs include (for the most part) more than 70 per cent of the members of each group. It is clear that the overwhelming majority of Negroes, whether rioters or not, hold low-skilled jobs. On the other hand, only a slightly smaller proportion of arrestees than potential rioters hold skilled or white-collar jobs.

Consequently, although our data clearly support the thesis that a large proportion of the rioters hold unskilled jobs, it must also be pointed out that about just as many potential rioters as arrestees have low-skilled jobs as operatives or laborers.

Closely related to the assertion that rioters consist primarily of the unskilled is the contention that a large proportion of the rioters are employed. Since we cannot use the 1960 employment figures of the riot areas, because of their sharp fluctuations from year to year, we can only make comparisons for the two cities for which we do have recent unemploy-

TABLE 7   Occupation of Male Arrestees and Residents of Riot Areas[a]

(In percent)

	Arrestees				Residents			
City[b]	White collar	Skilled	Semi-skilled	Un-skilled	White collar	Skilled	Semi-skilled	Un-skilled
Detroit	10.2	10.7	29.0	50.1	18.4	12.8	41.2	27.6
Newark	18.0		23.0	59.0	24.6		45.6	29.8
Cincinnati	9.4	6.5	16.7	67.4	18.0	10.8	22.9	48.3
Buffalo	10.6	3.5	33.3	52.6	10.9	13.9	36.8	38.4
Grand Rapids	6.4	14.2	27.4	51.9	7.7	15.8	34.9	41.6
Boston	29.4	11.8	11.8	47.1	20.3	13.5	29.7	36.5

[a] The above figures for occupation among the arrestees refer only to those arrestees who are Negro males 18 years and older; similarly, among the residents, the figures are given for nonwhite males 14 years and older. The "unskilled" category includes both laborers and all service occupations; the "semi-skilled" grouping includes only operatives; the "skilled" category includes only craftsmen; and the "white-collar" category includes sales, clerical, managers and proprietors, and the professionals.

[b] Since the occupations of the Detroit and Newark arrestees were not available to us, the figures presented in the above table were obtained from other sources. The Detroit figures are based upon a sample of 500 male arrestees interviewed by the Behavior Research Institute. We recomputed their percentages after excluding the "miscellaneous" category. See Sheldon Lachman and Benjamin Singer, *The Detroit Riot of July 1967*, Behavior Research Institute, Detroit, Michigan, 1968, p. 14. The figures for Newark were obtained from the Governor's Select Commission on Civil Disorder, *Report for Action*, State of New Jersey, February 1968, p. 271. Since the N.J. Commission included the "white-collar" figures in the "skilled" category, we have placed the figures midway between the two columns for both Arrestees and Residents to make them comparable.

ment figures—Detroit and Newark. In the New Jersey riot report, *Report for Action*, it was indicated that while 27 per cent of the arrestees were unemployed, 12 per cent of the Newark Negro population in the city as a whole were unemployed.[15] Similarly, whereas our arrest data reveal that 24 per cent of the Negro adult males in Detroit were unemployed, the Bureau of Labor Statistics estimated that 10 percent of the non-white residents in the central city were unemployed.[16] Thus, a higher proportion of the arrestees are unemployed than the potential rioters in the general population. But this discrepancy is not as large as it appears, for two reasons. First, since the Department of Labor includes in its count only those persons actively seeking a job, it severely underestimates the actual rate of unemployment. It excludes completely the "subemployed," which consists of a large proportion of men

in the ghetto who have given up looking for work.[17] Furthermore, since our arrestees are heavily over-represented by the young adults between the ages of 15 and 24, an age group which is itself greatly over-represented in the unemployed, it should not be surprising that our arrest data should indicate higher proportions of the unemployed than exist in the Negro population for the city as a whole. But, and more important, it should be noted that about three-quarters of the riot arrestees are employed. Hence the overwhelming majority of those who participate in riots are gainfully employed—even though it is usually in a

[15] *N.J. Riot Report,* p. 271. Governor's Select Commission on Civil Disorder, State of New Jersey, *Report for Action,* February, 1968 (hereafter referred to as the *N.J. Riot Report*).

[16] The Detroit figures were obtained from "Unemployment in 15 Metropolitan Areas," *Monthly Labor Review,* 91: v–vi, January, 1968, v–vi; the Newark unemployment figures were obtained from *N.J. Riot Report,* p. 271.

[17] Of course, our unemployment statistics are not really comparable to the U.S. Census' unemployment statistics since different criteria for inclusion are employed. All males 18 years and over who said that they were not working were classified as "unemployed." Whenever possible, full-time students were excluded. But even the Bureau of Labor Statistics criteria for estimating unemployment rates are being challenged by some observers. In a door-to-door survey of three Chicago poverty areas, it was found that an "actual" unemployment rate for these areas was more than a third higher than it would have been under the definition of joblessness used by the BLS. See "New Jobless Count Ups the Figure," *Business Week,* Dec. 10, 1966, pp. 160–162. Also *Kerner Report,* p. 257.

semi-skilled or unskilled occupation. Thus, although unemployment may be a factor in riot participation, it does not account for the riot participation of the three-fourths who are employed.

At the heart of the riffraff theory is the notion that rioters represent the criminal element of the Negro community. In fact, the arrest data tend to support this contention. With the exception of Buffalo and Newark, a sizable majority of the arrestees—ranging from 40 per cent in Buffalo, 45 per cent in Newark, 57 per cent in Detroit, 67 per cent in New Haven, 70 per cent in Grand Rapids and 92 per cent in Dayton—had prior criminal records.[18] But it is one thing to have a record and quite another to be a criminal; what is more, there are a number of reasons why these figures do not prove that the riot arrestees were principally criminals.

First, a criminal record in the United States simply means an arrest, as opposed to a conviction, record; probably no more than one-half of the arrestees with a record have been convicted, and probably no more than one-quarter for a major crime. Second, according to the President's Commission on Law Enforcement and Administration of Justice, which has made the only estimate we know of on the subject, roughly 50 to 90 per cent of the Negro males in the urban ghettos have criminal records.[19] Third, if the findings of the President's Commission on Crime in the District of Columbia are applicable elsewhere, convicted felons are much more likely

to be unemployed and to have criminal records than riot arrestees.[20] Fourth, our inspection of the prior criminal records of the riot arrestees revealed that their past arrests were for offenses which, on the whole, were much less serious than the offenses committed by the typical non-riot felons. The Bureau of Criminal Records in California's Department of Justice arrived at a similar conclusion after inspecting the prior criminal records of those arrested for participating in the Los Angeles riot of 1965.[21]

Hence, to label most rioters as criminals is simply to brand most members of the Negro community—and, particularly, the majority of Negro males—as criminals. Therefore, the criminal element is not over-represented among the rioters. Since the close surveillance of the Negro community by the police results in a disproportionately high number of arrests among male Negroes, it is to be expected that a majority of the rioters—who are predominantly young Negro males—would have criminal records.

The riffraff theory also holds that the riots were primarily the result of demagogic agitation by outsiders. Many first-hand descriptions of the riots do indicate that a few individuals and organizations—radicals as well as nationalists—encouraged some rioters and tried to exploit the rioting. Indeed, it would have been surprising if they had done

---

[18] Many of the Negroes with previous arrest records, technically, were not even arrested; as many were picked up for suspicious conduct and then later released. This is particularly true in the case of juveniles, many of whom were brought to the police station, but not arrested. Therefore, in many cases we are really referring to previous police "contact records" and not actual arrest records. The percentage for Dayton is higher than it ought to be; it resulted from an ambiguity in the coding instructions for that city.

[19] For nationwide estimates of the prevalence of arrest records, see President's Commission on Law Enforcement, *The Challenge of Crime*, p. 75 and R. Christensen, "Projected Percentages of U.S. Population with Criminal Arrest and Conviction Records" (August 18, 1966), report paper for the Commission. See also Jerry Cohen and William S. Murphy, *Burn, Baby, Burn* (New York, 1966), p. 208.

[20] Eighty per cent of the "typical" felons in Washington (who are 80 per cent Negro) have previous arrest records whereas only 60 per cent of the riot arrestees (who are 90 per cent Negro) have previous arrest (or "contact") records. About 50 per cent of the typical felons are unemployed, whereas only half as many (26 per cent) riot arrestees are unemployed. Furthermore, the typical felons more often have unstable marital relationships than riot arrestees; about 27 per cent of the typical felons are either separated, widowed or divorced, while only 7 per cent of the riot arrestees are either separated, widowed or divorced. Many of these differences are probably due to the age disparity between the two groups; the average age of the typical felon in Washington is 29 years old, whereas the average age of the riot arrestee is about 25 years old. See the *President's Commission on Crime in the District of Columbia,* Chapter 3.

[21] "Watts Riot Arrests," p. 37. Bureau of Criminal Statistics, California Department of Criminal Justice, "Watts Riot Arrests: Los Angeles, 1965."

otherwise. According to the arrest data, however, whether agitators or not, the overwhelming majority of the rioters were not outsiders. In seven of the nine cities for which information is available the proportion of the arrestees who were residents of the cities involved was 97 per cent or more. Ninety-seven per cent of the arrestees in Boston, Detroit and Grand Rapids, 98 per cent in Buffalo and New Haven, and 100 per cent in Cincinnati and Dayton were residents of the cities that experienced the rioting. And in Newark and Plainfield 92 per cent and 77 per cent of the arrestees were residents of those cities.[22] With regard to the role of conspiracy in the riots, the arrest sheets are, of course, less informative. On the basis of other evidence, however, it is clear that, whether outsiders or not, the agitators did not plan or organize the 1960s riots. This was the conclusion reached by the F.B.I. in 1964 and reiterated by its director J. Edgar Hoover and Attorney-General Ramsey Clark in 1967. This was also the conclusion confirmed a year later by the Kerner Commission, which made a thorough survey of the federal, state, and municipal reports on the 1967 riots.[23]

In sum, we have found that many of the social traits predicted by the second component of the riffraff theory to characterize rioters were over-represented among the arrestees, and in some instances, decidedly so. Much of this, of course, was due to the biases of the arrest data. But "over-representativeness" is quite a different matter from saying that the arrestees had predominantly riffraff characteristics. In spite of the heavy overrepresentation of young, single males, the striking facts are—again in view of the historic efficacy of the customary restraints on rioting in the United States, especially among

Negroes—that one-half to three-quarters of the arrestees were employed in semi-skilled or skilled occupations, three-fourths were employed, and three-tenths to six-tenths were born outside the South. So to claim, as the second point of the riffraff theory does, that the rioters were principally the riffraff and outside agitators—rather than fairly typical young Negro males—is to seriously misconstrue the 1960s riots.

FURTHER SPECIFICATION OF RIOT PARTICIPATION

Before concluding our discussion of the second point of the riffraff theory, however, it is necessary to evaluate it from a somewhat different perspective. For even though the theory is not confirmed when the arrestees are treated as a group, it may be confirmed when they are considered according to the type of offense, the day of arrest, the severity of the riot, the region of the country, or the year of the riot. In other words, even if the theory fails to account for the rioters as a whole, it may account for the rioters who were arrested for looting or arson, on the first or second day, in the more or less serious riots, in the North or the South, or in 1964 or 1967. Whether there were differences in riot participation from one region to another and from one year to the next is not possible to say in this report because the arrest sheets have been analyzed for too few cities and for none of those cities which experienced rioting in 1964, 1965, and 1966. But it is possible to say whether there are differences between one type of offender and another, from one day to the next, and from one kind of riot to another because the criminal charge and time of arrest are included on the arrest sheets and the riots were classified by the Kerner Commission.[24] And under these circumstances it is possible to evaluate further the accuracy of the riffraff theory.

[22] Altogether about 95 per cent of the 1967 arrestees were residents of the city in which the disorders took place; 4 per cent were residents of other cities within that state and only one per cent were residents of other states. Thus, the assertion that the riots were primarily the work of out-of-towners or out-of-state agitators appears to be without empirical foundation. In fact, most of the rioters were not only residents of the riot city, but also were long-term residents of the city. See the *Kerner Report,* p. 131.

[23] Federal Bureau of Investigation, *Report on the 1964 Riots* (September 18, 1964), p. 9; *Kerner Report,* Chapter 2.

[24] For the purpose of this analysis, we will focus upon the severity of only four of the "major" disorders—Detroit, Newark, Buffalo and Cincinnati, since we have sufficient comparable data for each of them. For the NIMH study we will more systematically relate the severity of all 19 riots in 1967 to the characteristics of their arrestees.

To begin with, the riffraff theory is not confirmed when the arrestees are classified according to criminal charge. For, as Table 8 indicates, the profile of the rioters—whether as disorderly persons, looters, arsonists, or assaulters—does not consistently resemble the profile of the riffraff. Those arrested for disorderly conduct were most likely to be young and unemployed and second most likely to be previously arrested; but they were also least likely to be born in the South. The looters were most likely to be born in the South; but they were also least likely to be young and unemployed and second least likely to be previously arrested. The arsonists were most likely to be previously arrested and second most likely to be born in the South; but they were also second least likely to be young and

unemployed.[25] The assaulters were second most likely to be young and unemployed; but they were also least likely to be previously arrested and second least likely to be born in the South. There are, of course, differences among the arrestees—perhaps the most striking of which is between the disorderly persons, who were younger, unemployed, and native-born, and the looters, who tend to be older, less employed, and Southern-born. But these differences cannot be explained by the second point of the riffraff theory.

Nor is the riffraff theory supported when the arrestees are classified according to day of arrest. Table 9 reveals, that males, the unemployed and those with prior criminal records are just as likely to participate on any one of the first three days of the rioting. However, there is a clear relationship between age and the day of involvement; 64 per cent of those under 25 years old were

TABLE 8 Characteristics of Negro Arrestees by Type of Offense

(In percent. Totals in parentheses)

Characteristics	Type of Offense			
	As-sault[a]	Arson	Loot-ing	Dis-orderly conduct
Sex: Male	92.0	92.9	93.8	93.1
Total	(499)	(85)	(6,099)	(1,344)
Age range:				
10 to 14	4.5	4.9	1.5	3.5
15 to 24	52.3	43.9	46.6	64.4
25 to 34	26.1	36.6	30.2	23.3
35 to 59	17.1	14.6	21.7	8.8
Total	(491)	(82)	(6,016)	(1,337)
Employment status:				
Unemployed	30.1	29.1	25.6	39.6
Total	(186)	(48)	(2,924)	(321)
Birthplace:				
In riot State	44.4	42.0	29.0	48.9
Outside South	21.8	17.4	21.4	11.9
Inside South	33.8	40.6	49.5	39.1
Total	(275)	(69)	(3,833)	(511)
Prior record:				
Previous arrest	56.6	69.4	59.4	63.8
Total	(251)	(62)	(4,093)	(652)

[a] The "Assault" Category consists primarily of persons arrested for throwing rocks and fighting with law enforcement officials, but also includes persons arrested for possession of weapons.

TABLE 9 Characteristics of Negro Arrestees by Day of Arrest

(In percent. Totals in parentheses)

Characteristics	Day of arrest		
	First day	Second day	Third and after
Sex: Male	89.8	86.8	92.0
Total	(1,240)	(3,285)	(2,302)
Age range:			
10 to 14	5.5	4.5	2.3
15 to 24	58.6	51.1	52.0
25 to 34	24.3	26.0	26.7
35 to 59	11.5	18.4	19.0
Total	(1,361)	(3,583)	(2,340)
Employment status:			
Unemployed	25.6	24.9	26.5
Total	(708)	(1,733)	(1,260)
Birthplace:			
In riot state	40.7	37.6	35.4
Outside South	7.1	6.9	6.8
Inside South	52.2	55.6	57.9
Total	(1,003)	(2,708)	(1,643)
Prior record:			
Previously arrested	58.5	56.9	57.3
Total	(1,063)	(2,835)	(1,970)

[25] *Kerner Report*, p. 130.

arrested on the first day, whereas 54 per cent of those under the age of 25 were arrested on the third or later days of rioting. Similarly, the highest proportion of native-born persons (41 per cent) and the lowest proportion of Southern-born persons (52 per cent) were arrested on the first day of rioting. However, the majority of these arrested on any one day were Southern-born. Consequently, these patterns cannot be accounted for by the second point of the riffraff theory either.

Whether the riffraff theory is more accurate when the arrestees are classified according to the gravity of the riots is more difficult to tell because the arrest sheets have not yet been analyzed for enough cities. Still, if the arrestees in Detroit and Newark, the sites of the two most serious riots in 1967, are compared with the arrestees in Buffalo and Cincinnati, the sites of two less serious, though not necessarily representative, riots, the differences are worth noting. For as Table 10 suggests, the arrestees in Detroit and Newark were less likely to be male, young, and unskilled—the information on employment status, birthplace and prior criminal record is not comparable—than the arrestees in Buffalo and Cincinnati. The differences in the age distribution of the arrestees may reflect, to some degree, the differences in the age distribution of the Negroes in these cities, but this is not so for sex distribution and occupational distribution. In any event, the available evidence suggests—and, it should be stressed, only suggests—that the second point of the riffraff theory is, if anything, more accurate for the less serious riots.[26]

[26] Other data not presented here indicate that the biggest difference between the more severe and less severe disorders is with regard to the most frequent type of offense. Over 75 per cent of the arrestees in both Detroit and Newark were

TABLE 10 Characteristics of Negro Arrestees by Severity of Riot[a]

(In percent)

| Characteristics[b] | Severity of Riot | | | |
| | "More severe" disorders | | "Less severe" disorders | |
	De-troit	New-ark	Buf-falo	Cincin-nati
Sex: Male	87.4	89.0	96.8	94.0
Age range:				
10 to 14	3.6	5.3	0	7.0
15 to 24	49.7	45.2	71.7	73.4
25 to 34	27.1	29.0	21.0	15.6
35 to 59	19.6	20.5	7.3	4.0
Male occupation:[c]				
White collar	10.2	18.0	10.6	9.4
Skilled	10.7		3.5	6.5
Semiskilled	29.0	23.0	33.3	16.7
Unskilled	50.1	59.0	52.6	67.4

[a] Although the Kerner Commision characterized the disturbance in Detroit, Newark, Buffalo and Cincinnati as "major" disorders, the number of deaths, injuries, arrests, and the amount of destruction was on a much larger scale in Detroit and Newark than in Buffalo and Cincinnati. See "Kerner Report," p. 113.

[b] The figures in this table refer to the characteristics of Negro arrestees only.

[c] The occupation figures for Detroit are based upon a sample of 500 male arrestees interviewed by the Behavior Research Institute. See Sheldon Lachman and Benjamin Singer, "The Detroit Riot of July 1967," Behavior Research Institute, Detroit, Michigan, 1968, p. 14. The figures for Newark were obtained from the Governor's Select Commission on Civil Disorder, "Report for Action," State of New Jersey, February, 1968, p. 271. The N.J. Commission included the "white-collar" figures in the "skilled" category. The occupation figures for Buffalo and Cincinnati refer to Negro male arrestees 18 years and older.

charged with looting, while less than 15 per cent of those arrested in Cincinnati and Buffalo were arrested for looting. Most of the arrestees (over 60 per cent) in Cincinnati and Buffalo were charged with disorderly conduct.

29

Riot ideology in Los Angeles: A study of Negro attitudes[1]

DAVID O. SEARS AND T. M. TOMLINSON

Each summer from 1964 through 1967 saw urban Negroes in America involved in a series of violent riots. Among the most critical consequences of the riots were the decisions made by the white population about the social changes required to prevent further rioting. These decisions rested in part on the whites' assumptions about the nature and extent of the Negro community's involvement in the riots. Matters of simple fact such as how many people took part in the riots, whether the rest of the Negro community repudiated the rioters and whether it viewed the riots as representing some form of collective protest against injustice and poverty, were initially quite unclear. Yet whites quickly made their own assumptions about such matters, and these strongly influenced their stance toward the riots and the entire racial problem.

There appear to be three widely held myths about the Negro community's response to

Reprinted from *Social Science Quarterly*, **49**, (3) 1968, 485–505, by permission of the authors and *Social Science Quarterly*.

[1] This study was conducted under a contract between the Office of Economic Opportunity and the Institute for Government and Public Affairs at UCLA, while both authors were members of the Department of Psychology, UCLA. The Coordinator of the research was Nathan E. Cohen. We owe a profound debt of gratitude to the many persons who worked on the Los Angeles Riot Study, with special thanks to Diana Ten-Houten and John B. McConahay. We also wish to express our appreciation to Esther Spachner for editorial help and to Peter Orleans for his comments on an earlier draft of this paper.

riots. The first is that the riots are participated in and viewed favorably by only a tiny segment of the Negro community. The figure often cited by news media and political spokesmen (both black and white) is between 2 and 5 per cent of the Negro population. Since riot supporters are thought to be so few in number, a further assumption is that they come from such commonly condemned fringe groups as Communists, hoodlums, and Black Muslims.[2]

The second myth is that most Negroes see the riots as purposeless, meaningless, senseless outbursts of criminality. Many white public officials certainly professed to see nothing in the riots but blind hostility and malicious mischief, drunkenness, and material greed. Perhaps because they held this view so strongly themselves, they tended to assume that Negroes shared it as well.

The third myth is that Negroes generally believe that no benefit will result from the riots. Negroes are supposed to view them with horror, seeing the physical destruction wrought in black ghettos, as well as the destruction of the good will patiently accumulated during early days of campaigning for civil rights. According to this myth, Negroes foresee "white backlash" and cities laid waste, rather than betterment in their life situations, as the main effect of the riots.

[2] See the attributions of the Watts riot to "young hoodlums," "the criminal element," and black nationalists by the mayor and police chief of Los Angeles, in the *New York Times*, Aug. 13, 1965, p. 26; Aug. 14, 1965, p. 8; Sept. 14, 1965, p. 22.

The response of the Negro community to the riots is a crucial consideration in determining how the society as a whole should respond to them. If these three myths are correct, perhaps the customary mechanisms for dealing with individual criminal behavior are not only morally justified but also the most practicable means for handling riots. If these myths are incorrect, if Negroes support the riots, see them as expressing meaningful goals, and expect them to better the conditions of their lives, then the responses traditionally used for dealing with criminals would be inappropriate. They would be impractical, ineffective, and likely to exacerbate an already difficult situation. Instead it would be essential to devise policies which took into account the fact that the riot highlighted a problem pervading the whole Negro community, rather than one limited to a few deviant individuals.

It is apparent that many Americans, black and white alike, have already rejected these myths. Others, however, retain them—those in positions of authority as well as those in the broader white community. Moreover, systematic data on them have not been widely available. Since these myths have had and will continue to have great influence in determining the white population's response to urban problems, it is vital that their validity be subjected to close empirical test. The primary purpose of this article is to present some convincing evidence of their inaccuracy, at least in the important case of the Los Angeles Negro community's response to the Watts riots.

METHOD[3]

The data on which this article is based were obtained from interviews conducted with three samples of respondents in Los Angeles County in late 1965 and early 1966. The

most important was a representative sample of Negroes living in the large area (46.5 square miles) of South-Central Los Angeles sealed off by a curfew imposed during the rioting. This sample, numbering 586 respondents, will be referred to below as the "Negro curfew zone" sample. The curfew zone contains about three-fourths of the more than 450,000 Negroes living in Los Angeles County, and is over 80 per cent Negro.[4] Hence it represents the major concentration of Negroes in the Los Angeles area. The sampling was done by randomly choosing names from the 1960 census lists, then over-sampling poverty-level census tracts by a cluster-sampling procedure to compensate for the underrepresentation of low-income respondents due to residential transcience. Another 124 Negro respondents, all arrested in the riot, were contacted principally through lawyers providing free legal aid. This "arrestee" sample was not representative but provided a useful reference point. Both Negro samples were interviewed by black interviewers living in the curfew zone. Though the interviews were long (averaging about two hours), interest was high and the refusal rate low. Checks were run on the possible biases introduced by the interviewers' own views and these do not give unusual reason for concern. The same interview schedule was used for all Negro respondents; it was structured, and included both open-ended and closed-ended items.

The third sample included 586 white respondents from six communities in Los Angeles County, half of which were racially integrated and half nonintegrated, with high, medium, and low socioeconomic levels. This sample is thus not wholly representative of the county, overrepresenting high SES and racially integrated areas, thus probably underestimating racial hostilities. Some, but not all, of the items on the Negro interview schedule were also used with white respondents. The main emphasis in this article is upon Negro opinion, so the white sample is not referred to except when explicitly indicated.

[3] For more complete accounts of the method, see T. M. Tomlinson and Diana L. TenHouten, "Method: Negro Reaction Survey," and Richard T. Morris and Vincent Jeffries, "The White Reaction Study," *Los Angeles Riot Study* (Los Angeles: Institute of Government and Public Affairs, University of California, 1967). See also R. T. Morris and V. Jeffries, "Violence Next Door," *Social Forces,* **46** (March, 1968), pp. 352–358.

[4] See U.S., Bureau of the Census, *U.S. Census of Population: 1960,* Vol. 1: *Characteristics of the Population,* Part 6: California (Washington, D.C.: U.S. Government Printing Office, 1963). Also David O. Sears and John B. McConahay, "Riot Participation," *Los Angeles Riot Study.*

THE THREE MYTHS

Data relevant to the first myth—that only a small fraction of the Negro community participated in the riot of August, 1965, and that nearly everyone else was antagonistic to it—show that it was clearly erroneous on both counts.

Furthermore, the Negro community as a whole was not overwhelmingly antagonistic to the riot. This point may be demonstrated in two ways. First, respondents were asked to estimate the proportion of "people in the area" (referring generally to the curfew zone) who had supported or opposed the riot. The mean estimate was that 34 per cent had "supported" the riot, and that 56 per cent had been "against it."

TABLE 1 Evaluation of Riot and Rioters[a]

	Overall Feeling about Riot	Feeling about Events	Feeling about Participants
Negro curfew zone (N = 586)			
Very or somewhat favorable	27%	29%	30%
Ambivalent or neutral	16	1	19
Strongly or moderately unfavorable	50	67	42
Don't know, no answer	7	3	8
Total	100%	100%	99%
Arrestee sample (N = 124)			
Very or somewhat favorable	52%	50%	57%
Ambivalent or neutral	10	4	12
Strongly or moderately unfavorable	32	45	23
Don't know, no answer	6	1	7
Total	100%	100%	99%

[a] The specific questions were as follows:
  For column 1, "Now that it is over, how do you feel about what happened?"
  For column 2, "What did you like about what was going on?" and "What did you dislike about what was going on?"
  For column 3, "What kinds of people supported it?" and "What kinds of people were against it?"
  These questions were not asked of the white sample.

The authors' best estimate is that approximately 15 per cent of the Negroes in the area participated in the riot. This was the proportion of curfew zone respondents who stated that they had been "very" or "somewhat" active in the riot and that they had seen crowds of people, and stores being burned and looted. The self-report of active participation, whether wholly accurate or not, indicates, at least, that numerous Los Angeles Negroes (22 per cent of the sample) were willing to identify themselves with the riot.[5]

Second, each respondent was asked his own feeling about the riot in a series of open-ended questions. He was asked directly how he felt about the riot, how he felt about the events of the riot, and how he felt about the people who were involved. Answers to these questions yielded three measures of feeling or affect toward the riot.[6] A little under one-third of the Negro curfew zone sample expressed approval of the riot on each of these three measures, and about half disapproved of the riot, as shown in Table 1. This finding

[5] For a detailed consideration of these data, see Sears and McConahay, "Riot Participation." Rates of participation in the Newark and Detroit riots of 1967 appear to have been similarly high, according to data published in *The Report of the National Advisory Commission on Civil Dis-* orders (New York: Bantam Books, 1968), p. 172.

[6] For a detailed description of the coding procedure, see Tomlinson and TenHouten, "Method: Negro Reaction Survey." The coding reliabilities were all over .95.

closely resembled the respondents' own estimates of public opinion in the area, as cited above.

Clearly, then, support for the riot was far more extensive than the public has been led to believe, numbering about a third of the area's adult residents, though a majority did disapprove of it. Even while disapproving, however, Negro respondents were markedly more lenient toward the riot's supporters than they were toward the destruction of life and property that occurred. Table 1 shows that 42 per cent disapproved of the participants, while 67 per cent disapproved of the events of the riot.

The Riot as a Protest

The second myth—that the riot was a meaningless, haphazard expression of disregard for law and order—was not commonly held among Negroes in Los Angeles. Many viewed the riot in revolutionary or insurrectional terms; most thought it had a purpose and that the purpose was, in part at least, a Negro protest.

Official utterances and the mass media, almost without exception, had described the events as being a "riot." Each respondent was asked what term he would use to describe the events. Table 2 shows that, given this free choice, over a third of the Negro sample selected "revolt," "insurrection," "rebellion," "uprising," "revenge," or other revolutionary term, thus flying in the face of the conventional definition. Other items given in Table 2 posed the question of a meaningful protest more directly, and show that a majority of the Negro community did indeed see the riot in these terms. Substantial majorities felt that

TABLE 2 The Riot as Protest

	Whites	Negroes (Curfew Zone)	Arrestees
What word or term would you use in talking about it?			
Riot	58%	46%	44%
Revolt, revolution, insurrection	13	38	45
Other (disaster, tragedy, mess, disgrace, etc.)	27	8	10
Don't know, no answer	2	8	2
Total	100%	100%	101%
Why were targets attacked?[a]			
Deserved attack	—	64%	75%
Ambivalent, don't know	—	17	21
Did not deserve attack	—	14	0
No answer	—	5	4
Total		100%	100%
Did it have a purpose or goal?			
Yes	33%	56%	56%
Don't know, other	4	11	13
No	62	28	29
No answer	—	5	2
Total	99%	100%	100%
Was it a Negro protest?			
Yes	54%	62%	66%
Don't know, other	3	12	15
No	42	23	16
No answer	—	2	3
Total	99%	99%	100%

[a] This question was not asked of white respondents.

it did have a purpose, that it was a Negro protest, and that those outsiders attacked in the riot deserved what they got.

Anticipating Favorable Effects

The third myth—that Negroes viewed the riot with alarm for the future—also was not subscribed to in Los Angeles. Most (58 per cent) foresaw predominantly beneficial effects, and only a minority (26 per cent) anticipated predominantly unfavorable effects. Similarly, more thought it would "help" the Negro cause than thought it would "hurt" it. These data are given in Table 3.

In fact, the participants and the community as a whole had rather similar attitudes about the riot. The arrestees were considerably more favorable toward the riot than was the community as a whole (see Table 1), but the community was equally optimistic about the effects of the riot, and as willing to interpret it as a purposeful protest (see Tables 2 and 3). Data presented elsewhere compare participants and nonparticipants within the Negro curfew zone sample, and yield almost exactly the same picture. Most participants tended to approve of the riot, while more nonparticipants disapproved than approved of it. However, in both groups a majority

TABLE 3   Expected Effects of the Riot

	Whites	Negroes (Curfew Zone)	Arrestees
What will the main effects be?[a]			
Very or somewhat favorable	—	58%	57%
Neutral, ambivalent, don't know	—	12	14
Very or somewhat unfavorable	—	26	27
No answer	—	3	2
Total		99%	100%
Do you think it helped or hurt the Negro's cause?			
Helped	19%	38%	54%
No difference, don't know	5	30	33
Hurt	75	24	9
No answers, other	1	8	4
Total	100%	100%	100%

[a] This question was not asked of white respondents.

Thus, a large minority of the Negroes in the curfew zone, about one-third, were favorable to the rioting, and the others' disapproval focused more upon the events than upon the participants. Over half saw the riot as a purposeful protest, many even speaking of it in revolutionary terms. Favorable effects were much more widely anticipated than unfavorable effects. This evidence indicates that the three myths cited above were invalid for the Los Angeles Negro community. It did not wholeheartedly reject and condemn its 1965 riot.

Participants' Attitudes

Negroes clearly had more sympathy for the participants than for the events of the riot.

expressed optimism about the effects of the riot, and interpreted it as a meaningful protest. In fact participants and nonparticipants hardly differed at all in the latter two respects.[7] This similarity of feeling between the participants (whether arrested or not) and the Negro community as a whole suggests both that the participants were not particularly unusual or deviant in their thinking, and that members of the community were not wholly willing to condemn nor to symbolically ostracize the rioters.

[7] See David O. Sears and John B. McConahay, "The Politics of Discontent: Blocked Mechanisms of Grievance Redress and the Psychology of the New Urban Black Man," *Los Angeles Riot Study*.

White Attitudes

The picture is quite different with respect to whites. As might now be expected, their attitudes toward the riot were considerably less favorable. Table 2 shows that whites thought it was nothing more meaningful than a "riot." Though most did feel it was a Negro protest, the consensus of opinion was that it was a purposeless, meaningless outburst. Table 3 shows that whites felt it definitely had "hurt" the Negro cause. Thus the cleavage in opinion that developed in Los Angeles after the riot was not so much between rioters and the law-abiding people of both races as between whites and blacks.

Other Riots, Other Communities

This is not the place to attempt a complete review of Negro opinion in other communities, or about other riots, but a brief discussion will indicate that results obtained here were similar to those obtained elsewhere in this nation.

Items directly analogous to those here evaluating riots and rioters have not been widely used. A *Fortune Magazine* national survey in 1967 did find that only 14 per cent felt the "violence and rioting that has already occurred" was "essentially good," while 58 per cent felt it was "essentially bad."[8] Similarly, a 1967 Harris national survey found that 10 per cent felt "most Negroes support riots" and 75 per cent felt that "only a minority" supports them.[9] These results indicate disapproval of riots by a substantial majority of Negroes. Yet the same Harris poll reveals that 62 per cent felt looters should not be shot, and 27 per cent felt they should be (in contrast to the 62 per cent of whites who felt shooting was appropriate for looters).[10] Clearly there are substantial limits on the strength of Negro disapproval and condemnation of Negro rioters.

Optimism about the effects of riots has also been characteristic. In several studies, Ne-groes have been asked whether riots "help" or "hurt" their cause, and the preferred answer has generally been that they "help." This was the result of a 1966 Harris national survey, a 1966 Harris survey of Negro leadership, and surveys of the Negro populations of Los Angeles (1966) and Oakland (1967).[11] The two exceptions have been a 1966 survey in Houston, a Southern city, where a slight plurality felt that riots "hurt," and the 1967 Harris survey (presumably national), which reported that only 12 per cent felt they would help—a result that is grossly out of line with all other surveys and thus difficult to interpret.

THE RIOT IDEOLOGY OF THE NEGRO COMMUNITY

Ambivalent evaluations of the riot, the feeling that it was meaningful, and optimism about its effects represent the simple elements around which a more complex belief system about the riot developed within the Negro community. This centered on a view of the riot as an instrument of Negro protest against real grievances. The substance of this view may be examined through the content of the protest and the grievances. First, let us consider in more detail the question of general community sympathy for the rioters.

Riot Events and Participants: The Community's Sympathetic Defense

Evaluations of the riot events and riot participants, shown in Table 1, gave the impression that the events of the riot were condemned more heartily than the rioters. Does the content of the respondents' attitudes support this impression?

The actual events of the riot were almost universally condemned. When asked "What did you like about what was going on?" 63

---

[8] Roger Beardwood, "The New Negro Mood," *Fortune,* **77** (Jan., 1968), p. 146.

[9] See Hazel Erskine, "The Polls: Demonstrations and Race Riots," *Public Opinion Quarterly,* **31** (Winter, 1967), pp. 655–677, for many of the results of these polls. This finding is given on p. 671.

[10] Erskine, "The Polls," p. 674.

[11] See W. Brink and Louis Harris, *Black and White* (New York: Simon and Schuster, 1966), pp. 264–265; *Federal Role in Urban Affairs,* Hearings before the Subcommittee on Executive Reorganization of the Committee on Government Operations, U.S. 89th Congress, 2nd Session, Senate, Part 6, p. 1387; William McCord and John Howard, "Negro Opinions in Three Riot Cities," *American Behavioral Scientist,* **11** (March–April, 1968), p. 26.

TABLE 4 What Did You Dislike About the Riot?[a]

	Negroes (Curfew Zone)	Arrestees
Crimes against property (burning, destruction, looting)	47%	26%
Crimes against persons	43	70
Negro attacks on white	(1)	(0)
Police shooting, killing, brutality	(14)	(32)
Killing, bloodshed, violence, shooting in general	(28)	(33)
Practical inconveniences	9	5
Negroes breaking law	1	0
Total	100%	100%

[a] Not asked of white respondents.

per cent of the Negroes sampled replied, "Nothing." The others gave widely dispersed responses. Crimes against property (such as burning and looting) and crimes against persons (such as killing and shooting) were cited about equally often as disliked aspects of the riot, as shown in Table 4. However, while the events of the riot were generally disliked and disapproved, they were not flatly repudiated. About 75 per cent couched their disapproval in terms suggesting sorrow and remorse (e.g., "regretful," "a sad thing," "a shame," "glad it's over") while only 25 per cent responded in a fashion suggesting repudiation of the riot (e.g., "disgusted," "disgrace," "unnecessary," "senseless"). Since disapproval of the riot did not necessarily in-

clude total dissociation from and repudiation of it, it is perhaps not surprising that the rioters and riot supporters were less harshly criticized than the event they created.

Indeed, the Negro community's description of the riot supporters, on the one hand, and the authorities on the other, reveal considerably more sympathy for those fomenting the riot than for those who tried to stop it. The descriptions of who had supported the riot, shown in Table 5, indicate that such sympathetic and understanding descriptions as "people who suffer" or "people wanting freedom" outnumbered such unsympathetic and repudiating responses as "hoodlums" or "Communists." The predominant conception of a riot supporter was not of a criminal, or

TABLE 5 What Kinds of People Supported the Riot?

	Negroes (Curfew Zone)	Arrestees
Sympathetic descriptions	45%	59%
Everyone	(10)	(15)
Good people (people wanting freedom, sympathetic people, etc.)	(5)	(8)
Deprived, mistreated (unemployed people who suffer, have-nots, poor people)	(30)	(36)
Unsympathetic descriptions	34	16
Anti-social (hoodlums, corrupt)	(12)	(10)
Political (Communists, Muslims)	(2)	(0)
Irresponsible (teenagers, fools, uneducated, thrill seekers)	(20)	(6)
Other	21	25
Estranged people (hopeless people, old people)	(5)	(9)
Middle class (business people)	(1)	(1)
Don't know, no answer	(15)	(15)
Total	100%	100%

[a] Not asked of white respondents.

TABLE 6 Did the Authorities Handle It Well or Badly?

	Whites	Negroes (Curfew Zone)	Arrestees
Well	66%	28%	15%
Badly	32	65	77
Should have stopped it sooner	(26)	(27)	(14)
They made it worse, were intransigent	(6)	(33)	(56)
Other	(0)	(5)	(7)
Don't know, no answer, other	2	8	9
Total	100%	101%	101%

of a disreputable or despicable person, but evidently of a person not so very dissimilar from respondent himself, though perhaps somewhat down on his luck.

In contrast, much antagonism was expressed toward the authorities' role in the riot. Only 28 per cent thought the authorities had handled the riot "well," and 65 per cent felt they had handled it "badly." The further breakdown of these responses is shown in Table 6; Negroes who thought the authorities had done badly were split between those who felt they should have put an end to the riot earlier, and those who felt the authorities had exacerbated the situation. Many Negro respondents did not like what had happened then, but their disposition was to defend and justify the actions of Negro rioters, and to criticize the actions of the white authorities.

Explanations of the causes of the riot also demonstrated a sympathetic defense of the rioters, as shown in Table 7. The dominant tendency was to blame the riot on legitimate grievances, such as discrimination, poverty, or police mistreatment (38 per cent), or on long-standing hostility and other pent-up emotions (26 per cent). Relatively few attributed the riot mainly to the incident that precipitated it, the fracas with the Frye family, or blamed any of the obvious candidates for a scapegoat, such as the Communists or gang members.

The contrast with opinions expressed by white residents of Los Angeles was a vivid one. By attributing the riot to grievances and to years of frustration, the Negro respondents suggested that the people who supported the riot had legitimate reasons for doing so. Whites, on the other hand, praised the work of the authorities, or even criticized them for

TABLE 7 What Caused the Riot?

	Whites	Negroes (Curfew Zone)	Arrestees
Specific grievances	20%	38%	51%
Discrimination, mistreatment by whites	(5)	(7)	(4)
Poverty, economic deprivation, inadequate services	(11)	(10)	(5)
Police mistreatment	(4)	(21)	(42)
Pent-up hostility, desire for revenge, fed-up	14	26	34
Frye incident	18	11	8
Undesirable groups	29	9	2
Communists, Muslims, civil rights groups, organized groups, KKK, agitators	(16)	(3)	(0)
Criminals, looters	(8)	(2)	(0)
Foolish people, teenagers, Southerners	(5)	(4)	(2)
Spontaneous explosion, accident, weather	10	0	0
Don't know, no answer	10	17	6
Total	101%	101%	101%

not being more punitive with the rioters (Table 6). Whites were much more inclined to attribute the riot to agitators, Communists, criminals, the weather, or simply to write it off as arising from the Frye incident (Table 7). The Negro community as a whole was much closer to the explicit sympathy for the rioters expressed by the arrestees. Both gave relatively sympathetic descriptions of the rioters (Table 5), harshly criticized the authorities (Table 6), and attributed the riot to legitimate grievances rather than to chance or whimsical or illegal and un-American factors (Table 7).

This contrast between black sympathy for the rioters and white condemnation of them, as reflected in explanations for the riot, has also been obtained in several more recent surveys made in other areas. For example, in Harris's 1967 survey, Negroes were about twice as likely as whites to attribute recent riots to grievances over jobs, education, housing, police, and inequality. Whites were more likely than Negroes to blame outside agitation, lack of firmness by government authorities, the desire to loot, or a desire for violence.[12] Negroes thought the riots were spontaneous; a vast majority of the whites thought they had been organized.[13] Negroes thought the looted stores had been charging exorbitant prices; whites thought they had not.[14] Among whites, 62 per cent felt looters should be shot; among Negroes, only 27 per cent felt that action was justifiable.[15] In other post-riot surveys, Negroes in Detroit and in Watts have generally explained the rioting in terms of a response to grievances about housing, jobs, the police, and poverty.[16] The most impressive difference of opinion about the rioters, then, is not between the law-abiders and

the law-breakers in the Negro community, but between blacks and whites.

The Purpose of The Riot: To Call Attention

Looking back on the riot, Los Angeles Negroes were largely agreed that it had been a purposeful, directed protest. But if Negroes saw the riot as a meaningful event, what was the meaning? What was the purpose of the riot; what was it supposed to accomplish? Negroes' perceptions on these matters may illuminate in what respects their hopes have subsequently been frustrated or fulfilled.

The dominant "purpose" of the riot, according to retrospective Negro perceptions, was to call the attention of whites to Negro problems. Fifty-six per cent of the Negro curfew zone sample had felt the riot had a purpose (see Table 2); of these, 41 per cent identified it as an attempt to call attention to Negro problems, and most of these saw the call directed specifically at white people. Smaller numbers saw it as an expression of accumulated hostility and resentment (33 per cent) or thought it was intended to implement some specific social or economic changes (26 per cent), e.g., to get more jobs, improve conditions, or get equal rights. The "message" from the Negro citizenry to the broader, predominantly white community is thus a two-edged one: a request for attention to their problems, and at the same time, an expression of accumulated angers and resentments from past grievances.

The specific problems being protested follow a line now familiar. The main targets of attack were seen as being merchants (38 per cent), white people in general (28 per cent), and the police (17 per cent). As already indicated (Table 2), most respondents felt these targets deserved the attacks they received. The predominant reasons given for the attacks had to do with justifiable grievances. Mistreatment of Negroes, in terms of discrimination or brutality, was the most common (31 per cent). Economic exploitation or disadvantage (e.g., overcharging, or unemployment) was next most frequent (19 per cent). These two categories accounted for the reasons given by half the Negro curfew zone respondents. "Chance" (10 per cent) and mere "criminal intent" (1 per cent) were

---

[12] McCord and Howard, "Negro Opinions in Three Riot Cities," Erskine, "The Polls," p. 662.

[13] Erskine, "The Polls," p. 666.

[14] Erskine, "The Polls," p. 665.

[15] Erskine, "The Polls," p. 674.

[16] Detroit Urban League, "A Survey of Attitudes of Detroit Negroes after the Riot of 1967," Detroit, 1967. See also *Federal Role in Urban Affairs*, p. 1387. The vivid contrast between whites and Negroes also appears in a Brandeis University survey: Lemberg Center for the Study of Violence, "A Survey of Racial Attitudes in Six Northern Cities: Preliminary Findings," Waltham, Mass., 1967, pp. 15–16. (Mimeographed.)

relatively rare responses. However, 17 per cent explained the attacks in terms of the rioters' longstanding frustration, anger, and resentment.

So, Los Angeles Negroes tended to interpret the riot as a purposeful protest. In retrospect, they saw its aims as twofold: a call for attention to their problems, and an expression of hostility and resentment over genuine grievances. Much of this interpretation must represent a rationale constructed after the fact for a violent and confusing series of events that almost certainly had no single cause and was not deliberately planned.[17] Nevertheless, the riot was a widely based outburst of Negro hostility, fed upon reservoirs of resentment and hatred that had not been perceived earlier or understood well by white people. It had a clear focus on racial antagonisms, the objects of hostility were not other Negroes, but white people, primarily merchants, and almost any symbol of constituted authority. Even if the "purposeful" quality of the riot was a rationalization, it described a moderately "rational" series of events.

Expected Outcomes of the Riot: Help for the Ghetto

In seeing the riot as a protest, a majority of the Negro population thought of it as a social-change action the principal aims of which were change in living conditions and aggression against the oppressor. Expectations about outcomes should thus serve as critical considerations in Negroes' thinking about the value of riots as instruments of social change. In the most general terms, these expectations were mostly optimistic, as seen earlier (Table 3). A further question is how Negroes expected the riot to affect the con-

[17] Some surveys may elicit a grander ideological structure than actually exists by utilizing a carefully designed Socratic progression of questions. However the section of the present schedule dealing with the riot began with only the simplest open-ended items; i.e., those listed in Tables 1, 4, 5, 6, 7, the first two items of Table 2, and the first item of Table 3. Only later were more leading structured questions raised (e.g., the remaining items in Tables 2 and 3). Hence most of the discussion of "riot ideology" rests on spontaneously reported responses, not on interviews "leading" the respondent on.

ditions of their lives, and, particularly, how they expected constituted authority and the broader white community to react.

By all odds the most salient expectation was that whites would begin to redress Negro grievances. The effect of the riot mentioned first by 43 per cent of the Negro respondents was help from outside the Negro community. An additional 13 per cent cited the effect of greater white awareness of Negro problems, and more comfortable relations between whites and Negroes. Thus, a majority thought first of favorable change among whites. These data are shown in Table 8.

TABLE 8 What Will the Main Effects of the Riot Be?

	Negroes (Curfew Zone)
Negroes will be helped or rewarded by others	43%
Negro-white relations will be changed for the better	13
Whites will be more aware of Negroes	(11)
Negroes and whites will get along together	(2)
Negro-white relations will change for the worse	13
Negroes will gain self-respect, get new leadership	2
Hope for something good	3
Nothing, no change	11
Don't know, no answer	14
Total	99%

Similar thoughts were expressed by those who thought the riot would affect the Negro's cause, or affect the gap between the races. Table 9 shows that the most common reasons Negroes gave for why the riot might help or hurt the Negro's cause had to do with white reactions to it. Similarly, of those who thought it would increase or decrease the gap between the races, 54 per cent expected some change in whites, 28 per cent expected change in both races, and only 12 per cent expected change among Negroes themselves. Hence the clearest expectation among Negro respondents was that the riot would effect favorable change among white people.

TABLE 9 Why Will It Help or Hurt Negroes?[a]

	Negroes (Curfew Zone)
Change whites for the better	42%
Greater attention to Negroes	(29)
More positive toward Negroes	(13)
Change whites for the worse, more prejudice, etc.	8
Change Negroes	15
For worse (give bad name, make worse off)	(12)
For better (greater self-confidence, morale)	(3)
Economic effects (fewer jobs, stores)	30
Other	5
Total	100%

[a] Asked of the 62 per cent of the sample who said the riot would help or hurt the Negro cause.

While Negroes expected a favorable response from whites, they did not expect a massive one. Table 10 shows that greater white awareness of Negro problems was almost universally expected, and most Negroes expected more sympathetic treatment. However, opinion was much more divided with respect to changes in the social distance between the races.[18] About the same number of Negroes felt "more at ease" (10 per cent) than felt "less at ease" (8 per cent) in the contacts with white people after the riot, and no change was reported in the frequency of contact with whites. So most Negroes seem to have expected more sympathetic attention to their problems, but relatively few expected more commitment from whites at the level of personal relationships.

Two possibilities Negroes rarely mentioned, curiously enough, were "white backlash" and greater Negro solidarity. Anticipation of greater white hostility or greater racial prejudice was mentioned by only 13 per cent as the most likely effect of the riot (Table 8) and by 8 per cent as the main reason why the riot might help or hurt the Negro cause (Table 9). Effects upon Negroes aside from

[18] An additional coding of the "increased gap" responses indicated that few Negroes thought increased separation a good thing, despite the popularity of separatist ideology among many activists.

effects upon whites were also rarely mentioned. Two per cent saw new self-respect or leadership among Negroes as a main effect of the riot, and 15 per cent and 12 per cent, respectively, cited change among Negroes as the main reasons why the riot might help or hurt the Negro's cause and increase or decrease the gap between the races.

In retrospect this seems surprising because these two effects seem to have materialized to a far greater degree than the generally predicted white sympathetic attention. At the time, whites indeed felt more aware of Negro problems, but scarcely more sympathetic, as shown in Table 10. And whites predicted a considerable widening of the gap between the races. The rise in Negro solidarity is more difficult to determine directly from these data, but it seems evident that the riot drew more support from Negroes than anyone could have expected, and that in many respects the community as a whole rallied behind the rioters.

Thus the changes described by both races follow a well-worn path in American race relations. The white population is mainly willing to adjust when it is easy and convenient to do so. Both races expected the riot to increase the awareness of Negro problems among the dominant majority whites, and it seems to have done just that. However, a misjudgment occurred on the more difficult issue of white sympathy with Negro problems. Here Negroes hoped for change, while whites frankly expected a deterioration of race relations. More helpful, perhaps, are the social distance data. Here Negroes' expectations may have been more accurate than those of whites. The white population's racial nightmares have traditionally been filled with the horrors of intimate social contact with Negroes, rather than the more ritualized contacts of occupational or political interdependence. So more pessimism on the social distance dimension than on the awareness or sympathy dimensions could reasonably have been expected. But these data (and Negroes' expectations) do not reveal an actual widening of the gap between the races, contrary to whites' expectations.[19] The "backlash" may mean a slowdown rather than an actual deterioration in race relations.

[19] See also Morris and Jeffries, "The White Reaction Study."

TABLE 10 Perceived Effects of Riot on Negro-White Relations

	Whites	Negroes (Curfew Zone)	Arrestees
Are whites more aware of Negro problems?			
More aware	79%	84%	80%
No change	18	13	17
Less aware	2	2	1
Other	1	2	2
Total	100%	101%	100%
Are whites more sympathetic to Negro problems?			
More sympathetic	32%	51%	49%
No change	27	31	38
Less sympathetic	37	12	9
Other	4	6	4
Total	100%	100%	100%
Did the riot increase or decrease the gap between the races?			
Increase	71%	23%	15%
No change	11	38	37
Decrease	13	24	22
Other	4	16	27
Total	99%	101%	100%

PREFERRED MECHANISMS OF GRIEVANCE REDRESS

A riot ideology appears to have developed among Negroes in the curfew zone, in part justifying the Los Angeles riot as an instrument of protest. To what extent did rioting thus become thought of as a legitimate and effective mechanism of grievance redress for the future? Not widely, apparently. Answers to the open-ended question "What must Negroes do to get what they want?" reveal a preponderantly conventional approach to equal rights, as shown in Table 11. Over half of the Negro respondents see some form of conventional middle-class behavior as the road to success (e.g., more education and hard work). Another 19 per cent see more efficient and active political participation as the answer, while only 3 per cent contend that violence is necessary for equal rights. So the majority of Negroes in Los Angeles, even after a riot they perceived as likely to have beneficial effects, still opted for moderate grievance redress procedures and for traditional methods of personal advancement.

The question still remains how strong this

TABLE 11 What Must Negroes Do To Get What They Want?

	Negroes (Curfew Zone)	Arrestees
Conventional approaches	56%	51%
Get more education	(27)	(15)
Work hard, strive and succeed	(23)	(32)
Get jobs, acquire wealth	(2)	(2)
Change stereotyped qualities	(4)	(2)
Political action	19	15
Vote more, follow their leaders, etc.	(6)	(6)
Protest, make needs known	(13)	(9)
Violent action	3	10
Increase morale	7	12
Remove self-hatred	(1)	(0)
Increase racial solidarity	(6)	(12)
Change whites, change both races	1	0
Other	5	7
Don't know, no answer	9	5
Total	100%	100%

preference for conventional mechanisms actually is, and whether or not the riot affected it. A sizable number of respondents expressed interest in demonstrations and nonviolent protest. Only a few (6 per cent) had participated in pre-riot civil rights activity, but 37 per cent said after the riot that they were willing to participate in demonstrations. Thirteen per cent said the riot had made them more willing to do so; so perhaps the riot made some Negroes more militant and unified.

It is hard to determine from the data whether it also increased their attraction to violence. However, when asked the most effective method to use in protest, given the alternatives of negotiation and nonviolent protest, 12 per cent selected violent protest (of the arrestees, 22 per cent did so). And 34 per cent thought there would be a recurrence of rioting in Los Angeles. Another 37 per cent felt they could not predict whether or not there would be another riot, thereby reflecting a lack of confidence in the durability of civic peace. While these data do not suggest that a majority of Negroes in Los Angeles advocate violence, the minority that does is rather sizable, and the expectation of further violence on the part of many others is an ominous sign; prophecies of that kind have a way of becoming self-fulfilling.[20]

CONCLUSIONS

This paper has been primarily concerned with the reaction of the Los Angeles Negro population to the Watts Riots of 1965. The principal findings follow:

(1) It is not correct that all but a small minority strongly disapproved of the riots, felt they were a meaningless and random outburst of violence, and felt deeply pessi-

[20] Particularly ominous, as might be expected, were the attitudes of the more militant respondents. Subdividing the curfew zone sample in terms of relative militance reveals considerably greater support for riots and higher endorsement of violence among the militants than among the more conservative respondents. For a detailed account of these data, see T. M. Tomlinson, "Ideological Foundations for Negro Action: A Comparative Analysis of Militant and Non-Militant Views of the Los Angeles Riot," *Los Angeles Riot Study.* See also T. M. Tomlinson, "The Development of a Riot Ideology Among

mistic about the probable effects of the riots on the welfare of Negroes. Actually, a large minority (about one-third) approved of the rioting, most Negro residents of the riot area felt it had been a meaningful protest, and most were optimistic about its effects on their life situation.

(2) A widespread "riot ideology" appears to have developed in the Negro community following the riot, with the following elements. The events of the riot were deplored, and the wish was expressed that the authorities had stopped it earlier. Yet the authorities tended to be criticized and the rioters defended. The causes of the riot were described in terms of genuine grievances with those who were attacked; e.g., a history of friction, discrimination, and economic exploitation with local merchants and police. The purpose of the riot was seen as being, on the one hand, to call the attention of whites to Negro problems, and on the other, to express resentment against malefactors. The riot was expected to bring help to the Negro population from whites, though major improvement in interracial personal relationships was not expected. This "riot ideology" seemed to justify and defend the riot, but violence was not often advocated for the future.[21]

Urban Negroes," *American Behavioral Scientist,* 11 (March–April, 1968), pp. 27–31.

Findings from other surveys on the level of endorsement of violence are not strictly comparable, because of different question wording. The range of estimates is substantial. In 1964, Kraft surveys in Harlem, Chicago, and Baltimore found 5 per cent saying violence was necessary, but one in Watts after the riot found that 14 per cent thought it was. See *Federal Role in Urban Affairs,* p. 1399. A complex question used by Harris in national surveys in 1963 and 1966 found 22 per cent and 21 per cent, respectively, thinking violence was needed. See Brink and Harris, *Black and White,* p. 260. After the Detroit riot of 1967, an Urban League survey found 24 per cent feeling there was more to gain than lose with violence (see Detroit Urban League, "A Survey of Attitudes"). And the 1967 *Fortune* survey found 35 per cent saying that riots and violence are necessary (see Beardwood, "The New Negro Mood," p. 148). Whether these represent secular changes or merely differently worded questions is unclear.

[21] There is considerable justification for speaking of this pattern of beliefs in terms of an

(3) The major cleavage that developed after the riot was between the white and black populations of Los Angeles, not between lawbreakers and lawabiders within the black population. Whites were much readier to condemn the riot, to see only purposeless violence in it, and to foresee a gloomy future for race relations. Whites were likely to ascribe the riot to agitators and criminal impulse, and less likely to attribute it to genuine grievances. These divisions of opinion along racial lines seem to be characteristic of the ways in which the two racial groups have responded across the country to recent race riots.[22]

Perhaps the most important fact of all is that so many Negroes felt disposed to justify and ennoble the riot after it was all over. It was not viewed as an alien disruption of their peaceful lives, but as an expression of protest by the Negro community as a whole, against an oppressive majority. Here perhaps lies one of the tragedies of the riot. While it was, in the eyes of many Negroes, an outburst against an oppressive social system, the response of whites to the call for attention and help was hoped to be favorable. Perhaps this was an analogy taken from the white response to the Southern civil rights battles of the preceding decade. However, relatively little help has in fact been forthcoming, and it is not clear that whites expect to give very much. Awareness of the problem seems obviously to have increased, but the retaliatory aspect of the "message" of the riot seems as salient to whites as the plea for help.

"ideology," based on the pattern of interrelationships between various of them. Approval of the riot, optimism about its effects, and perceiving the riot as a meaningful protest were all strongly correlated with one another.

[22] This observation of racial differences might seem to set a new record for banality in social science. The impressive finding here is not that whites and Negroes disagree, but that disagreement penetrates so deeply into each group, well beyond those that normally concern themselves

---

with public affairs. It could be, for example, that relatively few people care very much about riots, and that most people of both races reject them as they reject criminal behavior in general. That is not the case, however.

30

The uses of violence

A. CAMPBELL AND H. SCHUMAN

This chapter deals with Negro and white beliefs about, and involvement in, the riots that have occurred in Detroit, Newark, and many other American cities. We begin with a comparsion of Negro and white perceptions of the causes and character of the riots. Identical questions were asked of both Negroes

Reprinted from *Racial attitudes in fifteen American cities.* Supplemental Studies for the National Advisory Commission on Civil Disorders. Washington, D.C.: Government Printing Office, 1968, Chapter 5, pp. 47–59.

and whites and the results reveal a number of differences between the two samples. We next attempt to describe those respondents who indicate a willingness to participate in rioting or other related forms of violence. This second section replicates findings of earlier studies carried out by other investigators in Los Angeles, Detroit and Newark, with some extensions made possible by additional questions, a comparative framework, and larger sample sizes. The chapter ends with a brief look at advocacy of violence within the white population.

THE NATURE OF THE RIOTS

The differences between Negro and white definitions of the riots, perceptions of cause, and prescriptions for prevention are shown in the series of questions presented in Tables 1 to 5. The first question asked each respondent to characterize the riots as "mainly a protest by Negroes against unfair conditions" or "mainly a way of looting and things like that." White men are fairly evenly split

TABLE 1 "Some people say these disturbances are mainly a protest by Negroes against unfair conditions. Others say they are mainly a way of looting and things like that. Which of these seems more correct to you?"

(In percent)

	Negro		White	
	Men	Women	Men	Women
Mainly protest	56	59	38	48
Mainly looting	9	10	33	24
50/50 mixture	30	25	25	24
Don't know	5	6	4	4
	100	100	100	100

between viewing the riots as a protest and viewing them as largely criminal in nature, while white women choose protest rather than looting by two to one. Negroes were *not* so split: 58 percent regard the riots as mainly a protest and another 28 percent characterize them as partly a protest. Only 10 percent of the Negro sample saw the riots as mainly a matter of looting and similar offenses.

The main *cause* of the riots (see Table 2) according to spontaneous responses by nearly half the black sample lies in, or is associated with, unfair treatment of Negroes by whites. For example:

"Want to be treated like a human being."

"Unfairness to the Negro. The Negro has been pushed back for years. They are tired of being pushed around. They want better things in life just like the whites."

"Mostly Negroes want more in life and want to be treated the same as whites. Some of them have just as much sense and

TABLE 2 "What do you think was the main cause of these disturbances?"

(In percent)

Most frequent types of spontaneous response*	Negro		White	
	Men	Women	Men	Women
Discrimination, unfair treatment	49	48	22	27
Unemployment	23	22	13	13
Inferior jobs	13	10	5	5
Bad housing	23	20	15	15
Poor education	10	9	7	7
Poverty	10	8	11	9
Police brutality	10	4	2	1
Black Power or other "radicals"	4	5	26	21
Looters and other undesirables	11	11	34	34
Communists	0	0	8	5

* Each mention to this question was coded separately, and since some people mentioned more than one cause, the percentages do not add to 100. Only reasons mentioned by at least 10 percent of a group are presented here, except for the response "Communist" which is slightly under this limit.

education as whites and want to be respected just as much as they [whites] respect another one of their own. . . ."

Specific grievances often follow responses such as the above, particularly in the areas of employment and housing, but it is worth noting that they are frequently linked to words like "unjust" and "unfair" and sometimes to mention of "lack of respect." The phrases "want to be treated like anyone else" and "want to be treated the same as whites" recur frequently. A number of other specific grievance-type causes are also mentioned, such as police brutality, but in each instance by a relatively small part of the sample.[1]

Whites offer the same causes of the riots as do Negroes, but with only about half the frequency. On the other hand, while few Negroes perceive the riots as caused by

[1] We have shown earlier (Chapter IV) that direct questions on police practices indicate considerable resentment by Negroes and it is probable that specific questions relating police actions to the riots would have elicited more frequent perceptions of a causal link. But it seems clear that when Negroes are asked to think of the *main* cause of rioting, they more often think of general white treatment of Negroes and of specific economic areas.

"leaders"—black nationalist, Communist, or any other type—nearly a quarter of the white sample cite radical leaders as a major cause. Similarly, only one out of ten Negroes lay blame for the riots on criminal or other undesirable elements, but one out of three whites see this factor as important.

Since whites emphasize the role of radical leaders and of criminally inclined participants, it is not surprising that many believe the riots were "planned in advance" (Table 3): nearly half hold unequivocally to this belief and another third believe there was *some* planning. A much smaller proportion of Negroes (18 percent) see the riots as generally planned in advance, another third see some planning, but a third believe there was no planning at all.

TABLE 3 "Do you think the large disturbances like those in Detroit and Newark were planned in advance, or that there was some planning but not much, or weren't they planned at all?"

(In percent)

	Negro		White	
	Men	Women	Men	Women
Planned in advance	16	20	47	50
Some planning but not much	37	34	37	34
Not planned at all	38	30	12	10
Don't know	9	16	4	6
	100	100	100	100

A general "open-ended" question shown in Table 4 on the most important means to prevent future riots suggests a clear difference in focus by race. More than half of the Negro sample spontaneously mention improvement of social and economic conditions as the first solution, with more and better jobs the most frequently offered specific recommendation. Only one-fifth of the white sample think immediately in terms of such social and economic changes. On the other hand, nearly half the white sample call first for stronger police control, as against only one out of ten Negroes in the sample who mention police control as their first answer. ... When the long-term alternatives of police control *versus* improvement of Negro conditions are posed bluntly, a majority of white

TABLE 4 "What do you think is the most important thing the city government in (Central City) could do to keep a disturbance like the one in Detroit from breaking out here?"

(In percent)

First type of response mentioned	Negro		White	
	Men	Women	Men	Women
Better employment	26	24	11	9
End discrimination	14	15	2	3
Better housing	8	8	4	4
Other social and economic improvements	7	5	4	3
Better police treatment	6	1	0	1
Improve communications between Negroes and whites; show Negroes whites care	12	13	10	13
More black control of institutions	0	0	0	0
More police control	9	8	51	42
Can't do anything, have already tried everything	3	5	8	8
Don't know	15	21	10	17
	100	100	100	100

respondents choose the latter and another quarter say that *both* are needed. Likewise, some white respondents qualify their spontaneous first mention of police control shown in Table 4 by indicating support for economic improvements as well. The difference between races seems more one of salience and focus of attention than absolute opposition.

Finally, the long-term effects of the riots are viewed in very different ways by Negroes and whites (Table 5). Most whites (64 percent) believe the riots have hurt the cause of Negro rights and few believe they have helped. But a third of the black sample think that the riots have aided the Negro cause in America, while only a quarter think the riots have been mainly harmful in effect.

The reasons offered by Negroes for the belief that riots *help* are primarily in terms of tangible gains in the very same areas mentioned in response to questions about causes and prevention. About 20 percent of the Negro sample believe that in one way or another the riots have stimulated action to solve the major problems confronting Negroes. For example:

"They are making attempts to give us better jobs and respect."

". . . they are trying to make it so it won't occur again . . . helping Negro to

TABLE 5 "On the whole, do you think the disturbances have helped or hurt the cause of Negro rights, or would you say they haven't made much difference?"

(In Percent)

	Negro		White	
	Men	Women	Men	Women
Helped	37	30	13	14
Hurt	22	24	69	59
Helped and hurt equally	12	11	7	7
Made no difference	21	28	9	17
Don't know	8	7	2	3
	100	100	100	100

"Why do you feel that way?"
(In Percent)

	Negro		White	
	Men	Women	Men	Women
Find reason given:				
Helped:				
Tangible gains (e.g., more jobs)	19	20	8	8
Whites understand Negroes' problems better	14	10	8	8
Show of Negro power	9	5	2	1
Hurt:				
Destruction, injury	8	8	2	3
Increased anti-Negro sentiments	16	19	64	54
Made no difference:				
No tangible gain	19	23	5	12
Negroes are still not satisfied	0	1	7	10
Don't know	15	14	4	4
	100	100	100	100

start up retail business . . . trying to get more Negro national guardsmen."

"They are getting better jobs and better housing and better schools. That's what they were fighting for."

A smaller proportion of Negro respondents (11 percent) believe that the riots have awakened the average white person to an understanding of Negro problems in America, a perception shared by almost the same proportion of white respondents. Finally, a small number of Negro respondents (7 percent) evince special pride in the demonstration of black courage and power they see in the riots.

Negroes who see harm in the riots speak primarily in terms of the destruction and violence. White respondents, on the other hand, give overwhelming emphasis to anti-Negro sentiments aroused or stimulated by the riots. For example, white respondents reply in such terms as:

". . . it hurt because they got more people bitter . . . it's getting us a little more scared . . . Everyone is scared, you're scared to open your door now."

". . . they are doing harm to their real cause, as people forget the real thing and remember the wrong things they have done and stop helping them."

"Because of the vandalism and taking other people's property. This hurt them very much . . . People have bad opinions of them when they read about these things."

Sixty percent of the white sample report the rise in such anti-Negro sentiments, but only 18 percent of the Negroes mention this as an unfavorable consequence of the riots. Indeed, nearly as many black respondents perceive an increase in white understanding of Negro problems because of the riots as perceive an increase in white hostility.

Suburban white results have not been presented in Tables 1 to 5 but in general they are very similar to white city results. For example, where 33 percent of white city males see the riots as "mainly a way of looting and things like that," 35 percent of white suburban males choose that response; comparable figures for white females are 24 percent and 27 percent. As another example, more police control is mentioned first as the most important way to prevent riots by 51 percent of white city males as against 54 percent of suburban males, and by 42 percent of white city females as against 43 percent of suburban females. From a descriptive standpoint, city whites and suburban whites seem to perceive the riots in very much the same terms.

The findings presented thus far in this section add up to quite different—although not opposite—Negro and white perspectives on the causes, consequences, and prevention of urban riots in America. A solid, and at points overwhelming, majority of Negroes in these 15 cities see the riots as largely spontaneous black protests against unfair treatment, economic deprivation, or a combination of the two. The main way to prevent future riots is, in this view, to remove the underlying causes. Moreover, more Negroes think the riots helped in this direction than think the riots were harmful, although the division is close.

supported by the results in Table 7, which deals with whether the riots helped or hurt the cause of Negro rights. In this case there also appears to be a slight relation to education, with the *more* educated tending to perceive good coming out of the riots, especially among Negroes in their 20's and 30's. These results taken together suggest that, for the present at least, Negroes who take a wholly negative view of the riots represent the viewpoint of an older generation.

The white sample as a whole differs considerably from the black sample on the riots, but it does *not* present simply a mirror image of the nearly universal Negro definition. If that were the case, the white sample would hold an almost unanimous view of the riots as conspiratorial or criminal in nature, and

TABLE 6 "Some people say these disturbances are mainly a protest by Negroes against unfair conditions. Others say they are mainly a way of looting and things like that. Which of these seems more correct to you?"

By Negro age and education categories (results for men and women averaged) in percent

	Age 16–19*	Age 20–39					Age 40–69				
		8th grade or less	9–11 grades	12 grades	Some college	College graduate	8th grade or less	9–11 grades	12 grades	Some college	College graduate
Mainly protest	60	65	56	65	69	61	43	56	61	60	33
Mainly looting	11	5	10	5	4	4	12	10	13	9	13
50/50 mixture	25	21	26	27	24	35	30	27	23	30	54
Don't know	4	9	8	3	3	0	15	7	3	1	0
	100	100	100	100	100	100	100	100	100	100	100

* This group combines all educational categories.

Only about 10 percent of the Negro sample dissent clearly from this viewpoint and consider the riots criminal activity to be suppressed primarily by police control. Tables 1 to 5 indicate little sex difference for Negroes in this respect. The tables presented below allow analysis by age and education of three questions already discussed. Table 6 does not indicate any clear educational difference among Negroes with regard to perception of the riots as mainly protest or mainly looting, but does suggest a generally consistent trend by age, with a greater proportion of younger people than of older people seeing the riot as a form of protest. The age trend is

as responding only to police control. Instead, we find white respondents distributed over a range of positions and outlooks. This makes it more difficult, however, to describe them in summary fashion in this report. About a third of the white sample seem committed to a view of the riots close to that of most Negroes, namely, as protests against real economic and social grievances, protests that should be met by constructive attempts to remove these grievances. About a third see the riots as largely unjustified but conspiratorial assaults on law and order led by criminal, demagogic, or other undesirable elements, assaults that should be met first of all by firm

TABLE 7 "On the whole, do you think the disturbances have helped or hurt the cause of Negro rights, or would you say they haven't made much difference?"

By Negro age and education categories (results for men and women averaged) in percent

	Age 16–19*	Age 20–39					Age 40–69				
		8th grade or less	grades 9–11	12 grades	Some col-lege	Col-lege grad-uate	8th grade or less	9–11 grades	12 grades	Some col-lege	Col-lege grad-uate
Helped	36	33	33	39	40	67	24	24	34	36	28
Hurt	24	28	21	19	14	9	28	27	31	19	24
Helped and hurt equally	9	8	9	14	17	1	10	10	10	19	37
Haven't made much difference	25	25	29	23	16	18	24	31	19	24	9
Don't know	6	6	8	5	13	5	14	8	6	2	2
	100	100	100	100	100	100	100	100	100	100	100

* This group combines all educational categories.

police action. The remaining third or so of the white sample consists of people who combine both views more or less equally, as well as people who have no clear opinions on the matter.

A major purpose of later reports will be to describe and understand better these white divisions in perception. For the present, we can note from Tables 1 to 5 that men appear sightly more inclined than women to regard the riots as mainly "looting" and to favor primarily police control. Table 8 below indicates a strong trend, especially among younger persons, for the *more* educated to perceive the riots as mainly protests rather than as mainly looting. Age differences are somewhat less consistent and strong, but youth apparently has the same effect as greater education in making the riots seem to be purposive protests rather than simply episodes of mass criminal activity. Thus age trends for white city respondents are similar to those for Negroes. Indeed, a comparison of Tables 6 and 8 reveals that among teenagers and also among college graduates at older age levels, about the same proportion of whites and Negroes perceive the riots as protests. The young and the better educated of both races

TABLE 8 "Some people say these disturbances are mainly a protest by Negroes against unfair conditions. Others say they are mainly a way of looting and things like that. Which of these seems more correct to you?"

By white age and education categories (results for men and women averaged) in percent

	Age 16–19*	Age 20–39					Age 40–69				
		8th grade or less	9–11 grades	12 grades	Some col-lege	Col-lege grad-uate	8th grade or less	9–11 grades	12 grades	Some col-lege	Col-lege grad-uate
Mainly protest	62	30	32	48	56	60	32	36	35	41	49
Mainly looting	17	44	33	25	16	13	38	37	36	30	15
50/50 mixture	18	22	34	26	28	21	21	23	27	22	26
Don't know	3	4	1	1	0	6	9	4	2	7	10
	100	100	100	100	100	100	100	100	100	100	100

* This group combines all educational categories.

converge in their perceptions of the basic character of the riots.

Where white perceptions of the riots are in wholly negative terms, this is most obviously interpretable as opposition to violence, looting, and destruction. This is no doubt correct, but it is well to recognize also that a substantial proportion of the white sample is opposed to *non*-violent protest actions by Negroes as well as to violence. More than a quarter of the white sample (23 percent of the men, 32 percent of the women) believe Negroes are not justified in using *"orderly marches* to protest against racial discrimination" and more than two-thirds believe that "sit-in" protests are unjustified (tables not shown). Thus a substantial proportion of the white sample is against *any* active protest by Negroes.

Indeed, to a rather large segment of the white population the attempt to distinguish "violent" from "non-violent" demonstration is not very meaningful, as Table 9 indicates.

TABLE 9 "Some Negro leaders are talking about having nonviolent marches and demonstrations in several cities in 1968 to protest lack of opportunities for Negroes. Do you think such demonstrations are different from the riots, or that there is no real difference?"

(In percent)

	White		
	Men	Women	Total
Nonviolent demonstrations differ from riots	63	56	60
No real difference	32	38	35
Don't know	5	6	5
	100	100	100

Thus a third of the white population is so repelled by the idea of active Negro protest that it cannot or does not wish to distinguish between non-violent demonstrations and riots. The response "no real difference" is explained by white respondents in terms such as the following:

> "They're still just looking for aggravation. They're *looking* for trouble. They're just out looking to see what they can stir up, just hoping to aggravate people on the opposite side. That's all."

> "Even the peaceful ones get into big fights usually and a bunch go to jail before it is over."

> "Just plotting up a riot."

> "All I know is it's a mess. They are troublemakers."

In general, then, fully a third of the white population sees riots as simply the inevitable consequence of, if not the same as, the type of protests Negroes have engaged in from the late 1950's onwards. This helps explain why, not infrequently, white respondents join the names of Martin Luther King and H. Rap Brown as though they stood for exactly the same thing.

ADVOCATES OF VIOLENCE

Although the great majority of Negroes in this sample define the riots as spontaneous protests against real grievances, only a relatively small number say they would take part in a riot or similar violent action. A somewhat larger number—but still very much a minority—indicate positive approval of violence as a possible strategy for gaining Negro rights. *Most* Negroes in the 15 city sample, though they speak in terms that would seem to justify the riots, reject violence both as a general strategy and as an approach they would be willing to take part in themselves. *Riots are justified by most Negroes, but they are not recommended.*

Our findings in this area come from four questions that approached the use of violence from different directions, in different forms, and at different points in the interview. The question shown in Table 10 was quite general

TABLE 10 "As you see it, what's the best way for Negroes to try to gain their rights—use laws and persuasion, use nonviolent protests, or be ready to use violence?"

(In percent)

	Negro		
	Men	Women	Total
Laws and persuasion	39	39	39
Nonviolent protests	34	42	38
Be ready to use violence	20	10	15
Don't know	7	9	8
	100	100	100

and impersonal: about one out of six Negroes gave the response pointing toward violence, the highest such choice on any of the questions to be presented. It is difficult, however, to interpret the item alone because of the qualified nature of the phrase "be ready to use violence." Nonviolent protests receive much greater support, and while there is also some uncertainty as to how respondents interpret this phrase, both responses together suggest that for a majority of Negroes in these 15 cities, hope for change rests with protest of one form or another, not with legislative action or legal enforcement.

A second question in this area did not specifically offer an option of violence, but presented a discriminatory situation in open-ended form and asked the respondent to suggest his own solution:

> "Suppose there is a white storekeeper in a Negro neighborhood. He hires white clerks but refuses to hire any Negro clerks. Talking with him about the matter does no good. What do you think Negroes in the neighborhood should do to change the situation?"

No matter what the respondent answered the first time, he was then asked a follow-up question:

> "What if that didn't work, what should they do then?"

The categories into which responses have been coded are shown in Table 11, ordered

as far as practical from complete passivity to outright use of violence. Very few Negro respondents are willing to ignore such discrimination or rely on a mild protest such as a petition. Furthermore, despite the fact that the storekeeper's alleged behavior is probably illegal, only four percent initially suggest attempts to enlist government action—a finding consistent with the National Commission's conclusion that although "almost all cities had some sort of formal grievance mechanism for handling citizen complaints, this typically was regarded by Negroes as ineffective and was generally ignored" (*Report of The National Advisory Commission on Civil Disorders*, p. 4). The most obvious answer to the question for the nonviolently oriented person who wishes to do something is use of a boycott, and indeed three-quarters of the sample gave this as their first response. Only a very small percentage (two percent) of persons initially suggest out-and-out violence, usually in the form of burning the store.

The follow-up question postulated a more frustrating situation—the previous action "didn't work"—and as might be expected the percentage of people turning to violence shows an increase, although it still remains a relatively small proportion of the total sample. It might have risen higher, however, in another type of situation, for in the present case a large number of respondents adhered to the boycott response, noting quite logically

TABLE 11 Original and follow-up question about storekeeper incident
(In percent)

	Negro					
	Original question			Follow-up question		
	Men	Women	Total	Men	Women	Total
Do nothing; do nothing else	3	5	4	9	8	8
Gather a petition	1	2	2	3	2	2
Appeal to government (e.g., court, Civil Rights Commission)	4	4	4	9	10	10
Appeal to Negro organization (e.g., NAACP)	1	0	1	1	1	1
Open a cooperative or community store	1	1	1	2	2	2
Boycott the store	76	70	73	47	43	45
Nonviolent demonstration (e.g., picket, a march)	6	8	7	8	7	8
Get him out (implying violence but ambiguous)	2	3	2	2	2	2
Use violence (e.g., burn the store down)	3	2	2	7	5	6
Don't know	3	5	4	12	20	16
	100	100	100	100	100	100

that with community support a boycott in the situation described "just has to work." It cannot be argued, however, that the level of frustration simulated by the follow-up question inevitably results in a turn toward violence, since Table 11 shows that appeals for government help *also* rises from the initial to the follow-up question.

Our third type of question dealing with possible violence referred to a hypothetical riot and asked the respondent if he himself would probably participate in it (Table 12).

TABLE 12 "If a disturbance like the one in Detroit or Newark last summer broke out here, do you think you would join in, or would you try to stop it, or would you stay away from it?"

(In percent)

| | Negro | | |
	Men	Women	Total
Join in the riot	11	6	8
Try to stop it	11	7	9
Stay away	70	83	76
Don't know*	7	4	6
Other	1	0	1
	100	100	100

* "Don't know" responses to this question are separated from the residual "Other" category because they are fairly frequent and probably reflect genuine uncertainty rather than lack of understanding.

The proportion of persons saying they would join a riot is of the same order of magnitude as the proportion saying they would use violence in the follow-up question on the storekeeper reported previously. It is also interesting to observe that the proportion of about eight percent riot participants that we obtain to these two *hypothetical* questions is not far from the percentages of self-reported *actual* rioters obtained in previous studies of Los Angeles (4.5 percent to 17 percent, depending on criterion) and Detroit (11 percent) riot areas.[2] It is also important to note that about as many people say they would attempt

[2] On Los Angeles, see Raymond J. Murphy and James M. Watson, *The Structure of Discontent,* Institute of Government and Public Affairs, University of California, Los Angeles, 1967. On Detroit, see the Commission's *report,* p. 331.

to *stop* a riot as say they would join one, and of course that the great majority of people in the sample choose neither action but instead say they would try to avoid a riot altogether. The "don't know" percentage to this question is also high relative to most other questions, and probably indicates either genuine uncertainty or an understandable reluctance to speak frankly to the interviewer on this particular subject.

Individuals who said they would join in a riot were asked a series of follow-up questions about the type of action they would be willing to take in such a riot. Perhaps the most important finding of Table 13 is the fact

TABLE 13 Five Follow-up Questions for Those Who Said They Would Join in a Riot

(In percent)

| | Negro* | | |
	Men	Women	Total
Would be "one of the first to get into it," rather than "wait until it was already going strong"	4	1	2
Would "be likely to break windows of stores that treat Negroes unfairly"	4	2	3
Would "be likely to take things from such stores"	2	1	2
Would "be likely to burn such stores"	3	2	2
Would be likely to use other violence (e.g., "destroy anything the white man owns in the Negro community")	4	1	2

* Percentages are of the total Negro sample for each sex separately and for both sexes averaged. However, these follow-up questions were asked only of respondents who said they would "join in a riot." The maximum value a percentage in this table can take is the male, female, or total value, respectively, of the "join in" response reported in Table 12. For example, 11 percent of Negro men said they would join in a riot, and a little more than a third of these (four percent of all Negro men) said they would be "one of the first to get into it."

that slightly *more* people anticipate taking actions such as burning stores than anticipate looting ("taking things from such stores"). Yet pictures and accounts of actual riots strongly suggest that a far greater proportion

TABLE 14   Interrelations of Three Hypothetical Questions on Violence*

(In percent)

		"As you see it, what's the best way for Negroes to try to gain their rights— use laws and persuasion, use nonviolent protests, or be ready to use violence?"	
		Laws and persuasion, nonviolent protests	*Be ready to use violence*
"If a disturbance like the one in Detroit or Newark last summer broke out here, do you think you would join in, or would you try to stop it, or would you stay away from it?"	Would join in	6	29
	Would try to stop it, or would stay away	94	71
		100 (2158)	100 (442)
"Suppose there is a white storekeeper in a Negro neighborhood. He hires white clerks but refuses to hire any Negro clerks. Talking with him about the matter does no good. What do you think Negroes in the neighborhood should do to change the situation? What if that didn't work, what should they do then?"	Method involving violence (to follow-up question)	4	30
	Other methods (to follow-up question)	96	70
		100 (1924)	100 (439)

		"If a disturbance like the one in Detroit or Newark last summer broke out here, do you think you would join in, or would you try to stop it, or would you stay away from it?"	
		Would join in	*Would try to stop it, or would stay away*
"Suppose there is a white storekeeper in a Negro neighborhood. He hires white clerks but refuses to hire any Negro clerks. Talking with him about the matter does no good. What do you think Negroes in the neighborhood should do to change the situation? What if that didn't work, what should they do then?"	Method involving violence (to follow-up question)	31	6
	Other methods (to follow-up question)	69	94
		100 (251)	100 (2073)

* These cross-tabulations were run before weighting procedures used elsewhere in the report were available. In addition, "don't know," "other," and "not ascertained" responses are omitted entirely. The N's for each table are therefore given. Percentages may change slightly in later reports when weighting is used, but relationships should not change appreciably. The decision as to direction of percentaging was based on the item about "the best way for Negroes to gain their rights"; this is a more general question which should shape action but is not a commitment to personal action. The percentages in this case tell us what proportion of each philosophically defined group says it will act in terms of its beliefs, though, of course, exceptions can be explained logically as well as attributed to "error."

Symmetric measures of association for the three subtables, calculated from raw frequencies, are:

Q = .72, .90, and .75, respectively;

Φ = .29, .36, and .28, respectively.

of people engage in looting than in such deliberate destruction as arson.[3]

The resolution of this difference may lie in the fact that our hypothetical riot question, although worded as a prediction of probabilities of action, in fact probably taps ideologically-based intentions. "Burning a store" is a way of expressing conscious hostilities; looting is more apt to involve personal aggrandizement in a situation where this suddenly becomes easy and seemingly legitimate. The "looter" in many cases probably assumes this role as a result of the total situation; insofar as he may feel tempted in this direction beforehand, he is less likely to think it legitimate or want to admit it to an interviewer. The "burner" knows more clearly in advance of his intention, feels it legitimate in terms of his own values (rather than merely the immediate situation), and is thus able to discuss it more openly with an interviewer. An extreme example of this distinction is given in the Commission's *Report* (pp. 52–53):

> When a friend called to tell him about the riot on 12th Street, E. G. went there expecting "a true revolt," but was disappointed as soon as he saw the looting begin: "I wanted to see the people really rise up in revolt. When I saw the first person coming out of the store with things in his arms, I really got sick to my stomach and wanted to go home. Rebellion against the white suppressors is one thing, but one measly pair of shoes or some food completely ruins the whole concept."
> E. G. was standing in a crowd, watching firemen work, when Fire Chief Alvin Wall called out for help from the spectators. E. G. responded. His reasoning was: "No matter what color someone is, whether they are green or pink or blue, I'd help them if they were in trouble. That's all there is to it."
> He worked with the firemen for four days, the only Negro in an all-white crew.

Further evidence for the self-conscious character of the choice of violence in response to the three hypothetical questions we have discussed thus far comes from their high

interrelations. Although they differ considerably in specific content and format, Table 14 shows that the choice of violence on one is strongly associated with the choice of violence on another. There thus appears to be a small portion of the Negro population that is willing and perhaps eager to characterize itself in favor of violence as a way of solving racial problems in America.

We turn now to the last of the four questions asked about violence, this one not a hypothetical inquiry but a question about actual participation in past riots (see Table 15).

TABLE 15 "Have you ever taken part in a violent protest like a riot or a rebellion—I don't need the details, but just whether you did take part and how long ago?"

(In percent)

	Men	Women	Total
Yes	3	1	2
No	96	98	97
Don't know	1	1	1
	100	100	100

The total of two percent self-reported participants is smaller than the figures given to any of the hypothetical questions, presumably because actual riot participation can only have occurred to any substantial degree in cities that had had large-scale riots before March 31, 1968 (the end of our interviewing period). Evidence for this interpretation emerges clearly when we look at the results for the 15 cities following the classification presented in the Commission's *Report* for riots occurring in 1967[4] (see Table 16).

Although the differences are small here, the trend is quite consistent with the expectation that the greater the riot, the more people who should report actual involvement. The fact that some people report participation even in cities classified as having no riots in 1967 is probably due to the generality of the question and of the term "riot." Figures for the major riot cities are smaller than those re-

---

[3] Arrest data compiled by the National Advisory Commission on Civil Disorders also show that "the great majority of those arrested during the disorders were generally charged with a crime related to looting or curfew violations" (*Report,* p. 76). In fact, less than half of one percent of the charges brought against arrestees in 19 riot cities were in connection with arson (*Report,* p. 334).

[4] Both the Commission's classification and this survey took place before the April, 1968, riots in Baltimore, Washington, and several other cities on this list.

TABLE 16 Relation of Seriousness of 1967 City Disorders to Percentage of Self-Reported Participants in Actual Riots*

	Percentage of self-reported rioters
Cities having major riots (Cincinnati, Detroit, Milwaukee, Newark)	3.9 (based on 843 interviews)
Cities having serious riots (Boston, San Francisco)	2.7 (based on 258 interviews)
Cities having minor riots (Brooklyn, Chicago, Cleveland, Pittsburgh, Philadelphia, St. Louis, Washington)	1.9 (based on 1,290 interviews)
Cities classified as having no riots (Baltimore, Gary)	1.3 (based on 432 interviews)

* The classification of cities is from the "Report of the National Commission on Civil Disorders," p. 65 and pp. 323–324. The classification was based on a review by the National Commission of all recorded disorders which occurred during the first nine months of 1967. The percentage of self-reported rioters for each level of seriousness is the mean of the percentage for the cities at that level, based on answers in the present survey to the question in Table 15. The number of interviews used at each level is shown in parentheses. A small number of cases (9) used in these calculations were omitted in all other tables, accounting for the total N here of 2,823.

ported in previous studies, but this is to be expected since the present survey covered entire cities rather than specific "riot areas." (Not every city falls just where expected, but discussion of more detailed individual city differences must be deferred until later reports.)

What relation is there between self-reported actual riot participation and hypothetical riot participation? At the city level there appears to be no association, since city levels of hypothetical participation show little or no relation to the Commission's 1967 classification (see Table 17).[5]

[5] The rank order correlation between actual and hypothetical participation, using the 15 separate city percentages as units, is (Spearman) = −.04.

TABLE 17 Relation of Seriousness of 1967 City Disorders to Percentage of Persons Willing to Join a Future Riot*

	Percentage indicating they would join in a future riot
Cities having major riots (Cincinnati, Detroit, Milwaukee, Newark)	8.5 (based on 843 interviews)
Cities having serious riots (Boston, San Francisco)	11.6 (based on 258 interviews)
Cities having minor riots (Brooklyn, Chicago, Cleveland, Pittsburgh, Philadelphia, St. Louis, Washington)	8.2 (based on 1,290 interviews)
Cities classified as having no riots (Baltimore, Gary)	13.0 (based on 432 interviews)

* The classification of cities is the same used in Table 16 above. The percentages are averaged for the cities at a given level, based on replies to the question shown in Table 12.

Despite this lack of relation at the *city* level, however, there is a strong association at the *individual* level (Table 18). Of those who report having participated in an actual riot, 61 percent say, in effect, that they would

TABLE 18 Relation of Self-Reported Participation in an Actual Riot to Willingness to Join a Future Riot*

(In percent)

Probable participation in a hypothetical riot	Participated in an actual riot	
	Yes	No
Would join in	61	9
Would try to stop it, or would stay away	39	91
	100	100
	(62)	(2,715)

* The same considerations mentioned in the footnote to Table 14 apply here. Q for the above table is .89 and Φ is .26.

do so again. Of those who report never having participated in an actual riot, only nine percent say they would do so given the opportunity. Nearly as strong associations hold between self-reported actual riot participation and the other two questions discussed earlier that concern the use of violence. In general, people who report actual riot participation also tend to report a willingness to use violence in future situations involving racial issues.

We pointed earlier to evidence that persons who say they would take part in a hypothetical riot are probably more representative of the self-conscious and purposeful rioter than of the more casual or situationally determined looter. The associations we have just examined suggest that the same may be true of self-reported actual rioters. That is, surveys of actual riot participation may also tend to represent and describe most adequately the more self-conscious and probably ideological riot participants, but underrepresent others who may join for reasons they are less willing to discuss with an interviewer. This possible bias toward one type of riot participant rather than another should be kept in mind in later sections of this chapter.

But while we must recognize the distinctiveness of those who openly advocate violence as a way of solving racial problems, it is equally important to recall that they are not by any means a group standing sharply against or wholly apart from the dominant mood of the larger Negro population in these 15 cities. This is clear from the opening section of this chapter on the meaning riots have to Negro respondents. It is made even clearer by the question and results shown in Table 19. The question was asked of all respondents who said they would *not* join in a riot if one occurred in their city. The table indicates that the one out of twelve Negroes who say they would join in a riot have the sympathy of another five out of ten. Less than a quarter of the Negro sample voice a definitely unsympathetic attitude toward rioters.

Some examples of what people meant by "sympathetic" come from our set of special probes:

"Because they were fighting for what they believe in—justice."

"Because we have been mistreated. What they were revolting against was unjust. I just don't like their ways."

TABLE 19　"Even if you didn't join in (a riot) would you feel in sympathy with Negroes who did choose to join, or would you feel unsympathetic toward them?"

	Negroes		
	Men	*Women*	*Total*
Sympathetic	50	57	54
Unsympathetic	23	26	24
(Inapplicable: willing to join in)	11	6	8
Other, don't know, not ascertained	16	11	14
	100	100	100

"Because the colored man has got to fight for his rights in this country."

"I don't think they should do these things but I sympathize with them because of how they feel about things. They don't want to do it but they feel something should be done."

These and other similar responses make it clear that many people who are unwilling to commit themselves in an interview to active participation in a riot, nonetheless feel solidarity with those who do take part. They may disagree with, or be unwilling to risk, the method used by the rioters, but they define his goals as just, identify with these goals, and indeed often admire him for standing up for justice. In this sense, the small proportion of Negroes who participate in a riot are able, at least for the present, to count on a much wider context of moral and perhaps more tangible support from the black community. The rioter does not stand alone.

Support is not universal, to be sure, and the quarter of the sample who do not sympathize with rioters represent a sizable opposition within the Negro community. These people say such things as:

"Well, in my opinion, it just doesn't help to do these things. It's not right in any way."

"Actually I don't believe violence accomplishes much of anything. I would feel unsympathetic because as adults we should be able to settle things without violence . . . I feel that man can be made to understand the problems at hand. There would be no need for violence."

"Because they disturbed a lot of property, and people were not helped that way."

Whether this group grows or shrinks in size, prestige, and conviction may well be an important factor in the future of urban riots in this country.

THE BACKGROUND OF BLACK ADVOCATES OF VIOLENCE

Studies reviewed in the Commission's *Report* indicate that self-reported rioters are usually young and tend to be males. Our data for both hypothetical and actual participation show similar results (Figures 1 to 4). General levels of response vary by question but the age and sex trends are quite clear. Advocacy of violence is several times more likely among young people than among old and the decline is a fairly even one over the years, although sharpest from the teenage male group to men in their 20's. Favorability toward violence is about twice as great among men as among women on all four questions.

We noted earlier that the question involving a discriminatory storekeeper in a Negro residential area shows *both* a turn toward violence and a turn toward seeking government help when frustration is built into the situation. It is interesting to note that recourse to the government, like recourse to violence (and unlike other tactics), shows an inverse relation to age (see Figure 5). Thus younger

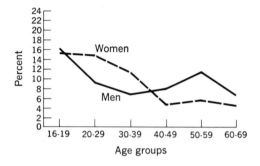

FIGURE 5 Relation of Age to Appeal for Government Intervention

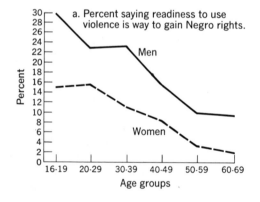

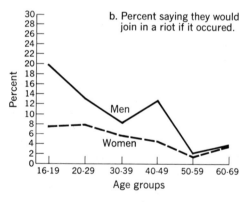

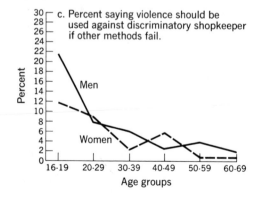

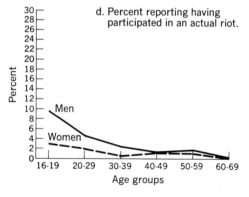

FIGURES 1 to 4 Relation of Age to Four Questions on Advocacy of Violence

TABLE 20 Percentage of Negroes Advocating Violence on Each of Four Questions by Age and Education (Results for men and women averaged)*

(In percent)

	Age 16–19**	Age 20–39					Age 40–69				
		8th grade or less	9–11 grades	12 grades	Some college	College graduate	8th grade or less	9–11 grades	12 grades	Some college	College graduate
Be ready to use violence to gain rights	22	19	16	17	24	24	9	11	7	14	1
Would use violence against discriminatory storekeeper if other methods failed	16	5	6	5	12	4	3	3	2	6	0
Would probably join in a riot	13	11	10	8	8	9	7	6	3	4	6
Report having actually participated in a riot	8	3	2	2	5	1	1	1	1	0	0

* The four questions and codes are given in full in Tables 10, 11, 12, and 15. Each percentage is based on the N for that particular age-education group; for example 19 percent of the Negro respondents ages 20 to 39 and with schooling of eight years or less gave the answer "be ready to use violence" to the question in Table 10.
** This group combines all educational categories.

Negroes are not only more apt to use illegitimate means, they are more willing to use legal means as well. This suggests that clear and effective legal action against perceived discrimination might appeal strongly to young people.

The relation of education to advocacy of violence within broad age categories is shown in Table 20. Although age continues to show consistent and rather substantial effects at each educational level, no clear relation emerges between advocacy of violence and amount of schooling. There is no evidence in Table 20 that any particular level of educational attainment either promotes advocacy of violence or moderates such advocacy where it would otherwise exist. Since education in turn is fairly closely related to income and occupational status, these results suggest that neither of the latter socioeconomic indicators taken alone will explain very much of the data on advocacy of violence.

Later analysis using differences among several socioeconomic variables may prove more helpful. Speculations by social scientists suggest, for example, that it may not be the absolute level of a man's education, income, or occupation that is important in creating dissatisfactions which in turn lead him toward violence, but rather the relations among these several factors. For example, men who attain high school or college educations but cannot find jobs of an expected status or income may become especially bitter. We plan to test these and other more complex models as rigorously as possible in later reports, but for the present we must note that preliminary analyses are not promising for an approach focused solely on economic or related personal status factors. For example, simultaneous controls for education and occupation within age groups produce little evidence that individuals with a high school diploma but an unskilled job are more *or* less likely to want to join a riot (or to sympathize with rioters) than persons of the same education located in skilled or in white-collar occupations.[6]

[6] There is a slight trend for adults intending to join a riot to hold lower status jobs when education is controlled, a trend suggested also in the Commission's *Report* (p. 36). In addition our small sample (N = 18) of teenage males who are both out of school and unemployed show about half inclined toward violence. These data will be presented fully in later reports.

Advocacy of violence appears to be surprisingly *un*related to measures of current socioeconomic achievement.

A wide range of perceptions, experiences, and attitudes, on the other hand, are associated with advocacy of violence. A sample of questions used elsewhere in this report are cross-tabulated in Table 21 with the hypothetical question about what the respondent would do and feel if a riot occurred in his city. The results suggest that those willing to riot tend to be high on dissatisfaction and also tend to attribute the source of dissatisfaction to whites. We cannot disentangle cause and effect in these relations, but clearly advocacy of violence is linked to a rationale that would seem to the individual riot proponent to justify violence and give it purpose.

At the same time it is important to note that many of the differences in Table 21 are small between those who say they would join a riot and those saying they would not. Looked at another way, Table 21 indicates that those who plan to join a riot include substantial proportions who are satisfied with their housing (59 percent), report no personal experience with job discrimination (57 percent), have had white friends (63 percent), and believe that race should *not* be a criterion in selecting a principal for a largely Negro school (70 percent). Thus the connection of intention to join a riot to other attitudes is far from complete at this point and we still have much to learn from the data before a more coherent picture can be presented of those who advocate violence.

THE POTENTIAL WHITE RIOTER

The attention focused on the recent urban riots easily leads one to forget that most *interracial* violence in American history has been directed toward Negroes by whites, rather than the reverse. Whether in the form of individual lynchings, mob terrorism, or quasi-legal local government actions, it is only within the last few years that such violence against Negroes has decreased substantially. That it is not gone completely is clear from incidents that sometimes occur when a Negro family first moves into a previously all-white neighborhood.

Our questionnaire did not explore the possibilities of white violence in detail. We did

TABLE 21* Relation of Negro Willingness to Join a Riot to Six Attitude Questions
(In percent)

"If a disturbance like the one in Detroit or Newark last summer broke out here, do you think you would join in, or would you try to stop it, or would you stay away from it?"
If Stay Away:
"Even if you didn't join in, would you feel in sympathy with Negroes who did choose to join, or would you feel unsympathetic toward them?"

	Join in	Stay away but sympathetic to rioters	Try to stop it	Stay away and unsympathetic to rioters
	(N = 258)	*(N = 1220)*	*(N = 228)*	*(N = 591)*
Dissatisfied with housing they presently have	41	32	30	29
Report they personally have been refused a job because of discrimination	43	34	37	21
Believe many Negroes miss out on jobs today because of their race	60	45	42	31
Believe black policemen treat Negroes better than do white policemen	14	8	9	6
Have never had white friends	37	32	22	29
Think schools with mostly Negro children should have Negro principals	30	17	13	11

* Each percentage is based on the N shown for that column and only one alternative is shown for each question: for example, of the 258 respondents who said they would join in a riot if it occurred, 41 percent answered a question on satisfaction with one's own housing by saying they were dissatisfied. The results in this table are based on unweighted data, as described above in the footnote to Table 14. Residual categories of response (don't know, other, not ascertained) are omitted from calculations of percentages.

include one question, however, that uncovers some of the potential for violence by whites lying just beneath the surface. The question we used (see Table 22) has a number of limitations, for example, the invidious meaning the word "rioting" has for most whites. Moreover, in some communities it is much easier for whites than for Negroes to express strong

TABLE 22 "Some people say that if Negroes riot in (Central City) next summer, maybe whites should do some rioting against them. Others say such matters should be left entirely to the authorities to handle. What do you think?"

(In percent)

	White		
	Men	Women	Total
Whites should do some rioting	8	3	5
Leave it to authorities	90	95	93
Don't know	2	2	2
	100	100	100

racial hostility *indirectly* by relying on "authorities," and so this choice is not necessarily as "legal" as its sounds. Despite these limitations, the results presented below are illuminating.

The total percentage (five percent) for white propensity to violence on this question is not high, but it is nonetheless almost two-thirds the size of the comparable figure obtained with the hypothetical question on riot participation asked of Negroes (see Table 12). Indeed, when translated into population terms, the absolute number of people of each race would be about the same, since there are nearly twice as many whites as Negroes in the 15 cities we sampled. Moreover, the figures given thus far are for city whites only: four percent of the suburban sample (5.5 percent men and 2.7 percent women) also accept the question's suggestion of counter-rioting against Negroes.

The results by sex for this question are very similar to those reported earlier for Negroes: the proportion of white men advocating violence is about twice that of white women. Age breaks by decade (not presented here) do not show a consistent relation between age and the advocacy of counter-riots by whites. However, there is one striking relation to age, especially when combined with sex, that is very similar for Negroes and whites: advocacy of violence is much more common among teenage males than among any other age-sex combination. When the white sample is divided on age by decade (males 16–19, males 20–29, males 30–39, etc.), 21 percent of the teenage males advocate a counter-riot, while no more than seven percent of any other age-sex combination do so. In fact, the figure of 21 percent for white male teenagers on the counter-riot question is essentially the same as the figure of 19.5 percent (see Figure 2) obtained for black male teenagers on the question about joining a future riot.

Thus what at first might have been taken as a racial phenomenon somehow peculiar to young Negro males seems now to be explicable more easily in terms of a conception of teenage masculine daring that has little to do with race. The riot figure drops off more sharply by age for white males than for Negroes, but this may be due at least in part

to the fact that white males in their 20's more easily and more quickly find a stable occupational role than is presently true for Negro males of the same age.

There is one respect in which the Negro and white "riot results" are less similar, namely, their relation to education. Table 23 suggests some relation of education to white propensity to riot, while Table 20 earlier showed no such trend for Negroes. It may be that this difference is due to ideological factors which make it more acceptable at present for educated Negroes to entertain violence as a strategy for change than for educated whites. It is also possible that here too in part similar mechanisms yet to be uncovered are at work for both Negroes and whites, but that differences in level of education obscure the similarity. These and other analytic issues will have to be deferred to later reports. It seems clear, however, from the results already presented in this section that research which focuses solely on black tendencies toward violence, without similar consideration of white tendencies, may lead one to miss characteristics which are common to most Americans, if not indeed to men everywhere.

TABLE 23 "Some people say that if Negroes riot in (Central City) next summer, maybe whites should do some rioting against them. Others say such matters should be left entirely to the authorities to handle. What do you think?"

Percent of whites advocating a counter-riot, by age and education (results for men and women averaged)

	Age 16–19*	Age 20–39					Age 40–69				
		8th grade or less	9–11 grades	12 grades	Some college	College graduate	8th grade or less	9–11 grades	12 grades	Some college	College graduate
Whites should do some rioting	12	10	10	6	1	0	4	6	5	1	1
Leave it to the authorities	88	88	84	92	98	92	93	92	94	94	95
Don't know	0	2	6	2	1	8	3	2	1	5	4
	100	100	100	100	100	100	100	100	100	100	100

* This group combines all educational categories.

Name Index

Subject Index